We both step and do not step in the same rivers; we are and are not.

—Heraclitus of Ephesus,
Fragment 12

About the Author

Najib Al Chamaa was a video game addict, spending up to ten hours every day in front of a screen for eight years. He was kicked out of his university for failing his first three semesters and was in the process of getting deported for it. He fell to daily substance abuse for two years, got himself into crippling debt, was misdiagnosed with bipolar disorder, and endured a year of medication, suffering side effects and withdrawal. He attempted to take his own life.

Today, Najib is a specialist in change management, Agile practices, business analytics, web/system design, branding, digital marketing, cybersecurity, and is currently pursuing a PhD in psychology. Having earned a Bachelor of Information Technology and Systems and a Master's of Networks and Security, he was appointed the role of lecturer by the age of twenty-six at the very university where his first enrollment was terminated. From developing and managing some of Oceania's biggest private game servers, to founding and growing a successful creative agency to a team of six, to directing chapters of one of the biggest professional referral networks in the world, to designing and composing master's degree units for Australia's most prolific university, Najib now seeks to bring change—real change—to those willing to commit to a unique lifestyle he formulated, called the Quasi-Chaotic Lifestyle, of which he remains a student; the answer he owes his life to.

NECESSITATING
CHANGE

A PRACTICAL GUIDE TO SELF-ACTUALIZATION

Najib Al Chamaa

First published in 2023 by Najib Al Chamaa

 A catalogue entry for this book is available from the National Library of Australia.

Paperback ISBN: 978-0-6457627-0-9
Ebook ISBN: 978-0-6457627-1-6

Printed in Australia by IngramSpark
Editing by Matthew Gilbert
Proofreading by Dave Valencia
Design by Storyfolk
Indexing by Maria Sosnowski
Publishing management and distribution by Publish Central

Disclaimer
The material in this publication is of the nature of general comment only, and does not represent professional advice. It is not intended to provide specific guidance for particular circumstances and it should not be relied on as the basis for any decision to take action or not take action on any matter which it covers. Readers should obtain professional advice where appropriate, before making any such decision. To the maximum extent permitted by law, the author and publisher disclaim all responsibility and liability to any person, arising directly or indirectly from any person taking or not taking action based on the information in this publication.

CONTENTS

FIGURES

INTRODUCTION

I shall bring to light the true riches of our souls, opening up to each of us the means whereby we can find within ourselves, without any help from anyone else, all the knowledge that we may need for the conduct of life.

—René Descartes, *Regulae Ad Directionem Ingenii (Rules of the Direction of the Mind)*

Heralded as the first modern philosopher, René Descartes conferred us perennial, axiomatic words that have yet to manifest themselves in a world distraught with distraction. "Je pense, donc je suis": *I think, therefore I am.* Descartes's intuition led him to value and place his faith in introspection and individualism rather than authority and tradition. How much of whom you know yourself to have become, and how much of your day-to-day conduct, mannerisms, goals, and preferences, are based on self-made realizations drawn from *personal experience*? Contrastingly, how much of it all is inherited, spoon-fed, and osmotically imparted?

The profession you identify with, the degree you've committed to, your political post, your religious affiliation, your moral compass, your sense of humor, how you dress, how you hold cutlery, how you hang toilet paper, what you think of the homeless, how you perceive other cultures, your mating checklist, your aspirations, your priorities, your idea of a happy family . . . How much of who you associate with, what you believe, and who you tell yourself to be is, in fact, derived from *intrinsic knowing*?

Our "normal" way of life is familiar to most; the status quo of a healthy lifestyle is a string of behaviors we seldom question. We set off with a primary, secondary, and tertiary education, followed by a few ratbag gigs leading to an internship and then, if we're lucky, a well-paying office job. There's a credit card awards menu of directives, a shiny car, prepackaged holiday travel, an investment house if we can manage, a family with a few problematic relatives we seemingly have no choice but to put up with, retirement at an age confining us to even more prepackaged itineraries, and, finally, a deathbed surrounded by friends and family assuring us of a Promised Land. A model we nod our heads in unison to as if to say, "They've lived a good life." The more prestigious, the more reputable, the more influential, the wealthier, and the faster one "succeeds" are the parameters we've been conditioned to use to judge our progress—a governing directive we all generally default to.

We often strive for "stability"—a point of certainty, convenience, and comfort. The thought of early retirement, the freedom to do as one desires, and the absence of obligation is an alluring fantasy we helplessly envisage. It's an end that justifies the means and the means by which we mature into independence, divorcing ourselves from nurture—or so we think. We assume the template stepping stones we have lived by have equipped us with the means to be autonomous, but how autonomous are we really?

With each passing day, we see further advancements in neuroscience, psychology, evolutionary biology, sociology, anthropology, and our understanding of the human species as a whole. Yet we unknowingly cling to prehistoric mannerisms that dictate our conduct. In generation after generation, ubiquitous in every corner of the world, tradition and culture bestow a psychological template along with expectations, hopes, and dreams. And while quality of life for most of us is at an all-time high, so, too, are depression and suicide rates. We inherit and assume a lifestyle which simply doesn't work in this age of constant change and uncertainty. Regularly confronted with an ongoing surge of novel opportunities in the form of people, places, and practices, our options seem endless. But our embrace of those options leaves much to be desired, and what resonates with us today will most likely not be the case tomorrow.

In a world riddled with pollution, epidemics, wealth inequality, warfare, famine, injustice, theft, homelessness, trafficking, corruption, oppression, prejudice derived of evil, ignorance, dogma, stigma, bad parenting, archaic administration, or sheer bad luck, we are compelled to make sense of it, understand it, work with it, and occasionally marshal our courage and ask for help. We turn to pseudoscientific self-help literature, self-proclaimed life coaches, inspirational TED talks, influencers, and entrepreneurial success stories for answers. Word salads that appear profound get passed for wisdom and often fall flat in practice, whether it's a list of virtues "you need to develop" or concepts "you need to rethink" or behaviors "you need to stop"—all of which *sound* good, but almost none of which are actionable or offer practical guidance. How does one work on their insecurities? How does one develop thicker skin? How does one recalibrate intuition? How does one "just do it." What's Step 1? What about the time, money, or support I don't have? What about the fact that I'm not you? A fleeting moment of motivation is often all there is to gain, leading us right back to where we started and feeling worse off than when we began—yet another failure to add to our list.

Now imagine a world void of disdain, void of expectation, void of capitulation, every moment sanguine. Imagine a world where your studies genuinely intrigue you, where the anticipation for the next class is unbearable, where education is as entertaining and lively as playing your video game of preference or a karaoke night out with friends or relishing a cheese fondue and freshly baked Älplermagronen in a small town in the Swiss Alps. Imagine if the work you financially depend on is perpetually fulfilling, intrinsically rewarding, and authentically enjoyable, where the weekends seem too long, the eagerness of mastery is insatiable, and the people around you are complementarily and equally driven. Imagine if your next workout is always a blast and the next meal always a delight. Imagine if every waking hour is *literally* one to look forward to. Imagine if success and living to our fullest is assured, a constant. What a world it would be.

What if I told you there is a way to *guarantee* such contentment, ensuring you *always* get what you want and, more importantly, what you need? What if I told you that every decision doesn't have to fear a convoluted and regret-ridden outcome? What if I told you that the existential thoughts keeping you up at night and haunting you between conversations at parties can be eradicated? What if I told you that you don't have to bend to the will of groups that "you should" (but would rather not) be affiliated with and still find success and acceptance? What if I told you that your mind-numbingly repetitive routines aren't mandatory to maintain the expectations, relationships, or ambitions you tell yourself are sentimental or necessary? What if I told you that what you believe to be intractable and disparaging personal attributes are in fact pliable? What if I told you that much of what is widely practiced and believed—what you have grown to accept and rely on—is precisely what is holding you back? What if I said that you have more cards to play than you've been dealt?

Do any of the following sound familiar?

▲ Anxiously waking up to the sound of an alarm, in a space in which you are reminded of how little you've accomplished, provoking the crippling thought of living through the same familiar day you've endured for as long as you can remember.

▲ Watching your friends seemingly progress through what you perceive to be the uninteresting and tedious humdrum, leaving you feeling alienated, different, and incompatible.

▲ Enduring endless judgment from family, cultural norms, and the competitive present, constantly feeling like you just can't keep up or do anything right—assuming you even care to.

▲ Dreading obligation—a task you can't stomach doing any more of but which still needs doing. An obligation so distasteful, you cherish the few moments you have left after awakening before your call of duty.

▲ Living a life of envy, never achieving or obtaining what you want, never feeling like you can, always despising those who do, subsequently questioning fairness.

▲ Deliberately allowing your mental problems to worsen because complete detachment from reality feels like the best option.

▲ Deprived of energy and/or motivation, neglecting your personal well-being, hygiene, and life savings.

▲ Going silent when someone asks you what's wrong.

This book is dedicated to the misfits, the unfulfilled, the misunderstood, the alienated, the unmotivated, the abandoned, and the distressed. To those without a purpose, without hope, without reason, and without support. To those who have lost their way, lost control, and to those who bear a weight on their shoulders they can't seem to shake off. To those who constantly make bad decisions and to those who have lost themselves. To those who have read the books, watched the videos, sat through the seminars, tested the spiritual, attempted therapy, and have yet to see a significant difference in their lives. This book is dedicated to helping you find the light today because you deserve a better tomorrow.

What this Book Isn't—and Is

This book is not an autobiography, a composition of abstract ideas open to interpretation, nor is it a motivational drama centered around woo-woo pseudoscience. It's not a soul-searching attempt at making you feel better about yourself. It's not another top ten list of what you need to know. It never mentions astrology. And, most importantly, it is *not* for everyone.

What is proposed in the pages to come is simply an alternative way of living: a *Quasi-Chaotic Lifestyle*—a life of constant change—with an emphasis on action and reflection. *Necessitating Change* outlines a practical and action-able model that is clear-cut, accessible, and inclusive. You don't need to be wealthy. You don't have to be living in a First World country. You don't need an existing support group. You don't have to be a genius. You won't need the will of a cross-country triathlete. You won't need to "free up a month." You don't have to be an extrovert. It doesn't require an unholy disciplined grind or anything you wouldn't enjoy. And, yes, if you are the routine type, this will work for you as well.

The first section covers shortcomings, oversights, and false beliefs of the twenty-first century psyche: *The Problem*. This is followed by what is possible and the how of: *The Theory*. The next section is dedicated to those who lack or have lost the capacity to reason or persevere, leading to *The Last Resort*. A concatenation of discussed concepts, ideologies, and informed values is presented as a framework of well-being that the Quasi-Chaotic Lifestyle hinges on follows, in what will become *The Purpose*. Following that is *The Means*: the cognitive tools you will need to sustain a Quasi-Chaotic Lifestyle.

We then turn to the means by which a Quasi-Chaotic Lifestyle is activated by dissecting a healthy decision's anatomy: *The Verdict*. We then meet *The Practice*, in which the practical guide to Self-Actualization is detailed. Finally, we arrive at *The Finish Line*, where we recap, reconvene, and redistribute opportunities a Quasi-Chaotic Lifestyle will afford us with.

Adopting a Modern Model Lifestyle

As described by Karl Weick, an organizational theorist, the efficacy of any model is confined to a three-way tradeoff between generalizability, accuracy, and simplicity, in which you can only have two of the three. What is to come in this book will be generalizable to most and simple enough to follow—though deliberately loose; emancipation through deliberation and reflection is an individual journey, not one that can be detailed in advance.

Don't expect to adopt this lifestyle overnight, though. Afterall, we have been raised to think, feel, and conduct ourselves in ways we have accepted unconsciously from the moment we are born. Adopting a Quasi-Chaotic Lifestyle will feel like learning to play the guitar. At first, the reality of not being able to "shred" sets in. Thoughts like "Maybe this isn't for me" or "This isn't going anywhere" may fuel your doubt. It will feel awkward, strange, alien, different, and sometimes painful. You'll read the material, make an attempt, fumble, forget, and reread it until you learn to play a jingle and get a taste for a tune. The sweet sound of progress becomes palpable, satiating desire, and sufficiently so to motivate perseverance and commitment. In time, as you begin to understand the fundamentals, you gain the ability to progress independently. And once you get the hang of it, you will learn to love it. Similarly, by the end of this book, you will become generously equipped and secure with the tools and knowledge you need to cultivate a life of change. Over time and with practice, you will find fulfillment and everlasting growth.

This journey, should you choose to commit to it, will also involve setbacks, confusion, and discomfort. You will find yourself retracing your progress and defaulting back to what you know best: the old you. At times like these, you will feel the need to reread particular chapters to stay on course. Keep this book close during times of uncertainty and even closer during times of doubt.

For the skeptical, references to empirical studies are provided to substantiate claims made. For the curious, a thorough application of the process is provided using three personas whose accounts are familiar to many and, perhaps, to you.

Let us begin.

To dare is to lose one's footing momentarily. To not dare is to lose oneself.

—Søren A. Kierkegaard, *Eighteen Upbuilding Discourses*

PART I

BREAKING BAD HABITS

THE PROBLEM

CHAPTER 1
THE TRADITIONAL PSYCHE

D*oxa*. It is a word ancient Greeks used to describe the domain of opinion, belief, and probable knowledge—in contrast to *episteme*, the domain of true knowledge or certainty. Philosophers have since wrestled with the term. Plato relegated doxa to a belief, unrelated to reason and the opponent of knowledge. Aristotle regarded doxa as a necessary first step toward episteme, extending a point of view and giving credence to tested and accepted truths passed down from generation to generation—what he called *endoxa*. More recent uses of doxa, such as that of sociologist and public intellectual Pierre Bourdieu, denote a society's unquestioned, taken-for-granted truths, or as Bourdieu (1977) put it, that which "goes without saying because it comes without saying," suggesting it sets limits on social mobility with a social space: "a sense of one's place."

Whatever the slant, for better or for worse, doxa refers to a particular state of *being* we willingly inherit. A state predisposing us to a demeanor of compliance, uninformed decision-making, and a socially conditioned outlook—the influence of which percolates through every facet of life. A disconcerting assertion, I know, but hear me out. Regret, failure, fear, doubt—where do they come from? Why are they so common? Life is hard, but does it have to be? Is everything we know a simulated reality configured in such a way that makes the "bad" pervasive and the "good" scarce? While this conjecture can make for a great Netflix series, the answer is this: life is only as hard as we make it for ourselves.

MISGUIDED POTENTIAL

Ancient Greece, highly regarded and considered the birthplace of Western civilization, would be a suitable axis from which to depart if we are to measure how far we've drifted from what seemed to work. From democracy, modern philosophy, and the Olympiad to modern medicine and the theater, what makes the ancient Greeks so appealing is their ability to utilize reason to understand and express the eternal and intelligible order of the world. "Know thyself" was carved into the pronaos of the temple of Apollo at Delphi, in which they seemed to have developed the art of interpreting the world, themselves, and life with the honesty and clarity we ought to be prioritizing as a people.

Instead, we find ourselves devolving into a world of polarized ideas, beliefs, aspirations, and viral trends—all inflated, exaggerated, and proliferated by social media. A hyperpartisanship of collectivism and social stigmatization—an "us versus them" mentality—has given rise to ideological dogmatisms, biased narratives, and backward policies that are choking our societies of independent, nuanced outlooks, freedom of speech, freedom of thought, freedom of opportunity, and freedom of autonomy. Whether its First World countries bearing Third World customs—oppressing women out of basic human rights such as governing their own bodies or the right to travel without a male "supervisor"—or cacophonies from the political spectrum's hypocritical motives promoting "cancel culture," a byproduct of the divide championing freedom of expression while policing our speech and our thoughts and which would have us fixate on how rabid, seemingly unhinged groups of keyboard bullies feel, we are frozen in fear as to how to respond to such temperamental and reputational terrorists.

An epidemic gone unnoticed is that of cultural rot, as authentic aspirations are further skewed by those who kick, swing at, catch, or throw a ball; those who decorate themselves with a façade of colors, contours, and exaggerated bodily anatomies with oils, silicones, and inserts to fit a naturally impossible image; and those who have nothing more to offer than staged "pranks," mumbles on stale tracks, or uniting provocation for baseless outrage. All of whom happen to be glorified and put on a pedestal for the world to mindlessly consume and idolize, to have red carpets rolled out in front of them and street names dedicated to them. It's a spasm of privileged lifestyles that leaves those in search of or practicing more meaningful pursuits, those actually making a charitable and benevolent effort for the benefit of others, such as essential workers (or any service involving compassion and care), teachers, researchers, and scientists, to name a few with existential dread, as many are barely able to make ends meet. What you end up with are blooming generations that are lost, misinformed, distracted, and pigeonholed as far as their conversation, interests, and values are concerned—a reflection of depressingly predictable lifestyles and osmotically predictable mimicry. It's not surprising to see that, in recent surveys, many children now aspire to be a "YouTuber" or a "social media influencer" (Parker, 2019; Akande, 2019). And if they were aspiring to become a lawyer, doctor, or teacher (often based on what their parents wanted for them), their top answers when asked why they wanted *that* particular career were "for money" (26%) and "for fame" (22%) (Akande, 2019). And it wasn't that long ago when most kids aspired to be pro athletes (Fatherly, 2015)—an aspiration that has steadily increased in popularity over the years (Mazzuca, 2003). Contrast these results to a social survey conducted in 1948 where 58% of boys and 73% of girls made "realistic" choices (*Guardian*, 1948). We seem to be headed toward a state of *Idiocracy*—the 2006 film where a former wrestler and porn star, President Dwayne Elizondo Mountain Dew Camacho, runs the new world order atop his four-seater trike, toting his brightly colored M248 SAW machine gun with his middle finger raised high to all the progress made by giants whose shoulders we ignorantly stand upon.

How did our values and virtues veer so far away from what used to be common principles? Perhaps it's a byproduct of rampant capitalism: an engineered consumerist psychology provoking wide-eyed commitments based on exaggerated claims and arousing our deepest primitive impulses, whether it's the salt and sugar in our food, media lined with erotic innuendo at every opportunity, irresponsible projections of wealth and power, or political parroting and tribalism. Maybe it's the exploitation of our evolutionary intuitions by fabricating scarcity with flash sales, clickbait, and loud advertisements—now common practice within economies—that edge laymen and laywomen into states of urgent decision-making. We are barraged by a nonstop broadcast of clips, spotlights, memes, and propaganda of what defines success or failure or bravery or ideals or whatever we know to be superficial but pursue regardless for the sake of belongingness and conformity. These new norms, alongside expectations derived of ethics, culture, and tradition, have shackled us to cookie-cutter templates that mold how we think, feel, act, and perceive the world.

The fact of the matter is that *who* and *how* you are is largely based on your upbringing. Where you've lived, who you spent time with, what your parents were like, and the events that took place shaped you into who you are today. Your mindset is generally inherited early on, and it's not until adulthood that you begin to form and cement your opinions on matters, morals, beliefs, and so on—only some of which are truly of your own. How often do you question your ways, your personality, your *inheritance*? Ever since the dawn of humankind, newer generations have been the unconscious successors to their parents' professions, beliefs, and mannerisms. You can be a blacksmith for half a century because your father was, and no one will bat an eye. It is the norm. You might come from generations of firemen, milkmen, cooks, carpenters, and so on. Your parents may have been conspiracy theorists; their aspirations may have been questionable and self-centered; their own idiosyncratic shortcomings may have been imprinted on you. How self-aware are we really?

Most people are other people. Their thoughts are someone else's opinions, their lives a mimicry, their passions a quotation.

—Oscar Wilde, *De Profundis*

Economies, communities, and societies as a whole influence who we are, a truism to consider and appreciate if we are to move forward. Awareness is the first step to change, and taking a step back to look at the absurdity of conventional norms from outside the box will facilitate the process of adopting an entirely new lifestyle.

▲ Education:

Designed in such a way that uninformed and costly decision-making is mandatory. How often are young adults forced to decide on what to major in with little to no intuition or experience on the matter? One day a child is raising their hand for a bathroom break; the next, they are making a three-to-five-year commitment costing hundreds of thousands of dollars of debt or hard-earned accumulated family savings with little or no understanding of the protagonist—themselves.

▲ Marriage:

How would you know who suits you best if you have only been in one, three, or even ten relationships? With every failure, you learn about yourself and how you respond to different personalities and traits: maturity, life skills, conflict resolution, dependability, responsibility, emotional intelligence. How many of these have you developed before submitting to a social construct's lifelong contract, assuming that love is eternal, your significant other will always be the person you fell in love with, and that you'll always be able and willing to fulfill each other's everchanging expectations? A beguiling fantasy, to say the least.

▲ Work:

With any form of contract, whether it's a subscription to a new-found hobby or a work contract, how confident are you with the commitment you are making? What is this confidence based on? Are you certain you know without a doubt that this is what you do best, that it's right for you, that it's what you want to excel in, that this is how you want to spend your youthful years? Or are you there because that is what is expected of you and/or the salary is too much to turn down—an end that justifies the means?

The list goes on, and rest assured, there are plenty of lists to come.
Not only do we inherit expectations, but the machinery of consumerism skews aspirations toward modes of ignorance, superficiality, and inauthenticity—antithetical to what was carved onto the temple of Apollo. How much of our modern-day individuality is an illusion and how much of it stems from informed and autonomous, self-made realizations about our true temporary self?

One may wonder how the Traditional Psyche (a term I will use to refer to inherited or societally imposed aspirational templates with rigid, linear, and oftentimes archaic ways of being) has held up in a world of modernity. In search of an answer, we refer to results of mental health surveys involving Gen Z and younger millennials. Psychologists and epidemiologists Praveetha Patalay and Suzanne H. Gage suggest an increase in depression from 9% to

15% in millennials between 2005 and 2015 in the UK. Similarly, a 2018 report from Blue Cross Blue Shield found that depression in millennials increased a staggering 47% since 2013 in the US. The Australian Bureau of Statistics reported that in 2019, suicide accounted for two in five deaths among those aged 15–17 (a 40% increase) and more than one in three among those aged 18–24 (a 36% increase)—a 25% increase in suicide over the last decade. The National Survey on Drug Use and Health (NSDUH), a nationally representative survey of U.S. adolescents and adults indicates rates of major depressive episode increased by up to 63% between 2005–2017 among adolescents and young adults. Major depressive episodes and suicidal thoughts also increased among young adults from 2008–2017, along with serious psychological distress that surged by a whopping 71% (see figure 1-1.) While we can deliberate the efficacy of methods for such research given the disparity of sensitivity and social stigmatization of mental health admission across generations, the totality of the findings within the last two decades should, at the very least, come as no surprise. One need only have a few honest conversations before arriving at a disconcerting realization: the correlation between depression and modernity.

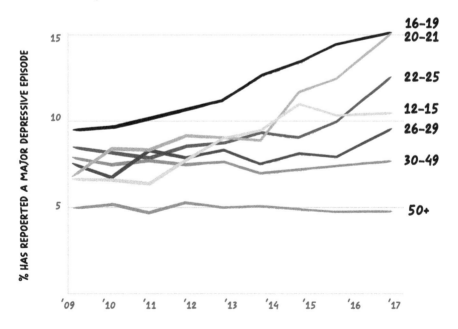

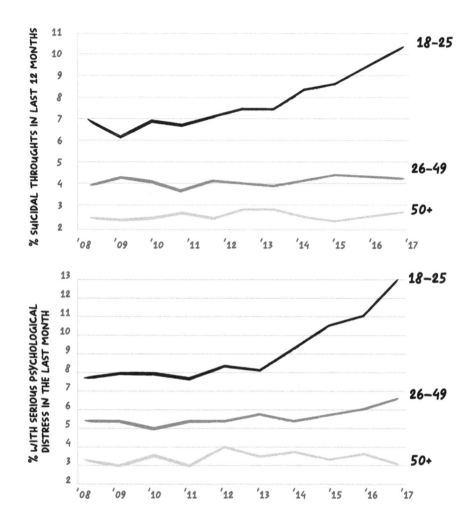

Figure 1-1: Depression, suicidal thoughts, and psychological distress
Adapted from Twenge et al. (2019)

How is it that in a world of ubiquitous opportunities, endless technological advancements, state-of-the-art education, seamless communication and interconnectivity, and a myriad of quality-of-life improvements we, as a species, have found ourselves in a world of hurt? Whether it's rising education (see figure 1-2), working shorter hours (see figure 1-3), declines in spending on necessities (see figure 1-4), increases in leisure hours per week (see figure 1-5), reduction in cost of air travel (see figure 1-6), or the increased accessibility to utilities, appliances, and overall reduction in housework (see figure 1-7), the correlate trend is apparent.

Another caveat worth highlighting: While much of the empirical substantiations presented in this chapter are largely based on US data with discrepancies in dates (a consequence of limited relevant dataset availability) that leave room for doubt and other correlate variables, one would not be surprised to find similar (if not more distressing) results with more concurrent, diverse, and geographically consistent datasets.

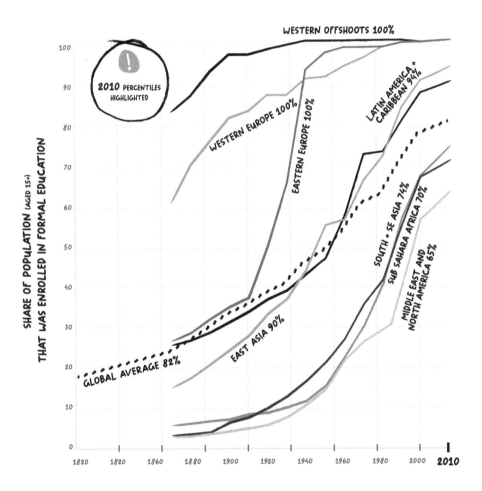

Figure 1-2: Global average rising of education
Adapted from Pinker (2018)

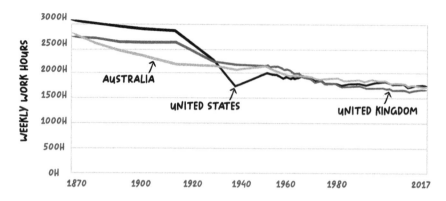

Figure 1-3: Working hours
Adapted from Giattino et al. (2018)

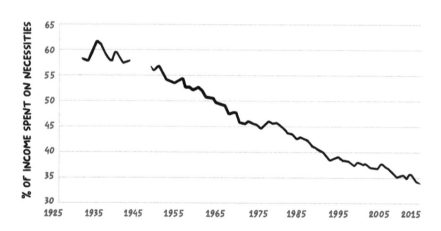

Figure 1-4: Spending on necessities
Adapted from Pinker (2018)

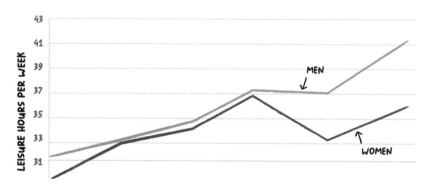

Figure 1-5: Leisure hours per week
Adapted from Pinker (2018)

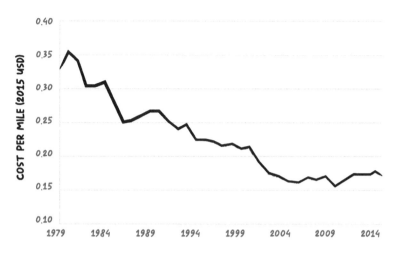

Figure 1-6: Cost of air travel

Adapted from Pinker (2018)

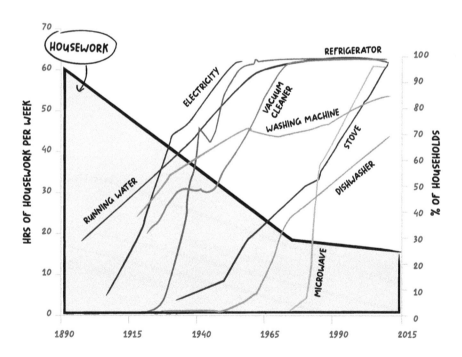

Figure 1-7: Utilities, appliances, and housework

Adapted from Pinker (2018)

Moreover, and generally speaking, some form of progression is expected with every generation, whether it's financially, reputationally or spiritually. Either way, and amongst the myriad of emergent problems newer generations face that we will explore, expectations and, ultimately, pressure continue to rise with every generation; its consequences correlating to depression rates. Social psychologist Thomas Curran and coauthor, sports psychologist Andrew P. Hill, (2022) concluded from a meta-analysis including twenty-one studies with data from more than seven thousand college students and another including eighty-four studies conducted between 1989 and 2021 with a total of 23,975 college students, that parental expectations and criticism are increasing over time (see figure 1-8.) It seems that we have arrived at a terminal in which "more" is no longer a plausible or necessary aspiration and instead detrimental.

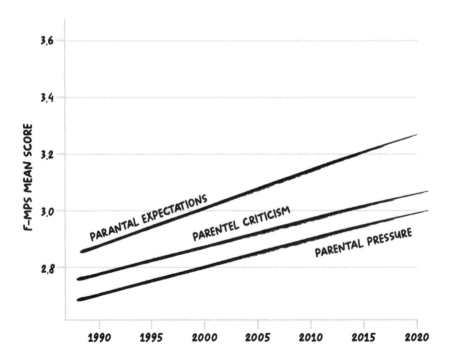

Figure 1-8: Parental expectations, criticism, and pressure
Adapted from Curran & Hill (2022)

The pervasiveness of a Traditional Psyche—the incompatibility of what it offers and the consequences of what it doesn't—raises deeper psychological problems we have yet to resolve. For example, we have a better understanding of the harsh realities of life and its black and meaningless inevitability, which has afforded us answers to lingering existential questions such as "What is the meaning of life?", "Are we just biochemical puppets?", and "Is a particular species of primate sacred?", deductively curbing plausibility of a Traditional Psyche's "divine plan" and further widening the expanse for a potential leap of faith. The fact that many religions in progressive Western civilizations are losing members while secularism is on the rise (Park et al., 2013; Smith et al., 2016; Smith, 2020; and what you'll find in most general/social consensus surveys) is testament to such tenable speculation. The quest for reason—to understand *why* things are the way they are—is a losing battle, forcefully necessitating capitulation and acceptance, both unsettling. It's a tough pill to swallow.

The pressure of time builds as we are left wrestling with social constructs, cornered into an office space fighting for what we are told is the right thing to do: study, work, start a family, and then pass into the abyss. A chilling thought, is it not? Which urges the mind to scavenge for reasons by any means necessary to justify the hardships, pain, and ambivalence as we push through to the next expectation life throws our way. It is a voyage of suffering one would expect a technologically advanced civilization to have mastered. Instead, beyond mystical explanations that offer little that one would consider honest solace or graspable answers, most are left with "That's just life," "That's how it's always been," or "When life gives you lemons . . ." The Traditional Psyche fails to deliver much-needed tools for navigating modernity, and yet most of us perceive the suffering we endure on a day-to-day basis as the norm. It begs the question of why such a critical condition isn't addressed with more rigor and guidance in schools.

Through globalization and digital interconnectedness, access to all the information (and contradictory outlooks) one can ask for are made possible. Curious minds wander, and newer generations are exposed to ever-growing possibilities of what they can do and become. And while parental and societal expectations still have a firm hold on their potential, this sudden change of circumstance, alongside an obstinate generational psyche, has proven to be troublesome for the young. We are apostates of tradition, dissenters of subjection, and nomads of reason, wandering in search of purpose with no map or signs as to what it is or where to find it . . . all while being forced to adapt to increasingly open, dynamic, and novel technological, environmental, economic, social, and political landscapes. Borders no longer exist. Distances are no longer out of reach. Ideas can no longer be obfuscated. Options are no longer limited. Attitudes are no longer landlocked by proximal influence. It's no wonder that youth inevitably grow dissent against inherited ideologies and then face resistance. *Who we are* was always in question and open for reconsideration, and since the turn of the century and its increasingly influential milieu, our identities have become more fluid than ever.

Think back to who you were a decade ago. What do you think of that you? If you were stuck in an elevator with *that* person, would you get along? Would you share the same sense of humor? Would you consider befriending them if you crossed paths at an event? Would your interests be aligned, and would you have much to talk about? How would you feel adopting that individual's priorities and lifestyle? This is the *illusion of the self*—that it endures, unchanging, over time. We are not who we were yesterday, nor who we will be tomorrow, but someone else entirely in this moment.

For if I try to seize this self of which I feel sure, if I try to define and summarize it, it is nothing but water slipping through my fingers. I can sketch one by one all the aspects it is able to assume, all those likewise that have attributed to it, this upbringing, this origin, this ardor or these silences, this nobility or this vileness. But aspects cannot be added up. This very heart which is mine will forever remain indefinable to me. Between the certainty I have of my existence and the content I try to give to the assurance, the gap will never be filled. Forever I shall be a stranger to myself.

—Albert Camus, *The Myth of Sisyphus*

As much as we hate to admit it, we live our lives making, and enslaved to, uninformed and misguided long-term commitments, blindly inheriting and capitulating to expectations, unknowingly limiting our individualistic potential, and, most depressingly, doing nothing about it. Living in "bad faith" as the twentieth-century Nobel laureate (though, declining the honor) philosopher Jean-Paul Sartre put it, is to deny one's freedom while relying on it to perform the denial. By disregarding individuality, circumstance, and our everchanging desires, we are setting ourselves up for failure and *assuming* its destiny. In the chapters to come, we will dissect the Traditional Psyche's incompatibilities with modern living and address emergent issues of an everchanging world-system. It's well past time to repudiate the psyche of social norms and the safety of broken convention. It is time instead to embrace the chaos and seek a higher ground of control and certainty.

CHAPTER 2
PESTILENTIAL GOAL-SETTING

The secret to success, the orchestrator of excellence, the path to glory, and the most overrated, counterproductive, and ineffectual way to get there is by what we all refer to as "goal-setting." The conventional use of the word refers to setting a deliberately challenging or ambitious objective—also referred to as a "stretch" goal—and taking the necessary measures to achieve the aim over an extended period of time. It will be strenuous, it will be demanding, but with discipline and grit, we endeavor to see it through. "Dream big!" you often hear. A big salary, a big house, and big experiences await you. We are encouraged to set our heart to what we believe we want and proceed with a grind until the goal is realized.

If realizing goals was that straightforward, I wouldn't have written this book, you wouldn't be reading it, and we'd be an interstellar species by now. But I did, you are, and we aren't. So, what gives? It seems to be what everyone's advocating, is it not? Don't goals improve performance and provide motivation to persevere and learn and stay focused? Truth be told, it is but the tip of the Traditional Psyche's insidious iceberg; much of what we have grown to rely on and accept is precisely what doesn't work in the twenty-first century. If personal experience hasn't definitively confuted the veracity of stretch goals' supposed benefits, let's examine the empirical findings.

Professor of business strategy and entrepreneurship Michael S. Gary and colleagues (2017) found that participants who were assigned hard-to-reach or long-term goals were much more likely to abandon them and resort to smaller self-set goals or adopt survival goals when faced with threat. The study found no improvements in performance when participants committed to long-term goals, and, worse, they generated attainment discrepancies that increased their willingness to take risks, undermined goal commitment, and generated lower, risk-adjusted performance. In fact, stretch goals, operationally defined as high-effort or high-risk goals, are attained less than 10% of the time—a definition that falls in line with the fanciful nature of the more ambitious goals we're encouraged to strive for. In behavioral analysis, the technical word used to describe the detrimental effects of stretch goals is *extinction*—the loss of reinforcement for previously reinforced behavior, which kills motivation. Missed goals are missed opportunities for such reinforcement, and given how unlikely it is to accomplish a stretch goal, one can only assume that stretch goals are, by definition, engineered to create extinction. Indeed, studies suggest that when individuals repeatedly fail to reach a stretch goal, their overall performance worsens (Kerr and Landauer, 2004; Fisher et al. 2003; Chow et al. 2001).

Professor of management and organizations Lisa Ordóñez et al. (2009) argue that the beneficial effects of stretch goals have been overstated, concluding that such goals can inhibit learning, distort risk preferences, and reduce intrinsic motivation (Sitkin et al., 2011; Mossholder, 1980; Rawsthorne and Elliot, 1999; Shalley and Oldham, 1985). Why? Because managers who pursued stretch goals were unrealistically optimistic about their position in a distribution of peers on almost every positive trait or ability (MacCrimmon and Wehrung, 1986). More so, stretch goals affected executive motivation because they perceived themselves to be "low-performing" for not reaching unrealistic objectives—a matter we will revisit in coming parts. The goal-setting literature also finds that the supposed benefits of goal-setting decrease with task complexity (Earley et al., 1989; Wood et al., 1987).

Always on the back foot, never good enough, and falling behind urge one to catch up and keep up by any means necessary. Generations are now driven by a "meta-mentality"—looking to game the system in any way possible to gain a competitive edge and get ahead. We resort to "the best way" of accomplishing X, Y, or Z, ignoring what's best for our respective present selves and abandoning autonomy. Why? Because we believe that winning is more important than living, and a goal unfulfilled is a life not lived. We bear a guilt-ridden conscience if we stray from what expedites our journey to the end we've set. And while we take notice of every orangutan's public regurgitation of the well-worn maxim, "It's about the journey, not the destination," it still doesn't change the fact that we feel outpaced and outdistanced. To make matters worse, we often find ourselves working toward familiar goals, whether it's a "shredded physique," mastering an instrument, or learning a new language, whose journey and benchmarks we've acquainted ourselves with by looking up "progress videos" on YouTube or tutorials that depict the "meta." We romanticize our goal as we envision ourselves in those dedicated peoples' shoes until the rubber meets the road and we find that we are tediously living through the motions. Analogous to watching a movie from its end to its beginning, we begin to question whether the countless hours are worth the effort for a vision we've imaginatively traced and retraced beginning to end, thinking it will make us whole.

This wavering desire evokes insecurities and disappointment, as we are quick to judge our character and not the cause. How do we even know this is the goal we want? What is it based on? How much are we willing to sacrifice for what we are not certain of? Did you happen to watch a two-minute clip of a street performer attracting everyone's attention and decided that's your goal for the year? Or was it your overachieving cousin whose academic prowess wowed everyone at the family dinner? Or was it Susan's popular entrepreneurial success posts on social media? Whether your spark of committal was derived of inspiration, envy, competitiveness, or curiosity, how informed is the pursuit of the goal you are setting?

Assuming you were certain of your commitment and the meta happened to be what you intrinsically enjoyed, wouldn't a stretch goal make sense? This is, unfortunately, a conjecture negligent of the increasingly plentiful opportunities of our everchanging world. By comparison, before and up to the nineteenth century, such opportunities were relatively limited. The extent to which you were able to explore your potential or confront challenges and obstacles that changed the course of your ambitions and dreams was limited to what was accessible—*not much* in a village of a few thousand people with defined roles and days that very much looked like the next. It was an era when the Traditional Psyche's goal-setting attitude seemed to have a place. This is no longer pragmatic in an aggressively progressive world of growing complexity and increasingly accessible possibilities. Ergo, centralizing our efforts toward a singular, ill-gotten purpose restricts our ability to capitalize on emergent realizations, discoveries, and changing circumstances.

Worst of all (and paradoxically), stretch goals disregard the fact that we are changing faster than ever, a fact that we will continue to substantiate and explore as we proceed. Committing to a stretch goal *knowing* the goalpost will assuredly move is not only fruitless but self-deceptive, especially if you are thinking, "This time, it's different," or assuming yourself to be an exception, falling victim to *main character syndrome;* believing you are *the* protagonist in a fictional movie of clichéd inevitable triumph.

One may find short-lived utility in dreaming of what can be as it infiltrates one's day-to-day behavior, emotions, and conduct. It is when the means by which the goal is achieved turns sour or the goal itself is no longer desired that we find ourselves reluctantly chasing a lost cause for no other reason than to fulfill a promise and avoid the consequences of surrender . . . Commendable stoicism or misguided masochism?

Our brain regulation systems were never designed to cope with efforts so long in duration, toward goals so large, with all-or-none outcomes that offer few alternatives. It is relatively easy to give up on looking for nuts when several days of foraging have proved fruitless. Giving up on a PhD program after five years, or a marriage after ten years, are decisions orders of magnitude larger, decisions whose costs often lead individuals to persist in the pursuit of hopeless or unwanted goals, creating the exact situations that disengage motivation and cause depression.

—Randolph M. Nesse (2004), founder of Evolutionary Medicine
  and Evolutionary Psychiatry

Psychological scientists Laura A. King and Chad M. Burton (2003) suggest that goals should be used only in the narrowest of circumstances: "The optimally striving individual ought to endeavor to achieve and approach goals that only slightly implicate the self; that are only moderately important, fairly easy, and moderately abstract; that do not conflict with each other; and that concern the accomplishment of something other than financial gain."

One can argue whether what King and Burton are describing would even be considered goals. You may be thinking that "smaller goals" are the way to go, but such "goals" don't offer what stretch goals promise: enduring motivation, persistence, direction, and deeper existential authenticity. Nevertheless, I submit that we can do away with stretch goals.

I would like to make it clear, however, that I am not suggesting we get rid of goals altogether but instead redefine—reframe—our relationship with the very idea of them. We are taught to think before we act—a maxim of generally great utility. But how much thinking is enough? How much thought justifies the means to an end? Is an end ever justified? Is there an end at all? Questions to entice your curiosity, but for now, let's further explore why the twenty-first century has unveiled a plethora of emergent issues we need to grapple with, unaware that they are hindering our capacities to grow and live to our fullest potential.

CHAPTER 3
THE TWENTY-FIRST-CENTURY DILEMMA

One major obstacle to our ability to take the first step and then sustainably and consistently pursue an endeavor is the shelf-life of motivation. The mental and emotional turmoil we often face when taking on something big can inevitably turn appealing visions into hopeless ventures. Overcoming challenges requires a willingness to *face the unknown* and *put in the work*. Procrastination and giving up are always the easier alternatives. Why make life harder than it needs to be? Understanding the constraints on our ability to *act on demand* and exert ourselves productively will enable us to better address and overcome them.

The distinction between *having* depression and *feeling* depressed is a predominant source of confusion for those self-diagnosing their woes. Almost everyone feels down from time to time; regretting a decision, facing a breakup, losing a job, laboring through exam prep, and even a rainy day can bring feelings of sadness, and sometimes there is no trigger at all. Then one day, circumstances change, and those sad feelings disappear. Clinical depression, on the other hand, also referred to as Major Depressive Disorder (MDD), is different; it's a mental disorder—with visible changes in the brain such as a reduction in the volume of the frontal lobes and hippocampus—that won't go away just because you want it to. While neuroscience fails to provide a complete explanation, there does seem to be a complex integration between genes and the environment. Research results from a large number of twin studies indicate that 40% of the risk of developing depression is genetic and the remaining 60% is associated with nonshared environmental factors—such as not living in the same household or hanging around different group of friends, etc. (Middeldorp et al., 2005). These studies also suggest that continuing difficulties such as long-term unemployment, living in an abusive or uncaring relationship, long-term isolation or loneliness, prolonged work stress, substance abuse, and a personality of high neuroticism (all of which are acquired and not innate) can increase the risk of clinical depression.

Feeling depressed, younger generations confuse their temporary symptoms with MDD and are quick to blame a "loose screw" or an inexplicable genetic "chemical imbalance," when in reality what they face are the consequences of being *insufficiently challenged.*

The Cambridge Dictionary defines challenge as "something that needs great mental or physical effort in order to be done successfully and therefore tests a person's ability" (to overcome challenge). The turn of the century has privileged newer generations across the globe with unparalleled education, shelter, sustenance, and a range of opportunities for flourishing (and yes, some parts of the world haven't progressed as far as others, but would have progressed nonetheless), all of which are taken for granted as it is in our nature to acclimate and pursue higher limits. The troubles facing youth today are incomparable to those of older generations; but of course, different times, different problems.

But how many times have you heard that story of your parents' journey to school every morning when they traversed vast distances in harsh weather with tattered shoes and rabid raccoons waiting around every corner? When they were obligated to work at an early age to provide for their family of seven that lived in poverty? By definition, those generations faced challenges *we* would consider abuse—challenges that weren't a choice but necessary for survival.

I would be remiss not to acknowledge the fact that newer generations are being handed the burden of opportunistic individuals, parties, and ideologies that have egomaniacally milked and exploited rampant technological advancements for power and control. They are bearing the burden of climate change; pension crisis; inflation; pandemic preparedness; nuclear security; degradation of animal welfare; maimed economies correlated with archaic geopolitical grudges; consequences of millennia of racial, cultural, and gender-sexual discrimination; the indoctrination of the masses in backward ideologies. And while such a macrocosm of inherited debt cannot be overlooked, what we have in fact been afforded with cannot be taken for granted either. Necessitating Change concerns the individual, and that is what we will focus on for now.

Nowadays, if the youth are able to make it through school and avoid getting run over by a bus, their chances of landing a stable job and living a twenty-first-century average life are almost certain. Life's on autopilot as they go through the motions, convinced they are doing everything they can, until one day, life comes knocking on their door, asking for more—more of their time, their nerves, their capacity—to no end, with an inevitable ponderance of "Why is everything out to take advantage of me or hurt me?" As an emptiness envelops their self, they begin to question the point of it all. Melancholy sets in, anxiety follows, and the likely comorbidity of feeling depressed takes its hold.

The amygdala is a collection of nuclei found in the temporal lobe and is considered part of the limbic system—a group of structures linked to the processing of emotions. It is prominently known for being in charge of fear and threat detection, and it's responsible for what you may know of as the "fight or flight" response; less known are the other two natural bodily reactions to dangerous, frightening, or stressful events: *freeze* and *fawn*. Not too far away are the frontal lobes of the brain, with functions that include problem solving, planning, working memory, sustained attention, and more. Now, imagine being a caveman faced with a saber-toothed tiger. Contemplating escape routes and the best plan of action would get you mauled, more often than not. Instead, your heartbeat and respiration rate immediately increase to provide oxygen and energy to the body, fueling a rapid response. Your pupils dilate to become more observant and aware of your surroundings. You begin to tremble as your muscles become tense and primed for action. The amygdala overrides the functions of the frontal lobe and forces you to *act* (fight or flight response)—commonly referred to as an "amygdala hijack." Alternatively, your skin might turn pale, and you may turn stiff, cold, heavy, numb with a decreased heart rate, to suggest to a threat you are dead and not a threat yourself (freeze response), or you may start to play nice, be in over-agreement, be overly helpful, and make your primary concern that your threat is happy (fawn response). Figure 1-9 provides examples of such emotional amygdala hijack responses to perceived threats. In evolutionary terms, animals with this fight, flight, fawn, or freeze response had a better chance of survival and were therefore "naturally selected."

Now, think of that job interview, therapy session, or homework you've been avoiding. Using that caveman's instincts when faced with a sabre-toothed tiger, you will quickly realize why your mind and body respond the way that they do. Clearly, your life isn't threatened—the world won't end if things don't go the way you want—and yet you begin to act irrationally. Think of the time you argued with your significant other and said something *you knew* you shouldn't have, or perhaps you capitulated and suddenly became overly apologetic and servile. Why do these things happen? What ought to be interpreted as a challenge is instead mistaken for a threat; the fear, guilt, pain, and shame that can follow trigger your amygdala to shut down your frontal lobe and force a *reaction* as it takes matters—and our autonomy—into its own hands.

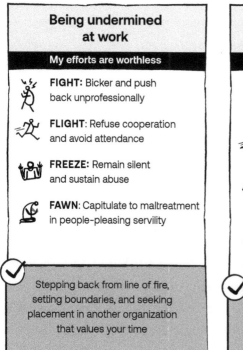

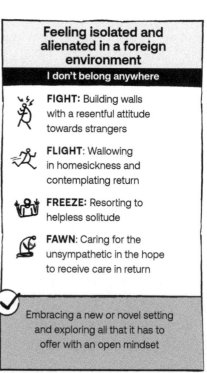

The consequences of prolonged perceived threat-induced reactionary instinct and endurance of cultivates habits of withdrawal, substance abuse, neurotic behavior, and extinction, the totality of which can cause Clinical Depression or Major Depressive Disorder (MDD)

Breaking a promise

I can never trust myself nor should anyone trust me

 FIGHT: Blaming others for your own shortcomings

 FLIGHT: Avoiding retrospection of personal development

 FREEZE: Foregoing commitment in fear of further disappointment

 FAWN: Placing emphasis on and wallowing over another's dismay

Constructively reflecting over what led to failure of commitment and setting measures to bolster self-assurance

Facing relapse of substance abuse

I'm destined to fail

 FIGHT: Projecting frustrations of strain of discipline onto others

 FLIGHT: Surrendering to further substance abuse

 FREEZE: Ruminating over justifications for further consumption

 FAWN: Appeasing urges with other forms of harmful habits

Leveraging support of specialized programs and others to address the issue pragmatically

Enduring the loss of a broken relationship

I'm undeserving of love

 FIGHT: Vilifying the opposite or same sex

 FLIGHT: Rejecting intimate and friendly relationships with others

 FREEZE: Wallowing in stagnation

 FAWN: Maintaining painful, conciliatory contact to lessen their suffering

Accepting the past, letting go, and moving on through counselling, self-empathy, and immersing oneself in the present opportunities

Failing to perform

I'll never be good enough

 FIGHT: Self-flagellation

 FLIGHT: Discontinuing the practice altogether

 FREEZE: Questioning the possibility of mastery in despondency

 FAWN: Constantly apologizing in regret

Assessing conduct, identifying areas for improvement, and setting sustainable action plans for further development

Figure 1-9: Fight, flight, freeze, and fawn emotional "amygdala hijack" responses to threats

Compounding the problem, becoming reactionary to hypersensitive threat detection as opposed to remaining calm, collected, and solution-oriented deprives us of opportunities to grow and mature. Challenge removes us from our "normal" selves and puts us into a state of focus—a space independent from who we think we are and our primitive nature of reacting impulsively. A space in which desire manifests itself. A space primed for growth without the biases that hinder our ability to go beyond what we already know. If you have ever felt like you were "in the zone" or "in the flow" when studying, performing, or taking part in any activity, your frontal lobes would have been fully engaged. If we are not challenged, we are not growing. The Industrial Revolution and the exponential nature of technological advances may have propelled the human species beyond its primitive evolutionary environment, but we are still at the mercy of our amygdala's sensitivities. What once ensured our survival is now threatening our livelihood and needs to be tamed.

This point becomes increasingly apparent in the process of overindulging—or spoiling—children. Researchers at the Overindulgence Project identified three types of overindulgences:

▲ Too much:

too many toys, privileges, clothes, entertainment options

▲ Overnurturing:

providing too much attention, doing their homework, rescuing them from uncomfortable emotions

▲ Soft structure:

not requiring chores, not enforcing rules (if there are any), not expecting children to perform

A study found that overindulgence led to poor self-control, a sense of entitlement and ungratefulness, overspending, goals of wealth and fame, preoccupation with image, disinterest in personal growth, irresponsibility, an inability to determine how much is enough, a need for immediate gratification, and much more (Bredehoft et al., 2002). Suffice to say, when these individuals grow up to be confronted with too little, undernurturing, hard structures, or, say, a stretch goal, you can imagine how their threat detectors would light up.

This pattern continues through schooling in the form of leniency (Blake, 2013) and lowered standards and "passing grade" thresholds (Lawton, 2015; Sheppard, 2017). Some regressive elements of First World nations are looking to eliminate standardized tests altogether (Williams, 2021). "Participation awards"—awarding participants of a competitive event just for being there, even if they do not win a place on the podium—are especially controversial. Many believe they hinder child development by teaching children the wrong life lessons, for example, indoctrinating them into believing that winning (competition) isn't important and showing up is all that matters. Social and developmental psychologists Carol S. Dweck and Claudia M. Mueller (1998) reviewed six studies to assess how different types of praise affected a child's willingness to challenge themselves and perform. Their analysis showed that children who were praised for their efforts (as opposed to their performance) tended to believe that intelligence is something that could be improved — *and they strived to do so*. It's worth clarifying that the efforts they refer to are *efforts* to do their best as opposed to simply "showing up" for stickers and trophies. Conversely, children who were praised for being smart were found to be more performance focused. This resulted in them displaying "less task persistence, less task enjoyment, more low-ability attributions, and worse task performance."

Another study found that children's schoolwork suffers when parents either over- or underpraise their performance—which also predicted higher rates of depression (Lee et al., 2016). By comparison, children whose parents provided accurate or slightly exaggerated praise saw the most beneficial results. This suggests several important realizations and reaffirmations. Children who were praised for their efforts and not their performance—in other words, rewarding the *relative* undertaking of a challenge regardless of whether they won or not—resulted in a willingness to further improve. These results also suggest that there is a place for participation awards. However, they shouldn't be one-size-fits-all or used to reward substandard accomplishments in the hopes of protecting a child's emotions—which would further deprive them of the benefits of being challenged.

We see further sheltering from challenge and the cultivation of fragility through a postmodern narrative that is best described as "What doesn't kill you makes you weaker" by social psychologists Jonathan Haidt and Greg Lukianoff in their book, *The Coddling of the American Mind*. Referring to "trigger warnings" and "safe spaces" as safeguarding based on "bad psychology," Haidt and Lukianoff write, "Avoiding triggers is a symptom of posttraumatic stress disorder (PTSD), not a treatment for it." They suggest that systematically avoiding discomfort is antithetical to the goals and process of cognitive behavior therapy (CBT)—one of the most effective treatments for a range of mental and emotional health issues. Which is to say, the best way to get over trauma, phobia, or PTSD (or challenge) is to face those reminders or triggers in a graduated, systematic, desensitizing way through "associative learning," a process similar to what you may know as *Pavlovian conditioning*.

A matter that may hit closer to home is social media and its consistent degradation of one's social faculties. Gone are the days when the only option for pursuing a potential mate was to literally meet them in person, usually in a place where others were watching (and perhaps judging), and then to blurt out a string of incomprehensible utterings that may or may not have lead to something more, if you managed not to throw up. We're talking about a blind, reckless, but brave attempt at not making a mockery of yourself, whether at school, a party, a mall, or a wedding. Now, it's a few weeks of chitchatting on Facebook, hinting at your status through Snapchat, or stalking issues she's interested in through her social media posts. Compare that to what is learned through more traditional social exchanges and adversity: social and emotional intelligence, conflict resolution, spatial awareness, confidence, initiative, courage, pride, and self-respect. Imagine navigating a professional environment or a relationship—or even self-perception—without these social faculties.

To make things even worse, this benign plight of challenge restriction comes benevolently disguised as social security programs and social welfare payments to those incapable or "at risk" such as retirees, the unemployed, families, caregivers, parents, and the disabled. If we were to explore the effects of such programs on those who are *willingly* unemployed and/or have treatable or manageable problems, one could speculate whether the extension of such safety nets is backfiring. What motivation will you have to solve your problems when you know you will always have a bonus plan B to lean on?

Upon graduating into independence and voyaging away from the comfort of "home," the insufficiently challenged are met with an ocean of challenges. Wave after wave crashes over them: remaining entertained, earning their privileges, being loved, doing their duties, dealing with their emotions, confronting conflict, abiding by the rules, performing competently, getting chores done, making sense of suffering, and so on. For many, it's too much to bear. Over time, they grow exhausted, weepy, easily irritated, overwhelmed by simple tasks, beyond the sympathetic understanding of others. The weight of the world paints every constructive challenge as a threat, discouraging pursuit of what tests one's abilities out of fear of facing yet another threat. The prolonged totality of such ordeals, as well as the increased tendencies toward substance abuse, neurotic behavior, and extinction (no reinforcement for previously reinforced behavior such as striving to be better, seeking to meet new people) can ultimately lead to clinical depression (Better Health Channel, 2012), necessitating medical and psychiatric intervention.

As a result, you can end up in an oxymoronic utopian dystopia of ubiquitous opportunity *and* suffering. Australian wine producers, for example, openly admit they rely heavily on backpackers—earning $250 a day—to pick their fruit (Carswell and Michael, 2015). They struggle to attract youth from the cities despite unemployment in Western Sydney peaking at 17%. The former chairman of Hunter Valley Wine Industry Association's viticulture committee, Ken Bray, blames social security, stating, "The problem is, our unemployed don't have to work. It's too easy for them; plus a lot of them come with baggage—real problems. They are too reliant on welfare and don't want to go where the jobs are."

In October 2016, 35,576 Australians perfectly capable of working refused suitable jobs. Out of these, some refused a job offer outright while others accepted the job but never turned up for work. For those who showed up, more than 22,000 quit their new job without a good reason to go back on unemployment payments. Whether social welfare cultivates indifference, however, is not in question. A study conducted by MIT and Harvard of seven welfare programs in Latin America, Southeast Asia, and Morocco suggested that welfare doesn't promote laziness (Banerjee et al., 2015). This question is the status quo and the ease with which we live, piggybacking from one safety net to another, sufficiently sheltered from challenge. The MIT and Harvard study's gauge of "success" was the number of hours worked per week. It didn't consider how participants' long-term social and mental well-being would be affected by the absence of challenges.

All that said, I'm not saying that social security for the *capable* does more harm than good. Circumstances vary and opportunities may be limited. Unfortunately, tradition, culture, and twenty-first-century privileges have not only starved youth of challenge but government-subsidized programs have facilitated "soft structure" paradigms for those *without* a permanent disability or disadvantage. This in turn curbs the urgent necessity of intrinsic contrived motivation, which further hinders their ability and willingness to grow and manage their biological shortcomings: their untrained amygdala; physical/emotional/personality differences and disorders; and all the confusion, ambiguity, and suffering a human life is bound to.

I resort to the words of a notoriously influential contrarian—a beau ideal of the public intellectual who harbors qualities we ought to strive for:

In life we make progress by conflict and in mental life by argument and disputation. The concept of the dialectic may well have been partly discredited by its advocates, but that does not permit us to disown it. There must be confrontation and opposition in order that sparks may be kindled.

—Cristopher Hitchens, *Letters to a Young Contrarian*

Learning to manage and control your amygdala's impulses does not necessarily involve pain, suffering, or some innate quality you may feel deprived of, but incremental practice you may have been benignly and systematically denied, ignorant of, or avoided. How many true mental, physical, and spiritual challenges have you willfully and independently overcome, and how many have you had the luxury of circumventing by having your hand held?

While the privileges of modernity and uninformed parenting can make for emergent issues of autonomy, lingering Traditional Psyche attitudes further impede our ability to adapt to an increasingly competitive world of ample opportunity. How many Traditional Psyche–derived excuses have you uninformedly resorted to in denying yourself autonomy of progression?

CHAPTER 4
SELF-LIMITING RELUCTANCY

We are often inclined to shy away from pursuing practices we assume will require traits we believe we don't or *cannot* possess. We are often quick to disparage our potential—for example, claiming an inferiority of "talent" or "genetics" compared to the *competition* to justify a failure of commitment, even while taking interest in what could possibly be a fulfilling practice. The "talent myth" is built on the idea that "innate ability" rather than practice is what ultimately dictates whether we have it within us to achieve competence, let alone supremacy. This Traditional Psyche's conniving idea robs individuals of control and the incentive to transform themselves through effort. Why spend time and energy when success is only available to people with the right genes?

Here are some excuses you may have recently heard or made yourself:

▲ "If I can't even maintain eye contact, how do you expect me to introduce myself to strangers and hold a conversation?"

▲ "Argh, let's order food online. I can't cook to save my life!"

▲ "Nah, I have weak knees. It runs in the family."

▲ "I'd love to give it a shot, but my hand-eye coordination is terrible."

▲ "I'm just not good at expressing myself. I can't articulate as well as other people."

▲ "I can't do anything about this stutter. I've had it for as long a-a-as I can remember."

▲ "I'm just not good at math; never have been!"

▲ "I can't help getting anxious during presentations as I always make a fool out of myself."

▲ "I'm far too old to start anything new."

I'm sure you can think of plenty more, and I'm willing to bet that your eyebrow is raised or you've taken offense, as some may have struck a familiar nerve. For each of the excuses listed, how many hours do you think these individuals actually spent trying to do something about it? How much of what and whom they surround themselves with have they considered to be detrimental or a causal factor of perceived deficiencies? How many experts have they consulted to improve on their self-proclaimed shortcomings? How far are they from believing that it doesn't have to be that way, that these issues can be dealt with, that the best orators, debaters, and presenters in the world were terrible at presenting, faced anxiety, and/or suffered a distracting quirk? That the best comedians got booed off stage dozens of times before earning a chuckle from the crowd? That the most resilient marathon runners couldn't manage a mile without stopping a few times along the way? That the best physicists were told they would never amount to anything when they grew up? That in leaving the war a captain and returning as a private and failing multiple business ventures, there was no way such a person would ascend the presidency? These are the accounts of Steve Jobs, Jerry Seinfeld, David Goggins, Albert Einstein, and Abraham Lincoln, respectively.

What natural aptitude *is* and *isn't* and how significant a role it plays in achievement is yet another concept woefully taught and sometimes neglected in schools. Many believe it's what sets one apart from the rest regardless of how much—or how little—training one has had. This lack of awareness has discouraged generations from believing in commitment and determination, causing them to give up before they even started. Think of the children you grew up with—that musically "talented" boy or the girl who was a mathematical "genius." There would have been a mutual consensus amongst the class that these kids were "special," and maybe it bothered you: "Why can't I be special too?" Little did you know that they spent countless hours every day and after school practicing, learning, and getting tutored, whether it was forced or out of interest.

In search of an answer, let's consider the vast body of scientific inquiry regarding natural aptitude. We begin by examining the work of psychologist K. Anders Ericsson. He conducted an extensive investigation involving several studies into the causes of outstanding performance, one of which involved three groups of children with different proficiencies in the violin, nominated by music professors at the Music Academy of West Berlin. The first group was composed of the outstanding students—those expected to become future soloists. Members of the second group were good enough to be parts of top orchestras but not soloists. Children in the third group were the least able, those who were undertaking a course to become musical teachers, which had far less onerous admission standards. The ability of each group was assessed by professors and by objective measures.

After a set of interviews, Ericsson found that that the biographical histories of the three groups were very similar and showed no systematic differences except one: a dramatic difference in the number of hours devoted to serious practice. The first group would have averaged around ten thousand hours of serious practice by the age of twenty; the second group, eight thousand hours; and the third group, four thousand hours. Ericsson also found that there were no exceptions to this finding. Top performers had learned no faster than those who only reached lower levels of attainment. Hour by hour, they improved at almost identical rates. The only difference was that top performers practiced more hours. Figure 1-10 illustrates this phenomenon as increasing levels of violinists expertise are directly correlated with the amount of time spent practicing.

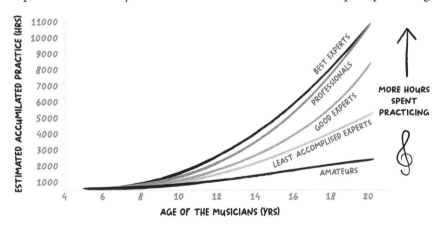

Figure 1-10: Practice and level of violinist expertise. Adapted from Ericsson et al. (2007)

You may wonder if this was only true in music and not in other fields of practice, but from art (Lehmann, 1953) and science (Simonton, 1988) to swimming (Kalinowski, 1985), tennis (Monsaas, 1985), long-distance running (Wallingford, 1975), and mathematics (Gustin, 1985), and even from the accounts of those willing to personally put it to the test, such as educational psychologist László Polgár, who raised all three of his daughters to play chess every day—all of whom ultimately became chess prodigies and grand masters—you will find that the "ten years–ten thousand hours" rule to reach world class status holds true. Like Ericsson and other psychologists of similar conviction, Polgár believed that "geniuses are not born, they are made" ("New documentary on the Polgár family," 2012).

OPPOSITION

The question of "nature versus nurture" has been an age-old debate. The findings of Ericsson and his fellow anti-natural-aptitude proponents contradict mainstream consensus, and as you would imagine, received a fair share of criticism (Sternberg, 1996; Anderson, 2000; Marcus, 2012; just to name a few). Award-winning educational psychologist Françoys Gagné—a particularly barbed academic critic (Gagné, 2007)—referred to the mainstream position of attributing significant natural impact to talent development as *Pronats* (pro-natural) and those who hold a strong opposition to naturalness (primarily two groups of scholars: Howe et al., 1998, and Ericsson et al., 2005) as *Antinats* (anti-natural). Gagné draws a distinction between talent and *giftedness* by referring to talent as "outstanding achievements" (with an emphasis on performance and achievement driven by *developed* competencies) and giftedness as "outstanding potentialities" (with an emphasis on potential and aptitude driven by *natural* abilities). In other words, the gifted are born with high talent potential, but the potential isn't realized without practice. For example, gifted but underachieving students have the intellect but are not *academically* talented—for reasons to do with how little time they have invested studying, researching, practicing, etc. (whereby intellect is the best domain that predicts academic achievement).

The use of the word "talent" from this point on will refer to "developed competencies" as opposed to how most interpret it: giftedness. Reference to its common use and interpretation will be indicated using quotation marks.

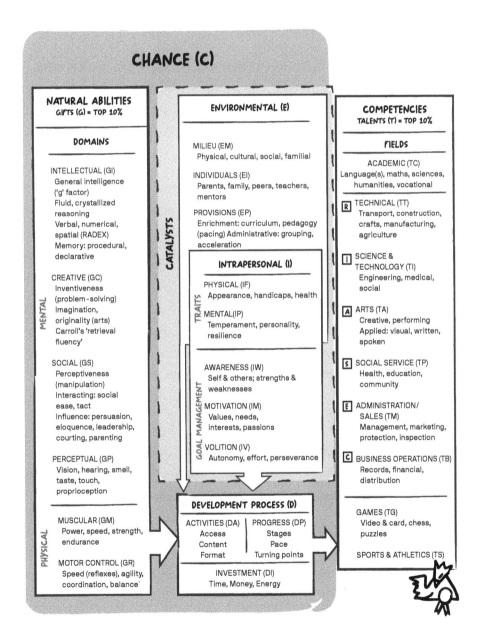

Figure 1-11: DMGT (Differentiating Model of Giftedness and Talent)
Adapted from Gagné (2010)

Gagné spent over thirty-five years developing his rigorous Differentiating Model of Giftedness and Talent (DMGT) (see figure 1-11) (which guides the Australian education department's policies on giftedness) that explains the causal influences that determine talent development (Gagné, 2010). What is not self-explanatory in figure 1-11 and requires elaboration is as follows:

▲ Gagné refers to the main causal influences as *components* (such as natural abilities or environmental components), which are broken up into their constituent parts, referred to as *subcomponents* (such as milieu, individuals, and provisions), which then constitute their own subcomponents, referred to as *facets* (such as physical, cultural, and social).

▲ The environmental subcomponents refer to the social environment (such as cultural expectations or household rules and structure), significant individuals (such as supportive peers or uneducated parents), and environmental "provision" (such as a talented group of friends or an effective school curriculum).

▲ Notice the overlap between the environmental and interpersonal components, indicating that the environmental component influences the intrapersonal component. For example, a passionate teacher (an individual) may invoke interest (motivation) that influences the development process for a given field. These two components are appropriately referred to as catalysts of the development process.

▲ There are literally hundreds of practices (what Gagné refers to as fields) to become talented in and six natural attributes (what Gagné refers to as domains) whose respective potentialities have genetic foundations.

▲ The shaded background refers to what Gagné suggests is out of our control and left to chance. For example, we don't choose our culture, neighborhood, or which kindergarten our parents enroll us in.

▲ The natural abilities, environmental, and intrapersonal components all causally influence the development process which determines competency in a given field:

▽ Talent development begins when a child or adult gains access (the first facet of the Activities subcomponent) through identification or selection to a program of activities (that involve particular content of a particular format—the other two facets), such as being accepted into a university.

▽ The progress of talentees from initial access to peak performance can be broken down into stages (the first facet of the Progress subcomponent—novice, advanced, proficient, expert). How fast the talentee progresses relative to others is referred to as pace. Finally, the course of the endeavor is marked with turning points (for example, being spotted by a coach or having a career-ending injury).

▲ Gagné states that natural abilities are not, by definition, innate—"Natural abilities need to develop progressively, in large part during a person's younger years; but they will do so spontaneously, without the structured learning and training activities typical of the talent development process" (Gagné, 2013a). In fact, he originally defines giftedness as "the possession and use of untrained and spontaneously expressed outstanding natural abilities or aptitudes (called gifts) in at least one ability domain, to a degree that places an individual at least among the top 10% of age peers" (Gagné, 2010). He refers to spontaneous learning as "acquired mostly subconsciously, that is, with little attention to its growth from day to day, or week to week." For example, when a parent assists their child with a problem from an activity that was unplanned.

While Gagné insists that natural abilities are developed, how they are developed has genetic foundations (what Gagné sees to be almost totally innate) that give rise to complex anatomical and physiological phenotypes (characteristics of an individual resulting from the interaction of its genetics with the environment—that are somewhat innate). These, in tandem with environmental and intrapersonal influences as well as maturation and informal learning, influence the development of natural abilities.

▲ Gagné uses a five-level bell curve classification (see figure 1-12) to differentiate levels of aptitudes and competencies. It is why he places the "gifted" among the top 10% of age peers as well as those who have systematically developed competency to a degree that qualifies them as "talented."

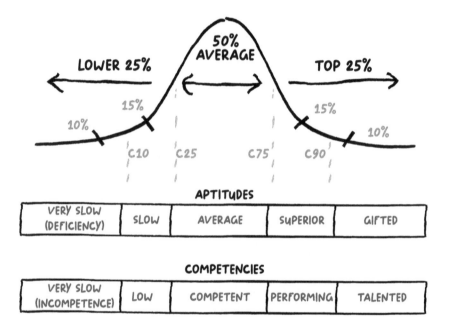

Figure 1-12: Five-level classification system
Adapted from Gagné (n.d.)

▲ Notice the language used to describe those with aptitude deficiency—very slow, as it is superior progression of talent development arising from natural abilities that Pronats credit the gifted with.

▲ "Individuals with natural abilities below the gifted level could still reach talent-level attainments through strong inputs from intrapersonal and/ or environmental catalysts, as well as from the development process itself (amount and intensity of learning and practice)" (Gagné, 2013b). Figure 1-13 illustrates how two individuals with the same level of competencies (talent development) could have achieved it differently. Emphasizing the caveat, he suggests, "This moderate relationship between gifts and talents also means that gifts can remain undeveloped, as witnessed by the well-known phenomenon of academic underachievement among intellectually gifted children. The causal components usually act through the development process, facilitating or hindering the learning activities and thus the performance."

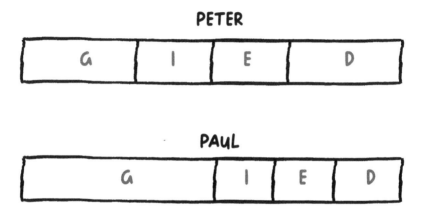

Figure 1-13: Talent development discrepancies of influence
Adapted from DMGT on YouTube (n.d.)

▲ Gagné's own review of existing literature brought him to propose the following hierarchy: Natural abilities, interpersonal influences, development process, and environmental influences (Gagné, 2010).

However, he ascribes a "moderate" predictive power of gifts as contributors to talent emergence given the catalytic nature of the environmental and intrapersonal components.

It is worth noting that Gagné transformed his framework to the "Expanded Model of Talent Development" (EMTD) (Gagné, 2013a). This expansion involved the addition of more columns to the figure to better depict the components that influence the development of natural abilities. The overarching concepts remain unchanged, however, so we will stick with the original DMGT to keep things relatively simple.

A STALEMATE

Empirical evidence exists to support causal interactions between any pairing of the five subcomponents in Gagné's model and in both directions. But as we have seen, significant evidence exists to suggest that practice plays an overwhelmingly significant role (or for some Antinats, such as Anne Anastasi, one of the past century's most prominent experts in psychometrics, *the only role*, going so far to suggest that the word "aptitude" be excised from psychology's vocabulary (Anastasi, 1980)). Pronats such as Gagné, on the other hand, like to regularly quote John W. Atkinson, a pioneer of the scientific study of human motivation, achievement, and behavior, to assert their position: "All human accomplishments can be ascribed to two crucial 'rolls of the dice': the accidents of birth and background."

Pronats insist there are upper limits of natural ability (Galton, 2006; Colangelo et al., 2001; Jensen, 2002); Antinats argue that accounts of the seemingly naturally gifted are in fact "perceived talent." An example of this is best represented in Robert H. Frank's book *Success and Luck: Good Fortune and the Myth of Meritocracy*. If you asked a professional hockey player what it took for them to reach the NHL, they would mention their coach's determination, their parents, and their own hard work, but they wouldn't mention the fact that they were born in January. Social, personality, and evolutionary psychologist Robert O. Deaner et al. (2013) found that 36% of all hockey players selected for top-tier leagues between 1980 and 2007 were born in the first quarter of the year compared to 14.5% in the fourth quarter— more than double the likelihood of being selected! (See figure 1-14.) The reason may be that the cut-off date for kids' hockey leagues is January 1, which means that children born earlier in the year would be older, faster, and stronger compared to those born later in the year. You would expect this disparity to dissipate over time, but kids that show the most promise are entered into more tournaments, given more time on the ice, and receive better coaching to grow their skills—and are therefore perceived as "talented." Antinats also point to massive historical changes in the highest levels of performance in other domains (Ericsson et al., 2007) to rebut arguments for varying upper limits of natural abilities.

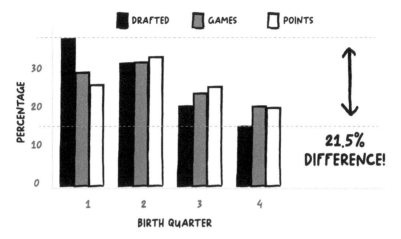

Figure 1-14: Perceived talent in hockey players
Adapted from Deaner et al. (2013)

In fact, Antinats deny that there is *any* appropriate way to measure a person's potentialities. The Pronats, for example, point to the predictive power of IQ for job performance and to physiological and metabolic characteristics for athletic performance. While many Antinats grant the existence of *fixed* physical genetic factors such as those determining body size and height to be an "innate advantage" (as opposed to dynamic body systems such as musculoskeletal, cardiovascular, respiratory, nervous, etc. that were found to only have a moderate genetic component (Malina and Bouchard, 1986; Guth and Roth, 2013)), they question any correlation of such factors to performance and point to systematic and socioeconomic causes that subject people to poor environmental, intrapersonal, and development conditions as playing a greater role in those findings.

As the celebrated rebel of evolutionary biology, paleontologist Stephen J. Gould, said in an interview regarding the nature-nurture controversy on IQ in 1995: "When faced with something very complex, we have a terrible tendency at trying to make things simple, to try and get a single number . . . There is no number that could capture the quality of mind."

What really added fuel to the flame of this debate was the debut of journalist Malcolm Gladwell's 2008 book, *Outliers*, that was largely based off on Ericsson's findings. It topped both the *New York Times* bestseller list in the

United States and the *Globe and Mail* list in Canada in 2008, holding the position on the former for eleven consecutive weeks. Between June 2011, when the paperback version was released, and February 2017, the book made the *New York Times* bestseller list for paperback nonfiction 232 times.

The growing popularity of "deliberate practice" (practice that is effortful in nature with the main goal of personal improvement rather than enjoyment) and nurture over nature in talent development sparked a meta-analysis of eighty-eight studies, which found that practice accounted for an average of only 12% of individual differences observed in performance across various domains (Macnamara et al., 2014). It wasn't long before Ericsson fired back, criticizing their definition of deliberate practice and questioning the criteria the data was based on. His re-analysis estimated that practice explained considerably *more* variance in performance, specifically 29% and 61% after attenuation correction (Ericsson and Harwell, 2019). They faulted the meta-analysis for overstating the importance of *quantity* of practice and not taking into consideration *quality* of practice. For example, given a task that can be repeated in similar circumstances with static rules and contextual implication (such as pressures to perform), anyone can attain a statistically comparable quality of performance compared to another. So, just because I invest ten thousand hours practicing chess doesn't mean I will be equally "talented" compared to someone who's invested the same amount of time. The original ten thousand–hour rule started with chess in the 1960s when researchers were unable to find grand masters who had invested less than ten thousand hours—roughly ten years (Simon and Chase, 1973). What changed? Online chess learning was far more efficient, while publicly available tutorials, cheat sheets, and videos accelerated the learning process. The saga lives on . . .

Both fronts present a respectable slew of evidence. Both fronts legitimately question the relevancy, interpretations, and validity of the other. Both fronts arguably pull to their respective extremities. As Gagné suggests of causal influences of talent development: "They all interact with one another and with the development processes in very complex ways; and these interaction patterns will differ significantly from one person to the next, as well as at different stages of that process." Alas, the question of nature versus nurture may never be definitively answered.

IGNORANCE UNRAVELED

Don't let this lack of certainty dishearten you, however! There is still much practical wisdom to extrapolate from these decades of research and inconclusive debates.

1. **The Critical Period overlooked:**

   A causal influence I believe to be understated and oftentimes overlooked is, in developmental biology, called *exuberant synaptogenesis*. When a baby is born, they have few synapses (connections between neurons in the brain), but by age 2–3, they will have twice as many as they will have as an adult. Synapses will continue to proliferate until ages 7–9 and then gradually fall until one is in their twenties (Petanjek et al., 2011). What's more, a study has shown that the *organization* of these connections also changes upon maturing. Instead of having networks made of brain regions that are functionally linked but distant from each other, the regions of a child's brain are tightly interconnected (Fair et al., 2009). This is why infants exhibit spongelike studiousness as the plasticity of their neural pathways have yet to establish separate "special nodes" or regions that reduce the number of steps that have to be taken when processing new information.

   Exuberant synaptogenesis is particularly important during an infant's critical maturational stage when its nervous system is especially sensitive to environmental stimuli, to learn a skill or trait, for example (Drachman, 2005). This is a developmental period of *synaptic pruning*—the process of eliminating/weakening irrelevant and inefficient synapses, which is viewed as a learning mechanism (Craik and Bialystok, 2006). Your body will prune or remove a synapse if it's not receiving enough environmental stimuli, because it assumes it doesn't need it to improve efficiency (efficient highways of connections instead of interconnected local clusters). In other words, it follows a "use it or lose it" principle. For example, constant environmental stimulation of motor skills as an infant (getting them to kick a ball around as opposed to playing with touch screen tablets) will cause particular synapses that influence muscular strength and coordination to grow and avoid pruning, making it an opportune time to capitalize on teaching correct technique/movement/skills for a particular field. (See figure 1-15.)

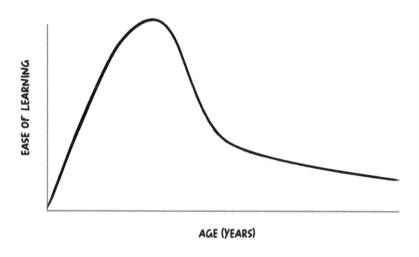

Figure 1-15: Critical period development curve

While Gagné does mention maturation to be a causal influence from birth to young adulthood or adolescence, he does not seem to acknowledge or give credence to the significance of environmental influence during an individual's critical period toward talent development: "These maturational processes have nothing to do, directly of course, with the talent development process; they mold the natural abilities that will become, in turn, the building blocks of talents" (Gagné, 2013a).

The Critical Period is another factor that can be mistaken for perceived talent. The age at which a child is regularly exposed to a given stimuli or practice (catalyzed by environmental influences, like parents) plays a larger, if not the most important, role to not only developing specific natural abilities *but to talent development itself.* The accounts of gifted exceptions that Pronats present and claim cannot be explained by deliberate practice or quality of practice *can* be explained by the alignment of optimal environmental influences and practice during the critical period. For example, Gagné demanded an explanation for violinist Sarah Chang, who began her violin studies at age four and promptly enrolled in the Juilliard School of Music, where she studied with the late Dorothy DeLay. Within a year, she had already performed with several orchestras in the Philadelphia area (Gagné, 2007).

2. No upper limit:

Gagné identified "ease and speed in learning as the trademarks of giftedness" and suggested that one can achieve a level of talent that rivals those
who are gifted. This suggests no upper limit to talent development besides
limitations influenced by fixed physical genetic factors. And just because
someone is gifted doesn't mean their potentialities will be realized. Nor
does it mean anyone with "very slow" or "deficient" aptitudes cannot
rival the accomplishments of the gifted. This is because environmental,
interpersonal, and development process components catalyze talent
development—as Gagné illustrates how the same level of competencies
can be achieved differently. (See figure 1-13.)

3. The role of chance:

Apart from fixed genetic factors, the remaining influences on developing
a given practice/field are controllable upon maturing into independence
or gaining sufficient control and freedom. Who and what we surround
ourselves with, for example, whether it's an ideal milieu of people, provisions, and activities or something less so, is a subject matter we will return
to. For the moment, it's worth appreciating our autonomy of control over
the influences we permit, forbid, and attract.

4. Giftedness misunderstood:

With shortening attention spans, clickbait headlines like "Sorry, Folks:
Study Says Musical Talent Mostly Comes from Your Genes" (Fingas, 2014)
or "Your Success Is Shaped by Your Genes" (Beard, 2017) lead us to believe
a disappointing fallacy. Given the effects of *anchoring bias* (the tendency
to rely too heavily or to "anchor" on the first piece of information acquired
on a given subject), the parroting of vernacular such as destiny or fate,
and curriculums (ACARA, 2021) that carelessly project the idea of "talent"
or "giftedness" without a second thought as to whether their true significance is being communicated effectively or not, you can only imagine
how quickly misleading exaggerations spread.

Consider *availability bias*—the tendency to draw conclusions and
create beliefs based on information that is most readily available and that
you are regularly subject to, and the majority's inclination to justify their

mediocracy such as by uninvolved parents, incompetent teachers, or simple indolence. You end up with a perpetual machine of misguidedness fomenting the assumption that anyone who excels must have a substantial unfair and unattainable *innate* advantage—yet another Traditional Psyche attitude.

Gagné himself expressed his frustration of such misconceptions by stating: "In another context, that same 'innate' label made me literally gnash my teeth. It came from its frequent use by well-intentioned fans of the DMGT and other presenters of the theory to describe the DMGT's gifts. They were comparing gifts and talents in terms of innate as opposed to acquired, in my view a clear misunderstanding of the DMGT's gifted-ness construct" (Gagné, 2013a).

5. Quality of practice understated:

Ericsson describes "deliberate practice" as being effortful in nature with a main goal of improving performance rather than enjoyment. In other words, mere experience, if not matched by deep concentration (which somewhat corresponds with Gagné's energy facet), does not necessarily lead to talent. This suggests a constant need for challenge, active learning, and reflection. When playing basketball, for example, one actively and attentively attempts to improve their free throw percentage by studying the angle at which the ball is released, the posture, the stance, and so on.

Quality of training is another causal influence often disguised as perceived talent—perceived by the public as an accelerated innate ability to achieve mastery. Quality of training involves (but is not limited to) the following:

▲ Ever-improving and more efficient training techniques with different technologies

▲ Proactively identifying areas of weakness and working on them

▲ Consulting others "ahead of the game" and leveraging their insights

▲ Harboring a growth mindset derived from intrinsic motivation and cultivated through changes of training routine, location, and instructor

▲ Investing time into auxiliary practices (different forms of fitness training, whether it be endurance or explosive workouts mixed with cognitive reaction training, or researching strategic theory to bolster your basketball performance)

6. Innateness overstated:

Given the body of evidence supporting the influential significance of deliberate practice (both quality and quantity), the lack of its emphasis by Pronats, the understated impact of environmental influence during the critical period of talent development, and the role of chance, one can only notice how diluted the influence of *innateness* becomes: to the point of insignificance or very little causal effect in the grand scheme of things.

> **If people knew how hard I had to work to gain my mastery, it would not seem so wonderful at all.**
>
> —Michelangelo, *The Instructor, vol. 39*

And if there is still any room for doubt, you may be under the following delusions:

▲ **You are reluctant or refuse to pursue anything that won't lead you to the cusp of competitive achievement because you *strongly suspect* or have come to realize (perhaps through sufficient experience) that you may not be particularly gifted in said pursuit's relevant domain.**

Assuming you are driven by intrinsic motivation, self-set aspirations, and/or genuine interest and love for competition or commercial/professional success but still resist, you might want to consider how well you fared in the environmental, intrapersonal, and developmental subcomponent-roulette. The question that naturally follows, then: What are the chances that the gifted top 10% were lucky enough to be born with the optimal environmental, intrapersonal, *and* development process components for the field *you* take interest in?

Yes, everyone *can* put in the hours of quantity and quality of practice, but not everyone will—including those genetically predisposed to having an edge in pace of progression. The next time you see a person demonstrating exceptional talent, recognize that they've almost certainly been raised practicing it, spent more time training, or enjoyed a superior-quality training regimen. Should you go through the same motions, you would eventually look, feel, and perform almost or just as well or even better! And if this isn't enough to convince you, ask them yourself! As the saying goes, "Medals are won in training, and tournaments are where you pick them up."

With all that said, it is common among populations harboring a Traditional Psyche and capitulating to evolutionary inclinations to become trapped in a systematic misapprehension of what, why, when, how, and with whom they should be doing things while striving to be the big fish, the head honcho, "number one." Whether it's blindly committing to a long-term pursuit with little to no understanding of themselves, assuming unchanging desires, romanticizing outcomes, becoming distracted by and/or longing for celebrity status and the validation of others, or always feeling on the backfoot, they uniformly set themselves up for certain gloom.

As we learned, focusing solely on winning (performance) leads to "less task persistence, less task enjoyment, more low-ability attributions, and worse task performance" (Lee et al., 2016). Some examples include:

▽ **Rushing** and not paying attention to constructive details, resulting in oversights and mistakes.

▽ **Harboring a "sore loser" attitude**, never enjoying the experience, focusing only on the win; being less willing to build productive relationships and leverage camaraderie; blaming and complaining as opposed to reflecting and growing.

▽ **Stressing** about losing, which discourages consistent participation or practice. Why risk a loss going after a win? A loss would damage self-esteem and future performance.

To make matters worse, the fabric of capitalistic society itself is systematized to favor "winners" while its propagators remain ignorant of what the development of talent supremacy actually involves. It's a toxic seed implanted by a hard-structured social, cultural, or household upbringing involving implacable demands, bullying, and punishment should one stray from religiously slaving to extrinsic selfish and apathetic expectations—to make *others* whose acceptance they are desperate for "proud." Children by the millions are forced into such regimes and/or deprived of developmental catalysts and ordered to excel anyway. Parents are quick to either shame or gaslight their children for not eventuating into superstars, or they blame the school. Instead, they should center their attention on providing the best causal influences they can manage, such as leading by example and role-modeling good habits, a healthy attitude, and virtuous values; immersing the family in a supportive community; and investing in a decent education with passionate teachers.

Instead, many parents argue, bicker, and road-rage in front of their children and then are shocked to hear that their little angels spent the day in detention for bullying kids at school. These parents are often glued to their TV screens or mobile phones, dismissive of self-growth or doing anything beyond the same job they've slaved at for decades. They don't study or upskill themselves out of curiosity or passion. They haven't found or shown excitement for sources of new knowledge. They often exhibit restrictive, oppressive attitudes and don't understand when their growing children aren't family-oriented and have no intention of maintaining a close relationship. How can they be surprised when their kids don't take interest in schoolwork or aren't filling up their time with constructive forms of leisure or productive hobbies?

This toxic seed of "existential winning"—an attitude of "I am either the best or a disappointment"—will flourish into provisional motivation and eventuate into everlasting imposter syndrome. The pursuit of self-fulfillment can only begin upon the uprooting of such limiting conditions. Recognize that the only reason you enjoy and are motivated to pursue endeavors that entail "winning"—rather than simply "participating" and immersing yourself in joyous and autonomously driven motives—is simply a consequence of old, bad habits. And as we know too well, old habits die hard. Rest assured, though, burying bad habits is a matter we will return to with a vengeance and a method.

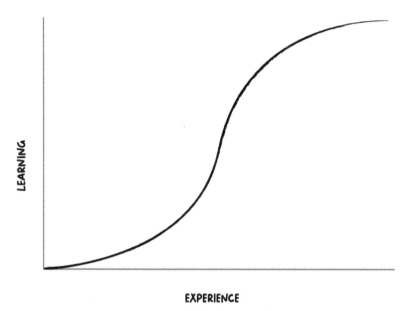

Figure 1-16: Sigmoid learning curve

In any case, you may very well be on your way to entering a competitive field and either planning out your tertiary education or questioning a practice you have committed yourself to excelling at. If so, allow me to present an idea worth considering using a typical learning curve. (See figure 1-16.)

With slowly accumulating small steps of progression at first and a plateauing of expertise toward mastery, the number of repetitions it will take to advance one more unit along the X-axis is greater than the total number of repetitions completed so far as represented in the Y-axis. In other words, proficiency increases rapidly at first, but at later stages, there are diminishing returns. Is your hobby or work intrinsically rewarding, or does the thought of winning keep you going? Are you willing to dedicate the rest of your life to this one practice that may not have been of your own provocation? For others and not for yourself? For reputation as opposed to living to your fullest potential? Are you ready to commit all your time to striving for competitive supremacy, or would you rather experience more of what life has to offer? Considering the inevitability of our everchanging selves, how likely do you see yourself wanting to go all the way, every step of the way, *willingly*?

▲ **You've chosen to pursue a field you've been gifted at progressing in or one that is lucrative to make the most of your time, instead of choosing what is most fulfilling for you.**

If so, then I suggest you read on. If your choice is driven by a knotted mess of unsavory obligation, expectation, financial circumstance, or what you may believe is a moral necessity, you should reconsider what may be lost: the freedom and autonomy you may have been ignorantly dispossessed from.

However, if you have the luxury of choice, then why consider the pursuit of a *truly* fulfilling practice to be a waste of time? The tracks of this line of inquiry will necessarily lead to existential questions—another matter we'll return to. For now, it is worth foreshadowing how different pursuits offer different perks to leverage, and some are worth more compromise than others.

▲ **You can't get over the fact that *chance* has favored others, and starting further behind is a gap you can't seem to square or accept.**

Whether you struck rock bottom with the initial roll of dice for natural abilities or environmental, intrapersonal, and/or development process components, or simply consider yourself in the "majority of average," you may find it easier to blame systems you have little to no control over, history you were not a part of, or populations that want the same thing as you do (such as equality), just not in the way you want to address it. You can try to push the onus of your shortcomings and *bad luck* onto everyone else, turning it into an identity and cementing yourself in stagnating denial, or you can make an effort and necessitate change!

Having made the case, I now solemnly ask: How difficult can it be to invest thirty minutes a day to improve your cooking skills? Or performing daily knee exercises to strengthen the joints you've rarely put to use? Or learning to juggle to bolster your dexterity? Or working on conversational skills to become socially adept? Or investing in a few speech pathologist sessions to fix that impediment? Or finding alternative, interactive, and interesting methods of improving your algebra? Or spending any significant amount of time rehearsing for your presentation? Did you know there are eighty-year-olds climbing Mount Everest and that picking up a new hobby or line of work at the age of forty-five won't collapse space and time? Just the opposite.

The sooner you stop lying to yourself about impossibilities, the sooner you permit yourself to grow. In his book *Lying*, neuroscientist and philosopher Sam B. Harris writes: "By lying, we deny others a view of the world as it is. Our dishonesty not only influences the choices they make; it often determines the choices they *can* make—and in ways we cannot always predict. Every lie is a direct assault upon the autonomy of those we lie to." Similarly, lying to ourselves about the possibility of competency or competitive mastery is a direct assault upon our own autonomy, as it undermines the best choices we can make for ourselves.

You may have noticed how I've mentioned that all components of the DMGT (apart from fixed physical genetic factors) are controllable to one extent or another. You may have also referred back to the DMGT with distraught skepticism and identified the second most prominent excuse after the "myth of talent": giving up on fields of interest due to personality "impediments" or supposed innate predispositions to remain idle or introverted or disinterested in intellectual development or emotionally unstable or *whatever*. But surely our personalities are immutable!

CHAPTER 5
THE MALLEABLE PSYCHE

Can people change? It's a question so simple, a measure so assessable, a science so thorough, yet most will either confidently conclude that it's an impossibility or modestly admit some ambivalence. It is mind-bendingly bizarre for such a momentous, life-altering query to not boast a global unanimity. The possibility of change is a point of view that governs many of the decisions we make—for ourselves as well as for others, and any decent being with a moral bone in their body would want such a question definitively answered given what's at stake. Instead, we rely on our "intuition" as we grow to accept our differences and form a stable psyche and identity to function constructively in society. However sensible this sounds, let's consult the facts to better understand what falls in the realm of the possible and what we can do about it.

When the topic of self-study and the definition of "self" are raised, it would be blasphemous not to address "the Big Five." Also known as the Five-Factor or OCEAN model, the Big Five is a taxonomy for personal traits that describe meaningful differences amongst people: what makes you you and me me. (Gagné refers to the Mental subcomponent of the Big Five as the Personality subcomponent as well, as there are an innumerable amount of descriptive qualities. He also sees temperance and resilience as stronger hereditary components and decided to list them as separate facets.) A result of the collective efforts of personality psychologists Ernest Tupes, Raymond Christal, J.M Digman, and Lewis Goldberg (Tupes and Christal, 1992; Goldberg, 1993) over a span of forty-three years, the Big Five identifies five cardinal personality traits:

▲ Openness to experience:

This trait concerns people's willingness to try new things, to think outside of the box and shy away from routine. It reflects the complexity and depth of an individual's mental life and experiences.

▲ Conscientiousness:

This trait has to do with controlling impulses and acting in socially acceptable ways. Those individuals characterized by this trait are very goal oriented,
delay gratification, work within rules, and plan and organize effectively.

▲ Extraversion:

This trait measures of your level of sociability and where you draw your
energy from.

▲ Agreeableness:

This trait concerns how well people interact and get along with others.

▲ Neuroticism:

This trait addresses one's emotional stability and general temperament, encompassing such characteristics as a proclivity to anxiety and
emotional pain.

You may ask, Where do these traits come from? The *lexical hypothesis theory*
states that when a certain behavior becomes prominent over time, we'll create
word for it. If we don't have a word for it, it must not be prevalent. Based on
this theory, the founding figures of personality psychology, Gordon Allport
and Henry S. Odbert (1936) studied the dictionary and found 4,504 words
that could reflect personality traits. Researchers such as Raymond Cattell
(1943) furthered this line of inquiry by looking for similarities among these
words to find trends and to narrow them down into the most influential
traits. He did this through a process of *factor analysis*, which is a statistical
method for determining correlated variables from large datasets. Through the
years, and as researchers further refined the terms to match modern terms in
dictionaries, the OCEAN model became one of the better and more credible
approaches for differentiating personalities.

There are a multitude of other personality tests out there, some of which
you may have done at school or possibly at work when your teachers or employers were figuring out which team to slot you in. You may have disagreed
with the results, or they didn't work in your favor the way you saw things. The
accuracy of such psychoanalytic approaches, particularly in social psychology,
has been a prominently controversial topic over the past few years, even rife

with scandals. What's in question here is the field of *psychometrics*—the science of measuring mental capacities and processes. If I am to persuade you to look into this matter and accept the significance of these traits without sounding absolute, we will need to rely on something a little more definitive.

Through further factor analyses into OCEAN, personality psychologist Colin G. DeYoung et al. (2007) proposed a statistical division that broke down each Big Five attribute into two additional aspects that improve on its reliability as a psychological measure (see figure 1-17):

BIG-FIVE
PERSONALITY TRAITS

Openness to experience composed of Intellect and Openness

Conscientiousness composed of Industriousness and Orderliness

Extraversion composed of Enthusiasm and Assertiveness

Agreeableness composed of Compassion and Politeness

Neuroticism composed of Withdrawal and Volatility

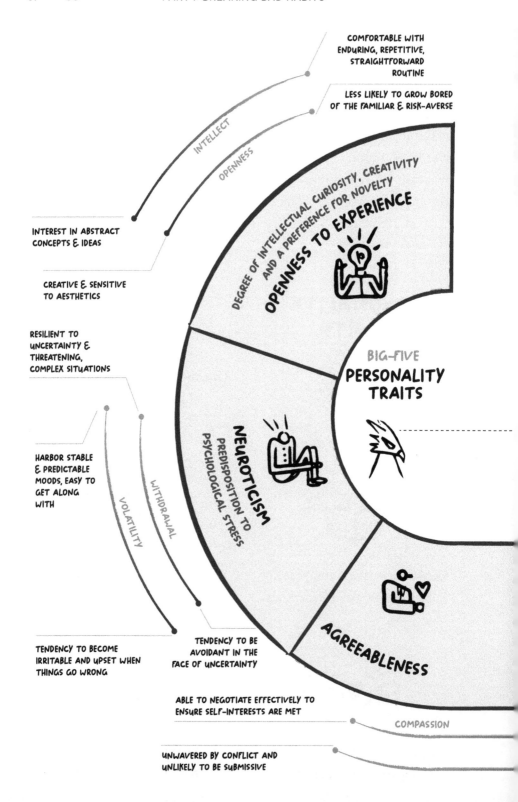

COMFORTABLE WITH ENDURING, REPETITIVE, STRAIGHTFORWARD ROUTINE

LESS LIKELY TO GROW BORED OF THE FAMILIAR & RISK-AVERSE

INTELLECT

OPENNESS

INTEREST IN ABSTRACT CONCEPTS & IDEAS

CREATIVE & SENSITIVE TO AESTHETICS

DEGREE OF INTELLECTUAL CURIOSITY, CREATIVITY AND A PREFERENCE FOR NOVELTY

OPENNESS TO EXPERIENCE

RESILIENT TO UNCERTAINTY & THREATENING, COMPLEX SITUATIONS

BIG-FIVE
PERSONALITY TRAITS

HARBOR STABLE & PREDICTABLE MOODS, EASY TO GET ALONG WITH

NEUROTICISM
PREDISPOSITION TO PSYCHOLOGICAL STRESS

VOLATILITY

WITHDRAWAL

TENDENCY TO BECOME IRRITABLE AND UPSET WHEN THINGS GO WRONG

TENDENCY TO BE AVOIDANT IN THE FACE OF UNCERTAINTY

AGREEABLENESS

ABLE TO NEGOTIATE EFFECTIVELY TO ENSURE SELF-INTERESTS ARE MET

COMPASSION

UNWAVERED BY CONFLICT AND UNLIKELY TO BE SUBMISSIVE

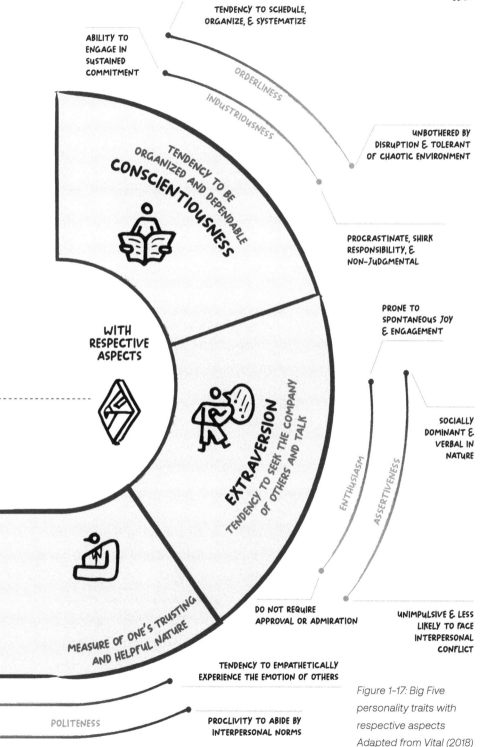

TENDENCY TO SCHEDULE, ORGANIZE, & SYSTEMATIZE

ABILITY TO ENGAGE IN SUSTAINED COMMITMENT

ORDERLINESS

INDUSTRIOUSNESS

TENDENCY TO BE ORGANIZED AND DEPENDABLE
CONSCIENTIOUSNESS

UNBOTHERED BY DISRUPTION & TOLERANT OF CHAOTIC ENVIRONMENT

PROCRASTINATE, SHIRK RESPONSIBILITY, & NON-JUDGMENTAL

WITH RESPECTIVE ASPECTS

PRONE TO SPONTANEOUS JOY & ENGAGEMENT

EXTRAVERSION
TENDENCY TO SEEK THE COMPANY OF OTHERS AND TALK

SOCIALLY DOMINANT & VERBAL IN NATURE

ENTHUSIASM

ASSERTIVENESS

MEASURE OF ONE'S TRUSTING AND HELPFUL NATURE

DO NOT REQUIRE APPROVAL OR ADMIRATION

UNIMPULSIVE & LESS LIKELY TO FACE INTERPERSONAL CONFLICT

TENDENCY TO EMPATHETICALLY EXPERIENCE THE EMOTION OF OTHERS

POLITENESS

PROCLIVITY TO ABIDE BY INTERPERSONAL NORMS

Figure 1-17: Big Five personality traits with respective aspects
Adapted from Vital (2018)

One of the better assessments of the Big Five's descriptive accuracy comes from the work of the controversial so-called "culture warrior," public intellectual, and clinical psychologist Jordan B. Peterson (a coauthor of the aforementioned DeYoung study) along with statistical modeling expert Robert O. Pihl and the distinguished psychologist Daniel M. Higgins ("Understand Myself," n.d.). It expands on the five-dimensional description while putting results on a spectrum and comparing them to those of ten thousand other people.

What's important to note is that these traits reflect *objective* behaviors, which means that each of them, as well as their subcomponents, are *not necessarily bad or good*. For example:

▲ Being competitive has its advantages when striving to better yourself at a particular practice, but it may not be as pragmatic when you're trying to cultivate meaningful relationships.

▲ Being extroverted can assist in one's ability to adapt to new places and meet new people, whereas being introverted can improve one's ability to be self-sufficient and independent.

▲ One may assume that being agreeable is a trait one cannot have too much of, but being excessively agreeable has its downfalls. Excessively agreeable people often don't know what they want because they are so accustomed to living for others—so focused on finding out what other people want that they find it harder to figure out what *they* need.

Therefore, the results of any personality test should not *necessarily* be an indicator of what should be worked on but an indication of what may work best for you now (with the exception of neuroticism).

What's particularly useful about Pihl, Higgins, and Peterson's expansion of the Big Five personality test is the substantiative statements that accompany the measures, explaining each score and its respective aspects. The meaning of this score is still open to interpretation, of course, and it won't perfectly reflect the true nature of your being. Most statements will hold true, but some may not. However, there is much to infer from the results and statements, and they will shape the direction and accompanying precautionary measures we explore later in the book. Here are a few more reasons why we ought to take a Big Five personality test.

▲ To understand the principal underlying determinants of what we perceive to be our "strengths" and "weaknesses"

▲ To reaffirm the fact that what we want and who we have become is unique to us and that "success" is in the eye of the beholder

▲ To recognize that different people operate to different standards, beliefs, mannerisms, and values in order to cultivate inwardly and outwardly consoling empathy

▲ To identify and address personality trait extremities hindering one's ability to progress and live a fulfilling life

FIXED OR FLEXIBLE?

It may have started to sound as though we are retracing our steps toward fixedness, as the results of a personality test may seem enduring. But before jumping to conclusions, we need to address the question that remains: Are personalities fixed from the moment we're conceived, or are they everchanging?

Such a question necessitates the mention of researchers who spent decades studying families, twins, adopted children, and foster families to better understand what influences our personalities. The most celebrated and widely cited investigation in this area, the "Minnesota Twin Study" (Bouchard et al., 2005), followed 350 pairs of twins between 1979 and 1999. Participants included sets of both identical and fraternal twins who were either raised together or apart. The results revealed that the personalities of identical twins were very similar whether they were raised in the same household or apart, suggesting that at least *some aspects of personality* (though not based on Big Five personality traits, and mainly IQ—a rather controversial measure of general practical intelligence) are largely influenced by genetics with a 70% heritability variance. This influential study has since sparked headlines, many of which exaggerated the finding and suggested the entirety of our identity is stamped on us from conception. Such a belief influenced scores of authoritative experts and television reports, as well as numerous books and print and online articles, and is reported as fact in most psychology textbooks. This, alongside archaic essentialist views (belief that a person is bound to innate characteristics that precede their existence), would explain the proliferation of misguided interpretations and why many of us believe in an "obstinate self." Other twin studies followed, whose findings suggested weaker correlations of around 40–60% heritability variance in the Big Five personality traits, though most did not involve twins that were raised apart (e.g., Jang et al., 1996; Bouchard and McGue, 2003; Vernon et al., 2008).

Of course, these and other similar claims triggered an explosion of criticism, the most recent from clinical psychologist Jay Joseph (2018), who details an impressive list of problems with TRA ("twins reared apart") studies, writing, for example, that "Many twin pairs experienced late separation, and many pairs were reared together in the same home for several years; most twin pairs grew up in similar socioeconomic and cultural environments; twins sometimes had financial and other types of incentives to exaggerate or lie about their degree of separation and behavioral similarity; their accounts are not always reliable. And in cases where evaluations and testing were performed by the same person, there was a potential for experimenter bias in favor of twin similarity."

Taking the matter one step further, geneticist Robert A. Power and developmental psychologist Michael Pluess (2015) used associated genetic variants to each of the Big Five personality traits to test for heritability on a *molecular* level. They found a correlation, though at considerably lower heritability rates: 15% for neuroticism and 21% for openness, with nonsignificant estimates for extraversion, agreeableness, and conscientiousness.

Veering away from twin studies, personality psychologists Brent W. Roberts and Daniel Mroczek (2008) refer to personality traits as "the relatively enduring patterns of thoughts, feelings, and behaviors that distinguish individuals from one another." They go on to explain that "Since 1994, cross-sectional and longitudinal studies have forced the revaluation of the assumption that personality traits do not change in adulthood" (e.g., Srivastava et al., 2003; Mroczek and Spiro, 2003; Roberts et al., 2006).

Performing a meta-analysis of ninety-two longitudinal studies covering ages 10 to 101, Roberts and Mroczek found that most personality changes occur between 20 and 40 but can continue into old age as well. (Later studies by others, including one that involved a massive cross-sectional sample of 1,267,218 children, adolescents, and adults—ages 10-65—also found that Big Five attributes change with age (Soto et al., 2011).) Roberts and Mroczek concluded that "Personality traits are developmental constructs, even in adulthood," referring to acts of "social investments" (such as adult roles in work, education, family, and community contexts) as catalysts for personality trait-change. For example, they suggest that becoming more invested in work leads to an increase in conscientiousness and agreeableness—traits that are typically rewarded in work settings (Lodi-Smith and Roberts, 2007; Hudson et al., 2012; Nye and Roberts, 2013).

IT IS VERY MUCH POSSIBLE

However inconclusive and contradictory the opinions *and* findings of experts in the field, and in light of the conclusions drawn from "Self-Limiting Reluctancy," it would be fair to deduce the following:

A significant amount of our habits, mindset, perceptions, behaviors, and feelings are derived of nurture and are not set in stone.

Even if we concede a conservative 50% heritability variance of personality traits, that leaves enough room for considerable and efficacious changes. As Peterson suggests, "The dice rolls when you're conceived and you're given a set of attributes . . . You're an entity with quasi-fixed attributes, but that doesn't mean you can't transform and learn." A perspective that coincides with Gagné's DMGT as well as the position of Antinats. If you think your attributes are holding you back, there is substantial scientific evidence to suggest real potential for intrinsic change. There is a way forward!

You may now be wondering if there have been any studies exploring the potential of *willful* personality change. (Is it really possible?) If you were, you're in luck.

Findings of a study conducted by personality and developmental psychologists Nathan W. and R. Chris Fraley (2015) suggest just such a possibility. They asked undergraduates to choose specific traits they wanted to change, make specific goals to accomplish that, and then spend four months working toward those goals. During this time, students would check in occasionally by taking the same self-guided personality test. In the end, participants were successful at boosting their levels of extraversion and emotional stability. A 2019 study led by Hudson with even more participants did something similar, but instead of having them set their own goals, researchers had them take on specific *challenges* each week to help them change their chosen traits. For example, someone who wanted to become extroverted might be tasked with starting a conversation with a stranger. The result? Most participants were able to increase their extraversion, emotional stability, and conscientiousness if they completed the challenges. (See figure 1-18.)

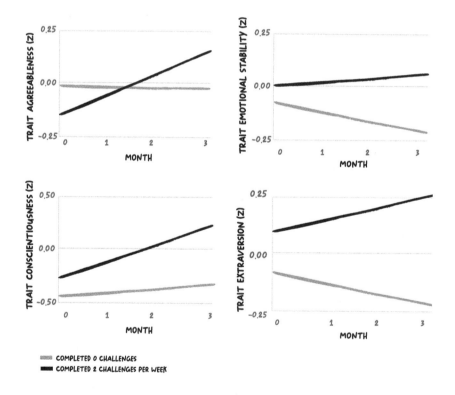

COMPLETED 0 CHALLENGES
COMPLETED 2 CHALLENGES PER WEEK

Figure 1-18: Emotional stability, agreeableness, conscientiousness, and extraversion through trait-change intervention
Adapted from Hudson et al. (2019)

The graph illustrating the total observed change in extraversion, for example, indicates a change of half of a standard deviation. This type of change represents someone who is moderately introverted moving to the middle point between introversion and extraversion—a substantial change indeed.

In yet another study (Jacques-Hamilton et al., 2018), another group of psychologists simply asked all participants—both introverts and extraverts—to act extraverted for a full week. The results were not all sunshine and roses. The introverts reported feeling less happy and authentic and more tired than the extraverted group. This tells us that *acting* a certain way—"fake it 'til you make it"—will not always end up with positive results. Instead, setting specific actions that can help you practice your chosen trait is the way to go.

So, like most developmental efforts, enduring change takes deliberate practice. But most importantly, it is very possible. Hudson (2021) went on to investigate the correlation between motivation and personality change. In two separate studies, students were recruited from psychology courses and offered the opportunity to change their personality traits for the better and asked to specify whether they wanted to improve their emotional stability or conscientiousness. Students in the first study were randomly assigned to change either emotional stability or conscientiousness; they didn't get a choice. In the second study, they did. For both studies, students were provided a list of prewritten "challenges" designed to help them change their assigned trait which they were asked to complete during the study (such as "Show up five minutes early for a class" to improve conscientiousness or "When you are worried about something, write it down" to improve emotional stability). Hudson found that even though students from the first study were not actively invested in the intervention's true aims (given they didn't have a choice which trait to develop), the challenges still had a beneficial influence on one of the two attributes: conscientiousness. Interestingly, changing emotional stability required that the participants received effective trait-change intervention (such as completing challenges on a weekly basis) *and* autonomously chose to work on emotional stability. (See figure 1-19.) Findings of great utility we will return to.

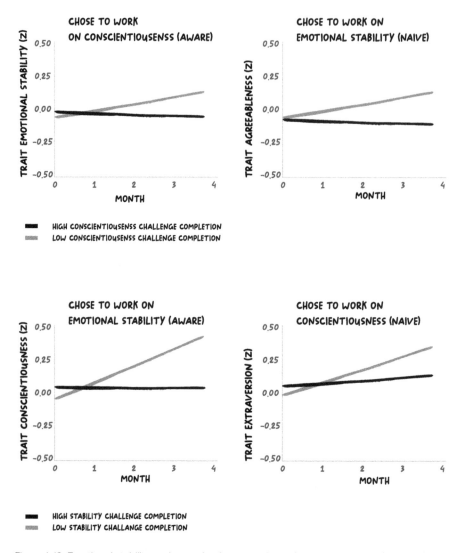

Figure 1-19: Emotional stability and conscientiousness through nonautonomous intervention. Adapted from Hudson (2021)

Given that it's possible for personalities to change, it should come as no surprise that this potential plays a significant role in, for example, long-term relationships. They are difficult to navigate because even if you feel you are with someone you *intrinsically* know to be "the one," this person may not be "the one" three years later because you would have changed and so too will they. This is almost always the case, and increasingly so in an everchanging twenty-first-century world. Yet the process of personality change is so slow that we don't notice. And so, to illustrate the utility of such an informed attitude and to foreshadow the principles of what *Necessitating Change* advocates, expect deviations of interest and personality to occur if you are looking to commit to a contractual long-term relationship. Regularly test for change, account for it, and adapt accordingly.

The next question, then, is this: What personality would I want if I could have any? A philosophical and perhaps a circular question to ponder! We know that people with different personality traits generally strive for certain things in their life. For example, more agreeable people will more likely want a family. But changing personality traits is a taxing endeavor and, more importantly, very time consuming. In one study, for example, interventions to induce personality trait changes took roughly twenty-four weeks on average to result in marked changes (Roberts et al., 2017). Nevertheless, personality psychologist Wiebke Bleidorn et al. (2019) suggest that such efforts are ultimately worthwhile. "The potential for producing long-term changes that would positively impact individuals across multiple domains suggests that personality traits are ideal targets for interventions designed to improve life success." So, apart from working on detrimental personality trait extremities (such as high neuroticism), it makes sense to focus on one particular trait that has the leverage for expediting what it means to live to one's fullest potential. But how do we know which one to choose?

Before we get carried away, the Traditional Psyche has many more attitudes to unpack. For now, the fact that *personal growth*, whether it's becoming funnier (more agreeable) or better at confronting and dealing with adversity (more conscientious), is almost never recognized in others is an attitude we ought to reform. We are generally quick to judge a book by its cover and assume lasting absolutes—who someone is in that moment will forever be that way, so to speak. On the flip side, you seldom hear anyone saying, "I'm going to work toward being more socially agreeable" or "I'm in the process of taming my volatility." You either are or you aren't and never in between. Polarized views and polarized distinctions subdue our awareness, willingness, and persistence in seeking intrinsic self-improvement, but it's time to acknowledge that people *can* change, that we can recognize and admit our collective shortcomings and encourage and support one another's initiatives to grow. It's okay to be "on the way"—everyone is. And while there are some with extreme personality traits who need a little more help and time, that is perfectly normal and human!

If you still believe you are eternally unmotivated, hopelessly socially incapable, permanently academically incompetent, or something else, you should reconsider. What you have become isn't fixed; it is subject to change, and don't let anyone tell you otherwise.

As we slowly reclaim control of our autonomy, you may yet fall victim to the Traditional Psyche's deluded pursuits—pursuits believed to be *authentic* but that are far from autonomous, and pursuits believed to be the best decisions but are in fact the worst. We've been distracted from what's best for our ourselves for far too long, and it's those very distractions that we need to confront.

CHAPTER 6
INCESSANT DISTRACTION

How often do you find yourself staring at a wall, fidgeting, restless, subconsciously sifting through your daily customs, contemplating which of the twelve things you routinely *depend* on and feel like doing, ultimately leading to the empty fridge–hungry stomach cycle of depreciating standards, eventually capitulating to a can of tuna you distastefully accept? Billions of people to interact with, thousands of hobbies to explore, hundreds of cultures/ideologies/cuisines/professions to contemplate and experience. Given all there is available to us, how is it possible to assume an ill-fated afternoon? I draw your attention, once more, to the following question: How much of what you do, how you do it, and why you do it is based on realizations drawn from *experience*, and how much is taught, expected, assumed, enforced, blindly adopted?

We grow worrisome with these routines, this lifestyle that the Traditional Psyche advocates. They become increasingly difficult to endure, and symptoms of depression begin to surface. "Why do I get bored of everything I do: this job, this relationship, this hobby? I can't do anything without this burden of boredom following me around!"—yet another symptom we often exaggerate, mistaking it with depression. One begins to question one's sanity, life choices, and whether there is something intrinsically wrong as opposed to what one has committed to: the outlook, the mindset, the motivations.

What is boredom anyway? Well, it's not a time in which you simply have nothing to do; it's when none of the options you have (or believe to have) appeal to you. Seeking to better understand the nature of the disengaged mind, social psychologist Timothy D. Wilson et al. (2014) gave participants in eleven separate studies a button and told them that pressing it would administer an electric shock. He asked them to entertain themselves with their thoughts for up to fifteen minutes, but they could press the button if they wanted. Despite being also told that they would be paid money to avoid the shock, 25% of women and 67% of men shocked themselves. As far as the participants were concerned, left with nothing but their imagination, many decided they would rather experience physical pain than boredom.

To make matters worse, a recent study conducted by network scientist Philipp Lorenz-Spreen et al. (2019) suggest that the collective global attention span is narrowing. The researchers studied numerous modes of media attention that included but weren't limited to the following: the past forty years of movie ticket sales; Google's index of books from the last hundred years; more modernly, Twitter data from 2013 to 2016 and how long hashtags remained popular; 2010–18 Google Trends; 2010–15 Reddit trends; and 2012–17 Wikipedia attention time. Coauthor, mathematician, and physicist Philipp Hövel elaborates on the matter, reaffirming that our collective amount of attention isn't any smaller. (See figure 1-20.) Instead, there is simply much more to pay attention to which exhausts our attention, cultivating an urge for "newness," which causes us to switch between topics more rapidly. ("Abundance of information narrows our collective attention span", n.d.) They go on to suggest other researchers investigate the consequences of the phenomenon on an individual level, but one can imagine how the fear of missing out ("FOMO"), the tribal need to "keep up," and proclivities to switch to the seemingly "next best thing" could erode one's capacity to remain engaged.

Box-plot representation of relative gains in different data sets: The values of the relative gains $\Delta L(g)i/Li$, shown in a box-and-whisker representation for A Twitter, B Books, C Movies, D Google, E Reddit, F Publications, and G Wikipedia. The median is shown as a gray bar and the mean as a black diamond. Whiskers are chosen to show the 1.5 of the interquartile range.

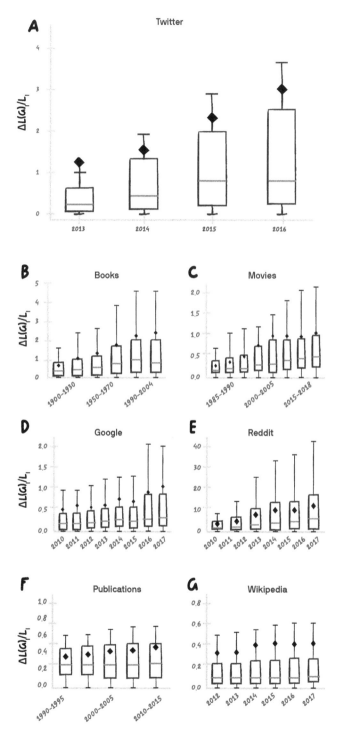

Figure 1-20: Collective global attention span
Adapted from Lorenz-Spreen et al. (2019)

Access to bigger, better, faster, stronger, cuter, and crazier modes of media attention generates one viral trend after another. Each movement, each story leads to another and then another and another, each finely tuned to stimulate our deepest primal instincts of shock and awe to hijack our attention away from any of the "mundane" experiences we take for granted. We board a bandwagon and jump from one to the next, indifferent to the last. Our senses grow numb, quickly acclimating to each new high, unimpressed with the status quo. In psychology, there is a name for this: *hedonic adaptation*, as we helplessly tread a *hedonic treadmill*, desperate to maintain a state of perpetual satisfaction. Given how our appetite for interest has grown increasingly diffi-cult to satiate while our attention spans deteriorate, how narrow-sighted our options of interest have become, and how repelled of boredom we've grown to be, what you end up with from all these twenty-first-century issues is a recipe for addiction and self-harm. Studies such as that published by organizational psychologists John D. Watt and Stephen J. Vodanovich (1999) suggest that de-pression, anxiety, drug abuse, alcoholism, bad grades, and poor social skills are a consequence of extended boredom. This may explain the vicious cycle of poor decision-making, binges, poor performance, lack of motivation, and indiffer-ence we endure that further exacerbates the effects of boredom. Our bodies need stimulation to remain healthy, and as Norman Doidge, a distinguished psychiatrist, suggests: "Nothing speeds brain atrophy more than being immo-bilized in the same environment: the monotony undermines our dopamine and attentional systems crucial to maintaining brain plasticity." To put it another way, *variety* and stimulation encourage *neurogenesis* (the generation of new brain cells) and extend the lives of brain cells that already exist.

The next controversial headline, the next Netflix series, the next AAA video game release, the next tragedy, the next election, the next Hollywood scandal, the next witch hunt, the next six-second viral clip, the next overly dramatized reality TV show, the next hysteria we desperately depend on for a fix. The contrast of what there is to consume with what present reality has to offer is a growing disparity evident with our increased attachment toward the surreal. Another hit of dopamine to spare us the pain of solitude and feeling underwhelmed. Figure 1-21 illustrates an increase of hours spent watching TV by individuals and households over the years. Figure 1-22 shows how much more time we spend on social media, with adolescents and young adults increasingly "connected." Figure 1-23 depicts how much of our active leisure time is being substituted for screen time. Figure 1-24 highlights how much more we have been captivated with "news." Figure 1-25 lists statistical facts of cell phone usage and habits, a normalized addiction. Given what is available in the absence of distraction, it is, for many, about avoiding underlying emotional pain. Maybe it's loneliness, anxiety, frustration, a lack of fulfillment or meaning. It may be a stale, miserable long-term relationship you're in; the memory of falling short of what would have, should have, could have been; or the thought of the steep climb toward a goal you insist on but detest pursuing. If you remain preoccupied, you don't notice.

And no, screen-time is not the only escape we resort to that is in question; it is anything whose absence reveals the pain. Being a workaholic, for example, doesn't mean you're exempt from mindless distraction. Oftentimes, it is precisely why a workaholic works so hard: because when they aren't, they're hurting. In such cases, it's not boredom that's painful; it's the absence of distraction revealing the pain that's already there. In other words, succeeding to whatever (often extrinsic) productive measures one designates to oneself wouldn't solve their problems; it would simply reveal them. After failing to fulfill what was assumed would bring lasting contentment, all they are left with is the emptiness they've been unconsciously or consciously avoiding.

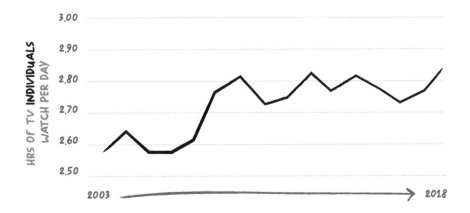

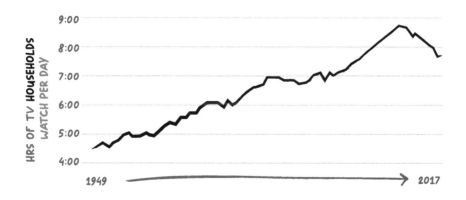

Figure 1-21: Hours spent watching TV for individuals and households

Adapted from Ingraham (2019)

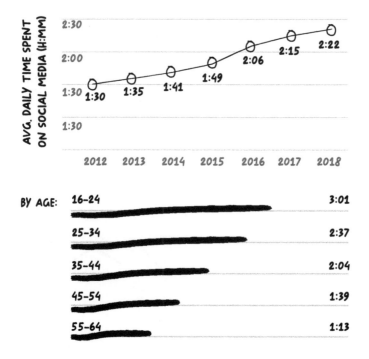

Figure 1-22: Daily time spent on social media

Adapted from Salim (2019)

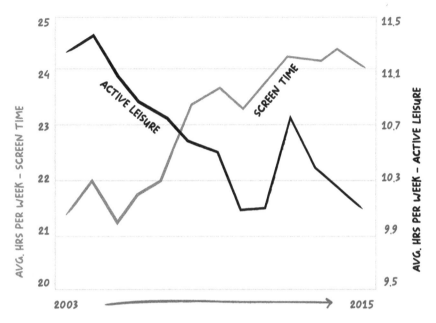

Figure 1-23: Free time to screen time

Adapted from Emily (n.d.)

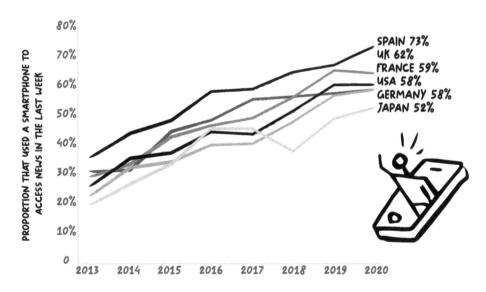

Figure 1-24: Access to news via smartphone

Adapted from Newman (n.d.)

74% of Americans feel uneasy leaving their phone at home

71% of Americans check their phones within the first 10 minutes of waking up

53% say that they have never gone longer than 24 hours without their cell phone

47% consider themselves "addicted" to their phones

35% use or look at their phone while driving

70% of Americans check their phones within 5 minutes of receiving a notification

43% use or look at their phone while on a date

61% have texted someone in the same room as them before

48% of people say they feel a sense of panic or anxiety when their cell phone battery goes below 20%

45% say that their phone is their most valuable possession

64% use their phone on the toilet

ON AVERAGE, AMERICANS CHECK THEIR PHONES 344 TIMES PER DAY

THAT'S ONCE EVERY 4 MINUTES!

HOW ABOUT YOU?

Figure 1-25: Cell phone usage and habits

Adapted from Wheelwright (2022)

Cognitive neuroscientist Benjamin Baird et al. (2011) suggest that when bored, people's brains showed greater activity in regions responsible for recalling autobiographical memory, conceiving the thoughts and feelings of others, and conjuring hypothetical events—that is to say, boredom induces reflection, empathy, and creativity. Boredom gets you thinking about why it is you are bored, what led you to be bored, your life choices and the events that got you to where you are, and what steps may get you to where you'd rather be in the future—a process referred to as *autobiographical planning*. Boredom is what spurs creative action and may very well be what has driven us to accomplish much of what we've achieved (Mann and Cadman, 2014) and should therefore not be seen as the problem.

There are times, however, when boredom *does* seem to be detrimental, for example, when there is work that needs doing. You may find it difficult to focus. You'll yawn and grow lethargic. It turns out that the part of your brain that influences motivation and pleasure also affects drowsiness (Oishi et al., 2017). If the source is actual boredom, that's your brain chemistry telling you that whatever you've been distracted by isn't stimulating, engaging, or catching *your* interest. (In other words, it's not for you.) Drowsiness is often mistaken for boredom; it comes from emotional fatigue caused by the stress (Grafe and Bhatnager, 2018) of worrying about the task itself and/or avoiding the effort the task presents. This can then lead to procrastination, the thief of time, and is also associated with depression, anxiety, fatigue, and reduced satisfaction across life domains (Beutel et al., 2016). Therefore, what may seem to be the detriments of boredom are in fact the consequences of drudging through unstimulating tasks, insufficient challenge, or procrastination—all of which exacerbate the consequences of emotional fatigue. Surrendering to a lifestyle and commitments spurring boredom but never engaging with the truth of reality it brings to bear and doing nothing about it is living in bad faith. You are free to surrender, and it is when you do it that you deny your freedom to do otherwise, distracting yourself in denial of your freedom to change.

The real worry, then, is not perpetual boredom but meaningless *Incessant Distraction*. Distraction from not only the underlying pain we both unconsciously or consciously avoid but, as sociologist and philosopher Theodor Adorno suggests, distraction from what could otherwise be productive, constructive, growth-catalyzing experiences we should be making time for instead of the vapid, inauthentic dead ends of fruitless and unfulfilling activities.

You may be quick to retort and suggest that *any* time enjoyed is time well spent, but is it really? We will forego the consequences of hedonistic outlooks for now, but ask yourself this: Is shooting heroin time well spent? The "but" is on the tip of your tongue, but how far is binge-watching 435 episodes of an anime, soap opera, or a forensic investigation series; religiously devoting hours every day to brain-melting video game grinds; or endlessly browsing through social media and public forums from ingesting a slow-brewed opioid? All are addictive, and the abuse of any is detrimental to personal growth by an order of magnitude relative to everything else there is to experience.

You are effectively embezzling welfare from your future self and justifying it by what every other prisoner of distraction spouts. How far has it gotten you? And what are you imagining the alternative to be? (We will progressively discover just how much you have truly been missing in the sections to come.)

You may assume I'm referring to anything you perceive to be time *not* enjoyed but time well spent. It is curious that most don't consider that alternatives can correspond with time enjoyed *and* time well spent, thinking such privileges are exclusive to a productive minority. And even more peculiar is how so few question what is, in fact, "time well spent" and whether there are levels to what we describe as "time enjoyed." These are the questions we will seek to answer, but for now, it is worth emphasizing that rewatching season 4 of *The Office* or binging on a buy-one-get-one-free order of pepperoni pizzas every now and again isn't the problem. The issue is when we default to the same damned twelve things we reliably *depend* on for "good feelings." They keep us Incessantly Distracted from everything else there is to experience, leaving us in a docile state of *being* instead of a driven state of *doing*.

> **There is no such thing on Earth as an uninteresting subject; the only thing that can exist is an uninterested person.**
> —Gilbert K. Chesterton, *Heretics*

Robert Nozick, an award-winning political philosopher, posed a thought experiment where people had a choice to plug into a machine that simulates preferred reality and induces nothing but pleasurable experiences, which I will exaggerate for artistic reasons. You could, for example, be the president of a lush green continent and, in your free time, an award-winning Hollywood actress who morphs into an Andean condor to watch everyone's facial expressions as they walk past the Starbucks cafés you now own and notice how you jacked the prices of every item to a million dollars while contracted Navy SEALs protect the now-superexclusive Frappuccinos—because you thought it was funny. You would never know the anguish of heartache, an upset tummy, second-hand embarrassment, or the loss of a pet iguana—you are guaranteed experiences of pleasure, never pain. Nozick found that what dissuaded many people from "plugging in" was the fact that it wasn't based in reality.

Pursuing this line of inquiry, I present to you the following dilemma to consider: Mikayla is head over heels and has never felt happier; however, she's oblivious to the fact that her significant other has been cheating on her for the duration of their relationship. Since Mikayla lives in blissful ignorance, and assuming she would never find out, would it be better leaving her in the dark? Which reality is best for Mikayla?

Similarly, many live in their own personal *Experience Machines.* They get so involved, entranced, captivated, and distracted by an identity, orientation, group, or belief that they slowly begin drifting into pseudoreality, in constant need of affirmation of what they desperately want to be real—so much so that their sensitivities are cranked to maximum, highly prone to offense-taking should anyone attempt to burst their bubble, question their ways, challenge what they tell themselves to be justified, proven, or real. Remaining distracted in a familiar state of satisfaction—a consequence of how shallow and ungrounded their sources of meaning—denies their progression in *reality*, ultimately eliciting the pain their routines paradoxically and temporarily alleviate. Are they, too, best left in the dark? How long before the false glow of their willful ignorance loses its luster? And by then, will it be too late?

On an evolutionary basis, boredom is a state that encouraged our primal ancestors to seek new ground, tribes, land to harvest, and mates to increase their chances of survival. Our shortening attention spans may be a further evolutionary adaptation in a world overwrought with ubiquitous opportunities; one is obligated to grow bored given the proliferation of opinion, misinformation, and questionable options to pick and choose from. Whatever the reasons for our surrender, we have no choice but to confront our cognitions, face reality, and seek stimulation elsewhere in pursuit of time *intrinsically* well spent, whether we remain connected to the grid or practice meditation with a yogi in a cave. Symptoms of extended boredom are a sure sign that change is overdue as I now call upon the person you could become to awaken its past self from hypnotized slumber, rub its misty, starstruck eyes, and rebel. This is a new age—the age of personal revolution!

CHAPTER 7
PROCREATIVE PREDISPOSITION

Distractions come in many shapes and sizes, and perhaps one of the most enduring, accepted, and, in some places of the world, sanctioned within the Traditional Psyche, is childbearing. Continuing the line of evolutionary insights, we refer to the work of evolutionary biologist, ethologist, and popular-science writer C. Richard Dawkins's award-winning book *The Selfish Gene*, from which we'll be able to see through the lies we've been fed—lies that have robbed us and continue to strip us of autonomy and informed aspirations.

In his search for the origins of altruism, Dawkins explains that we are survival machines in which our genes' sole purpose is to live on so that they, and they alone, are immortal. The genes that make it through impose their characteristics on their vehicle—the body—allowing it to survive and therefore pass those same genes on. The survival of the fittest really means the survival of genes, because a gene that didn't look after its own interests would become extinct.

The experience of bearing and raising children delivers an overpowering sense of fulfillment unlike anything an individual has or potentially will ever experience. This sense of purpose is closely entangled with their kin. If we are to consider Dawkins's insight, it would suggest that this is what the gene has longed for, as we would expect the reward of biochemical stimulus to be second to none. The vehicle—the body—has served its purpose and the gene's goal has been achieved. The reward is an experience we all naturally gravitate toward: a deeply seeded, biologically induced inclination I will refer to as "Procreative Predisposition."

Dawkins emphasizes the power of *kinship*. Think of a father who is willing to risk his life to save his child from a burning building. He also champions *reciprocal altruism*. Think "you scratch my back, I'll scratch yours," in which doing a favor and expecting one in return can improve one's chances of survival. We see this behavior in chimps, for example. However, it seems that humans have gone beyond kin selection and reciprocal altruism. For example, we empathize with strangers who are unlikely to return the favor, we weep at fictitious dramas, we donate blood. All of this has to do with people who don't share our genes. Dawkins suggests that our genes are misfiring and evolving beyond prehistoric evolutionary necessities—rising above our origins.

And so we are in a constant battle with our ancestral predecessors' evolutionary mechanisms and the means by which they survived. Our technological advancements have thoroughly changed the environment we live in, and as a result, we have outgrown our dependance on many of those cognitive reactions and survival instincts that now work against us. This is another particularly important realization because it demands that one train the mind and question one's impulses and intuitions. We are no longer primates whose sole purpose is to reproduce and care for our offspring so our genes can live on. It's time to cease aping our ancestors and emancipate ourselves from this primitive inclination and live by our *own* values.

Evolving into something more than a primate, we find ourselves in unfamiliar waters of genetically independent sovereignty. What parents feel toward their children—their "purpose"—is mostly genetically induced euphoric bliss, a state of being that can be garnered through other means. Our genes don't care; they are predisposed to reward their host with reason and meaning simply for fulfilling their purpose. How often have you met a parent who belittled you by saying, "You won't know what struggle/purpose/life is until you bear children of your own."? Considering what we know now, this self-congratulatory and patronizing assertion comes off as ignorant vanity. There is more to life than life itself, so to speak. Bearing children is certainly a direct pathway to purpose, but this does not make someone better than you, nor does it justify a moral high ground or overshadow other profound experiences life has to offer. A committal of a third of one's life is to be taken with caution, consideration, and scrupulous deliberation; it's a commitment whose impetus and consequences are obfuscated by stigmatizing the very idea that childbearing could be questioned. Acknowledging what most people default to in search of purpose—often to remedy the emotional pain of a meaningless life—I will now unveil the ugly truth of what many of us seemingly capitulate to without question.

We often hear that parenting is the hardest job, and if we are to treat it as such, then why not consider one's suitability for the job? For those so eager for parenthood, how well do you know yourself? Do you harbor qualities that make for a great parent? How sure are you of this? How experienced are you? Do you have any references to show? Would you consider yourself a role model for a child to look up to? Will you have the time to share meaningful moments and to express affection and love on a daily basis? Or will you keep them perpetually distracted with tablets, phones, and consoles and rely on every external support system available such family, friends, and childcare or the largesse of social security, adding more burden to society? These are the questions we seldom ask. Many victims of bad parenting and traumatic, troubled childhoods (a result of soft or hard structure upbringings, as mentioned on page 27) often end up with a need for immediate gratification; poor self-control; a sense of entitlement; ungratefulness; goals of wealth, fame, and image; disinterest in personal growth and responsible behaviors; and/ or an inability to determine how much is enough. For those who have yet to realize their personal limitations or understand what works for them and what doesn't, the certainty of parenthood as a lifelong commitment that will serve all involved is a bit of a stretch.

To stigmatize the means by which anyone seeks fulfillment in their own individualistic way—to express moral outrage or even disappointment with another's choice, such as to eschew reproducing (described by Leslie Ashburn-Nardo, industrial psychologist and coauthor of a study investigating childbearing stigma in the workplace (Trump-Steele et al., 2016) who elucidated her findings in an interview (Stern, 2020) as "violating strong-held values or expectations")—is taking the lower road. Being child-free is usually derided as "unnatural" and often subjected to unsolicited questioning by friends, family, colleagues, acquaintances, and strangers. Some parents pressure children for grandchildren, sometimes threatening disownment for denying them the retirement pleasures of caring for more kin. Sometimes the reasons are religious. Family-support and -legacy proponents suggest the primary purpose of bearing children is to secure financial support or assistance in old age. The fact of the matter is that the twenty-first century has granted conveniences, safety nets, securities, and health proxies that void the need of family caregivers for most. Once a prehistoric necessity—and one still relevant in developing countries—to eschew childbearing begs the question of self-centeredness. And yet saving for one's own retirement and comfort instead of "investing" in a child with expectations of a return would spare another life of obligation and undesired devotion. Of course, this is a multifaceted issue, but under the circumstances I have outlined, I suggest it is an absurd choice nonetheless.

"The childless are perceived to be psychologically unfulfilled, that they'll have regrets and lead less meaningful lives," Nardo adds. And so how dare we question the difficulties and limitations a parent faces, undermining what they tell themselves to have been a meaningful decision leading to a life of fulfillment? Again, let's consult the facts.

A study conducted by andrologists Maja Bodin et al. (2019) found that there were five reasons men wanted children:

1   **Ideal image (51%):**
    longing for children, parenthood, and family and the joy and uncondi-tional love it was assumed to bring

2   **Legacy (22%):**
    something to pass on, leaving a trail in the sand

3   **Personal development (12%):**
    burnish their self-image and enrich their lives

4   **Relationship (8%):**
    assumed to bring happiness and strengthen the partnership

5   **Practical circumstances and prerequisites (2%)**

The sample size was relatively small (191 men aged 20-50 years old), but, again, the findings should come as no surprise. We generally associate fulfillment with parenthood despite it being for most their first genuine, grueling, and harrowing attempt at it.

Sociologist Rachel Margolis et al. (2015) found, on average, the effect of a new baby on a person's life in the first year is devastatingly bad — worse than divorce, worse than unemployment, and worse even than the death of a partner. Their research found that couples had an uptick in life satisfaction leading up to childbirth, but only 30% maintained that same state of happiness two years in. The effects were worse for parents older than thirty with a higher education. Surprisingly, gender was not a factor. The study, with a sample size of 2,016 German citizens, did not consider cultural differences, social welfare, public support, social security, and long-term effects, but the results are noteworthy. "Needless to say, most parents would say otherwise," remarked family sociologist Nicholas H. Wolfinger (2018). "Although willing to acknowledge the hardships of parenthood, they are generally quick to tout its rewards." This is a good example of *Fading Affect Bias*, in which emotions associated with unpleasant memories fade more quickly than those associated with positive events.

And while childbearing norms remain overbearing, they have begun to shift. The University of Michigan's Health and Retirement Study revealed that, in 2016, 18% of people in their fifties had never had children, nor did 15% of those in their sixties and 10% of those in their seventies (2016 HRS Core, n.d.). Richard Johnson, director of the Program on Retirement Policy at the Urban Institute in Washington, DC, attributes the growing number of childless couples to several factors, including "Women's increased educational attainment and increased employment." The second-wave feminism of the 1960s and 1970s, and the consequent move toward a more equitable society, gave women more control of their reproductive faculties. They were no longer beasts of childbearing burden. Investigating drops in fertility in developed countries, evolutionary biologist Lonnie Aarssen and evolutionary psychologist Stephanie T. Altman (2012) concluded that women who wanted fewer or no kids had a greater interest in a career, fame, and generating new ideas and discoveries in pursuit of an enduring personal legacy. Again, this should come as no surprise. Poorer countries, by comparison, lacking such education and burdened by misogynistic dogmatism whether through cultural or religious oppression, have little to no access to contraception, are less likely to use it, and don't know any better as a result of early marriage and gender roles, the need to care for elders, and the need for extra labor.

Part of a multi-institution team of researchers studying the relationship between happiness and parenthood (Glass et al., 2016), sociologist Jennifer Glass wrote: "The negative effects of parenthood on happiness were entirely explained by the presence or absence of social policies allowing parents to better combine paid work with family obligations. And this was true for both mothers and fathers. Countries with better family policy 'packages' had no happiness gap between parents and non-parents." Policies such as guaranteed minimum paid sick and vacation days also positively impacted the happiness of everyone in that particular country. The same pattern held for policies like childcare. "Countries with cheaper out-of-pocket costs for childcare," she reported, "had happier nonparents as well as parents, perhaps because everyone benefits when children are well-socialized and their cognitive development is prioritized in early childhood."

Imagine selfishly making a decision with little to no experience in the matter, with little to no understanding of oneself, and oftentimes without the time or resources needed to fully provide for the child—putting the onus onto others—*and still* being audacious enough to insist on parenthood as the high moral path. The restrictions of extraneous support systems and the subsequent outrage of parents who suffered the burden of their *own children* during the 2020 global pandemic says it all.

Sociologists Ranae J. Evenson and Robin W. Simon (2005) found no correlation between differences in parental status and levels of emotional well-being or enhanced mental health. Family demographer Tanya Koropeckyj-Cox (2002) found little evidence of psychosocial disadvantage among childless middle-aged and older adults. Another study conducted by the aforementioned Nicholas H. Wolfinger (2018) examined the relationship between children and happiness using over forty years of data from the General Social Survey, a national American omnibus survey. He concluded that older parents with minor children still at home are less happy than their empty-nest (childless) contemporaries. And while children in the house tend to make some men less happy, just being a parent has no significant impact on men's happiness. For women, bearing children is marginally associated with a *decline* in happiness. Nobel laureate economist Angus Deaton and clinical psychologist Arthur A. Stone (2014) found that both nonparents and parents have similar levels of satisfaction, but parents experienced more spikes in daily joy and stress than nonparents.

Other researchers, such as the aforementioned Jennifer Glass (2016), have also highlighted how financial stress impacts parental happiness. Further elaborating in her research brief for the Council on Contemporary Families, she called it a "happiness penalty" and listed related stressors for parents: "Time and energy demands; sleep deprivation; work-family conflict; difficulty finding high-quality, affordable childcare; and financial strain."

The most recent Consumer Expenditures Survey data from the USDA (US Department of Agriculture) estimated the average cost of raising a child from birth to age seventeen in the US to be $233,000 USD (around $335,200 AUD) in 2015. Labor economists David G. Blanchflower and Andrew E. Clark (2019) found the presence of children to be associated with lower levels of life satisfaction and markedly lower satisfaction for the divorced, separated, and widowed. They also found the happiest group, on average, to be the married with no children. Parents that are financially secure with higher education *were* correlated with increased overall happiness, suggesting that they may very well be living in commensurate bliss and/or have the most to gain from our Procreative Predisposition. With divorce-to-marriage ratios at roughly 70% in Russia, 57% in Spain, 51% in France, 45% in the United States, 43% in Australia, 41% in the United Kingdom, and 39% in Germany (Statista, 2017; "Marriage and Divorce Statistics," n.d.; NVSS, 2019; Australian Bureau of Statistics, 2021), one can only *cringe* at the "benefits to risk" balance and lost opportunities associated with parenthood but available to nonparents whose savings are spent on living a free and meaningful life, as they see fit.

It would be fair to say that parenthood *should not* be the first—and perhaps not even the last—attempt to find purpose. Those who have yet to understand themselves or find an individualistically meaningful and fulfilling pursuit (often far from it) do not make great parents. Given what we know about ever-changing desires, you can imagine what becomes of these individuals when their children mature and eventually move on with their lives. You will notice how some of these people attempt to vicariously live *through* their children to make up for what they themselves never achieved. This adds to the pressure, expectations, and social complications children face. Once their children decide to move out, and with that distraction now gone, emptiness quickly ensues. A longing for their children takes over, with constant calls to visit and perhaps a request to reside nearby or even continue living in the same household as one big happy family. Although a beautiful image to envisage, you would *also* notice how children find it emotionally draining to live with their parents. Clinging to what once was their purpose, such parents tend to veer from that empowering sensation toward a world of judgment and unwarranted imposition. This may all sound very familiar to you, someone you know, or perhaps something you've experience firsthand. Of course, it goes without saying that this doesn't describe all cases, but it is clearly not uncommon.

That all said, it is worth noting that becoming a parent is perhaps the most selfless and commendable challenge one can endure: committing a third of one's life working to give and living to work for another to thrive. It would be heartless to discount the efforts of parents who might be making the most out of a bad, premature, uninformed, forced, or imposed decision. And of course, it goes without saying that for those who conceived children for all the right reasons while accepting the "happiness penalty" and offering their kin freedom of choice, support, and unconditional love without the expectation of a return—they make the world a better place.

While many default to childbearing for purpose or drive, others lean on another predictable inclination.

CHAPTER 8
A CURSED GRAIL

"Do what makes you happy!" We see and hear this phrase everywhere, whether on a bumper sticker, in a fortune cookie, tattooed across a backpacker's arm, being shrieked from a convertible Shelby Mustang, chanted at psychedelic music festivals, or blared on every morning talk show. It's a directive that goes without saying for most, another ideal broadcasted on every medium: a happy couple, a happy family, a happy birthday, a happy Halloween, a happy graduation, snapshots of the happiest moments of everyone's lives. We've been beaten over the head with this concept for decades with varying, vague, and questionable ways of achieving it, though plenty of recent and bestselling books claim to have the answer: Martin E.P. Seligman's *Authentic Happiness* (advocating a focus on what he calls "signature strengths"), Daniel T. Gilbert's Stumbling on Happiness (suggesting we evaluate how happy we ought to be by comparing ourselves to those of similar background and experiences), Shawn Achor's *The Happiness Advantage* (championing "Learned Optimism"), Norman Vincent Peale's *The Power of Positive Thinking* (encouraging goal visualization and positive thinking), and of course Rhonda Byrne's *The Secret* (claiming the secret to happiness is "positive energy," which attracts positive things into your life).

We've already touched on the correlation between modernity and depression, but what about modernity and happiness? With quality of life being at an all-time high for most, the proliferation of "positive psychology," and the seemingly unending surge of guides to happiness, are we really getting happier? Steven A. Pinker (2018), an experimental cognitive psychologist, would be the first to tell you that we are. He concluded, rather controversially, that we are all in fact happier than at any previous time in (researched) history, referencing longitudinal studies such as those concerning GDP, life satisfaction, and student loneliness trends while reconciling disproportionate gaps in wealth, generational differences, and other historic trends. Pinker suggests the ultimate measure of happiness would be the weighted lifetime sum of periodic probing for how one feels several times a day, every day, but concedes it would be too laborious and expensive to organize. This leaves us with evaluations of how people *generally feel*, and it is from here on that the measure's efficacy fails. Any individual's judgment is subjective, biased, and relative for innumerable reasons, including the very language they associate with particular emotions and the fact that such judgments are often made on the spot, left to the mercy of transient contextual factors (Schwarz and Strack, 1999).

Other psychologists, along with a landmark survey of the state of global happiness, suggest we have reached a point where average life satisfaction is stable at best and possibly declining rapidly (Kahneman et al. 1999; "Changing World Happiness", 2019). For now, I ask: How far has the pursuit of happiness gotten you and those you know?

The impracticality, blindness to reality, tone-deafness, and in some cases pseudoscientific mysticism of self-help literature aside, they all assume the same thing: we *ought* to pursue happiness and judge our courses of action by what we believe will make us happier. After all, happiness is commonly seen as a hallmark of psychological health (Fredrickson, 1998) with social philosophers offering various schemes and policies that provide greater happiness for the greatest number (Bentham and Mill, 1973). And why wouldn't we all assume the same? Feeling happy feels great, so striving for more happiness makes the most sense, right?

All men seek happiness. This is without exception. Whatever different means they employ, they all tend to this end. The cause of some going to war, and of others avoiding it, is the same desire in both, attended with different views. The will never takes the least step but to this object. This is the motive of every action of every man, even of those who hang themselves.

—Blaise Pascal, Pensées (Thoughts)

I can feel your resistance: "Happiness? Really? You're now going to tell me that pursuing happiness is nonsensical?" Once again, the Traditional Psyche has instilled beliefs so deeply rooted that even though we know as given fact that life could be better, we persist on the same paths that we *know* don't work. Let's turn back the clock to get a better grasp of why we bear the capacity to be happy to begin with.

While there is no concrete answer (as you might expect) from the mindlessness and complexity of natural selection, evolutionary psychologist William von Hippel (2018) offers a simple explanation, suggesting that happiness is a mechanism of motivation. It's how we once rewarded ourselves for doing "good things" such as adding sugar, salt, and fat to our diet (as opposed to feces and dirt) and signaled "attractive qualities," such as suggesting to our tribe and potential mates that we didn't have a crippling disease that left us and them at the mercy of angry mammoths.

In 1971, social psychologists Philip Brickman and Donald T. Campbell coined the term that was referenced earlier: *hedonic adaptation*—the tendency of humans to return to a relatively stable level of happiness despite major negative or positive life-changing events. (See figure 1-26.) Brickman and Campbell studied two sets of people, one of which won large lottery prizes and a group of accident victims who were paralyzed. They found that in the long term, neither group ended up being any happier than the other (Brickman et al., 1978).

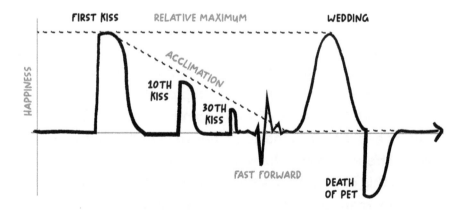

Figure 1-26: Hedonic adaptation

Von Hippel goes on to suggest that we can't be permanently happy because it would defeat its intended purpose. If you were able to be happy forever from one achievement (say, finding a loaded berry bush), then you wouldn't be motivated to improve on yourself, which goes against sexual selection (mate competition) and maintaining your place in a tribe where your chances for survival are that much better. As Randolph M. Nesse put it: "They (happiness and unhappiness) are aspects of mechanisms that influence us to act in the interests of our genes."

Now, fast forward back to modernity. While we still feel compelled to *belong* and find a mate, it is by no means a matter of primitive survival anymore. It's no longer about sugar, salt, and fat. It's no longer about whether you're eating feces or dirt (though this may very well still concern some politicians) or having to protect yourself from angry mammoths. It is much, much more than that. Like every other evolutionary mechanism we possess, our capacity to feel happy or unhappy is yet another evolutionary tool we attempt to force-fit and repurpose into modern life. If it's not about survival anymore, then what is it about? Alas, happiness is as nebulous as a dream. We all like to think we know what it is, how it happens, how long it lasted, and who was involved, but we don't. What is happiness to you? To others? A week ago? A year ago? Perhaps most importantly, how well does it serve as a goal?

Daniel Kahneman, Nobel laureate and arguably the most influential living psychologist, suggests that happiness has two sides: an experiential or emotional side (what he refers to as the *experiencing self*) and an evaluative or cognitive side—the "constructed story" we save in memory and base future decisions on (what he refers to as the *remembering self*). Wanting to demonstrate how people retrospectively evaluate experiences and how different the interpretations of each self can be, Kahneman et al. (1993) had participants submerge their hand in painfully cold water for sixty seconds (the first trial) and then again for sixty seconds with an additional thirty seconds where the water was minimally warmed from 14°C to 15°C (the second trial). When asked which trial they wanted to repeat, the majority chose to participate in the longer trial. And although the first trial was technically "easier," almost everyone prefers the second! It's for the same reason most would rather wait in a long line that moves fast than a slow-moving line that takes less time.

Kahneman's own peak-end theory implies that what we remember most about experiences are their high (or low) points and how they end—which has been empirically validated in numerous domains and is precisely why the retrospective summary judgment of happiness (our evaluations of happiness) often differs greatly from the extrapolated total of experienced happiness through ESM (Experience Sampling Method)—the total weighted sum of experience Pinker was referring to. (See figure 1-27.)

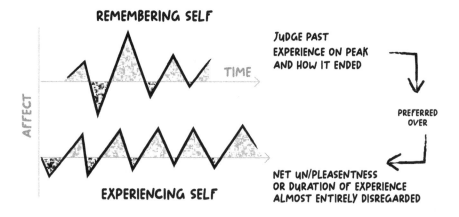

Figure 1-27: Peak-end theory

And while recent studies suggest peaks and ends aren't the best predictors of remembered experience for more complex experiences, the certainty that evaluative happiness is what people value is not in question (Strijbosch et al., 2019).

Kahneman submits that for many years, he was convinced he had a right answer—that the experiencing self is reality, and if you want to make people happy, you should improve their experiences (Harris, 2019). He eventually gave up on this answer as he found that people prefer good memories over good experiences; they want to be satisfied with their lives. Kahneman elaborates by saying memories are all you get to keep and that people think of the future not as experiences but as anticipated memories.

But how does one evaluate the peaks of an experience or the profundity of an end? Nat Ware, a renowned business leader, entrepreneur, economist, and prolific inventor, suggests that happiness and its evaluation relate to expectations: "We are unhappy when our expectations of reality exceed our experiences of reality" ("Why We're Unhappy," n.d.). He calls this the *expectation gap* and suggests there are three ways we form our expectations:

▲ Imagination:

This occurs when what we imagine to be the best decision does not live up to our expectations, leading to disappointment: "When imagination exceeds reality." Social media, for example, sets false expectations with the latest and greatest fitness supplements and photoshopped before-and-after pictures. Travel videos may romanticize an experience, showing you the best a destination has to offer as opposed to the busy mess and littered streets that surround its landmarks. Ware also refers to how online search engines present the most liked images and content, effectively skewing our expectations of experiences that could not possibly live up to the images.

Which is why when we tell kids they are going to be the most famous, richest, or prettiest, we're setting expectations that simply cannot be fulfilled. The goals they then value determine not only what they want to achieve but also the standards against which they evaluate their achievements (Carver and Scheier, 1981). What they imagine to be their valued destination is in fact a goalpost set so impossibly far that whatever progress they make in its direction is trivialized. You would have noticed this with people who are disappointed with what *you'd* consider to be outstanding achievement; it still fell short of the standard they set for themselves. In most cases, this disappointment does not interfere with the goal of being the richest or prettiest; their self-set imagination gap keeps spurring them forward.

What's especially paradoxical here is what happens when happiness *itself* is the goal; a directive many ignoramuses will have you strive for. Because being disappointed when falling short of a goal is incompatible with achieving happiness—the more you strive for happiness, the more likely you will be disappointed, in turn making you even more unhappy! As for positive thinking, comparing realities, anticipating future outcomes, or whatever you want to call it, their causal link to well-being remains contested (Horowitz, 2017). Across cultures, happier people were those who more often experienced emotions they *wanted* to experience, whether these were pleasant (e.g., love) or unpleasant (e.g., hatred) (Tamir et al., 2017). And what bears repeating is that the more aggressively people pursue happiness, the less they seem to be able to obtain it (Kesebir and Diener, 2008).

What you imagine *ought* to be taking place in specific situations can further exacerbate the futility of a goal. For example, in situations that are perceived as conducive to high achievement (where your chances of doing well are better), one is more likely to be disappointed with their achievements (Wiese, 2007). Let's say you value academic achievement. You are more likely to feel disappointed if you get a low grade in an easy class compared with a hard one because that goal seemed easily obtainable. Similarly, if you don't wake up with gleeful joy on your birthday or show up at the party everyone was invited to with a big smile on your face, you're going to feel bad just for feeling bad—because you believe you *ought* to be happy. The more you value—and pursue—happiness, the less likely you are to obtain it, *especially* when happiness appears to be within reach (Mauss et al., 2011). This study found that the higher people valued happiness, the more mental health difficulties (including depression) they experienced, especially during times of low stress (your average day), because if they weren't happy, they couldn't attribute the reason to external circumstances.

▲ Those around us:

This refers to the expectations derived of comparisons we make of our reality to the reality of others, which Ware calls the *interpersonal gap*. Perhaps your parents constantly compared you to your cousin: "Why can't you be more like her?" Or your group of friends finds success and love while you watch from afar in despair. Or maybe it's the media's ceaseless idolizing of the most popular, sexiest, happiest people, provoking a sense of inferiority and dejection.

We often (and sometimes unknowingly) gauge our standing on the social status ladder—a particularly self-deprecating habit and a byproduct of an evolutionary mechanism (for example, mate competition to improve one's chances of survival) catalyzed by the competitive fabric of capitalistic societies. It has become a psychic norm to compete from the day we are born: "You were such as a beautiful baby compared to your siblings." Then it was how well you performed in school compared to your peers and, not long after, how you faired against your colleagues at work. Our natural inclination to compare ends up trivializing minor victories we ought to be proud of.

More importantly, the interpersonal gap leaves us at the mercy of external circumstances; it relies on outside situations, people, or events that influence our expectations at a given time (for example, growing up in the slums as opposed to a high-end neighborhood). Denying the autonomy of happiness, we remain dependent on environmental influences: the milieu, the individuals, the provisions.

▲ Past experiences:

We often compare how we're feeling now to how we felt in the past, wondering whether or not we are happier. Ware calls this the *intertemporal gap*. Do you feel better off? Does your remembering self construct a story of present-day triumph of being self-made or suggest that the highest point in your life was making that game-winning three-point shot at the buzzer, a moment you were never able to supersede?

Depriving generations of challenge through soft structures and twenty-first-century privileges, we consequently deprive them of what Ware calls a "positive intertemporal gradient": making it harder to improve over time because their starting baseline is substantially higher than what their talents can afford or sustain. (See figure 1-28.) You can foresee how expecting more and more from succeeding generations will not only make it harder to triumph but would considerably diminish every succeeding generation's happiness.

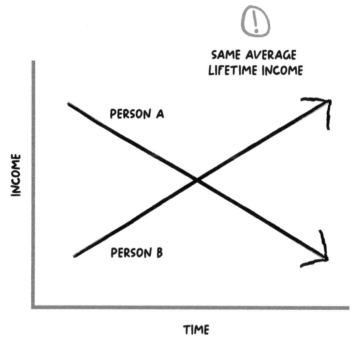

Figure 1-28: Intertemporal gradient

Here's a question: How do you know when you've had the happiest day of your life? You would only have your previous happy experiences to compare to, and by that measure, you usually believe you can confidently say, "*This* is the happiest day of my life." The same can be said about the worst days of your life. Put differently, the height of personal happiness can only be measured by the depth of personal sadness; it is a comparative emotion. Ironically, avoiding emotional sadness limits one's ability to experience the heights of happiness (Schafer, 2016).

This is why elders often tell you, "Oh, you're still young, so keep your chin up" when they see you upset, or they shake their head when they see how excited you get about the purchase of a new phone. They know that that *particular experience*, relative to what you will likely experience in the years ahead, is relatively trivial. The best and worst are yet to come, though for that point in time, it may be the worst (or best) you've ever felt. As far as you're concerned, your first "break up" would have likely been the worst experience you've ever had. You *will* experience worse that will overshadow that feeling, but until then, you would have every right to feel the way you did.

And while Ware's expectation gap helps address questions of desire and unhappiness, fundamental uncertainties remain: What exactly *is* happiness? How do we best pursue it? What do we need to be happy? Is happiness simply a comparative measure? Should I stop pursuing happy things to avoid making it harder for myself to be happy in the future? These lines of inquiry give rise to a debate that has spanned centuries but has advanced substantially in recent decades. We inevitably find ourselves in the realm of philosophy—the "philosophy of happiness" that has produced a number of "theories of happiness" we will now explore.

NUANCE

We cannot begin our exploration without first trying to define happiness—though as you may have anticipated, there is no straightforward answer. Happiness could be an idea, a vision, or a memory; it could be how you're feeling in the moment or how you remember yourself feeling in the past. To make our lives easier, we will refer to how philosophers discern it, namely in two ways:

▲ **A state of mind:**

Refers to psychological states of positive emotional condition, pleasure, etc., and what Kahneman's "experiencing self" encompasses. Such an interpretation pertains to how one "*is* happy," suggesting a certain psychological condition as opposed to saying, she's leading a happy life.

▲ **Well-being:**

A value term in which happiness concerns what benefits the person, what serves their interest, what Kahneman's "remembering self" encompasses. To ascribe happiness in the well-being sense is to make a value judgment given the subjective nature of what benefits our individual selves: what you think is best for you may differ from what is best for me. And continuing from our last example, the idea of "*being* happy" seems to have more to do with the characteristics of the person herself as opposed to a psychological state.

Theories of "affect-based" happiness and well-being exist in various forms and dimensions with plenty of nuances, overlap, and descriptive anomalies. Generally speaking, there are four main flavors, which we will briefly cover, as well as credible hybrid theories under each classification to contrast the implications and shortcomings of what "the best" of each has to offer:

1. Hedonism:

A theory that places a premium on pleasure over pain, in which the pleasantness of our experiences is the only thing that matters and is worth pursuing. There are a number of hedonistic variations, some of which justify the pursuit of pleasure to the *pleasantness* of the sensation, others to nature, some with explanations, and others without. The eighteenth-century philosopher Jeremy Bentham (1988), for example, offers the simplest form, in which the more pleasantness one can experience, and the less painfulness one encounters, the better life will be. Bentham measures these aspects by their duration and intensity. Plain and simple, right? A common and more nuanced perspective amongst philosophers in the last decade is ethicist and political philosopher Daniel M. Haybron's (2010) "emotional state" theory:

▲ EMOTIONAL STATE THEORY:

Haybron argues that happiness is not such a simple notion as a favorable balance of pleasure and unpleasure. He argues that to be happy, one's emotional condition as a whole must be positive—also referred to as *emotional well-being* (Haybron, 2010). The emotional state theory focuses on what Haybron refers to as *central affective states*—psychological states that are deeper, more profound, and more lasting to one's psychology and behavior, such as contentment and confidence or anxiety and loneliness. You can still be happy when you're sad because this form of happiness is deeper. In contrast, *peripheral affective states* are short-lived and superficial, like stubbing your toe or an orgasm.

Haybron suggests there are four major emotional dimensions that matter for happiness. (See figure 1-29.)

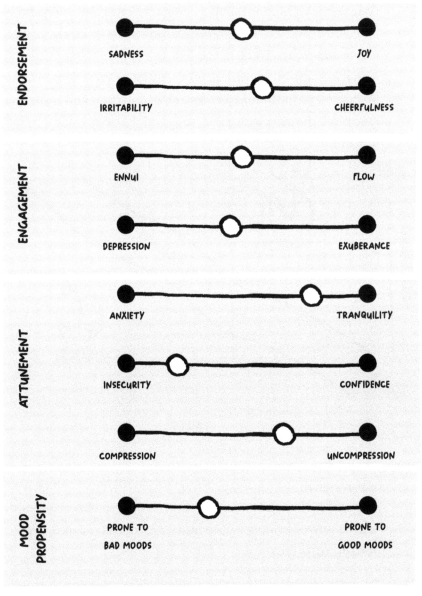

Figure 1-29: Emotional state theory

▽ **Endorsement:** The "feeling" part of the emotional state theory and what is most visible. To be cheerful and joyous, as opposed to irritable and sad. These have depths as well, though; for example, winning the lottery versus running into a friend on the street— neither of which are everlasting.

▽ **Engagement:** Embracing life, being interested and energetic as opposed to bored or withdrawn. Exuberant (buoyant) rather than depressed (vital). To be in the flow as opposed to stagnating in ennui (dissatisfied from a lack of occupation or excitement). Notice in figure 1-30 the balance between skills (or talent) and challenges and recall the issue with goal setting and the twenty-first-century dilemma.

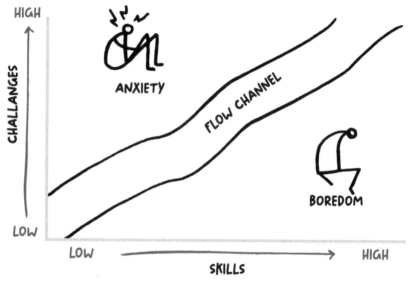

Figure 1-30: Flow

▽ **Attunement:** To be tranquil (as opposed to anxious), confident (as opposed to insecure), uncompressed (as opposed to compressed, e.g., consumed by work or responsibilities, tunnel visioned, seldom looking up at the stars).

▽ **Mood propensity:** Refers to an individual's disposition to experience moods. It's psychologically deeper than any mood or emotion per se—deeper in the sense that it refers to one's *unconscious* tendency to fall into bad moods, which counts against happiness. Negative mood propensities correlate with high levels of neuroticism, a common consequence of difficult life circumstances such as abusive parents, a rocky relationship, or an expectation gap too big to square.

Ergo, happiness in Haybron's emotional state theory is when all four dimensions are maxed—a state referred to as *robust psychic affirmation* (robust because positive mood propensity is resilient to negativity).

While some may not consider the emotional state theory to be a hybrid, one can argue that a positive, enduring, psychic affirmation state—a lasting experience in a broad sense—must have an evaluative element. Regardless, this is hedonism's best dog in the race.

Arguments against the emotional state theory:

▽ Relative to other theories of happiness, it doesn't reflect the quality of one's life as a whole. The subjective nature of interpreting whether one is attuned or not is a comparable measure as governed, for example, by the expectation gap.

▽ The emotional state theory isn't linked with priorities that one can feel, endorse, engage with, and/or attune to with extrinsic desires both knowingly and unknowingly. Whether someone can arrive at robust psychic affirmation with uninformed motivations is debatable, but prioritizing a particular emotional state may deny that person the best that life has to offer.

2. Desire-fulfillment theories:

Equating happiness with fulfillment of one's specific desires as opposed to just having experiences (Griffin, 1986). Variations mainly concern temporality and scope: some focus on fulfilling present desires, others on a level of desire-fulfilment in life as a whole, others seek a more global outlook, and still others pursue intangible functional attributes. Ludwig Wittgenstein, known to be one of the greatest philosophers of the twentieth-century, said in his last words: "Tell them it was wonderful!" This after a life of negative emotions and even downright misery. He sought illumination, truth, struggle, and purity but did not much desire pleasure. A desire theory *would* suggest his life was wonderful; a hedonistic theory would not. More specifically, we now refer to political and ethical philosopher David Sobel's (1994) comprehensive "informed desire" theory:

▲ INFORMED DESIRE THEORY:

The best life is the one we would desire if we were fully informed about objective facts of what will be best for me and you.

Arguments against desire-fulfillment theories:

▽ You can imagine how subjective and questionable one's evaluation of desires is and how their value can turn such a theory upside down. Award-winning moral and political philosopher John Rawls's (1999) imagined case of a talented intellect who has an overwhelming desire "to count blades of grass in various geometrically shaped areas such as park squares and well-trimmed lawns" is commonly used to argue the position. So even though she may be fully informed of her options, an informed-desire theorist would have to submit that counting grass is best for her.

▽ Suppose this intellect's "true fulfilling desire" was to count flavors in wine to become a sommelier, though she presently dislikes the taste of it she would have to acquire. Would this be the best path for her? It may benefit her *idealized* self, but would it really benefit her given how much she desires to count blades of grass?

▽ Focusing on priorities doesn't mean we're focusing on feelings, so you can be fulfilling your desires but still feel upset, anxious, or miserable—much like Wittgenstein.

▽ Setting challenging values and ambitious desires might undermine one's ability to achieve them. How were these goalposts intuitively set to begin with?

3. Objective list theories:

The two aforementioned classifications are subjective, in which what one ascribes pleasure to or what one desires are individualistic. Objective list theories place happiness outside of how *we* feel and what we necessarily want and more on things that benefit us independently of our attitudes, feelings, or what we think (Nussbaum, 1992). These theories list items that are generally agreed to constitute well-being such as love, safety, security, freedom, academic accomplishments, or a lucrative career. They can even include emotional states such as happiness. You may be familiar with Aristotelian values—this is an example of an objective list theory. A broadly acclaimed hybrid nature-fulfillment theory would be moral and political philosopher Martha C. Nussbaum's (1992) "capability approach":

▲ NUSSBAUM'S CAPABILITY APPROACH:

In short, it claims that the freedom to achieve well-being is of primary moral importance and that well-being should be understood in terms of people's capabilities and functionings. Capabilities are the doings and beings that people can achieve if they so choose, whereas functionings are capabilities that have already been realized. Nussbaum refers to the things that an individual can choose from as their capability set which depends on "conversion factors" such as personal, sociopolitical, and environmental conditions and "basic capabilities": innate traits—natural abilities—as described when addressing Self-Limiting Reluctancy. Nussbaum goes further and identifies ten "central human capabilities" (Nussbaum, 2011):

1. **Life:**
   Not dying prematurely or before one's life is so reduced as to not be worth living (suggesting euthanasia is morally just).

2. **Bodily health:**
   Having good health, including reproductive health with adequate nourishment and shelter.

3. **Bodily integrity:**
   Being able to move freely from place to place, secure from violent/sexual/domestic assault; having opportunities for sexual satisfaction and choice in matters of reproduction.

4. **Senses, imagination, and thought:**
   Being able to use the senses; to imagine, think, and reason in a way that is informed and cultivated by an education. Using one's imagination and thought to produce works and events of

one's own choice. Using one's mind—protected by guarantees of freedom of expression—for political and artistic speech and the freedom of religious exercise (though many religious practices contradict much of what is in the list).

5. **Emotions:**

   Being able to have attachments to things and people outside ourselves, to love those who love and care for us and to grieve in their absence, not having one's emotional development blighted by fear and anxiety.

6. **Practical reason:**

   Being able to conceive "the good" and to engage in critical reflection about the planning of one's life.

7. **Affiliation:**

   Being able to live with and toward others; to recognize and show concern for other humans; to engage in various forms of social interaction; to imagine the situation of another and empathize; having a social basis of self-respect and non-humiliation, entailing provisions of non-discrimination on the basis of race, sex, sexual orientation, ethnicity, caste, religion, national origin, and species.

8. **Other species:**

   Being able to have concern for—and be in relation with—animals, plants, and the world of nature.

9. **Play:**

   Being able to laugh, play games, and have fun; freedom from having one's enjoyment and recreation criticized or prevented.

10. **Control over one's environment:**

    Being able to participate in political activities, making free choices, and joining with others to promote political views; to own property and goods on the same basis as others; to seek and accept work and be treated reasonably at work; to be free from unwarranted search and seizure.

You can see how Nussbaum's capability approach was designed as a broad, normative framework, one that it is commonly used in the development of political philosophy, public health ethics, environmental ethics, climate justice, and the philosophy of education (and in Australian energy vulnerability policies (Willand et al., 2021), indigenous policy (Klein, 2016), and curriculums (Skourdoumbis, 2015)—just to name a few).

Arguments against the capability approach:

▽ While an objective list may lead one toward conventional (or some other defined ideal) success, an individual may still not resonate with those "objective" goods and may even believe that some go against their personal desires (such as having children). For a theory of well-being to be institutionalized in a capitalistic society is to imply utilitarian conformity to a particular socioeconomic ideal. Thus, on the spectrum of subjectivity, Nussbaum's capability approach seems to be more demanding.

▽ Most people don't have the freedoms of such capabilities, which rely on democracy, education, employment, freedom of employment, healthy family life circumstances, and so on. And given the *relatively* prescriptive nature of such a list, it does suggest a narrower view of potentialities.

▽ Objective list theories are bound to a question with a necessarily elusive answer: What should the list consist of? Who gets to say? Why does anyone get the authority to make the list anyway? Why not include exploration of space or relationships with technology instead of animals? Proponents of such theories are considered elitist as they are claiming that certain things are good for people and they know best. For example, if an individual is not as concerned with the arts or other species, does that make them deficient humans? At the same time, a list can be elitist *and* true.

4. Life-satisfaction theories:

Equate happiness to having a favorable attitude toward one's life as a whole (or some aspect of it, such as career), achieving what they see as important, believing the conditions of their life are excellent, and that if they could do it over, they wouldn't change much (Diener et al., 1985). The life-satisfaction theory would have you evaluate your life with respect to its value for *you*—and not, for example, in terms of whether it is valuable according to some expectations. One ambitious proposal that promises to strengthen the position of happiness in the well-being sense is ethicist and political philosopher Leonard W. Sumner's theory:

▲ **SUMNER'S LIFE-SATISFACTION THEORY:**

Identifies well-being with what Sumner calls *authentic happiness*—a happiness that is informed and autonomous (Sumner, 1996). Authenticity is achieved when a person's values are central to their evaluation of well-being—that is, what's important for *their* happiness, aligned with values that are truly their own (autonomous) as opposed to some aesthetic ideal or ethical standard—and those values survive critical reflection (informed). Such an outlook thwarts the arguments raised earlier by Nozick's Experience Machine and submits that keeping Mikayla in the dark (see page 78) is denying her authentic happiness. One is happy in this account if their evaluation of satisfaction is based on facts or at least beliefs which are justified given the available evidence.

Arguments against life-satisfaction theories:

▽ The issue of informedness in this account is based on *informed evaluation*—by the individual's own standards as opposed to outside measures of an "idealized life." However, being more informed in this sense doesn't necessarily mean you'll act rationally or have the capacity to. The extent to which "facts" influence the decisions you make and how well your life goes is up to your own assessment.

▽ Sumner regards external standards that evaluate well-being to be incompatible with individual sovereignty, even though they could still serve as constraints or conditions that genuinely benefit a person without alienating what they desire. Such a stance has caused philosophers to regard his theory to be an "extreme subjective" as opposed to a "moderate subjectivist" theory as he claims it to be.

▽ Given that evaluating one's life is not a straightforward process, one can question whether people have realistic attitudes of life satisfaction or dissatisfaction. As we have previously highlighted, some people make life-satisfaction judgments on the spot based on whatever comes to mind. So, one may be overly joyed by a life that *could* be much better, and contrastingly, one may be disconcerted by a life the majority could only wish for.

You can imagine how literature that doesn't make a distinction about what kind of happiness they're referring to can invalidate the intelligibility and efficacy of whatever it is they happen to be preaching. Anyone who tells you how you ought to be feeling or what you ought to be striving for is prescribing their own (often uninformed) objective-list theory, which has to be taken with a grain of salt—especially if their prescribed objective goods conflict with your desires. Anyone suggesting that you live in the moment and do what you feel is best *now* is clearly disavowing any sense of prudential value. Anyone telling you to pursue your dreams and be steadfast with the effort is turning a blind eye to uninformed or changing desires. These are only a few examples of how ignorant and impractical much of what gets passed for wisdom truly is.

WHAT DOESN'T WORK

As we tread toward a lifestyle superior to that of the Traditional Psyche that is compatible with the twenty-first century while addressing its emergent issues, we must thwart all that doesn't work. Drawing from what the Kahneman, Ware, and most credible happiness theories have to offer, we can deduce and reaffirm that the following don't work:

▲ Incessant Distraction:
Consider those who spend their nights partying, having mindless sex and/ or taking drugs that "feel right in the moment," only to break down in

tears during quieter times. From a hedonist's perspective, that balance is still tipped in the right direction, but are they really happy? Similarly, if you remain Incessantly Distracted with video games, TV, or a workaholic attitude, you may be happy or not unhappy in the moment, but overall, are you really happy? Finally, given the paradoxical nature of setting hedonistic happiness as a goal, it has been argued that hedonism undermines happiness, especially, as we know, if we depend on it to subdue underlying pain. Consider Nozick's Experience Machine thought experiment and how the majority rejected the idea of imagining an ideal future even if their circumstances were terrible. No matter how experimenters parsed the proposition of the experience to make it more appealing, and given how much more there is to consider to satisfy both interpretations of happiness (state of mind and well-being), a growing consensus seems to be that there is more to life than pleasure, which is why many philosophers have lowered the importance of happiness (as a state of mind) in the great scheme of what defines a good life.

▲ Permanence of desire:

Richard B. Brandt, one of the most influential ethicists and moral philosophers of the second half of the twentieth century (1982), suggests that the main problem with desire theories is that desires change over time. Merely fulfilling past desires is what we referred to earlier as misguided masochism. This suggests that desire theory overemphasizes only what is going on at the time of the desire, actioning desires while they are still fulfilling.

▲ Heteronomy:

Consider the subdued housewife who tries to make the most of a situation by adapting her expectations and satisfactions to available opportunities. Even though she knows she lives under manipulation, she can still sincerely say she feels that she's happy. Similarly, you may be making the most of limiting attitudes inherited from indoctrination and oppression while growing up (whether it be extrinsically directed aspirations like childbearing or a career path your parents wanted for you) and still say that you are happy. But how long do you think these "welfare evaluations" will last, especially when confronted with alternative paths, truths, and experiences that beckon exploration? Have these adaptations affected your mood, perhaps even to the point of clinical depression, or at least caused you to keep justifying your choices?

▲ Ignorance:

Consider the case of an orphan who has been training to be a monk since a very early age, leading to a life sheltered from other lifestyles, opportunities, and experiences. He is now offered three choices: he can stay on the monk's path, become a waiter, or work as a landscaper outside the monastery in the outskirts of the city. He has no conception of the latter two alternatives, so he chooses to remain a monk. But surely it might be possible that his life would be better if he were to live outside. But how would you know how much better you could have it? Similarly, think of a depressed, overachieving person who believes their life is a failure, that nobody likes them, and that they haven't accomplished anything meaningful. You can point out the fact that they're wrong and show them how amazing they are, how many friends they have, and so on. You may also suggest that ignorance is bliss. But is it really? Would you really want to be Cypher from *The Matrix* and be plugged back into an Experience Machine? As distastefully put by screenwriter Paul Abbott's fictious character Frank Gallagher: "If ignorance is bliss, Down syndrome must be euphoric."

How much of the aforementioned sounds familiar? With all the problems we've described, dissected, and explored thus far—are you beginning to connect the dots? Whether its authenticity of pursuits, autonomy of desires, being informed of what is possible, confronting the expectation gap, emotional-state propensities and their underlying causal factors, happiness as a goal and the absurdity of such an attitude . . . We seem to be focusing on out-of-date list theories which harken to Traditional Psyche sentiments and relying on hedonistic pursuits to patch up the pain of detachment—both efforts lack autonomy and informedness, and are, ultimately, inauthentic.

Amongst the few voices that go against the grain is Russ Harris's best-selling book, *Happiness Trap*, which acknowledges the futility of pursuing happiness and suggests we "act on values, not emotion." While it is a step in the right direction, we must again recognize the fact that our values are constantly changing as well. Harris will repeatedly have you "dig deep" and figure out what your values are using a questionnaire from which you then set meaningful goals. If we have learned anything, however, it's that we should avoid setting guardrails to our potential as "we both step and do not step in the same rivers, we are and are not."

> **I may venture to affirm of the rest of mankind, that they are nothing but a bundle or collection of different perceptions, which succeed each other with an inconceivable rapidity, and are in a perpetual flux and movement. Our eyes cannot turn in their sockets without varying our perceptions. Our thought is still more variable than our sight, and all our other senses and faculties contribute to this change; nor is there any single power of the soul, which remains unalterably the same, perhaps for one moment.**

—David Hume, *Treatise of Human Nature*

So, what should dictate our direction if it's not values or happiness? If it's not about passion? If there is no purpose? If our desires and our self-concept regularly change? These are the golden questions that we will work our way toward answering. But whatever framework of happiness and well-being we pursue, know at the very least what it ought to address and what it should exclude.

The Traditional Psyche's incompatibilities with an everchanging twenty-first-century milieu work against us in more ways than we can intuitively realize: from how we manage our ambitions, to how we interpret threats, to the belief or myths of what we can and can't do and become, to how we spend our time, and, ultimately, how we spend our life. The issue of defining "time well spent" and topics of purpose, reason, aspirations, and fulfillment have all been presented. And so, once we rid ourselves from all bestowed expectation, what are we left with? Where do we go from here? Having now explored various theories of happiness and well-being, you may be reminded of *Necessitating Change's* subtitle and the book's promise of a practical guide to "self-actualization." Is it a desire-fulfillment theory? An objective list of objective goods? Does it consider how we feel in the moment? All will be revealed in due time, but it is worth appreciating the clarity and scrupulousness we now advance with.

CHAPTER 9
SHORTSIGHTED LIMITS

One of the most legendary ideas in the history of psychology takes the form of an unassuming triangle divided into five sections and referred to universally as Maslow's "hierarchy of needs." Published in an academic journal in 1943, it has since become a mainstay of psychological analyses. From the start of his professional career, prominent psychologist Abraham H. Maslow sought nothing less than the meaning of life. He wanted to find out what made life purposeful for people in modern day America, where the pursuit of money and fame eclipsed interior or authentic aspirations. The hierarchy depicts five different levels of needs, from the physiological to the psychological to the arguably spiritual (without any trappings of mysticism). (See figure 1-31.)

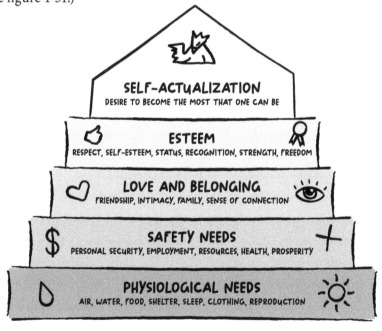

Figure 1-31: Maslow's hierarchy of needs

Maslow pursued questions with particularly evasive answers: What do we long for? How do we arrange our priorities? We can't live by spiritual callings alone, but we also can't be focused only on the material. Both realms need tending. We often meet spiritual types who suggest we forget about money, housing, a good insurance policy, and how to pay for lunch. Pragmatists, on the other hand, focus on feeding their family and putting money in the bank. It bears repeating: we are complex, multifaceted creatures.

Maslow categorized human motivation in the following order: First, meeting physiological needs such as food, water, warmth, rest, and safety. Then we aspire to belongingness and love, friends and lovers, esteem and respect. Lastly, we are driven by what he calls *self-actualization*: achieving one's full potential by finding meaning and fully engaging in creative self-growth—a process by which we discover, become, and affirm our identity.

Maslow attributed the following characteristics to self-actualized people:

▲ **They have a comfortable acceptance of self—flaws and all.**
They accept who they are, understanding their shortcomings as natural personal characteristics. They can laugh at themselves and lack defensiveness or artificiality.

▲ **They prioritize and relish the journey rather than focusing on a destination.**
They regard as ends in themselves the many experiences and activities that are, for others, only means. They are able to make the most out of seemingly trivial and routine activities.

▲ **There is frequent occurrence of peak experiences.**
Maslow referred to a peak experience as: "[an] oceanic feeling. Feelings of limitless horizons opening up to the vision. The feeling of being more powerful and more helpless than one ever was before. A feeling of great ecstasy and wonder and awe . . . And the conviction that something extremely important and valuable has happened." (Maslow, 1964). Historically, a peak experience is associated with such psychological phenomena as "flow," though given Maslow's assertions, it is better described as the quintessential embodiment of euphoric being—a highly valued experience

characterized by depth of feeling or profound significance in contrast to other experiences. It is worth noting that one need not be self-actualized to have peak experiences; a self-actualized individual simply experiences them more often.

▲ **They are motivated by personal growth and not the satisfaction of needs.**
They accept the absence of a finish line and know there is more to life than fortune, fame, and family. They expect nothing more at whatever summit they reach than more "cyclical growth"—not bliss, stagnation, or retirement but further evolution and peak experiences.

▲ **They rely on their own experiences and judgment, independent of cultural norms and social constructs, to form opinions and views.**
They neither accept all, like sheep, nor reject all, like rebels, and have their own individualized code of ethics.

▲ **They are spontaneous in their internal thoughts and outward behavior.**
They *can* conform to rules and social expectations but tend to be open and unconventional.

▲ **They constantly indulge in continued freshness of appreciation.**
They don't take their blessings for granted and have a sense of continual wonder and awe at even the simplest of experiences such as a sunset or a blossoming flower.

▲ **They are autonomous, resourceful, and independent, free from relying on external authorities or other people.**
Despite being socially compassionate with choosing profound interpersonal relationships, they are comfortable with solitude and don't feel the need to conform to other people's ideas of contentment or happiness.

▲ **They are able to judge situations correctly and honestly and are sensitive to the superficial and dishonest.**
Their sense of realism allows them to view life as it unfolds both logically and rationally. While they may participate with the ceremonies and rituals of convention, they recognize them for what they are and do not

allow artificiality to take precedence over what they see to be internal or essential.

▲ **Self-actualized individuals embrace the unknown and the ambiguous.**
They do not feel threatened by it nor are they afraid of it and simply accept it; they are comfortable with it and are often attracted to it.

▲ **They choose only a few profound interpersonal relationships.**
As opposed to many perfunctory relationships.

▲ **They are socially compassionate and possess social interest, community feeling, and a sense of oneness with all humanity.**
This is what Maslow referred to as *gemeinschaftsgefühl* (human kinship).

It's important to address the fact that there have been revised versions of Maslow's hierarchy, most notably the work of Douglas T. Kenrick et al. (2010), a well-respected evolutionary psychologist who attempted to generate an empirically validated hierarchy. His contemporary renovation substitutes self-actualization with reproductive goals such as parenthood, mate retention, and mate acquisition. An empirical outlook indeed, it would be safe to assume these motivations to be a form of self-actualization (the result of the Procreative Predisposition, as we have recognized) and therefore not in conflict with the premise of Necessitating Change. It is also worth noting that toward the latter years of Maslow's life, he was working on a theory of transcendence that involved liberation from egocentricity, altruism, and "unity of being." Feel free to read up on it, but for the issues addressed here, anything beyond self-actualization is beyond the fundamental course correction we are seeking to bring to bear. Or to put a "Spinoza" on it: As far as Necessitating Change is concerned, we are limiting our reach to sub-specie durationis ("under the aspect of time"), signifying the limited satisfaction of an individual's perspective. In other words, given our cosmologically infinitesimal and short-lived presence, we will focus solely on an egotistical outlook that is temporarily necessary to break our bad habits and enable any chance of reaching eternal or global aspirations.

In most capitalistic societies, the focus has primarily resided in the lower three tiers of the hierarchy and the more superficial levels of the spiritual, in which wealth, a big house, a happy family, and even fame are highly sought after as attributes of ultimate achievement. Mainstream media and social constructs set a precedent for each generation, and given how every channel, magazine, newsfeed, forum post, and so on is riddled with updates of which hip-hop artist has the biggest diamond-encrusted necklace, which NBA player has the biggest family, or which soccer-club owner owns the biggest yacht, it's not surprising to see that recent generations have come to believe that the purpose of their endeavors resides in materialism, prestige, and childbearing. Historically speaking, older generations were comfortably embedded in the lower tiers of the hierarchy, and while a few may have attained the qualities of self-actualization as defined by Maslow, it's abundantly clear that their primary purpose was survival: putting food on the table, providing for their family, and seeking safety and protection from environmental, political, social, and natural threats. Faced with the daily challenges of getting by, their acquaintance with the upper echelons of Maslow's pyramid of needs was either scarce or resided in the *superstitious*—in the religious dogma that dominated the social fabric of communities. Although the struggle for survival persists to this day, its attributions have ascended to higher levels of the pyramid.

As Steven Pinker explains in his book *Enlightenment Now*, quality of life has been on a steady incline, especially in the last two decades, whether it be measured by literacy, general health, freedom, education, sustenance, wealth, equality, safety, democracy, or expanding rights. Whether these privileges have been inherited or are simply more ubiquitous and accessible, newer generations seldom face issues akin to those of previous generations. Their salient dilemmas have more to do with personal progress than meeting life's basic necessities: "I'm doing everything I should be doing, yet I still feel as though I am on the back foot." "What am I doing wrong? I did well in college, I'm getting my exercise, and I love my partner, yet I still have trouble staying motivated."

In addition to the myriad of problems we have explored thus far shedding light on the juxtaposition of unparalleled quality of life and depression and suicide rates, we arrive at a particularly pertinent issue worth unpacking.

Examining Maslow's hierarchy elucidates a predicament beyond the intertemporal progress the aforementioned privileges afford. With preliminary necessities fulfilled through inheritance, social securities, technological advancements, and economies of scale, newer generations are left with higher tiers to strive for. Unfortunately, what ends up happening is the "reach for more" remains stuck in the middle tiers of the pyramid. More fame, more wealth, more love—most of which are ultimately trivial, unfulfilling, or short lived. There is certainly *some* truth to the idiom that "money doesn't buy happiness," which creates a disformed, bottom-heavy pyramid.

This quest for *more* and the endless staircase of ever-growing expectations has left us in a vicious cycle of self-dissonance. What it means to become self-actualized is blurred, subjective, contextual, and individualistic, making it difficult if not impossible to plant a flag when one has truly "arrived." Indeed, there is no destination but a space of fulfilled application. As the saying goes: "Life is not a noun; it's a verb."

Anyone climbing the corporate ladder usually does so because they "ought to," often exhausting their freedom and quality of life in the process. Investors invest and continue investing because they ought to, amassing wealth to no end. Do you ever stop and wonder, "How much is enough?" The dichotomy between the means to facilitate self-actualization and self-actualization itself is often naively overlooked. Consider the segregation of social classes. The working class strives to be middle class, the middle to be upper middle, the upper middle to be millionaires, the millionaires to be multimillionaires, and so on. You often find that we acclimate to whatever standard of living we attain and then seek higher ground—what we now know to be the hedonic treadmill, a recurring theme. You may be telling yourself now that winning a million dollars in a lottery is all the money you could ever need, but how do you know this? How do you know, for example, that your standard of living or what it is you're after won't change, or how new friends or a significant other might influence how you choose to live your life? Money makes money, so wouldn't you reinvest it and live a frugal life until you can retire off your returns? Maybe it's enough for you *now*, but will it be enough for you in five years? Recall the problem of stretch goals. And tangentially, would you feel as euphoric if you received five thousand dollars after hitting the jackpot?

Figure 1-32: Salary, life satisfaction, and experienced well-being

Adapted from Killingsworth (2021)

In 2010, an annual income of $75,000 USD (around $108,000 AUD) was often referred to as the minimal cut-off for happiness. (See figure 1-32.) You might have heard about this through one skewed narrative or another. Chances are, that's probably all you know of the widely misquoted study conducted by Kahneman and Deaton (2010). As you would expect from journalism bound by metrics and advertising revenue and, consequently, sensationalism, deception, and misleading narratives that exploit cognitive biases for clicks, they left out the meat from the potatoes. Kahneman and Deaton made abundantly clear (including in the title!) that there is a delineation between experiential and evaluative well-being (here we go again) and how survey participants were questioned. In fact, the study found that evaluative well-being *did* continue to increase with incomes beyond $75,000, though with diminishing returns. This makes sense considering what we now know now when evaluative judgments are taken into consideration: the reality of interpersonal and intertemporal gaps. And while Kahneman and Deaton found a plateau of experiential well-being at the $75,000 mark, a recent study identified a limitation in the scale used to measure it (a binary measure which leaves no room to register improvement).

Drawing on 1,725,994 experience-sampling reports from 33,391 employed US adults, positive psychologist Matthew A. Killingsworth (2021) found that experienced well-being did *not* plateau past $75,000 and continued to rise—again, with diminishing returns and less so compared to evaluative well-being. Lower income didn't cause sadness directly, but as you might imagine, it would be hard to be consistently happy if your physiological and safety needs were under constant threat—paying your rent, feeding your family, settling medical debts. After the $75,000 threshold, individual temperament, life circumstances, or individualistic X-factors had more of an influence on a person's outlook than money itself. And it's also worth pointing out that if you take inflation into consideration, that 2010 income of $75,000 equates to $96,000 (around $138,000 AUD) in 2022. While you may be thinking, "Well, I'm nowhere near that, so I ought to prioritize 'money-making,'" simply recognize that you may not be *that* far off the upper limit and compromising freedom of experience to inch closer may be counterproductive, all things considered. Self-actualization does not, indubitably, come with a $96,000 price tag, and compromising, endless wealth accumulation does not equate to endless happiness.

A 2018 study on the correlation between worldwide happiness and income yielded some affirming insights. Based on a global sample of 1.7 million people (using the same polls as the aforementioned survey on the state of global happiness), it found that income satiation occurs at $95,000 for life satisfaction with incomes of $60–$75,000 necessary for emotional well-being (Jebb et al., 2018). As the researchers explain, the findings "point to a degree of happiness adaptation, and that money influences happiness through the fulfillment of both needs and increasing material desires."

However, most interesting was the finding that in the world's wealthier regions, *income satiation* extends beyond the $95,000 mark, and in some areas that number is actually associated with lower life evaluations and levels of well-being (such as in Western Europe, East Asia, and Latin America). The authors posit that after this threshold, people may be chasing after material gains and engaging in social comparisons that could lower their sense of well-being—inflating a discontented bottom-heavy pyramid.

While we cannot be surprised with contradictory conclusions given study limitations, the difficulties of trying to measure life-satisfaction and emotional well-being, and the countless variables that cannot be controlled with certitude, we can confidently deduce the following:

▲ Avoid costly, uninformed commitments that deprive us of autonomy, otherwise the consequence will be compromise: doing what we'd rather not do for lack of choice and giving up emotional well-being out of constant fear of meeting basic necessities.

▲ These findings indicate correlation, not causation. That is to say, evaluations of happiness and well-being are multi-faceted. So just because you earn more money than another won't necessarily mean you're happy in the experienced *and* evaluative sense, as the well-being you reap after tending to your basic necessities is almost entirely based on your circumstances, expectation gap, and whatever theory of happiness you naturally respond to. For example, you may have a lucrative though stressful job, an inherited expectation gap too vast to bridge, poor spending/investing habits, or suffer the consequences of every other human shortcoming you can imagine.

▲ Given diminishing returns, we now have a ballpark figure to circumvent unnecessary compromise; that is to say, should you find yourself lucky enough to be earning anything around $90,000, you need not feel desperate for more and ought to invest time in other, *more* intrinsically rewarding pursuits. But is it really that simple?

To help answer this question, radical financial planner Paul D. Armson put it best when he offered this straightforward approach to seizing financial independence (Armson, 2016):

Step 1: Sell your car, or sell your house, assuming you have one.

Step 2: With the proceeds, get yourself a cheap flight out to Kathmandu, Nepal.

Step 3: Take a short, cheap internal flight out of Kathmandu to Lukla. You'll enjoy the landing experience.

Step 4: Pop on your walking boots and head north. You'll eventually come to a little village called Jorsalle on the west side of the Dudh Kosi River, just south of Namche Bazaar, in the spectacular Khumbu region.

Step 5: Take a right turn. You'll now be off the beaten track. After another thirty minutes, you'll come to another little village. Your new home! Here you can buy yourself a little shack for next to nothing. What's more, with most of the sale value of your car or house still in the bank, you'll probably be the richest person in the village!

And yet while you would have met your basic necessities and have the spending power to ensure safety, love, and belonging, you will likely still be left longing for more. Contrastingly, you may find the opposite with individuals harboring structurally unsound *top-heavy pyramids*—those who've exhausted all their efforts to pursue self-actualization and esteem while neglecting the rest. Think of passionate activists, monks, and artists who set aside their well-being and personal life in pursuit of purpose.

Although Maslow never intended for this model to take the shape of a pyramid, the structure and direction of this sacred geometry highlights his intent. One would assume the climb to be linear, where each base is accomplished and then you're on to the next. And perhaps after reaching the summit, the credits start to roll. But as you would expect, "Life ain't a movie." Every level in the pyramid plays an increasingly important role, but neglecting the supportive foundations below will only make successive levels increasingly hard to attain *and* maintain.

A HARROWING ASCENT

It goes without saying that academic institutions do a good job at teaching useful, pragmatic practices such as chemistry, biology, physics, math, and so on. Unfortunately, the study of the self is woefully—and sometimes entirely—neglected, and as a result, understanding the nature of higher aspirations is alien to most. Considering that instructions for attaining higher echelons isn't as forthcoming as the apple pie recipe that slipped your mind, this is a serious problem. In other words, the higher you reach, the more challenging it gets. Think of the pyramid as Mount Everest where the summit is the pinnacle of a life of fulfillment. The higher you climb, the harder it is to navigate, coordinate, communicate, and manage. Aspiring to ascend without guidance, support, method, and the right tools can be dangerous. For example, one may commit to lifelong sacrifices for the sake of misguided self-esteem such as "social status" or what one may sincerely (though ignorantly) insist to be "what I'm made for." This then leads to a vicious cycle of unwanted responsibilities such as childbearing, early marriage, onerous loans, risky investments, or refusing to pivot from an unfulfilling career. One would assume that a society with any interest in its well-being would place a heavier emphasis on studying the self. Maslow's hope was to see businesses make more profits by not only addressing our basic needs but our higher psychological and spiritual ones as well: truly enlightened capitalism.

Think, for example, of meditation (the absence of distraction), counselling, and therapy as Sherpas—the means to make the ascent probable and risk-free. However, Sherpas expect some form of climbing expertise, an understanding of altitude and how to acclimate to it, teamwork, emergency protocols, and so on. In short, they expect some level of *experience*. The same can be said about meditation, counselling, and therapy: experience is critical. The more you acquire, the higher the likelihood of figuring out what's best for you. There is only so much you can learn about yourself if your experiences are limited, and only so much information to work with at any given time. Still, the more life experience you have, the more likely you will solve the riddle that is your individualistic sense of self-actualization.

Uncertainty is another element that makes its presence known the higher you climb. Every component in the spiritual realm is unique to that of the beholder, which means that its acquisition is gained through the beholder's initiative and conviction. What you resonate with is neither given nor foretold. You are essentially climbing blind, in heavy fog, not knowing if what you are climbing toward is in fact the peak. We consequently need to accustom ourselves to the potential absence of certainty and learn to strive for and embrace uncertainty, as the signposts leading to or away from self-actualization lie deeply hidden somewhere within that shrouded mist.

How often have you come across a lost soul, in turmoil, without purpose? Often following—or preceding—a long-drawn-out sigh, their conversation reveals feelings of inadequacy and defeat. Perhaps a consequence of one's inherently competitive nature, there may be a sense that, "She's found meaning and I haven't, therefore I am inferior." The reality is that purpose is elusive for most of us, and it's perfectly *okay* to not have found "the one" or "what gets me out of bed in the morning." You will often hear, "Just give it some time and you'll find it" or "You just need to be patient; it'll come when the time is right." Absolute drivel! Hollow hope is a recipe for a disaster and a subject I dissect in upcoming chapters. Instead, set your sights on a practical call to action: a Sherpa on steroids riding an Apache helicopter who comes in the form of change!

You might still be scratching your head at what it will take to pursue self-actualization. "What is my full potential? Potential in what sense? How do I discover or become my identity? How does such an outlook square with an everchanging self? And you still haven't answered the question of which theory of happiness ultimately rules self-actualization." And so, it may seem as though we are left with more questions than answers—answers we aren't yet ready for. And while you may have noticed commonalities between Maslow's attributions of human motivation and theories of happiness, I would very much like you to take a moment, a day, or even a week to ruminate over how we've all been ignorantly and inauthentically conducting ourselves in light of the issues I've brought to your attention and what you think I'm leading you toward.

If you've already begun to speculate on what the Quasi-Chaotic Lifestyle may involve and are questioning the feasibility or practicality of what you're imagining—seeing it perhaps as too controversial or contentious or even ridiculous—then allow me to retort. Simply set aside such presumptions; the only matter you will increasingly find absurd is how pigeonholed we've become and how much we've been missing out on.

PREQUEL TO PART II:

REVELATIONS OF PROMISE

A few questions, a few insights, and a few studies are all it takes to reveal our unconscious blueprints: symptoms that may sound all too familiar, references that perhaps hit too close to home, patterns of predictable outcomes. Start instead with self-awareness to recognize and liberate yourself from extraneous constructs restricting your thought and conduct. Examine the present to find your footing. Consciously navigate a brighter future toward the pinnacle of *being*: self-actualization. More importantly, put sensible theory into practice with a realistic, actionable, and practical approach. We can always delve deeper into such esoteric dynamics as our neuropathological inhibitions, but at the end of the day, what do you do with this information?

How do we make up for all the time, opportunities, and challenges we've wasted? How do we course-correct our way out of an inauthentic and unfulfilling existence? As you might have guessed by now, it's through accelerating the accumulation of experience! A Quasi-Chaotic Lifestyle foregoes long-term goals and instead presents a reliable surge of illuminating, welcomed challenges. With every new experience and exposure to the unfamiliar, you are training your prefrontal cortex to inhibit the amygdala's response and remain in a state of flow. The experiences *you* choose will shape your talents and personality in ways that will bring you the most value. A Quasi-Chaotic Lifestyle will minimize meaningless Incessant Distraction, ridding proclivities of procrastination and escape. It will reveal interests and aspirations to rival your Procreative Predisposition. Most importantly, it's not a matter of thinking harder, hoping, or waiting, but an approach you can act on *today*. I will now present the foundations of the Quasi-Chaotic Lifestyle and demonstrate its potential. Revelations of promise, revelation of self!

PART II
REVELATIONS OF PROMISE
THE THEORY

CHAPTER 10
THE WATERFALL METHODOLOGY

Maslow's hope for enlightened capitalism, one that primarily profits from addressing higher psychological and spiritual needs, unveils a truth we ought to exploit: a capitalistic society invests far more of its resources into advancing efficiencies that support organizational success instead of individualistic self-actualizing motifs. However, distilling these capitalistic developments of operational efficiencies, one discovers pearls of wisdom that are applicable to personal, day-to-day conduct. It is from the information technology (IT) industry and, specifically, software development, that we derive the foundation of the Quasi-Chaotic Lifestyle. You might be wondering, "What on Earth does software development have to do with the Traditional Psyche, stretch goals, consequences of insufficient challenge, self-actualization, genetic inclinations, false beliefs of intrinsic potentialities, meaningless perpetual distraction, or happiness?" Without getting ahead of ourselves, let's take a step back and explore what the IT industry has invested billions perfecting.

We begin by exploring the software development model known as the Waterfall methodology. First introduced in 1970 by computer scientist Winston W. Royce (2017), this model describes a linear software development process consisting of defined stages that encompass activities, requisites, and responsibilities for meeting the particular requirements of a system to be built. In other words, it's a rigid method for developing a product sequentially, consisting of stages that lead one to the next—from beginning to end. Much like a waterfall, phases in the Waterfall methodology flow from one pool to another, filling one completely before spilling into the next. (See figure 2-1.)

This model is strict; it emphasizes planning, documentation, predefined phases (with contextual indifference, I might add), structured organization, stringent rules and regulations, a rigorous hierarchy of communication and decision-making, and a well-defined goal whereby all requirements must be known prior to development. A project's *initiation brief* defines the deliverables one should expect to receive by the end of the development process; no more, no less.

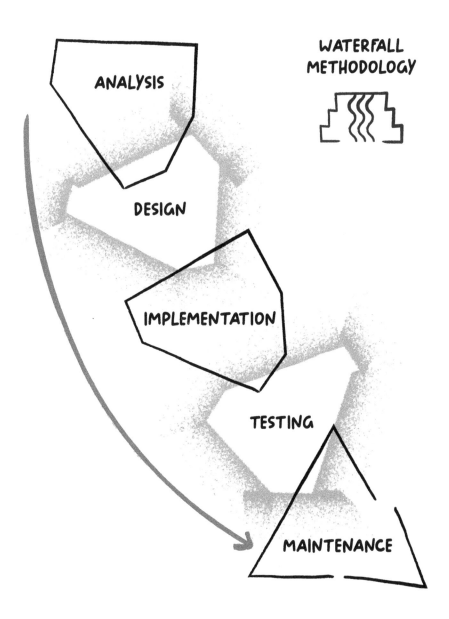

Figure 2-1: Waterfall methodology

In software development, such endeavors are confined within what econo-mists call the *iron triangle* or "triangle of objectives," as its creator, project management pioneer Martin Barnes, coined it. It consists of three constraints. (See figure 2-2.)

1. Scope:

Requirements specified to achieve the expected outcomes. For example, a CRM (customer relationship management) system that tracks customer engagement and retention.

2. Resources (cost):

The cost of said scope, including (but not limited to) funding, personnel, competencies, and assets necessary to meet all project deliverables.

3. Time:

The estimated time required to fulfill said scope.

The Waterfall methodology is designed to exhaust time and resources to fulfill the desired scope. The "iron" element to this trifecta suggests the sides cannot be bent or broken without degrading the quality of scope, underdelivering, delivering late and/or overbudget, or cancelling the project altogether. In other words, if you are looking to increase the scope of a given project, you must increase the resources and the time dedicated to it as well.

Given the profundity of what there is to extrapolate from the Waterfall methodology's exercise, we will now explore a holistic application of its methods. It is worth noting that, for the sake of succinctness, I have simplified much of the process, making use of its traditional form as opposed to its modern/hybrid adaptations. I must also warn you that while the following case study might feel like a digression, its implications are paramount for what is to come.

PREDICTIVE PROCESS
(WATERFALL)

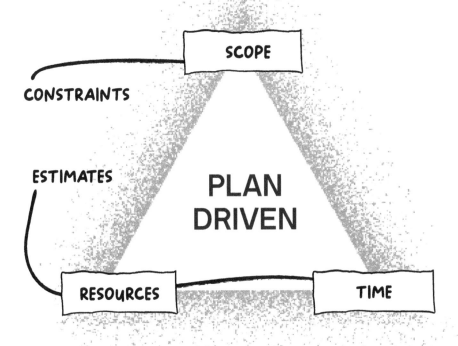

**THE SCOPE CONSTRAINTS CREATE
RESOURCES/TIME ESTIMATES**

Figure 2-2: Iron triangle

A MODEST UNDERTAKING

Let's take the example of a local-yet-sizable medical clinic that has been operating for the past decade. The managing director, Jane, has decided it's time to upgrade their systems of operation to capitalize on newer technology in order to optimize their performance and offer an improved quality of service to their loyal customers. After all, the community has flourished, the queues are getting longer, and staff are spending too much of their time working through trivial administrative formalities that could be automated.

Jane has hired a software development company utilizing the traditional Waterfall methodology to custom-build a system to fit their needs. The clinic was advised that development would consist of the five following stages:

▲ Requirements gathering:

A small team of business analysts and consultants interview clinic staff of varying roles and assess costs, benefits, and risks to establish a comprehensive list of "requirements." This process also involves documenting how things currently operate, what the problems are, and where the clinic wants to be—all to produce the initiation brief. They had just weathered end-of-year seasonal celebrations while mourning the retirement of two of their most senior employees. Given the clinic's budget and schedule needs, and preparations that need to be ready for their busiest months of the year (November and December), the clinic and team have ten months to get this system built and up and running.

▲ Design and building:

Once the initiation brief is finalized and signed off by leading stakeholders, the system-design process kicks off with brainstorming sessions, from which the development team starts producing logical, infrastructural schematics and detailing dataflow with concrete specifications. In other words, what the system will look like and how it will to work. Once design is complete and approved, the actual software is built.

▲ Verification:

Upon completion of the software, the system's features, functionalities, and usability are verified and tested by a control group in a controlled environment to ensure it meets the requirements listed in the initiation brief.

▲ Deployment:

Once all verification assessments are complete and the system is approved for release, it is deployed into the clinic's IT working environment.

▲ Maintenance:

And finally, once deployment is finalized and signed off, the clinicians and staff provide feedback and raise issues they confront in the live environment to verify acceptable deployment and amend any issues that arise.

The project commences. The business analysts and consultants organize times to visit the clinic and observe their operations. They take note of staff roles and break down the responsibilities, influence, and importance of key stakeholers. They ask each stakeholder to describe problems they face and particularly time-consuming tasks in order to generate a list of functional priorities. They also hire an SME (subject matter expert) to advise on how healthcare sectors typically operate. The requirements document is constructed: a stack of 142 pages. Jane, impressed with its dimensions and heft, signs off her approval as do the project managers. So far, so good! However, four months have already passed, and all the clinic has seen are multiple interviews and documents to sign. As tension mounts, the project managers assure Jane that their competent team of sixteen—all offshored—are more than capable. After all, this isn't their first CRM-rodeo!

While the system is designed, Jane is called in for meetings, though they are few and far between. Still, as far as she's concerned, everything is adding up, and while much of what is conveyed to her sounds like jargon, she trusts the development team and eagerly nods along. They are now six months deep; everything's been signed off and development commences. A month, two months, three months pass. November is around the corner, and Jane begins to worry. She's been told that everything is on schedule and there is nothing to worry about. A few of her staff, including herself, are called in to test completed modules of the system. During those sessions, they identify a number of inconveniences, one of which is how long it takes to amend notes to a client entry. They insist that this feature be more accessible.

Jane is advised that the infrastructure would not be able to facilitate the change request, as small a change as it seemed to be—but she and her team know it still has to happen. Otherwise, staff would resort to physical notetaking, which would substantially undermine the efficacy of the system. The team either needs to go overbudget by working overtime or extend the schedule by another two weeks. Jane and her team decided to expand the budget, but that isn't the end of the delays. The development team did not anticipate the time-consuming act of balancing various compliance regulation procedures that require rigorous inspection and meeting standards with what the clinicians were asking the system to produce. They also realize that digitizing all the existing analog records would require a substantial amount of time, since relying on manual input is not practical. What's worse, none of the existing system was salvageable, as it was all written in legacy code. The development team had no choice but to build the infrastructure and logic from the ground up. They were eight months in and not even 30% through the specified requirements. Jane receives the bad news: the project's budget needs to be doubled, and it will take twice as long to deliver. When asked to explain what happened, the project managers complain they were not aware of all the issues they would run into, blaming lack of maintenance and the technologically archaic state of the clinic. Jane, taken aback, has no choice but to seek financial support from their local council.

Nine months later, Jane gets a call and is told the system is ready for deployment. How exciting! Her team is to spend the next two weeks in training before the system will be deployed for all to use. It isn't ten minutes into the training before Jane hears the huffs and puffs, the sighs, and shrugs. "You can't expect us to pick this up in a week, can you?" "I can barely make out what this figure says." "When does it print a file for me to stow away in cabinet C20?" The invigilators monitoring the staff's use of the "finished system" run from one desk to the next trying to explain where things should be done and how. They came prepared with a neatly laminated eighty-two-page user manual whose coarse pages no one in that room would be caught dead licking their thumbs and flipping through. They neglected the age difference of most of the clinicians and, most importantly, their potential resistance to new tech and new modes of operation. The existing system works perfectly well and has done so for years. Why fix what wasn't broken? One issue after another crops up, and it's clear they won't be able to launch the new system anytime soon.

The training facilitators suggest a further three-week delay that would push the clinic into the busiest time of the year, which would mean a mid-January launch. The project is already a year past its original projected date of completion, and at this point they have no choice; they are far too deep into their commitment to turn back now. To make matters worse, the two senior employees who had retired left with specialized knowledge that was critical for unique cases their clinic often faced. They are somewhere between the Caribbean and Honolulu, and the development team is forced to wait for their return before progressing any further.

As the clinicians slowly begin to realize the potential a new system could offer, a number of "a-ha moments" ensue. What if they had an internal communication system, a chat feature that would allow the GP to directly ask one of the front-desk consultants a question? That would save trips to and from the office. When such ideas are put forward to the development team, Jane is always met with resistance, followed by a slew of new documents that are to be curated and approved and then pushed on to the team, which has to reprioritize their growing list of change requests. This leads, once again, to further delays.

January comes around, and the entire team, though apprehensive, nods hesitantly when asked if the system is good to go.

Jane was told the development team would be deploying the new system directly, since the clinic could not afford a phased transition. Running the old and new systems simultaneously would be a logistical impossibility given the nature of their business and how the system was built. On Monday night, a team of five is to spend the night at the clinic setting up the new system across all devices, and on Tuesday morning, they should be able to hit the ground running!

Tuesday morning arrives: *disaster.* While working the previous night, the team realized that almost half the devices employed in the clinic were too outdated to run the system without it consistently crashing, which meant they would have to operate at half the capacity. This was a nonstarter given the "safety critical" sphere of work they operate in. Eight computers are replaced, the "overnight roll-over" is completed, and on June 16—roughly two-and-a-half years after the initially proposed day of completion—the system is finally ready for use. The sliding doors are unlocked, the phones start to go off, and the team rolls up their sleeves and gets to work. What happens next should come as no surprise: *chaos.*

▲ Records are missing, as data transposition was not completed because system validation prevented particular entries with missing information to be registered.

▲ Their old system's patient identification protocol relied on photos often stapled to paper files that are no longer accessible—photos deemed too costly to digitize. Regular patients are not accustomed to presenting forms of identification the system requires, some of which (like a driver's ID) are not even present in a patient's listing.

▲ GPs and those at the front-desk find themselves frantically sifting through the manual, trying to work around system errors that prevent them from actioning items such as bookings and subscriptions, as mandated input is either unavailable or foreign to their knowledge of how they used to operate.

▲ Some of the staff resort to jotting down notes on sticky notes when receiving phone calls or face-to-face correspondence, which means the system has no trace of contact. The inconsistent use of the CRM system leads to distrust of the information logged, which in turn results in numerous misunderstandings and miscommunications between patients, doctors, and counsellors.

▲ Even considering the best-case use of the system for a straightforward patient interaction, the efficiencies of what the new system has to offer are not apparent. They aren't really saving that much more time, considering how efficient they had grown using a paper-based system. Maybe all they needed were taller, wider cabinets after all?

By the end of the day, it dawns on Jane that there is no turning back. The old system is now defunct and getting everything reinstated, as well as any further work on their shiny new system, isn't going to happen. It is, in short, an investment nightmare. What seemed like an obvious improvement turns out to be a calamity, and everyone is left wondering, "What went wrong?"

If you think the hypothetical clinic case study was self-servingly exaggerated, thinking to yourself, "Surely oversights of that nature for a project of that scale and budget aren't possible . . . ," then I draw your attention to the Victorian government's initiative of introducing a new transportation "smart card" ticketing system called Myki to replace the existing Metcard in Australia. Prep-work commenced in late 2002, and three years later a consortium was awarded the $500 million contract to develop the system, with completion date set for 2007 (Operational Effectiveness of the Myki Ticketing System, tabled 2015). After unending delays caused by deficiencies in governance, project planning, and contractual arrangements, Myki finally went into full operation in 2012. In 2014, an article published in Melbourne's The Age referenced the Public Transport Ombudsman (PTO—an agency assisting individuals with complaints about public transport in Melbourne and Victoria) newsletter: "Over the past two years, cases have remained at the highest level since the PTO began operations in 2004. Myki continued to be the main cause of inquiries and complaints, making up 33 per cent of case receipt in July to December 2013." From console bugs to slow card-processing times to unreadable vending machine screens in sunlight to unwanted receipt information to poor education of how the new system worked—the list of problems was and is still extensive. Costing $1.52 billion and nine years to roll out, the Myki bungle went $550 million overbudget, was delayed two years, and is only one of many botched Waterfall projects of this scale.

PRESUMPTION, NEGLIGENCE, RIGIDITY

With an increasingly evolving, diverse, interconnected, and chaotic economy — a consequence of proliferating technological advancements—it wasn't long before criticisms of the Waterfall methodology started to surface and the cracks began to show.

1. **Often, customers realize what they wanted is not what they need. Identifying root issues, bottlenecks, and desires of business processes is usually underpracticed and overlooked, and a knee-jerk judgment is made based on the most apparent but often misunderstood problem.**

   Referring back to the case study, the medical clinic's old system was essentially digitized and modernized. Sure, there wasn't much paperwork to push around, but the way information was passed and processed created bottlenecks. Approval of screenings always required a certified GP to meet a patient face to face, but technology capable of automating this process (by providing the GP with virtual images and readings, voiding the need for face-to-face diagnoses) already existed.

   Even with an SME assisting the development team, no one took human nature into account with as much rigor as they should have—the staff members' shortcomings, workarounds, exceptions, beliefs, and preferences. Such considerations should have also been extended to the unique customer demographic the clinic predominantly served as well as its particular mode of operation. For example, interactions with patients were built on trust as opposed to stringent compliance procedures.

2. **There is little to no room for deviation once a project has commenced, meaning that if circumstances change at the midway point, changing the plan would either be impossible or very expensive.**

   During the project, opportunities to capitalize on a-ha moments were met with pushback. Further changes and costs meant that the system's delivery would be delayed, discouraging Jane and her team from providing insights to the development team that would have added much needed *value*.

3. **Customer feedback is limited throughout the development process, meaning the impression and the general feeling of the customer is not taken into account until the end of the system's development—once everything is done and dusted.**

    Not only did staff feel detached from their own system's development, but this disconnect meant that everything was being built for whomever the development team was imagining it was for and not for the people who were actually going to use it. How they felt using it, what they would change, and what they struggled with were potentially fruitful but neglected insights.

4. **Integration of the finished product into existing operations usually occurs with a "big bang" launch, which makes it difficult to identify bottlenecks or challenges during development.**

    Whether it was the outdated technology that the clinic was utilizing or stress-testing the system's efficacy during rush hours, the real bottlenecks that were deeply intertwined with workplace culture, policy, and habits never surfaced until the theory was put into practice by directly inserting it into the working environment it was intended to be used in.

5. **The system being built isn't tested in what will always be a complex working environment until the very end.**

    Although the team tested the system after it had been built, it took place in a controlled and static environment. The test cases and acceptance criteria were limited to what the development team had initially scoped for and not for the challenges and conditions a complex working environment would present. As far as anyone was concerned, the new system ticked off all the boxes.

6. **A lot of effort is spent—usually 20–40% of a project's total time—on planning and documentation. This is valuable time that could have been better spent building and testing.**

Those first eight months focused on planning and then replanning every time the development team was faced with a change request, a setback, or an unforeseen realization. Most of the effort was invested in writing, editing, approving, signing off, and circulating documents instead of real development and more contact with those who would ultimately use the system.

7. **Much of this planning often leads to redundant and suboptimal solutions that get replaced or simply discarded.**

Simply digitizing their old workflow did not lead to a better mode of operation. The ability to cross-check and integrate their CRM with third-party ID verification technology, for example, proved to be of little use considering that most patients presented their overseas drivers licenses and other international identification paperwork. The development team essentially wasted three months of work when they could have prioritized for other sought-after and salient features.

8. **The estimated time required to complete a project is often understated; unforeseen delays are all too common.**

Realization after realization, setback after setback, one request for more funding after another—these all seemed to be unfortunate and unlucky mishaps, leading to a version of Stockholm Syndrome as the clinic grew empathetic with the development team's frustration, even as they began to realize the scope of their own now ill-fated investment.

9. **The utility of the system isn't realized until the very end. Throughout development, the organization seeking the benefits of "tailored tech" have no choice but to keep operating inefficiently while waiting for delivery. By the time the project is finished and maintenance is underway, competitors are already working on the next big thing, capitalizing on rapid technological advancements and the nature of an everchanging industry.**

None of the features being developed were readily deployable, which meant the clinic would have been left with *nothing* had they decided to pull the plug due to financial constraints. To add insult to injury, by the time the system was fully developed, an off-the-shelf software package specifically designed for clinics was released overseas. It seemed to promise everything the clinicians hoped of this shiny new system and was readily available for a fraction of their investment—now a liability.

10. **The sheer number of requirements along with the complex interactions between people, business processes, and reality combine to create an escalating number of possible scenarios to be handled.**

The operational nuances and considerations the system had to account for far exceeded what they had initially planned to address. No amount of planning, investigation, or discussion would have revealed truly valuable features that facilitated such complex interactions.

So, how does a software development's life cycle for a clinic in an urban suburb have anything to do with consistently getting you out of bed at 6 a.m. with vigor and will? Well, let's piece the puzzle together.

For each of the ten points raised, take a moment to consider what *you* would have done differently to prevent these lapses from occurring. What do you think led to the issues that *emerged*? Assuming it wasn't the clinic team's or development team's incompetency that led to this multimillion-dollar disaster, how is it possible that, given enough time and resources, this project failed? Could they have seen the warning signs and put a stop to it a few months in? What measures could they have taken to estimate the constituents of the now-broken iron triangle with greater accuracy?

Some of the solutions may have seemed blatantly obvious to you. "Surely they'd consider the possibility of oversights and bias." "Why didn't they ask their customers what they thought along the way? How naive!"

Now consider your life as one big project that involves a scope (aspirations, obligations, responsibilities), resources (active/passive income, friends and family, your tools and technology), and time. Consider how a Traditional Psyche, one that relies on expectations, the status quo, blind assumptions, and overzealous commitments, would relate to the Waterfall methodology, and then read through the ten aforementioned issues once more. Think of an endeavor you set out to accomplish that fell flat, you gave up on, or eventually failed to accomplish. Are you beginning to make the connections? Do you see the similarities?

Thinking about your own particular endeavor (whether it be a malfunctioning relationship, a university degree you aren't enjoying, or questioning your expensive investment in a hobby you recently took up), go through each of the ten issues one last time and consider what you might have done differently and *should* do differently moving forward to avoid such predicaments.

Going back to software development, you would be right to assume that experts in this field would have developed an alternative approach that addressed such matters as changing, incomplete, or nonexistent scope/requirements while anticipating blind spots. The approach or philosophy (a generalization of the practice) I'm referring to is known as the Agile philosophy. Before we explore its nuances, it's worth acknowledging its success. Two of many studies were conducted to compare the efficacy of Waterfall versus Agile: the Ambysoft 2013 Project Success Survey and the 2015 Chaos report by the Standish Group. It is apparent in figure 2-3 that Agile development teams are doing something right.

COMPARING IT PROJECT SUCCESS RATE

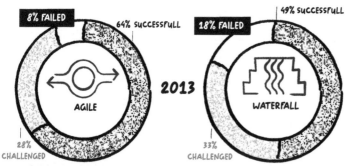

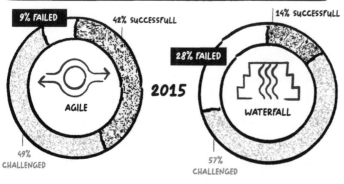

Figure 2-3:
Waterfall versus Agile
Adapted from 2013
IT Project Success
Rates Survey Results
(2013) and Chaos
Report (2015)

While somewhat inconclusive given the disparity of the studies' sample sizes and diversity of projects considered, it is interesting to observe how the failure rate of Waterfall projects has increased over time. Given the increasingly chaotic and changing technological landscape of the twenty-first century, one would imagine this trend to continue and worsen.

A few more studies published between 2016 and 2017 further demonstrate the efficacy of Agile. The Global Project Management Survey, run by the Project Management Institute (and involving 3,234 project management professionals, 200 executives, 510 project management office directors from a range of industries, and interviews with 10 corporate leaders), reported that 71% of companies are implementing Agile. VersionOne, a leading provider of Enterprise cloud development products and services, revealed in its eleventh annual "State of Agile" survey that 98% of respondents (which include hundreds of organizations ranging from manufacturing to healthcare, 26% of which employ at least twenty thousand people) said their organization has realized success from Agile projects. PwC, one of the biggest accounting firms in the world, reported that Agile projects are 28% more successful than traditional projects in meeting market demand. And one more for good measures: the *Harvard Business Review* declared that 60% of companies using an Agile approach experienced revenue growth and higher profits.

There is beauty in what makes sense. In a world cluttered with emotional, physical, and spiritual turmoil, one often finds solace in matters that add up, in rational thought and logic, in a story with a beginning and an end, in a poem that satiates an appetite, in a symphony that resonates with chords of intuition. I hope to provide a line of sobering observational summations that add up to what will become a clear path to follow. The journey begins here, with the Agile philosophy.

CHAPTER 11
THE AGILE PHILOSOPHY

The basis of any model generally relies on the system it is bound to. Its efficacy and utility are directly correlated to its *suitability*, which in turn urges an understanding of the environment it is to be used in. The case study detailed in the previous chapter is fairly complex—the number of considerations, nuances, and unforeseen complications seem to be, at their very best, typical, and at their very worst, arbitrary. Enter stage right: the theory of *complex adaptive systems*. In a nutshell, it is an interdisciplinary concept that attempts to blend insights from the natural and social sciences to develop system-level models that allow for heterogenous agents, phase transition, and emergent behavior. In other words, it's a matter of understanding how unique (heterogenous) and independent entities (agents) independently react (phase transition) to inputs such as environmental changes or imposed conditions while operating together in a dynamic ecosystem and then predicting outcomes (emergent behavior) that might also be perpetuated by further unique phase transitions. Complex adaptive systems encompass a dynamic network of interactions while recognizing that the behavior of the ensemble may not be predictable based on the behavior of the individual components, e.g., how a butterfly's wing flap can lead to a hurricane (referring to an element of chaos theory called the *butterfly effect* in which small changes can lead to much larger changes). John R. Turner and Rose Baker, both professors of applied technology and performance improvement (ATPI), synthesized the characteristics of complex adaptive systems as follows:

1. **Path dependence:**
    Complex adaptive systems tend to be sensitive to their initial conditions— the smallest deviances can lead to significantly unexpected outcomes. The same force might affect different systems differently.

The initial state of affairs at the hypothetical clinic described previously —the technology, the individuals, the general demographic of their patients —led the development path down a tangent of modernity that would have been entirely different for another clinic that may have had newer tech and more tech-savvy clinicians in a rural town with a primarily local demographic.

2. System history:

The future behavior of a system depends on its initial starting point and subsequent history.

The history of how this particular clinic operated, the leniency of its compliance policies, how clinicians adapted their sticky-note taking over the years, and the diversity of its patient base influenced their working methodology.

3. Nonlinearity:

Complex adaptive systems react disproportionately to environmental perturbations. Outcomes differ from those of simple systems.

The busiest time of year for this particular clinic, how staff reacted to change upon commitment of the overhaul and throughout development, and the impacts of the senior clinicians' retirement and subsequent unavailability significantly affected the system's development.

4. Emergence:

Each system's internal dynamics affects its ability to change in a manner that might be quite different from other systems.

Emergent realizations of opportunity proposed by clinicians based on whatever arbitrary sequence of events transpired that lead to a-ha moments, which otherwise would not have occurred had they been designated a different part of the system to test or if another clinician was called in to test.

5. Irreducibility:

Irreversible process transformations cannot be returned to their original state.

The depth of commitment to the system's development and the sunken cost created a situation in which there was no turning back.

6. **Adaptability:**
   Systems that are simultaneously ordered and disordered are more adaptable and resilient.

   Clinicians handled disorder by developing their own paper-based system of communication which cultivated habits and agency.

7. **Operation between order and chaos:**
   Adaptive tension emerges from how much energy the system is required to exert in order survive within its environment (also known as energy differential).

   The system and its predefined workflow (how the clinic operates) are obligated to deal with patients regardless of attitude, circumstance, idiosyncrasies, and contextual consideration.

8. **Self-Organization:**
   Complex adaptive systems are composed of interdependency, interactivity, and diversity.

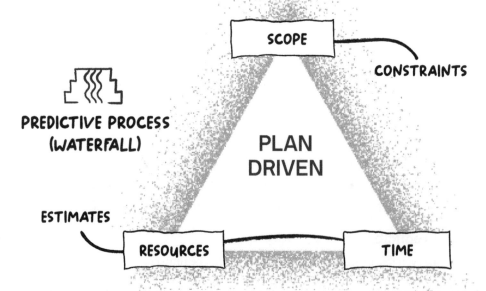

Figure 2-4: Predictive versus adaptive iron triangle

> *The clinic was composed of various technologies and dynamic relationships between clinicians and patients, GPs and patients, and patients and patients.*

Our clinic is an example of a complex adaptive system, and the means by which the Waterfall methodology was applied did not anticipate most of the eight aforementioned characteristics and their consequential chaotic implications. What would have? The Agile philosophy.

Popularized by the "Agile Manifesto," published in 2001 by seventeen software developers, the Agile approach discovers requirements and develops solutions through the collaborative effort of self-organizing and cross-functional teams alongside their end users (the people who will eventually use the system).

What distinguishes the Agile philosophy from the Waterfall methodology is its orientation toward scope. (See figure 2-4.) Where the Waterfall methodology is constrained to a fixed scope, the Agile philosophy is not. The adaptive process takes resources and time as fixed constraints and leaves the scope open to reiteration, pivots, and *change.*

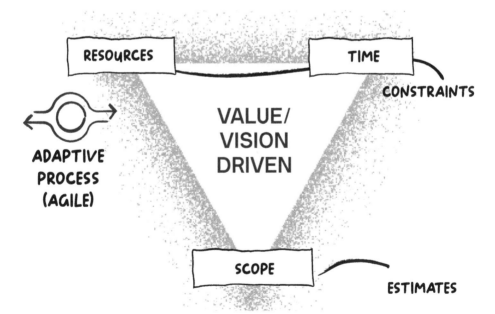

THE RESOURCES/TIME CONSTRAINTS CREATE SCOPE ESTIMATES

The manifesto is based on the twelve following principles (both general and team-specific).

1. **Ensure customer satisfaction by early and continuous delivery of valuable software.**

   Early and continuous exposure to *value* from any developments increases the likelihood of commitment, avoids second-guessing and the stress of doubt, and validates whether the development team is on the right track.

2. **Welcome changing requirements, even in late development.**

   Seizing opportunity from new realizations throughout the endeavor. One small a-ha moment can eventuate into a considerably valuable feature. Better late than never!

3. **Deliver working software frequently (in weeks rather than months or years).**

   The key word here is "working." If the project is cut short due to budget or cancelled for any reason, stakeholders are still left with software *of value* that can be readily utilized and deployed as opposed to scrapping and discarding all progress.

4. **Develop close, daily cooperation between businesspeople and developers.**

   Build the project *around those for whom the system is intended*, bit by bit, piece by piece. Regularly question and consult end users so that by the end of the project, the development team understands how the customer *thinks* and *feels*—how the customer runs and interacts with the business inside and out, every caveat and bottleneck.

5. **Working software is the primary measure of progress.**

   Not meetings, not half-functioning features, not transactions nor document writing. This converges all efforts on maximizing working software by any means necessary.

6. **Focus on sustainable development and maintain a constant pace.**

   Prioritize for a healthy working environment to avoid insidious, stress-inducing stagnation or conflict that would disturb overall progression.

The following six principles are development team-specific. While our case study did not concern the troubles the development team faced, I will leave the debacle of miscommunication, misunderstanding, finger-pointing, stress, and exhaustion to your imagination. All remaining six principles, however, are equally relevant and serviceable for our Quasi-Chaotic initiative.

7. **Reflect frequently on how to become more effective and adjust accordingly.**

   The Agile development team pays great attention to self-reflection or retrospectives in order to establish an everimproving and efficient working environment and understand the system they are operating within—whose dynamic is adapted to each project and its unique challenges.

8. **Continuous attention is paid to technical excellence and good design.**

   Remaining acutely aware of what's working and what's not, and the best method or meta for the team in question to consider and deliberate; remaining open to new and creative ideas and relationships.

9. **Simplicity—the art of maximizing the amount of work not done —is essential.**

   Overcomplication of processes and conduct impedes the ability to capitalize on opportunistic change, but, more importantly, it obscures the means to deliver work effectively.

10. **Best architectures, requirements, and designs emerge from self-organizing teams.**

    Agile teams that are motivated and collaborative know to draw the best ideas and input from whomever is best at that particular task, and to share useful skills and practices to upskill the entire team. This is a proactive approach to mitigate the risks of dependence on an individual and ensure continuity and sustained productivity in the event of an unexpected absence.

11. **Projects are built around motivated individuals who should be trusted.**

Build a team with the right level of technical ability and experience and then trust and support them. Why would you have them on your team otherwise?

12. **Face-to-face conversation is the best form of communication (colocation).**

To avoid miscommunication and misunderstanding and minimize "noise."

AGILE TECHNICALITIES

By this point you may have already realized the applicability of such a model to the complexity of day-to-day conduct in the twenty-first century. But this philosophy's serviceability is further accentuated by its practical derivatives. Scrum, FDD, Extreme Programming (XP), Kanban, and RAD—just to name a few—are Agile development *methodologies* that share all twelve aforementioned Agile principles. We are not looking to contrast each of their pros and cons but rather to adapt their commonalities and efficacies to how a Quasi-Chaotic Lifestyle is conducted. You will find a lot of overlap between the various applications, and in some cases teams incorporate practices from two or more.

Please note that the application of the practices detailed in this chapter are not the Quasi-Chaotic Lifestyle itself. They are merely constituents of the method outlined in detail later in the book.

We'll focus on the most popular combination: Scrum and Kanban. The main difference between the two is that Scrum is iterative and involves ceremonies, processes, and artifacts, whereas Kanban is a noniterative "flow-based" approach involving a visual project management method to improve flow of work. While there are nuanced differences between the two regarding their practical application, team roles, the tools they commonly use, and their scheduling systems, and while professionals in this line of work will argue over the semantics, I will resort to their simplest definitions, adaptations, and conjoined uses.

Scrum was introduced by professor of management practice Hirotake Takeuchi and organizational theorist Ikurijo Nonaka in their 1986 *Harvard Business Review* article, "The New New Product Development Game," aimed at optimizing manufacturing-firm speed and flexibility. The term "scrum" is an abbreviation of "scrummage," often used to describe a tightly packed but *disorderly* crowd; in rugby, it defines a united and tightly organized formation. The name poetically encapsulates the chaotic nature of a rather harmonized team. Software developers Ken Schwaver and Jeff Sutherland later popularized its use in a greater range of companies in the 1990s, as it became the most widely deployed productivity tool among high-tech companies.

Kanban, on the other hand, which translates to sign, signboard, or billboard in Japanese, was a scheduling system for "lean" manufacturing introduced by Taiichi Ohno, an industrial engineer at Toyota. Kanban became an effective visual tool to help run many kinds of development projects and is used religiously in Agile teams as an industry standard. Its use is ubiquitous and found in varying industries including the most reputable and successful companies in the world such as HP, Pixar, Zara, and Spotify.

The agile, cyclical, and iterative nature of Scrum uses time-boxed development *Sprints*—chunks of work delivered periodically, where the product of each chunk is referred to as an "iteration." Each Sprint is conducted as such (with the exception of Initial Scoping, run only once in the beginning):

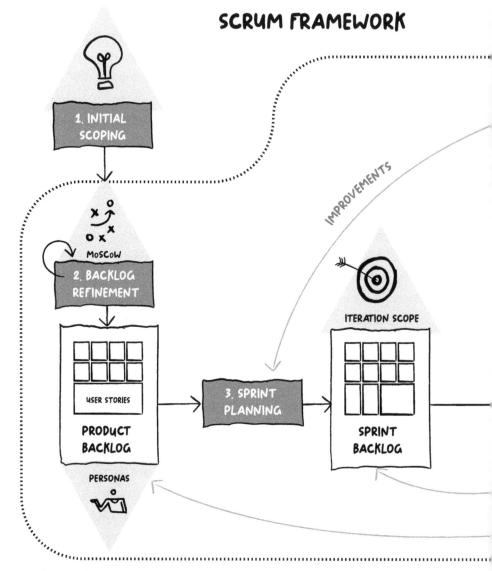

Figure 2-5: Scrum framework

1. Initial Scoping:

End users are consulted and *personas* are constructed. These are fictional descriptions of actual end-user archetypes to ensure the specific needs of all involved with the project's lifecycle will be addressed: their age, their role, their interests, hobbies, and technical prowess, daily routines, problems, frustrations—anything and everything that informs design, development, testing, deployment, and future maintenance. High-caliber

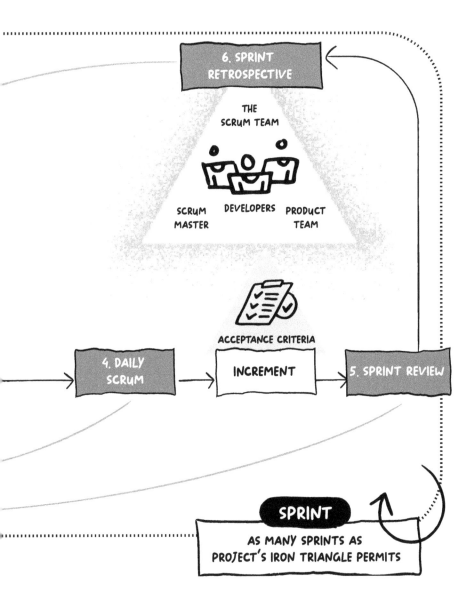

tech companies leading the fringe of cutting-edge practice and service go as far as to create and erect life-sized cutouts of their personas so that developers can work empathetically while remembering whom the system is for.

Brainstorming sessions are conducted with clients to develop a base list of "must haves," "should haves," "could haves," and "won't haves"

(MoSCoW for short, a popular prioritization technique), though the level of detail is not nearly as rigorous as that of Waterfall methodology requirements gathering. Functionalities (features) are organized into *user stories*, which encapsulate a valuable feature to be built while ensuring awareness of who it's for and why. If you cannot explain who a feature is for and why they need it, then it shouldn't be built. User stories are often expressed in a simple sentence, structured as, "As a [persona], I [want to], [so that]." An example of a user story would be this:

As Jane (or the managing director), I would like to know when my clinicians are busy so that I do not interrupt their work unnecessarily when I need to have a word with them.

Used conjunctly with user stories, the Kanban board is a canvas composed of silos or lanes that vary depending on how a team operates and the nature of their work, but at the core of any Kanban board are the following. (See figure 2-6.)

▲ **Backlog:**
a column of user stories and associated tasks a team aims to ideally complete over the course of the entire project. User stories that weren't completed in a Sprint are returned to this column for later reassignment.

▲ **To-Do:**
a column of user stories and associated tasks a team plans on completing in a Sprint.

▲ **Doing:**
a column of user stories and associated tasks team members are currently working on.

▲ **Done:**
a column of user stories and associated tasks completed for the current Sprint.

▲ **Archive:**
a column of completed user stories and tasks of concluded Sprints.

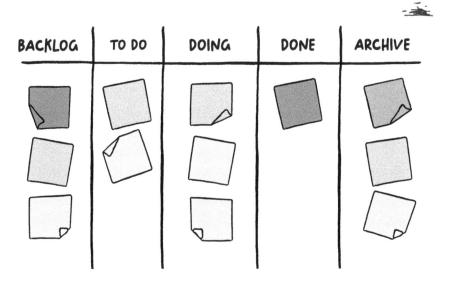

Figure 2-6: Kanban board

2. Backlog Refinement:

Also referred to as "Backlog Grooming," helps Agile teams improve their development process by ensuring project tasks are well defined and readily actionable without the need for more information, deliberation, or research—they are "ready to go." It is best practice to see this step as an ongoing process. It involves:

▲ Breaking down user stories into even smaller chunks—work that ultimately results in the completion of the story. These chunks of work are often referred to as "cards" or "tasks" (similar to Kanban). A general rule of thumb is to limit each chunk of work to around 2-4 hours. This is important for a number of reasons:

▽ Cards not progressing through the board hint at a problem. Self-organizing teams are then quick to support whatever is stuck so work can continue.

▽ Cards that move are a visual sign of progression, giving individual developers a sense of accomplishment and productivity.

▽ The team can quickly see how the project's overall development is fairing and swiftly address early signs of stagnation before it's too late.

▲ Assigning user stories a unit measure to suggest priority (influenced by agreed-to MoSCoW directives). This dictates what the team will focus on first to ensure their end users get what they *need* regardless of what delays or speed bumps they face along the way.

▲ Assigning user stories another unit measure related to "workload estimates": how long a task might take based on educated observations in order to set a feasible scope of work (and realistic client expectations) for each iteration.

▲ Amending user stories with acceptance criteria—an agreed list of conditions that the scope encompassed by the user story must satisfy in order to be considered done and of value to the end users.

Backlog Refinement also involves incorporating insights and realizations drawn from the Sprint Review (a subsequent phase) once a Sprint is complete. The Backlog is modified with user story reprioritization, new user story additions, reclarification of acceptance criteria, and identification and investigation of dependencies.

3. Sprint Planning:

Each Sprint should take no longer than 2–4 weeks. At the beginning of every Sprint, the development team discusses and agrees on a set of user stories they see as feasible within this time frame, which is then commucated to their end users so they know what to expect by the end of the Sprint. Accepted user story cards are moved from the Backlog lane to the To-Do lane. This cements the iteration's scope, and the Sprint commences.

4. Daily Scrum:

The developers hold a daily Scrum that is often restricted to fifteen minutes to minimize time spent in meetings and maximize productivity (which is why it's often referred to as a "Stand-Up meeting" because everyone can't wait to sit back down!). No detailed discussions transpire, no vapid conversations, no wasted time; the focus is simply on "Here's what I've been up to since our last Stand-Up," "Here's what I'm planning to do today," and "Here's what's blocking my ability to complete my work." This ensures that the entire team is on the same page but, more importantly, prompts a collective effort to unblock whatever roadblock any individual may be facing to sustain productivity. Team members ensure that their cards are up to date and reflect what was said.

5. Sprint Review:

Once the Sprint is complete, it is presented for review to stakeholders in the form of a deployed, working, and polished product (though representing a fraction of all features that will end up being delivered) to ascertain validity of utility, customer satisfaction, and (potential) changes. Feedback is invited, the impact of any uncompleted work is discussed, and insights into value (what end users see as most beneficial for a given feature and *why*) are elaborated on. If all goes well, the end users are able to capitalize on the efficiencies the product has afforded thus far as it is deployed to the live, working environment.

6. Sprint Retrospective:

This is perhaps the most valuable Scrum exercise, when the team reflects after each completed Sprint to identify and then agree on process improvement actions. They discuss what went well during the Sprint, what didn't, and what they could do differently in the next Sprint.

And the cycle repeats, producing one iteration after another, until the end users receive a complete, holistic, tailored, informed, and optimal product that satisfies all the prioritized needs and wants their iron triangle permits. By the end of the project, end users would have already familiarized themselves with how their shiny new system works, as they have been making use of each incremental improvement in their working environment throughout the process. Success!

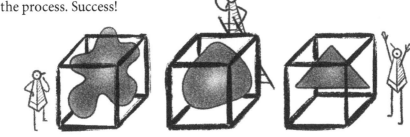

PROACTIVE AND ADAPTIVE MEASURES

I sincerely hope that by now, you can see *why* the Waterfall methodology did not perform well in a complex adaptive system, and how the Agile philosophy, specifically the Scrum + Kanban methodologies, would have increased the chances of success for the clinic's pursuit of tech-driven optimization.

▲ Had the development team worked in Sprints and built the system itera-tively (in chunks) for their end users to test, the clinicians would have been able to gain a sense of where true value lay, refining their Backlog as they proceeded to the next Sprint. It would have also helped dull resistance and voided skepticism and stress once the clinicians were able to see and use what they had asked for.

▲ Had the development team relied on modular user stories as opposed to detailed and hefty requirement documents, they could have spent those first few months developing working software. It would have also enabled efficient and swift reprioritization and the addition of new features without the need for the tedious process of issuing request changes, document rework, and approvals.

▲ Had the development team constructed personas, or at the very least made an effort to fully understand the nature of the clinicians —who they are, their motivations, their technical prowess, their attitude to change, their daily workflow, their pain points and opinions—the clinicians would have felt involved and been able to contribute more to priorities and utility of features than any business analyst could spin out of thin air or a questionnaire could elicit.

▲ Had the development team insisted on figuring out a way to run the working iterations in parallel to the existing software (such as instructing an extra clinician to mimic the inputs of a real interaction), the clinicians would have been able to test the system earlier on in a working environ-ment in the heat of busy hours. This alone would have made apparent the importance of nuance and need for insight from the senior clinicians who had retired. This would have also revealed the antiquity of the current tech.

▲ Had the clinic been able to exploit incremental deployments of the system, they would have been able to benefit from its efficiencies from the very first iteration, further promoting change willingness, ideation, and the identification of design oversights.

▲ I am sure you can think of many, many more improvements.

I would now like to take a moment to congratulate you for soldiering through two relatively technical chapters! Rest assured, these technicalities form the basis of the Quasi-Chaotic Lifestyle; their utility will become clear as you read on. For those who were able to make the connections, you may be inclined to stop reading now and find ways to incorporate learnings from these chapters into your daily routine in a meaningful, useful way. But as we know all too well, putting theory into practice is a problem in itself, as we are often deprived of practical instruction. A truly informed model is what *Necessitating Change* aims to deploy, one that takes into account the fact that we cannot simply act on demand with what does not resonate and that heartache, depression, highs and lows, reason or the lack of it, personality patterns, mental/physical challenges, and other human baggage will skew our commitment and, more importantly, our outlook on our ability to change.

We will now take a giant leap across the chasm of opportunity—the leap from software development to daily life—and bridge the gap to Quasi-Chaotic efficacy!

CHAPTER 12
THE NEXUS OF CHAOS AND DEVELOPMENT

As the puzzle pieces slowly fall into place, you might have realized by now that the world itself is a complex adaptive system in which you are an acting heterogenous agent with a fractal disposition that suggests your life is its own complex adaptive system. Recall the characteristics that define such systems: systems with history, nonlinearity, emergence, irreducibility, and adaptability, operating between order and chaos, path dependent, and self-organizing—all qualities that correspond with the conduct of life. *This* is the dynamic and increasingly chaotic environment we are all bound to.

What we have learned from the problem of goal setting and the issues that arise from the presumptuous, negligent, and rigid Waterfall methodology and its corresponding Traditional Psyche is that this approach simply *doesn't work* or, at the very best, is suboptimal for use in complex adaptive systems. Its staged, planning-heavy, and change-resistant characteristics do not suit the increasingly chaotic nature of the system we reside in.

Now consider the definition of a "project": any undertaking that is carefully planned to achieve a particular aim. Recognize that your life is a series of mini projects, such as pursuing a promotion at work, maintaining a difficult relationship, or going to sleep. Knowing what you know now regarding the industry-proven Agile philosophy, do you see how we have been doing it wrong all along?

We have been systematically and repeatedly predisposing ourselves to failure with an insidious attitude in perpetual dissolution—completely out of tune with the main protagonist: our respective selves. Disregarding our sense of individualism and expecting we will get it right the first time leaves little room to pivot, and should any issue arise, the problem is always the character, the environment, luck and not the *method*.

Given what we have learned of the Waterfall methodology and its short-comings, and the Agile philosophy and its suitability for complex adaptive systems, all that's left is to splice the ends of what software development has to teach us to the ends of what our livelihoods have to gain. To address these matters, we will resort back to the iron triangle that encompasses the constraints our self-development projects are bound to: scope, resources, and time.

Scope:

What does your heart desire? Relative to your past achievements, how does this goal compare? Is it attainable? Is it feasible? Is it even possible? Scope will outline measures that will dictate how much time and how many resources your projects will require. Whether it's a fancy watch or admitting your interest to your crush or finally committing to that black belt, how much you take on to achieve your self-set objectives defines your scope.

Resources:

How much will it cost to attain the objectives you've defined in your scope? Resources doesn't necessarily equate to financial capacity. It also relates to nerves, physical wear, health deterioration, stress, and any other "expense." However, in order to gain, we must lose, and some compromises and payments are to be expected. How much and what is reasonable compromise will be further explored throughout the chapters to come.

Time:

"Time is what we want most, but what we use worst," wrote the English nobleman William Penn. It is often neglected and not taken seriously until it's too late. When you work yourself into the ground looking to make your parents proud, you're left with little to no time to simply enjoy their presence while they're still around. When you live a frugal, mundane, and restrictive life to save up for a dream car, you will have wasted your youth of experience and left yourself wondering which engine is going to die out first. When you willfully neglect your mental health, reassuring yourself that you'll address it someday, the consequences will have already manifested, permanently altering your trajectory. Time is free, but priceless. Time, above all, will be your primary adjudicator.

As for the twelve principles of the Agile philosophy, here they are once more, adapted to an individual's endeavors:

1. **Ensure protagonist (your) satisfaction by early and continuous attainment of valuable experience.**

   Early and continuous exposure to the value of any committed endeavor will increase the likelihood of commitment, void second guessing and stress, and validate whether you are on the right track or not. This includes but is not limited to prioritizing short-term commitments, tracking progress, reflecting on novel experiences while contemplating and proactively identifying room for improvement, and then *acting on* self-made realizations.

2. **Welcome changing requirements, even in late development.**

   Anticipating changes in needs, values, priorities, aspirations, and preferences and/or better alternatives for maximizing the attainment of self-actualizing endeavors. A pivot is better late than never. Even if you have been committed to a specific person, place, or practice, worrying about the right time to pivot, that time is always now. Laboring through a long and arduous project that adds little to no value is wasted effort; pivoting to deliver something that adds *worthwhile* value trumps. Similarly, persevering with what has exhausted value is a losing bet in the quest for self-actualization.

3. **Attain valuable experience frequently (weeks rather than months or years).**

The key word here is "valuable." If an endeavor is cut short due to changing circumstances, you have at least gained valuable experience that can be reflected upon and is readily serviceable and leverageable. This may come in the form of new and constructive relationships, settings/practices of interest, or transferrable skills.

4. **Pursue individualistic endeavors.**

Leverage your curiosity and untapped interest. Cultivate experiences around *yourself* (as opposed to around what others are imposing/expecting of you)—bit by bit, piece by piece, questioning and reflecting along the way so that by the end of the endeavor, you understand what worked for you, what didn't, and what you were able to take away from the experience. Create a habit of setting valuecentric commitments and prioritize for those that are most beneficial to you as opposed to what others think are valuable.

5. **Valuable experience is the primary measure of progress.**

Not more of the same, not compromises, not empty promises, not over-planning or vapid conversation. This converges all efforts to maximize valuable action and experience—by whatever means to make the project happen. I am not advocating a blind jettison of planning all together. By assuming a sufficient consideration of risk instead of excessive pondering over the *best* approach, you will often find that acting on the "suboptimal" with relatively minimal planning, along with regular introspection and a welcoming of change, *is* the ideal approach to take given the increasingly chaotic nature of the everchanging world and self we are bound to.

6. Pursue sustainable scope, maintaining a constant pace.

Maintain a healthy working environment rather than forced, stress-inducing, stagnation-prone practices that would disturb overall progression. The best diet is not necessarily *the best diet* but a sustainable one. What and how much we decide to take on ought to be both feasible and appropriate to our relative, individualistic iron triangles.

7. Reflect on the means to optimize effectiveness of pursuit and adjust accordingly.

Practice self-reflection to establish everimproving and progressive conduct, a healthy working environment, and deeper understanding of the system you are operating within. In order to move forward, you need to know where you stand. If you don't have a well-defined baseline, you wouldn't know how far you've gotten, how well you're doing, or whether you're advancing in the right direction. As psychologist Jordan B. Peterson reminds us, "Compare yourself to who you were yesterday and not to who someone else is today. That is a game you can win." Remember: what matters most, regardless of scope, is that a meaningful, valuable project be achieved for the end user—you!

8. Maintain continuous attention to what works for oneself and what does not.

Remaining acutely aware of what's working, what isn't, and *why*; the best method or *personal meta* for you to consider, deliberate, and ultimately capitalize on; and remaining open to new and creative ideas for self-governance.

9. Strive for simplicity—the art of maximizing the amount of time not wasted—is essential.

"A designer knows he has achieved perfection not when there is nothing left to add, but when there is nothing left to take away," said Antoine de Saint-Exupéry, literary laureate of both France's and the United States' highest awards. In other words, identify and repudiate *anything* or *anyone* that does not add value or stands in the way of your self-actualization.

10. Refer to approaches, advice, and opportunities from the experienced.

Leverage insight from experienced others whose individual characteristics as well as contextual considerations closely relate to yours. Understanding that one size does not fit all and paying close attention to *whose* advice you are acting on.

11. Surround yourself with motivated individuals who can be trusted.

Build a team with the right level of technical ability or experience and trust and support them. A team to encourage, motivate, assist, protect, teach, guide, and challenge you along the way.

12. Face-to-face conversation is the best form of communication.

To void miscommunication, misunderstanding, and minimize noise in communication. An incredibly influential principle to be taken seriously with valuable individuals we cross paths with.

Each item's nuance, utility, and considerations are further explored in chapters to come, but for the moment, and in light of all that's been revealed, reflect on what your life has amounted to and ask yourself whether adopting these twelve Quasi-Chaotic principles makes sense and is possible. If not, ruminate over why.

A practical guide wouldn't be practical if it wasn't simple enough to summarize in one single breath. In fact, I can do one better. By simplifying and synthesizing the essence of what drives the success of the Agile philosophy into one practice, one word, you will have a better chance at taking the first step in the right direction. That ultimate, almighty, and feared word—and discipline—is "change."

We will now take a deeper look into what ties everything together and essentially *drives* the Agile philosophy and its relevance to your life.

CHAPTER 13
ITERATIVE DIVERGENCE

When you think of "change," what is the first thought that comes to mind? Uncertainty, fear? Or perhaps: "Why?" "Why fix something that isn't broken?" "What if I'm not made for it?" "What if it turns out to be a wasted effort?" "What if it's not something I'd enjoy?" "What if I end up worse off?" The fact that the word is commonly associated with negative connotations and risk says a lot about the way we live our lives. More importantly, it suggests that the "discipline of change" itself is seldom practiced and its potential not fully realized—*yet*.

The essence of the Agile philosophy resides in—you guessed it—its agility! The ability to swiftly pivot and adjust depending on changes in circumstances or requirements based on continuous feedback and constructive experiences—minimizing cost and maximizing value. Treading informedly, one must remain conscious of the duality at play: understanding that change is necessary and assumed while also facilitating the process of change with minimal repercussions. The former is addressed in this chapter; the latter will be explored in Part V: The Tool Kit.

Why is change necessary and assumed? Because suggesting you will get a project and its nonlinear and emergent implications right the first time is naive and irresponsible. Every project is complex in its own way, whether it's a booking system you are developing or your pursuit of becoming a competitive yo-yo slinger. Besieged by uncertainty and facets completely out of our control, every project is a learning endeavor with lessons for correcting *velocity* (course correction and shifting level of commitment) that lead to valuable realizations. So much can go wrong that you make whatever informed guesses you can based on the facts available and give it your best. The key is to anticipate change, welcome it, and act on it.

Perhaps this is stating the obvious, but change is a product of action. The entire premise of this Quasi-Chaotic ideology is to fixate our attention on action rather than contemplation and rumination—on *doing* more than *planning*. Instead of assuming what can or can't work, simply attempt the alternative and find out. Elementary at face value but deeply understated and sorely unpracticed.

What drives progress in Agile software development, for example, is starting with a base that is composed of informed guesswork, available facts, and *experience*, and then progressively iterating (changing) the understanding of what is required based on continuous feedback attained from the end users. More often than not, unfortunately, is that what analysts, designers, and developers believe is the best approach to fulfilling specified requirements is far from what the end users actually need and/or what works best for *them*. And sometimes, inefficient functionality makes for better systems as it is better suited to the workflow/style/characteristics of end users. That is to say, "best practice" is not always what's best for a given team or organization, as we previously learned when considering the travails of the medical clinic.

So, how does this tie in with our day-to-day lives? Simple. You are the end user of your project. If you commit to a substantial undertaking and assume you will get it right the first time with the plan you have in mind, you will most likely fail. Constantly consulting your end user (yourself) and determining what is working and what isn't—and taking it seriously—leads to better chances of success. Anticipating change and remaining leery of what can get in the way (such as inauthentic pursuits) will heighten self-awareness and keep you *proactively on the lookout* for better alternatives. Keep altering your approaches and evaluate your experiences until something clicks, while remaining open and attentive to further uncharted potential. Keep opening new doors as you tread forward. Pick and choose what you see as best for you: *you decide*, not the world. Regularly iterating and building on the people, places, and practices you involve yourself with—or drop entirely—will allow you to better home in on exactly what works best for you while minimizing the risk of wasted efforts, stagnation, grief, or regret. And, what worked for your friend may not work for you, as relying on inauthentic pursuits to force your way to success using someone else's process is a recipe for disaster.

**Failure is simply the opportunity to
begin again, this time more intelligently.**

—Henry Ford, My Life and Work

The wisdom that comes with experience cultivates certainty. Hypothetically speaking, if you have sufficiently sampled *everything* there is to experience, you would know precisely what works best for you, what doesn't, and why. Your decisions toward self-actualization thereafter would be obvious. This is the ultimate goal. And while this is a hypothetical impossibility restricted by our respective iron triangle's primary adjudicator (time), we have no choice but to strive for as much valuable experience as our time on this blessed planet permits. And the quickest route there? Change. People often take months, years, even decades to change particular aspects of their lives, and then only do so at times of desperation. The quicker we iterate, the more agile we become and the faster we are able to attain quality. When asked about the countless failures he had when trying to create the light bulb, Thomas A. Edison, one of the most prolific inventors of all time, famously said, "I have not failed. I've just found ten thousand ways that won't work."

A shift of focus to change itself as a driving force ensures maximum exposure to novel experiences. The quicker you experience the best and the worst of what is to come, the better able you'll be to manage challenge and times of crisis. Figure 2-7 illustrates how the Traditional Psyche is generally slow to adapt. As it lives through the motions, opportunities come and go, most of which it may not even recognize and some of which it cannot ignore. The ups and downs are drawn out, and its ability to adapt to changing circumstances and dilemmas takes longer than it should.

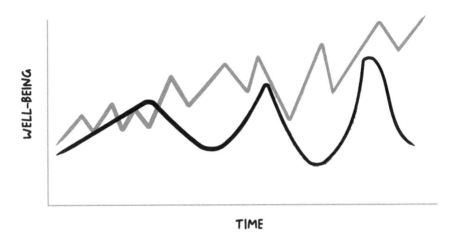

Figure 2-7: Traditional lifestyle versus lifestyle of change

With a lifestyle of change, the highs and lows come swiftly and regularly. You will notice, however, that the lows aren't as low, because we catch ourselves—through change—*before* we lose control and spiral into depression. We constantly pivot. What's more important is that every point presented in the graph encompasses an experience, an event, a catalyst for a change in your state of mind. Each point suggests lessons and reflection that permit growth as an individual at an unprecedented rate relative to that of a Traditional Psyche. It's common to acknowledge a particular individual's maturity as a reflection of how much they've experienced, whether they have been put through a ringer or fought a war at an early age or travelled the world with their parents. They would have been exposed to a vast number of opportunities that enabled them to evolve into a confident, experienced, and perhaps self-actualized persons.

Here's a quick question: What is your favorite ice cream flavor? Pistachio? Or maybe vanilla? How do you know it isn't apple crumble? Or perhaps pickled mango? The answer is, *you don't.* You are going to live the rest of your life not knowing that pickled mango is truly your favorite ice cream flavor. Why? Because you have settled for what is in fact your eleventh-favorite ice cream flavor!

Now let's apply this logic to everything else in your life. This is where it starts to get fun (or depressing).

Your haircut:

You've had a temple fade for six years, and you're wondering why people never look at you differently or why a different crowd doesn't take interest in you. If you only tried short, permed hair, you might catch the attention of a photographer, eventuating into a gig as the clothing model you've always wanted!

Your daily morning routine:

You've been waking up at the same time, eating the same breakfast, and taking the same route to work every day for years now. The first two hours of every day is a haze of muscle memory and déjà vu. If you tried waking up later, blasting through a cold shower, and taking a breakfast you prepared earlier in the week, you might feel more energized and save up to an hour each day—extra time you could later fill by starting a knitting hobby!

Your diet:

You have completely disregarded the science behind nutrition and eat whatever is at your disposal. You assume that eating well is a chore and then wonder why you feel like a sack of potatoes after lunch. If you only attempted the FODMAP diet, you could effectively negate insulin spikes and become twice as productive for the three-hour period after lunch that, which could ultimately lead to a promotion. And guess what? Your eczema flares may also subside!

Your friends:

There are nearly eight billion people around the world, yet you have dedicated your attention and efforts on four of them who always cancel on you last minute and are never there when you need them. If you'd only expanded your circle, you could create the best support group you could imagine!

Your career, your significant other, your accent, your car, your vocabulary, your hobby, your holiday plans, your handwriting, your gym workout, the perfume you use, the brand of kitchen knives you have, the way you brush your teeth, your posture, how you sneeze. It boggles the mind how so many believe they are destined to *be a particular* someone or *live a particular life* when, in reality, they can be anything and everything they ever *needed*. Don't wait for desperate times and desperate measures, for you will only make irrational decisions that will often lead to unfavorable outcomes. Think of it this way: Is it best to grocery shop while full or on an empty stomach? Decision-making on a satiated appetite results in responsible purchases of the correct ingredients that will last the longest. Grocery shopping on an empty stomach is a wasteful effort often leading to a stacked pantry of expiring biscuits, moldy bread, a fridge full of green cheese and wilting vegetables. You take on more than you can manage because you are desperate to fill the emptiness. You can't think straight because you are starved of the self-possession and contentment that generally come with a "healthy" lifestyle.

Acclimating to mediocrity and routine may, in the long run, be the biggest threat to one's pursuit of self-actualization. As soon as we arrive at a state of comfort, we tend to retire into a slumber of convenience. The longer your stay at Camp Comfort, the harder you will find it to leave. Your knees grow weak, your fire dies out, and any desire to reignite the flame is doused by a myriad of lame excuses and emotional distress. Years can pass before depression sets in, and any chance of climbing out of the hole you dug yourself becomes ever so much more impossible—often requiring the aid of others. We have all been there and wondered how we let things get that bad that quickly.

That fire I speak of is a byproduct of change. The excitement that comes with trying something new keeps us lively and driven. Anticipating the fun, productivity, and perks that come with a newly adopted activity/characteristic/project gives us a reason to wake up in the morning and jump out of bed. It's the coffee to kick-start our day, the cigarette to sooth our mind, the drug that keeps us high. It's the challenge we look forward to. We often pair these feelings with the undertaking itself, but what's really firing up the dopamine is *change itself* and the mystery that comes with new experiences!

If you happen to find a person, place, or practice that sparks a long-lasting flame, then you've managed to find yourself your very own pickled mangoes. A delight indeed! But does it stop there? Of course not! Remember, our focus is change and not the pickled mangoes. Enjoy them as long as you can. Tell your friends about your pickled mangoes. Make a career out of pickled mangoes! And if you become the Pickled Mango Queen, you've surely gotten a taste of quality and fulfillment, *but what if . . .*

What if you could have been the Horseradish Empress? This is where change becomes ever so valuable. Always keep your options open. Build on what you know and regularly adopt something new. This allows you to pivot if the new entices you more than the old, but it also leaves a base for you to fall back to in case the new doesn't specifically tickle the cockles of your heart. It's a fool-proof approach that negates heavy risk, minimizes the consequences of what little risk is left, and keeps you on your toes with the fire of self-improvement constantly burning. Perfection.

That said, change is forever and can be unforgiving. After all, we don't live in a world of static circumstances. We are invariably influenced by external elements that constantly shape and reshape who we are, however unaware we are of the process. To make matters worse, and as we already know, our very own aspirations and desires change regularly as well. What we want now can be vastly different from what we'll want in three, five, ten years. How does one ascertain commitment? Through change. Recall the Agile philosophy and the problem with fixed plans: Change is assumed to be necessary and inevitable, and one must anticipate it, welcome it, and prepare for it. It is this realization that will void doubt, fear, and dissonance. If we have learned anything about the dangers of goal setting, it is to assume that what works for us today may not work for us tomorrow. Our taste changes over time, so when your "Horseradish Delight" ice cream wears on you, you already know better than to question your fealty. Once you establish an Agile mindset, you have practically insured your sanity. You will be ready for anything in the name of change.

If you wonder what a change-oriented way of living *feels* like, consider the ketogenic diet as an analogy. The premise of such a diet suggests that if we deplete our system of carbohydrates, adaptive changes to brain energy metabolism will take place in which ketone bodies become the primary source of fuel instead of glucose. You would effectively be substituting fat for carbohydrates as an energy source, resulting in *fat-adaptation*. Similarly, with a Quasi-Chaotic Lifestyle, we are replacing stretch goals (ends that justify suboptimal means) and the journey to achieve them (means that justify an unreliable end) with change itself as our new energy source—a process or state we will refer to as *Change Adaptation/Adapted*.

The success of a Quasi-Chaotic Lifestyle hinges on this very concept and is worth reiterating. We aren't particularly centering our attention on *means that justify the end*, per se (because there are no ends when it comes to self-actualization) but on *change itself*. All one would need to justify an experience is for it to be novel and considerate of one's iron triangle. That's it! I would be fooling you if I said that such a transition can happen overnight. Like any change in habit, it takes time and effort before it actually starts to work—just as you would expect when adopting, say, a ketogenic diet: There are stages of adaptation accompanied by a "keto flu"!

A lifestyle of change is going to be quasi-chaotic; we are abandoning stability and embracing the expediency of chaos. You know that anxiety attack you have every time you go through an ethnic food menu? *Where do I even start? How do all these food options differ? How can the kitchen possibly store enough ingredients for three hundred dishes? And what if the one I order tastes weird?* The answer? Start anywhere. Every new experience offers a new opportunity to consider, to capitalize on, to leverage for growth, and to draw and accrete realizations in order to make increasingly informed and self-actualizing decisions. That is to say, *change catalyzes serendipity*.

Change is a gift that keeps on giving. Figuring out what is best for you is just the tip of the iceberg. As you will now discover, its real value lies in the opportunities it reliably delivers on a silver platter as you pick and choose your path toward self-actualizing success. Onwards and upwards!

CHAPTER 14
SHADES OF SERENDIPITY

Ask yourself this question: How do the "successful" triumph? What does your reasoning gravitate toward? Merit? Luck? One is generally inclined to assume inherited wealth, an abundance of support, or sheer luck to justify the discrepancies between one's personal achievements and that of celebrities and titans of industry—winning the "ovarian lottery," as Warren E. Buffet, one of the most successful investors of all time, put it.

> **I entirely abandoned the study of letters. Resolving to seek no knowledge other than that which could be found in myself or else in the great book of the world, I spent the rest of my youth traveling, visiting courts and armies, mixing with people of diverse temperaments and ranks, gathering various experiences, testing myself in the situations which fortune offered me, and at all times reflecting upon whatever came my way so as to derive some profit from it.**

—René Descartes, Discours de la Méthode Pour bien conduire sa raison, et chercher la vérité dans les sciences (Discourse on the Method of Rightly Conducting One's Reason and Seeking the Truth in the Sciences)

Descartes' explanation of how he wrote one of the most influential works in the history of modern philosophy, with importance to the development of natural sciences, is quite revealing.

On his expedition, Descartes also met Isaac Beeckman (at the time considered to be one of the most educated men in Europe), who sparked his interest in mathematics and the new physics, in particular the problem of falling bodies (gravity). On November 10, 1619, while traveling in Germany and thinking about using mathematics to solve problems in physics, Descartes had a vision in a dream through which he "discovered the foundations of a marvelous science." This became a pivotal point in young Descartes's life and the foundation on which he developed analytical geometry. He dedicated the rest of his life to researching the connection between mathematics and nature, and arguably lived to his full potential.

What do you perceive to be the reasons for and constituents of Descartes's ability to fulfill his potential? Here are a few more stories of those you may be more familiar with:

▲ Bruce Willis:

If you had asked Bruce Willis if he ever planned to become a movie star, he would have scoffed. He may be the most unlikely action hero to have been conceived, owing to a relentless stutter that began at the age of nine. At seventeen, he was cast in a high school production, but "A miraculous thing happened," Willis told *Reader's Digest*. "I was doing this goofy play, and when I got onstage, I stopped stuttering. When I stepped off the stage, I started stuttering again. And I went, 'This is a miracle. I got to investigate this more.'" Had he not tempted faith and auditioned for the role, he would have never had the epiphany that made him who he is today.

▲ Harrison Ford:

His stature and good looks were only leading to bit parts in minor television shows when he first moved to Hollywood in the early sixties. Tired of unavailing cast calls, he resorted to carpentry to survive, until one day a man hired Ford to install cabinets in his home. That man happened to be George Lucas. He invited Ford to an audition, where Ford won the part of hot-rod bad boy Bob Falfa in the surprise 1973 hit, *American Graffiti*. The very next year, a director named Francis Ford Coppola hired Ford to expand his office and thereafter cast him in his Oscar-nominated thriller, *The Conversation*. Out of all the alternatives one would expect blockbuster film opportunities to arise from, carpentry would be the last on the list!

▲ Oprah Winfrey:

Success struck for Winfrey when she won the Miss Black Tennessee beauty pageant. In her interview, amongst her answers that caught the audience's attention (most of which were contrary to expectations), she shocked the crowd by saying she hoped to become a broadcast journalist. After, returning to the radio station to pick up her award of a watch, she was offered a part-time job to read the news while she completed her high school education. After that, at the age of nineteen, Winfrey landed a job with a CBS-affiliated news station, becoming the first African-American, female coanchor in Nashville, which initiated her journey of becoming an iconic TV figure.

I now ask, what commonalities do these celebrities have with Descartes? Was it entirely luck? You can probably tell where this is leading—to a point I will further elaborate on by adding the notion of contrast to what one perceives as luck.

A study conducted by professor of theoretical physics and mathematical models Alessandro Pluchino et al. (2018) found that some degree of talent is necessary to be successful but also that the most talented people almost never reach the highest peaks of success, overtaken instead by mediocre and luckier individuals. In their study, the authors accumulated a plethora of evidence from other studies about the fundamental role of chance, luck, and other random factors in determining personal and professional success or failure. Here is some of what they found:

▲ Scientists have the same chance of publishing their biggest hit at any time throughout their career. That is, the highest-impact work can be, with the same probability, anywhere in the sequence of papers published by a scientist. It could be their first, it could be written midcareer, or it could be their last paper.

▲ Those with surname initials that are earlier alphabetically are significantly more likely to receive tenure at top departments.

▲ One's position in an alphabetically sorted list may be important in determining access to oversubscribed public services.

▲ Roughly half of the variance in incomes across people worldwide is explained only by their country of residence and by the income distribution within that country.

▲ Middle-name initials enhance evaluations of intellectual performance.

▲ People with easy-to-pronounce names are judged more positively than those with difficult-to-pronounce names.

▲ Innovative ideas tend to result from a random walk in our brain network.

▲ Individuals with noble-sounding surnames are found to work more often as managers than employees.

▲ The probability of becoming a CEO is strongly influenced by your name or your month of birth.

Seeking to find the missing ingredient that explains a Gaussian distribution (an emergent bell-shaped pattern of distribution observed in nature, similar to the five-level bell curve classification referenced on page 39) of talent and distribution of wealth following a Pareto law (or what you may know to be the 80:20 principle, a phenomena in which 80% of outcomes come from 20% of causes), the researchers produced a model that simulates the reality of the patterns we see today. Their findings suggest that *randomness* is the secret ingredient working behind the scenes.

If you think this phenomenon is limited to a particular practice or industry, many researchers, including investment strategist Michael Mauboussin (2012), statistician and risk analyst Nassim N. Taleb (2016, 2017), and economist Robert H. Frank (2017), have explored (and described in several successful books) the relationship between luck and skill in financial trading, business, art, music, literature, science, and many other fields. They concluded that chance events play a much larger role in life than many people have imagined, and that talent and effort are not enough.

One can only imagine how deep such roots run beneath the seemingly arbitrary and innumerable agents of chance in complex adaptive systems. Recall the astonishingly mundane case referenced in "Self-Limiting Reluctancy" (see page 41) where hockey players born in the first quarter of the year were more than twice as likely to get selected for top-tier leagues compared to those born in the fourth quarter. Ask yourself this: "How much of my success, what I care about, love, and am driven by was achieved through careful planning?" You may be humbled by what you find if you follow the trail of contemplation far enough.

How do these studies contrast with the success of Descartes, Willis, Ford, and Winfrey (among many others)? And what does this mean for success? Is it even worth the effort if success is governed by forces out of our control?

Let us put aside karma, destiny, and fate for a moment and investigate this matter *objectively*. We do so to consider the possibility that success, as we know it, is in *our* control and not entirely left to chance. Although we are born with different privileges and into unique circumstances, what we become is ultimately of our own doing and no one else's. Accepting the cards we have been dealt and making the most of what is available. Taking responsibility and appreciating the fact that we have no one else to blame for what we decide to do from this point forward but ourselves. It's a double-edged sword, though, in the sense that you are in control of everything that goes right *as well as* everything that goes wrong. You will no longer feel defenseless or powerless, at the mercy of the arbitrary. The simple principle of "causation"—cause and effect—will be your life-long mentor, abolishing ambiguity and laying out a road of certainty and self-confidence.

Living an aimless life with little or no direction and expecting everything to fall into place because of some divine plan is gloomy to say the least. When faced with adversity and despair, one must feel helpless trying to justify reality with "I suppose this is my fate" or claiming the influence of some supernatural power. Nonsensical and disheartening, such justifications lack any sense of reason, logic, and contextual understanding of how the world works. And if we are looking to take control of our *destiny* (a subject matter we will revisit), such mindsets and beliefs will prove of little use. It's a trade-off between control and compromise—the former a constant, the latter a choice. Neglecting choice and the power to change, though, can only lead to self-inflicted desolation and stagnation.

MANUFACTURING SUCCESS

Okay, I suppose the band Fort Minor was wrong all along: it certainly was more than 10% luck, and it might have been about 20% skill. The next obvious question is, well, "What exactly am I in control of?"

To address the practical value of these realizations, it is best to define the constituents of success in a form that's applicable to however one chooses to work with it:

▲ **Luck:**
  success or failure brought about by chance rather than through one's own actions.

▲ **Chance:**
  the probability of an occurrence taking place.

▲ **Randomness:**
  an occurrence without method, lacking a pattern; unpredictable.

▲ **Opportunity:**
  a time or set of circumstances that makes it possible for an occurrence to take place.

▲ **Serendipity:**
  an unexpectedly favorable occurrence.

▲ **Merit:**
  the quality of being worthy enough to warrant praise, reward, or an opportunity.

And to simplify matters, we will refer to chance as the probability of a *realistic occurrence*, and randomness as the probability of an *unrealistic occurrence*. In figure 2-8, three main domains are mapped out: unrealistic occurrences, realistic occurrences (both sized to the realm of probabilities), and merit (sized to the extent of an individual's practical faculties). The union of the occurrences is the field of opportunity, and the intersections between occurrences and merit is the opportunity the individual is capable of seizing, which we refer to as serendipity.

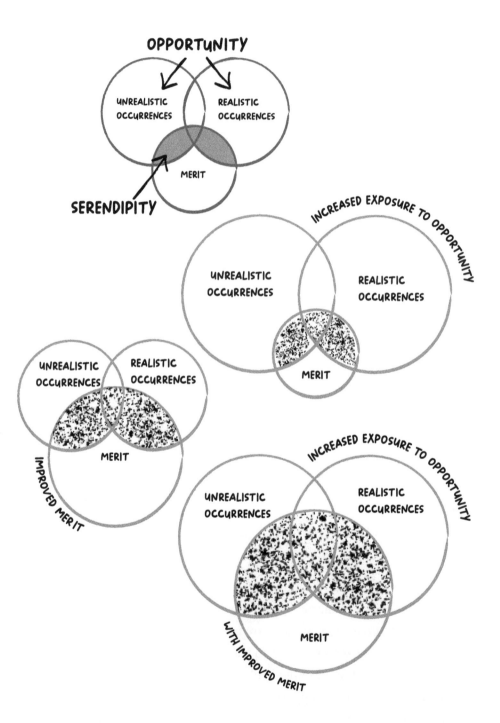

Figure 2-8: Manufacturing serendipity

Luck has been best described by the stoic Seneca, a Roman philosopher and tutor to Nero: "Luck is what happens when preparation meets opportunity," whereby preparation refers to merit (the product of practice) and opportunity is derived of exposure (the quantity and diversity of people, places, and practices we present ourselves to). The beauty of this poetic trichotomy as illustrated in the diagram is its practicality: we can, in fact, catalyze serendipity. We cannot control what occurrences we face, but we can control our exposure to unrealistic and realistic occurrences as well as how much opportunity we seize to improve the likelihood of serendipity.

Facilitating serendipity is the art of conceiving opportunity and capitalizing on it—a process we will refer to as *manufacturing success*. You cannot find the right place at the right time, but what you can do is drastically increase the chances of this occurring. In the words of Milton Berle, the first major American television star: "If opportunity doesn't knock, build a door." Essentially, opportunity finds those looking for it. How do you start looking for opportunity? Through change! Change of location, change of attire, change of contacts, change of hobbies, change of careers, change of tech. Change of everything!

How can you expect to find a partner if you spend all of your free time at home? How can you expect to get a promotion if you don't know anyone at work besides those in close proximity of your desk? How can you expect to discover your next favorite type of ramen noodles if you always order the same kind? How can you expect to become a blockbuster movie star if you aren't willing to wait tables in a restaurant in Hawaii to impress your customer who happens to be a director who casts you in her short film? (Chris Pratt's story.) You should not expect to get anywhere other than right where you are if you do not submit to the forces of change. Albert Einstein defined insanity as "doing the same thing over and over again and expecting different results." Refusing change, grinding through the pain of the vacuous tedium and expecting anything to happen other than what you can no longer stomach is truly insane! René Descartes and the celebrities I mentioned were not only honing their skills but seeking opportunity and seizing it. Interestingly, the authors of the study "Talent versus Luck: The Role of Randomness in Success and Failure" defined talent as whatever set of personal characteristics allow a person to exploit (seize) lucky opportunities.

FRACTAL RABBIT HOLES

So, what should you do when faced with an opportunity? Think back to a time when your friends or family insisted you attend an event, to which you adamantly refused. You were forced to go, but once there, you quickly realized you were having the time of your life and eventually met lifelong friends. We've all been there. What held us back is what we need to overcome, and the best way to do that is through practice! Every once in a while, take a chance. See where it takes you and learn from it. In time, you'll get better at capitalizing on opportunity, and before you know it, you'll look back at how far you've come and think to yourself, "Wow, I really am lucky, aren't I?"—thanks to the role of chance in tilting the balance of talent development and success in your favor!

Now that we know how important a role opportunity plays and what it *can* look like, it's imperative to learn how to recognize its many forms, as it is often disguised. As Thomas A. Edison put it, "Opportunity is missed by most people because it is dressed in overalls and looks like work." There are three channels in which opportunity is found, all of which are interconnected: people, places and practices. The more people you expose yourself to, the more likely you will be introduced to new places and practices. The more places you expose yourself to, the more likely you will be introduced to new people and practices. And so on. Additionally, understanding *how* opportunity delivers value is worth exploring, as it will enable awareness and an open mind. Opportunity offers the following:

1. **CHALLENGE:**
   opportunities to train the mind, build character, and test and improve one's abilities and limits.

2. **EPIPHANY:**
   opportunities to learn about what works best for us.

3. **SERENDIPITY:**
   opportunities to expedite success.

Here are a few examples of how people, places, and practices can individually offer challenge, epiphany, and serendipity:

▲ People:

Harnessing the power of good relationships and becoming a good net-worker is a practice we never hear enough of, yet most of us are terrible at it. The word "networking" gets a bad rep for being associated with "white collar" networking events, insipid dialogue, and the tooting of horns. "Big" people (must) = big opportunity. You will soon realize (or may have already realized) that this is far from the truth, and the quicker you stop shrugging off "average people," whether they're a bartender, an office jockey, or your substitute P.E. teacher, the sooner you'll be able to facilitate serendipity. The benefits and opportunistic possibilities are endless (recall the nature of complex adaptive systems). There are hundreds of books detailing how and why networking can help and even how to do it. It should come as no surprise to learn that many employers are growing more skeptical of online applications with bloated, fabricated-experience-littered résumés and are increasingly reliant on word-of-mouth referrals and graduate programs. Here are a few examples of how opportunity is disguised through people:

1. **CHALLENGE**

   ▽ **Confrontation:** What better way to build character than through argument and discussion. Recall Cristopher Hitchens's view on disputation: there must be confrontation and opposition in order that sparks may be kindled. Whether it's improving your artic-ulation, your nerve, your patience, or perhaps growing thicker skin—whether it was a positive or negative experience—you will find no short-age of opportunities for challenge than through confrontation.

   ▽ **Competition:** What's more fun, having a paper plane convention or a paper plane competition? Assuming you aren't a sore loser (and if you are, there's a challenge to overcome!), going head-to-head with other motivated individuals is another opportunity to learn how to better work under pressure while building confi-dence, integrity, and sportsmanship.

▽ **Charisma and emotional intelligence:** Given what we now know of the umpteen variations personalities can take—their unique attitudes, mannerisms, preferences, and inclinations—all offer challenges of camaraderie, companionship, and congeniality. If you have ever done a DISC or Myers-Briggs personality test (even though their scientific validity is contested), you will know what I am talking about!

2. EPIPHANY

▽ **You don't know what you don't know:** Asking acquaintances, friends, and even strangers (when appropriate) what they did over a holiday or what they are looking forward to can unveil a plethora of interesting insights into personal ventures you may take interest in. Mountain biking just fifteen minutes from here? Why have I never heard about it?

▽ **Standing on the shoulders of giants:** Seek help and advice not just from your best friend or your family but, again, from acquaintances, weekend friends, and strangers when appropriate. That tradesman you met at a pub has probably experienced more highs and lows with wisdom to share than your middle-class, overly protected, attractive high school friend you always go to for a nag. What's easier: learning on your own how to invest from scratch or having that friendly mortgage broker guide you on the journey based on their own experience and tribulations?

▽ **Yin-yang gang:** Who works best for you as a friend, a mentor, a family member, or a significant other? The more time you spend with people of various cultures, attitudes, situations, and mindsets, the more you know what works best for you. What makes you think you are destined to be tied to those you now know? How will you know they aren't the best or the worst society has to offer if you don't expand your connections?

3. **SERENDIPITY:**

▽ **A friend of a friend of a friend of a . . .** Are you looking for someone? Someone to employ you or share a hobby with or to date? Your chances of finding that person are exponentially higher the more people you know. Six degrees of separation—and less.

▽ **A bend to a bend to a bend . . .** Have you ever been on a pub crawl and ended up joining another crawl and then another? And somehow ended the night with fourteen new contacts in your phone, seven different pubs experienced, and an awesome story to share around the office? The permutations of a complex adaptive system are endless; people offer bends to no end.

▽ **A friend to a bend to an end . . .** Running into a friend who happens to work at the café, school, hotel, or vet you're visiting usually brings a moment of surprise, coincidence, and, more often than not, a tour around the venue, a conversation with the manager, insight into how a clinic operates—all of which can lead to a sense of appreciation, interest, and awareness.

▲ **Places:**

Location, location, location. Suffice to say, where you are puts you in contact with varying people and practices, but the place itself, the environment, deeply impacts one's well-being, mindset, and compulsions. Close your eyes and imagine the following: the kitchen, your bedroom, the office, a library, your lawn, the balcony, on a train, on a beach, the interstate, Madagascar, and/or any place you haven't been to. What does it *feel* like? You could be anywhere in the world right now instead of right where you are. How will you know if the way you are, what you've become, what you aspire to, or anything you despise is deeply associated with your location unless you give more of them a try?

1. **CHALLENGE:**

▽ **Atmospheric pressure:** Operating in an environment outside of one's comfort zone has its perks, not by only training one's fear response but building the capacity to adapt when necessary.

Learning how to tune out background chatter, getting used to people chomping with their mouths open, navigating a dangerous or precarious situation, or, at the very least, finding your limit and knowing when to remove yourself from a situation.

▽ **A legal alien:** Cultural incompetency is a matter we are seldom aware of. We mistake other cultural practices, habits, and norms for shortcomings as opposed to simply being different. By stereotyping and biasing our interactions, we overlook what could be a slew of new opportunities. Place yourself in a space in which *you* are the odd one out, and it won't be long before you start questioning your own ways.

▽ **Gaia and I:** How far into the pit of materialism have you fallen? How disconnected are you from the wonders of nature and space? How engrossed into an ego have you gotten? How irritable, pedantic, and overly sensitive to the trivial have you become? A breath of fresh air, the surreal splendor of burbling streams, the rich hues of autumn leaves under a golden light, a warm and a sweet-smelling breeze flowing between your toes. The opportunity to reconnect awaits.

2. EPIPHANY

▽ **Productivity:** Different spaces put you in different moods and states of mind. What space works best when you need to study, relax, work out, reflect, get a confidence boost—or just want to be left alone?

▽ **Long-Haul call:** Where do you live? What's the neighborhood like? Is what you need in reach? Does it provide an environment you can thrive in? Is the community restrictive or open? Do the people you live with make for a space that promotes change? Would it work better to live alone, with family, with motivated strangers or slouches? Environmental osmosis is real.

▽ **Online terrain:** The virtual world is composed of a daily routine of web pages, forums, news outlets, social media platforms—spaces we gravitate toward. When was the last time you looked for a *new* website, or are you content with the echo chambers you have found yourself in? Polarizing views are found within every tribe, but have you considered consuming content of "the other" just out of curiosity? Did you know there are sites out there that allow you to tune in live to any radio station anywhere in the world? Did you know there are subforums for every practice you can think of, and that if you ever needed expert advice, it's always a click away?

3. **SERENDIPITY:**

▽ **Hidden gems:** An oasis at a park, a rustic soul food restaurant down an alley, a quiet village in Bombay, a forty-minute drive to a bungalow on a peninsula—how else will you find personal serenity or an exotic experience if you don't take a different route to work once in a while or turn off your GPS and drive in one direction just for the hell of it?

▽ **Different spaces, different faces:** If you've been looking for that Easter egg in an Easter egg hunt in the same six spots for the last three years, guess what? The egg ain't there, so start looking elsewhere! The love of your life, your forever friends, or your most astute and caring mentors may be slugging through a marathon, building a sandcastle on a beach, stuck in a queue getting their license renewed, or ambling down a mountain path!

▽ **Lost but found:** The genuine excitement of getting lost and finding a way back is an unforgettable experience that switches on primal instincts we never knew we had. It doesn't have to be eighty miles from the nearest city in a sub-Saharan desert; it could start with a count to one thousand Mississippis on a tram, disembarking, turning off your phone, and finding your way back on foot. What you find on the way will be obstacles and opportunities you will never forget: street names, helpful acquaintances, friendly cats and dogs to pet and play with, dollar coins on the side of the road. How far you can traverse in a single day will leave a memory that will last and a heel blister that will not.

▲ Practices:

A hobby, an obligation, a habit, work, a responsibility, entertainment—any and every action you take. I ask once more: How much of what you do is based on self-made realizations drawn from *experience*? How much of it is based on how you were raised, the status quo, what you picked up from watching a movie or deliberating life with a friend? We almost never ask ourselves these questions. Instead, we occasionally, and usually through shear accident (or forced), try something new, and *if* we happen to be in the right state of mind, we *may* pick it up as a habit. How depressingly narrow and insular of a life that would be. Out of everything there is to experience, to work, to experiment with, how do we manage to tell ourselves that *this* is the only way?

1. CHALLENGE

▽ **Mental:** Garnering intellect, experience, and wisdom to make informed, logical, sensible decisions is a no-brainer. To exhibit excellence, integrity, and discipline toward oneself and others ensures the merit required to capitalize on opportunity, whether it's defragmenting the work of Edward Thomas's poetry, reading up on better ways of conducting yourself at work, or studying different or opposing ideologies.

▽ **Physical:** Experience is taxing, there is no doubt about it. Cultivating the stamina to act on opportunity is paramount. To be physically capable of coming back home from a long day of work and still having the energy to continue to another workout, another meal prep, another outing, another activity . . . Mental *and* physical fortitude are optimal for maximum experience!

▽ **Spiritual:** Overnurturing and the twenty-first-century dilemma of curtailed real challenges impedes on our holistic well-being. How often do you challenge yourself spiritually, if at all? The benefits of mindfulness and a grasp of reality are plentiful, liberating, and self-actualizing. Take ten minutes out of your day to meditate.

2. EPIPHANY

▽ **Fitness monotony:** Imagine actually looking forward to your next workout. How easy would it be to lose the weight you've been meaning to lose and stay fit if you genuinely couldn't wait to do it every day. It doesn't have to be four sets of high-volume reps of bench presses, inclines, and cable crosses. And it doesn't have to be a hundred crunches a night. Have you tried skipping rope overlooking a lake? Hiking through a lively redwood forest? Skating around a park? Martial arts with your best buddies? Surfing with dolphins? Hot yoga? Competitive tap dancing?

▽ **Self-actualization:** Arguably the most important opportunity of all: taking on a self-actualizing practice. What form of practice motivates you, provides a sense of reason, gives your life meaning? A practice you wake up and go to sleep thinking about? What practice do you intuitively sense a will to excel in and offers you the ability to *apply* yourself to your fullest potential?

▽ **Just better:** How well do you clean your dishes? How well do you brush your teeth? How well do you remember where you left your belongings? How well are you able to express yourself? The biggest lie we tell ourselves is, "Ah, that's just how I am." No. You are wrong. And you should be ashamed for denying yourself the opportunity of change. Watch a YouTube video of how to best wash dishes. Ask a dentist how to best brush your teeth. Delegate certain areas to leave your earphones or car keys. Pick up a dictionary and build your vocabulary.

3. SERENDIPITY:

▽ **Autopilot greetings:** We are often asked, "How's your day going?" And regardless of what hell or epiphany that may have transpired, we smile and say, "My day's going well. And yours?" Any other response is bound to startle. The next time someone asks, tell them how your day is *really* going. You'll be surprised to find that you will often be met with reciprocal sincerity that may lead to newfound shared interests and/or insights that would generate much needed empathetic connections!

▽ **Itchy backs:** Doing favors is not only a good deed that is rewarding emotionally; it's one that pays dividends in the long run. Not necessarily in an immediate favor in return but in prestige, support, and/or respect that earns you the right to more opportunities through trusted communion—opportunity that is second to none. Givers will gain!

▽ **Communities:** Most activities often have communities that share the practice, collaborate, and hang out. Consider the number of people and places you can potentially expose yourself to with every hobby or internship you attempt. Group-based activities always build strong relationships that can influence your future.

To say that all the aforementioned possibilities is all one can expect of opportunity is an understatement.

> **We are never somewhere in relation to the horizon since the horizon moves with our vision. We can only be somewhere by turning away from the horizon, by replacing vision with opposition . . . To be somewhere is to absolutize time, space, and number . . . Every step towards the horizon presents a new vision, a new range of possibilities.**
>
> —James P. Carse, Finite and Infinite Games

Opportunity is ubiquitous, whether one chooses to believe it or not. Build your merit to warrant eligibility of opportunity. Pursue new opportunities by experiencing the different. Be open to opportunities when they present themselves. Learn to associate the prospect of a novel experience with a positive outlook instead of a negative one. It may not turn out to be a pleasant experience but remain conscious of what value there is to derive from it. Consider what you've learned, how you've grown, whom you've met, and how and what has changed; oftentimes, what people call serendipity is just a matter of exposure and curiosity.

PREQUEL TO PART III:
DESPERATE MEASURES

The commonalities and implications of conventional "project management" along with life constraints, the Waterfall methodology, and the Traditional Psyche have revealed a bridge of opportunity to traverse. The field of software development has afforded us the means to manage and navigate complex adaptive systems toward value, however obscure and elusive it may be.

The Quasi-Chaotic Lifestyle is not only predicated on the fact that we, as individuals, have regularly changing traits, behaviors, preferences, and aspirations, it addresses incompatibilities and emergent issues of the Traditional Psyche with the twenty-first-century's privileges. The fact of the matter is that the everchanging technological, environmental, economic, social, and political landscapes of modernity proliferate opportunities of experience to challenge, to garner epiphanies, *and* to facilitate serendipity—all of which are necessary agents in our quest for self-actualization!

How much closer do you feel to an answer—to the *means* to self-actualize? You may have recognized what the *how* entails. Perhaps you've noticed a list of objective goods to leverage. You might have even begun to contemplate where your potentialities lay and ruminated over what serendipitous chain of events could get you there. However, after realizing what this journey may encompass, even more specific questions may have crossed your mind: "How do I attain mastery if I am to constantly change what I pursue?" "How do I effectively pick up favorable traits and rid myself of unfavorable ones?" "How do I break my bad habit of lethargy?" "How do I overcome my fear of failure and embarrassment?" And others . . .

Toward the end of Part I: Breaking Bad Habits, I asked of you to take a moment, a day, or a week to reflect on what we have been exploring. Yet you may not have. You may have been reading thus far without any intention of taking the invitation seriously or contemplating its actual use. If so, I wouldn't entirely blame you. It's a big ask, and not all of us *feel* in control. Still, I have fleshed out the facts and detailed the realm of relative possibility given our individual circumstances. The nexus of chaos and development is awaiting your initiative! Yet after all that's been said, you may *still* have no intention of taking action. *What is stopping you?* Perhaps your questions remain unanswered: "Why *should* I change?" "Why fix what isn't broken?" "Why not remain safely a cog in a system that offers a livable life for the modest price of losing autonomy and self-actualization?"

Allow me another moment.

To proceed to the actionable—to truly appreciate and act on what there is to gain *as well as* to understand how much there is to lose— one must be willing, committed, and receptive. While the following section may serve as intermission to some of you, it might serve as an epiphany for others.

It goes without saying that each of us harbors widely differing needs, backgrounds, attitudes, outlooks, ambitions, resources, and available time. And so, regarding one's "openness" to embracing a Quasi-Chaotic Lifestyle, you will likely find yourself in one of the following categories:

1. **EAGER:**

   You may be convinced, curious, and hopeful of what is to become your practical guide to self-actualization. If so, the following section may not be as relevant to you, but it will certainly offer a perspective for boosting your self-governance as you prepare to adopt a psyche and a lifestyle befitting an everchanging self and world.

2. **HELPLESS:**

   Perhaps you are cynical, suspicious, apathetic, or self-proclaimed to be incorrigible. Since you did make it this far, you may have rolled your eyes a few times, perhaps with a furrowed brow, feeling patronized for being categorized in any way, shape, or form. You may have a chip on your shoulder, or perhaps melancholy has dulled your senses to even considering the thought of regaining control. And that's okay. It's your prerogative to feel any way you choose. But I sincerely hope you give the next three chapters the time they deserve and yourself the chance you deserve.

3. INDIFFERENT:

You may be doing well for yourself, enjoying the read but with no intention of acting on what is being proposed. To you I say, *You have more to lose than those who have lost it all.* You may have a stable job, a healthy relationship, and a clear conscious, but if one is to bet on life and its twists and turns, assume a curve ball when you least expect it. Such is the nature of Murphy's Law: "If anything can go wrong, it will." Don't act out of desperation; seek to adopt a lifestyle that will serve as your well-being's insurance.

If there is any precept to live by, it would surely be to *strive for the better.* Living to one's fullest potential, whatever that may be, must be the highest denominator of any *good life* and a conviction to never let go of. Again, I ask, *What is stopping you?* You may or may not know. It may be extrinsic or self-inflicted. It may be an obstacle or obstruction. Whatever the issue, the prospect of change demands the liberation of doubt and self-deception. In Part III: Desperate Measures we address three possible culprits for what may be preventing your committal to change. I must warn you, however, that some of what I propose may not be what you want to hear, but I assure you it might very well be what you need to hear.

PART III
DESPERATE MEASURES
THE LAST RESORT

CHAPTER 15
A SENSE OF URGENCY

In times of emotional or energetic stagnation, the thought of getting out of bed feels like a wasted effort: What's the point? After all, the hole you may have dug yourself into may *seem* too deep, and the thought of taking initiative is a start to an ending you probably can't see. Perhaps you harbor a nihilistic sense of despondency: "We'll all die eventually, so why bother? Why should I spend more energy than I have to for some Quasi-Chaotic-Quackadoodle lifestyle that *supposedly* works?" Allow me to propose a perspective worth considering.

To begin, why are we even here? On Earth, as a species? Where is the source of our consciousness? Who or what put us here and then left us with no answers? Without delving too deeply into existential speculation (for now), let us consult the facts.

To put things into perspective, current estimates suggest that there are as many as two trillion galaxies in the observable universe, each with roughly 250 billion stars, most of which host planets of their own. Within the Milky Way alone, we know of roughly three hundred million planets that lie in a potentially habitable zone—the right distance from a star that shines brightly enough to generate the correct temperature, with a size and gravity that is sufficient for life to appear. What we don't know, however, is whether these planets do, in fact, harbor simple, let alone *intelligent*, life.

On Earth, it took around 3.8 billion years to go from the origins of life to a civilization—more than a *third* of our universe's 13.8 billion years of existence. Not only that, but for life to emerge, you would need an unbroken and stable line of life that evolved in the right way, in the right environment, with the right conditions—not too hot, not too cold, and without interruption, stray comets, gamma rays, solar flares or a supernova that blows our atmosphere out of existence. The conditions literally have to be *just* right—the *Goldilocks principle* of the perfect storm for sparking and sustaining life. Those odds are difficult to imagine. What *are* the chances? Assuming it has been nearly four billion years since the origin of life, we can speculate over how many worlds in the "habitable zones" of the universe remained stable for (a fact worth reiterating) *a third of the universe's age*. The chances are immensely unlikely, especially given how the planets in our own solar system happen to be in a stable orbit around a stable star. If this arbitrary "luck" weren't enough, consider also our interplanetary structure and how all the planets "fell into place," permitting the harmony of balance needed for life to blossom—for example, Jupiter's role as our planetary guardian whose gravitational pull protects us from stray, life-threatening asteroids and comets.

The Grand Tack hypothesis attempts to explain the evolution of our solar system; it notes that four rocky planets close to the Sun and four gas giants farther out is an unusual configuration rarely seen amongst other solar systems. Current theories and computer simulations suggest that gas giants form and tend to gravitate close to a primary star—in the case of Jupiter, it was found to have been orbiting about 1.5 AUs (astronomical units: a unit of measurement equal to the distance from Earth to the Sun) from the Sun, close to where Mars is today! Its gravitational forces then cleared out the region around Mars from debris, gas, and rocky material that could have interfered with life's development. But as Saturn approached—according to computer models—the orbital resonance between Jupiter and Saturn dragged Jupiter out to where it is today. Again, what are the chances? I submit they are alarmingly miniscule.

If we added one sufficiently sized planet to our solar system, it would disrupt the complex adaptive system that has evolved, destabilizing orbits and potentially pulling Earth out of its life-supporting "Goldilocks zone" and rendering it inhabitable. Considering the conditions required to maintain stability, our solar system's particular configuration relies on terrifyingly low probabilities—so low that we may well be the only intelligent life form in our galaxy. A chilling thought indeed.

Roughly 541 million years ago, life on Earth seemed to make a drastic change in direction in which fossil records show signs of an unprecedented surge of major animal *phyla*—referred to as the "Cambrian explosion." For the prior three billion years, there was nothing you would consider as complex life, specifically, multicellular organisms. There was suddenly an abundance of oxygen. Scientists speculate it to be the result of a boom of phytoplankton in oceans, their photosynthetic abilities contributing one of the building blocks for the emergence of complex life. Still, *Homo sapiens* (anatomically modern humans) only showed up around two hundred thousand years ago. So, for the vast majority of Earth's history, there was no such thing as "thinking."

Intelligence is rare because it took so long to happen on Earth. One thing for certain is that all complex creatures seem to be *eukaryotes*—organisms with cells, cell nuclei, and membranes. We are all ancestors of single cell goop—a merger two billion years ago speculated to be between two simple life forms: a bacterium cell and an Archaean cell. They survived as a symbiotic organism and miraculously managed to reproduce and replicate in the configuration, and that seems to be the origin of all complex multicellular life. This is called the "fateful encounter" hypothesis. If true, then our very existence has been the result of sheer dumb luck!

Our own civilization has only been around for forty-three thousand years or so—a mere blink of an eye in the grand scheme of things. The idea that no civilizations arose a hundred or two hundred million years ago is mind boggling, especially when considering that it took *this long* for life to take the form we see today. In just the past half millennia, we have experienced extraordinary technological advancements and are beginning travel around our own solar system pursuing interplanetary occupation—and perhaps beyond.

Imagine a civilization that is five million years ahead of us; they should have written their presence across the sky by now. Assuming the technological advancements we've achieved in such a short amount of time, imagine what we would have been capable of if we'd been around another million years or even just a few thousand. We would be exploring other galaxies and leaving behind a signature signal that would be hard to miss for other intelligent life! Yet we do not see it. This disconnect between the probability of extraterrestrial life and the lack of evidence for it is called the *Fermi paradox*. Perhaps they don't want to be seen, or their technology is so advanced that we can't detect it. Perhaps.

In 1961, Frank D. Drake, a radio astronomer and astrophysicist, was involved in the search for extraterrestrial intelligence. He presented an equation that summarizes concepts scientists must contemplate when considering the question of other radio-communicative life (what we can refer to as "intelligent life"). The hypothetical aforementioned timeline is but a single variable in Drake's equation which goes like this:

$$N = R_* \, f_P \cdot n_e \cdot f_l \cdot f_i \cdot f_c \cdot L$$

Where:

N = the number of civilizations in our galaxy with which communication might be possible

R_* = the average rate of star formation in our galaxy

f_p = the fraction of those stars that have planets

n_e = the average number of planets that can potentially support life per star that has planets

f_l = the fraction of planets that actually develop life at some point (the lifeline that has already been detailed)

f_i = the fraction of planets with life that go on to develop *intelligent* life (civilizations)

f_c = the fraction of civilizations that develop a technology that releases detectable signs of their existence into space

L = the length of time for such civilizations release detectable signals into space

Now, we could have explored the wonders that eventuated into each of the equation's variables, but for the sake of succinct delivery, we will leave the rest to your imagination as well as further study by respectable geologists, paleontologists, astrophysicists, astronomers, and biologists. Still, should you feel the need to explore this matter, here's an example of a low estimate, combining NASA's star formation rates, the "Rare Earth" hypothesis value of $f_p \cdot n_e \cdot f_l = 10^{-5}$, biologist Ernst W. Mayr's view on intelligence arising, Drake's view of communication, and historian scientist Michael B. Shermer's estimate of lifetime:

$$R_* = 1.5{-}3\,yr^{-1}, f_p \cdot n_e \cdot f_l = 10^{-5},$$
$$f_i = 10^{-9}, f_c = 0.2, and\ L = 304\,years$$

GIVES:

$$\bigtriangledown$$

$$N = 1.5 \times 10^{-5} \times 10^{-9} \times 0.2 \times 304 = 9.1 \times 10^{-13}$$

The result suggests there are 0.00000000000091 intelligent civilizations in the Milky Way—indicating we may very well be alone in this galaxy and possibly in the observable universe. Drake's equation has received its fair share of criticism, most of which has to do with the fact that several variables are largely based on conjecture. Calculations with a more optimistic set of assumptions suggest there could be 1,000–10,000 technologically advanced civilizations out there, which sounds promising! However, when one realizes that the Milky Way Galaxy is about a hundred thousand light years across, the futility of contact is clear. Assuming radio-communicative intelligent life willing to make contact is an average of fifty thousand light years away, our attempt to communicate through radio transmission would take fifty thousand light years one way and another fifty thousand to come back. In comparison, the next closest galaxy, Andromeda, is 2.5 million light years away. The Milky Way is the boundary of our aspirations.

Of course, intelligent life *could* be closer, unless they haven't already obliterated themselves by self-inflicted means such as nuclear warfare, pollution, or the consequential effects of resource depletion or by extrinsic catastrophe such as a solar flare, stray pulsar beam, or asteroid impact (which is much more likely than you think—12,600 years ago, one almost wiped out the entire human species). The odds are enough to make one rather inconsolable.

So, imagine that we are on our own. What an astounding responsibility we have! Think of what that knowledge should do to our political agendas, what we think of ourselves, how we get along with one another. Imagine how ridiculous it is to divide our world into countries or to wage war because of someone else's fanatic ideology or to descend into weeks, months, or years of cavernous melancholy from falling short of perfection, academic expulsion, or heartache by not meeting another expectations every step of the way; or to fall into outrage and endure torment of regret because our inanimate, well-marketed, shiny new Air Jordans, Patek Philippe, or Tesla were gashed. Imagine if there is no one else we can possibly engage with who thinks like us or looks at the stars or has the privilege of *being*. Imagine *if this is it?*

Every decision to spend time wallowing, worrying, and/or grieving over the cosmologically trivial is a decision not to spend it on countless other potentially self-actualizing directives. You might be telling yourself that real life will begin when you finally graduate, get a promotion, attain citizenship, or get married. It won't—not really. The past is interpreted memory; the future is a figment of your imagination. What is real is always *now*; it is all that you can ever be certain of. We have roughly four thousand weeks to live—make them count.

We cannot help but feel the effects of loss; we are hardwired to be that way, and that's okay—but the lingering grief is not. What there is to lose by allowing the menial, the superficial, the extraneous, the speed bumps, and so on to take control of where we lead our finite lives far outweighs the immediate, emotional present. We ought to remain conscious of reality: why we are here and what we are doing. Cosmology gives us a humbling perspective, but you don't need to be depressed about it. On a cosmic scale, our tininess and uniqueness make us special!

If you wish to make an apple pie from scratch, you must first create the universe.

—Carl Sagan, *Cosmos: A Personal Voyage*

We emerged from chemical reactions and, after 3.8 billion years, have reached a point where you are reading a book and contemplating life. Is that not enough? Why does there have to be a point? Purpose isn't predestined; its discovered! When looking for purpose, you're not looking for the meaning of life; you're looking to *give your life* meaning. Too many people give up on this pursuit, dying by the age of twenty-five though they aren't buried until they're seventy-five.

We are small, finite, rare beings with a limited amount of time on Earth because the laws of nature forbid us from being immortal. From the early years of the universe, the second law of thermodynamics has consistently demonstrated *entropy*—a gradual movement into disorderliness. What physicists strongly suspect is that in the process of going from order to disorder, complexity naturally emerged as part of the evolution of the universe. So, we exist *because* the universe is decaying, not in spite of it. The certainty of inevitable annihilation is *necessary* for our existence and need not provoke a sense of despondency—quite the opposite!

Everything you are composed of is made of carbon, an element produced from decaying stars—perhaps from a single star but more likely from many. Stars unimaginably larger than anything anyone could truly comprehend, at a scale so vast that it dwarfs anything that ever happened in human existence. To want anything more than mere existence—an infinitely rare anomaly, along with a consciousness that has yet to be understood, all constructed from star dust—is a downright absurdity. Contemplate this idea; give it the time it deserves.

A man who dares to waste one hour of life has not discovered the value of life.

—Charles R. Darwin, *The Voyage*

If the fact of your utter uniqueness is not a good enough reason to pique your interest in making the most of your temporary existence and accepting the privilege and prospect of self-determined *meaning*, then I don't know what is. You are special. You are one of a kind. Don't waste this precious opportunity because of a memory, an unfortunate event, a breakup, or a lousy upbringing. The universe compels us to shed our despondency and invigorate a sense of urgency!

CHAPTER 16
PERPETUAL DISSONANCE

Attitudes generally shape our behavior, and most people naturally seek consistency between the two. For example, if you believed eating meat to be immoral, were trying your best to be a vegetarian, and then staggered to Hungry Jacks after getting plastered at a local footy game to wolf down a burger, you would feel a sense of *cognitive discomfort.* Enter stage left: *cognitive dissonance,* a phenomenon proposed by social psychologist Leon Festinger in 1954. Dissonance at its most basic level is *inconsistency.* Cognitive dissonance is inconsistency in thought. Simple, right? Contradictions in our values, attitudes, and/or behaviors lead to cognitive dissonance. It's the discomfort—or, as social psychologists prefer to say, the pain—experienced when holding two or more conflicting cognitions, be they beliefs, ideas, biases, or emotions. The discomfort can manifest in a variety of ways including anxiety, regret, embarrassment, shame, or stress. So, we sublimely change these cognitions to find a consistency and equilibrium that makes us feel better about ourselves. A common example for explaining this phenomenon is the smoker's dilemma.

Jimmy knows that smoking leads to cancer, yet he consciously decides to keep smoking. There is a contradiction between what he knows and what he does, which leads to several possible cognitive "adjustments" in Jimmy's subconscious:

▲ **Simple denial:**

"The evidence that smoking leads to cancer isn't defiitive!
I read this article about a man who lived until the age
of one hundred and five, and he was a smoker."

▲ **Comparing:**

"I don't smoke half as much as my aunt, and she's still kicking!"

▲ **Minimizing:**

"Well, I don't really smoke that much."

▲ **Rationalizing:**

"It's okay because I only smoke when I get stressed."

▲ **Scapegoating:**

"You'd smoke, too, if your life was difficult as mine."

▲ **Justifying:**

"I work out and do cardio two times a week, so
it doesn't even matter that I smoke!"

▲ **Grandiosity:**

"I can quit whenever I feel like it. Besides, I have iron lungs."

And here are some other examples of cognitive adjustments someone you know may be resorting to:

▲ **Remaining in an abusive relationship while knowing it's toxic:**

▽ **Simple denial:** "It's not abusive. This is normal in any relationship."

▽ **Comparing:** "It's not as bad as Suzy's. She
showed up to work with a black eye!"

▽ **Minimizing:** "It only happens once in a while."

▽ **Rationalizing:** "Considering how rough an upbringing
he had, I can see how he'd react like this."

▽ **Scapegoating:** "It's always those girls who dress the way they
do. They make it difficult for even a decent man to ignore."

▽ **Justifying:** "I deserved it. I shouldn't have
said those things to begin with."

▽ **Grandiosity:** "I can figure this out on my own. I can deal with it"

▲ **Struggling with an eating disorder, eating poorly, and knowing what is causing most of your grief:**

▽ **Simple denial:** "It's not a disorder. It's just a phase I'm working through."

▽ **Comparing:** "Some of my friends eat junk food for breakfast, lunch, and dinner. I'm not nearly as bad."

▽ **Minimizing:** "My diet isn't *that* unhealthy."

▽ **Rationalizing:** "I work incredibly hard, so I deserve this meal."

▽ **Scapegoating:** "If my boss wasn't causing me such grief, I wouldn't feel the need to eat this way."

▽ **Justifying:** "It's okay because it's just comfort food. Everyone needs comfort food once in a while."

▽ **Grandiosity:** "I can lose this weight whenever I feel like it."

I'm sure you are already thinking of a few people you know whose cognitive adjustments are causing you grief: the worst people you know, everyone who has let you down, or someone who is presently being a nuisance. Think of the times you were at your lowest and how the people you depended on were nowhere to be seen and when subsequently confronted, had nothing but lame excuses. Think of the naysayers, the judgmental, the haters, the stubborn, the irrational, the illogical. Think of all the people you could have done better without and what your life would have been like without them.

A lifestyle of change giveth, but it also taketh away—but for your own benefit. We have a nasty habit of tying ourselves to what may seem like "necessities," be they financial, emotional, or spiritual. A habit of giving a little bit of ourselves away for the sake of reassurance and insurance, even though we are often left disappointed, unfulfilled, and longing for something different. These shackles hold us back from better alternatives. The puzzle pieces you have forced together form a picture you tell yourself looks right, but that's a lie most of us live with every day. And we *know* this and wonder "What if?" late at night. So, you imagine different scenarios of how things *could* turn out, grinding, crumbling, grating what's left of your sanity, trying to convince yourself that things will get better. But they never do.

You may have lived a life of servility, taking blame and submitting, constantly giving others the benefit of the doubt. Pushing back or expressing anything insinuating oppression, alienation, or hurt feelings only made matters worse, leading to guilt trips, patronization, scapegoating, and every other form of cognitive adjustment. The fact of the matter is, how you feel doesn't matter to *them*, because they are deeply engrossed in a bubble of self-loathing, void of any sense of reason, hopelessly irrational, perpetually dissonant.

Everyone has their priorities, their responsibilities, their problems, their demons—their lives to deal with—*and so do you*. But people who constantly add to the load of your life should not be tolerated. If they aren't willing to adapt, you cannot help them. Considered one of the founders of humanistic psychology, Carl Rogers once pointed out that there are necessary preconditions for entering into a therapeutic relationship. One of them, for example, is that both individuals must *want* "therapy" to happen. If these conditions aren't met, then what you are doing isn't helping and possibly even *making it worse*. Similarly, should those standing in the way of you and change remain perpetually dissonant and unwilling to cooperate, any form of reconciliation or attempt to "meet the other halfway" will be futile.

How, then, do we emancipate ourselves from burden and abuse, especially if we have little hope or drive for progress? We abandon everything that's holding us back. Anything maliciously hurting, castigating, and/or demoralizing us or that impedes our efforts to live to our fullest or doesn't add value to who we are and where we want to be. "When I let go of what I am, I become what I might be. When I let go of what I have, I receive what I need," said the ancient philosopher Lao Tzu. Letting go in this way may hurt more than you think, but pain for freedom is a bet you should be willing to make if you have any intention of turning your life around.

You are the prize; *you* are the one that opportunity should seek; *you* are the person people fear to lose. Until you realize your self-worth, you will always be on the back foot, begging for attention, love, security, and belongingness. And when you do, you will have everything you need; you will have yourself, *and that's good enough.* You will learn to love the visage of a transient, familiar self staring at you from the mirror. You will seek to improve yourself any way you can because that reflection is the home of your consciousness, the carrier of your existence, one that shouldn't be neglected or undermined. Your time is precious, your seconds are counting down. Are you going to drape yourself with a cloak of pity or make a stand and take that first step to rejuvenation?

A CHANGE OF PERSPECTIVE

Since you've made it this far into the chapter, you should now know why *you* may be left behind. If you have found yourself in a place of hurt, stagnating for months or years because nothing has worked for you thus far, it is likely that you are the fly in the ointment, living in your own perpetual cognitive dissonance. I suggest you reread the chapter with the perspective of, say, your significant other, a best friend or colleague, or anyone you may have potentially been imparting grief to. Whether it's endlessly wallowing in self-pity, radiating negativity while rejecting any advice, or denying, comparing, minimizing, rationalizing, scapegoating, justifying, or avoiding the problems besieging you, consider *their* turmoil, *their* personality differences, *their* hardships, *their* situation and how you may have been impeding *their* own quest for fulfillment.

If you don't add value to other people's lives, if you don't constructively contribute, if you don't carry your own weight—and, most importantly, if *you* do not change—you *will* be left behind. If you resort to grandiosity and conclude, "Well, I don't need them anyway!", you will be left behind. If you expect any other outcome from the next person you lean on, should you refuse change—you will be left behind again. The foundations that have kept you afloat thus far are crumbling with each passing minute you remain stagnant and keep doing what you have always been doing. This, again, is what Einstein defines as insanity: doing the same thing over and over and expecting a different outcome. If you don't take action, you *will*, over time, grow bitter, jealous, hurtful, and increasingly incorrigible, making things worse for yourself and the people around you.

You can try every cognitive acrobatic adjustment you can manage—and you will remain precisely on the same path to self-wrought desolation until there is no one left to help pull you out of the hole you've dug for yourself. You will read about an actionable counter to this cognitive stalemate in the coming chapter, but for now, it is imperative to acknowledge the high possibility that cognitive adjustments are preventing the self-awareness necessary to liberate yourself from who you now know to be your worst adversary—*you*. Don't underestimate the influence of such cognitive maneuvers as they are precisely what makes good, ordinary people do wicked things. How the Crusaders raped and massacred cultures and entire nations; how the Ottomans, Japanese imperialists, Nazis, and others engaged in genocide, ethnic cleansing, and war crimes too numerous and inhuman to list; how psychopaths live in a reality void of dissonance; and how scammers, thieves, con artists, fraudsters, criminals, and anyone committing immoral or unethical acts can often live with themselves. As Nobel laureate Richard P. Feynman, pioneer of quantum electro-dynamics and one of the greatest theoretical physicists of all time, asserted, "The First Principle is you must not fool yourself. And you are the easiest person to fool."

I would like to preface the following chapter by asking you to ruminate over the tribulations you are currently facing—be they a consequence of the past, present, or what you anticipate your future to bear—and answer one simple question: How bad do you want change? Write your answer down and save it for later. You will need it.

CHAPTER 17
SUFFER

Sorrow is not an individual failing but a basic inevitability for our entire species. We are fragile constructs, in constant battle—often blindly—with adversity and with little intuition of reality, yet also hopeful, with an unquenchable need for sympathy and affection. Our tribulations are symptomatic of being human, not a curse to endure. Being miserable doesn't exclude us from the human community. It's actually a sure sign that we are normal and that life is progressing in its own convoluted way, more or less exactly to plan. What does exclude us from community, however, are perpetual cognitive adjustments that we have come to rely on to keep us from changing.

We deny, minimize, rationalize, scapegoat, justify, and/or lean on grandiosity to elude change. That dissonance is the means by which we arrive at a solitary personal terminal, one that does not permit anyone but the individual's reception. Escape from what I will refer to as an "Unreachable Terminal" is only permissible by the individual and the individual *alone*. What prevents departure is excess emotional baggage: an insurmountable expectation gap, when expectations of reality *greatly* exceed experiences of reality. It is this Unreachable Terminal that some of us find ourselves in, a forlorn state necessitating a list-ditch effort, one that is practical, actionable, indiscriminate, and one we will now explore.

The ancient Grecian mythical figure Pandora and her gift of curiosity tempted her betrayal of what her father Zeus asked of her: to never open the box (scripturally, a jar) he had given her, as its contents were not for mortal eyes. Seeking to punish humans for accepting the gift of fire her brother-in-law, Prometheus, rebelliously equipped them with, Zeus had secretly used the jar as a vessel for all forces of evil—mutant descendants of the dark and evil children of the primordial deities Nyx, goddess of the night, and Erebus, god of darkness: Apate, Deceit; Geras, Old Age; Oizys, Misery; Momos, Blame;

Keres, Violent Death; Ate, Ruin; Eris, Discord; Ponos, Hardship; Limos, Starvation; Algos, Pain; Dysnomia, Anarchy; Pseudea, Lies; Neikea, Quarrels; Amphilogiai, Disputes; Makhai, Wars; Hysminai, Battles; Androktasiai and Phonoi, Manslaughter and Murders. Of course, she opened the jar, and thus came the end of the Golden Age, a period of peace, harmony, stability, and prosperity—a time before the evils existed, when men lived amongst the gods in a world of abundance and serenity. Pandora, in a panic, was able to seal the jar shut, leaving behind one last little creature: Elpis, Hope. A matter of debate amongst scholars across the ages, some maintain that Elpis (the final spirit a spiteful Zeus wanted for man) was in fact the worst of them all. To existentialist philosophers like Friedrich W. Nietzsche, hope prolonged man's daily suffering with the false expectation of something good to come.

This false reality you have tied yourself to, then, is anchored to hope. Hope that one day a miraculous epiphany or a serendipitous opportunity will show up on your front porch. A hope your support group will reassure you that "It will come; it takes time" and "You are deserving; keep your head up" along with thoughts and prayers. It is this very hope that casts you into gloom—not by negativity but by false beliefs regarding your career, your love life, your hobbies, your planet. Hope is to blame for embittering and angering us and for generating endless corrosive disappointments. Such was the realization of Blaise Pascal, the great seventeenth-century mathematician and philosopher, in his work *Pensées* (a position the Stoics deeply aligned with). Hope is the cause of the expanse between the possible and the phantasmagorical, what I will refer to as the "Imagination Gap." Hope, instilled by extraneous influences, blinds us to what our respective iron triangles permit.

How, then, do we become liberated from a particular social milieu and its rigid attitudes, archaic prejudices, and practical "necessities" not of our own making? How do we overcome what Martin Heidegger, a revered though controversial philosopher, called *geworfenheit* ("thrownness" or "being thrown into the world")? The vast majority fail dismally at this task. Instead, we surrender to a socialized, superficial mode of being he called "they-self" (as opposed to "our-self"). We follow *das Gerede* ("the chatter") which we read or hear about in newspapers, on TV, on social media, and in the large cities Heidegger hated to spend time in. We wear our masks and play our roles unconsciously or at times consciously and willingly—desperate for comfort and acceptance, in fear of alienation and uncertainty. To overcome this thrownness, Heidegger suggested that we should pursue an understanding of our psychological, social, and professional provincialism and then rise above it to a more universal perspective. We shall attempt to make the classic Heideggerian journey away from *Uneigentlichkeit* (inauthenticity) and toward *Eigentlichkeit* (authenticity).

So, again, what's stopping you? Liberation through a Quasi-Chaotic Lifestyle is at your disposal, in this very book! Perhaps you remain perpetually dissonant (especially if you've been inconsolably stagnating), stuck at an Unreachable Terminal, willingly despondent, feeling like it's easier to wallow than work your way out. You, and no one else, are the prime mover of your own undoing—and redoing. So, what is there to do?

To answer the question, I refer to a global expert on organizational change and transformation, Jen Frahm, who describes five pillars of "organizational change" in her book, *Conversations of Change: A Guide to Implementing Workplace Change* (2017), particularly for organizations aspiring to become Agile: *change capability, change readiness, change resistance and stakeholder engagement, change communication, and change leadership.* Much like the Agile philosophy, we as individuals have much to gain from industry's investment in perfecting (in this case) change management. Of these five, two-and-a-half are relevant to one's personal efforts to overcome obstacles preventing the authentic desire to adopt a Quasi-Chaotic Lifestyle:

1. **Change capability:**
   "Anything an organization does well that drives meaningful business results."

2. **Change readiness:**
   "The cognitive precursor to the behaviors of either resistance to, or support for, change effort."

3. **Change resistance:**
   "The refusal or unwillingness to adapt to altered circumstances."

For example, if an organization and its people do not have the right attitude toward change or the financial, material, and/or human resources necessary to execute change efficaciously (are not change ready), then they are very likely to be change resistant.

The first, change capability, is central to the Quasi-Chaotic Lifestyle and the means to drive meaningful results. You are *change-capable*: the means to achieve change is at your fingertips. Next comes knowledge of what is stopping you, which we can boil down to change readiness and change resistance.

The prolific social psychologist Kurt Lewin, one of the founding fathers of "change management," developed what he refers to as *force field analysis,* which provides an overview of the balance between forces driving change in a business and the forces resisting change. He suggests that change occurs "when the forces for change are greater than the forces against change" (1951). You know what there is to be done. You've done some homework, watched TED talks and YouTube videos, listened to advice based on highly rated Reddit comments, and perhaps paid close attention to what your circle recommends. Just take baby steps, you're told. "I know this. I get it. I know what I can do. I know what needs to be done. But why don't I want to? Why is it so hard to be motivated and energetic and do what everyone else seems to do on a whim?" Alas, your "forces against change" outweigh your "forces for change." And while change readiness is precursory to change resistance, it doesn't mean you can't be change resistant even when ready for change, unwilling for whatever reason to action those first few steps.

What's the point, then, if everything feels arduous and tedious—whether it be action toward change or the enduring routines that keep you on the edge of sanity but ultimately take you nowhere? Such an outlook invokes change readiness, which we will address first.

He who has a why to live can bear almost any how.

—Friedrich W. Nietzsche, Götzen-Dämmerung; oder, Wie man mit dem Hammer philosophirt (Twilight of the Idols or How to Philosophize with a Hammer)

CHANGE READINESS

Ancient Greece, circa 399 BCE. Aristotle and Plato took it as a given that everything has an essence, a specific set of core properties that are essential for a thing to be what it is, that gives something its defined function. They also applied that principle to people, believing that before we are even born, we are destined to fulfill our *essence* or predesignated purpose. This outlook is known as *essentialism*, one that many of us unknowingly accept or assume by way of social vernacular, tradition, or religion. We often hear "They were born/destined to be . . ." or perhaps there are family expectations: "Their parents were doctors, and they should be too." It's a rather appealing concept, summoning a vision of triumph, esteem, purpose, and pride, and effectively justifying the suffering we are all subject to.

It wasn't until the twentieth century that Jean-Paul Sartre formulated the work of preceding philosophers and declared to the world that "existence precedes essence"—a mantra suggesting that after birth, we are left to find our own essence/purpose. This idea came to be known as *existentialism*. A rather revolutionary conjecture to make at the time, it proliferated through societies by virtue of World War II's conclusion and fallout, and why wouldn't it? The *angoisse* (anguish) of existence, as Sartre put it, was inconsolable, as the horrors of war wrought unresolvable moral confusion and perennial dilemmas. The thought of *preordained angoisse* was impossible to square as the masses began to challenge the meaning and purpose of human life. Any ideologies that attempted to anthropomorphize nature's causality (eventualities of a war-ridden reality), to attribute and justify egregious human behaviors and raw consequences to a god, animal, or object and assume answers in what was revealed to be an answerless macrocosm was deemed to be *absurd*. This is a concept derived of existentialism: to live "the life of the absurd" is to reject any pursuit of meaning, as there is nothing to be discovered—the core sentiment to what is known as *absurdism*. Its origins are linked to the "father of existentialism," the philosopher Søren A. Kierkegaard, and later popularized by the second youngest recipient of the Nobel prize, philosopher-absurdist Albert Camus, in his essay *The Myth of Sisyphus:* "Many people die because they judge their life is not worth living; paradoxically, others die for ideas or illusions that give them a reason for living." In other words, reasons for living and reasons for dying are one and the same: an oxymoronic absurdity.

In Greek mythology, Sisyphus was banished after cheating death twice and then punished by Zeus to push a boulder up a steep hill with the promise of freedom should he push it to the top. Each time Sisyphus drew near to the peak, the weight of the stone grew too heavy to bear, and it rolled back down, only for Sisyphus to make another attempt, and another, and another. "One last push. I'll get it this time." Believing he can do it, Sisyphus is left rolling the boulder up the hill for eternity. Some philosophers associate the futility of Sisyphus's efforts with the absurdity of human life and the remorseless cruelty of fate.

In cheating death twice, Sisyphus was the prime mover of his own undoing, realizing the consequences of his actions. How, then, did *you* get to your own point of absurdity? What unfortunate chain of events led you to precisely where you are now? Did you *will* it or did the threads of fate determine your present situation?

This dilemma gives rise to the debate between *free will*, the belief that human action is freely chosen and that you are the author of your fate, and *determinism*, the belief that all events are caused by past events, such that nothing other than what does occur could occur. For example, the outlook of a determinist would suggest that your preferences are shaped by past experience, perhaps more so in earlier years as you cemented your moral, ethical, societal, and other beliefs. Insecurities and paranoia might have roots in a difficult or abusive upbringing. If you've been raised amongst thieves, who is to blame if you become one? Are you in control of the next thought you think, or does it simply emerge? Was Sisyphus "at fault" when he grew up rivaling his brother Solmaneous for his parent's affection, which led him down a spiral of deceit and treachery? Alternatively, the autopsy of Charles Joseph Whitman, an infamous serial killer, revealed a brain tumor that may have influenced his spontaneous frenzy. Should Whitman be held responsible for his actions, or was he destined to kill without willing it? What about anyone suffering from a mental disorder such as schizophrenia? In the case of a violent drunk, what do you blame: the booze or the drinker? What about your own upbringing? Did you choose the family you were born to, the social class you were raised in, your religious affiliation, the color of your hair, your sense of humor? As Sam Harris put it, "There is not a cell in your body or brain that you—the conscious subject—created. Nor is there a single influence coming from the outside world that you brought into being. And yet everything you think and do arises from this ocean of prior causes. So what you do with your luck, and the very tools with which you do it, including the level of effort and discipline you manage to summon in each moment, is more in the way of luck."

Such lines of inquiry can be taken to extremes when considering Einstein's *theory of special and general relativity:* an effect cannot occur from a cause that is not in the past. Given sufficient computational power and assuming you were able to know the precise position and momentum of every atom in the universe, you would be able to infer the past and future of their values, effectively ruling out free will altogether. We bow to Pierre-Simon Laplace, a polymath pioneer and scholar whose quote in "A Philosophical Essay on Probabilities" (often referred to as "Laplace's demon") made the case for *casual determinism:* "The future is entirely predictable from the past."

This rather puzzling and frustrating dilemma beckons thoughtfulness but also offers some valuable realizations. If you do in fact possess free will, you are then the author of your actions, ergo, your actions bear meaning, and your *will* possesses promise and suggests control. You are responsible for all that has become and consequently at fault for your own demise—as are Whitman, Sisyphus, and anyone else authoring grief regardless of their past and extraneous influences. A determinist, however, lives through the motions, accepting fate as it comes and the absence of control. This may also impel a sense of understanding and forgiveness of themselves and others. "How could I blame my father for not knowing how to be one. His own father died young, leaving him to help raise a family of eight in poverty and a civil war."

"Man may do what he wills, but he may not will what he wills," said "philosopher of pessimism" Arthur Schopenhauer, also known as the "artist's philosopher." In other words, while you may often be free to act according to a motive, the nature of that motive has already been determined. Such is the outlook of *compatibilists,* who separate internal and external causes and believe that free will and determinism can exist simultaneously. Sean M.

Carrol, a theoretical physicist and compatibilist, boils it down to 1) how the world works (pointing to the intrinsic random nature of quantum mechanics), and 2) what words to attach to how the world works. In other words, *we are more or less free*. While all internal factors can be *technically* derived (assuming Laplace's demon that every thought, judgment, and memory is derived of "brain wiring," whose own constituents of atoms can be measured and mapped and their subsequent interactions and effects predicted), we have no choice but to separate obvious external factors from *seemingly* internal factors. So, I will blame you if you drink and drive, but if you uncontrollably sneeze on my plate of food, I will not. Neuroscientist and philosopher Patricia S. Churchland suggests that asking whether one is "free" is the wrong question. Instead, it comes down to how much *control* we have. The more control, the more responsibility we bear.

At this point, it is in my conviction that we have no choice but to adopt a dichotomic perspective, one that takes the best that both free will and determinism have to offer and produce a spectrum of reasoning without the need for faith or false belief. You *are* in control, though not entirely of your own doing—a quasi-utilitarian outlook that coincides with the practicality of a Quasi-Chaotic Lifestyle.

Where then, do we find meaning in a meaningless world? Camus tells us the answer is to embrace the meaningless. He defined an *absurd hero* as someone who truly knows that life is absurd and goes through it with a smile. "We must imagine Sisyphus happy," for the absurd hero's life is as meaningless as endlessly rolling a boulder up a hill and finding enjoyment in it anyway. Not because of hope, but notwithstanding of it; the search for meaning is *itself* meaningful. It is not up to Zeus to determine whether Sisyphus finds meaning in his task. In doing so, Sisyphus revolts against the gods. Likewise, we respond to a meaningless universe with our own subjective meaning and revolt against the absurd. In turn, we accept and champion the fact that meaning is ideal, not real. Heidegger helps us pull away from "they-self" by insisting that we focus on our own inevitable death and *das Nichts* ("the nothing") that awaits. Awareness of our *Sein-zum-Tode* ("being-toward-death") will liberate us from angst and wasting our energies on capitulation and sacrificial acceptance to recover our version of Eigentlichkeit—authenticity. Birthdays, for example, ought to be a reflective celebration of the experiences one has garnered thus far—a reflection on how far one's come and how much more there is yet to do—not a stoic succumbing to *das Nichts*. It should be a yearly ritual to motivate an individual to continue living to their fullest, as they see fit. If anything is *not* worth celebrating, it's the fact of growing old, that our life is finite and temporary. You may scoff, but this is precisely why we stop celebrating birthdays around the age of thirty-seven, as a study commissioned by Interflora, a flower delivery network, concluded after examining the attitudes of two thousand people across the UK (Anon, 2019).

Letting go of what we presumed to be an inevitable, ill-fated future would effectively lay the foundation for a *realistic* outlook. We are reclaiming control, correcting our relationship with meaning, and now willing to revolt against the absurd. We are change ready! We will now turn to change resistance wherein the unwillingness to adapt to altered circumstances is maintaining our "forces against change."

CHANGE RESISTANCE

You were right all along! The effort isn't worth it. The anxiety and nauseating thought of having to take that first step, then the next step, and then the next, precisely as you have imagined it to be, is what you have grown to despise: an intangible, intrinsically meaningless, and presumably requisite process for traversing your Imagination Gap.

You have fallen so far behind the hope you still cling to that the journey paradoxically turns hopeless in perpetual dissonance. In this frame of mind, you have every right to tell yourself it isn't worth it, because to live in bad faith while pursing the impossible—or at the very least, an undertaking you abhor—*is absurd*. Whatever undesired expectations society or your family have of you aren't worth it. That meta diet, that optimal gym workout, those particular parties you're invited to, that PhD, that salary—everything and anything you loath—*are not worth it*. Stop forcing meaning onto what is meaningless to you. Stop deliberately searching for meaning where it does not exist. Let go of this *hope* and resist surrendering to *das Gerede*: the trivial, the grind. Give your time meaning *or it will give you hell in return*. A life of change offers achievable initiatives that are suited to *you*, that *you* choose to pursue, that will propel *you* toward *your* self-actualized potential.

Of course, I would not have you think for a second that this change of mindset and eventual epiphany will "switch" overnight. To which we arrive at the final resort: *Suffer.*

Before you boot this book across the room, hear me out. In every epic action film, there comes a moment where all the odds are stacked against the protagonist. She's lost her family, her dignity, her job, her hope, and she is faced with a decision: give up or change. On the flip side are people who have had a near-death experience that motivated them to make the most of every day they have on this blessed planet. What these people have in common, fictitious or not, is that they share a distinct and definitive moment—a point of epiphany—when they realize it's do or die, that everything from that point on will be a fight they will go the distance with. They make a promise to never revisit mediocrity or half-assed attempts at anything they do. In theater, this moment is referred to as *anagnorisis*: the moment one discovers the true nature of their own circumstances.

How do you reach such a moment of revelation? Simple. Stay right where you are. Continue doing exactly what you're doing. Go to sleep and wake up and with that same empty feeling in your heart and weight on your shoulders. Drink your coffee and smoke your cigarette outside the office at 7 a.m. Go back home after working overtime with no compensation and run to mommy and daddy for a whine. Watch the next trending Netflix series and spend the week chatting about it with your conditional friends. Have another drink, take another puff, switch your Xbox back on, and remain perpetually distracted. If you have it in you to live like this to the end, then do so. Put this book aside and keep telling yourself that things will change—somehow. Keep suffering in solitude, unwilling to force change, unwilling to say enough is enough, unwilling to adopt a Quasi-Chaotic Lifestyle. Just know that the universe in all its glory and scale could not care less about your situation or whether you leave nothing behind other than the memory of someone who pushed paper around.

With the abundance of information available on the internet, many have self-diagnosed the source of their problems, ascribing it all to some hereditary, idiopathic, or chronic disease and naively cementing their fate. Thinking they are biologically predetermined to be this way and letting life pass them by. Fortunately, this is not the case for most, so if you find yourself in doubt, you are obligated to proactively seek and capitalize on any and every form of support society has to offer. Whether you think support systems will work for you or not, cast aside any presuppositions. If you refuse to give therapy, counselling, anti-depressants, meditation, hot yoga, and so on a chance, you have only yourself to blame. There are ways to manage, mitigate, and live with your mental-emotional discomforts while still moving forward. Change demands it. If you aren't trying every possible solution available to you, you are willingly heading down the path of despair. Perhaps (and you'll know this) you deny your autonomy and refuse to accept responsibility because placing the blame on what is out of your control is easier than having a thirty-minute conversation with a therapist.

Not making a decision is a decision in itself. If you decide not to act, imagine how your life will turn out. Draw it out, map it. You will know because you are living it right now. Try to imagine how far you'll go and how much you'll be able to accomplish if you refute the possibility of change. Picture yourself three, five, even ten years from now. Will you be content to losing a limb to diabetes, your significant other to greener pastures, your children to a divorce, a lifelong friend to extended depression, or, most worrisome, losing yourself?

It starts and ends with you. There *is* an answer a few pages away. You are change capable. The illusion of self (see page 15) compels us to perceive our past self as another person full of addressable shortcomings. Let go of *that* person; you are no longer *that* failure, *that* liar, *that* procrastinator, *that* selfish/abusive/oppressive/ignorant/careless/irresponsible/untrustworthy husband/wife/father/mother/sibling/colleague/friend. Don't let *that* person determine how you live the rest of your life. You are who you choose to be *now*. If you do choose to suffer, do so knowing that it is *you* who refuses to act. Let your bills accumulate, your relationships deteriorate, your opportunities and time pass you by. Let your physical and mental well-being degenerate and keep suffering, knowing that you could have done something about it but didn't.

However, there will come a time in which you tell yourself that you've had enough. The not-so-very-well-known poet and novelist Heinrich Karl (Charles) Bukowski put it this way: "When you get the shit kicked out of you long enough, you will have a tendency to say what you really mean." This is your anagnorisis—discovery of the true nature of your own circumstances.

Eventually, the routine you are presently bound to—the people, places, and practices that have kept you barely afloat—will either depart, bore you, or become too heavy a burden to maintain, whether it be for financial, health, or other dependencies. This is the point at which you are no longer change resistant as your "forces for change" begin to outweigh your "forces against change" and you become *Change Receptive.* This overwhelming sensation of determination will ignite a fire—a roaring inferno!—that will echo through the false shell you once were. And *now* when you are faced with the question once more, "How bad do you want change?", you and every bone in your body will know the answer: *Pretty fucking bad.*

It is not death that a man should fear, but he should fear never beginning to live.

—Marcus Aurelius, *Meditations 12.1*

You will no longer hesitate, you will no longer procrastinate, you will no longer second-guess yourself. From this point on you, you are the maker. You are your own prime mover as you depart your Unreachable Terminal and pursue a Quasi-Chaotic Lifestyle that will change your life forever and for the better. Now in control, you will be ready to make up for the time you wasted—informedly considerate of your iron triangle, *willing* to pursue what is meaningful to *you.* And the fastest way there is on the premium express train that is a Quasi-Chaotic Lifestyle.

For the same reason general advice doesn't instantaneously exculpate you from your woes, my approach, beliefs, and intrinsic values will differ from yours. In other words, there isn't anything anyone can tell you, nothing anyone can do to motivate you, and nothing anyone can teach if you are unreachable. But some can show you a way out—if you allow it.

PREQUEL TO PART IV:
DIRECTION

A miracle, a turn of the tables, and a one-way ticket toward anagnorisis will inflame the pyre—not of hope but of control. The first step toward a Quasi-Chaotic Lifestyle is often the hardest to make, but once you take it, you will quickly realize that they are steps in the right direction.

From the roots of dysfunction (where we began), we addressed the numerous critical incompatibilities and emergent issues arising from the Traditional Psyche; we curbed, busted, rebutted, confuted, denounced, and discredited most of the overarching attitudes, outlooks, and methods that simply no longer work. Along the way, we unearthed revealing truths of what is possible: success, control, talent, self-development, autonomy, informedness, happiness, and self-actualization. We proceeded to glean the pearls of wisdom afforded by the Information Technology industry and bridged the gap from software development systems and delivery to a philosophy to daily life by recognizing principles and practices to productively employ for our own personal benefit. The iterative and serendipitous nature of the proposed Quasi-Chaotic Lifestyle, finely tuned to thrive in a complex adaptive system, has been demonstrated to offer revelations of promise. And now, with the philosophical and rational underpinnings of meaning itself, all that's left is to bring it all together into a cohesive theory of happiness: the Quasi-Chaotic View, a frame of well-being that the Quasi-Chaotic Lifestyle hinges on.

PART IV
DIRECTION
THE PURPOSE

CHAPTER 18
THE QUASI-CHAOTIC VIEW

It is now time to marshal our facts and consider all that has been brought to light to inform a twenty-first-century "adapted" theory of happiness and well-being. We begin by answering the most pressing question: What theory of happiness does Maslow's hierarchy of needs fall under, and does it stand the test of time? Given what we know now, we can make the following observations:

1. **The components of Maslow's hierarchy of needs and the twelve characterizations he attributes to self-actualized individuals read very much like an "objective list of goods" to strive for.**

2. **The peak experiences that Maslow associates with self-actualized individuals closely relate to "hedonistic expression."**

3. **His definition of self-actualization suggests that it rests on "subjective desire"—that is, living to one's fullest potential.**

Given the various theories of happiness and well-being as described in Chapter 8: A Cursed Grail, each of these reflections suggest Maslow's framework to be a hybrid of sorts. The literature on the innumerable theories available is deep and broad, and the language, definitions, and classifications associated with them can be—and often are—disputed. To simplify matters and regain our bearings, given how much ground has been covered, we will refer to a broader taxonomy and leverage a diagrammatic representation of what moral and well-being philosopher Valerie Tiberius (2013) sees as *current* theories of personal well-being. (See figure 4-1.) The work of social and political philosopher Malcolm Thorburn (2015) will provide further direction to help navigate what may at first be intimidating but will quickly make sense. It is worth reemphasizing that none of the items illustrated are specifically singular theories, but categorizations.

Thorburn explains: "The inner circle is designed to show how informed values and desires can connect subjective theories with objective well-being theories. The outer circle is designed to portray the same relationship through highlighting the connections between subjective-informed desire fulfillment and life satisfaction theories and objectively informed target-driven theories. The connecting (broken circle and lower case) links around the outer periphery indicate the key elements that can help bind subjective and objective theories of well-being together."

Take a minute to consider figure 4-1 and guess which categorization Maslow's hierarchy of needs would fall under.

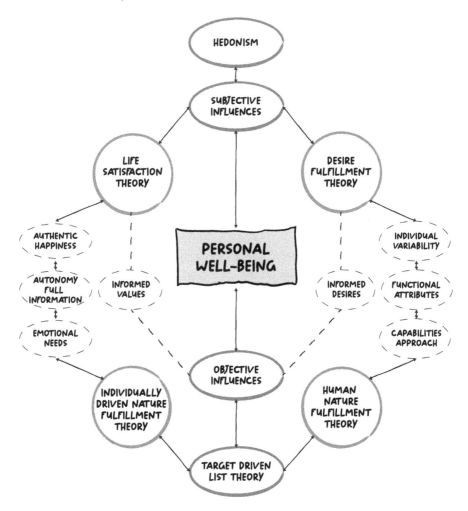

Figure 4-1: Theories of personal well-being. Adapted from Thorburn (2015)

What was your hunch?

Maslow's theory is in fact widely regarded to be a *nature-fulfillment theory*, which postulates that there are two ways to understand the achievement of human potential—fulfilling our own individual nature (e.g., our unique and specific gifts, talents, and capacities) or fulfilling our universal human nature (e.g., our capacity to love, be creative, and exercise reason). Maslow's sacred pyramid seems to have concatenated the two definitions with "high-level" descriptions of what he regards to be "living to one's fullest." But which of the following two related categorizations Tiberius identified would it correspond with: human nature fulfillment theory (where list items are determined by necessary functional outcome-based attributes that are instrumentally good for us) or individually driven nature fulfillment theory (where list items are determined by the extent to which they match people's emotional needs and contribute to their subjective happiness)?

To make it easier, refer back to Nussbaum's capability approach (see page 102) for contrast. What do you think of Maslow's hierarchy of needs now? Here are two more hints.

1. Gagné

2. Nietzsche

Give up? The fact of the matter is that Maslow et al. (1979) looked to biology as a basis for psychology and ethics. His criticisms of the shortcomings of scientific psychology were accompanied by unwavering biological essentialism in which "truth, goodness, beauty, [and] justice" would ultimately be explained through "biochemical, neurological, endocrinological substrates or body machinery" (Maslow, 1971). Maslow was a humanist but also an essentialist who suggested what humanistic psychologist Christine N. Winston (2015) succinctly tabulated as the underlying themes to Maslow's interpretation of "living to one's fullest potential." (See figure 4-2.)

Theme	Existential psychology	Humanistic psychology
Subject of inquiry	Human existence	Human self
Ontological position	Existence precedes essence	Essence precedes existence
Temporal orientation	Future gives the present meaning	The "here and now" gives the present meaning
Therapeutic goals	Awareness and acceptance of the human condition	Awareness and acceptance of the human self
Growth motivator	Anxiety	Actualizing tendency
Optimal functional	State of Being	Process of Becoming
The good life	The search for meaning	The search for self

Figure 4-2: Existential psychology versus humanistic psychology
Adapted from Winston (2015)

So, the answer (if you haven't gathered it by now) is that Maslow's hierarchy of needs is, like Nussbaum's capability approach, a *human* nature fulfillment theory. And the potentialities Gagné was referring to are the same ones that Maslow meant when suggesting, "What a man can be, he must be. This need we call self-actualization" and adding "It refers to the desire for self-fulfillment, namely, to the tendency for him to become actualized in what he is potentially. This tendency might be phrased as the desire to become more and more what one *is*, to become everything that one is capable of becoming" (Maslow, 1987). Whether these are innately driven tendencies or spontaneous realizations of desire, neither matters to a Quasi-Chaotic Lifestyle. The difference is that the Quasi-Chaotic View opposes the pursuit of what may seem to be an innate predisposition toward a particular field, considering it to be inauthentic if one capitulates to expectations by, for example, reluctantly pursuing a career as a basketball player if seven feet tall.

Given the criticisms raised of essentialism and the exaggerated significance Pronats attribute to innate "natural abilities" influencing talent development, we are left with what Winston is using as humanistic psychology's counterpart: *existential* psychology—a perspective in line with conclusions drawn from the preceding chapter. What we are after, then, is what we will refer to as *Existential Self-Actualization* that operates under the following themes:

▲ The subject of inquiry is human existence and not the human self, given the illusion of self.

▲ The ontological position is that existence precedes essence.

▲ The temporal orientation is of a future that gives meaning to the present, leaning toward prudential value, informed decision-making, and peak-end memories.

▲ Therapeutic goals are the acceptance and awareness of the human condition—the absurdity of life and *Sein-zum-Tode* (being-toward-death).

▲ The growth motivator is anxiety, which Heidegger contends is the awareness of nothingness and one's finitude driving anxiety (Heidegger, 2008). In other words, what shifts the "forces against change" toward the "forces for change" is the accumulation of angst as one remains conscious of control at an Unreachable Terminal.

▲ Optimal functioning is a state of being anchored in what Heidegger referred to as Eigentlichkeit (authenticity). Moving away from estrangement, extrinsic motives, and pursing individualistically driven values and toward engagement. In other words, rejecting a state of "becoming," as its pursuit is nothing more than a red herring.

▲ The good life is a one that is fully engrossed in the search for meaning, the search itself being meaningful.

The underlying psychological and philosophical themes I will associate with the term "self-actualization" will be in reference to themes of existential psychology; rejecting essentialist views and pertaining to self-set aspirations irrespective of what is purportedly innate. To differentiate between the two, references to "Existential Self-Actualization" will henceforth be indicated by capitalization: "Self-Actualization."

Let's now look to *individually driven* nature fulfillment theories for an answer, where "objective list" items are determined by the extent to which they match peoples' emotional needs and contribute to their individually determined happiness (well-being). Haybron's "emotional state view" theory and Sumner's "theory of life satisfaction" both tend to the different definitions of happiness (in the well-being and state-of-mind sense) and to different capacities, but both fall in line with the individually driven nature fulfillment theory outlook. And here is where our metal detector for Self-Actualizing gold goes off. We are getting closer!

For reasons articulated in Chapter 8: A Cursed Grail, whereby arguments against each of the most credible theories of well-being and happiness were highlighted—along with realizations drawn from the identification and exploration of salient emergent issues of the twenty-first century's everchanging landscapes—further objective elements could, if linked to what the IT industry has afforded us with (e.g., an understanding of how the complex adaptive system we are bound to operates), represent the most efficacious prospect for proposing a modern Self-Actualizing theory of well-being.

To do so (while also constructing the Quasi-Chaotic View), we will incorporate the following:

▲ the truths we have deduced from examining the Traditional Psyche and the truths revealed upon their close examination

▲ the twelve Agile Principles adapted to individualistic endeavors

▲ Haybron's emotional state view

▲ Sumner's theory of life satisfaction

▲ affirmations of Nussbaum's capability approach

▲ Maslow's hierarchy of needs

TO SUBSCRIBE TO A QUASI-CHAOTIC VIEW . . .

First and foremost, we must redefine Self-Actualization, remaining mindful of its underlying existential themes: *the cyclical process of re-creating, testing, and flourishing off an identity toward transient self-desired potentialities while engaging one's fullest capacity—all governed by psychic affirmation.* In other words, through the diversification and proliferation of experience, one autonomously pursues and continually pivots off of perceived potentialities that provide a sense of endorsement, engagement, attunement, as well as the fulfilling opportunities of growth the fruits of their labor offer—knowing all too well they and the self are transitory.

Submitting to this new definition in the absence of an "ending," the dearth of a destination, and the reality of an everchanging world with an everchanging self requires constant change, both inwardly and outwardly. To be Self-Actualized in this regard is to be a hoarder of meaningful experiences and a minimalist in what one authentically immerses oneself in. And while the analogy of climbing Mount Everest to illustrate the climb for Self-Actualization is true to Maslow's interpretation of the process, definitions, and underlying themes, it does not correctly reflect what Self-Actualization entails. And so, we return to whence we began.

We both step and do not step in the same rivers; we are and are not.

—Heraclitus of Ephesus, *Fragment 12*

Heraclitus of Ephesus (540 BC) was one of the most enigmatic pre-Socratics; his paradoxical aphorisms were some of the most difficult to understand, earning him labels like the Riddler and the Dark (Diogenes and Robert Drew Hicks, 1979). Heraclitus, a polymath, was seen as a "material monist or a process philosopher; a scientific cosmologist, a metaphysician and a religious thinker; an empiricist, a rationalist, a mystic; a conventional thinker and a revolutionary; a developer of logic—one who denied the law of non-contradiction; the first genuine philosopher and an anti-intellectual obscurantist" (Graham, 2008). He considered himself as self-taught, relinquishing his hereditary title of "king" to his younger brother (Heraclitus et al., 1979) in order to search for truth and wisdom.

Heraclitus observed that the moment we step into a river, the water is displaced with new water; reverberations are caused by other elements such as rocks, branches, fish, and wind; the temperature, appearance, taste, and composition are as fluid as the river itself. Moreover, we are everchanging as we step into the river. Wettened by the river, shedding skin cells, we have aged ever so slightly, the sensations on the soles of our feet changing as well while pressed against the bottom of the dynamic streambed. The river is in constant flux, and so too are we as we both step and do not step in the same rivers; we are and are not. Said Heraclitus, "Nothing endures but change"—given that everything is in flux, the only thing that doesn't change is change itself.

Ergo

There is no peak to climb toward,
For the peaks are ever-changing.

There is no essence to discover,
For your self is temporally locked—
Constantly acclimating.

Every step you take in the river of life—
Influences and restricts the next step to take.

Hindsight seems obvious,
Foresight seems probable,
Counsel seems questionable,
But none can offer you certainty of stride,
Commitment or fate.

Take a leap and risk a fall,
Stand idle and watch the river pass you by.

In Lieu

Find your footing, test the next, the next . . .
And the next.
Shift your weight, test the next, the next . . .
And the next.
Only the next step dictates the next,
The rest we leverage the experience of,
And of others we defy.

Tread informedly, awake, and conscious,
With tools of improvision and adaptation at hand.
Follow the river of flux and experience
In the one direction of time—
Making the most out of what you are permitted
As far as change will take you,
As far as you can.

The purpose of life is change. Change is synonymous with the proliferation of experience. With experience we approach certainty. In contiguity of certainty, we discover reason—the reason that justifies the purpose and the reason to strive for an ideal respective of individualistic potentialities. The search for transitory meaning is itself meaningful—congruent with the meaninglessness of reality, revolting against the absurd.

> **Experience is, for me, the highest authority. The touchstone of validity is my own experience. No other person's ideas, and none of my ideas, are as authoritative as my experience. It is to experience that I must return again and again, to discover a closer approximation to truth as it is in the process of becoming in me.**
>
> —Carl Rogers, *On Becoming a Person*

A Quasi-Chaotic Lifestyle would have you excel in different fields until interest in all the ways you can gratifyingly put them to practice fades *or* if the value/benefits of those efforts no longer outweigh the value potential in another field. Regular change and regular exposure to challenge, epiphany, and serendipity will skew the influences on your developmental process in your favor. And if you choose to commit to a given practice with the intent of reaching the cusp of its competitive edge, change will again expedite your course: change of training, change of education, change of mindset, change of what and whom we surround ourselves with.

BUT WAIT, THERE'S MORE

To further the significance of change, we will perform a literary technique referred to as *analepsis*: a flashback that takes the narrative back in time from where it is now. More specifically, let's return to the following question raised in Chapter 5: The Malleable Psyche: *Given that personality change is taxing and time consuming, which one trait would you focus on to expedite what it means to live to your fullest potential?*

The fact is, there has been little empirical evidence suggesting a direct correlation between particular personality traits and the characteristics Maslow attributes to self-actualized individuals. This is mainly because it is difficult to measure self-actualization to begin with—it is highly subjective. The few studies that have been conducted either have sample sizes too small to validate definitively or use unreliable instruments to conduct their experiments. However, one attempt to conceive better psychometrics to measure self-actualization stands out.

In the study, educational psychologist Guy R. Lefrançois et al. (1997) used a method they coined MAP (Measure of Actualization of Potential) to synthesize traits associated with successful and functioning individuals based on a literature review, an international panel of twenty-eight experts, and two focus groups. Their findings boiled self-actualization down to two major components: "openness to experience" (open to new and creative ideas of self-governance) and "self-reference" (awareness of what is taking place in one's personal experience—in other words, reflection). What a convenient coincidence! Do openness to experience and reflection sound familiar? These two traits define Agile practitioners *and* are the necessary ingredients for Manufacturing Success—each of which are at the crux of unlocking our full potential. What's more, these very same traits enable the constructive malleability of the self as illustrated in the following analogy.

Consider forging: how a blacksmith transforms metal into a desired shape. Hammering on cold metal will get them nowhere; only when the metal is sufficiently heated does it grow malleable enough that with every hammer strike, it mutates iteratively in the direction the blacksmith desires. Too much heat and shear lines begin to appear, making the metal more prone to cracks; too little heat and the blacksmith will be hammering all day to exhaustion. Similarly, exposing oneself to challenge to promote a desired mutation is the metaphorical heat. Too much challenge and one is prone to break; too little and commitment and progress will wane. How we *practically* forge our way toward "openness to experience" is detailed in Part VII: Execution.

You may have also noticed that openness (the first of the Big Five personality traits) coincides with the two traits associated with successful and functioning individuals. Bingo! Openness is the trait we will aim to bolster. Use this measure to gauge how far into the deep end you can dive while adopting a Quasi-Chaotic Lifestyle. The higher you score, the more likely you'll be comfortable taking on bigger instances of change. Think of attending a big event you've never been to alone as opposed to trying on a differently colored shirt!

If you recall, personality trait extremities can be disadvantageous. When it comes to "high" openness, for example, psychologists associate the following "problems" with it: issues with social or professional functioning due to excessive fantasizing, peculiar thinking, diffuse identity, unstable goals, and nonconformity with the demands of society (Piedmont et al., 2012). What say you to that? The Quasi-Chaotic Lifestyle does not require extreme openness nor does it advocate it. However, a moderately high level of openness will help you sustain an efficacious life of change while enabling sufficient conformity to societal norms to maximize realizable opportunities. The bonus? Openness is also used as leverage to expedite conditioning of personality trait extremities hindering Self-Actualizing initiatives.

If you've been recoiling from the thought of straying off the beaten path, you now have every reason to exercise your cognition and start hammering your traits into Self-Actualizing shape!

A PYRAMID REINTERPRETED

Maslow's pyramid presents objective needs that are sufficiently generalized to include what most people desire—as opposed to more restrictive lists of conditions for happiness and well-being such as those proposed by moral philosopher Derek A. Parfit's (involving childbearing, 1984) or Catholic philosopher Mark C. Murphy's (involving religion, 2001) indiscriminate of varying iron triangle capacities. While Maslow may not have explicitly described his underlying rationale for pursuing self-actualization, one can interpret these objective needs through a *rational egoistic* lens. In other words, *why* we pursue particular physiological needs, for example, is dictated by whether that pursuit (such as for a big house) will maximize our own *individual* well-being. Such an outlook contrasts with a utilitarian one which aims to maximize the well-being of everyone involved. So, overspending on an unnecessarily big house or material possessions, overeating, or ignoring one's physical and emotional health actually undermines our individual well-being as it curbs one's freedom of and the capacity to exercise change.

Arguments against rational egoism raise issues of temporal selves (for example, how can you evaluate the value of a commitment for a future self) as well as ambiguity surrounding human rationality itself. Addressing the first, we acknowledge the illusion of self that we have already taken into consideration, resorting to a Piagetian perspective that to act in one's own self-interest, one must take into consideration one's present self and future selves as well as the present and future selves of others (if one is to flourish, that is). We will address the second argument regarding rationality in Part VI: Decisions when addressing decision-making.

Building on Maslow's foundations, our adaptation of the pyramid now bears a few more nuances:

▲ **Constraints:**

The overall scale of the pyramid (e.g., relating to how ambitious one's physiological or safety pursuits can be) is limited to one's circumstances. The pyramid can grow or shrink depending on changes in the pyramid's constraints.

▲ **Scaffolding of change:**

Scaffolding is, by definition, a temporary structure—so, too, are our respective pyramid of needs. Seeking change involves the reinvestment of resources and time: discontinuation followed by adoption and then dismantling and temporary reconstruction.

▲ **Iron scaffolding:**

Equivalent attention is to be invested in the maintenance of each component and the interdependencies of component associations to sustain the pyramid's structural integrity. This is to prevent bottom-heavy or top-heavy pyramids that neglect the significance of either supporting foundations or higher aspirations. Changes in a person, place, or practice permeate through all other interdependent needs with some impacts more significant than others.

▲ **Scaffolding maintenance:**

The scaffolding itself requires constant upkeep; think of the iron rusting as one's waning and changing identity, wants, and needs. The structural integrity of each layer of the scaffolding must be maintained.

▲ **Vibrance of color:**

Each layer is gauged by *sufficiency of quality* rather than quantity; in other words, more is not necessarily better. Color suggests diversity, depth, and profundity. The process of Self-Actualizing change paints each respective component with a vibrance of color. The pyramid will then grow saturated, then fade, grow saturated again, and fade once more, progressively getting more saturated over time as one discovers *lasting* Self-Actualizing change.

▲ **Pyramid brightness:**

Refers to the state of one's *psychic affirmation* as driven by the life a pyramid represents. A state of being that is driven by interest, exuberance, and engagement will cultivate a flow and/or peak experiences that induce a spike of brightness, causing the pyramid to emanate and glow. A *pulsating* pyramid suggests that all component needs are fulfilled, facilitating regular peak experiences.

Note: To clarify what such a state feels like, the positive psychologist who coined the concept of "flow," Mihaly R. Csikszentmihalyi (1990), explains its nine dimensions as encompassing the following:

1. challenge-skill balance
2. action-awareness merging (automaticity)
3. clear goals (understand what needs to be done)
4. unambiguous feedback (whether internal, such as finger tension when a drumstick falls in place at the right time, or external, such as the nodding of heads in a crowd)
5. concentration on task (focused, not distracted)
6. sense of control (feelings of liberation from the fear of failure)
7. loss of self-consciousness
8. time transformation (for some, time seems to stop or pass quicker than usual)

9. autotelic experience (the end result of the other eight factors, referring to how the experience is so enjoyable and rewarding that one is
motivated to repeat it)

And so to represent temporary Self-Actualization, we are left with a very
bright, highly saturated, and structurally sound pyramid with significant
intertemporal growth—a pyramid whose regular reconstruction is necessary
for maintaining the state. (See figure 4-3.)

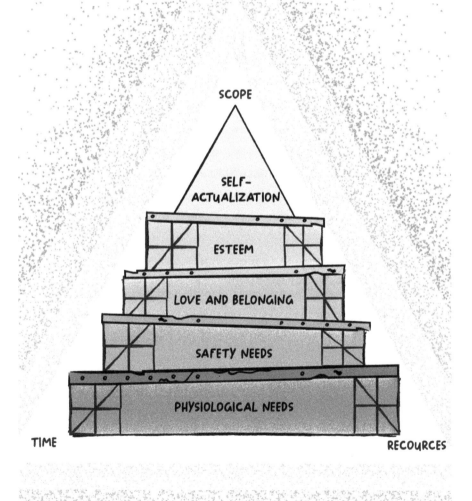

Figure 4-3: Maslow's hierarchy of needs revisited

ADAPTED CHARACTERISTICS OF A SELF-ACTUALIZED INDIVIDUAL

Coupled with Maslow's five objective goods comes a different flavor of objective goods: a list of virtues also referred to as aretaic values (very much like Aristotle's list of moral values and, once again, based on Maslow's characteristics of a self-actualized individual) to guide us toward Self-Actualization.

1. **They have a comfortable acceptance and pride of self—flaws and all.**

    They accept who they are, understanding their developmental shortcomings as natural characteristics derived of influences that were once out of their control, are able to laugh at themselves, lack defensiveness or artificiality, are proud of what they have self-reliantly become.

2. **They constantly indulge in continued freshness and appreciation, even for the most trivial or routine activity.**

    Often in "attunement" (see page 98), they don't take their blessings for granted and have a sense of continual wonder and awe for even the simplest experiences such as a sunset or a flower; they appreciate the miraculous absurdity of life's experiences—the positive and the negative. They relish experiences that for other people are only means to ends.

3. **They are motivated by personal growth and not the satisfaction of needs, prioritizing for early, frequent, and continuous attainment of valuable and diverse experience—their primary measure of progress.**

    They accept the absence of a finish line and therefore don't regard destinations as sources of motivation. Instead, they immerse themselves in "cyclical growth"—prioritizing and amassing experiences of personal value from which to garner transferable knowledge and skills. They understand that further development of talent and merit promotes serendipity, unlocking additional Self-Actualizing opportunities to capitalize on.

    After an act of change, they are sensitive to and mindful of their progression and even more so of regression to avoid ill-informed or unsatisfactory initiatives. They are acutely cautious of costly commitments with delayed prudential value (regardless of how great the reward *could be*) and gauge certainty of their initiatives through further acts of change as means to achieve it. They remain proactive with change, reactive to opportunity, and open to challenge.

They gauge forward movement by tracking their progress respective of where *they* started and not by the measures of others. They evaluate their trajectory based on what they can control, reflect on novel experiences while contemplating and identifying room for improvement, and then act on self-made realizations. They track intrinsic traits such as habits and personality extremes and opportunities to develop more openness to change.

4. **They rely on their own experiences and judgment, independent of cultural norms and social constructs, to form opinions, views, and individualistic motives.**

They neither accept all, like sheep, nor reject all, like the average rebel. They have their own code of ethics. They accrue experiences, questioning and reflecting on what they believe to be true, wary of the dishonest, the ignorant, and the malevolent.

They don't overplan or make decisions based on assumption, influence, or extrinsic pressures. They achieve authentic judgment through experience, favoring action, introspection, and change over planning, extrinsic validation, and commitment. They are attentive to what's working, what isn't, and why, relying on personal meta to deliberate—and ultimately exploit—paths forward, remaining open to new and creative ideas for self-governance.

5. **They are spontaneous in their internal thoughts and outward behavior, endlessly curious, embracing the unknown and the ambiguous.**

They can conform to rules and social expectations but tend to be open and unconventional, not confined by traditional norms. They don't feel threatened by the unknown or ambiguous; they simply accept it, are comfortable with it, and are even attracted to it, understanding that it's precisely where opportunity lies.

They anticipate changes in or better alternatives to particular needs, values, priorities, aspirations, and preferences from what they have yet to experience. They do not fear a pivot toward the unknown even if they are nearing a goal of their past self which has exhausted its value in practice for their present self.

6. **They are self-sufficient by remaining autonomous, resourceful, independent, and free from reliance on external authorities or other people and by pursuing sustainable scope.**

They are comfortable with solitude and don't feel the need to conform to other people's ideas of contentment or happiness; however, they may strategically leverage any knowledge and opportunities available to them. They surround themselves with motivated people who can be trusted—a team to encourage, motivate, assist, protect, teach, guide, and challenge though without being reliant on anyone in particular.

They maintain an "uncompressed" (depressurized) working environment of practices to keep a consistent pace of change and progression. They pursue only what is both feasible and in their self-interest, mindful of what their iron triangle permits to ensure independence and autonomy.

7. **They are able to judge situations correctly and honestly, sensitive to the superficial and conducting themselves to what a situation requires in order attain value.**

Their sense of realism allows them to view life both logically and rationally rather than being fearful of nonacceptance. They approach conflict earnestly and prefer face-to-face conversation to allow for complete expression of ideas and avoid misunderstandings while forming sensible and well-informed conclusions to act on.

What Aristotle referred to as phronesis (*practical* wisdom) is the ability of an individual to judge what is the right amount of virtue in any particular situation. They understand what means to certain "good" ends entail and whether they are worth pursuing, and they have better measures to weigh the potential worth of particular ends.

8. **They are affable, well-presented, and captivating to benefit themselves first, but their benefit depends on the benefit of others.**

Despite possessing *Gemeinschaftsgefühl* (social interest, community feeling, a sense of oneness with all humanity), they act in their own interest that is also dependent on the benefits to others. This includes one's future selves *and* the future selves of others, as the totality of influence on the decision one makes always returns to one's present self-benefit; facilitating valuable opportunities to capitalize on.

They exhibit an attractive aura of authentic confidence, amiability, and mystery, are mindful and adaptive with what and how they communicate, and behave not only to create enjoyable experiences for themselves but also for others.

9. **Striving for simplicity—the art of maximizing engagement with one's authentic state of being—is essential.**

Recall Antoine de Saint- Exupéry's quote: "A designer knows he has achieved perfection not when there is nothing left to add, but when there is nothing left to take away." They identify and repudiate anything or anyone that doesn't add value or stands between them and Self-Actualization.

They understand the limitations to one's capacity for experiencing the fullest of each moment, and therefore don't overencumber themselves with more than what their iron triangle permits.

10. **They prioritize change, are Change Adapted, and naturally and regularly transform their identities.**

Given that change is the focal point of their efforts, they have grown accustomed, over time, to its practice as well as its inward and outward impact. They find comfort, solace, and affirmation with change and are repelled by stagnation, inactivity, and complacency—the essence of being Change Adapted.

Consequently and purposefully, their identities—being memories, experiences, relationships, and values—naturally and regularly transform. While there is always a central backbone of people, places, and practices they associate themselves with to remain embedded productively in a structured world, they consistently test, prod, experiment, challenge, validate, invalidate, and change the constituents of their identity through further change.

And with all that said—and to put it plainly—the Quasi-Chaotic View associates well-being with one's evaluation of their progress toward Self-Actualization and happiness with one's emotional condition as they head toward Self-Actualization.

A THEORY OF WELL-BEING AND HAPPINESS, NOT *THE* THEORY OF WELL-BEING AND HAPPINESS

It is worth emphasizing the need for compassion and humility when it comes to any objective list of goods, whether they are concerned with a hybrid theory or not. There is no one Tolkienian theory to rule them all, nor should we ever expect there be one, for such an attitude or prospection is to make a mockery of all that has been said.

Embrace "the different," including people whose lives are governed by differing theories of well-being and happiness that seem incompatible with how the world runs. To do otherwise is to be an elitist, ignorant to the nature of diversity and its creative, innovative, and human emanations.

The people you most respect, enjoy, or are in awe of are themselves precisely that way because they approach life differently. If we all were to conform to the same desires, preferences, and modes of operation, we may as well live in an Orwellian society, coerced, indoctrinated, brainwashed, and peer-pressured to become colorless blobs without flavor, scent, or the idiosyncrasies that make the world as mysteriously serendipitous as it is. We wouldn't have as much depth of nuance in architecture, theater, dance, sculpture, painting, poetry, or music if there weren't different slants on life and beliefs that took each artist down their rabbit hole of devotion, drama, and imaginativeness. If not for unique value systems, we wouldn't have those pursuing honest and humble lives, settling for life's simplest fruits of experience such as baking the bread, painting the ceiling, maintaining an orchard, caring for cattle, or ensuring that a household's plumbing is in order—or those pursuing daring, audacious lives, testing the boundaries of human limits, summitting peaks, freefalling from space, surrendering their life to charity, or earning medals of honor. We wouldn't have centuries and millennia of generations compromising their liberty to honor culture, tradition, and lasting ideologies. No, if not for fundamental dissimilarities, we wouldn't have much of what makes the world so special. And while much of this diversity is what the Quasi-Chaotic View advocates and facilitates, it is still the product of prolonged uninformedness, authentic compromise, or Suffering.

The Quasi-Chaotic View is one of many theories, most of which the masses default to, none of which can assure objective truths, and only some of which propose objective goods. That is to say, there is no one "correct" mode of life. We are to remain conscious of all "truths" such lists project and accept the nihility of *objective* objective goods. The sciences suggest there is no such thing as objective morality, objective truth, or objective reality. Neither I nor anyone else can offer such things. To that end, I encourage you to adapt them and the Quasi-Chaotic View as you see fit.

However, different theories are better accustomed to different state of affairs. More specifically, *Necessitating Change* proposes that the Quasi-Chaotic View is especially well-suited for a globalized, interconnected, and everchanging twenty-first century world; and it is very much finely tuned to bolster a Quasi-Chaotic Lifestyle and what it has to offer.

IF THE QUASI-CHAOTIC VIEW DOES NOT RESONATE WITH YOU . . .

. . . then I suggest you read on anyway, as there is much to gain that may still be of use to you, however you decide to live your life. The values, attitudes, behaviors, and goods defined within the Quasi-Chaotic View and central to the Quasi-Chaotic Lifestyle are required to be of sustainable use.

To live a life unconstrained by convention, doing precisely as you desire, with certainty and control, fully engaging in actions that your iron triangle permits that are morally good and that promote your ability to live to your fullest potential, is not a matter of chance but method—the method we will now explore.

They see poetry in what I have done.
No.
I apply my methods, and that is all there is to it.

—Georges Seurat, Seurat: Correspondances, Témoignages, Notes Inédites, Critiques (Seurat: Correspondences, Testimonies, Unpublished Notes, Critiques)

THE TOOL KIT

Now equipped with an informed and adapted theory of well-being and happiness, we are better able to home in to the *practice* the Quasi-Chaotic Lifestyle entails. We know what is wrong, why it's wrong, what is possible, why it's possible, and now we know what we are aiming for.

Reclaiming sovereignty and breaking away from the status quo provokes adversity, whether in the form of social judgment, self-doubt, stagnation, roadblocks, or emotional distress. We will thus need tools to keep us on track, protected, resourceful, and efficient—a tool kit we will keep at the ready. Rather than accepting circumstance, let us shape reality as it comes and take control once and for all.

The kit I refer to is not a physical box with screwdrivers and wrenches that I will ship for $19.99. Rather, it consists of cognitive and behavioral tools for cultivating an environment, mindset, and attitude congruent with the Quasi-Chaotic View and capable of nurturing a Quasi-Chaotic Lifestyle—all of which correspond with and promote Gagné's DMGT catalysts for developmental success. *The Quasi-Chaotic Tool Kit* consists of the following: *Curiosity* for when we are uncertain; *Osmosis* for when we are helpless; *Accountability* for when we consider surrender; *Momentum* for when we stagnate; Ambition for when we're complacent; *Failure* for when we face defeat; and *Pride* for when we're demoralized. They are the necessary ingredients of a healthy, Quasi-Chaotic Lifestyle and an arsenal to mitigate and manage emergent issues you will inevitably face activating a Quasi-Chaotic View and remaining consistently and sustainably on course toward Self-Actualization!

PART V
THE TOOL KIT
THE MEANS

CHAPTER 19
CURIOSITY

They say curiosity killed the cat. I say the cat put itself in a precarious position because of poor decision-making and a lack of spatial awareness. An idiom used to keep children out of harm's way; an untruth to keep adults at bay.

Perhaps you've played an endless game of "Why?" with a young child, only to be led down the path to an existential crisis of contemplative dread: "Dad, how are rainbows made?" is followed with "Dad, why does the spectrum of light give off those colors?" to "Dad, why do the receptors in the back of our eyes perceive different colors depending on their wavelengths?" only to end by questioning reality itself and a "Go ask your mother." Children seem to exhibit a level of curiosity that is curious to say the least and is perhaps why children are better problem solvers than we are (Lucas et al., 2014). Their undeveloped prefrontal cortex (where working memory, reasoning, logic, planning, and pursuit of goals—to name a few—are managed) induces un-conventional "parallel thinking" and, consequently, creativity. For example, an adult will see a golf club exactly as it is. In contrast, a child will see a broomstick as a javelin or a sword. This creative interpretation gives them the ability to be cognitively flexible, inventive, and ultimately great problem solvers. The full development of a prefrontal cortex in adulthood (around the age of twenty-five) leads to functional fixedness and a level of certainty that lessens one's inclination toward inquiry and increases reliance on beliefs and expectations—often to our detriment (Thompson et al., 2009). The negative impact of *functional fixedness* on fostering creativity was the focus of a NASA study which found that 98% of 1,600 four- and five-year-olds tested at the "creative genius" level, a number that depreciated to 30% five years later and to 12% five years after that. When the same test was administered to adults, it was found that only 2% scored at this genius level (Ainsworth-Land and Jarman, 1993).

This finding is beautifully demonstrated by the Marshmallow Challenge designed by Peter Skillman, a product-design veteran. It involves the task of constructing the highest possible freestanding structure with a marshmallow on top. The structure must be completed within eighteen minutes using twenty sticks of spaghetti, one yard of tape, and one yard of string. Kindergarten graduates performed consistently better and built taller and more interesting structures than the average team of adults and, specifically, groups of business school graduates. Skillman explains it's because of the tendency for children to immediately stick the marshmallow on top of a simple structure, test the prototype, and continue to improve upon it. (Sound familiar?) The fact of the matter is, nowhere in the rules of the challenge are the participants told how to approach the puzzle, but children were quick to default to a focus on the objective and then *incrementalize* toward it. (See figure 5-1.) Business school students, on the other hand, tended to spend time planning for the tallest possible structure, vying for power, and finally producing a structure to which the marshmallow is added—assuming this is how the experiment organizers *expected* them to operate.

NOT OPTIMAL BUT WORKS!

Figure 5-1: Marshmallow Challenge

Humans seem to have a habit—a need, even—to exploit, to get ahead by any means necessary to maximize immediate reward and avoid costs, hyperfocused on a goal and blind to peripheral value. Research finds that adults fall into a "learning trap" where too much weight is placed on an initial generalization from a given stimuli (Fazio et al., 2004; Rich and Gureckis, 2018). For example, if an adult infers from one negative experience that, say, eating a banana pizza is a bad idea, they may generalize and relate the experience to all fruit pizzas—failing to explore other related stimuli such as pineapple pizza (which is *also* a bad idea, but you know what I mean). Similarly, you may know someone who has forever excluded a genre of music, a cuisine, a culture, a people, or a country because of one bad experience, ignorant to experiences that could have been their best. In four elaborate studies, cognitive and developmental psychologists (respectively) Emily G. Laquon and Alison Gopnik (2022) confirmed that adults underexplore following negative outcomes while children "are motivated to explore despite all costs," allowing them to reach accurate final conclusions to experimental challenges (compared to adults) by testing stimuli even if it was relatively costly.

Pair a developing nervous system with a curious, creative, and explorative mind unbound by narrow-sighted assumptions, expectations, and *knowledge*, and you end up with enhanced erudition. This is the "critical period" we have previously discussed (see page 44) which produces an infant's spongelike studiousness until adulthood when the plasticity of their neural pathways tightens and the questions begin to fade.

And why is that? Why do we cavalierly stop asking questions? Why do we capitulate to whom we believe we've become and how we perceive the world to be? Why do we cement our ideologies, mannerisms, judgment, and sentiments with obstinance? Is it a result of social norms, the Traditional Psyche, a lacking milieu, Incessant Distraction, or perhaps all the above? How did we become so sure of ourselves, what we want and what we need? Perhaps it's the need for confidence and certainty to perform in a professional work environment. But is this a valid argument? It's true that we change—everyone changes—which is the premise of *Necessitating Change*. But what needs to change is what *prompts* change, our *attitude* toward change, and *how often* we change.

Psychologist and well-being researcher Todd Kashdan, who studied curiosity for over twenty years, developed alongside colleagues a comprehensive model to understand and measure curiosity (Kashdan et al., 2020). They suggest there are five dimensions of curiosity:

▲ Joyous exploration:

The recognition and desire to seek out new knowledge and the subsequent joy of learning and growing.

▲ Deprivation sensitivity:

A dimension with an underlying emotional tone of anxiety and tension more prominent than joy—pondering abstract or complex ideas, trying to solve problems, or seeking to reduce gaps in knowledge.

▲ Stress tolerance:

The willingness to embrace doubt, confusion, anxiety, and other forms of distress that arise from exploring new, unexpected, complex, mysterious, or obscure events.

▲ Social curiosity:

Wanting to know what other people are thinking and doing by observing, talking, or listening in to their conversations.

▲ Thrill seeking:

The willingness to take physical, social, and financial risks to acquire varied, complex, and intense experiences.

All of these ingredients are tied to the very definition of what it is to be Self-Actualized. Curiosity is to a Quasi-Chaotic Lifestyle what phototropism is to a plant; it leads a plant toward sunlight, while curiosity leads us toward our new source of energy: change.

Here are three ways Curiosity is used to sustain a Quasi-Chaotic Lifestyle:

1. FALLIBILITY CURIOSITY:

"The greatest obstacle to discovery is not ignorance—it is the illusion of knowledge," said historian Daniel J. Boorstin. The cornerstone to the Quasi-Chaotic Lifestyle is that of Fallibility Curiosity. Everything and anything you know, think, feel, and believe along with (equivalently) anything and everything you don't know, don't think, don't feel, and don't believe is *information*. How we process and interpret this information shapes the world into how we each perceive it to be.

What you know is what you think you know because you believe it to be true. You believe it is true through knowledge acquired at some point in time through observation, education, or instinct. These sources of information are *mostly correct* if you are to use this information in the system they were conceived. To say the piece of land you are standing on is flat because you were taught that a flat surface has a horizontal surface with no depth is true to an extent, as far as the eye can see, but is untrue from a different frame of reference. And so on. Such is the cognition of "pessimistic epistemological fallibilists," in which they believe with certainty that absolute knowledge is impossible. Always, there remains possible doubt as to the truth of a belief, a consequence of our limited human cognitive capacities.

Believe none of what you hear and only half of what you see.

—Edgar Allan Poe, "The System of Dr. Tarr and Prof. Fetcher"

Karl Popper, one of the greatest philosophers of science of the twentieth century, was particularly interested in the different methods scientists were using to make their predictions. He examined the work of Sigmund Freud, the father of psychoanalysis, who was concerned with the individual psyche and predicted that our childhood experiences are deeply corelated with who we grew up to be. Popper noticed how Freud was able to extrapolate whatever suited his theory from seemingly any evidence, whether it was rationalizing dreams with repressed memories of childhood (usually of a sexual context) or how getting hugged too little or too much as a child influenced intimacy as an adult. Karl and other critics referred to Freud's work as "pseudoscience," seeing that Freud could always read the past differently to validate his theory, making it unfalsifiable. Whether there is truth behind psychoanalysis is not the matter in question but *how* we arrive at such a truth. Contrastingly, Popper also observed the work of Albert Einstein and how instead of looking backward and using past data to predict the present, he was looking ahead and predicting future states of affairs. This is how Einstein proved general relativity—by predicting where the stars would be during an eclipse. In so doing, he put his theory at risk of being disproven.

Popper, an ambassador of the scientific method, maintains that the only genuine test of a theory is one that attempts to falsify it; in other words, scientific theory must be *prohibitive*. Where pseudoscience attempts to confirm a theory, science attempts to disconfirm it—suggesting that any genuine theory must be testable, refutable, and falsifiable, all of which are contingent on the data that gives rise to it (while it's method of procurement must itself be replicable, testable, refutable, and falsifiable). (See figure 5-2.)

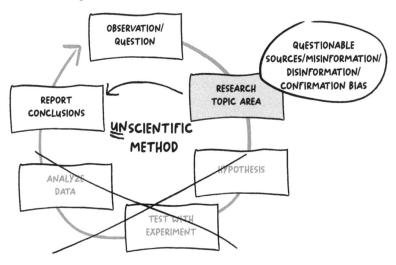

Figure 5-2: Unscientific method

Unfortunately, this reliable, equitable, and constructive method to arrive at *objective truth* has been increasingly neglected in the twenty-first century as misinformation proliferates, wreaking havoc on economies, healthcare systems, and families worldwide. The chasm between what is known to be true and what is claimed to be true has widened because of polarized views, exaggerated and misleading headlines, hyperpartisanship, and tribal, social, and ideological stigmatization and dogmatism—all of which have given rise to "cancel culture," moral relativism, backward (regressive) cults, and so on. Political figures and corporate cowards skew their narratives toward the loudest unhinged minorities, the greatest financial gain, and the most convenient political agendas. In the search for objective truth, one finds it exceptionally difficult to arrive at a point of certainty. To make matters worse, what we often rely on—the scientific method—itself has limitations, contingent on the data being evaluated and validated. Issues arise from data quality, data literacy, data sovereignty, data provenance, statistical power, sample sizes, scientific bias, and suboptimal publishing incentives (to name a few), which only scratch the surface of the hairy problem that is misinformation.

Of course, I am not advocating for anarchy or suggesting we shun institutional instruction or academic and scientific insight and progress. Nor am I questioning the melting point of steel beams or the species of our leaders. What I *am* advocating, however, is that we occasionally subject our cognitions to the following question: "What if I'm wrong?"

What if you were wrong about your definition of a good life and your impression of anyone else who chooses to live differently; about a rival's intentions; who's at fault; a political position you avidly support; what you thought your friend meant when he said that thing in that weird way; what you think is best for you, your children, your family, and society; how you're justifying your prejudice toward a person or people; a belief driven by a fear rhetoric without any compelling evidence; what you think someone's first impression of you is; the spiritual path you are devoting your life to; controversial medical advice from someone without any qualifications who spends too much time on Facebook; the hill you're willing to die on because you read a few articles contradicting a body of work that professionals spent a lifetime amassing and peer-reviewing; believing you're smarter, know more, or are more capable than you actually are, falling victim to the Dunning-Kruger effect (a cognitive bias in low-ability people who don't possess the skills or self-awareness to recognize their own incompetence); giving your spouse yet another chance to keep their promise. What if you were wrong all along? Think of all the people you may have wrongfully hurt, alienated, or dismissed. Think of all the re- markable experiences you may have wrongfully overlooked, ignored, or missed. Think of all the pain, hardship, and tension you may have unnec- essarily experienced and unjustly imparted—everything that could have been avoided. Think of all the time you may have wasted. *Think about it.*

And rest assured, there is still time for change.

Theodore Millon, a highly regarded personality psychologist with awards named after him, put personality on a continuum, suggesting that the personality disorders in *DSM-5 (Diagnostic and Statistical Manual of Mental Disorders,* which he had helped develop earlier versions of) are just extreme accents within said continuum. In other words, we are all a little bipolar, a little paranoid, a little schizophrenic, sadistic, antisocial, narcissistic, and everything in between. Millon's (2004) dimensional theory establishes fourteen personality disorders, each of which every person has with their own differing intensities. How often do we brush off emotional patterns we endure? How much attention do we pay these emergent feelings we carelessly neglect? Do you know the extent to which your clinical personality patterns and syndromic intensities affect your livelihood? How many of these accents have you recognized and estab- lished the means to subdue and manage? What if you were wrong about *why* certain events transpired the way they did?

One must, at the very least, entertain "the contrary," as there is much more to lose than face: experience; opportunity; and Self-Actualizing, serendipitous realizations. Popper realized that every false belief we discover brings us closer to knowing what is true. It is through Fallibility Curiosity and regularly iterating and testing our beliefs—and then attempting to falsify them through further iteration—that we can arrive at some proximation of objective truth: more specifically, what works best for us and what it means to live to our own individualistic life to its fullest potential.

2. SERENDIPITOUS CURIOSITY:

In a nutshell, Serendipitous Curiosity would have you proactively pursuing a seemingly arbitrary motive and seeing where it takes you! It would have you ask how someone's day has been *and then listen*. It would have you pick up a conversation in an airport lounge and *reciprocate*. It would have you introduce yourself to your neighbors and *learn* how they keep their lawn crisp and trimmed. It would have you travel and *experience* other cultures (especially those your family detests!). It would have you *spontaneously act* on novel experiences for no reason other than the fact that they are novel—taking you down the rabbit hole that is life and its wonderous serendipitous surprises. If you've ever wondered, "He looks quite jolly; I wonder what's on his mind!", introduce yourself! Openly admit why you are asking the question, initiate a friendly conversation, and see where it takes you. Follow your thoughts and your curiosity and act on them in any way possible. Set yourself up for what's to come. "You will *not* believe what I did today!" The more random the act, the more you'll know you are exercising Serendipitous Curiosity to its fullest extent.

3. DEVELOPMENTAL CURIOSITY:

Looking to better understand the role of curiosity in learning and memory, psychologists and cognitive neuroscientists Matthias J. Gruber and Charan Ranganath (2019) explored its effects on learning and retention in academia. Drawing on a range of ideas from psychology, cognitive neuroscience, and systems neuroscience, they concluded that one who is curious about a particular subject enhances memory encoding through increased attention, exploration, and information-seeking and the consolidation of information. This explains the difficulties many students face when they commit to and/or are confronted with subject matters that don't intrigue them—that don't immerse them in a curious state. Whether it's the teacher's fault or the fault of the student is beside the point. What matters is that our best chance to strive, learn, and grow (the individual's meta) is to pursue matters that engage *our* curiosity.

You will know when you have found a matter that spikes your child-like curiosity. You will find yourself hungry for answers and starved of an understanding. Unfortunately, how we act on that curiosity is often emotionally driven, skewing our motivation to pursue rational, constructive truths. Developmental Curiosity is the means by which we counteract such resistance.

An incredibly effective approach for understanding why enigmatic problems continuously arise is the iterative interrogative technique called the Five Whys. Developed by Sakichi Toyoda, founder of Toyota Industries Corporation, it is a process that identifies the underlying root causes of a problem. For example:

Problem:

My partner and I aren't talking because we argued about who we'd invite to the wedding.

1. Why? Because she wanted to invite someone she used to date in high school and I'm not okay with that.

2. Why? Because it's not something I would do.

3. Why? Because bringing someone you used to have feelings for hurts.

4. Why? Because it makes me feel insecure. I am insecure around people she used to have feelings for.

5. Why? Because I can't help comparing myself to them and feel inferior.

You could spend an entire afternoon arguing with your soon-to-be-bride or spend your time constructively drilling down to the core of the issue itself. Why justify your resentment with a blanket statement claiming, "That's just not something you do!"—a close-ended defense leaving no room for a half-met solution? While a functioning relationship is (ought to be) a matter of interest-justifying reconciliatory responses, we often resort to an emotional reaction. If you recall, this is primarily a consequence of an untrained amygdala reacting to what it perceives as a threat—a reaction that over time turns into habit. Instead, we ought to collect ourselves, note our interest, and present the matter to Developmental Curiosity.

In his book, *Atomic Habits,* James Clear suggests that habits are the compound interest of self-improvement in which automatic, subconscious behaviors play out like a cognitive script. Behavioral economist Jason Hreha defines a habit as a solution to a recurring problem. The Five Whys technique allows us to distill and bring to light the causations of underlying problems that give rise to negative feedback loops. Whether it's a problem, a solution, or simply a line of inquiry we take interest in, the Five Whys is worth employing to help subside emotional responses, attain constructive and reflective understanding, and further inform the velocity of our Self-Actualizing trajectory.

We will revisit the Five Whys in Part VII: Execution when we adapt it to suit Quasi-Chaotic initiatives. While its ultimate utility may not yet be clear, guardrail rules of conduct will be detailed that makes its use more than just a simple series of "whys." For now, it is worthwhile to appreciate the power of causality and our ability to reverse-engineer issues we fail to understand.

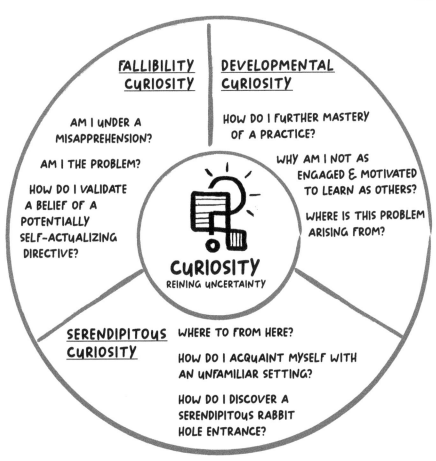

Figure 5-3: Curiosity

How curious are you really? How often do you ask yourself questions you can't answer? Do they keep you up at night? Do you do doggedly pursue explanation? Or do you brush them off and return to Incessant Distraction and confirmation bias in fear of popping the myopic bubble you may have incarcerated yourself in? The curious mind wanders often, guiding us into the unknown, into uncertainty, toward unfamiliar places, people, and practices. Everything you would want for cultivating a lifestyle of change!

CHAPTER 20
OSMOSIS

Do you recall a time you befriended a new circle of people and noticed changes in yourself after a while? You may have started picking up their sense of humor, parroting their vocabulary, mimicking some of their reactions, or adopting some of their day-to-day practices and behaviors. Such an influence harkens back to Gagné's updated DMGT—the Expanded Model of Talent Development (EMTD) that suggests exactly what you would have experienced: environmental catalysts playing an important role in your personality's development. (See figure 5-4.)

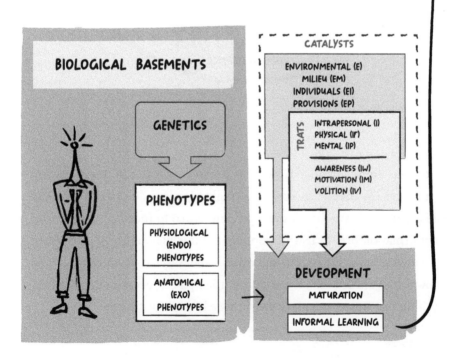

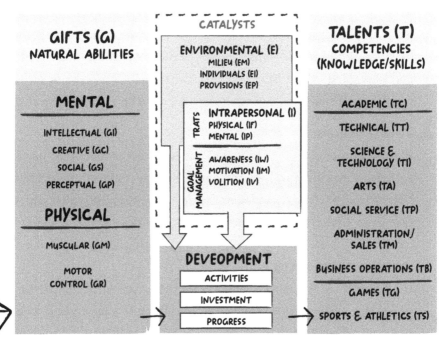

Figure 5-4: EMTD (Expanded Model of Talent Development). Adapted from Gagné (2013)

Given what we have come to know about the "malleable psyche" (see page 62) and how the development of talent and the self are very much under our Quasi-Chaotic control, you might have ascertained what an effective method of altering your traits, habits, and behaviors could look like.

Osmosis is the process of gradual or unconscious assimilation of knowledge. We naturally pick up (and impart) habits, mannerisms, and mindsets from (and to) the people around us, although there is much debate as to why this happens. Some explanations include:

▲ Tribalism:

Human beings needed to invent socially acceptable behavior in order to fit in, be accepted, and increase both their and their tribe's chances of survival. A sign of respect to those with a higher social status would be to imitate—to "mirror"—their mannerisms to increase affiliation and foster relationships (Lakin et al., 2003). For example, people who are given a conscious affiliation goal such as "You will be interacting with this person as part of a cooperative task in which it's important to get along and work well together" or a nonconscious affiliation goal by using suggestive words like "affiliate," "friend," or "together" were found to be much more likely to mimic behaviors than those who did not have such a goal (Lakin and Chartrand, 2003). In other words, when there is a *desire* to affiliate, mimicking the behaviors of others was found to be a natural response.

▲ Peer pressure:

Feeling left out or being the "odd" one does not provide that sense of belonging we all naturally want—arguably the result of our tribalistic tendencies. Whether it's today or the next, it is very likely that you will give in to whatever you've been refusing to take part of, whether it's capitulating to feelings of alienation or mirroring the bravado of a role model—as the following study found.

Across three different academic years and involving 543 first-semester university students aged nineteen to twenty-two, labor and behavioral economists Xiaoyue Shan and Ulf Zölitz (2022) had three separate cohorts of students take personality tests, assigned them to randomized study groups, and, at the end of the semester, conducted another personality test. They found that the students became more similar to their peers along several dimensions across the OCEAN measurement of personality traits. These findings suggest that we pay closer attention to who we surround ourselves with as we may be subconsciously leading ourselves astray by remaining loyal to decisions we made yesterday.

▲ Perception-behavior link:

Subconscious mimicry works like social glue to help pairs bond and, once again, reflects an evolutionary inclination to remain socially cohesive. Social psychologists Tanya L. Chartrand and John A. Bargh (1999) detailed three experiments that roughly mapped out how this "chameleon effect" works. In group activities, they used an actor who would intentionally smile, jiggle their foot, or rub their face. Researchers observed that participants would mimic their behaviors—and specifically the more empathetic ones—as empathy is yet another evolutionary advantage suggesting that much of this happens at a subconscious level.

And given how ingrained this "fixed personality myth" is in societal attitudes, it is worth beating the proverbial dead horse. Changes in personality traits have been documented, from mentoring programs designed to make one more prosocial, more honest, and more competitive (Kosse et al., 2020; Abeler et al., 2021; Boneva et al., 2021) to a socio-emotional skills intervention that reduced one's impulsiveness and disruptiveness (Sorrenti et al., 2020), to virtual coaching apps that can change personality in a desired direction (Stieger et al., 2021), all the way to how reforms in pedagogical structures can have a significant impact on personality—such as the case of a German schooling reform in which reducing years of schooling by a year increased openness and decreased emotional stability (Dahmann and Anger, 2018). So, let's put on, tighten, and wax-seal the lid on this jar of fixed-personality baloney and shift our focus to the very possible and attainable intrinsic changes many of us desire—and need!

Here are three ways Osmosis is used to sustain a Quasi-Chaotic Lifestyle:

1. **SELECTIVE OSMOSIS:**
   Proactively surround yourself with people whose characteristics and knowledge you wish for yourself, whether it's their kindness, hospitality, ambition, financial literacy, fitness, or expertise in a particular industry. Whatever change you seek to enact, surround yourself with those who have fulfilled it themselves or are aspiring to do so. In time, you will realize how much of what they do has been imparted on you! This selective effort also extends to how places affect one's general well-being as well as practices that expose you to desired people and places!

   ▽ **Where you are:** Living in the city versus living in the suburbs affects what we do in both noticeable and subtle ways. The buzz of the city, the constant motion of businessmen and women hurrying to meetings—you will feel a sense of urgency to act. There is so much happening all the time and everywhere that you find yourself constantly distracted with more to do. Whereas if you lived in the countryside, you may feel a lot more relaxed and content with nature's serene presence.

Over time, either setting will inevitably influence the way you speak and interact, what time you wake up, how many people you meet, and so on.

▽ **Who you're with:** Besides the obvious, such as picking up a daily smoking or boozing habit, there are many more subtle changes of mannerisms you inherit unconsciously depending on who you surround yourself with on a day-to-day basis. Go-getters versus couch potatoes—the group you are with plays a significant role with what you do with your free time. Do members of your circle spend much of their time loafing around recording bottle flips and six-second dance clips? Or are they up at sunrise every morning getting ready for a hearty run around a freshwater lake? Over time, you will naturally grow accustomed to any repeated experience, whether you choose to participate or not; your standards and inclinations *will* shift, and, before you know it, you're either adopting unhealthy regimens and cultivating cognitive adjustments to justify them or being buoyed by the energy of positive change. As the late entrepreneur and motivational speaker E. Jim Rohn once said, "You are the average of the five people you spend the most time with."

▽ **What you're doing:** Although this component goes hand in hand with the previous two, it is still worth considering its collateral effects. For example, CrossFit is popular primarily because it's a group effort. Most classes you see consist of ten plus individuals sharing hardship, commitment, and camaraderie as they encourage one another to persevere. Contrast this with the lonely, repetitive, and monotonous nature of soloing a nightly gym routine. Which of the two would offer lasting motivation? And yes, this is a trick question.

In addition to what is osmotically imparted by the people and places that various practices immerse us in are the practices themselves. In Chapter 5: The Malleable Psyche (see page 64), we explored studies demonstrating the efficacy of personality trait interventions in which regular engagement with behaviors associated with a trait increases its expression even without being explicitly psychologically invested. One thus ought to exploit Selective Osmosis by investigating practices that necessitate behaviors aligned with a particular trait for improvement!

2. DIVERGENT OSMOSIS:

Immerse yourself in a diverse group of individuals who may not be actively seeking the specific changes you are looking to achieve but whose various qualities are interesting, appealing, or generally uplifting. Ask about their passion, how they are acting on it and why. We don't know what we don't know, so remaining curious and questioning the unknown may lead to new people, places, and practices we wouldn't have otherwise thought to pursue! Different personalities who work in different industries with different aspirations and affiliations. Sure, your values may not align entirely with theirs, but fixate your attention on what is progressive and enjoyable and grow!

3. REFLECTIVE OSMOSIS:

Have you ever wondered how you'd treat your clone? How you'd perceive your other self to be from an outside perspective? Have you ever thought what you actually looked and sounded like and what it felt to be around someone like you? You may have seen footage of yourself and thought, "Do I really sound like that?" "Do I really make those faces when faced with incompetence?" It can be terribly difficult to assess our own faculties because we only have our own perspective as reference.

Reflective Osmosis suggests you surround yourself with those who share similar characteristics and observe how *others* respond to them. Similarly, it encourages us to throw ourselves in the line of fire and contemplate how we feel on the receiving end, whether we're left with a welcoming and wholesome impression or a cold and estranging one. Reflective Osmosis compels us to act on and grow from what we learn through the lens of those we may already be familiar with.

The truth of the matter is that we are a lot less forgiving of others than ourselves. If we lash out, we're able to justify it with a "bad day" or a difficult upbringing. We may be quick to pardon ourselves for making a scene, or upsetting another, or violating a rule because we know we have good intentions, harboring memories of all of those we've supported, all the favors we've done, all the charity we've dispensed, and so on.

Should you ever find yourself the victim of wrongdoing, injustice, or the pointed end of a someone's bad-day stick, then do yourself a favor and reflect on a time you may have been *that* person and ask yourself how you would have liked to have been approached. You may know not to be confrontational, because that's not how you positively respond to conflict. Maybe you respond better to a constructive conversation revolving around the facts of what transpired and how, or to words of encouragement that imply a willingness to reconcile, or through bartering of what one had to gain or lose, or perhaps to a setting that may inflame or dampen the hostility of a situation—for example, if a conflict is taking place in a crowd, some people are much more cooperative if they aren't shamed publicly but instead critiqued in private.

Conversely, recognize how you felt by any act of compassion or generosity, whether it be someone opening the door for you or presenting you with a homemade banh mi during a rest break at work or a simple, "I'm headed to the grocery. Can I get you anything?" You know how impactful such gestures can be, compelling one to reciprocate and potentially leaving a lasting, powerful impression the recipient feels impelled to bestow on to others.

How we are emotionally impacted by another's actions and what Reflective Osmosis draws from such experiences are Self-Actualizing lessons as raw as they come.

The Greek philosopher and sage Epicurus, born in 341 BC, committed himself to helping people attain a happy, *eudaimonic*, tranquil life characterized by *ataraxia* (peace and freedom from fear) and *aponia* (the absence of pain). He recognized the fruitfulness of friendships and how nonpossessive and decent people acted with their friends, concluding that we did not see our friends enough. So, he ended up buying a big house and living with all his friends! They all stopped working for other people and traded better pay for freedom to do as they wished. They devoted themselves to calming their

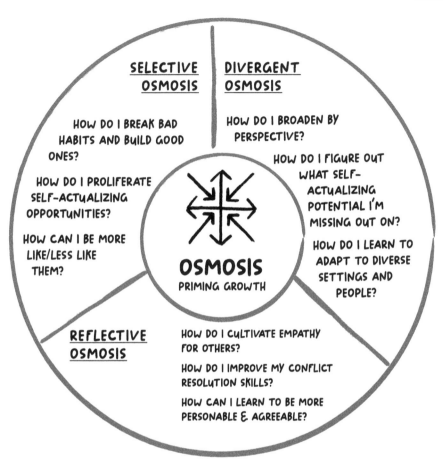

Figure 5-5: Osmosis

own mind, spending time alone, writing, reflecting, and meditating. This idea was so successful that Epicurean communities emerged throughout the Mediterranean with up to four hundred thousand people living in communes from Spain to Palestine.

Who do you surround yourself with and how much of who they are and what they do aligns with what you know is best for you? Do you consider the people and groups you've committed yourself to as good candidates for your very own Epicurean community?

CHAPTER 21
ACCOUNTABILITY

The truth about substantial, intrinsic change is that we don't get to relish the fruit of its accomplishment throughout its pursuit. Whether it's the weight loss our new diet will bring or Beethoven's "Moonlight Sonata" we wish to learn after starting piano lessons or learning to socialize amongst strangers. The benefits of certain changes take time; it's a covertly gradual and oftentimes challenging process marked by temporary disconnection from what the endgame promises. Of course, our Quasi-Chaotic sights are fixated on change throughout the journey and not the destination, but even the most highly regarded and driven intellectuals, connoisseurs, and *successful* face speed bumps, setbacks, dissuasion, and demotivation along the way. They get bored, burned out, and fed up from time to time, but where others gave up, they persevered.

The rush of excitement that comes with novel experience is addictive, but it doesn't take long to realize how much more there is to learn or *how much more* repetition is necessary or *how much more* time we are going to have to spend failing before it starts feeling right. Whether it's the soreness of our muscles after a first workout (that fades after subsequent visits) or the painfully slow process of learning major scales on a piano (that eventuate into muscle memory) or overcoming our resistance to striking up a conversation with a stranger (that eventually starts feeling natural). In psychological terms, I'm referring to the process known as *automaticity*: when the quality of a behavior, mental process, or activity can be carried out rapidly and without effort or explicit intention.

A study conducted by health psychologist Phillippa Lally et al. (2010) found that it takes an average of sixty-six days to form a new habit (with a range of 18–254 days). A behavior that study participants wanted to "automate" was an asymptotic process; in other words, it necessitated significant explicit effort and attention at first, which, after time, plateaued as the habit took hold—further substantiating those first few months of required perseverance. (See figure 5-6.)

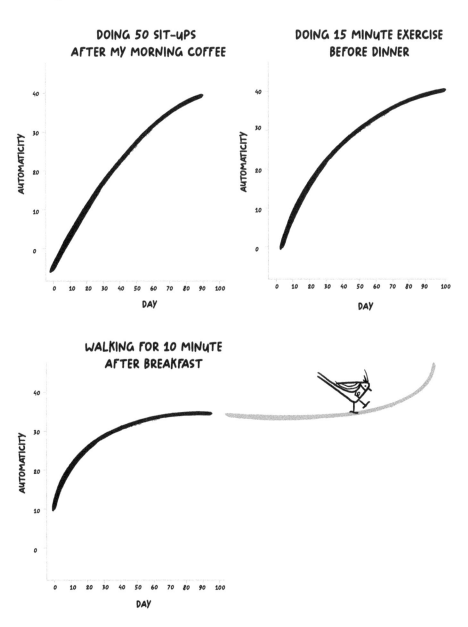

Figure 5-6: Automaticity of habit
Adapted from Lally et al. (2009)

So how does one persevere? How does one remain sufficiently motivated to make it through the first hurdles of struggle and apprehension? By being accountable and willing to accept responsibility for what one has committed to do.

Blame, on the other hand, has an inverse relationship with accountability and deprives us of important lessons that promote Self-Actualization. This doesn't necessarily mean you must take on the weight of the world and avoid providing constructive criticism to those who may be at fault. But centering the focus on ourselves and what we could have done better is substantially more productive and circumvents the callousness that often accompanies blame, whether it be a projected or internalized grievance.

You might, for example, blame your terrible day at work with "I earned it" as justification for breaking your diet. Or you succumb to poor self-esteem and discontinue your piano lessons after watching a child prodigy. Or you blame the unrealistic body images that social media propagates and decide that the pain of working out isn't worth conforming to the status quo. You may even feel inclined to blame your past, your mistakes, your laziness, your parents, the people around you, the environment you're in . . . *anything* to avoid the challenge of substantial, intrinsic change.

A vivid example is subject matter experts in areas they repeatedly fail to walk their talk. Think of certified nutritionists and personal trainers, for example, who in the pursuit of fitness have learned about the ins and outs of every enzyme, cardiovascular component, diet, workout routine, and optimum combination of all the above but fail to realize any results them-selves—always giving up, giving in, or growing complacent. Or relationship pundits who have invested countless hours mastering relationship frame-works, communication models, sexual strategies, or pick-up lines but refuse to put in the fieldwork, take on the challenge, and/or build attractive relational traits and behaviors in themselves. You know who I'm talking about.

When we shift blame, we submit to the forces out of our control and disempower our ability to *make a difference*. Shit happens, there's no doubt about it, whether it's your colleague's incompetence, stubbing your toe on a chair at night, or slipping on a puddle of urine your new kitten left you. If we blame our colleague for not finishing a job our work depends on, then what have we accomplished? Besides demoralizing the team, ruining the work atmosphere, and stressing ourselves out, very little. The job still isn't done, your colleague is still incompetent (and now insecure), and the chances of such a predicament arising again is very likely! Instead, take accountability and set measures to ensure it never happens again. Consult your supervisor to work out mitigation strategies. Provide constructive feedback and support your colleague. As for that chair, what will cursing in the dark and blaming your significant other for asking for a glass of water accomplish? Besides upsetting them, very little. They're still thirsty and your toe is still bruised. Turn on the lights the next time you enter a dimly lit room barefoot, remember to stow away the chairs, and ice your toe immediately! And what does punting your kitten over the fence for peeing on the carpet accomplish? A restraining order, perhaps. If you allow a moment of rage and blame to take over, how does that fix anything? You've riled yourself up, urine is still seeping deeper into the floor, and Mr. Whiskers will probably do it again! Get your kitten tested for urinary tract infection or place another litter box around the house so it never happens again.

Here are three ways Accountability is used to sustain a Quasi-Chaotic Lifestyle:

1. SELF-ACCOUNTABILITY:

Accepting responsibility and becoming accountable seems like unnecessary work and may open you to blame or criticism. But the sooner you take accountability for what's wrong, the sooner you permit yourself to grow, learn, and become a person that people can trust and appreciate—and more importantly, a person that you can trust and appreciate. What is your word worth? When you promise yourself you'll get out of bed at six the next morning, when you tell yourself you'll attend that boxing class five days in a row, when you promise a friend you'll be there at two o'clock to help him with his luggage? If your word is worthless, how do you expect anyone to rely on you, recommend you, refer you, promote you, or commit to you. The same applies to what you tell *yourself*: what you commit to, what you aspire to do. Imagine where we would be if everyone fulfilled whatever they set out to achieve, void of doubt and stocked with certainty.

But are you entirely to blame for your blame-game? Social psychologists Nathanael J. Fast and Larissa Z. Tiedens (2010) demonstrated how blame is very much socially contagious. They observed that an individual making a "blame attribution" increased the likelihood that people would make subsequent blame attributions for their own unrelated failures, ultimately cultivating what they term a *blame culture*. If we have learned anything from Osmosis, it's that what, where, and who we surround ourselves with shapes us into what we become, so it would make sense to identify chronic blamers and be the first to claim responsibility and make a difference, or distance ourselves from them. Below are some examples of what Self-Accountability compels us to do:

▽ Avoid blaming others when it's their fault. Provide constructive criticism (if it would make a difference), but always contemplate what you could have done better.

▽ Avoid making excuses for why things are the way that they are. Figure out what's wrong and *do* something about it.

▽ Avoid blaming others for incompetence. Instead, consider assisting them and improving their skill set. Everyone has to start somewhere.

▽ If your relationship is not going as well as you thought it would, consider how you may be exacerbating the challenges and conflicts you face.

▽ If your message is hurtful to another, examine how and why *your* style of communication may have been unhealthy and unproductive.

▽ In times of conflict, empathize with and understand another's perspective even if you vehemently disagree with their sentiment.

▽ When you make a mistake, ensure it never happens again. And if it does, iteratively change the means by which you are attempting to achieve the objective.

2. GROUP ACCOUNTABILITY:

As self-sufficient as the Self-Actualized are, they are equally as resourceful. Social psychologists Priyanka B. Carr and Gregory M. Walton (2014) concluded that even subtle suggestions to work as a team dramatically increased people's motivation to take on difficult tasks, leading to greater enjoyment, perseverance, and engagement and even higher levels of performance. In the study, participants were asked to solve a puzzle. One group was told that each member would receive a hint from the experimenter; the other was told the study was investigating "how people work on puzzles together" and that they would later receive a hint from one of the participants. The second group, who felt like they were working on it "together," worked on the puzzle 48% longer than those who thought they were working alone. Additionally, the second group rated the puzzle as more interesting compared to the other group, reflecting an increase in *intrinsic* motivation (the act of doing something without any obvious external rewards). Put this together with the extrinsic motivation one gets when working in a group (through esteem, a reward, a bump in salary) and what you end up with is the means to persevere!

With that said, it's important to note that working with a group may have negative effects if one feels *obligated* to work with others or if one's contributions go unnoticed or if one doesn't have ownership over their work. But of course, we know better with change!

3. PARTNERED ACCOUNTABILITY:

Think of someone you look up to, someone you know. Whether it's your parent, your significant other, your mentor, your teacher, your financial planner. How would you feel knowing you let them down? How would you feel breaking a promise you made or failing a favor? It's not particularly encouragement we're seeking but an *accountability partner* to hold us accountable for promises we've made to others (including our future selves)—to check on us the day we said we'd get it done, and if we haven't, to explain ourselves. You could even extend the onus to someone you recently met, someone you want to give a positive impression, perhaps someone you're infatuated with or your boss or a friendly neighbor whose conversation you enjoy. If not for us, let's do it for them!

Figure 5-7: Accountability

To possess the means to see through any change our iron triangles permit is exceptionally liberating. Knowing we are able to fully experience what a particular endeavor has to offer without a premature surrender will reward us with a sufficiently informed outlook to reflect and deductively iterate toward Self-Actualization. Said one of history's greatest military commanders, the Carthaginian general, Hannibal: *"Aut inveniam viam aut faciam"* ("I shall either find a way or make one").

CHAPTER 22
MOMENTUM

As we now know, small changes or perturbations within complex adaptive systems can lead to significantly different outcomes. Equivalently, commencing and sustaining a life of change requires one potentially small event, one promising domino to fall, to kickstart a chain reaction that can lead in many directions—a chain that mustn't be broken as the fall of dominos must not stall. Consistently discerning value in swift disorder is not only productive and rewarding but you never know what serendipitous plot twist the next day will present—though, in the case of developing any new skill or healthy habit, practice and consistency are essential to attain mastery (assuming its pursuit is what you believe to be Self-Actualizing). And one would be foolish not to acknowledge the adversity that the chaotic nature of life will inevitably and reliably thrust upon us: we will face valleys of despair, despondence, and desperation—engendering stagnating distractions, breaks, and even the potential surrender of a skill, healthy habit, or Quasi-Chaotic commitment. Would it not make sense, then, to set a measure in place to safeguard against inertia?

Recall the months following a newly adopted practice (a new job or a hobby, for example) when you were on an absolute tear, experiencing accelerated growth, and kicking ass on a daily basis. You would have been driven by the awe of the novel experience you sought to perfect or the motivation to please your newly acquainted supervisors and colleagues, or competitiveness and ambition urging you toward earning the esteem you felt you deserved and were capable of. You would have felt unstoppable, reaping the benefits of unbeknownst change and the surge of excitement that accompanied it. You would have felt productive, driven, content, on top of the world, perhaps even succumbing to momentary blissful comfort: "Now this is the life!" However, discovery turns to routine, social proactiveness turns to social capitulation, and challenge turns to monotony. The excitement faded and that drive seemed to vanish.

You may have tried to persevere, justifying your malaise as "just a phase" that would pass, but it never did, leaving you wondering, "What happened?"

For most, change is only provoked out of servitude or desperation—whether it's blindly taking on the next commitment the status quo compels of us or an unexpected opportunity we frantically grab on to. Regardless of the reason, the benefits are quick to manifest, but soon after, feelings of assuredness dissipate and we are left feeling perplexed. "No, really, what happened?" As we have come to realize, the prime mover is *personally motivated* change; the act of change is what gives rise to that fleeting period of determination and progression. A life of constant change will reliably invoke a proactive attitude and a productive drive, which is why we ought to *necessitate* change. It is worth reemphasizing: change *itself* is the reward. The key is to maintain a constant loop of novel experience and feedback, propelled by perpetual change to guarantee long-term dividends. (See figure 5-8.) It is thus in our best interest to generate and maintain Momentum.

Figure 5-8: Feedback loop of change

At this point, you may be thinking to yourself, "But at what point do I settle?" If you are, I urge you to question why you're asking such a question to begin with. Why do you feel the need to settle? Do you truly believe in a utopistic end—a final destination where you are sipping a piña colada on the golden shores of the Caribbean Punta Cana as the credits roll? Do you honestly think that constant change entails exhaustion? Do you doubt change to be anything short of perpetually gratifying, enjoyable, and insatiable once you're Change Adapted? I encourage you set aside such negative connotations and assumptions, because the only proof is experience itself. The proof is in the Caribbean bread pudding!

The falsities of the Traditional Psyche play a ubiquitous role in modern life—the misguided expectation of a utopian destination being one of them and aversion to the very means of arriving at a utopian *state of being* another. This quest to find the "one true love" or "dream job" has been tattooed onto our conscience. We have this unexplained need—urge—to strive for what we seldom question. It is only when we start asking the bigger questions or achieve the goal we set ourselves to, expecting ultimate satisfaction, that we realize how misled we've been. This is commonly referred to as a "midlife crisis."

We are everchanging: physically, mentally, emotionally, and spiritually. *Settling* is simply incompatible with this hard fact. Most of our goals and wishes change with each experience and moment that passes. Appreciating this inevitability implores us to embrace the need for constant change, eliminating the need for constant battles against inertia. In other words, once you've built Momentum (the means by which are detailed in Part VII: Execution), the "automaticity for change" (from being Change Adapted) voids the need for explicit attention and the cumbersome effort of unshackling the chains to the now undesired life you've bolted yourself to. Once again, the longer you remain in Camp Comfort, the harder you will find it to leave.

Here are three ways Momentum is used to sustain a Quasi-Chaotic Lifestyle:

1. **ANGULAR MOMENTUM:**

    Fulfilling change necessitates further change, reworking and progressing what we have already achieved. For example, if you picked up a new hobby, persevered through the effortful process preceding automaticity, and found it to be fulfilling, how you continually exercise the hobby warrants room for still more change. Which setting best supports your newly adopted practice of reading a topic of newfound interest? At home? Your partner's home? The botanical gardens? Try them all! Or if you have found a new group of friends, consider what changes these new friendships could give rise to. How much of what they do, how they do it, and whom they do it with might interest you? Recall the question regarding exercise: CrossFit or soloing a nightly gym routine. Which of the two would offer lasting motivation? The answer is change! CrossFit for as long as you feel driven, cross over to soloing a nightly gym routine, and then go on a mountain hike or try rock climbing. *This* is how Angular Momentum ensures lasting fitness motivation, and you can bet your bottom dollar that it works in almost every other domain.

    Angular Momentum promotes *horizontal* change to further an experience or an endeavor to its fullest potential while also helping us maintain iterative and serendipitous divergence. No, you don't have to drop your hobby after sixty-six days, and you don't need to exhaust every possible setting to read a book. As long as you commit to change before interest in a desired person, place, or practice dies out, and maintain the momentum of change, you're on the right track!

2. **VERTICAL MOMENTUM:**

    Periodically and proactively force categorical change. How long has it been since your last substantial change? Vertical change generally encompasses *bigger* and *bolder* moves, launching ourselves into a different orbit of experience, so to speak. New practices, new places, new people! It cultivates the courage we need to make the changes we've been avoiding over fear of the consequences of choosing the unknown. The more distant the orbit, the further we are from comfort. Have you spent a decade laboring through the *same damned* job? In the same industry? With the *same* people? Catapult yourself out! Your future self will be indebted to you. And if you're thinking, "That's easier said than done," you're dead right! Don't fret, though. How to work your way up to bigger, bolder moves will be detailed as you read on.

Alternatively, there will be periods in which difficult circumstances constrain your iron triangle's scope for change to a minimum. Under such circumstances, be advised to dial back your momentum of change to a lower, though still novel, orbit to retain your budding Quasi-Chaotic habits. For example, you may choose to meet new people through social media, explore remote areas in Google Maps, or pick up hand lettering. Remain considerate of your iron triangle and adjust accordingly, but always, *always* maintain that momentum of change. It doesn't matter how slow or modest the effort as long as you remain as agile as your capacity permits.

3. **SPONTANEOUS MOMENTUM:**

If you cannot recall the last time you attempted something truly *different*, then it's time to act impulsively on the first seemingly arbitrary opportunity that arises.

Ever consider trying out the coffee shop another block further from where you normally default to? Ever try inviting a colleague home for dinner? Have you ever sat on a tree branch and inspected the life its bark harbors? Have you ever worn your shoes the opposite way at work (be careful which ones you choose!) and waited to see how long it took before someone noticed? Imagine the conversation that would transpire:

> "So you're telling me that you intentionally wore your shoes the other way around and waited to see how long before anyone noticed?"

> "Yes, for two hours and thirty-six minutes."

> "You can't be serious. That's ridiculous! What's next? Replacing pictures of Rose's husband with Brendan Fraser?"

> "Count me in!"

NBD (Never Been Done) is a term we'll revisit as we explore the application of the Quasi-Chaotic Lifestyle. How many NBDs are you able to achieve in a month? Set a goal and then break it!

**In his heart, every man knows quite well that,
being unique, he will be in the world only once
and that there will be no second chance . . .
he knows it but hides it like a bad conscience—
why? From fear of his neighbor, who demands
conformity and cloaks himself with it. But what
is it that forces the individual to fear his neighbor,
to think and act like a member of a herd, and to
have no joy in himself? Modesty, perhaps, in a few
rare cases. For the majority it is idleness, inertia,
in short, the propensity for laziness
. . . men are even lazier than they are fearful.**

—Friedrich W. Nietzsche, *Unzeitgemässe Betrachtungen*
(Untimely Meditations)

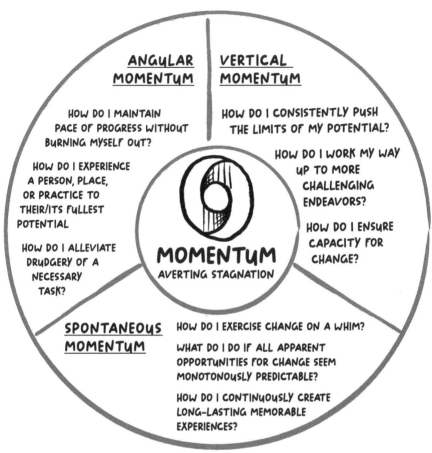

Figure 5-9: Momentum

Once you build Momentum, change effortlessly emerges. The automaticity of change—the muscle memory, the intuition—will become second nature. Resist worries of exhaustion. There is nothing more exhausting than laboring through more of the same.

CHAPTER 23
AMBITION

The next tool we are going to make use of is the most ravenous and merciless of the bunch: Ambition. Ambition is the antithesis of appreciation; one demands tenacity, the other adjures reflection. Ambition is what will keep you up at night when others sleep. It's what gets those five extra reps out. It's what has you mingling after work in search of new connections. It's why you'll climb up a hillside because why the hell not? Ambition is what conjures the courage to work out of your comfort zone. But to ride a wild horse, one must first tame the beast of its celerity. It needs to be treated with respect and handled safely to ultimately ride far and fast. Ambition is very much like that.

Ambition will have you asking yourself, "Is what I'm doing *now* getting me closer to where I want to be?" If the answer is no, Ambition will help you find something that does. If you aren't sure, Ambition urges you to try something else for reassurance. Asking the question keeps you attentive. It reminds you of your aspirations and keeps you acutely sensitive to the potential for further change. Focused and eager, you learn to not waste another minute until you get what you want: change! And when life throws its curveballs and your flame dies down, Ambition is the dimly lit kindling that remains, ready to pick you back up and flare into another exciting experience to pursue!

And, as you might have guessed, Ambition is a double-edged sword. Marching ambitiously negligent can turn one toward self-centeredness and narcissism. You may begin to question every action you make: time spent with friends and family, a faster way of accomplishing a mundane errand you were already finishing up, beating yourself up for inefficiencies. Ignoring the experience of the moment and what it has to offer is, ironically, more inefficient than you think. And while Ambition seeks to propel us toward a target at all costs, we must learn to pull back to what our respective iron triangles permit. And while we may not be taking the "optimal" route that others may be traversing, we must remain mindful of the risks of the Waterfall methodology, wherein the feasibility and sustainability of a development reliably beat the risks of a broken iron triangle.

Indeed, research offers mixed opinions of whether Ambition promotes "success." Some studies find that it's positively related to career satisfaction (El Baroudi et al., 2017), others found a negative correlation (Judge et al., 1995), and some found no significant correlation at all (Zimmerman et al., 2011). Some studies suggest that ambition improves one's ability to attain their desired career path (Ashby and Schoon, 2010), while others did not (Ng and Feldman, 2014). And while these discrepancies can be attributed to the veracity of measures of ambition (Hirschi and Spurk, 2021), it goes without saying that how Ambition is managed and projected is not just a binary choice. In other words, Ambition is not something you simply switch on to become a devout Buddhist David Goggins or switch off to binge-watch *Friends* again.

One may ask, "Well, I don't have that drive to any significant degree. I don't have dimly lit tinder or kindling, let alone a fire. What do I do?" I'm sorry to say that ambition isn't something you can simply conjure out of the ether. It's the aftermath of an epiphany, a realization of passion for an experience. And the only way to experience these realizations is by pursuing the unknown and finding what really stokes your flame. And although this may feel out of reach right now, know that it's impossible to be uninterested in *everything* (unless you have found yourself in a state of clinical depression). Allow this fact to saturate your intent with ardor and impatience. Your passion is out there, waiting for you. You just need to go looking for it!

And if this is all starting to sound demanding, remember this: Ambition does not necessarily mean more effort, more work, more hardship. Ambition is simply the desire to achieve something, or, as organizational psychologists Timothy A. Judge and John D. Kammeyer-Mueller (2012) put it, "the persistent and generalized striving for success, attainment, and accomplishment." Ambition may lead you down the path of minimalism, for example, striving to do less—to rid oneself of excess and anything that obfuscates what you have realized to be your fullest potential. Perhaps it leads to a spiritual odyssey or being one with nature, living in a cabin in the middle of nowhere.

Here are three ways Ambition is used to sustain a Quasi-Chaotic Lifestyle:

1. **COMPETITIVE AMBITION:**

   This dyad is synonymous with the combination of nitrous oxide and jet fuel. Competition drives ambition and vice versa, provoking motivation and further propelling growth. Of course, too much of anything is hazardous, and being overly competitive with the wrong outlook gives rise to haughty and suspicious attitudes, prompting envy or bitterness and restricting one's ability to employ Osmosis. Sportsmanship is paramount, and if *the other* is striving for a similar ideal and seems to be ahead, they probably know something you don't. Perhaps the two of you could consort and bolster each other's progress. Said Sir Isaac Newton: "If I have seen further, it is by standing on the shoulders of giants." Harness the power of competition and cooperate with those striving to be the best.

   How often do we ask our colleagues how they operate? How often do we consult other families and ask how they've got it so *right*? How often do we email the people we look up to and ask for advice? Similarly, have you thought of organizing a cook-off for those with culinary ambitions? Or setting up a leadership board for those who wrap burgers the quickest at work, meditate the longest, or make the most people smile in a day? It's incredibly fun, amazingly constructive, and a catalyst of growth like no other!

2. **GOVERNING AMBITION:**

   As previously stated, Ambition keeps us acutely attentive of where there is room for improvement. We know to constantly seek *more* of what we want (quality *and* quantity to the extent that our iron triangle permits), whether it's more time, more practice, more people, more places, more peace and serenity. "A man's reach," said the poet Robert Browning, "should exceed his grasp, or what's a heaven for?" The power of potential or an unfulfilled wish spur us to strive for the ideal. A general governing direction, which should be our default, directs us toward experiential crests—the best that life has to offer.

Agile teams often face the misconception that retrospectives exist to resolve conflicts and differences. This is not what they are primarily for. The principal purpose of a retrospective (essentially a ceremony to enable the team *as a group*) is to evaluate their past working cycle and figure out what went well, what didn't, and what they could be doing better. Conflicts, on the other hand, are addressed as they arise to maintain momentum of development. Some Agile teams struggle to identify items to address when there is *always* a matter that can be improved upon. For example, is information communicated across members in the best possible format? Is it sent in the timeliest manner? Is it inclusive of all the considerations that are relevant to other parties involved? Similarly, is the tea you're sipping the best it can be? Are you ironing your shirts in the fastest and most efficient way? Are you driving in a way that is most fuel efficient? Are you and your partner resolving conflicts in the most constructive, considerate, and decisive manner possible? Questions to ponder, with answers to propel!

3. CONTEMPLATIVE AMBITION:

The ambitious are swift to identify those who negatively question, restrict, or prevent change, shedding light on who or what hasn't been identified as a *Detractor*. Once we have our sights set straight, those standing in the way are in plain view, subjugating optimal Osmosis. It may be a person, place, or practice exhausting precious time that our ambitious intentions require. It may be a bad habit, a bad diet, an addiction, unrealistic expectations, a restrictive setting, emotional baggage, or an oppressive group or individual. The Quasi-Chaotic Lifestyle demands that we rid ourselves of Detractors (and how we do so is detailed in Part VI: Decisions).

The Traditional Psyche and the status quo skew our interpretation of the word "ambition" and what it entails. If we have learned anything about Self-Actualization, it's that we ought to strive for our *own* definition of what it means to live to *our* fullest potential. Ambition doesn't compel you to be someone you are not or toward an end in which you do not resonate with the means.

Figure 5-10: Ambition

It is simply a tool that obliges us to experience the best of what is meaningful to us, in our own individualistic way. And while striving for an ideal that exceeds one's grasp is bound to lead to some failures, be conscious of the sacrifices you make. Rest assured, each tool has a purpose, each with a counterpart, each providing balance to an unbalanced lifestyle (the Quasi-Chaotic Lifestyle!) tipped in your favor.

CHAPTER 24
FAILURE

Most of the people you often hear about are the triumphant, but how many *billions* live lives of mediocrity—years and years of failure, rejection, and frustration, never striking gold? How many of those with *unremarkable* lives do we hear about? Instead, media cues up a daily selection of violent exceptions, instilling a "normative baseline", swaying many to believe that *everyone* is successful with a pain-free narrative of achievement—a baseline we morosely compare to our own. We cannot forgive ourselves the horrors of our own iterations because we have not seen the iterations of those we aspire to become. Look no further than the anguished laments and tear-soaked scripts of your favorite writers before they received their first commission. Or the early stories of your favorite comedians who faced a nightly buffet of hecklers while living in their car before earning their first Netflix special. Or entrepreneurs with a history of bankruptcies who finally turned a profit.

The normative baseline *ought* to represent those seeking to improve, those somewhere in between, and those who are on their way. We often associate improvement with a sport, an instrument, or a hobby but seldom with *the self*. We've been led to believe that adulthood assumes *cementation* of the self—a "final form" with invariable traits. If a joke falls flat, that person isn't funny. If someone overweight shows up at the gym, some see their presence as out of place. We often default to polarized judgments: they're funny or not, they belong in the gym or not—nothing in between. What if they're working on their improv game? What if they're familiarizing themselves with gym equipment? What if they're practicing? We ought to applaud those seeking to improve and support them on their way. It's time to bring attention to those in between.

Our most important tool is Failure. *It will make the difference.* Our aim should be to fail and to fail fast. The more we fail, the more quickly we learn and reap the benefits of an informed pivot. How does muscle grow? It has to fail in order to grow back stronger. Systematic microtears in muscle fibers through stress and load when lifting weights lead the body to repair itself by fusing together new myofibrils. Muscle growth occurs when the rate of muscle protein synthesis is greater than the rate of muscle protein breakdown (induced by a caloric surplus). In other words, we cannot grow unless we take on an *excess* load of action, challenge, responsibilities, and aspirations. While challenge can be taxing, we are gaining more in the grand scheme of things; there is net growth. Additionally, muscle growth doesn't occur when you lift the weights (when you are amidst the struggle); it occurs while you rest (when you reflect afterward).

It bears repeating: *If we do not fail, we will never grow.* Recall the lessons of the Agile philosophy regarding software development. How would the end user know what they need if they don't know what they *don't want*? Show them what you think they'd value, await the feedback, and iterate until you get it right. When a client comes back with criticism, this is music to a developer's ears because they know with certainty which direction to avoid if they are to deliver value. Again, fail and fail again until you get it right. This approach is an industry standard, so if it works when millions of dollars are at stake, why wouldn't it work for you?

Not convinced? Well, in a study involving the analysis of 776,721 grant applications submitted to the US National Institutes of Health from 1985 to 2015 and 170,350 terrorist attacks carried out between 1970 and 2017 (rather dark, but hey, science is science), researchers sought to create a mathematical model that could reliably predict the failure or success of an undertaking. What ultimately differentiated the losers from the winners was not persistence. The study found that the faster the subjects failed, the better their chances of success, *only* if they learned from their failures. And the longer the delay between attempts (not maintaining Momentum), the more likely the subjects were going to fail again (Yin et al., 2019). Computational social scientists regard failure rather definitively as "the essential prerequisite for success" (Noonan, 2019).

Of course, failure has a temporary cost. But what would you rather endure: four months of heartache after a break-up or a ten-year relationship nightmare that ends up divorce and financial obligations that take 50% of your belongings? And yet our mind is easily swayed into pessimism when we think of change and the risk of failure. We think of immediate repercussions and ignore long-term gains because of how we feel in the moment. How we feel in that moment is more real than the possibility of crisis ten years down the road that we evade the thought of. And for this reason, failure is not appreciated as much as it should be.

Here are three ways Failure is used to sustain a Quasi-Chaotic Lifestyle:

1. ITERATIVE FAILURE:

How do you feel when you fail? When you drop the jar of mayonnaise? When you fail your driving test? When pull a no-show to that kickboxing class? Sorrow, regret, hatred, resentment, vindication?

Be happy that you'll *never* drop that jar of mayo again because you've learned your lesson to not handle glass jars with greasy fingers. Be happy that you rectified the error you made during the driving test which may avert an accident in the future. Be happy that you've realized kickboxing was never something you enjoyed and now you have another combat sport to look forward to.

What do you enjoy failing at the most? Where a failed effort turns from an "oopsie" into an "a-ha" instead of a "f***'s sake!" How much more enjoyable would a learning experience be if all the discomforts were in fact epiphanies or gratifying realizations? How seamless would those hours of commitment be? *Who* do you enjoy failing with the most? A discussion leads to an argument in which the first thing that comes to your mind is, "Oh my goodness. Here's our chance to learn about one another!" as opposed to blame, condescension, or patronization. *Where* do you enjoy failing the most? In a space where others visibly fail, a competitive setting, or perhaps in solitude?

Iterative Failure is the metal detector leading us to Self-Actualizing gold. Every failure is another opportunity to dampen our over-sensitivities to anything other than perfection, as failure is requisite to perfection itself.

2. REINFORCING FAILURE:

"Why do we fall, sir? So, we can learn to pick ourselves back up," said Alfred Pennyworth. Rejection is another form of failure. We construct stories in our mind, whether it's imagining a perfect day-in-the-life of the job you're hoping to win or the loving family you will have with the crush you haven't yet approached, only to be followed by a rejection letter and an "It's not you, it's me" to quash the hope of it all. We subsequently regard ourselves as failures—failing to star in the imagined movie we have been mentally playing on repeat. We'll never get everything we want, *and that's okay.* When one door closes, another opens. In hindsight, you may tell yourself, "Imagine what it would have been like if . . . ," but what's done is done. You may not have gained anything, but you likely didn't lose much either except maybe an opportunity, and there will be plenty more of those.

So why does rejection feel the way it does? Because we cling to the fictitious story; we conjure what could've, would've, should've happened. And so, the act of moving on is an invaluable tool that will help us get through the plethora of setbacks we must expect. Reinforcing Failure will numb the pain of rejection and build calluses of resilience to be proud of. If we are to learn by failing fast, we better get used to rejection, and we do this by failing fast!

3. OPPORTUNISTIC FAILURE:

Those who avoid or do not have the privilege of failing often miss out on serendipitous detours. Failing demands *proximal* change: how you made the attempt, with whom, in what setting, and so on. Seeking support and alternative methods of accomplishing the task at hand will lead you to exploring new people, places, and practices, all of which can catalyze diverse opportunities to exploit. Opportunistic Failure insists we continuously expose ourselves to risk and test our limits—an intrepid approach that nevertheless leads to relishing the fruits of failure and the opportunities it gives rise to.

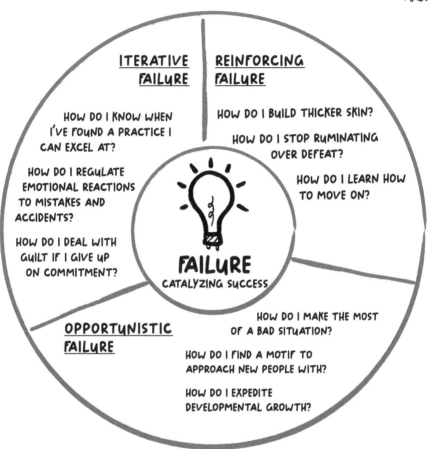

Figure 5-11: Failure

Life is about perspective, and the quicker we realize that failure is normal, healthy, and productive, the quicker we'll be able to employ it constructively and become who we've always wanted to be. We are accustomed to only celebrating our successes, but I think it's high time to celebrate our failures. So, take pride in the stuff-ups, slip-ups, face-plants, disappointments, miscalculations, misjudgments, mistakes, and missteps, and delight in the improved, wiser, new you!

Ever tried. Ever failed. No matter.
Try again. Fail again. Fail better.

—Samuel Beckett, *Worstward Ho*

CHAPTER 25
PRIDE

You might be feeling apprehensive about issues arising from spontaneity, ambition, and the positive attitude one *ought* to associate with failure—anticipating feelings of embarrassment, judgment, humiliation, discomfort, and so on. Given the significance of Failure's role in a life of change, failing fast without feelings of personal degradation can be a logistical tightrope for those not yet accustomed to *living*. It is therefore in our best interest to prevent failure from impeding our ability to live to our fullest. The means to accomplish this is through Pride.

Psychologists see pride as a positive emotion that confirms or enhances social worth (Lazarus, 1991), which is tied to our own sense of worth, also known as self-esteem (Leary and Downs, 1995). Social-personality psychologist Jessica L. Tracy (2017) found that if you convey your pride through nonverbal expressions (such as a puffed-up chest, head back, knowing smile, and expanded posture—see figure 5-12), others cognitively associate this with success and, in return, give you esteem. This consequently leads to believing that we deserve the status and reaffirms that what we have done was something to be proud of. And here's a little-known fact: pride is Darwinian and universal (across cultures, beliefs, races). Even infants as young as four months and congenitally blind athletes who could not have learned such expressions from nonconscious mimicry (Osmosis) are able to exhibit recognizable traits of nonverbal pride.

Figure 5-12: Authentic pride stance

Tracy distinguishes two types of pride: *authentic pride* and *hubristic pride* (also known as "narcissistic pride," one of the seven deadly sins in religious scripture). Those with hubristic pride are normally associated with being aggressive and manipulative, engaging in misbehavior, and seeking power and control. They are low in perceived social support and low in implicit self-esteem, which suggests their pride is a defensive mechanism to cover their insecurities.

Those with authentic pride, by comparison, are often quick to credit those who led to their success. They exhibit a sense of humility. Authentic pride relates to the second-to-last need in Maslow's hierarchy and inherently promotes a primal, evolutionary stimulus: esteem that encourages us to do bigger, better, and greater things, to gain a sense of accomplishment, to *feel* like we've made a difference, and to *want* to belong—helping us maintain our self-worth while we fail fast.

Personality and social psychologists Lauren Eskreis-Winkler and Ayelet Fishbach (2019) asked participants to answer binary choice (yes-no) questions and were then told whether they answered correctly (success feedback) or incorrectly (failure feedback). Both types of feedback showed the correct answer because there were only two choices. In a follow-up test that consisted of only questions which the participants had previously received feedback to (questions that had the same answer choices as the initial quiz questions, but the questions themselves were phrased in reverse), it was found that they learned more from success feedback than failure feedback. This held true even when learning from failure was less cognitively taxing than learning from success, and even when learning was incentivized. Participants who received failure feedback also remembered fewer of their answer choices. In short, they learned more from personal success than personal failure yet learned just as much from other's failure as from their success. "When failure feedback is inevitable, our results suggest that people will learn more if failure feedback can be separated from the ego. No matter the precise method for reducing ego involvement—for example, positioning people as vicarious learners or instructing people to reappraise feedback in less threatening terms—our results suggest that reducing the degree to which failure involves the ego will promote learning." Authentic pride detaches us from our ego—then all failures become successes and the means to progress.

Here are three ways Pride is used to sustain a Quasi-Chaotic Lifestyle:

1.   LOSSLESS PRIDE:

If we've learned anything thus far, it's that the status quo often works against our deepest integrities. Any deviation from the norm generally results in a sense of despondency when one commits a socially unacceptable act witnessed by or revealed to others. Complete disregard to social norms will get you fired, alienated, and/or ostracized, all of which would detract from one's potential opportunities.

However, opposing the status quo is not what's in question here. The question is *how* to break from social norms and defamatory judgment. Recall that time at prom when you and your pre-pubescent friends hit the dancefloor for the very first time? You never really learned how to dance and assumed everyone else was in the same boat. You look around, awkwardly swung your limbs about, and immediately realized it's a lot harder than it looks. You then promptly retreated to the buffet for the rest of the night while watching everyone else awkwardly swinging their limbs. Those who stayed on the dancefloor either already had a bit of practice or were conscious of how badly they danced but did it anyway and had the best night of their life. They kept their pride, and you did not. By shamefully leaving the dancefloor after a failed attempt at something you'd never practiced, you lost your dignity and, consequently, self-esteem.

The alternative would have been to find pride in that very first attempt, laughing off the awkwardness and asking your friends to teach you a move or two that would have demonstrated confidence and warranted respect. You are broadcasting the fact that you *know* you're bad at dancing because you've *never* learned how, but you're doing it anyway because you're enjoying yourself with those who have. The bonus? You're building a fun rapport and relationships while you're at it! The difference between giving up and taking it on in this example is *humility*. Pride plus humility oozes confidence that warrants esteem and, in turn, allows you to break social norms while maximizing opportunity. In other words, we have nothing to lose when we fail and only ourselves to blame when we do.

And when it comes to other spontaneous acts of curiosity or unconventional behavior that prompt something along the lines of, "You're weird," take it as a compliment! Take Pride in your courage with an "I know, right?" As far as you're concerned, there's nothing weirder than the conventional!

2. **ATTRACTIVE PRIDE:**

Another perk of authentic pride is that when people are seeking knowledge or support, they are much more likely to choose it from someone exhibiting authentic pride—more so than any other emotional expression, as Tracy concluded from her studies. As we have come to learn, leveraging serendipity often takes the form of exposing oneself to more people. The more we seem approachable, authentic, and proud, the better able we are to *exert merit* (demonstrate desired traits or abilities) and make the most from an opportunity!

3. **REFLECTIVE PRIDE:**

The German word *Schadenfreude* was first documented in the 1740s. It's a compound of *Schaden* (harm/damage) and Freude (joy) which translates simply to "harm-joy" or the experience of pleasure, joy, or self-satisfaction that comes from learning of or witnessing the troubles, failures, or humiliation of another. Social psychologist Richard H. Smith (2014), suggests that "Schadenfreude is a natural human emotion" and that "The way we compare ourselves to others plays an important role in our self-esteem . . . Competition itself is a kind of comparison process."

To substantiate his point, Smith cites evolutionary psychologists Sarah Hill and David Buss (2010) who suggest that "individuals appear to be acutely attuned to diminutions in rank or attributes" (Kalma, 1991; Mazur and Booth, 1999). This explains how envy compels us to improve conditions in which we rank lower than others in areas that are crucial for survival and reproductive success. These ideas had been previously explored in *social comparison theory*—proposed in 1954 by renowned psychologist Leon Festinger—which suggests that people have an innate drive to evaluate themselves, often in comparison to others.

Our biological inclinations and the media's projections of violent exceptions subject us to unfair comparison to those beyond our social circle and beyond our knowledge of what afforded *their* success—further widening the expectation gap. The hedonic treadmill, mischievous as it is, leads us to misremember our progress of personal development as confined to our respective iron triangles. Reflective Pride involves recognizing not where one stands relative to others but how far one has come relative to where one used to be, as well as to making an effort to measure and celebrate the *distance traversed*. Recall Jordan B. Peterson's quote: "Compare yourself to who you were yesterday and not to who someone else is today. That is a game you can win."

Figure 5-13: Pride

Ambition is to progression what Pride is to recognition. Self-appreciation of one's accomplishments enables self-sufficiency; you no longer need anyone to validate your achievements. It's a self-perpetuating cycle that enhances and sustains social status while promoting divergence and opportunity!

PREQUEL TO PART VI:

DECISIONS

You now have the Quasi-Chaotic Toolkit—an assembly of tools you will very much need for what's to come. Tools that will pull you back, push you forward, pick you up, keep you going, and keep you growing and contented every step of the way. The issues that will arise in the process of adopting and sustaining a Quasi-Chaotic Lifestyle are thematic; with practice, you will know which tool and its applications to use when the time comes.

Unraveling the knotted mess you may be in is a matter I promised we'd return to. The question of who or what is holding you back and what you ought to do about them or it, however, is not one we are ready for just yet. Regaining control throws everything and everyone, including who you know yourself to have become, on the table. We therefore need to start by overcoming what you may be dreading by starting on the path of a Quasi-Chaotic Lifestyle: loss, regret, and grief.

You are the prime mover; the decisions you make are the moves you take. Moving toward Self-Actualization is what we intend to do, but the first decision is whether you truly want to commit to a Quasi-Chaotic View and/or what the Quasi-Chaotic Lifestyle has to offer. Unearthing choices you never knew you had and revealing doors you never knew were unlocked will open up a new world of opportunity and challenge. Regardless of where you are in this process, it's now time to learn how to make the best decisions for our respective self-interests and live with them!

PART VI
DECISIONS
THE VERDICT

CHAPTER 26
HARD PROBLEMS

A*Hard Problem* is a problem with no clear resolution. It is a daily itch you can't scratch, a nightly buzz you can't swat, a growing pressure you can't relieve. It involves inexorable pain and grief, no matter the path taken. It is an obstacle with no happy ending.

Some examples of Hard Problems:

▲ Realizing after working for six years in an industry you invested advanced education into that this line of work is not for you and the competitive salary and benefits don't cut it anymore.

▲ Letting go of a lifelong friend who has grown dependent on you, which has significantly impacted your well-being—so much so that you find little emotional time for yourself.

▲ Arriving at a potentially relationship-ending moral deadlock whereby what you believe and insist to be an inadmissible transgression necessitating authentic apology is met with vehement repudiation by your significant other.

There is no avoiding the issue, and fear of a regrettable decision, joined by a myriad of doubts, insecurities, and, most prominently, uncertainties, immediately manifests. Each option presents its own slew of consequences that you endlessly contrast and deliberate. You are torn between doing the "right thing" and "what's best for me"—a rather hairy problem when the two oppose one another. Moral and ethical considerations incite dissonance, and "what ifs" wash over you:

▲ What if I'm not able to get as good a position if I change my mind after resigning? What if I don't enjoy the next career I commit to? What will my family and friends think of me?

▲ Will [lifelong friend] ever forgive me? What will they do without me? Will I ever forgive myself? What if my absence throws them over the edge? Does this make me a bad person?

▲ What if I never find anyone else like them? What if I concede and compromise? What if the problem is with me and not them? Should I just give it a few more months?

The problem with Hard Problems is that they don't give any clear indication as to *why* they are there to begin with; they seem to chaotically emerge, which is what you'd expect from complex adaptive systems. The question that often follows is, "Why me?":

▲ Why did I have to choose accounting? Everyone else seems to have gotten their first pick right. Why did I only just realize this after placing a mortgage?

▲ I have enough problems in my own life. Why can't they just get it together? Why am I always the one helping and never the person being helped?

▲ Why is this happening now? Why do I get so upset when they talk about their past relationships? Why do I always end up with someone still in touch with their ex?

The fact of the matter is that the problem you had to face was always there; you just didn't know it or did but decided to put up with it to the point of intolerability until effectuating Murphy's Law. Do you recall the underlying pain we subdue by remaining Incessantly Distracted? It is this very pain that Hard Problems evoke. Living a life of constant change will force us to address matters we may be carelessly avoiding that have eventuated into Hard Problems.

A Quasi-Chaotic Lifestyle necessitates action, and those looking to adopt it will need to reconsider—and overcome—the role of *passivity* to avoid those Hard Problems. Though if you have one now, it's already too late. The only way past the issue is through it. In this section, we will learn how to confidently work through Hard Problems and how to make and live with Self-Actualizing decisions that are void of regret. By the end, you will no longer fear Hard Problems. In fact, you will learn to welcome them with an outlook centered around the opportunities for growth and self-fulfillment that come with change!

REGRETS? I'VE HAD A FEW

Regret is pernicious because it elicits a sense of helplessness and vulnerability. No matter how much wealth we've accumulated, how much power we bear, how much influence we have, how much bereavement we express, how much we are willing to change and do from this point on, we cannot undo what has been done. When stuck in regret, we are at the mercy of decisions fixed in the arrow of time, ruling the future we inevitably face.

Daniel Pink, the author of five bestselling books on subjects of motivation and business, and a team of survey research experts carried out the American Regret Project. They surveyed 4,489 people and then launched a website called the World Regret Survey, which has collected more than sixteen thousand regrets from people in 105 countries. Writing in his new book, *The Power of Regret*, Pink reports that when participants were asked, "'How often do you look back on your life and wish you had done things differently?' . . . Only 1% of our respondents said that they never engage in such behavior—and fewer than 17% do it rarely. Meanwhile, about 43% report doing it frequently or all the time. In all, a whopping 82% say that this activity is at least occasionally part of their lives, making Americans far more likely to experience regret than they are to floss their teeth" (2022). This finding coincides with an earlier study conducted by neuropsychologist Isabelle Bauer and developmental psychologist Carsten Wrosch (2011) which showed that 90% of its adult participants have deep regrets about their lives, and that the more they dwell on them, the worse their quality of life tends to get. And the determinant of the level of regret? The size of the gap between an individual's perception of what happened as opposed to what *could have* happened (Das and Kerr, 2010). Yet another gap to add to our evergrowing list of self-imposed detrimental suppositions; gaps affecting our happiness, our willingness to change, and, in this case, our ability to move on.

Regret can be all-consuming, and it can destroy lives. We see it all around us, whether it's over immigration, career choices, affairs—the list is long. It leads to self-flagellation and the cessation of Self-Actualizing initiatives. Economic psychologist Marcel Zeelenberg et al. (2002) suggest there are two ways to experience regret: the "action path" (regretting the things we did) and the "inaction path" (regretting the things we did not do). A simple question to ask is what induces more regret? Action or inaction?

We begin by questioning our natural tendencies. One study found that soccer goalkeepers in penalty kicks *believe* action (jumping to one of the sides) is more normal than inaction (staying at the center of the goal) and that a failed inaction produces more regret than a failed action. As a result, goalkeepers will almost always choose action over inaction even though, statistically, it reduces their chances to stop the ball (Bar-Eli et al., 2007).

Other studies show that a decision to act leads to greater regret than a decision not to act when both resulted in failure *and the latter is the norm* (Miller and Taylor, 1995; N'gbala and Branscombe, 1997). In some cases, however, when the norm is to act, the pattern is reversed (Gilovich and Medvec, 1995; Zeelenberg et al., 2002). There seems to be a correlation between what one *believes* to be the norm and patterns of regret. In other words, the disparity between belief in a norm and the choice you make dictates whether you regret action or inaction that leads to failure. Furthermore, how regret-table a decision is depends not only on the type of decision we make but on the type of decision that is the societal or contextual norm. There seems to be an underlying irrational subjectivity to it all!

When it comes to decision-making motivations, consider the work of Edward Tory Higgins (1997, 1998), one of the most highly regarded and influential researchers in social psychology and the science of motivation. Higgins formulated the Regulatory Focus Theory, which proposes that human motivation in decision-making consists of two regulatory orientations:

1. **PROMOTION-FOCUSED INDIVIDUALS**

   are motivated to achieve aspirations, accomplishments, and ideals. They are sensitive to the presence/gain or absence/non-gain of positive outcomes in situations.

2. PREVENTION-FOCUSED INDIVIDUALS

are motivated toward duty, responsibility, and security. They are sensitive to the presence/loss or absence/non-loss of negative outcomes in situations.

Economic psychologist Adi Itzkin et al. (2016) found that whether action or inaction leading to failure was more regretful depends on the decision-maker's regulatory orientation. One of their interesting finds is how promotion-focused individuals attributed less regret than prevention-focused individuals to action decisions that failed *and* the same amount of regret to inaction decisions that failed. The finding concurs with other studies that suggest prevention-focused individuals might be more vulnerable to reduced well-being, whereas promotion focus is related to more resiliency (e.g., Van Dijk et al., 2013). A parsimonious explanation is provided by a study that found action-related regrets, though painful, spur people to learn from their mistakes and move on. Inaction-related regrets, on the other hand, are much more likely to lead to anxiety, depression, stagnation, and a feeling of longing over not knowing what could have been (Davidai et al., 2018).

Another curious find was how a *trigger for change* decreases regret following action (Itzkin et al., 2016). Given a negative prior feeling or event (a "prior"), such as not being happy with the university one is currently enrolled in, there is less of a chance of regretting the action of changing universities. This is because the negative prior creates a trigger for a change, increasing the *normality* of choosing action. Elementary at face value, but what one associates negativity with is a controllable mechanism we can benefit from, and one we will return to. As authors of the study state: "Moreover, we believe that not only a prior negative outcome but also a change in the environment may create a trigger for change, increasing the normality of action and reducing the normality of inaction, and therefore reducing the regret from action decisions compared to inaction decisions."

For example, working in the dynamic but turbulent high-tech industry of everchanging technologies, products, and talent, an action decision will be less regrettable given that it is an environmental expectation—one that looks very much like the one we are looking to cultivate with a life of change!

But wait, there's more! Recall the need to prioritize openness to experience for personality change? Research indicates a close fit between this very trait and promotion-focused individuals (Friedman and Forster, 2001; Vaughn et al., 2008; Groeneveld, 2012)! Yet another reason to forge our psyche toward openness!

The aforementioned studies compel us to bridge the could-have-been gap of contrition, overcome passivity, question norms of conduct, employ decisions of action, cultivate triggers for change, and immerse ourselves in an environment where change is the norm. All steps in the right direction, but we aren't out of the woods yet!

THEN AGAIN, TOO FEW TO MENTION

We have traversed philosophical, psychological, technological, sociological, anthropological, and neurological landscapes; there is much to draw upon to rule out any rationale for regret. Whether it be the topic of free will, how our past couldn't have led to any other outcome, the justifications of an untrained amygdala, the centeredness of change, or environmental influence, it all converges toward one ultimatum: *acceptance*.

Consider this: Making an informed decision requires information. Hard problems involve insufficient information—no clear way of ascertaining where our decisions will lead us given the chaotic nature of the system. (If there was, the decision would be obvious.) If we accept these two simple facts, whatever decisions we make will come with a condition: to act on them and never look back. Stay true to the decision you've made and accept the fact that you made the best one possible given everything there was to know *at the time*. In hindsight, you'll appreciate the careful consideration and precautionary measures you devoted to contemplating your options before choosing an act of change you can be proud of!

"If I'm sincere today, what does it matter if I regret it tomorrow?" said the Portuguese writer José Saramago. If you are sincere with yourself and take the time to evaluate all possible options, eventually arriving at what you truly believe is the best decision and commit to it, there will be *no rationale for regret*. Lingering on the could've/should've/would've is feckless when there is nothing else you could have done!

If you recall, cognitive behavioral therapy (CBT) is one of the most effective treatments for a range of mental and emotional health issues. Central to the treatment is what is referred to as *cognitive reappraisal*. It refers to subjective reinterpretation to change how you respond to a situation. You learn to reframe or *reappraise* a situation with the aim of achieving a better emotional response. For example, someone who stresses easily can learn to focus on how much worse things could be by comparing themselves to others less fortunate. CBT is most effective when you learn to reinterpret a situation before an emotional response is fully developed. In our case, we will be looking to reappraise the act of change and the loss that may sometimes accompany it as an opportunity for growth. It is certainly easier said than done, but rest assured, the Quasi-Chaotic Lifestyle garners habits that will naturally cause you to reappraise your tendencies toward Self-Actualizing action.

Voiding regret necessitates reappraisal but even more importantly, requires some self-compassion. To accept whatever outcome emerges within a Quasi-Chaotic Lifestyle during its adoption involves the following:

1. **To be understanding of ourselves, our shortcomings, the inevitability of outcome owing to prior conditions, and of the necessity of failure to Self-Actualize;**

AND THEN

2. **To further reappraise the situation as the best you could have done, to be proud of the efforts you have made, and to focus on what change made possible.**

What will start off as deliberate reappraisal, in time, will become naturally coalesced with acceptance. Not only does acceptance mitigate anxiety better than suppressing or controlling of your emotions (Levitt et al., 2004); accepting negative emotions has correlates longer term with positive well-being such as lower levels of anxiety and depressive symptoms (Tull et al., 2004; Roemer et al., 2005; Kashdan et al., 2009; Shallcross et al., 2010). In fact, research by behavioral psychologists Kohki Arimitsu and Stefan G. Hofmann

(2015) suggests that self-compassion (acceptance) and cognitive reappraisal reduce negative emotions (including regret) more than reattribution and self-deflection.

That said, acting on a decision is only half the solution. Making a regret-free decision doesn't instantly or indefinitely exculpate us from grief—grief that may breed dissonance and subsequent cognitive adjustments and even a relapse of regret. For example, you may have ended a relationship on mutually agreed terms and with sufficient information to be content with the decision, but that doesn't mean heartache won't be quick to follow along with irrational second thoughts.

I DID WHAT I HAD TO DO, WITHOUT EXEMPTION

Grief is a natural response to loss. It is inevitable and there is no escaping it. As far as the science is concerned, there is no shortage of theories about grief (Weiss, 2001), and consensus on why grief exists remains elusive.

You may be familiar with the Kübler-Ross model (otherwise known as the Five Stages of Grief). It is worth quickly mentioning how George A. Bonanno's large body of peer-reviewed studies debunked its utility by showing how the vast majority of people who have experienced loss are subject to multiple trajectories (Bonanno and Galatzer-Levy, 2012) that involve resilience, recovery, chronic dysfunction, or delayed grief or trauma.

Whether natural selection shaped our capacity for grief is yet to be definitively verified (Nesse, 2005), but there is no doubt that it shaped the mental mechanisms that give rise to grief. If we understand them, we will be better equipped to minimize it's deep-seated and stagnating pain.

Without delving further into the realm of behavioral ecology, ethology, and evolutionary biology, the answer to where the emotion of grief comes from is still up in the air. One thing we know for certain: grief is, from a Darwinian perspective, a detrimental epiphenomenon that seems to oppose the act of kin selection. It's a disadvantageous "Darwinian fitness" characteristic that one would assume to have been naturally *deselected* because it causes painful responses, disrupts livelihoods, and leads to depression, all of which would have impeded our ancestors' survival.

The best understanding we have of this paradox comes from the work of John Bowlby, a psychoanalyst who developed the *theory of attachment* in the 1940s and 1950s, which is still influential today. He suggests that young children are motivated to stay close to their caregivers in order to ensure their survival. In a healthy attachment, the caregiver is sensitive to the infant's needs, and the child feels comfortable roaming, knowing that safety is nearby. However, if the roaming child disappears and dies, the loss cannot be remedied, which results in grief—genetically induced perpetual melancholy, if you may. It's as though natural selection can't shape a mechanism that gives the benefits of attachment without the extraordinary cost of grief. We see broken relationships as the end of the world, a broken attachment that cannot be remedied, in which we ruminate over recursive and dead-end potential attempts to reunite, spelling what we misconstrue to be the end of our gene line (if we refer back to C. Richard Dawkins's work).

What is especially useful here, from an emotional standpoint, is the realization that despair and sadness are responses to *broken attachments*. Natural selection preserves our genetic tendencies to respond to separation with distress and motivation for reunion. To further the point, if we are to transpose the contextual influence of our ancestral evolutions to modernity, it would explain how broken attachments and their subsequent grief have migrated to other aspects of modern human life. Whether it's grief over a divorce after a long marriage, giving up a long-term habit due to injury or growing responsibilities, or migrating from a country of deep-rooted belonging—essentially anything we have regularly *depended on*—we are naturally inclined to ignore any negative influence we may have experienced from that relationship, that habit, that home and focus on one simple truth: we are experiencing a broken attachment in the form of losing a person, place, or practice that may have otherwise been (or what we *believe* to have been) "selectively advantageous." We are systematically configured to focus on the loss itself and not the contextual justification or epistemic influence or what we have gained—a cognitive bias we will revisit.

Referring back to our evolutionary origins once again gives us a better understanding of why we react the way we do. We cannot completely mitigate the feeling of grief, but we *can* make an informed effort to assure ourselves that whatever the loss, it is not the end of the world, and that this recursive infinite loop to reunite is a systemic malfunction (denial) and can be interrupted through *action*. Reminding ourselves of why the loss took place and making the most out of what good came out of the decision will dissolve lingering grief that would otherwise impede our quest for Self-Actualization.

In taking back control of our lives, we will face a wall of Hard Problems that require a robust decision-making model to void regret, minimize grief, and maximize the likelihood of making the best Self-Actualizing decisions we can for ourselves—a model we will now explore.

CHAPTER 27
THE THREE PILLARS
OF CONVICTION

Decision-making generally implies consideration. *How* we utilize considerations and how much we consider often go unquestioned. Each of us seems to have our own way of contemplating a decision, whether it's consulting a friend, pursuing our gut feel, flipping a coin, ruminating over hypothetical scenarios, or some inconsistent combination of strategies. Most perplexing is how most of us do not employ a consistent method from which to *reliably* draw efficacious decisions.

For the question at hand, there is a multitude of decision-making models that behavioral and organizational psychologists, as well as economists, have developed. Adhering closely to the Quasi-Chaotic View, I will simply mention them and which insight our *Quasi-Chaotic Decision-Making Model* adopts from each.

▲ Leon Mann's **GOFER Decision-Making Model** (Mann et al. 1988): influencing a values component

▲ Adam Smith's **Rational Decision-Making Model** (Boudon, 2003): influencing an emotional motive component

▲ Victor Vroom and Phillip Yetton's (1973) **Vroom-Yetton Decision-Making Model**: influencing an informed guidance component

▲ Gary Klein's (2017) **Recognition-Primed Decision-Making Model**: influencing a high-stakes consideration component

▲ Chris Argyris's **Ladder of Inference Decision-Making Model** (Argyris and Schön, 1992): influencing an assumption recognition and verification component

Some are one-dimensional and/or don't place emphasis on *our* individualistic best interests/preferences nor are they attuned to the fact that we are human beings, cursed with limited faculties, fluctuating desires, and self-sabotaging proclivities. Before we incorporate them into what will ultimately become the Quasi-Chaotic Decision-Making Model, we must first set the foundations upon which to build.

You will be familiar with the different centers we use to approach a decision. Littered throughout our vernacular are idioms like "Use your head," "Follow your heart," and "Listen to your gut." And a robust body of research into the nature of decision-making indeed recognizes the roles of cognition, emotion, and intuition in human decision-making (Burke and Miller, 1999; Schwarz, 2000; Bohm and Brun, 2008; Lerner et al., 2015; Sinclair, 2016). These three "pillars of conviction" will provide the structural support for a Self-Actualizing certitude.

1. Cognition—The Head

In 1947, the economist Oscar Morgenstern and the legendary mathematician John von Neumann, whose influential contributions to varying fields are too numerous to list, developed "axioms of rationality" (Neumann and Morgenstern, 1953)—a set of truths for rational behavior, namely:

▲ **Completeness:** assumes an individual has defined preferences

▲ **Transitivity:** assumes that preferences are consistent across options

▲ **Continuity:** assumes there are defined points where one option is better than another

▲ **Independence:** assumes that a preference holds independently of the possibility of another outcome

By checking the boxes of these axioms when making a decision, we can be thought of as rational beings. It was long believed that rational people use information and measurement rather than emotion or intuition, but is this really how people make decisions? How rational are we? Nobel Laureate statistician and economist Milton Friedman (1953) quashed such questions with a simple rationale: "As if . . ." Using the analogy of an expert pool player, he argued that they aren't calculating all the angles and frictions when they line up a ball but act as *if* they know and exercise those formulas. In other words, it doesn't really matter if the pool player *isn't* calculating the angles and frictions before they pot a ball because it's as *if* they did. As long as the model we use has predictive power, then unrealistic assumptions don't matter.

Similarly, we evaluate situations using seemingly sufficient information, contemplative rigor, and complex hypotheticals and act *as if* we are rational beings. Unfortunately, how we interpret what we see around us and what we have learned to expect from ourselves is far from what Neumann or Morgenstern would consider rational.

We are faced with situations in which behaving as if we're rational individuals leads to what almost always seems to be, in hindsight, *irrational* behavior, as briefly illustrated by our goalie decision-making example mentioned earlier. Confronted with a dilemma, we overlook how potentially ignorant we may be of past and present circumstances of others. Emotions further skew the truth, the facts, and the reasons, whether it be time constraints, a pet peeve, a trigger to deeply seeded trauma, a series of unfortunate events, or even an agitating hot summer's day. Our emotions are viscerally with us all day and night and, as a result, feel more real than those of others—narrowing our perspective even more than it is pigeonholed already. We mask our irritation, envy, disgust, and sorrow, yet we seldom give others the benefit of doubt for enduring hardships and struggles unbeknownst to us. We run the events that took place exactly as we remember them and chew the cud of ethical arithmetic that doesn't seem to add up. We then find ourselves engrossed in a vicious cycle of negative associations, blinded by feelings of betrayal, hatred, and vengeance that lead to the abandonment of what could have otherwise been a successful relationship, a fruitful hobby or career, constructive epiphanies, or a serendipitous rabbit hole.

Upon confronting a quarrelsome friend for example, we often invest a few hours of emotionally charged deliberation and then impulsively commit to a decision of excommunication whose positive and negative consequences are out of our intellective reach. Our actions may bring out sides of people we never knew existed and reactions we never thought they were capable of. Our decision may trigger a chain of events sparking collateral we could have never predicted. Subsequent events may reveal opportunities that could have never come into existence if it wasn't for the grief that ensued, dependencies we never knew we relied on, or bad habits we never knew we had. As the saying goes, we really don't know what we have until it's gone.

What is known as "using one's head" generally involves an accounting of pros and cons, risks versus rewards—an objective attempt to rationalize a decision. But how much are we willing to rely on our logical judgment of what there is to gain or lose or who is wrong or right? Quantifying the weight of each consideration and foreboding the mental arithmetic that follows is another problem that certain decision-making models may have you attempt—suggesting you flesh out the potential results of each solution and analyze preferentiality. But in study after study, researchers have found that we are terrible at predicting our future emotional states (Wilson and Gilbert, 2003), our future behavior (Dunning, 2007), future spending (Peetz and Buehler, 2009), how long it takes to complete a future task (Buehler et al., 2010), how long we'll have a happy relationship (MacDonald and Ross, 1999), the likelihood we'll engage in healthy behaviors (Lipkus and Shepperd, 2009), how we'll perform on exams and tests (Helzer and Dunning, 2012)—pretty much everything!

We need to accept that we are not entirely rational. We operate in rational and irrational ways. We have to work *with* our nature rather than against it. And while weighing what we perceive to be the pros and cons of a decision will ultimately form the central pillar of our Quasi-Chaotic Decision-Making Model, we must also incorporate other considerations to thwart our irrational tendencies before verifying a Self-Actualizing verdict.

2. Intuition—The Gut

Every day, you make decisions and judgments. You spend more time on some than others, and you often make them on the fly. Think of when you were deciding which insurance plan to invest in versus the time you had to pick a pair of socks. Life would be exhausting if we had to deliberate over the hundreds of choices we make every day, so instead, our mind uses shortcuts to make judgments about the world around us. We commonly refer to this as "gut instinct," as if we already know the answer before the question is asked. This phenomenon arises from heuristics and what often leads to irrational decision-making.

While it is common for psychologists, philosophers, and neuroscientists to equate intuitions with heuristics, some do propose a clear difference between the two (Hilbig et al., 2010)—a difference that we will pass over, as it's of peripheral irrelevance.

Heuristics are problem-solving approaches that rely on previous experience and intuition rather than careful analysis. The concept was originally introduced by Nobel laureate Herbert A. Simon in 1957, who coined the term "satisficing" to denote a situation in which people make judgments that are "good enough." And the limited knowledge and intellective reach that makes our suboptimal decisions feel *as if* they were the best decisions to make he referred to as "bounded rationality."

If you recall, our regulatory orientation (promotion-focused or prevention-focused), what we *perceive* to be the norm, and what we feel *inclined* to do dictate how regrettable a failed decision is. One study investigated people's tendencies to overemphasize the value of their intuitions (or what they feel inclined to do) and then how they felt about the eventual outcome of the gut-instinct-decision they make (Kirkebøen, 2017). It found that intuitive choices intensify positive emotions, both anticipated and real, after successful outcomes much more than negative emotions after failures. These tendencies matter.

It wasn't until cognitive and mathematical psychologist Amos N. Tversky and the aforementioned Daniel Kahneman further developed this field of study in the 1970s and '80s that a plethora of cognitive biases (following heuristics) governing how we conduct ourselves on a day-to-day basis were identified.

Cognitive bias refers to a systematic error in thought that affects judgment. We are all inherently biased, whether we like to admit it or not. Everything that has led up to this point has shaped you into what you are today, and every experience you've had, whether good or bad, has influenced your preferences and tilted your perspective in a particular direction. How you feel about anything is entirely subjective. The only reason you like anything in particular is because the experiences you've had with it were positive, whether due to circumstantial, environmental, or even genetic influence (such as a temperament that influences events positively or negatively through involvement, commitment, and/or agreeableness. The consequences would influence what you end up liking and disliking and alter your trajectory). Accounting for cognitive bias forces us to remain acutely aware that we have consequential predispositions in some way, shape, or form.

The list of cognitive biases is quite extensive and still growing; we will, however, explore a few that are most relevant and actionable:

LOSS AVERSION:

Under *rational economic theory*, decisions should follow a simple mathematical equation that weighs the level of risk against the amount at stake. But Tversky and Kahneman (1992) found that for many people, the negative psychological impact we feel from losing something is roughly twice as influential as the positive impact of gaining *the same thing*. And if you didn't know why economists take great interest in the topic of decision-making, it's for the same reason that insurance providers typically have a long list of unlikely and costly outcomes that individuals may be vulnerable to if not insured (Putler, 1992).

In short, our gut fears loss more than it looks forward to gain. How do we manage this bias? It can be as simple as rephrasing the narrative you are using to define risk and reward: "I'm going to gain my freedom" rather than "I'm going to lose my significant other" can make a world of difference—what we have learnt as cognitive reappraisal.

ANCHORING BIAS:

Broadening the previous definition, this epiphenomenon of evolutionary mechanisms has us place heavier emphasis on the first piece of information that draws our attention, unduly influencing subsequent judgments. It's the automatic process of leveraging immediately available information as a focal point for decision-making. In another study, Tversky and Kahneman (1974) had participants spin a roulette-style wheel and were subsequently asked to guess the percentage of U.N. countries that are in Africa. Those who got a high number on their spin guessed higher percentages. The takeaway? Insistently avoid impulsive decision-making regarding Hard Problems, remain skeptical of what initial information you have to work with, and then question it with more rigor.

SURVIVORSHIP BIAS:

A form of selection bias, the effects of survivorship bias have us overlook those whose decisions did not lead to a favorable outcome. It's the logical error of spotlighting those who survived, assuming we have the full story. Common examples would be the risk of starting a new business. Estimates suggest that a third of all businesses fail within the first year, yet we single out the successes of a friend, an acquaintance, or a viral entrepreneur we see on TV to justify our decision to make a substantial investment. Or we may be drawn into "penny stock" success stories or lottery winners who make it to Reddit's front page when in reality there are thousands if not hundreds of thousands of others burning their hard-earned savings with nothing to show for it. How we counteract survivorship bias is detailed in the following bias.

AVAILABILITY BIAS:

Here's a question: Do you think the world is getting better or worse over time? You may be inclined to assume the latter because of seemingly endless wars erupting around the world, ubiquitous poverty, novel and resurgent terrorist groups, pandemics, political dilemmas, and so on. However, if you were to consult the facts:

▲ **Life expectancy:** For most of human history, life expectancy at birth was around thirty years. Today, worldwide, it is more than seventy, and in the developed parts of the world, more than eighty (Roser et al., 2013).

▲ **Child mortality:** 250 years ago, in the richest countries in the world, a third of the children did not live to see their fifth birthday. This number has been reduced to 6% even in the poorest of regions (Roser, 2013).

▲ **Poverty:** Two hundred years ago, 90% of the world's population resided in extreme poverty; today, fewer than 10% do (Roser, 2013).

▲ **War:** Great powers *constantly* waged war in the past; the last such battle (prior to the major escalation of the Russo-Ukrainian War) took place sixty-five years ago (Levy and Thompson, 2010).

▲ **Battle deaths:** Wars of all kinds have been less deadly; the annual rate has fallen from 22 per 100,000 a year in the 1950s down to 1.2 in 2019 (UCDP, 2019).

▲ **Democracy versus autocracy:** We have seen democratic setbacks in Venezuela, Russia, and Turkey and threats of authoritarian populism in Europe and the United States, yet the world has never been more democratic. More than two-thirds of the world's people now live in democracies (Marshall et al., n.d.).

The list goes on. And yet what is made available to us on the daily news and elsewhere skews our impression. Information has become more accessible than ever, and a constant surge of doomsday coverage stalks us from across the globe, all at once, all the time, further exaggerated by clickbait headlines and polarized narratives. There is no avoiding it. Such "news" is projected on TVs everywhere you go, discussed on your favorite podcast, talked about on most social media platforms. It feeds the next bandwagon that everyone is on and which you will inevitably be confronted with, one way or another. Why wouldn't we reasonably assume the world is worse off than ever? We confuse what seems to be a proximal proliferation of economic, political, societal, environmental, and cultural deterioration brought to our attention with the proliferation of global information, misinformation, and sometimes, disinformation.

In other words, how much and how often we are exposed to a piece of mis/dis/information will determine the likelihood that our minds see it as truth. What further exacerbates availability bias is confirmation bias, which reaffirms our (mis)beliefs. The more one surrounds oneself with flat-earthers and reads about flat-earth "proof," the more likely they will be assured that the world is flat!

How do we circumvent anchoring, availability, and survivorship bias? By exposing ourselves to unfamiliar people, places, and practices offering opposing views that *broaden* cognizance of heuristics. Proactively consulting *the different* will flatten the bias and enable better-informed decisions. Of course, a Hard Problem may not offer you the leisure of time to gain these insights, so then what do we do?

A primary constituent of a healthy decision lies with *relevant experience*—what we will refer to as *Informed Perspectives*. Not what you hear from your partner in crime, your best friend, and certainly not your ragdoll cat whom you've named Experience. These people (and cat) may have your best interests at heart (maybe not your cat), but if they or someone they're closely attuned with were never faced with the same dilemmas you have (with similar contextual considerations) and lived to tell the tale, their opinions and instruction will have little to offer (especially your cat's). Unwarranted confirmation bias, white lies, and uninformed guidance serve little to no purpose for what we are seeking achieve. Rest assured, whatever you're experiencing, whatever decision you're having to make, is almost certainly not unique to you. Given the hyperconnectivity that comes with twenty-first-century tech and the general abundance of support nets available, you will find someone in your effort to attain the wisdom you need who has been-there-done-that.

Bigger decisions require more Informed Perspectives. Each source of insight would reflect their own gut feel, risk versus reward, and post-decision analysis. This suggests the following:

▲ **Know what questions to ask when consulting these individuals. Circumstances differ, but we will know how much to rely on the advice of those with an Informed Perspective depending on how relatable their situation was. Some questions to ask:**

> ▽ What was your gut telling you and why?
>
> ▽ What did you think there was to gain and lose?
>
> ▽ What did you end up gaining and losing?
>
> ▽ Who did you consult with to help reach a verdict? Did it help?
>
> ▽ Did the decision lead you toward a more fulfilling life?
>
> ▽ What would you have done differently knowing what you know now?

▲ **Refine your pros and cons into "absolutes" by cross-checking the veracity of your assumptions with what the Informed Perspectives had to offer.**

While intuition may only account for some of the insights you consider, you sure as hell will have less of a reason to regret a decision you make once you gain input from a diverse set of experienced individuals. Now onward to the third and final pillar!

3. ~~Emotion~~ SAAC (Self-Actualization Auxiliary Coefficient)— The Heart

While there is no doubting the influence of emotion when making a decision, a Hard Problem necessitating a decision *cannot* hinge upon hedonistic temptations or ill-informed desires.

To further emphasize the impact of emotion on decision-making, not only do expectation gaps skew our perception of what it would take to make us happy but emotions triggered by one event can spill over and affect other, unrelated situations. Studies have shown that they produce a prior that can completely influence judgment and perception in irrational ways (Wiltermuth and Tiedens, 2011; Lerner et al., 2015). For example, in a study conducted by behavioral economist Francesca Gino and professor of operations and information management Maurice E. Schweitzer (2008), a group of participants were asked to estimate the weight of a person based only on a picture and would be paid for the accuracy of their guess. They were then asked to watch a short video. Some watched a clip of a young man being bullied (which was found to make people angry in a pilot test); the rest watched a National Geographic special regarding the Great Barrier Reef. All participants were then given "another participant's" estimate—which were in fact values close to the true number the researchers had slyly predetermined—and asked whether they wanted to revise their initial guess. Only 26% of those who watched the young man being bullied trusted the estimate they received and adjusted their own accordingly, which led to greater accuracy in their judgment (a matter to be mindful of when consulting Informed Perspectives.) How much credence, then, should we give to our feelings when drawing judgment or making a decision or what we passionately desire in the moment?

Plato encouraged us to subject our ideas to examination rather than acting on impulse. He compares our feelings to being dangerously pulled along by a group of wild horses and advises Socratic Discussion (a constructive and cooperative *argumentative* dialogue) with yourself or another. Through questioning the fragilities of our minds, ancient Greek sceptics recommended that we develop an attitude of what they called *epoché*, translated as "reserve" or "suspension of judgment": being aware of our proclivities to error, never rushing into decisions, letting ideas settle and then reevaluating them at different points in time. Recall Richard Feynman's precept advice: "The First Principle is you must not fool yourself. And you are the easiest person to fool."

Upon confronting a Hard Problem, one must accept the certainty of emotional priors and the potential for misguided desires. Rest assured, though, we are not disregarding emotion or individualistic desires altogether but focusing on the one constant we are certain of: the desire to Self-Actualize, which necessarily involves emotional well-being. Assume that whatever is leading you toward this aspiration will be found on numerous paths, some of which you may know to be enjoyable and others which are not. You wouldn't be pursuing Self-Actualizing actions if you weren't in touch with your motives. Therefore, assume that any decision being made is always in favor of what propels you toward Self-Actualization and thus worth any compromise. To put it more plainly, as long as

Self-Actualizing motives are involved, whatever the outcome of action you take to a Hard Problem will lead you in the general direction you desire—and this, you will find, is always enough.

Unfortunately, many have yet to realize what is worth compromising for, which is why this third pillar—the Heart—was coined SAAC (Self-Actualization Auxiliary Coefficient). Committing to a decision that *supports* your quest for Self-Actualization (by any means, to proliferate opportunities to cultivate challenge, epiphanies, or serendipity), whether, for example, by freeing yourself of restrictive people, places, or practices, or by gaining the freedom to amass diverse experiences, void of a matter worth compromise, should be weighed as *equally* valuable as another's decision toward what they have found to be a matter worth compromise. In other words, if one has nothing to lose, one ought to favor a decision that maximizes freedom of choice *and* exposure to diverse opportunities. We refer to anything else as *Less Permitting*.

This coefficient refers to the means by which we construct our baseline of refined pros and cons. The SAAC compels us to exploit the learnings of loss aversion and populate our cons list with at least twice as many forfeitures of what acting against Self-Actualization would lead to. While it may sound like a trivial number derived from Tversky and Kahneman's contributions, it still bears weight we ought to leverage. It should not be misconstrued with the profundity of the "heart's deliberations" but seen as an effort to rebalance our biased scale to a *sufficient* degree and test bounded rationality. In other words, if we can't be perfectly rational, given what we know of our human limitations, we can try to be *reasonable*.

Staying true to our empirically substantiated initiative, we will now take our understanding and insights of regret, grief, the three pillars of conviction, credible decision-making approaches, and the Quasi-Chaotic View and formulate a truly informed model from which to reliably draw Self-Actualizing decisions, void of regret, with minimal grief!

CHAPTER 28
THE QUASI-CHAOTIC
DECISION-MAKING MODEL

Change—real change—implies decision-making. The fact of the matter is, we always have options; we just don't know it. As the saying goes, "Our lives are the sum total of all the decisions we have made," and I will go further and add *and haven't made.* Many never decide, never change, and unsurprisingly, never realize their full potential.

Time and time again we meet those who are stagnant, going through the motions, dead from within, so to speak. What led them down that precarious path to their demise is in the past. What is most worrying is their certain belief of impending doom, a future in which change seems stranger than fiction. Taking a stand and *deciding* to break out of despair and/or inactivity becomes an impossibility that very few manage without costly external assistance. Overcoming this seeming impossibility is, of course, contingent on a particular attitude, one that relies on "deliberate Suffering." How quickly we regain autonomy and control depends on *how* one is reminded of why one suffers. The Quasi-Chaotic Decision-Making Model not only expedites this transition but prepares our next act with the diligence needed to see a Self-Actualizing decision through, for we now know better than to act out of desperation.

In light of the Quasi-Chaotic View, we will now construct what we'll be referring to as the *Receipt of Sufficient Consideration,* or RSC for short. As previously mentioned, voiding regret necessitates acceptance—accepting that there is only so much information, thought, time, and effort one can commit when considering a course of action. A visual record of our best effort to invest in making a Self-Actualizing decision—an RSC—will serve as a conduit of reassurance. At the same time, voiding regret does not exculpate us of lingering grief and its corrosive outgrowth—exacerbating postdecisional dissonance and overwhelming the cognitive adjustments we make to relieve the discomfort of loss, often leading to what-could-have-been regret. Which is why the RSC is also composed of affirming directives to action, serving as a bulwark against regressive cognitive inclinations.

The Quasi-Chaotic Decision-Making Model involves three stages, each with a defined purpose:

1. **REALIZING THE DECISION:** WHERE WE CONSTRUCT THE RSC TO

   ▽ Thwart cognitive biases

   ▽ Negate emotional baggage

   ▽ Prioritize Self-Actualizing motives

   ▽ Extend our intellective reach

2. **ACTING ON THE DECISION:** WHERE WE ACTION THE RSC'S VERDICT AND

   ▽ Prepare a plan of action to blunt negative collateral

   ▽ Overcome hesitation

3. **LIVING WITH THE DECISION:** WHERE WE ACTION THE RSC'S AFFIRMING DIRECTIVES TO

   ▽ Minimize grief

   ▽ Void postdecisional dissonance and regret and bridge the could-have-been-gap

Staying true to the practicality of the *Necessitating Change* narrative, I will apply the model to a dilemma many of us have faced or may yet face: moving out of our parents' house and living independently. In this exercise, you have identified that remaining there has been unbearably aggravating and is limiting your Self-Actualizing efforts.

To elucidate the model's application, we'll be making the following assumptions and disregarding a lot of contextual consideration, at least for now:

▲ Identifying the matter as a Hard Problem suggests it is already a trigger for change.

▲ Consciously deciding to lose (something) in order to gain.

▲ Prioritizing self-interest, prioritizing Self-Actualization.

▲ The decision to move out comes at an age (seventeen) considered to be abnormally early within the community we reside in; the norm is to remain at home.

▲ Holding you back is gut instinct: fear of regret, failure, abandonment, guilt, and so on.

We press on.

STAGE 1: REALIZING A DECISION

So, what pathways are we comparing? The truth is, there is only one path— *through* the Hard Problem. The alternative is not working through it (whether by inaction, compromise, or circumvention), but that's a decision—or an indecision—more likely to be regrettable.

The RSC we construct in Stage 1 consists of four steps:

1. **Write out what you are contemplating in favor of inaction.**

   (In this example, it is staying at your parent's house despite the intolerance)

   While counterintuitive, and while we assume moving out is the right decision to make, we favor loss aversion by flipping the narrative around. (See figure 6-1.)

STAYING AT PARENTS HOUSE

Figure 6-1: RSC: realizing a decision—step 1: Spelling out inaction

2. **List all the advantages of inaction (the pros).**

   Think of all the reasons that compel you to stay right where you are. You're not paying rent, laundry and food are taken care of, you won't have to work as many shifts to afford rent if you decide to stay, and perhaps there's a sense of belonging.

STAYING AT PARENTS HOUSE

PROS	CONS
1. DON'T HAVE TO PAY RENT	
2. CAN SAVE UP EXTRA CASH FOR SAVINGS	
3. LAUNDRY TAKEN CARE OF	
4. MUM TAKES CARE OF COOKING	
5. I WON'T HAVE TO DEAL WITH WORKING LONGER HOURS	
6. IT'S A NICE HOUSE, I WONT BE ABLE TO AFFORD ACCOMODATION THIS GOOD.	

Figure 6-2: RSC: realizing a decision—step 2: Listing advantages of inaction

3. **List all the disadvantages of inaction (the cons); include the advantages of action—at least twice as many as the advantages of inaction.**

Since the norm is inaction and gut instinct compels us to avoid loss, this counterintuitive approach is exactly that: to counter the intuitive. We will exploit what we learned from loss aversion and reappraise the situation to make explicit all there is to lose—anything relevant that would catalyze your quest for Self-Actualization—should we side with inaction. (See figure 6-2.) Amassing a list of negative priors serves as a trigger for change and minimizes chances of regret.

For example, what would have been, "I'll be able to invite my friends or crush over," becomes, "I'll never be able to invite my friends or crush over out of embarrassment" in remaining where you are and thus siding against Self-Actualization.

This list may take some time to build; it's often easier to own your cognitive adjustments. Whatever shortcomings you've been attempting to justify would be appropriate to add to the list. What's been stopping you from pursuing Self-Actualization? Dig deep and question why you feel the way you do. Do you fear independence? If so, why? Is it too easy at Camp Comfort? What's so appealing about the house you presently live in that you wouldn't be able to get from an affordable replacement? Where does your shame stem from? Why do you fear judgment? Recall the lessons in Incessant Distraction. What underlying pain are you avoiding by staying? Are you staying out of laziness? Is it *really* because you're lazy? The SAAC (Self-Actualization Auxiliary Coefficient) compels us to ideate everything that would arise—including potential opportunities—from a change of environment, such as the new people and practices whose discovery would have otherwise not have been possible.

STAYING AT PARENTS HOUSE

PROS	CONS
1. DON'T HAVE TO PAY RENT	1. I'LL ALWAYS BEAR THE SHAME OF LIVING IN MY PARENTS' HOUSE
2. CAN SAVE UP EXTRA CASH FOR SAVINGS	2. I'LL ALWAYS BE A DISAPPOINTMENT TO MY PARENTS
3. LAUNDRY TAKEN CARE OF	3. MY MOM WILL NEVER BE ABLE TO TURN MY ROOM INTO A KNITTING ROOM FOR HER TO ENJOY
4. MUM TAKES CARE OF COOKING	4. I'LL NEVER BE ABLE TO INVITE MY FRIENDS OVER OR MY CRUSH OUT OF EMBARRASSMENT
5. I WON'T HAVE TO DEAL WITH WORKING LONGER HOURS	5. I'LL ALWAYS FEEL BAD FOR USING UP HOUSEHOLD AMENITIES
6. IT'S A NICE HOUSE, I WONT BE ABLE TO AFFORD ACCOMODATION THIS GOOD.	6. I'LL NEVER BE ABLE TO COME BACK HOME LATE AS IT WOULD WAKE UP MY PARENTS
	7. I'LL NEVER FEEL INDEPENDENT
	8. I'LL NEVER GET A CHANCE TO FIND A PLACE WITH A GOOD AND DIVERSE SUPPORT GROUP
	9. I'LL ALWAYS FEEL LIKE SOMEONE'S LOOKING OVER MY SHOULDER, JUDGING ME
	10. I'LL NEVER HAVE COMPLETE PRIVACY
	11. I'LL ALWAYS HAVE TO PUT UP WITH MY DAD'S BICKERING THAT ALWAYS SEEMS TO BUM ME DOWN
	12. I'LL ALWAYS HAVE TO TIP-TOE AROUND THE HOUSE WHENEVER MY PARENTS INVITE GUESTS OVER
	13. I'LL ALWAYS HAVE TO PUT UP WITH MY MOM'S SOUL-CRUSHING PASSIVE AGGRESSIVENESS

Figure 6-3: RSC: realizing a decision—step 3:
Listing twice as many disadvantages of inaction

4. **Consult Informed Perspectives and verify your lists. Amend, modify, and/or remove entries that are unlikely based on *their* experience and how relatable it is and record their initials after each modification; this will serve as a seal of approval. Don't make a decision until you consult at least two Informed Perspectives to thwart risk of anchoring bias, especially when you have limited experience in the matter.**

J.H. was shocked to hear you don't pay for rent, food, or any household expenses. He shared the story of his own upbringing and the pain his parents had to endure that provoked a sense of guilt. M.T., your best friend's dad, shared his story of how it was difficult getting kicked out of his home at fourteen back in the day and how it ultimately led him on a serendipitous journey. C.S., your high school janitor, explained how the comfort and privilege of his parents' house compelled Incessant Distraction from the shame that lingered. T.C., the high school teacher you kept in touch with, corrected your impression of what seemed to be parental regret. She shared her story of having to put up with her own sons' resistance to independence. She was disappointed in herself for not having the time to raise children that were capable and willing to seek independence themselves. After openly asking her how she felt about them staying home, her kids were taken aback when she said, "Your dad and I don't want you to leave! Why would you say that? We're not disappointed in you; we are disappointed with ourselves because you're always upset, and we feel like we're to blame!" (See figure 6-4.)

STAYING AT PARENTS HOUSE

PROS	CONS
JH 1. DON'T HAVE TO PAY RENT	1. I'LL ALWAYS BEAR THE SHAME OF LIVING IN MY PARENTS' HOUSE
2. CAN SAVE UP EXTRA CASH FOR SAVINGS	2. I'LL ALWAYS BE A DISAPPOINTMENT TO MY PARENTS
3. LAUNDRY TAKEN CARE OF	3. MY MOM WILL NEVER BE ABLE TO TURN MY ROOM INTO A KNITTING ROOM FOR HER TO ENJOY
4. MUM TAKES CARE OF COOKING	4. I'LL NEVER BE ABLE TO INVITE MY FRIENDS OVER OR MY CRUSH OUT OF EMBARRASSMENT
5. I WON'T HAVE TO DEAL WITH WORKING LONGER HOURS	5. I'LL ALWAYS FEEL BAD FOR USING UP HOUSEHOLD AMENITIES
6. IT'S A NICE HOUSE, I WONT BE ABLE TO AFFORD ACCOMODATION THIS GOOD.	6. I'LL EVER BE ABLE TO COME BACK HOME LATE...
	7. I'LL NEVER FEEL INDEPENDENT
	8. I'LL NEVER GET A CHANCE TO FIND A PLACE WITH A GOOD AND DIVERSE SUPPORT GROUP
	9. I'LL ALWAYS FEEL LIKE SOMEONE'S LOOKING OVER MY SHOULDER, JUDGING ME
	10. I'LL NEVER HAVE COMPLETE PRIVACY
	11. I'LL ALWAYS HAVE TO PUT UP WITH MY DAD'S BICKERING THAT ALWAYS SEEMS TO BUM ME DOWN
	12. I'LL ALWAYS HAVE TO TIP-TOE AROUND THE HOUSE WHENEVER MY PARENTS INVITE GUESTS OVER
	13. I'LL ALWAYS HAVE TO PUT UP WITH MY MOM'S SOUL-CRUSHING PASSIVE AGGRESSIVENESS
	TC. MY SOCIAL LIFE WILL ALWAYS BE LIMITED GIVEN THE OPPORTUNITIES THAT LIVING WITH ROOMMATES WOULD OFFER
	MT. I'LL NEVER EXPERIENCE THE FREEDOM AND MOTIVATION OF HAVING TO LIVE SELF-SUFFICIENTLY
	CS. I'LL ALWAYS FEEL COMPELLED TO DISTRACT MYSELF WITH UNPRODUCTIVE ACTIVITIES BECAUSE OF MY SHAME

> TC. MY PARENTS WILL ALWAYS FEEL DISAPPOINTED IN THEMSELVES

Figure 6-4: RSC: realizing a decision—step 4:
Amending lists with Informed Perspectives' insights

The hairier the decision, the more likely the chance you gravitate toward irrational and illogical assertions. How certain are you of the claims you are listing? This is when you would need to dedicate more time to seeking out more Informed Perspectives.

> ### What can be asserted without evidence can also be dismissed without evidence.
>
> —Christopher Hitchens, *God Is Not Great: How Religion Poisons Everything*

There will be times when discussions with Informed Perspectives reveal gaps of knowledge you ought to bridge through further action (whether it be additional conversation or further exploration of a place or practice). You may also come to realize that you've been viewing the situation through a skewed lens that is worth correcting before concluding that you've made the best decision your iron triangle permits.

Just because your heart, gut, or mind becomes fixated on something doesn't mean you need not question it. Don't let your predisposed prejudices and preferences influence a decision entirely, but do listen to what they have to say. Question long-term commitments without short-term experience and give weight to these impulses accordingly. Understanding the dynamic nature of our intuition may give you the reassurance you need to reconsider. That is to say, dissecting all that influences a decision, whether it be emotions, extraneous influences, or cognitive biases, and utilizing a robust and consistent model of decision-making will cultivate the confidence you need to *move* on in favor of what's best for you—Self-Actualization. And with that, your RSC is ready!

STAGE 2: ACTING ON A DECISION

You will be faced with decisions that may flip your life upside down, decisions that may result in cutting out what you have relied on for years, decisions that make the hair on the back of your neck stand stiff. I'm referring to outcomes like:

▲ Severing long relationships and dealing with the aftermath
▲ Quitting work, updating your resume, and grinding interviews again
▲ Going back on promises

You may feel selfish, coarse, and even heartless at times, but the key imperative for any of this to work is that the actions you commit to are *nonnegotiable*. The process of thought and time you devoted to realizing a decision will lead to a plan that must be followed—to do otherwise is to live in bad faith. Any potential transgression is diminished through verified consideration and assertive conviction. What needs to be done for you to move on, to hoist yourself out of the remorseless pit you may have found yourself in, is now crystal clear. All that's left to do is to act on it.

You may be asking, "How? How do you expect me to turn my back on my parents who have raised me? They have nothing else to do but care for me." Simple. You just do it. The fact of the matter is that as long as negative influences control your life, whether it's the place, the people, or the practices, you will *never* find the change you seek. Would you rather continue the arduous, endlessly stagnating path you are on, or grit your teeth, endure the loss, and make the best decision for yourself? It should come as no surprise that a seemingly self-focused decision can turn *your* life around, but the chaotic and serendipitous nature of complex adaptive systems can often bring about positive consequences to agents other than yourself. For example, accepting an abusive relationship and offering unconditional support no matter the cost deprives the other person of critical realizations they might draw from their Suffering if you leave. You may very well be the lifeline preventing a tilting of their "forces against change" toward their "forces for change"!

Such reasoning may still not be enough for some of us. You may hesitate to take action because of one or more of the following:

▲ FEAR

If you're afraid of potential strife or inciting turbulence, I suggest you avoid making big decisions until you are better accustomed to facing the unknown and are more confident with your conflict resolution abilities. As always, practice makes perfect, and if you've had little to no experience in working through Hard Problems, confronting individuals, letting go of old practices, or leaving familiar places behind, it's very likely your anxiety is the result of inexperience.

If you start with smaller changes and decisions, you will feel more comfortable making bigger decisions when you realize that change isn't all that bad. That one severed relationship (a friend as opposed to a best friend, partner, or family member) turned out okay, and when you moved out of the house, it surprisingly nudged your parents to take on new hobbies! Moving in with a group of productive and positive individuals encouraged you to be more proactive and sociable. You were able to navigate through the hardships and still visit your parents from time to time. Oh, how proud they've become! Familiarize yourself with uncertainty before you jump into the deep end. Like any diver, you need to decompress before you dive deeper!

Rest assured, there are tools and mechanisms we have yet to explore that will offer practical conflict resolution instruction to minimize collateral effects and guide you through such fears.

▲ GUILT

The difference between guilt and regret is that guilt is felt when we intentionally do something we know is ethically or morally wrong, whereas regret is felt after looking back on an action and feeling we should or could have done something differently—not knowing at the time we were doing something "wrong."

If you have given your RSC sufficient consideration, we can assert the following:

1. You've made an informed decision, the best you could have made given the information you were able to gather, which you have done to the best of your abilities. This comes with the assumption that

Informed Perspectives were consulted and the majority pointed in a particular direction.

2. You have realized that what you are addressing is a Hard Problem and that you must lose in order to gain.

Guilt is a powerful emotion that is difficult to entirely mitigate. Use it as a lesson to motivate better decision-making in the future, to understand the repercussions of poor decision-making, and to set measures in place to avoid misguided decisions from happening again. My old man once said, "We all make mistakes. We are human. We must make mistakes if we are to grow. Most of the time we have no choice but to make the mistake, and so it's not our fault, even if it is. But it's when we make the same mistake again that we have ourselves to blame."

And if all else fails: if you find yourself inexperienced; if you haven't been able to overcome fear or guilt; if you happen to be prevention-focused, introverted, and unopen to experience—then you know very well your last resort awaits you—Suffering. You are change capable, if you've read this far, one assumes you are *Change Receptive*, yet you remain change resistant. Your RSC will catalyze the transfer of influence from "forces against change" to "forces for change" by demonstrating *on a daily basis* that you are in control, that you *can* leave a space that has been provoking grief or shame, limiting your liberty and impeding your quest for Self-Actualization.

Referring back to the case we began with, you have realized and verified a decision, and it's time to act. Engage your parents, face to face, with your RSC, and explain how much there is to lose if you don't move. Tell them what your Informed Perspectives had to say and share their stories. You'll still visit, and they can now focus on taking on change for themselves! You'll give yourself a month to pack, find a shared flat, and ask for more shifts at work—all of which you will reassess once you've settled in. It may be a difficult pill to swallow, but you must do what is best for you, your future selves, and the future of others, in this case, your parents'—given that your well-being influences theirs (and theirs yours).

STAYING AT PARENTS HOUSE

PROS	CONS
JH 1. DON'T HAVE TO PAY RENT	1. I'LL ALWAYS BEAR THE SHAME OF LIVING IN MY PARENTS' HOUSE
2. CAN SAVE UP EXTRA CASH FOR SAVINGS	2. I'LL ALWAYS BE A DISAPPOINTMENT TO MY PARENTS
3. LAUNDRY TAKEN CARE OF	3. MY MOM WILL NEVER BE ABLE TO TURN MY ROOM INTO A KNITTING ROOM FOR HER TO ENJOY
4. MUM TAKES CARE OF COOKING	4. I'LL NEVER BE ABLE TO INVITE MY FRIENDS OVER OR MY CRUSH OUT OF EMBARRASSMENT
5. I WON'T HAVE TO DEAL WITH WORKING LONGER HOURS	5. I'LL ALWAYS FEEL BAD FOR USING UP HOUSEHOLD AMENITIES
6. IT'S A NICE HOUSE, I WON'T BE ABLE TO AFFORD ACCOMODATION THIS GOOD.	6. I'LL EVER BE ABLE TO COME BACK HOME LATE...
	7. I'LL NEVER FEEL INDEPENDENT
	8. I'LL NEVER GET A CHANCE TO FIND A PLACE WITH A GOOD AND DIVERSE SUPPORT GROUP
	9. I'LL ALWAYS FEEL LIKE SOMEONE'S LOOKING OVER MY SHOULDER, JUDGING ME
	10. I'LL NEVER HAVE COMPLETE PRIVACY
	11. I'LL ALWAYS HAVE TO PUT UP WITH MY DAD'S BICKERING THAT ALWAYS SEEMS TO BUM ME DOWN
	12. I'LL ALWAYS HAVE TO TIP-TOE AROUND THE HOUSE WHENEVER MY PARENTS INVITE GUESTS OVER
	13. I'LL ALWAYS HAVE TO PUT UP WITH MY MOM'S SOUL-CRUSHING PASSIVE AGGRESSIVENESS
	TC. MY SOCIAL LIFE WILL ALWAYS BE LIMITED GIVEN THE OPPORTUNITIES THAT LIVING WITH ROOMMATES WOULD OFFER
	MT. I'LL NEVER EXPERIENCE THE FREEDOM AND MOTIVATION OF HAVING TO LIVE SELF-SUFFICIENTLY
	CS. I'LL ALWAYS FEEL COMPELLED TO DISTRACT MYSELF WITH UNPRODUCTIVE ACTIVITIES BECAUSE OF MY SHAME

TC. MY PARENTS WILL ALWAYS FEEL DISAPPOINTED IN THEMSELVES

It may not be as easy a conversation for some of us, but rest assured, in Part VII: Execution, I demonstrate three practical applications of the Quasi-Chaotic Lifestyle that apply to such situations. How to enact your decisions will be elaborated on and exemplified using varying personas in dire circumstances with contextual and personality differences. For now, appreciate the versatility of an RSC, whether it's for realizing a decision, acting on it, or living with it!

Figure 6-5: RSC: acting on a decision

Now that we have acted on the decision and done what is assuredly Self-Actualizing, there is no turning back. You can now proceed to cross out the left column! (See figure 6-5.) The focus now shifts to newfound, actionable, affirming directives. All that's left is to live with the best decision there was to make!

STAGE 3: LIVING WITH A DECISION

The criticism expressed earlier in the book about the innumerable self-proclaimed life coaches, influencers, and motivational hoo-hahs arises once more. They would have you *generally think* about what means the most to you and what changes you seek, urging you to follow your dreams, pursue your goals or your heart or your gut instincts when it comes to making a rational decision, and then taking action, all effortlessly, without pushback. Nonsense, *expect pushback*. The banal impracticality of such wishy-washy encouragements sounds good at face value, but conveniently leaves out that what prevents most people from pursuing their heart's desires often necessitates some form of moral dispossession, heresy, going against the grain, giving up long-term commitments, or contending with family values, just to name a few! Such rah-rah narratives are not only useless but pernicious, further expanding the gap between one's imagination when attempting change and the slamming reality of norms, consequence, and conflict. One must expect natural transgressions provoked by grief and postdecisional dissonance.

How do we mitigate our cognitive inclinations—inclinations that induce grief, grief that exacerbates postdecisional dissonance? By revisiting our RSCs regularly, hanging them prominently in front of us so they will be clear as day, reading them out loud, and consulting our Informed Perspectives once more to support our efforts to realize and act on the best possible Self-Actualizing decisions we can make. Any attempt to revise or reconsider is trivialized as the facts are evident and the uncertainties are unveiled. Anything other than a wholehearted commitment would be a conscious step backward. This is the cornerstone to suppressing regret. What comes of subsequent events are out of our control, so the point is to be confident about the *method* and not the outcome.

It is assumed that what gives rise to a Hard Problem (consequently necessitating an RSC) restricts our ability to become truly Self-Actualized and realize the benefit from any negative influence. With that said, not acting on a decision can also facilitate opportunity (such as learning to deal with mom's passive-aggressive behavior, growing thicker skin to be immune to judgment, building character, and so on.) However, in the grand scheme of things, we know to refer to such a trade off as Less Permitting.

Ultimately, how a decision sits with you matters the most. Whether the final outcome is for better or worse, how a decision is perceived—how close you get to *equanimity*—makes all the difference. Reappraising what doesn't go your way as "At least I can say I gave it my best" instead of "I knew I shouldn't have listened to Karen!" can mean the difference between bitter regret and sanguinity. In other words, how we respond to the aftermath of a decision; how we *feel* about it on the day we made it, a week after, or a year later; and how we capitalize on the change we have afforded ourselves with is just as important as making the decision itself.

And thus we have the two ingredients of the remedy to living with a Self-Actualizing decision: *acceptance* and *action*.

What remains is to act on and manifest the newfound opportunities that arise from making the hard decision. Wallowing in what we have lost will paralyze our ability to move on, which is precisely why we shift our attention to what has been permitted (all that is listed under the right column) and fulfill those opportunities—realizing and celebrating all there was to gain. We cross out each opportunity we act on and keep doing so until we have crossed out twice as many opportunities as there were benefits of inaction. We must gain, at the very least, twice as much as we have lost.

We'll throw a party and invite our friends and our crush. We'll make full use of our new kitchen and iterate through new recipes. We'll go out on binges and return home at odd hours. We'll get to know our new roommates. We'll meet their friends and socialize. We'll help our parents set up the new knitting room. We'll walk with pride of independence. We are manifesting the change that our decision permitted.

A shared flat of four and two more days at the café. I can manage that. I'll make it work! The sheer excitement of change that comes with moving in the right direction is stimulating. You're on our own now, there's no turning back. Oh boy, what's next? Where do I even start!

STAYING AT PARENTS HOUSE

PROS	**CONS**

JH

PROS

1. DON'T HAVE TO PAY RENT
2. CAN SAVE UP EXTRA CASH FOR SAVINGS
3. LAUNDRY TAKEN CARE OF
4. MUM TAKES CARE OF COOKING
5. I WON'T HAVE TO DEAL WITH WORKING LONGER HOURS
6. IT'S A NICE HOUSE, I WONT BE ABLE TO AFFORD ACCOMODATION THIS GOOD.

CONS

1. I'LL ALWAYS BEAR THE SHAME OF LIVING IN MY PARENTS' HOUSE
2. I'LL ALWAYS BE A DISAPPOINTMENT TO MY PARENTS
3. MY MOM WILL NEVER BE ABLE TO TURN MY ROOM INTO A KNITTING ROOM FOR HER TO ENJOY
4. I'LL NEVER BE ABLE TO INVITE MY FRIENDS OVER OR MY CRUSH OUT OF EMBARRASSMENT
5. I'LL ALWAYS FEEL BAD FOR USING UP HOUSEHOLD AMENITIES
6. I'LL EVER BE ABLE TO COME BACK HOME LATE...
7. I'LL NEVER FEEL INDEPENDENT
8. I'LL NEVER GET A CHANCE TO FIND A PLACE WITH A GOOD AND DIVERSE SUPPORT GROUP
9. I'LL ALWAYS FEEL LIKE SOMEONE'S LOOKING OVER MY SHOULDER, JUDGING ME
10. I'LL NEVER HAVE COMPLETE PRIVACY
11. I'LL ALWAYS HAVE TO PUT UP WITH MY DAD'S BICKERING THAT ALWAYS SEEMS TO BUM ME DOWN
12. I'LL ALWAYS HAVE TO TIP-TOE AROUND THE HOUSE WHENEVER MY PARENTS INVITE GUESTS OVER
13. I'LL ALWAYS HAVE TO PUT UP WITH MY MOM'S SOUL-CRUSHING PASSIVE AGGRESSIVENESS
TC. MY SOCIAL LIFE WILL ALWAYS BE LIMITED GIVEN THE OPPORTUNITIES THAT LIVING WITH ROOMMATES WOULD OFFER
MT. I'LL NEVER EXPERIENCE THE FREEDOM AND MOTIVATION OF HAVING TO LIVE SELF-SUFFICIENTLY
CS. I'LL ALWAYS FEEL COMPELLED TO DISTRACT MYSELF WITH UNPRODUCTIVE ACTIVITIES BECAUSE OF MY SHAME

TC.
MY PARENTS WILL ALWAYS FEEL DISAPPOINTED IN THEMSELVES

Figure 6-6: RSC: living with a decision

Once the SAAC coefficient reaches a factor of two—once you have crossed off twice as many cons as pros—you should find yourself liberated from the emotional burden of the decision you've made. If not, keep going until the urge to retrace your steps dies out, until the recursive infinite loop to reunite with a broken attachment is interrupted. Make it your mission to cross off every last item! You'll be able to talk about what you acted on, hear about it, even confront what was lost without the discomfort that would otherwise seem to linger. Once you're satisfied that you have successfully lived with the decision you've made, cross out the right column to signify triumph. (See figure 6-6.)

And, most importantly, you will reflect about what took place, how it came to be, and how to avoid similar dilemmas in the future while recognizing, capitalizing, and improving on what you have learned about yourself. If you take this step seriously, with honesty and conviction, you will have realized intrinsic growth, taking you one step closer toward becoming Self-Actualized!

And with that, you are now equipped with a Quasi-Chaotic Decision-Making Model fine-tuned to facilitate your overcoming of big, hairy, Hard Problems. Congratulations!

PREQUEL TO PART VII:

EXECUTION

We have now equipped ourselves with the cognitive, behavioral, emotional, and intellectual attitudes, tools, and truths to engage the adoption of a Quasi-Chaotic Lifestyle. However, before we proceed, another intermission is called for.

I now speak directly to you, reader. Yes, you.

I KNOW WHAT YOU MAY BE THINKING:

▲ You've read this far and may not be so convinced as to have become invigorated with impatience and zeal for what a life of change has to offer.

▲ You've been inspired by an idea or two and may ruminate over them in the coming weeks.

▲ You may have decided to give it the old college try, and for that I commend you.

Regardless, I want to make this next point explicitly clear, and if you could hear me, I am beginning the following sentence with an audible throat-clearing:

I will not have you think for a second that anything I imply in this book will miraculously exculpate you from your woes, relieve you of strong impulses to capitulate to social expectation or be a slave to extrinsic motives, or heal the pain of judgment and self-flagellation you may have faced. You've been raised and have lived to think, feel, and conduct yourself in ways you had no choice in but perceived to be the only reality. We can sift through all the literature of the sciences and review and contrast what worked for whom and why, but we will remain right where we are, with what we have, surrounded by who we know, in a place we've grown all too familiar with. The fact of the matter is, facts don't matter.

A group of undergraduates were invited to take part in a study about suicide (Ross et al., 1975). They were presented with pairs of suicide notes where one had been composed by a random individual, the other by a person who had subsequently taken their own life. The students were asked to distinguish between the fake and genuine ones. After making their judgments, the students were connected to electrodes and given feedback. Some were told they had a genius for the task, identifying twenty-four out of twenty-five pairs correctly. Others were told they only identified a few correctly.

As you would expect from psychological research, the entire study was a setup. Although half the notes were indeed genuine and obtained from the Los Angeles County coroner's office, the scores given to the students were fictitious. The truth is that all participants performed, on average, very much the same.

In the second phase of the study, the researchers revealed the deception and told participants that the point of the experiment was to gauge their physiological responses to *thinking* they were right or wrong (which is, in fact, a double bluff—those pesky psychologists). The students were then asked to estimate how many suicide notes they had categorized correctly and how much the average student would get right. Well, the high-scoring group said that they had, in fact, done very well—much better than the average student—even though *they had just been told they there was no basis for such a belief.* Conversely, the low-scoring group thought the opposite. "Once formed," the researchers observed wryly, "impressions are remarkably perseverant."

Again, the facts don't matter. Whatever it is you are waiting for, whatever answer you or your future self may be searching for, whatever change you are longing for, will and can only begin with *action*. True change—a change of circumstance, a change of pathways, a change of trajectory, a change of belief, of values, of behaviors, of attitudes, of traits, of heart, of scenery, of whatever—true change *begins and ends with action.*

The real value of *Necessitating Change* is therefore *not* in any of its empirical insights, revealed truths, or clever cross-disciplinary connections. Indeed, you may be tempted to overlook them anyway and proceed with what you've been telling yourself to be "good enough." The value to gain from *Necessitating Change* is actually in the pages to come—the practical guide to Self-Actualization: *the method of continuous action* that incorporates all the theory, so that you don't have to think or worry about it. You will find an easy-to-follow, step-by-step approach so you don't have to make it up as you go. It offers inclusivity, feasibility, and sustainability, so you don't have to grind through every step of the way.

But for any of what I am proposing to work, *you must follow through.* Referring back to the ketogenic analogy: you can't half-ass ketosis; you either are fat-adapted or not. If you are not fat-adapted, the ketogenic diet will not work. Similarly, you either are Change Adapted or not. If you are not Change Adapted, the Quasi-Chaotic Lifestyle will not work.

I won't sugarcoat the fact that becoming Change Adapted takes effort. You must be willing and ready to put in the time for any of this to work. Consider all there is to lose, all there is to gain, and take seriously the question prefacing Chapter 17: Suffer: *How bad do you want change?* If you don't have the clear-cut response you know to be the answer, you know what to do—Suffer. And yes, the first step is often the hardest. But much of the journey to adopting the practice is easier than you think, and once you are Change Adapted, sustaining a Quasi-Chaotic Lifestyle will feel like anything but work!

To reiterate: The process described in Part VII: Execution is designed to help you adopt the Quasi-Chaotic Lifestyle and must not be taken lightly. Breaking out of what we have grown to rely on and embarking on the transition toward Self-Actualization will require thought, effort, time, and action. You will be confronted with problems—Hard Problems—from which you will draw decisive conclusions that will shape the stepping stones of progress to come. Every realization, every lesson, every tool, and every multidimensional concept presented so far will come into play in the chapters to come. Once you are Change Receptive—and you will know when you are—proceed to liberty!

Now is the time we rise, together. Keep this book close—and closer in times of doubt. Now is the time to turn things around for good, to adopt a life of change and transform who you once were into who you are destined to be: the best version of *you.*

PART VII
EXECUTION
THE PRACTICE

CHAPTER 29
LEARNING BY EXAMPLE

We will now initiate the transition and adoption of a Quasi-Chaotic Lifestyle through three personas. Each one distinctive, the accounts of the three will encompass emblematic lifestyles at different stages in life with their own personal slew of complications, self-asserted limitations, and adversity.

1. **Mike:**

   Seventeen years old, out of shape, faces social anxiety, unable to admit interest to his high school crush, plays video games up to seven hours a day, falling behind academically, soon to graduate from high school but doesn't know what tertiary degree to pursue, bullied and teased, chronic procrastinator, culturally inept

2. **Andrew:**

   Twenty-eight years old, grew up in a restrictive household with an oppressive family, financially strained, smoker, facing an existential crisis, in an abusive relationship, envious of the successful, has not openly admitted his homosexuality to his conservative mother, has a tedious and repetitive part-time job, despises the tertiary degree he is pursuing

3. **Rachel:**

   Thirty-six years old, overweight, juggling work and two children (one of whom is particularly troublesome), unsupportive husband, dreams are dying, always wanted to pursue tertiary education but doesn't have the time, facing a midlife crisis, always running 200% 24/7, grapples with archaic management at work, in a social group that spoils her children, not a good listener

We will assume that all three of these hypothetical people have read through Necessitating Change and are seeking to adopt their version of a Quasi-Chaotic Lifestyle under the Quasi-Chaotic View.

These personas and their lives need not resemble you and your lifestyle exactly to be useful, so refer to the one you most resonate with—the one that offers relatable scenarios for reinforcing your comprehension and practical understanding of Quasi-Chaotic learnings, considerations, and tools. It is also worth mentioning that we will not cover every aspect of each persona's profile nor will each and every question, motif, and initiative they face be fleshed out. Feel free to assume what may be underlying reasons and eventual outcomes for what is not detailed comprehensively, based on what you have personally experienced and/or what you would expect to happen. After all, we have collectively grown all too familiar to one another, and worryingly predictable.

The structure of the following chapters and respective subsections will be as follows:

1. **Mike's initial lifestyle overview**

2. **Andrew's initial lifestyle overview**

3. **Rachel's initial lifestyle overview**

4. **Execution: Step 1 detailed**
   - ▽ Step 1 applied to Mike
   - ▽ Step 1 applied to Andrew
   - ▽ Step 1 applied to Rachel

5. **Execution: Step 2 detailed**
   - ▽ Step 2 applied to Mike
   - ▽ Step 2 applied to Andrew
   - ▽ Step 2 applied to Rachel

6. **And so on**

Should you choose to track only one persona's journey, there will be a sign for which page to skip to at the end of each step's description and the end of each respective persona's step application. Such an approach would allow you to digest a first run's bearings, enabling greater attention to detail as you go through the remaining persona journeys (as you would rewatching a movie, for example). Alternatively, reading through all three at once would deepen your focus on Quasi-Chaotic tools, methods, and exercises and their flexible use—which would interrupt your immersion with an individual's journey. I recommend the former, as immersing yourself in a familiar world and visualizing the traversal of a difficult situation into liberty will give you the confidence you need to commit, but of course, do what you think works best for you! Either way, I encourage you to eventually read the accounts of all three personas as each offers challenges that fall within a genre of issues that may be relevant to you and your understanding of the process's holistic application.

Pay close attention to the connotational narrative your imagination defaults to as you immerse yourself into the worlds of Mike, Andrew, and Rachel. Remain wary of the lens through which you interpret their trials and tribulations, the good and bad actors involved, and how scenarios play out. If you sense underlying skepticism, cynicism, or pessimism, I suggest you read on, because all is not as it seems; the chaotic nature of the complex adaptive system that is life is facetiously and deceptively unpredictable.

Be sure to refamiliarize yourself (as needed) with the process from beginning to end before attempting to adopt the Quasi-Chaotic Lifestyle. References to tools, concepts, and frameworks detailed in preceding sections will be made throughout the following chapters, so refer to the Glossary and Essentials (page 553) or the Index (page 595) for quick reference to definitions and concepts to make the most of what these next steps have to offer.

One more thing: If you find yourself questioning the veracity of our personas' accounts, I urge you to ask the people you know of their own journeys, how costly their important realizations were, where their problems emerged from and how, and by what means they were able to find relative success. It will clear up any doubts you may have.

Enough preamble. *C'est parti!*

MIKE'S ODYSSEY

Mike, seventeen, lives with his parents as an only child. He's the "average kid on the block," not really known for anything other than being "that guy with the hoodie," the one you'd see at a birthday party shuffling his feet, glued to his phone. Mike is finishing up his final year in high school with an international baccalaureate. He's had a record of substandard grades, and much of his time is spent playing online multiplayer video games. He likes to think he's competitive and in fact does relatively well, but it takes up to seven hours of his time *every day* and even longer hours on weekends.

How did it all start? Well, as an only child, his loving parents benignly indulged him with all that his heart desired. They both work full-time jobs, and the fact that interest in "character building computer games" kept Mike off the streets and out of trouble made parenting that much easier. Content with his online adventures, Mike doesn't ask for much, requiring only a paid subscription and a fast internet connection. How lucky his parents must be! But what started off as a Christmas present ended up as an all-encompassing religion of detachment from reality.

Mike is what you would call a "professional gamer" if he was sponsored with a salary, but he isn't. Instead, like the other 99% who *sacrifice so much* for pixels, he is what you would call an addict. If Mike is ever accused of addiction or spending too much time gaming, you would be quick to notice every form of cognitive adjustment possible: "I don't play all that much." "Why is it a problem if it makes me happy?" "I'm doing well in school and in everything else my parents want me to do." "I have tons of friends! They're all online. You just don't see them." "My parents ought to be proud I'm not a drug-addict like some people I know!" And so on . . .

His day typically begins with a jolting start to the sound of his alarm. He stayed up late the night before, finishing up "click-and-collect" quests with his online gang of friends. A sharp, familiar pain strikes his chest after awakening from another fantastical dream cut short. "You'll be late for school, Mike. Hurry up!" his mother yells as he staggers down the stairs with his half-tucked shirt, scruffy hair, and pubescent stubble. Cereal is his go-to meal for breakfast and dinner, signifying his way of "min-maxing": a character-building strategy of optimizing (maximizing) a specific desirable action, behavior, or endeavor by minimizing everything else. It's a common concept in the world of competitive video games. Mike has been engrossed in this way of playing for so long that it has spilled over into his day-to-day life, where he attempts to minimize the time spent on anything other than maximizing his ability to better himself at his game.

Mike recently started facing some troubles. He's worried about the overseas bachelor's degree he's expected to pursue. He doesn't have the slightest idea what program to enroll in, and it's starting to bother him. Most of his chums at school know precisely what they want and seem to have a real-world drive that Mike simply can't relate to. A sense of panic is beginning to set in as he realizes that soon he'll be on his own, left to compete against those he has grown to envy because of their commitment to a practice he has been minimizing: studying.

Mike tends to avoid looking at himself in the mirror; his haunted image reminds him of how feeble he comes off to his high school crush, and he is ashamed of himself. He's never kissed anyone before. He wants to, but he lacks the courage and charisma to manage anything more than eye contact whenever the opportunity arises. "I think she likes me," he'll tell himself occasionally, only to cull any hope of it with pessimism and self-pity. Mike has always felt misunderstood and can only relate to his online pals who respect his commendable understanding of game mechanics and strategy. In his mind, Mike feels as if he is constantly being negatively evaluated or judged when attempting to conform with a particular "group" at school, leaving him alienated.

At the same time, he is deeply narcissistic, feeling as though the world revolves around him—the protagonist, the hero, much like his online avatar. Everyone else isn't good enough, confused, disgusting, selfish, or lucky. Anything other than what he sees to be the *optimal* way of living and behaving is substandard, subhuman. It's no surprise that he is culturally incompetent, repelled by any other way of life that does not fall in line with the one he has ignorantly formed through forum-surfing in communities full of those holding similar values and attitudes. The path he treads in complete oblivion will inevitably lead to pain and suffering that that will leave an indelible mark.

ANDREW'S ODYSSEY

Andrew, twenty-eight, is currently pursuing his master's degree at a reputable university. He's lived a life common to most, going through the motions, shackled by social constructs that have led him to where he is today. He shares a flat with frat boys he met during orientation week in his first semester. They're good friends, though not particularly ambitious. They spend their free time smoking, watching series and movies, and partying whenever they get the chance.

Andrew has an "average" office job three days a week liaising with the elderly and selling retirement plans. He doesn't care much for the work or anything else for that matter. His daily routine consists of waking up late, sipping a double-shot Americano and smoking a "Winnie Blue," and then making his way to university (though only to classes with mandatory attendance). Barely awake, he hears what his lecturers have to say, sometimes actually listening, and then rushes back to the comfort of yet another Netflix series with his roommates. They share a chuckle as he texts his boyfriend, Travis, who lives interstate. Those conversations generally revolve around Travis's daily frustrations, such as how irritated he gets watching people in the cafeteria chewing with their mouths open. Travis was Andrew's first true love, but three years on, their long-distance relationship is crumbling as they independently question where to go from here.

Travis is facing a "premature" midlife crisis, though Andrew can't recall the last time he wasn't. You see, Travis's aunt, who had taken care of him after he was abandoned by his parents at an early age, passed away two years ago, leaving him scarred, spiteful, and irritable. Travis's attitude has turned their relationship sour and borderline abusive. He justifies it all with the loss he's endured, and the chip on his shoulder doesn't help. Andrew understands—he's been empathetic all along—though the beginning to the end of Travis's trauma is neither apparent nor possible given that Travis refuses counselling and denies there's a problem to begin with. They've spoken about it once or twice before, but Andrew is always left feeling guilty, always the one to blame.

Andrew comes from a family of tradition and pride. His mother expected a lot from him, given the poverty she grew up in. Her aching joints and back are a testament to the pain and hardships she's faced providing for Andrew and his brother while offering them a future—with an expectation of prosperity and support once they've graduated. Every day, he feels the building tension and pressure. Andrew is stuck between a rock and a hard place: deprived of freedom, of care, of meaning, he is bound to decisions without choice, to individuals without unconditional connectedness, to initiatives without significance—all imposed or inherited, whose repudiation bear consequences too stifling to even consider. What exacerbates his constraints is envy; his older brother, Jeremy, is a well-established architect who is married and has paid off his house mortgage—the "ideal" outcome his mother never ceases to expect from Andrew. Jeremy has always wanted the best for his little brother, regularly reminding him that he's always a phone call away, but Andrew never calls. He chooses to live in poverty, refusing his sibling's support. If it wasn't for his brother, Andrew thinks, his mother may have seen him differently, accepted him, and given him the validation he needed to justify soldiering through to the end of his academic journey.

Andrew isn't what you'd call a "macho" man. He shies away from confrontation, avoids trouble, and abides by the rules and regulation he's aware of. His idea of a happy life is finding a stable job, getting married, having kids, and retiring—though this idea scares him; it's mundane, expected, *boring*. But he doesn't know of any other path that may offer him purpose or peace; it is all that he feels he ought to strive for.

Andrew dislikes being in public for too long because he always finds himself comparing his progress with that of others. All the happy faces he walks by, the happy couples, the wealthy studs, children playing with careless glee. "Why can't I be happy like them?" he mumbles under his breath. The sight of contentment and optimism embitters him.

The lens through which Andrew interprets life is that of a compulsive depressive. His mental dialogue never fails to deliver a daily dose of negativity that paints any sensory reception black. In bed late at night, he browses his social media feed to see what his friends and acquaintances are up to. Selfies at the beach, posts of joyous announcements, celebrations, videos of success and triumph. He feels inferior, unwanted, mediocre, inadequate, belittled. "How did it come to this?" He has done what everyone else has: he went to school, partied hard, has a job, and is pursuing a tertiary education. "What am I missing?" He doubts his sanity. "Maybe I'm bipolar. Maybe its ADHD. There must be a screw loose. Maybe I'm destined to be a miserable, good-for-nothing meat carcass, just another reason the M1 is jammed." What little motivation he had to sustain his impressively mundane routine is flagging, and the thought of giving it all up is becoming more alluring than ever.

RACHEL'S ODYSSEY

Ah, good ole Rache'. You can always count on her! She's that friendly neighborhood character who always seems to attract the envy of other moms. Rachel seems like she has it all: a big house, a faithful husband, two boys (Dewy and Danny, ages eleven and thirteen), a career as a sales rep copywriter, and a wardrobe that makes her stand out in a crowd. She's intelligent, she's beautiful, and she's had enough.

"When will this stop? When will I ever catch a break?" Rachel has been running for most of her life, constantly pushing herself to maintain what she already has. She's tired of having to put 200% into every waking minute of her life to keep it all afloat. The thought of it is a pressure point that induces a state of rage, quickly reducing her to tears as she puts the kids to sleep or anticipates having to prepare the next day's school lunch at midnight before finally collapsing into bed.

Rachel is now thirty-six with a birthday coming up—a day she dreads because it's another reminder of dreams slipping by and how quickly her energetic days are flying. She seems to have it all, but it is far from what she wants, from the dreams she remembers having. She wants to be free, free of chores, obligations, expectations, and routine—free to do as she wishes. She's never tasted adventure, never taken a risk, never travelled on her own, never seen the world absent of distraction. She's come to realize that the fantasy she envisaged a decade ago has turned into a nightmare.

You couldn't tell, however. Most of the time, she enjoys her job and the people she works with. She can't imagine a life without Dewy and Danny—although Dewy has been a particularly difficult child to raise. Her husband, Lewis, was her high school love and now lifelong husband. He's been good to her but offers nothing more than the minimum you'd expect from a significant other. Something is missing—a thought that has been creeping up on Rachel in the worst of ways. Lewis makes little effort to help with household chores and the kids. Sure, he occasionally picks the kids up from school and is the one to organize fast-food pickups—but only after Rachel's repeated instructions. It seems that an altercation is always needed before he budges on helping with even the simplest of parental or spousal responsibilities. "Why can't he just recognize my efforts, see how hard I'm working, take some initiative, or show some appreciation?" Their love along with their sex life has dwindled into little more than the occasional peck on the cheek. Things were never the same after Dewy was born.

Dewy was their attempt to relive the happy moments they once shared, to rejuvenate their stale marriage, to feel like a functioning, loving couple again. The fact that they both work 9–5 jobs meant that any last bit of freedom went out the window with Dewy's arrival. What little time Danny got to spend with his parents was replaced with tablets and smartphones so he could busy himself and void the nagging. Dewy grew up deprived of attention and resorted to crying and whining before the crack of Rachel's voice was heard. He wasn't a broken child; it was just the only way he could get his parents' much-needed attention.

Not a day goes by that Rachel and Lewis aren't having an argument, whether it's about the overcooked chicken, the mess Lewis or the children had left, who's fault was it that Danny fell and grazed his knee, etc. Irritation turns to anger, anger to melancholy, and melancholy to depression. She has had enough, and is now facing questions that burn from within: "If it had never been Lewis . . ." "Was Dewy a mistake?" The thought of a mother being repelled by her child terrifies her. In a world of hurt, she can only blame herself for the decisions she's committed to, with seemingly no way out.

CHAPTER 30
STEP 1: THE SETUP

Life can only be understood backward but must be lived forward.

—Søren A. Kierkegaard, *Journals IV A 164*

A Quasi-Chaotic Lifestyle is sensitive and reactive to informational input. We therefore require the following means to track, manage, drive, ensure, and maintain our progress based on the decisions and actions we make and take and their eventual outcomes:

▲ To appreciate *distance*, an odometer that provides the reassurance of gradational intertemporal development—incremental personal growth (cultivating Pride).

▲ A readily available list of tasks to action (promoting Momentum and fostering Accountability).

▲ Consolidating realizations (drawn of Curiosity) to reap growth-catalyzing rewards (of Failure).

▲ Developing instructional insights (for Osmosis) and self-realized guidance (for Ambition).

How we accomplish all the above is by exercising what the Agile philosophy and its practices have to offer, namely, the Scrum framework and Kanban!

If you recall, user stories encapsulate chunks of value-driven work in the Agile framework. Given the serendipitous nature of unpredictable Quasi-Chaotic conduct and trajectories, however, we will not be making use of conventional user-story structure. Confining ourselves to a particular "purpose for action" limits what we could otherwise serendipitously discover or exploit in opportunities that arise as we go forward. Our primary objective is change—nothing more, nothing less.

That said, let's kick things off by constructing your very own Kanban board!

Your Kanban board should posses the following qualities:

▽ **Availability:** It is readily available for use at all times.

▽ **Accessibility:** Its management and access are convenient and efficient.

▽ **Amenability:** It is customizable, with the ability to move and amend cards.

You have the choice of two formats for your Kanban board:

▲ **PHYSICAL KANBAN BOARD:**
Sticky notes, a marker, a wall/mirror/board with enough space, string, and tape (see figure 7-1) to form five lanes of which the first and last will grow increasingly congested.

▽ **Availability:** Ensure the board is located in a space you visit regularly. Avoid discarding any cards.

▽ **Accessibility:** Avoid a setup that requires excess packing and unpacking or tinkering so you can make amendments conveniently.

▽ **Amenability:** Attach sticky notes to each other or tag sticky notes with labels that reference a separate booklet page number where its related notes are written.

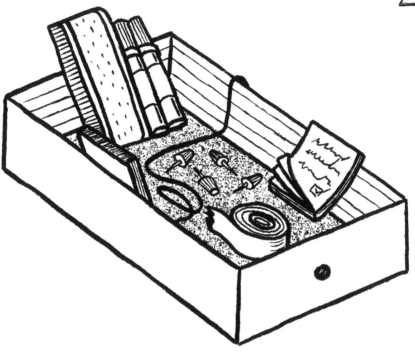

Figure 7-1: Physical Kanban board box set

▲ **DIGITAL KANBAN BOARD:**

One of several free online Kanban tools or digital canvases that offer Kanban features such as Trello and Miro.

▽ **Availability:** Bookmark the web app and download the phone app if it has one. Avoid permanently deleting cards.

▽ **Accessibility:** If using a computer to access the web app dedicate a separate monitor just for it, or leave it open on a separate device if possible. Make use of macros, shortcuts, and productivity features on offer.

▽ **Amenability:** Make full use of the app's tools such as card descriptions, comment sections, checklists, and attachments.

It's worth noting that neither a physical nor digital Kanban board is better than the other. There are advantages and disadvantages to each, with varying perks and implications that suit some people more than others. For example, a physical

Kanban board offers a ceremonial location to revisit, it is significantly more visible, the movement of cards has a visceral and emotional impact, it's more flexible, and it has a lot more room for creativity. A digital board offers remote access, has the ability to add attachments and links, allows you to search and audit, and has a slew of automations to streamline repetitive actions. How do you figure out what works best for you? I think you know well enough by now!

Availability, accessibility, and amenability are paramount for an effective Kanban board, so take your time and incrementally improve said qualities as you proceed. Personalized modification of the process, further Kanban/Self-Actualizing tips, and Quasi-Chaotic habits to substantiate your Kanban board endeavors will all be detailed in later chapters.

With your Kanban board set up, you are now ready to set sail! We will begin with some basic steps for growing accustomed to coordinating your Kanban board with day-to-day undertakings. Our primary objective for now is to facilely adopt the fundamentals of a Quasi-Chaotic Lifestyle. We will therefore only populate and manage our boards with *current* responsibilities, at least for now. In other words, use your Kanban board to implement the seven following stages for whatever routine you are presently bound to—no more, no less. I suggest you give yourself a week or two to carry out enough daily Sprints to familiarize yourself with the process and some of the tools at your disposal.

1. Initial/Continuous Scoping:

Populate your Backlog with all that needs doing, whether it be household chores, an upcoming event, small errands, work-related matters, self-set existing goals, Kanban exercises, and so on.

Once you do get the hang of it, Initial Scoping need not take place only when a Sprint is completed; instead, you can see this as a continuing exercise (Continuous Scoping) where you populate your Backlog as you go as ideas, responsibilities, challenges, and, eventually, directives and opportunities for change arise during subsequent Sprint Planning sessions. And yes, serendipitous or impromptu experiences are to be added retroactively and reflected upon!

2. Backlog Refinement:

Refine your cards to a point when they are readily executable. Amend them with whatever detail, indicators, or directives will ensure visibility, clarity, and actionability. I offer a few ideas and tips below, but feel free to refine your cards in a manner that works best for you!

Consider labeling your cards to help differentiate between categories. For example:

▽ **Categorize by location:** Where do you expect the task to take place? At home? At work? Somewhere else? This will help you quickly locate a suitable task to action depending on where you are.

▽ **Categorize by outcome:** Consider a scale of how well a completed task resonated with you. This will offer a visual overview to assist with insightful pattern-finding.

▽ **Categorize by willingness:** Which tasks are you looking forward to, and which ones would you rather avoid? This will help match your changing physical and mental capacities with what you're capable of at any given time through careful Sprint task allocation.

It is of utmost importance that the tasks we write are sufficiently specific, measurable, achievable, and time limited. "Eat healthier," for example, is not particularly actionable by itself. How, exactly, will you achieve this? Does it involve hours of research looking up nutritional facts? If so, shouldn't this undertaking be a card of its own? Above all, how will you know when the task is complete? You could live the rest of your life not knowing when to move that card from Doing to Done; it will sit there, motionless. The transition of a card across the board signifies progress as its motion is a reward in itself—a sense of achievement that will never fail to motivate you!

Instead, try "create a list of five healthy and delicious meal prep recipes." It is much more actionable, it seems reasonably achievable, and we know exactly when to mark it complete! If a task is particularly hairy, break it down into granular, manageable chunks. How do we eat an elephant? One bite at a time! So instead of "clean the house," try "clean the living room," "tidy the kitchen," "dust the garage," and so on. If it still feels overwhelming, break it down even further: "clean the sink," "polish the cutlery," "tidy the pantry."

You do not need to refine all your cards at once. Simply refine enough of them for a Sprint and continue refining them when you have the time. Of course, the more cards you've refined, the more there are to choose from in your next Sprint!

If you weren't able to complete a card by the end of your Sprint, leave a status update (by amending your sticky note with another or leaving a comment if you're using a digital board) and move it to your Backlog to pick up for the next Sprint. Moreover, reexamine the existing cards you have in your Backlog. Given the lessons this completed Sprint has afforded, how might you alter your Backlog of tasks? Will you pivot away from commitments? Will you pursue them differently? Consider how you would alter and/or correct velocity (change of direction, trajectory, and level of commitment) based on what you now know.

3. Sprint Planning:

Every day, pick a few cards (suited to your capacity) and move them from your Backlog into your To-Do lane. These cards will encompass your Sprint—the ones you feel ready to take on. For cards that feel like chores (which may often be the case at this stage of "pre-Quasi-Chaotic adoption"), harbor them until you're ready. If you've been avoiding a readily actionable card for too long, the card now becomes a challenge (which deserves its own label!). Don't forget to exploit lessons drawn from Partnered and Group Accountability by leveraging a friend, colleague, a group environment, etc.

4. The Sprint:

Action Sprint-allocated cards by moving them to your Doing lane and then to the Done lane once they're finished! A few things to consider:

▽ Ideally, you want no more than one card under the Doing lane at a time, as it promotes focus and helps mitigate a sense of overwhelm.

▽ It is best to exercise these motions as soon as the occasions arise. (When you are about to commence a task, for example, move your card and then begin.) Updating your cards throughout the day helps maintain Momentum as opposed to moving swaths of cards at one time.

▽ If you've decided to employ a physical Kanban board, move any cards you wish to action from the To-Do lane to the Doing lane before you depart the premises. Once you return, move whatever tasks you have completed to the Done lane. Alternatively, take whatever cards you plan to action with you and maintain three separate paper-clipped (To-Do, Doing, Done) stacks of sticky notes. Slap them on your board when you're back! Otherwise, if you're using a digital board, you'll be able to manage your cards in transit.

5. Sprint Review:

After your Sprint is complete, update the cards sitting under your Done lane with a brief summary of what happened. From there, take note of how you feel about what and how the events transpired, such as whether or not you enjoyed the task, how you felt before/during/after the task was completed, what you liked and didn't like about it, etc. Take record of who was involved, perhaps some notable quotes, what you learned about yourself, and what you would have done differently. How much you write depends on how significant the task was. It's entirely up to you, but the more, the merrier! After a while (and like brushing your teeth), you will naturally feel uncomfortable falling asleep without keeping your board in tip-top shape. Think of it as a form of journaling!

Examples of thorough Sprint Reviews will only be provided throughout Step 1's persona application. Sprint Reviews in Step 2 and beyond will only address the task detailed in its respective step. Your Sprint Reviews ought to encompass as many Sprint tasks as possible however!

6. Sprint Retrospective:

Reflect on the completed Sprint. Pay close attention to what it is you are reflecting on and how. With Sprint Retrospectives, we aren't interested in resummarizing what happened as we have already done or shifting blame. Instead, we are interested in optimizing processes; identifying what worked and what didn't will tell us what to do more of, what to do less of, and what to do differently. The ultimate aim here is to arrive at meaningful realizations that will improve our overall productivity, efficiency, and sense of fulfillment throughout further Sprints. The way to get there is by asking yourself the following questions:

▲ **WHAT WENT WELL? WHY/HOW?** SOME EXAMPLES:
   ▽ **What went well:**
     I managed to complete all tasks in a timely manner.
   ▽ **Why/how:**
     Because I did the tasks I knew I'd enjoy in the morning when I'm most grouchy. Because I used a timer and pushed for a finish without the need for perfection.

   ▽ **What went well:**
     I took my losses like a champ.
   ▽ **Why/how:**
     I focused on the consequences that would have occurred had I not been given the opportunity to fail and learn from my mistakes. I compared my situation to someone else's whose consequences did manifest—instantly relieving me of guilt of failing and invoking gratitude for the lessons I've learned.

▲ **WHAT DIDN'T GO WELL? WHY/HOW?** SOME EXAMPLES:

▽ **What didn't go well:**

I kept procrastinating.

▽ **Why/how:**

The task I took on was too intimidating, and every bit of me wanted to avoid it. I was in a space that was incredibly distracting, feeling constantly tempted to deviate from my work.

▽ **What didn't go well:**

I didn't feel entirely engaged with my accountability partner.

▽ **Why/how:**

I didn't keep them posted throughout the task. I needed more contact from my accountability partner.

▲ **WHAT SHOULD I CONTINUE DOING AND WHAT CAN I DO TO IMPROVE?**

Often gleaned from realizations made in the previous two questions, these answers should result in more actionable tasks to fill our Backlog. Addressing the aforementioned examples in chronological order:

▽ Continue doing tasks I enjoy in the morning and label cards based on what I enjoy and don't enjoy doing.

▽ Download a timer app and keep it handy to avoid a vicious cycle of perfectionism.

▽ Amend failed tasks with the consequences I would have faced had I not learned my lesson.

▽ If tasks are extra-hairy, search online for what those consequences could look like and amend the card with photos.

▽ Avoid populating the Backlog with excessively intimidating tasks. Instead, break them up into one-hour chunks of work.

▽ Identify all distractions and figure out ways to avoid them. Otherwise, relocate to a different setting that may encourage task completion.

▽ Consult my accountability partner and ask for more contact; otherwise, find a new accountability partner.

Take note of your answers in a separate card/s and feel free to compile every other Sprint Retrospective's findings into a document or within a separate column on your board. They will come in handy! Most importantly, don't forget to celebrate the completion of your Sprints with a hearty fist pump and a "Let's go!"

7. Archive actioned cards:

Move all of your now-amended cards from your Done lane to the Archive lane. This final lane will serve as our repository of triumph, a visual representation of progression. Each card is a testament to the distance traversed and a reason to be proud. A digital board will make it easy to search and filter through cards actioned months, even years ago! Otherwise, you can organize and label piles of sticky notes, make use of booklet card sleeves, or stock them for quick reference using other creative means.

And the cycle (see figure 7-2) repeats with every Sprint. Rest assured, the cyclical flow of Sprints will become second nature in no time. Your first Kanban setup may take a couple of hours to organize and a few days to get used to, but managing your board shouldn't take longer than 10–30 minutes a day once you get into the swing of things—a ritual you will very much grow to love and look forward to!

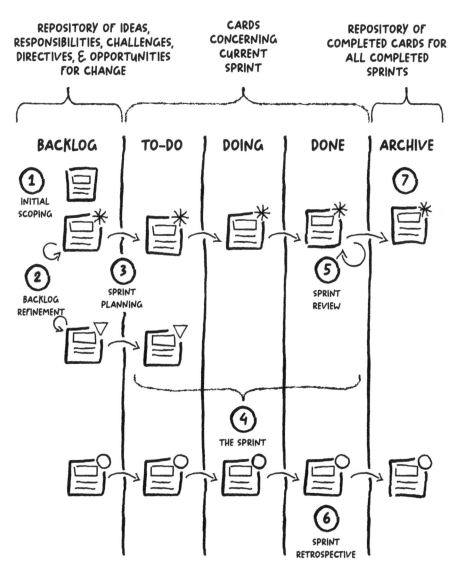

Figure 7-2: Running a Sprint on Kanban

Tracking Mike's journey? Read on.

Tracking Andrew's journey? Skip to page 366.

Tracking Rachel's journey? Skip to page 371.

APPLIED STEP 1: MIKE

During downtime between gaming, Mike works on setting up his Kanban board. He decides to try a digital board he found on a top ten list and goes on to explore its features: "Labels, due dates, checklists, uploading images . . . Yeah, this will do, I guess." Mike proceeds to gradually, though grudgingly, populate his Backlog. (See figure 7-3.)

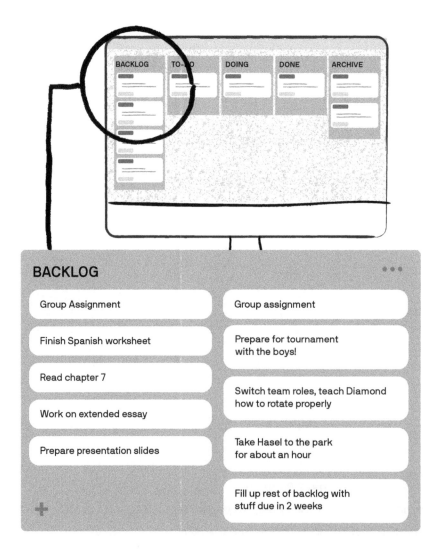

Figure 7-3: Mike's Backlog

He decides to label his cards based on his school subjects. After all, there isn't much else in his life apart from academic drudgery and video games. So, he half-heartedly allots due dates for most and, as you might have noticed, many tasks aren't particularly actionable, specific, or measurable. He can be careless, but that's Mike in a nutshell! He does find his digital Kanban board easy to use and doesn't mind having it all in one place, though he grows anxious knowing how much needs doing. It's all there, on the board, and he can't avoid it.

As the days pass, Mike never manages to plan his Sprints consistently. Instead, he sees his Kanban board as a calendar. He only works through items the night before they are due. The fact of the matter is, there is *never* a good time, as the process always feels forced, abrasive, and painful. For him, they are all chores except, of course, preparing for the upcoming video game tournament whose card includes a relatively (relative to what he's written in his other cards) detailed review he manages to muster up. Most interesting, however, is the realization he makes when reflecting on his English and IT-related cards. He feels slightly more compelled to do a better job with *their* respective tasks, wanting to impress Elly, his crush, who happens to be in the same class for those particular subjects. It is a source of motivation unrelated to the subjects themselves, but a source that indirectly justifies the means, which is . . . interesting. Other card reflections aren't as insightful. (See figure 7-4.)

Figure 7-4: A card from Mike's Sprint Review

He does manage a decent Sprint Retrospective (see figure 7-5), however, without any actionable improvements to address his anxiety and how little he cares for his academic work.

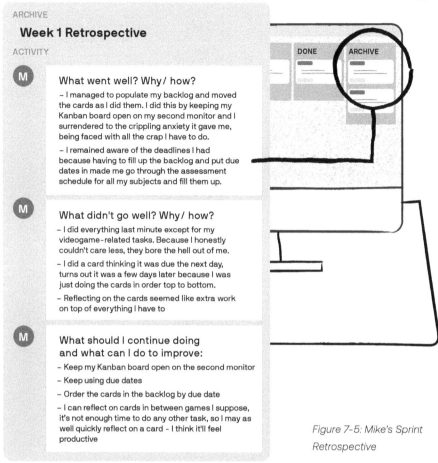

Figure 7-5: Mike's Sprint Retrospective

Within a week, Mike is starting to get the hang of the tool but not the method. (See figure 7-6.) It still feels like yet another chore to maintain, as he doesn't feel he is gaining much value from it. He knows why but just doesn't want to admit it: another minute spent making a genuine effort to write and manage his cards correctly is another minute of revealed angst and a minute not spent on his precious online grind—a "malpractice" that will eventually backfire. Mike attempts to get a separate Kanban board going with his online team members to work on better competitive video game strategies, but they never get around to setting it up. Mike is still deeply immersed in his bubble—the upcoming tournament taking priority—and gives little attention to the other tasks. He ends up asking for an extension for his Spanish homework and accepts the 10% penalty he'll receive.

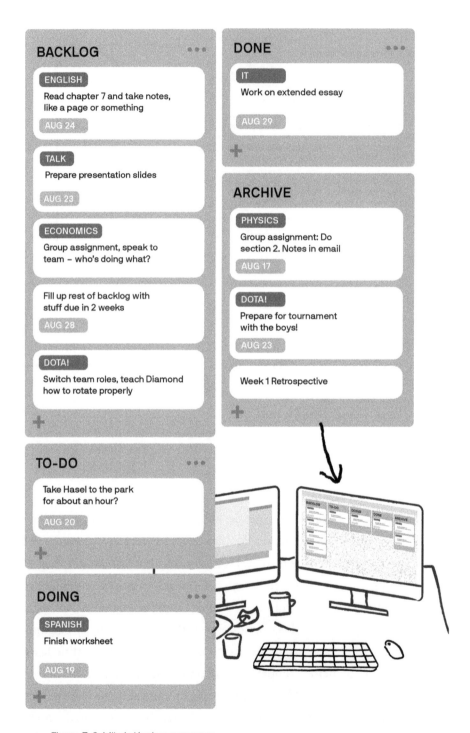

BACKLOG   ...

> ENGLISH
> Read chapter 7 and take notes, like a page or something
> AUG 24

> TALK
> Prepare presentation slides
> AUG 23

> ECONOMICS
> Group assignment, speak to team – who's doing what?

> Fill up rest of backlog with stuff due in 2 weeks
> AUG 28

> DOTA!
> Switch team roles, teach Diamond how to rotate properly

DONE   ...

> IT
> Work on extended essay
> AUG 29

ARCHIVE

> PHYSICS
> Group assignment: Do section 2. Notes in email
> AUG 17

> DOTA!
> Prepare for tournament with the boys!
> AUG 23

> Week 1 Retrospective

TO-DO   ...

> Take Hasel to the park for about an hour?
> AUG 20

DOING   ...

> SPANISH
> Finish worksheet
> AUG 19

Figure 7-6: Mike's Kanban progress

If you're only tracking Mike's journey, skip to page 377.

APPLIED STEP 1: ANDREW

Late at night, after a cigarette and a few episodes of yet another action-thriller remake, Andrew puts some thought into what type of Kanban he'll build. He figures he is already familiar with a digital canvas he's used for work, and since the visual flexibility the tool has to offer works well with his visual learning style, he thinks, "Why not!"

Andrew begins by listing everything that is on his mind. (See figure 7-7.) And since he already relies on a calendar, he doesn't feel the need to use due dates, though he does sense that maintaining both systems is somewhat redundant. He then decides to categorize tasks by location as he only finds himself in the same five places at any given time. He often plans his day in advance—a routine type of guy—so depending on where he is going to be, he picks a card or two for the day. Like Mike, there isn't much happening outside his routine. It's university, work, home, and the occasional weekend outing.

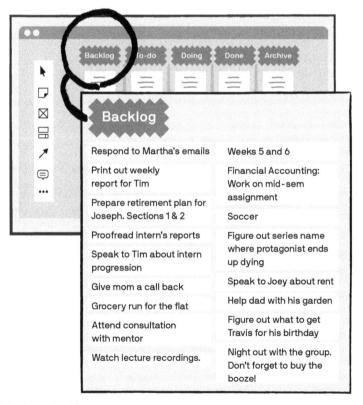

Figure 7-7: Andrew's Backlog

Andrew doesn't stop there, though. He color-codes his cards to represent how happy he is with the outcome. This allows him to revise what doesn't go well and why. The pattern is predictable, but again, that's the type of person Andrew is: predictable. He is a little confused, though. "How much do I record? Every little thing? Breakfast, lunch, dinner, the loo?" He leaves it at "obligations" and doesn't think much more of it for the time being. "There's only one way to find out!"

Throughout the week, Andrew picks a few cards after his morning routine and gets down to it. He finds it difficult to refer back to his Kanban while on the move as its interface isn't designed for what he is attempting to achieve. He can log in at work and from home, but when he's out, he resorts to a screenshot he's taken earlier in the day for reference. An inconvenience, but he doesn't like being "on the move" anyway. Regardless, he enjoys the act of moving cards, and while he doesn't necessarily feel like he is getting anywhere in life, he does feel a sense of progression. "What's that you've got there, Andy?" Tim, his supervisor, asks. "Oh! This is my Kanban board. I'm taking on a Quasi-Chaotic Lifestyle!" "A what?" "A Quasi . . . err, I'm changing things up, Tim. You know, for the better!" "Good on you, Andy. You're a good lad. Keep at it!"

Andrew very much looks forward to his Sprint Retrospectives. He feels like a detective, connecting dots using bits and pieces of obscure information to formulate the bigger picture he believes to hold an answer. His Sprint Retrospectives reveal incremental, productive realizations (see figure 7-8), and his Sprint Reviews are turning into diary entries (see figure 7-9) as Andrew realizes that getting it all out makes it easier to sleep (as opposed to late-night ruminations). Given how he is used to overthinking what transpired throughout a day, he is already a little more attentive to detail and how even the smallest occurrences affect him.

What went well? Why/ how?

- Labeling the cards by location made it convenient to visualize the work I had to do and whether I could do other tasks in the location in tandem.

- Having finished cards by the end of the day made my leisure time a lot more enjoyable and bearable. I often get anxiety thinking I didn't accomplish enough which ruins some experiences I have.

- A continuation of the last point - I was a lot more at ease at the end of the night, not needing to replay the day over in my head to make sense of what happened and how I felt about it. Since the cards are there and I can see them, they gave me that peace of mind which really helped.

What didn't go well? Why/ how?

- Maintaining tasks in two different systems was redundant, whilst I didn't take too much time to rewrite things over, I did, however, have some inconsistencies between the two which led to missteps, having to rush a forgotten card I needed to get done on the day. I can see how this can turn into a bigger problem the more tasks I add.

- Since I wasn't able to move cards on the go, I feel like I'm missing out on the great feeling of moving a card. This also didn't bode well with the previous point because by the time I got access to my board, I had forgotten what the inconsistency was.

What should I continue doing and what can I do to improve:

- I could also label the cards with urgency to figure out which cards I can postpone if another task is taking too much time. Some didn't really need due dates, but its better if I can get them sooner rather than later.

- Continue labeling using locations and potentially pair cards that can be done in tandem.

- Have a quick gander at the Done lane at night for that peace of mind.

- I should copy/paste work-related cards into my Kanban board before I leave work to avoid any more accidents.

Figure 7-8: Andrew's Sprint Retrospective

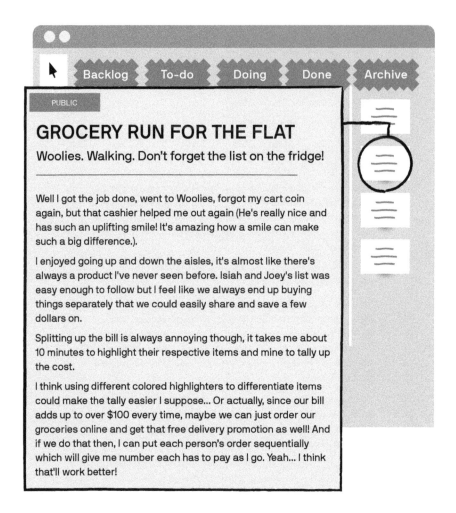

Figure 7-9: A card from Andrew's Sprint Review

Standing outside his university mentor's room one day, he notices other students waiting their turn and decides to strike up a conversation. He notices that all of them are in fear of failing. They all find solace with one another knowing they are in the same boat, and they figure they'll eventually meet again. Andrew realizes he should've asked for their contact details. "Gosh, why didn't I? So much potential lost. I'll make sure I do it next time."

A week in and Andrew is already getting the hang of his Kanban ritual (see figure 7-10), with new ideas of managing his daily commitments cropping up as he goes through the motions.

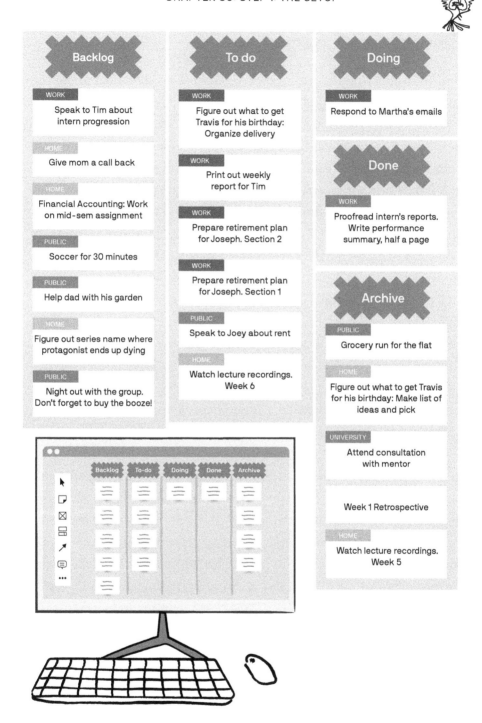

Backlog

WORK
Speak to Tim about intern progression

HOME
Give mom a call back

HOME
Financial Accounting: Work on mid-sem assignment

PUBLIC
Soccer for 30 minutes

PUBLIC
Help dad with his garden

HOME
Figure out series name where protagonist ends up dying

PUBLIC
Night out with the group. Don't forget to buy the booze!

To do

WORK
Figure out what to get Travis for his birthday: Organize delivery

WORK
Print out weekly report for Tim

WORK
Prepare retirement plan for Joseph. Section 2

WORK
Prepare retirement plan for Joseph. Section 1

PUBLIC
Speak to Joey about rent

HOME
Watch lecture recordings. Week 6

Doing

WORK
Respond to Martha's emails

Done

WORK
Proofread intern's reports. Write performance summary, half a page

Archive

PUBLIC
Grocery run for the flat

HOME
Figure out what to get Travis for his birthday: Make list of ideas and pick

UNIVERSITY
Attend consultation with mentor

Week 1 Retrospective

HOME
Watch lecture recordings. Week 5

Figure 7-10: Andrew's Kanban progress

If you're only tracking Andrew's journey, skip to page 377.

APPLIED STEP 1: RACHEL

With what little time she has to spare, Rachel has no choice but to use her lunch break at work to get the ball rolling. She pulls out a stack of sticky notes from her drawer and gets to work. She plans on using the back of her wardrobe at home as a board: A bit of masking tape for the lanes, sticky notes for the headers. "Yeah, that'll do, I suppose. A few differently colored marker pens should help with the labeling, too . . ." She gives it a quick think and decides to label her cards based on how eager she is to do them: "Looking forward to it," "Bearable," "I'd rather not," "Just do it." She foresees how this approach will come in handy, enabling her to balance out a day with a few tolerable tasks mixed in with the rest of her many commitments.

As she begins to populate her Backlog (see figure 7-11), she lets out a quiet, enervative sigh. Chore after chore after chore. "This can't be normal," she thinks to herself as she begins to wonder what everyone else's week will look like. She grows increasingly frustrated with the way her week is shaping up, questioning her life choices as she finishes her Sprint Planning. While she knew her days were difficult, it is now explicit; this is what it has come to. She stacks the cards, emphatically shoves them in her bag, and gets back to her duties.

It isn't long before Lewis notices her frequent visits to the bedroom and eventually catches her in the act, moving cards around. "What's this, honey? Your secret plan to take over the world?" He is clearly proud of his clever sense of humor. Rachel ignores him and continues sifting through her cards, hanging them up with care. "No, really, what are you up to?" Rachel turns her head. "Change. This is change. It's quite a private matter, so I'd really appreciate it if we kept it that way." "Yeesh, fair enough. You seem to have woken up on the wrong side of bed today. It was just a question." "I'm sorry, I . . ." "Don't worry about it. Just let us know when dinner's ready, okay?"

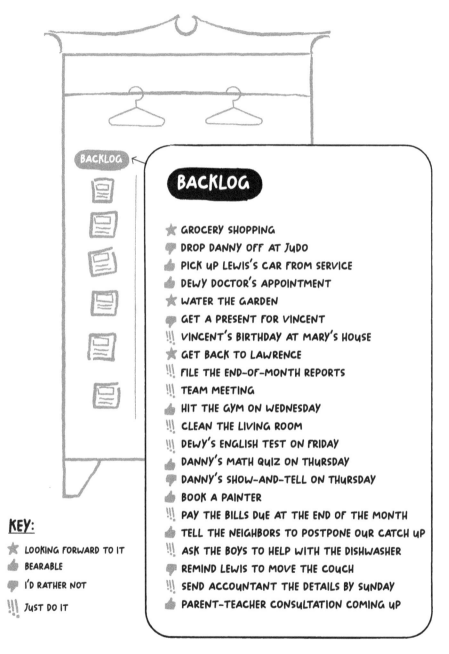

KEY:

⭐ LOOKING FORWARD TO IT
👍 BEARABLE
👎 I'D RATHER NOT
‼️ JUST DO IT

Figure 7-11: Rachel's Backlog

In between consultations at work, Rachel decides to call her best friend, Katie, and apologize for how long it's taken to get back to her. "I'm so sorry, Katie. You know what my days are like." "No need to apologize, Rachel. I totally get it. I just wanted check and see how you were doing!" "Ups and downs; you know how it is. Actually, I've got to tell you about this thing I'm trying out. Maybe you can help . . ."

Rachel is pragmatic with her approach; if she is going to do something, she does it right—her Retrospective reflecting her fastidious nature. (See figure 7-12.) Each day she wakes up, stumbles to her wardrobe, and scopes her daily Sprint. She decides to amend her sticky notes with different colored ones representing reflective summaries.

WEEK 1 RETROSPECTIVE

WHAT WENT WELL? WHY/ HOW?

- Labeling the cards with what I was and wasn't looking forward to allowed me to balance out the day making my week a lot more bearable, lowering the chances of burn out.

- Adding descriptions and checklists to tasks made it so I wasn't forgetting as many things as I used to, whether it's an envelope, spare clothing for Dewy, or a matter I need to raise with someone I'm going to run into on any given day.

- Reflecting on what I'd normally see as unbearable made it somewhat more bearable. I found myself focusing on what I'm learning in the moment, which distracted me from what I normally think about (the fact that no one's helping usually).

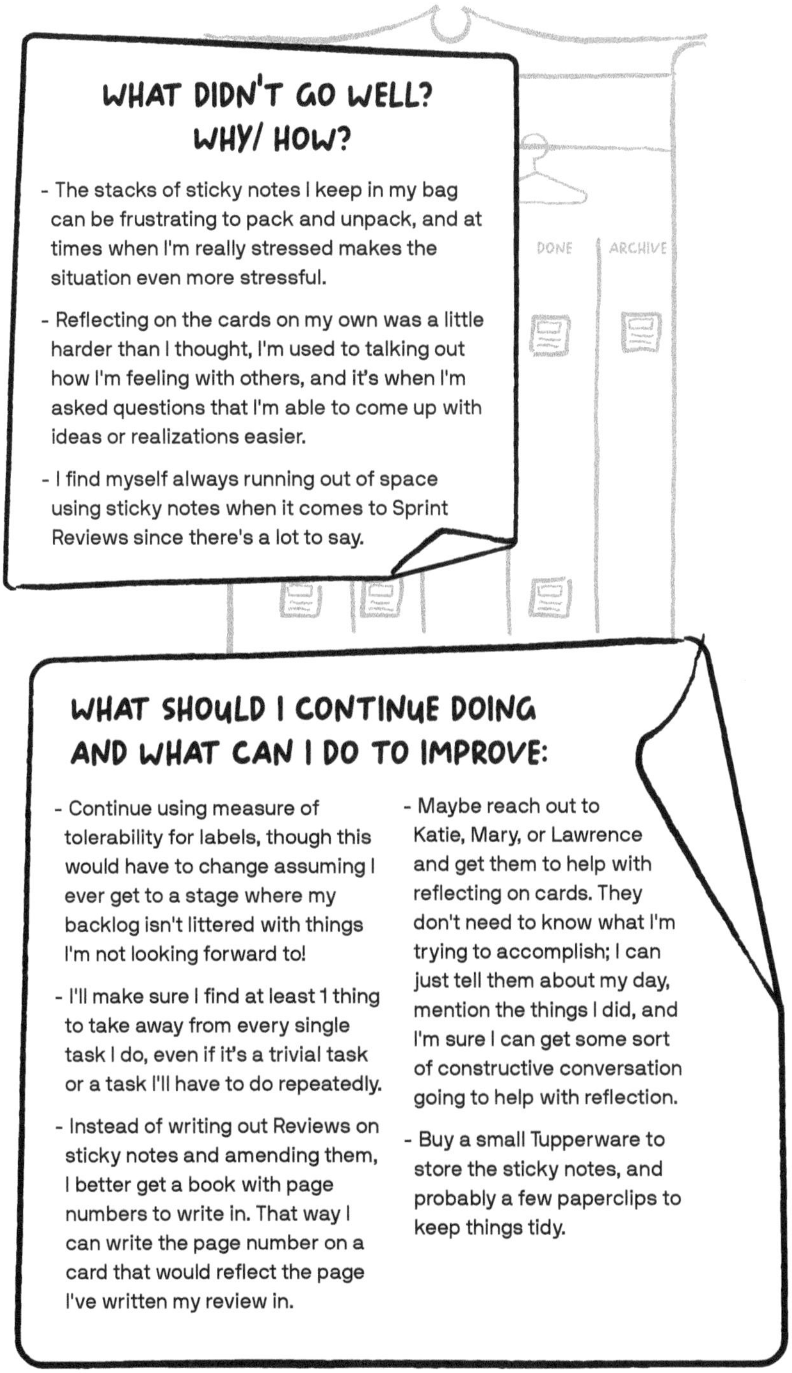

WHAT DIDN'T GO WELL? WHY/ HOW?

- The stacks of sticky notes I keep in my bag can be frustrating to pack and unpack, and at times when I'm really stressed makes the situation even more stressful.

- Reflecting on the cards on my own was a little harder than I thought, I'm used to talking out how I'm feeling with others, and it's when I'm asked questions that I'm able to come up with ideas or realizations easier.

- I find myself always running out of space using sticky notes when it comes to Sprint Reviews since there's a lot to say.

WHAT SHOULD I CONTINUE DOING AND WHAT CAN I DO TO IMPROVE:

- Continue using measure of tolerability for labels, though this would have to change assuming I ever get to a stage where my backlog isn't littered with things I'm not looking forward to!

- I'll make sure I find at least 1 thing to take away from every single task I do, even if it's a trivial task or a task I'll have to do repeatedly.

- Instead of writing out Reviews on sticky notes and amending them, I better get a book with page numbers to write in. That way I can write the page number on a card that would reflect the page I've written my review in.

- Maybe reach out to Katie, Mary, or Lawrence and get them to help with reflecting on cards. They don't need to know what I'm trying to accomplish; I can just tell them about my day, mention the things I did, and I'm sure I can get some sort of constructive conversation going to help with reflection.

- Buy a small Tupperware to store the sticky notes, and probably a few paperclips to keep things tidy.

Figure 7-12: Rachel's Sprint Retrospective

Late at night, as she packs Dewy's and Danny's school lunches, she reflects. "Telling Katie about this Kanban thing felt reassuring. I think she'd make a great accountability partner. I wonder what she'd think of my day-to-day. I wonder what her day-to-day looks like. I doubt it's worse than mine." She then scribbles it all down. "The dishwasher? Not much to say about that, I guess, though I'm not sure why I detest it. It does feel productive, but I suppose the fact that Lewis could at least offer to do it—but doesn't—makes it that much less tolerable."

Figure 7-13: A card from Rachel's Sprint Review

By the end of the week, Rachel grows accustomed to the structure her Kanban board brings to her chaotic life. She realizes that planning out the week isn't as easy as planning out the day. She manages to get her team meeting notes done in advance, feeling like she could get it out of the way after her uplifting chat with Lawrence, a close friend. While her Kanban alleviates the overall stress of her day by balancing the good with the bad, and although she is making a few important realizations along the way (see figure 7-13), Rachel is still desperate for change, and her weeks still feel like more of the same. (See figure 7-14.)

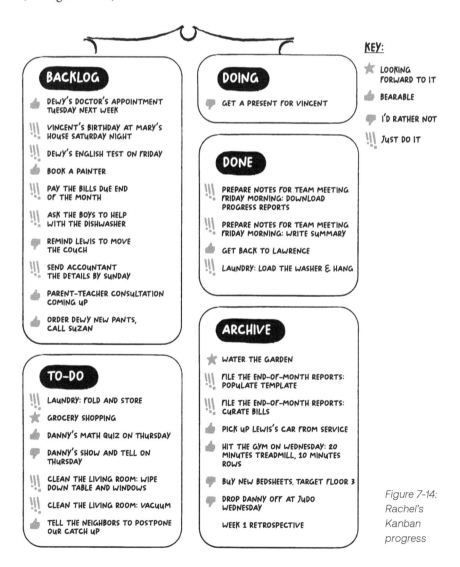

Figure 7-14: Rachel's Kanban progress

CHAPTER 31
STEP 2: SCOPE OF INFLUENCE

**Success is a science; if you have the
conditions, you get the result.**

—Oscar Wilde, in a letter to Marie Prescott

Now that you've familiarized yourself with and gotten into the habit of using Kanban, we will take the next step and introduce what we will be referring to as the *Scope of Influence* (or SOI for short). To make any sense of one's predicaments, one must first evaluate situational and contextual *influence*. Amidst the turmoil of transition, the deeply seeded consequences of a Traditional Psyche, and the general commotions of any given day, far too many factors and caveats come into play to draw clear-cut conclusions about what we can act on—delineating causation from correlation. In other words, what may be associated with an issue may not necessarily be responsible for it. Obligation, emotion, and distraction intertwine into what can be described as a hopelessly entangled fishing line we are using to fish for facts. We must pinpoint the ends and work our way backward to have any chance at disentangling the knotted complex-adaptive-system-of-a-mess we have found ourselves in and are helplessly bound to.

Recall the Imagination Gap and the broken iron triangle and how we are to compare ourselves to who we were yesterday instead of who someone else is today and focus on what is in fact achievable given our respective capacities. The SOI sets the foundation that encompasses our being—our "summary relative self"—and neatly captures Gagné's DMGT and the differing forms that influence can take. It's a table we will regularly revisit, leverage, and action as it will comprise every feasibly actionable significant point of influence relevant to us, organized into three simple categories:

▲ People:

Individuals (not groups) that *significantly* influence one's welfare.

Your two thousand Facebook friends do not count unless you regularly meet with each of them individually and they directly influence your well-being. The list can also consist of people in your memory and reminiscences that crop up every now and again that influence your daily moods and/or decision-making.

Listing primary (kin, neighbors), social (coworkers, a fanbase), collective (audiences, bystanders), or categorial (ethnicities, religion, nationality) groups and overgeneralizing and consequently lumping individuals into points of influence is counterproductive, as that can reflect prejudice, neglects nuance of character, and, more relevantly, limits specific action. It is often one's shared place or practice with another that you may detest or feel a sense of belonginess to, so identify it as such.

▲ Places:

Settings that *significantly* influence one's welfare.

Your bed, the beach, school, an airport, the slums, a restaurant, your parents' house, the shower. Maybe it's that Pilates class you attend once in a blue moon even though you're still paying the full subscription price.

▲ Practices:

Any process or activity that *significantly* influence one's welfare.

A hobby, an obligation, entertainment, a habit, and anything in between. Perhaps it's the trivial act of grabbing a coffee during work hours, an experience you look forward to and enjoy or a particular effort that keeps you motivated and energized. On the flip side, maybe it's self-deception, white lies, or the act of pursuing negative thoughts ad nauseam.

Include any person, place, or practice that consistently makes you cringe, grin, dread, hysterical, agitated, self-conscious, insecure, excited, bored, etc. Any point of influence that affects your daily welfare to a noticeable degree, whether positively or negatively, and that can (and *will*) be addressed independently, should go on the list.

The purpose of the SOI is to set the record straight, to detach that black cloud from who you really are. Lay it out, dissect it, and focus on the facts rather than opinion and emotionally driven filters. This is an objective initiative to set a scope to tackle. Constructing an SOI that completely encompasses one's truly significant influences will take time, certainly a few hours and perhaps a few days, to differentiate significant influences from one-offs and to distinguish which *category* of influence they are arising from.

Instinctively identifying what influences our daily welfare is a bootless errand littered with red herrings that obfuscate deeper causations. Whether it's a consequence of cognitive adjustments or a matter we have simply grown to accept as a part of who we are—"just something we do" or who we feel obligated to associate with—some points of influence will require a number of reflective iterations to unearth. An influence may be sitting right next to you this very moment, or it's the environment you're presently surrounded by or even something as innocuous as a tic you're expressing. By proactively and attentively *searching*, points of influence become that much more forthcoming. As for the question of how time-consuming this and other preliminary activities of adopting the Quasi-Chaotic Lifestyle may be, think of it like this: You spend thirty minutes trying to figure out what to order on Uber Eats and another thirty figuring out what to watch while you eat it. Are fifteen minutes of deliberation and trigger-tracking a day too much to ask given what's at stake? How do you know when to stop, you ask? You stop when you've identified *enough* items to action relative to what your iron triangle is able to consider, contemplate, and address in a given Sprint.

Remain acutely aware of your thoughts, feelings, sensitivities, and reactions and the connotative associations you subliminally default to throughout the day, taking note of any behavior, feelings, or thoughts that may unveil another point of influence. The best time to anticipate such triggers is during your highest and lowest emotional states. As you have urges to speak to someone, are reminded of an expectation, or *react* with automaticity to a specific situation, you will start to notice patterns. Given what could possibly be the most important undertaking of your life, your future deserves such acute thought and consideration. It's impossible to determine routes to desired destinations if we don't know where we currently stand. These raw, unfiltered inclinations will thus form the basis of your benchmark, the data that will instruct your next steps, the beginning of who you want to become and the end of who you don't want to be.

The word "actionable" will continue to crop up, as it is the crux of this lifestyle and why it works. Quantifying influences will allow you to envision *achievable* objectives you can count on your fingers! Recall a time you had an argument with someone who was being completely unreasonable. A person who argued with emotion rather than fact, with unstructured retorts rather than constructive reasoning, who would change the subject before putting each point to rest. This is what we are attempting to avoid with our SOI: carving the facts into a cinder block we are about to shatter our respective glass houses with. And of course, don't forget to amend your Backlog with this task and action it as you would any other!

Tracking Mike's journey? Read on.

Tracking Andrew's journey? Skip to page 383.

Tracking Rachel's journey? Skip to page 385.

APPLIED STEP 2: MIKE

"A list of influences? I can do that," Mike confidently mumbles to himself as he amends his Backlog with the card. To say it was an effort would be an understatement. It takes Mike nearly two weeks of anxiety-ridden procrastination before he is able to peel himself off his "gaming" chair (with a slumped backrest that perfectly resembles his posture, I might add) and muster the courage to give it a solid ten minutes of honest thought.

Figure 7-15: Mike's SOI

What you may first notice is the dimunitive scale of Mike's table (see figure 7-15), as its scope of influence is limited by what he's exposed himself to—there really isn't much beyond his desk at home and school. After he is done, Mike doesn't know what to make of it, unknowingly making cognitive adjustments, reassuring himself that a small circle is better than a bigger one, reflecting his "min-maxing" outlook.

With the SOI in mind during his gaming sessions, Mike realizes he's always gravitated toward "Top 10" videos on YouTube, where he spends a lot of his time when he's multitasking the tedious grinds his game necessitates or shoveling in a meal before getting back to it. Apart from that, the only household duty Mike has ever taken on is helping his mother cook, especially when it involves a bake. Growing up, he'd watch the Food Network on his mother's lap instead of the usual animated series other children were fond of. "Hmm, I suppose that's worth noting," he thinks to himself.

Elly, his crush, is an obvious entry, whose encounters make school more bearable. Savoring her proximal company whenever he gets the chance, the thought of Elly is often accompanied with a sigh of despair. "I guess I'll take note of that too . . ."

He's grown close to Chris, his online friend whom he's known for three years and one of the few people he resonates with. He often shares his day-to-day grievances with Chris, and they've had several memorable moments while gaming—moments of companionship and connectedness he has never experienced with others. They understand each other—"It's us against them"—and predictably reassure their shared perspectives.

The mocking of Jimmy, an insensitive and sarcastic Varsity ruffian, makes it difficult for Mike to converse with others. He's a bully who shoves Mike around every now and then, teasing him for taking interest in Elly. Mike's grown accustomed to this sort of treatment and resorts to indifference, feeling that in some way he deserves it. Mike writes Jimmy's name down, hesitant for what's to come.

Reflecting on the task during his Sprint Review, Mike takes note of how certain influences obstruct his flow (and increasingly so) when he's deeply immersed in intensive game play. He figures that what works best is to passively let realizations come to him as opposed to intentionally pursuing them, and then take note as soon as they arise. This is the extent of his initiative, and while it works, you wouldn't have expected anything other than minimal effort from Mike!

If you're only tracking Mike's journey, skip to page 387.

APPLIED STEP 2: ANDREW

Andrew amends his Kanban board with the SOI task and proceeds to busy himself with a list. Being a nocturnal overthinker, it doesn't take him long to make one. (See figure 7-16.) He isn't significantly influenced by anything other than the routine he is bound to.

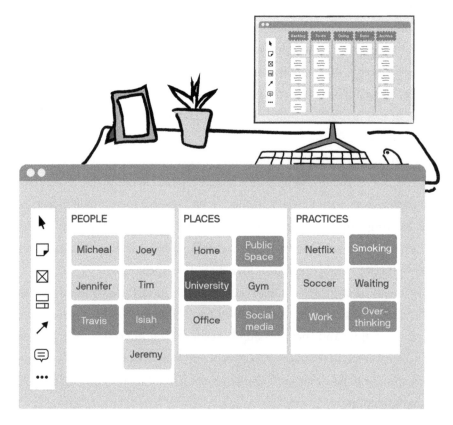

Figure 7-16: Andrew's SOI

Andrew is older than Mike, so you would naturally expect him to have netted more points of influence: his mother and father, Michael and Jennifer; his boyfriend, Travis; his two roommates, Joey and Isiah; and Tim, a work mentor-supervisor Andrew looks up to.

With the SOI in mind, he starts paying closer attention to what has been impacting his day-to-day psyche, and a few more points of significant influence emerge over the following days. Victim to a vicious cycle of overthinking, Andrew harbors a masochistic way of justifying and falsely validating the black cloud he's convinced he toils under. He plays and replays imaginary scenarios, hypotheticals, and thought experiments until they feel as real as the pain they invoke. It's a self-fulfilling prophecy that Andrew remains unaware of. He isn't *entirely* oblivious, though; he's aware of how ritualistic this habit has become and takes note of it. He believes it to be the means by which he is able to fall asleep: getting lost in his thoughts until he drops into unconsciousness.

In a rather unusual realization (he thinks), Andrew recalls a number of times he almost collided with a lamp post or a pedestrian or found himself as a deer caught in the headlights, literally getting honked at by oncoming traffic. He never seems to look up as he walks, and he almost always walks with his head down and his eyes on the pavement. He knew why, though; he despises public spaces. Having to digest all that he sees and hears publicly is exhausting, as he gets easily overwhelmed around groups and crowds and requires time alone to recharge. He would rather minimize the breadth of those experiences as much as possible.

Andrew takes notice of his impatience one day as he waits for an elevator to arrive at a busy hour. The wait seems to provoke deeply seated animosity; more than that, he realizes that he despises waiting in general! He takes note of it. As he does, he is immediately reminded of upcoming school assessments that he very much is *not* looking forward to. "I can't wait to graduate; I just can't," he murmurs. He is keen to move on to the next expectation.

Reflecting on the SOI task during his Sprint Review, Andrew finds that what works best for him is to identify what he'd rather be doing or feeling and take note of anything that prevents or hinders their fruition.

If you're only tracking Andrew's journey, skip to page 387.

APPLIED STEP 2: RACHEL

You may have been taken aback by the fact that Rachel finds her toilet to be a significant point of influence! During the week, as she tries to piece together her SOI (see figure 7-17), she realizes that she often looks forward to paying the toilet a visit, often for no other reason than to browse through her social feed. "That *is* kind of weird," she thinks to herself.

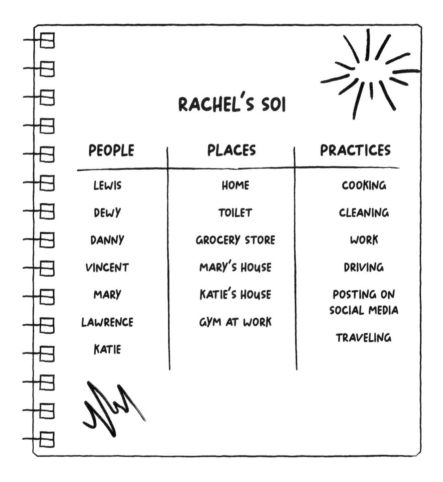

RACHEL'S SOI

PEOPLE	PLACES	PRACTICES
LEWIS	HOME	COOKING
DEWY	TOILET	CLEANING
DANNY	GROCERY STORE	WORK
VINCENT	MARY'S HOUSE	DRIVING
MARY	KATIE'S HOUSE	POSTING ON SOCIAL MEDIA
LAWRENCE	GYM AT WORK	TRAVELING
KATIE		

Figure 7-17: Rachel's SOI

Not only that, she catches herself daydreaming again about that trip to Spain eight years ago while accompanied by her pals Mary, Lawrence, and Katie. The fond memory of freedom, solitude, and negligence of any consequence. She looks back at photos and asks herself how it all got so complicated, so fast.

Rachel likes to drive, and sometimes she'll take a detour just to add another kilometer to the odometer. She enjoys the sound of the tires meeting the asphalt, the rumble of the engine, listening to the radio, and cruising along.

While it took her a few days to notice, she realizes that her first instinct when having to wait for something or someone is to pull out her phone and review the likes she's received on social media. Whether leaving a wholesome or sarcastic comment on another post or posting her own showcase of how loving a family she has, she likes to reopen the app just to monitor how much praise she's received.

Deep in thought, Rachel recognizes how often she misunderstands topics in conversation. She isn't sure why, but she feels as though she is either forgetful or the information she's receiving is not being parsed well. Right before dozing off to sleep one night, it clicks; she recognizes how bad of a listener she has become. Rachel actively tries to be patient with people. She always waits for others to finish speaking before she begins. But she realizes it is the way she unconsciously tunes out in conversation that is causing the issue. Maybe it has something to do with being consistently surrounded with noise, whether in the office or at home. Whatever the reason, she writes it down.

With the SOI done, she makes a Kanban card, pastes it to her wardrobe wall, and tapes her SOI right above it. During her Sprint Review, Rachel finds that proactively identifying problems that besiege her is the easiest method of ascertaining influence. Any person, place, or practice that gives rise to an issue, and, similarly, anything that might alleviate it, is deemed a significant point of influence.

CHAPTER 32
STEP 3: NAVIGATING SOI

Dare to be honest and fear no labor.

—Robert Burns, in a letter to Robert Graham

Now that we have our Scope of Influence set, the question that follows is how much positive or negative impact these people, places, and practices have on our welfare—whether it be our social, mental, spiritual, or physical well-being—and whether there are aspects to each that we are taking for granted or overlooking. The next step, then, is to simply rank our lists of influences by order of significance.

The subjective nature of such evaluations is exactly that: subjective, and it must be. If we are to conduct ourselves in line with the Quasi-Chaotic View, we must learn to judge situations correctly and honestly, unswayed by expectation, norms, or extrinsic constructs. Revealing our individualistic Self-Actualizing directives begins with self-sincerity. Forcing deliberation over what authentically resonates with ourselves and what doesn't relative to everything else—realizations that are often veiled by cognitive adjustments—will provoke profound realizations to further leverage. For now, reserve speculation as to how much credence we give our intuitions, though as you may recall, they might be foreshadowing!

It's important to note that, at least for now, minimal thought should be invested into *why* these influences make you feel the way they do. Don't excessively brood over your affinities and aversions; don't let empathetic, moral, or ethical implications get in the way. Simply label and order based on impulse. Just because kin, home, or a career you've recently committed to happen to be negative influences, and similarly, just because those of differing cultures or the same gender (in a manner that opposes ideologies or attitudes you've been raised to practice) or spending time alone happen to be positive influences, doesn't justify a recoil from labeling them as such, because these points of influence are considered potentially regrettable, taboo, or blasphemous. It doesn't make you a bad person. Living in bad faith, however—in other words, yielding to the external pressures of society by adopting false values—does underscore who your worst enemy is. Deceiving yourself into thinking you don't have the freedom to make choices, let alone admit "the facts" out of fear of potential consequences, is a recipe for self-inflicted desolation and (as described in Chapter 4: Self-Limiting Reluctancy) a direct assault on your own autonomy. That said, each point of influence may be associated with a dichotomy of implications both positive and negative. A "but" is usually quick to emerge and always worth consideration. As the expression goes, "Don't throw the baby out with the bathwater!"

I must warn you, however, that upon adopting the Quasi-Chaotic Life-style, it is highly likely that your negative influences will outnumber the positive. And given how "cutting things out" is a more convoluted process than "adding things in," we will spend more time exploring those influences as we track through our personas' journeys. You may feel inclined to interpret an SOI dominated by negative influences as a consequence of *who you are*, believing that you are incompatible with all the world has to offer. I urge you to reconsider, as the reality is quite the contrary: what you have been unwittingly associating, surrounding, and immersing yourself with may very well be incompatible *with you.*

So don't default to self-flagellating condemnation. While self-pity and self-loathing do offer a masochistic identity and a sense of safety with others who will affirm such a view, it is, again, denying one's autonomy. It denies the opportunity to work our way out of the Traditional Psyche and its confining directives skew and twist the lens through which we interpret reality. With a Quasi-Chaotic View, we now know better.

That's not to say that some negative influence indicators may very well be the result of your own shortcomings, whether it's narcissism, low social competency, unaddressed trauma, or being stuck in negative feedback loops. But these are actionable matters and by no means showstoppers. And while overhauling our respective imperfections takes time, that journey doesn't imply temporary destitution. All is not lost! There are people, places, and practices suited for everyone wherever they are on the path, even if you happen to be a forlorn outcast!

Newfound influences will continue to crop up while you navigate your SOI and throughout your journey. A point of influence may reveal itself in the moment as you experience its effects, or it may spontaneously surface by way of hindsight when you least expect—even awakening you at night! Whenever it happens, jot it down and amend your SOI to keep it up to date. And again, don't forget to amend your Backlog with this step and then action it as you would any other.

Tracking Mike's journey? Read on.

Tracking Andrew's journey? Skip to page 392.

Tracking Rachel's journey? Skip to page 394.

APPLIED STEP 3: MIKE

After mulling over what negatively influences his daily well-being, Mike realizes that an influence can be subtle—so much so that it becomes a part of who we are, and we accept it without question. Over the years, he has developed a stutter that has impeded his ability to communicate with confidence, which Mike feels is one of the reasons no one takes him seriously. He evaluates its relative impact and amends his list. Now fixating on what really gets his blood boiling, he figures he may as well get it all down and decides to give his SOI deeper thought. (See figure 7-18.)

What immediately springs to his mind is how much he despises the yearly visit his family makes to their hometown overseas to reunite with extended family. He isn't proficient enough with his mother-language to have any meaningful conversations with the other teenagers at the gatherings, frequently feeling estranged, unable to interconnect and express his frustrations. The judgments and comparisons he faces at these gatherings have become an annual dose of unnecessary and upsetting antagonism—a familiar alienation.

MIKE'S SOI

PEOPLE	PLACES	PRACTICES
③ MONICA	① BEDROOM	① VIDEOGAMES ④
THOMAS ②	③ SCHOOL ②	SLEEP ③
① ELLY	UNIVERSITY ①	② YOUTUBE
② CHRIS	② KITCHEN	④ COOKING
JIMMY ①	HOMETOWN ③	STUTTERING ②
④ HASEL		STUDYING ①
EXPATS ③		③ MIN-MAXING

Figure 7-18: Mike navigating SOI

He also discovers that what seemed to be the backbone of his school's social circles is a pervasive shared interest in social media: who is engaged in the latest trends, who is putting on the best show of superficiality, which peacock is spreading its feathers. "Pathetic, all of it." Mike doesn't fit in, nor does he want to.

School is both a blessing and a curse. Mike leans on the fact that he is doing reasonably well, given what little time he spends studying (which is practically nonexistent) and that he only has to listen in class to pass his year. He enjoys the thought of bettering others while making much less of an effort, giving him a sense of superiority. He justifies his mediocrity and unwillingness to study by telling himself he would top the grades if he put *any* effort into it. But saying he despises studying is an egregious understatement. He is so repelled by the act of reading, memorizing, and regurgitating what he couldn't care less about that hard labor or solitary confinement would be more tolerable. Studying always feels forced. It is always left to the last minute, always accompanied by desperation and anxiety. Upon reflection, Mike realizes how much more anxious he's become as the days draw nearer toward assessment deadlines, but what is more interesting is how much more he then engages in competitive gameplay. He can't help notice that he relies on his games for emotional support, release, and escape. This thought intermittently emerges in his mind. Mike tries to shake it out of his head, but it is already too late.

Now more self-aware, feeling disillusioned by what he sees now were cognitive adjustments, his patience, sensitivities, and nerves in flux, Mike's angst is beginning to spill over into his daily gaming routine. Tinges of toxicity and vitriol begin to accompany his reactions to misplays and defeat. His team's missteps trigger outbursts and damnation, making the entire experience unnecessarily tense and unpleasant as a sense of self-hatred bubbles up from within. He has no choice but to amend his SOI accordingly.

As much as his parents' love outshines that of his friends, his father is difficult to converse with. Thomas isn't a particularly good father, but he provides, ensuring that Mike never feels deprived of anything (as far as he is aware of). But that is the extent of their father-son relationship. Although Thomas always lets Mike do whatever his heart desires (which is never more than staying plastered to his monitor), he teases him about his insecurities, such as how Mike's first and last kiss will probably be from their household pup, Hasel. He jokes about Mike's stutter around his friends. He sees no issue with that. He's just trying to be funny!

Mike's Sprint Review of navigating his SOI involves a prioritization approach that takes on *levels* of negative emotion. He first addresses negative influences that provoke disgust, followed by those that trigger hatred, contempt, fear, guilt, and nervousness. Congruently, whatever he despises less is the highest positive influence!

If you're only tracking Mike's journey, skip to page 396.

APPLIED STEP 3: ANDREW

The approach Andrew takes is to ask himself, "If I were forced to immediately sever one of my influences, which would it be? How much better or worse off would I be? How would I feel if waiting were no longer unbearable versus eliminating the urge to smoke? How different would my life be if Travis were to vanish from the face of the planet tomorrow instead of my roommates?" These questions and the constructive inner dialogue that follow, suggest possibility and breakthrough—an encouraging prospect to envisage, and one that Andrew desperately needs. The appeal of eradicating negative influences is beginning to take over. Andrew feels ready. His realizations proliferate while he deliberates what is necessary to move to the next stage. Asking himself what is worse and what he'd rather not do opens his imagination to every aspect of his life. (See figure 7-19.)

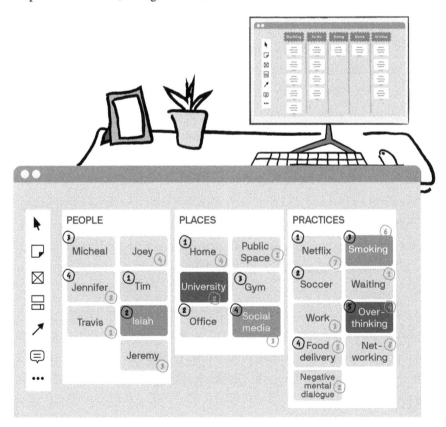

Figure 7-19: Andrew navigating SOI

His mentor, Tim, has encouraged him to network, to acquaint himself with everyone in the office and beyond. However, Andrew's shy and introverted nature always makes for aimless and awkward introductions. It feels nearly impossible to maintain a relaxed exchange, as he never understands what he wants from an interaction or how much he ought to value the opportunity of getting to know someone new. As a result, such interactions are difficult to navigate, making networking a horrifying experience—synonymous with public self-immolation. It often leaves bad impressions and pushes him even lower on the social scale as yet another conversation ends with a limp handshake and an "Uhh, you too . . ."

Netflix is Andrew's main source of joy and interest: a laugh, a tear, a rush of adrenaline. Without it, he has nothing better to do with his spare time (besides exercising a childhood habit of dribbling a soccer ball every week or so). He also feels it is his go-to getaway as soon as problems arise. His mind immediately gravitates toward the next episode of whatever he is binging on whenever he is confronted with hard decisions or bad news. To his credit, Andrew recognizes the escape and figures it warrants action. He also realizes the similarities Netflix has with smoking—another quick fix to dull his senses. And while smoking does alleviate some of the stress, the horrid odor it leaves on his fingers and facial hair are a repelling but "necessary evil."

Michael and Jennifer raised and cared for him, with dad the good cop and mom the bad—obvious influences to note. Tim and Isiah always extended an olive branch; they listened and genuinely took interest in Andrew's well-being. They share their meals from time to time, knowing Andrew couldn't cook to save a life if he had to. Speaking of cooking, much of Andrew's monthly expenses involve meal takeaways or home delivery—which goes straight onto his list.

As for Travis, he realizes there isn't any positive influence left to consider. It is negative throughout; even his joyful memories lose their positive glow. It is at this point that Andrew knows what needs to be done, though he doesn't have it in him to make it happen. "What would he do without me? What would he do to himself?"

If you're only tracking Andrew's journey, skip to page 396.

APPLIED STEP 3: RACHEL

Rachel's SOI is less straightforward to compile. Her approach to enumerate her influences is to count the number of times an influence plays a role in her day-to-day. She gives herself a week to estimate priority and increments the prevalence of an influence in a note app on her phone as they arise.

She quickly realizes the sensitivity of information she has been jotting down, so sharing her SOI with anyone other than her best friend, Katie, would not bode well. Her son and her husband being at the top of the list of negative influences is a bitter truth to accept, but Rachel understands that if she is to have half a chance at moving forward, then brutal honesty is necessary. (See figure 7-20.)

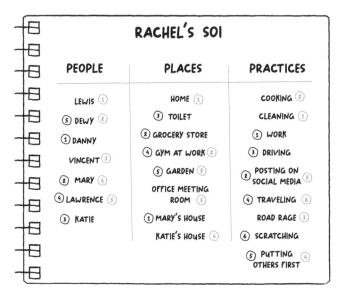

Figure 7-20: Rachel navigating SOI

Vincent, her brother in-law, uncle to her sons, and husband to Mary, is always a nuisance during shared excursions or family dinners. He always spoils her children, going against Rachel's will and instruction. When they ask for another can of soda or another pack of sugar-laced chocolate bars, Vincent always complies, even though Rachel tells them they've had enough. It sabotages her attempt to nurture discipline in her boys, always feeling like a slap in the face. What makes matters worse is how the boys perceive those experiences. They see Rachel as strict and difficult and Vincent as giving and loving, when in reality she is only trying to ensure healthy eating habits. Vincent obviously doesn't give a hoot.

This is another reason why a visit to Mary's house is an event she never looks forward to. Vincent and Mary's children are as spoiled as they come, and her boys pick up nasty habits Rachel has to spend weeks trying to undo. Whether it was the latest and greatest gaming console, tablet, or phone they had; table manners they didn't have; or messiness galore, it felt like a losing battle.

Truth be told, Rachel doesn't mind cooking and cleaning; she likes nurturing her family and being productive. Over time, however, it all turns into an exhausting chore accompanied by nagging, disruptions, and sometimes tears as her children play and flail in their chaotic ways. She always feels like she is in the way as her boys and husband whine about any noise her household responsibilities entailed. And then they give her more to do as she is doing it! How ungrateful.

Rachel has a love-hate relationship with her garden. While it helps her build self-esteem (knowing she can, at the very least, raise plants properly), there is never enough time to keep up with the many floral variants she has. The household keeps her busy enough!

At work, meetings at the office never fail to upset her. Each one is atrociously run, the chairperson always arriving underprepared with a slew of excuses. Every meeting is a free-for-all of agenda items with proponents talking over and louder than everyone else. No one is taking minutes, and irrelevant conversations take up most of their time. "How does this business even run?" she often wonders. Her tendency has been to put others first, to give another the benefit of doubt, to resort to compromise as opposed to negotiation. She is proud of this quality, but it always seems to relegate her to the sidelines.

As she contemplates these negative influences, she realizes how much maltreatment she's been putting up with. The thought of . . . Her phone buzzes, and as she snaps out of her musing, she discovers how hard she has been scratching her eczema. Her arm now bleeding, Rachel sobs in solitude, in her car. She's had enough. It all ends now.

CHAPTER 33
STEP 4: FIVE WHYS

The greatest enemy of any one of our truths may be the rest of our truths.

—William James, *What Is Pragmatism*

Nobel laureate physicist Richard P. Feynman was once asked in an interview why magnets repel. The interviewer, not satisfied with his answer that it's just what magnets do, edged Feynman on. Feynman shifted in his seat and responded with his own question: "How does a person answer *why* something happens?" He then gave an example (roughly recalled) "Aunt Minnie is in the hospital. Why? Because she slipped on the ice and broke her hip. That satisfies the answer. But it wouldn't satisfy someone who came from another planet and knew nothing." When the interviewer looked confused, Feynman went on. "Why did her husband take her to the hospital? Why did she slip on the ice? Why is ice slippery? Why does ice expand under pressure? You have to know what is *permitted* to be understood and known and what is not (restricted to our relative capacities of intellect, wisdom, cognition, knowledge, etc.). There are many different levels. In this case, it depends on whether you are a student of physics or someone who doesn't know anything. All I can say is that there is a magnetic force that makes them repel."

As frustrating as it is to be presented with an answer that doesn't satisfy our curiosity, we must also consider why we don't pursue and insist on answers to phenomena we are happy to accept as truth, whether consciously or unknowingly. Feynman emphasizes this point by suggesting, "You are not at all disturbed that you can't put your hand through a chair even though the electromagnetic force that prevents you from doing so is very similar to magnetic repulsion. It is simply taken for granted." With our respective iron triangles in mind, we have no choice but to pick our questions, understand our limits, and pursue answers we are permitted to understand or be known and that are worth our limited time and available resources.

The difficulty Feynman faces in attempting to resolve a "why?"—let alone communicate his answer to others—is precisely what we face in our attempt to understand *why* an SOI item imparts the influence it does to the degree it does. The context in which we allow something to be true is subjective, circumstantial, and relative. Our relative capacities limit our understanding of *why* we behave the way we do, contingent as it is on our age, our experience, the scope of our contextual understanding, and our people skills, among other influences. Similarly, upon confronting a question, another's ability to explain themselves adequately or behave themselves in a manner that appeals to you—assuming they understand the underlying reason of why they do/did what they do/did—also depends on *their* age, their experience, the scope of their contextual understanding, their people skills, and a plethora of other considerations. So *why* an influence is what it is to you, and why another may interpret that same influence differently, is entirely dependent on your capacity to understand and take diverse considerations into account as well as their capacity to understand, take diverse considerations into account, communicate effectively, *and* behave empathetically. We may as well be from different planets.

How, then, do we arrive at answers that satisfy our curiosity and our dilemma? This is yet another liberating virtue the Quasi-Chaotic Lifestyle has to offer. A "satisfactory answer" is one that is understood (that we allow to be true) or one that is actionable, or both—that's it. We aren't so much interested in understanding the forces that give rise to exhaustive/terminal existential questions but in what permits our own progression. "You have to know what it is that you are permitted to understand and be known and what it is you're not." Self-awareness and awareness of what we are "permitted" to understand, precludes what could otherwise be Incessant Distraction of the trivial. In other words, the questions you may be asking, the questions you feel need answering, and to whom and from whom you need answers, may simply be nonstarters given your capacity to make sense of them or another's capacity to constructively engage with them—resulting in what can only be described as a wild goose chase.

Let's take the hypothetical example of a friend whose lack of punctuality never seizes to disappoint you. After another night of waiting, you express your frustrations and demand an apology, only to receive pushback. "I'm sorry you're so upset about it, but I think you're overreacting. Suggesting that I'm disrespecting you or your time is a bit much." You then ask yourself the following question: "Why can't my friend understand that they are wrong?" What we are seldom mindful of is the nature of the topic at hand and knowing what we are and are not permitted to understand and know. For example, their obstinacy may be the result of underlying trauma (a defense mechanism triggered by confrontation—the aftermath of a difficult upbringing) whose effects have yet to be understood by them, let alone by you. Their position and reactions may be a consequence of different values, morals, or ethics derived from a disparate cultural upbringing. It may also be the result of varying intellectual or emotional capacities, not permitting a level of consideration you may *expect*. And so on. You are both experiencing life through differing lenses and consequently interpreting "objective" facts with subjective variance. Asking yourself such a question, then, would likely lead nowhere, and demanding an adequate answer would be a futile struggle bound to muddy your relationship. You are therefore required to accept a subjectively axiomatic conclusion: "That is what my friend believes, and I have no choice but to believe him," which is akin to Feynman's conclusion, "That is just what magnets do."

So, what do we do about it? How do we tackle uninformedness that is potentially hindering our authentic pursuits? We unearth the facts and face them: behaviors are a consequence, not a cause, as we have understood from a compatibilist outlook. Because our cognitive biases and cognitive adjustments shroud the truth, it is imperative to devote sufficient time and consideration to arriving at meaningful, sufficiently accurate, and actionable realizations. It's not a matter of determining the best possible outcome but an actionable, progressive, intermediary step in the right direction—inducing an iterative and potentially serendipitous exertion to arrive at what works.

We will thus resort to *Developmental Curiosity* and apply the Five Whys to the highest prioritized negative and positive influences and then work our way down. What is arguably the most time-consuming step as you pursue a Quasi-Chaotic lifestyle is mastering the fluency of self-reflection, which *will* get easier over time. You will find that our highest prioritized influences can be a little too hairy to tackle from the get-go, so as always, address what your relative capacity permits. As René Descartes suggests, "Divide each difficulty into as many parts as is feasible and necessary to resolve it." Divide and conquer! Bear in mind, it is essential to address positive influences with equal rigor to avoid oversights, in accordance with Feynman's cognizance. (This is also a method of "Cartesian doubt"—a form of methodological skepticism that grounds our ruminations in experience and reason rather than expectation and unsubstantiated belief.)

Before we press on, we must first adapt the Five Whys to what is most relevant at this stage in the process of adopting a Quasi-Chaotic Lifestyle. We are seeking to understand *why* items within our SOI influence us the way they do. There's a reason the SOI was not called Scope of Justifications! So, we will restrict our answers to why we *feel* the way we do and not *why we think another person behaves the way they do* or why a place or a practice is the way it is. The burden of justification is on all those in question, and how the problem is dealt with comes down to a cooperative initiative. From negotiations to compromise, some negative influences can be a temporary but necessary evil, binding two people to each other's iron triangle and giving rise to educational moral dilemmas.

Applying the Five Whys correctly can be challenging depending on how we're answering each consecutive Why. A few rules are provided to promote self-sufficiency and to help you avoid going too far off track. Practice makes perfect, so don't expect to get it right from the get-go or arrive at meaningful realizations in swift order.

The Quasi-Chaotic Five Whys Rules of Conduct:

▲ There will be alternative routes to answering the question; some will lead nowhere while others will sound shallow. So consider iterating through a few routes.

▲ What matters most is that you end up with a realization that warrants something actionable. So don't stress if the Why you act on does not turn out to be the actual root cause.

▲ Avoid repetition of points.

▲ If you haven't arrived at anything particularly profound after the fifth Why, keep going until you do.

▲ Avoid explaining *how* something happens but rather *why* it happens. Don't get stuck at one level; you need to go deeper.

▲ Avoid blaming others. The focus is on "I." Begin every answer with "I."

▲ If you get stuck on a Why and aren't sure how to proceed, leave a question mark and seek an Informed Perspective to help you go further.

▲ Use the *Therefore Check* to check your work, starting from your final Why and working your way upward. This will act as a troubleshooter to check the logical flow of the chain and force you to revise it if it isn't.

Below we apply the Five Whys to the aforementioned example regarding the punctuality of our friend:

▲ **Why?** Because I feel disrespected when someone isn't punctual.

▲ **Why?** Because I feel belittled to know my time is not being taken seriously.

▲ **Why?** Because I'm made to feel like my time isn't as important as others when others don't show up at the time that was agreed upon.

▲ **Why?** Because I take the time to get ready in advance and plan ahead to avoid wasting other people's time.

▲ **Why?** Because I value time more than anything.

Exercising the Therefore Check:

I value time more than anything, *therefore* I take the time to get ready in advance and plan ahead to avoid wasting other people's time, *therefore* I'm made to feel like my time isn't as important as others when others don't show up at the time that was agreed upon, *therefore* I feel belittled to know my time is not being taken seriously, *therefore* I feel disrespected when someone isn't punctual. The final Why revealed a subjective belief that is actionable. Assuming good intentions (what we ought to expect from a friend), you cannot fault them for what is subjective, especially if it's a matter they aren't aware of or believe in. How we action these realizations and confront those in question will be detailed in the following chapter.

For now, take your time as you work through each point of influence. Some items may take a day or two, and sometimes a week. Sometimes the Why isn't as forthcoming and will require additional support to draw out the truth. Counselling is recommended if you find difficulty making sense of the true nature of a problem. We are intrinsically biased, and the support of a professional, neutral third-party will help draw these realizations out. And while we aim to eliminate negative influences from our SOI, some seemingly positive influences may be derived from unfavorable sources or negative influences. Each point of influence warrants its very own card in our respective Backlogs, and as always, action them as you would as any other!

The SOI holds secrets we will endeavor to uncover, and we will do so by questioning each and every point of influence. What we may have otherwise relied on or assumed to be beneficial, seen to be an axiomatic or shared belief, or told ourselves to be a necessary evil may—and often is—not be the case, whether partially or entirely. The Five Whys will unveil the truth of your influences one way or another—whether or not these truths implicate matters we are not presently permitted to understand or know. Indulging in temporary fixes will not mix well with a lifestyle of change. As you know (or have yet to realize), expediency is suboptimal and stagnation is the enemy. All of these obstruct freedom of change and exposure to opportunity, impeding our quest for Self-Actualization.

Regardless of what the status quo has to say about your interpretation of an influence, stay true to yourself and state the facts, as they come. It's about how you *actually* feel and not what you think you *should* feel.

Tracking Mike's journey? Read on.

Tracking Andrew's journey? Skip to page 407.

Tracking Rachel's journey? Skip to page 412.

APPLIED STEP 4: MIKE

Mike goes on to add the Five Whys tasks to his board, creating a separate card for each of the positive and negative influences. In the last two weeks, Mike actioned most of the cards in his Backlog and managed half-decent reflections, but failed to deliver three assessments, worsening the dire situation he's already found himself in. Even though much of it is forced, he does feel a sense of progression; he *is* trying. His video games now increasingly anxiety-inducing, Mike grows desperate and nauseated.

Amidst the turmoil, however, he does make several important realizations. In attempting to apply the Five Whys, he faces a few deadlocks but iterates and perseveres. Some of his answers are shallow, others don't feel right, and a few are downright naive. Mike has to dig deep. "I'm better than this. Whatever it comes down to, I can handle it." He isn't quite ready to give up on his ego.

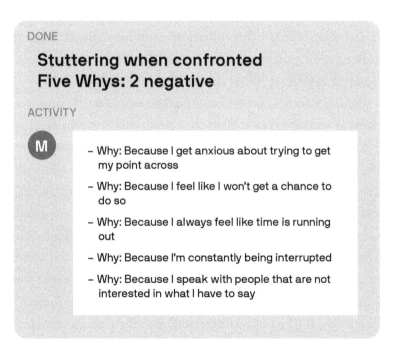

Figure 7-21: Mike stuttering (negative influence) Five Whys

Upon reflection, Mike comes to realize his stutter worsens whenever he is confronted. Whether it is a teacher at school putting him on the spot, having to deal with Jimmy's mischief, an online discussion escalating to an argument, or facing off with his father. He's always felt immense pressure trying to get a point across and realizes he's never been given enough time to elaborate. Mike needs that extra time to gather his thoughts and formulate an answer, but given how it seems he is always spoken to in a rush, every confrontation feels like a losing battle. His final Why came down to his upbringing and the fact that his father never gave him a chance to speak his mind, since he obviously knew better. (See figure 7-21.) Every interruption breaks Mike's train of thought—and with it, his confidence—and whenever he attempts to reiterate, his father speaks over him again, further diminishing his morale. Over time, his stutter developed into a habit that manifested in his day-to-day conversation. The bottom line, however, is that those he converses with don't take him seriously; they simply aren't interested in what Mike has to say. He starts to sense deeply seeded emotions bubbling up again; what he believed to be an idiopathic behavior (his stuttering) turns out to be the consequence of cowardice and inconsideration. The unraveling of this predicament leads Mike to a silent epiphany: "What else have I been missing?"

The sense of gratification and accomplishment Mike derives from his video games is second to none. His online peers cheering him on, his name atop the scoreboards—it's all that ever mattered; it's all he has. But he knows, deep down, that excessive hours spent on video games *are* a waste of time, restricting his opportunities, offering a depressing modicum of transferrable skills, and curbing his intrinsic growth. He's come to admit his passion is in fact an addiction, one that is threatening what he vaguely understands to be Self-Actualization. And with his Five Whys conclusion at hand (see figure 7-22), he now knows why he just can't move on. Why leave behind the only practice he sees himself to be proficient at? "Without my video games," Mike thinks to himself, "I'd be just another loser." Since he's hardly spent any time doing much of anything else, he would have nothing else to lean on!

DONE

Videogames
Five Whys: 1 positive

ACTIVITY

M

– Why: Because its so much fun compared to everything else I can do.

– Why: Because I love being better than others at something I'm good at

– Why: Because it makes me feel like I'm doing something right

– Why: Because everything else I do, I don't care much about since I'm not good at it

– ~~Why: Because playing games growing up was just fun~~

– Why: Because I'm afraid of failing

– Why: Because I don't want to let my parents down

Figure 7-22: Mike video games (positive influence) Five Whys

Mike is so far behind what he wants to achieve that the climb appears hopeless—a peak too distant and high. Even worse, not only has he realized a deep fear of failure; he worries about what his parents really think of him, for as much as they shower him with love, this very love is the impetus for his addiction. He cannot bear the thought of letting his parents down after everything they've done for him, and so he escapes to the comfort of his hedonistic pleasure. The soft structure of his upbringing left him insufficiently challenged, though it's not a matter he would fault his parents for entirely; after all, they wanted a better life for their child, given how difficult an upbringing they faced. It's a harsh actuality to face, one he cannot deny, but he is now aware of it.

The truth of his addiction reveals the underlying reasons for his disdain of studying: being forced out of hedonistic incapacitation and into quite the antithesis of it. The displeasure of drudging through what seems pointless to him exposes the truth he is running away from. It is why he procrastinates endlessly, wanting to avoid overwhelming anxiety, preferring to remain Incessantly Distracted. He's always blamed his inability to focus on how easily he's bored or distracted by the smallest of things around him. He's blamed the teachers, social expectations, the system, and the world for being backward and alienating. After years of religiously immersing himself in video games—a "harmless" activity he's enjoyed since he was a little boy—Mike now feels like he is too far behind his peers at school. He never really retains information, as he has always resorted to memorizing his subjects' contents the night before assessments. Every time he picks up a book, he is reminded of how utterly meaningless it feels, how he has to go through another night of tedious and mind-numbing recitation only to forget it all the next day. The weight on his shoulders growing heavier with each passing day, like a ticking time bomb, and with final exams just around the corner, Mike feels helpless.

In the two weeks that it has taken him to complete his SOI, Mike suddenly finds himself unwilling to continue with his online adventures. He is not quite sure why, but it just doesn't feel right anymore—a pain too visceral to describe. The thought of willingly choosing to go down this path of failure is now engraved in the back of his head. He is no longer carefree; he has now begun to Suffer. As a result, he updates his SOI to match how he feels.

As for addressing the negative influence of considering tertiary education, it takes Mike a few goes, but once he feels like he's arrived at an item worthy of action (see figure 7-23), he reads it back to himself. "I've never bothered to find out what the nature of work that field of study would lead to is like, therefore I've never seen if the theory's application is a matter that excites me, therefore I don't understand what the point of all the theory is, therefore I'm not overly enthusiastic about any topics, therefore I don't know what I should pursue . . . Wow." What may seem obvious to you often isn't the case for those living with cognitive adjustments or in angst. More importantly, Mike is well aware that the problem remains, but the simplicity and actionability of his realization make his emancipation seem *possible*. The mere fact of knowing what he could be doing makes the influence that much more manageable.

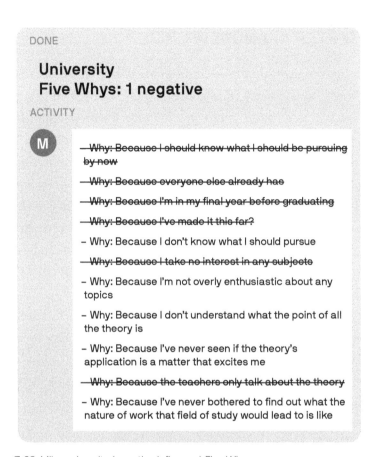

Figure 7-23: Mike university (negative influence) Five Whys

Not sure of how the rest of his peers figured out what they wanted to do, he decides to ask around, anonymously posting questions on public forums. It isn't long before he realizes the majority are in his shoes or are simply fulfilling their parents' wishes! It is a matter ubiquitous amongst individuals of his age, giving him some solace to leverage. He didn't know any better because he never considered to ask what the endgame would look like—the strategy he has always employed while gaming in the online realm he now seeks to let go. Mike knows what must be done.

If you're only tracking Mike's journey, skip to page 415.

APPLIED STEP 4: ANDREW

Andrew decides to dedicate the weekend to his Five Whys; he has nothing better to do anyway. He starts off by addressing his mother's influence. Who do you know that never fails to bum you out after a conversation? Perhaps someone who never ceases to lecture you, question you, and provide "advice for your benefit." A conversation that always seems to be one-sided and stale, to which your only response is, "Yeah, I know" or "Yeah, I guess," and any rebuttal risks provoking another thirty minutes of criticism. Andrew realizes that what his mother is constantly asking of him is not something he can possibly do. Advice is to be appreciated, but there is a line to be drawn, and it seems as though this line has been nonexistent throughout Andrew's relationship with Jennifer.

Andrew concludes that he cannot live up to his mother's expectations because his life has become intolerable. He's never been able to make a decision for himself, always capitulating to what was asked of him. While not deeply profound, Andrew arrives at a why with a somewhat actionable directive (see figure 7-24): "That's good enough for now, I suppose."

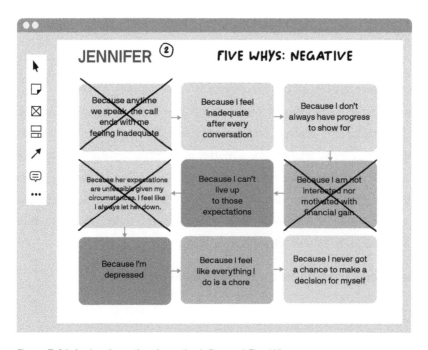

Figure 7-24: Andrew's mother (negative influence) Five Whys

Andrew then turns his attention to why he feels Jennifer has a *positive* influence. (See figure 7-25.) He has to reiterate a few times, scratch his head at the Rules of Conduct once or twice. All the while, his phone has been buzzing with social media updates; they are starting to get under his skin. "Why is this so difficult!?" But he keeps going until it sounds right, leading to a rather straightforward realization: his mother truly does care, it just isn't expressed in a manner that feels like it. He decides that what is actionable is his appreciation. He can't remember the last time he expressed appreciation for his parents' commitment and figures it's about time he did. He doesn't understand *why* their care feels so restrictive and authoritative, but now feels compelled to make sense of it, one way or another.

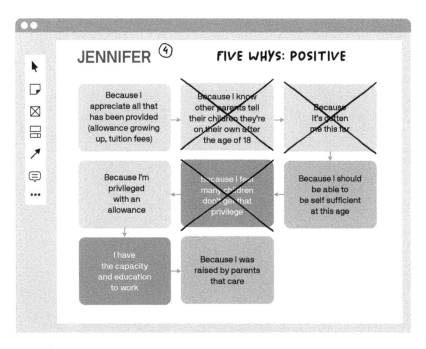

Figure 7-25: Andrew's mother (positive influence) Five Whys

Andrew proceeds to work through his next prioratized negative influence. (See figure 7-26.) "I don't have a reason to be happy, therefore I feel like something's wrong with me, therefore I get anxious around happy people, therefore I feel alienated from others." Everywhere he looks, he sees reasons. Everyone has somewhere to go, someone to meet, something to look forward to . . . but Andrew doesn't. Still, the spite that once seemed to bubble and boil anytime he saw a happy couple or a cheerful family seems to fade away. It doesn't make him feel any better about the fact that he hasn't found a reason to be happy yet, but it makes outdoor errands that much more bearable. He realizes that to be comfortable in public, he has to find a reason to be happy—plain and simple.

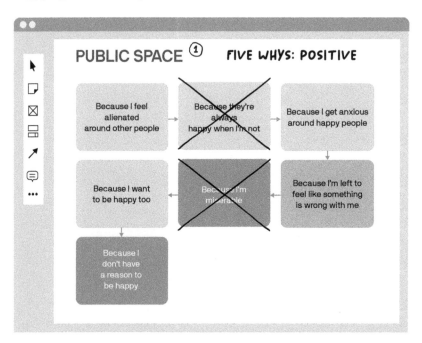

Figure 7-26: Andrew public space (negative influence) Five Whys

Andrew realizes he's been conforming to extrinsic desires and none of his own—at least none with an authentic drive. To make matters worse, he is never able to commit to anything other than what he believes to be the routine tasks he has to do to fit the image of what his mother regards as "successful." For every waking hour he isn't studying, exercising, practicing an instrument, or learning a third language, he feels he is letting his parents and himself down.

As for Travis, the outcome catches him by surprise. Given how much Andrew feels like he has to put up with, being forced to focus on himself leads to a realization that seems to explain all that is wrong with the relationship: the slew of negativity is a consequence of the distance that separates them. They've never stopped chatting on the daily, but ever since Travis moved interstate, there isn't much left to talk about. And given how hard circumstances are for both of them, all there is to talk about is the difficulties they both face. Andrew realizes he hasn't been contributing much positivity to the conversation anyway. Maybe it's just the distance compounding with circumstance? Andrew's epiphany leaves a lump in his throat. (See figure 7-27.) His phone buzzing, he heavy-handedly turns it off, tucks his notebook away, and leaves for a walk.

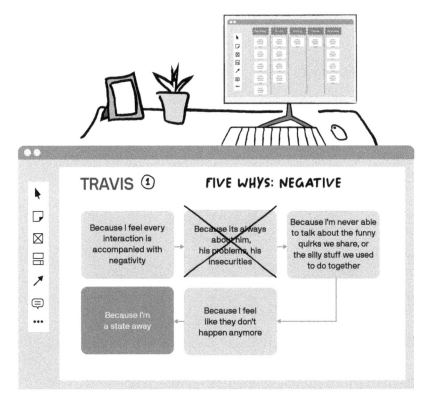

Figure 7-27: Andrew boyfriend (negative influence) Five Whys

Upon returning home, feeling a little refreshed and determined to muster through, he turns to the next negative influence: his impatience. (See figure 7-28.) Andrew can't fight the facts. The reason he despises waiting is a product of cognitive adjustment: he rationalizes his rage with the industrious inefficiency provoked by any inconvenience—even though he knows he is only rushing back to the comfort of home and his nightly, vapid routine. The sense of captivity he desperately wants to rid from his life is a self-fulfilling prophecy: living in bad faith, denying his own freedom while relying on it. Waiting leaves him with his thoughts—and two conflicting demands that provoke the discomfort: he needs to do what he feels he ought to be doing but doesn't want to, and yet that is all there is for him to do. Ashamed and disgusted with how much autonomy he's conceded, he knows it's over. He is now aware. He is now in control.

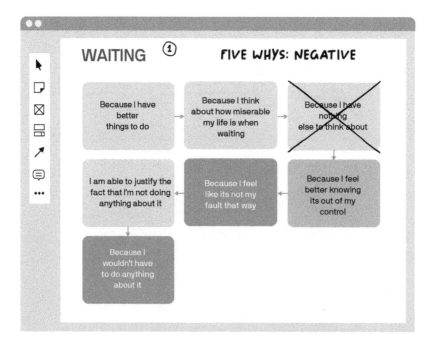

Figure 7-28: Andrew waiting (negative influence) Five Whys

If you're only tracking Andrew's journey, skip to page 415.

APPLIED STEP 4: RACHEL

What appears clear in retrospect may not be readily apparent in the midst of chaos. An impression that may have seemed innocuous could be covering an ugly truth that we are compelled to face, should we pursue Self-Actualization. Rachel's first Five Whys application takes place, ironically enough, in the toilet. It has been a particularly difficult day, but she decides to make the time and lock herself in to get it done. The screaming and thumping taking place outside—"Mom! He took my phone! Dewy took my phone!"—gradually set fire to the frustrations she has been putting up with. Her hands now trembling, she contemplates her fourth Why: "Why am I left alone? Why is this so difficult? I'm left alone because I'm in the bog, for goodness sakes! The only bloody place I get to myself is in the toilet, and I still need to justify it!" Rachel gathers her breath and lets out a deafening screech: "Will you two knock it off!?" She scratches off the fifth and gives it another shot. (See figure 7-29.) Now on the cusp of outrage, it finally clicks: the toilet is the last place at home where Rachel feels like she has boundaries. Writing her fifth and final Why comes with an outburst of tears. "Rachel, are you alright? Honey?" asks Lewis as he shuffles by the door. "I'm fine, just leave me be, please . . ." she helplessly pleads in despair.

Figure 7-29: Rachel toilet (positive influence) Five Whys

It is now crystal clear: her family has become entirely dependent on her, making her feel like an abused caregiver. Dewy, Danny, and Lewis's first tendency when confronted with hunger, conflict, a mess, or any discomfort is to call out for Rachel rather than addressing it themselves. Being a mother doesn't warrant such treatment. Rachel is now more determined than ever. She sobs into her pillow that night and decides to revisit her SOI when she is ready.

Figure 7-30: Rachel gym (negative influence) Five Whys

The very next morning, instead of using her lunch break for a quick workout, she decides to take on one more item: the gym! (See figure 7-30.) She doesn't feel like pushing through another high-intensity routine, so she thinks, "I may as well figure out why not." Rachel does enjoy the workouts, especially with her colleagues. Feeling a sense of productivity, it is one of the few practices she does for herself. There's always a bit of friendly banter and nostalgic songs playing in the background that they all sing to. But her lack of progress comes down to the fact that her family's bad eating habits osmotically affect her ability to stay true to her diet. She's always had to cook separate meals, which means more washing and more nagging to put up with. It's either that or an uphill battle trying to get her family to eat healthy again. Also obstructing her way, however, is a myriad of bad influencers she knows she has to work through.

POSTING ON SOCIAL MEDIA ②

WHY: BECAUSE I ENJOY SHARING JOYFUL MOMENTS WITH OTHERS

WHY: BECAUSE I VERY MUCH ENJOY THE LIKES AND COMMENTS TO MY POSTS

WHY: BECAUSE I GET A SENSE OF VALIDATION FROM THEM

WHY: BECAUSE I NEED TO FEEL LIKE I'M LIVING A MEANINGFUL AND HAPPY LIFE

WHY: BECAUSE I HATE MYSELF

WHY: BECAUSE I REFUSE TO ACCEPT ALL MY HARD WORK HAS AMOUNTED TO ANYTHING LESS

Figure 7-31: Rachel social media (positive influence) Five Whys

She has time for one more item on the list. (See figure 7-31.) She is just about to open her Facebook feed and thinks she'll address it there and then. Posting the latest and greatest "happy" portrayal of her family and day-to-day achievements, she realizes how much she depends on validation from her friends and family to feel like she's living a meaningful life, that her life isn't overburdened with constant hardships and heartaches. A "happy family" is how Rachel evaluates how she is faring—an evaluation based on values she's grown up with. Living in denial and depending on validation to affirm her cognitive adjustments, she's accepted the normalcy of always giving 200%. She lives a lie to avoid the question any mother would shudder to consider: "What if . . . ?"

CHAPTER 34
STEP 5: CUTTING

It isn't positions which lend one distinction, but one who enhances positions.

—Agesilaus II, *Plutarch on Sparta*

You may be familiar with "cutting" and "bulking" when it comes to bodybuilding. It's the process of adopting a nutrient-dense diet of caloric deficit followed by a calorie-dense diet of caloric surplus. The former stimulates fat loss to retain lean muscle; the latter promotes muscle gains but involves fat gain as well, depending on how strict the diet is. (A lenient, unhealthy bulk is referred to as a "dirty bulk.") Cycling back and forth between the two can ensure an optimal bodybuilding venture. Similarly, we have "dirty-bulked" the points of influence populating our respective SOIs, and it's time we shed the excess holding us back. Such cutting can be physically and emotionally demanding, but the benefits are only realized if we go the full nine yards. Time is of the essence, and Detractors who impede our quest for Self-Actualization are to be eliminated. This is *nonnegotiable*!

To begin, we must rid ourselves of two presumptions:

1. Cutting does *not* imply impulsive termination of relationships or leaving everything behind and voyaging to mid-Atlantic archipelagos. With the hard facts our Five Whys conclusions afford, we will seek to address the roots of negative influences and not necessarily the points of influences associated with them. The focus is on causation, not correlation.

2. Cutting does *not* involve cutting everything that *makes us feel bad*. To avoid falling into hedonistic territory, we must fixate our perspective on a more constructive outlook. Given what we know of the *twenty-first-century*

dilemma, it would be counterproductive to place ourselves in an environment void of challenge. Just because that lousy treadmill we bought on eBay evolves into a routine we despise, for example, doesn't mean we drop walking or exercising altogether. Challenge doesn't necessarily involve people, places, or practices you loath; it is simply anything that requires great mental or physical effort. Now primed for change, we know better and continue iterating through other means of achieving fitness, such as finding a worthy challenge that is also something we look forward to.

With that out of the way, let's take a seemingly benign example of a nuisance you've been hypothetically having to put up with. Let's say you're fed up with your friend Kyle for teasing you about a matter that never fails to elicit a reaction he finds funny (a matter that gets under your skin for personal reasons he is unaware of). The most rational next step is to bring your pain to his attention before resorting to drastic measures. Minimizing collateral damage and fixating our attention on what is truly detracting value will prevent us from throwing the baby out with the bathwater. But *how* we take action can certainly make for awkward, sticky, or in some cases intimidating situations given the unpredictability of outcomes—all the more reason to invest in a little preparation.

Now, before you ask, "Isn't careful planning the antithesis of what the Agile philosophy preaches: to fail fast?" Rightfully so. However, when it comes to big decisions and Cutting, big risks are to be expected. Agile organizations cannot drop departments, shrink business operations, or relocate their headquarters on a whim. The thought and time required for any given decision depends on the severity of the repercussions requiring consideration, as there is no turning back once action is taken. Remember: we're not contemplating ways to live with, work around, or alleviate the effects of a negative influence. We're cutting out root causes of negative influences entirely. The decision is always in favor of Self-Actualization. Recall the SAAC—Self-Actualization Auxiliary Coefficient (see page 318): "What are all the Self-Actualizing potentialities I lose if I don't cut this negative influence?"

Cutting Gracefully

Cutting places and practices is *relatively* easy. They don't offer resistance; your conviction will suffice. When it comes to people, however, it's another story. Assuming shared good intent, it is imperative to approach the matter in a considerate and empathetic manner to avoid coarse or confrontational reception. If you recall, characterizations of a Self-Actualized individual include independence and freedom from reliance on others. One who harbors a Quasi-Chaotic View is also repelled by experiences that *hinder* Self-Actualization, and this includes conflict when it's unnecessary (if one is truly independent) and unconstructive.

To mitigate adversity when Cutting involves people, we refer back to conclusions drawn of our Five Whys to form a dialogue (expressed face-to-face with a tone of conviction) that will reinforce the bottom line: enough is enough. Thomas Gordon, an American clinical psychologist, developed a concept called the *I-statement* in the 1960s. The structure of an I-statement goes something like this:

I feel [insert feeling word] when [describe what is causing the feeling]. I would like [what you would prefer to happen instead].

The intent is to enable a level of assertiveness in conflict resolution without blaming or pointing fingers, which reliably elicits defensive reactions.

A common response (also referred to as a *You-statement*) to Kyle's maltreatment may be, "Can you please knock it off?! You know how much that topic irritates me, and you can see it's only funny to you! How would you like it if I yapped the same damned line that pissed you off around other people every single time we met?" Or, if you have a little more self-control: "Mate, can you please stop? You're not funny and now you're being childish about it."

In either example, you will *feel* the impact of the words by the tone. You-statements are interpreted as hostile because being accusatory is threatening. One may feel as though their morals, values, or egos are being attacked; the aforementioned You-statements would have therefore been interpreted in overexaggerated ways, such as "Are you saying I'm a bad person? Are you saying I'm immature? Are you saying I don't have a sense of humor?" The amygdala overcomes critical thinking. Kyle, not recognizing the emotional distress of another as the result of genuine pain, may decide to double down by repeating his one-liner or retort with, "Why can't you just take a joke?!"

Instead, using an I-statement will sound a little more like this: "I feel genuinely upset every time this topic is brought up—especially in public—because I've asked for that to stop several times already. It's doubly worse when I react this way in public, as it's embarrassing. I'd really appreciate it if friends can be considerate of each other's honest asks."

You may be skeptical, but an accusatory tone does no more than raise tensions while neglecting the other's perspective and the fact that everyone has a past, a present, and their own capacities to work with. (Recall the topic of free will [see page 211] and Feynman's dilemma.) I-statements present good intentions. They not only bring the wrongdoing to the wrongdoer's attention, but they shift the focus to oneself and suggest a willingness to fix the situation without attack or shame. You have to try it to believe it, and yes, it does take practice. You may have to plan out and memorize I-statements in advance, but as with any other new skill, the automaticity of its use will come. Once you get the hang of it, you will learn to restrain yourself when you feel the "you" bubbling up as an incident occurs. And there's more! If necessary, feel free to use your Five Whys breakdown (tidying up the language used if it was excessively emotional) to further elaborate on the "because" part of your I-statement if you find the Detractor in question unconvinced. Read your list bottom to top (as you would with a Therefore Check), and you'll be surprised to see how your sincerity will (usually) be received.

Now, if we are to assume the other is understanding (which is what we want from those we surround ourselves with!), we should expect empathy *and* support to rid the relationship of inflictions brought to light. If they aren't, they will have consciously decided to neglect our genuine attempt to rectify a negative influence that is impacting our welfare, our effort to better the relationship, and, more importantly, our quest for Self-Actualization.

Assuming our grievance with Kyle has been made explicitly clear, you may come to realize after an honest discussion that he didn't value his public image as much as you did and therefore didn't see it as a problem. He also may not have been aware of how deeply seated the topic was for you, provoking a pain point of a difficult past. Kyle now must decide if he wants to respect what is subjectively important to *you*, which ultimately comes down to priorities. In most cases, the issue is resolved, and if your friend is a true friend, they may be willing to help you address whatever shortcoming, sensitivity, or insecurity made the negative influence as impactful as it was!

However, should they choose to disregard your sincerity and continue with the maltreatment *after the matter*, we can safely conclude that Kyle values a moment's chuckle more than your important values and deeply seated triggers. The fact of the matter is, the decision was already made. The root cause of the negative influence was going to be cut, one way or another, even if it meant losing a friend.

Every actioned iteration of a Five Whys conclusion will bring to light newfound negative influences to deal with. If this is the case, simply amend your SOI with a new item to address. We are peeling back the layers of seemingly knotted predicaments and addressing them one layer at a time. Now knowing the attitude this person holds in rejecting your sincerity, and depending on how far down their list of priorities you turned out to be relative to where you place them in yours, it would be incontrovertible to suggest this relationship to be Less Permitting (not as Self-Actualizing, as someone else you could invest your time and attention into). Such a realization instructs labeling this point of influence with negative association in your SOI. Applying the Five Whys once more, now informed, you conclude that "I can't befriend anyone that doesn't hold me to a similar standard as I to them," which suggests a dead end. The negative influence is no longer *correlated* to Kyle; the negative influence *is* Kyle. Depending on how impactful cutting this particular Detractor would be, you may have found yourself in possession of a Hard Problem. If so, you know precisely what comes next: an RSC.

Be who you are and say what you feel, because those who mind don't matter, and those who matter don't mind.

Bernard M. Baruch, *Long Island Star-Journal*

Regardless of how important you tell yourself a person is, facts are facts. The fact of this matter is that you've been hurt, disrespected, and overlooked—so much so that it began to negatively influence your welfare. You took the time to recognize it, attempted to make sense of it, gave them the benefit of the doubt, and then tried to rectify the matter in a nonaccusatory manner with a constructive outlook. Kyle was given a chance to control how the negative influence would be cut, but his response left you with only one path forward. If you want to make the most of what you are permitted, you know better than to settle for anything less than what is best for you. No single person is worth the degradation or pain. Everyone has their stories, quirks, and mannerisms you find cute or funny, and similarly they have their shortcomings, issues, and behaviors you find irritating or aggravating. So, resist the temptation to view what you are thinking of giving up as irreplaceable or the act itself as a moral dilemma.

Let us now address a few common taboos about cutting people:

▲ **A soulmate:**

There are almost eight billion people on this blessed planet. The chances that you only resonate with one person and one person alone is statistically damn near impossible. The chance that you unknowingly walk past "the ones" you are most compatible with *on a daily basis* is almost certain. Sure, circumstance make the moments you share more special than others, but such moments are ubiquitous—but those moments won't exist unless you're willing to move on after the relationship has ended.

▲ **Family:**

Whether you adhere to social constructs or not, the weight of "bloodline" and the responsibility expected with family does not need to be as sacrificial or morally obligatory as you think. A controversial topic, we must sometimes question the role of family in our life. How big of an influence does family play? This differs from culture to culture, but you only have this one life to live. Will you live it in the shadow of people you had no choice to call your own, or will you take a stand on what may be toxic, restrictive, choking customs and traditions that keep you caged in the thought of what could've, should've, or might've happened if you had chosen your freedom?

▲ **Your clique:**

> If a person in the group becomes a Hard Problem and their contact
> is unavoidable, then it may be time to part ways with it all. Sure, you
> share history and memorable experiences. And yes, it may be a shame to
> discontinue the regular catch-ups and get-togethers. And of course, you
> can still reach out and meet the rest. But don't think for a second you
> have any obligation to put up with Detractors. All too often, we feel the
> need to stick with those we had no choice but to acquaint ourselves with.
> Much like family, the friendships that formed may have been the result of
> nothing more than setting—whether it was attending the same school or
> university, living in the same neighborhood or dorms, or regularly visiting
> a household because your parents or friends knew theirs.

Further impulses of resentment may fester and corrode your sanity, breeding
scathing questions such as "How could she?" or "If it wasn't for him, I'd still
have . . ." or "After everything I've done for them" or "I can't be around this
group anymore because of her . . ." as you wrestle with the dissonance of what
you would have done in their place. As the saying goes, "Resentment is like
drinking poison and hoping it will kill someone else." Resentment is death.
We know better than to stagnate. We know to change.

What comes next need not entail a ceremony or even an explanation.
All that follows should be graceful detachment. What does that involve, you
may ask? Very little. Everything that could have been said was said, all that
could have been considered was considered, and all that we could have done
was done. We move on, and continue living life to the fullest with the aid of
RSC instruction!

LESS PERMITTING POSITIVE INFLUENCES

Equally as important as cutting negative influences is cutting Less Permitting
positive influences.

*It is worth noting that cutting such influences is carried out precisely as with
negative influences. Furthermore, addressing Less Permitting positive influences
is better deliberated after working through negative influences (and in some*

cases after you've hit your Quasi-Chaotic stride)—which is what Mike, Andrew, and Rachel will be doing. Remain conscious of "how much is enough" and what your iron triangle permits to avoid cutting out a positive influence that may very well be Less Permitting but sufficiently Self-Actualizing in the interim. If, with all things considered, you believe that you lean on the influences to necessitate change, then consider Bulking (adopting new people, places, and practices, detailed in the following chapter) before cutting them out to minimize collateral and regret and to maintain a sustainable and healthy psyche.

The following questions and considerations will help you determine whether a positive influence is Less Permitting or not:

▲ **Scope:**

If a positive point of influence is one-dimensional (a well-paying, enjoyable job that is stringent, restrictive, routine-heavy) and doesn't offer a scope in which opportunity can flourish, then question it:

▽ Does it (and will it continue to) permit change?

▽ Does it (and will it continue to) facilitate opportunity?

▽ Does it (and will it continue to) challenge me?

▽ Does it (and will it continue to) support my quest for Self-Actualization?

▲ **Time:**

If a positive point of influence's "opportunity-versus-time" factor (frequency of exposure to opportunity) is relatively low, you will want to consider iterating while remaining wary of restrictive routines.

▲ **Resources:**

If a positive point of influence is too costly, and resources can be better utilized to catalyze even more change, then it may not be favorable.

The ideal ratio is to invest minimal time and resources for maximum Quasi-Chaotic value! Use this rule of thumb to evaluate your positive points of influence.

In summary, the diagram below (see figure 7-32) illustrates the routes of Cutting depending on the complexity of the problem we are confronted with. It begins with either a simple or a Hard Problem (think of a simple problem as a one requiring an errand, a conversation, or a few clicks of a button, like unsubscribing from newsletters that litter your inbox) that we realize through the use of the Five Whys. Some Five Whys conclusions will be straightforward to address, others will not. In the case of cutting negative influences relating to people, first assume cooperation and attempt to resolve the issue using an I-statement. If an I-statement doesn't do the trick, then we are presented with a new negative influence—which may ultimately be the person themself. Upon working through another Five Whys, you may either arrive at a nonnegotiable dead end or decide to give the Detractor a chance to reconsider using a new I-statement and Therefore Check based on a the newly targeted Five Whys. If this fails to abolish the negative influence, then we are left with a Hard Problem to address by: formulating an RSC, acting on the decision, and living with it.

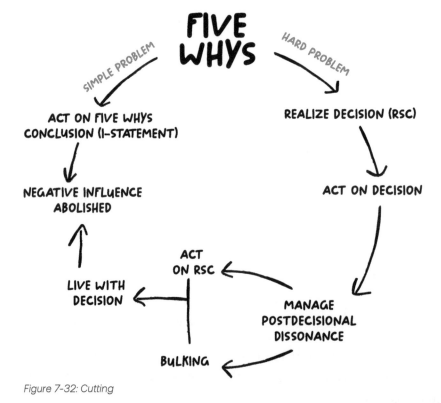

Figure 7-32: Cutting

The product of the Cutting phase is a list of To-Dos: mandated items of action we will seek to fulfill with ardor and with certainty in the name of Self-Actualization! Each item will detail how you plan to rid your SOI of negative influences and Less Permitting positive influences, which can consist of:

▲ **Generating and acting on straightforward solutions**

▲ **Preparing and delivering I-statements**

▲ **Preparing, acting on, and living with an RSC**

Each item makes for a card to amend our Backlog with. All stagnating influences *will* be addressed eventually—the sooner the better, as soon as your iron triangle permits. Once there is *enough* to action (and a few to select from), we will make the time to execute the promises we've made to ourselves, holding ourselves accountable to bask in the serenity that comes with our subsequent liberty. "How bad do I want change?" should always be foremost in your mind.

As we pop the bubble we've been blowing for as long as we can remember and expose ourselves to the harsh truths of a reality that isn't working (depending on how dirty your natural bulk has been), you may have to put in more work than you thought. Consider this Buddhist proverb: "Pain is inevitable. Suffering is optional." The end to your Suffering is only a few hard facts away. If you want it bad enough (and I trust that you do if you've made it this far!), muster up the courage to see it through. I promise you will not regret it.

Tracking Mike's journey? Read on.

Tracking Andrew's journey? Skip to page 432.

Tracking Rachel's journey? Skip to page 438.

APPLIED STEP 5: MIKE

His exams are now two weeks away and Mike is experiencing overwhelming anxiety. He notices how many more toxic comments he's been leaving in forum threads and comment sections of videos. In an attempt to cope with unbearable distress, he tried to play a game or two, but it only ended up exacerbating his condition, resulting in more frequent outbursts. His escapes are turning into aggravating, soul-crushing spaces. He can't sleep, finds it difficult to eat, and the lump in his throat persists. "His forces for change" are now beginning to outweigh his "forces against change" as Mike is now boarding the first departure out of his Unreachable Terminal.

It is down to either his list of To-Dos or studying, and of course Mike chooses the former. Some take more thought than others as he paces back and forth in his room, overthinking the consequences he'll face. "It can't get any worse than this. I may as well get it over with." He jots down his list on the back of a pizza brochure and decides to act on each throughout the week. (See figure 7-33.)

Figure 7-33:
Mike action plan
from Five Whys
conclusions

Anticipating the need to use I-statements for influences that are likely to turn confrontational, he decides to prepare one and test it with someone he's a little more comfortable with. The first negative influence he addresses is his father and his stutter. Mike understands that his father has good intentions and is not maliciously bullying him, however, he seems unaware of how his unwelcome comments and constant interruptions affect Mike. It takes him about half an hour to scribble and rescribble an I-statement that makes sense, one that doesn't sound too robotic. He takes his cue card to his father and cautiously begins. "Dad, can . . . can I talk to you for a minute?" His father is startled; he's never heard his son utter those words. "I get s-stressed out and anxious when . . . when I'm interrupted, and because of that I-uh stutter. I have a hard time formulating my s-sentences. I'd apprecia . . . I'd appreciate it if I wasn't interrupted and was not made f-fun of so that I can express myself clearly and work my way out of th-this stutter." The silence that follows is deafening, Mike's heart races as he waits. "I'm sorry, son. I . . . I didn't know." Thomas stands up and embraces his teary-eyed son. "I'm sorry I made you feel this way. I didn't mean to." It must be months, maybe years, since their last genuine hug. Mike, overwhelmed with emotions he has been bottling up for years, wipes his tears and shuffles back to his room in melancholy.

The very next day, Mike decides to make a proposition to his parents. He gets them together and suggests he skip his visit to his hometown until he is better able to communicate with his extended family. He then suggests that he spend the time during the holidays attending a supplementary language course of his native tongue and insists that his parents speak to him in his native tongue at home as well. His parents look at each other, confused but pleasantly surprised and genuinely moved by his will to connect with his uncles, aunts, and cousins. "You could learn the language while we're there, you know, but I suppose one trip wouldn't hurt."

The next negative influence he addresses is school and how interacting with his peers never fails to spark a feeling of inferiority, given his inclination to compare himself unfavorably. He decides to focus his attention on himself until he reaches a plane of confidence. He deactivates his social media accounts, sits at the front of every class with his peers out of view, and spends his time in the library during breaks. Toward the end of the week,

Mike decides it's time to confront Jimmy the bully, having avoided Elly out of fear of further snarky remarks. Encouraged with how his last I-statement went, he has high hopes.

Nervous, his hands trembling, Mike walks up to Jimmy with cue card in hand and begins. "I feel, uh . . . I feel s-self-conscious and uh . . . insecure when . . ." Jimmy's forehead furrows as he straightens his long frame. "What?" Mike takes a gulp and continues. ". . . when I g-get made fun of in front of everyone when trying to s-speak with Elly. I'd appreciate it if you . . . I mean, I'd appreciate it if . . ." Jimmy snatches the card out of Mike's hand and proceeds to recite it out loud in a mocking voice, shattering what is left of Mike's pride. He shoves him into a locker and walks off. Defeated, Mike sobs while most of the class watches, stunned with second-hand embarrassment. His eyes watering, Mike shakes himself off and walks straight to the principal's office. He receives a few snide leers in the following weeks but isn't bothered again. Later, at prom, Mike is sitting alone near the buffet when Elly sits down next to him. "You know, I thought you were brave walking up to Jimmy like that. I didn't know you liked me." What comes next is a moment Mike will never forget: Elly reaches out and puts her hand in his, and as he clasps it firmly, a wave of ecstasy washes over him. What he feels that night is *purpose*, something *real* worth fighting for—his first taste of meaning. On cloud nine for the rest of the night, Mike forgets about his problems, his insecurities, and all the hardships he knows he has yet to face.

With what little time is left, and as distracted as he is with the cutesey back and forths he is having with Elly throughout the day, Mike turns his attention to the most pressing matter on his To-Do list: university. It is worse than not knowing what to enroll in; it is the imminent exams Mike wants to desperately avoid, whose results will dictate whether he is eligible for enrollment. He thinks long and hard of ways to overcome his inability to study and curb his video game addiction. In the past, after facing a stretch of defeat and drama in the video games he plays, he tried to cut gaming entirely—cold turkey—but it never lasted.

If he is going to resolve this dilemma, it would start by constructing an RSC he could lean on. As for Informed Perspectives, he searches online for others struggling with a video game addiction and is relieved by the number of those with similar battles. He reads through their stories and desperate attempts to overcome—accounts that sounded all too familiar. He reads through anecdotes describing how challenging the transition was but how it was all worthwhile after they managed to quit for good. He reads about the inevitable consequences he's been trying to avoid, and realizing there is nowhere to run, genuine fear runs up his spine. Writing out the pros, he knows it would be an uphill battle trying to minimize the hours while battling his addiction. (See figure 7-34.) Stumbling across a few Russell Brand videos online, it seems as though abstinence is the best way of escape.

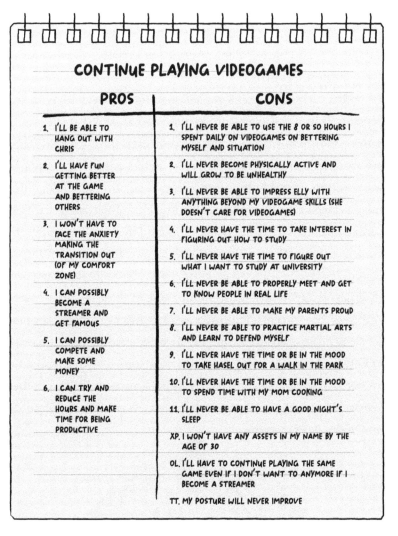

Figure 7-34: Mike video game RSC

He isn't ready to act on his RSC just yet; after all, quitting cold turkey is easier said than done, considering he's been playing games religiously for the last eleven years. But Mike knows he wants change more than ever, and he knows he can't do it on his own.

His anxiety is an amalgamation of his competitive nature, capitulating to what he's been denouncing for as long as he can remember (studying), and the life-altering dilemma he's now up against: his looming final exams. Trembling, he consults his mother as a desperate plea for help; the clock is ticking. He confesses his guilt, his faults, his arrogance, his fears, and the precarious position he's found himself in. He breaks down in tears. "I'm sorry I'm such a disappointment. I don't know how it's come to this. I want you to be proud of me, but I haven't done anything to earn it." All this and more as he sobs in his mother's arms.

His mother, in shock, comforts her son and asks why he is saying such things. She tells him she loves him no matter what, and that she is willing to do anything to help him get through the difficult times. "Everything is going to be okay, Mikey. Don't you worry." She shares a few of her own teenage failures, rejections, speed bumps, and lessons, and how everything turned out just fine—as long as she learned from her mistakes. They decide to hire a tutor while Mike leverages what the Quasi-Chaotic Lifestyle has to offer. He asks his peers, he sweeps through forums, and he watches videos to learn of how others study. Everyone seems to do it differently. Some jot down notes in their tablets, others study in groups, some sit alone in libraries, a few recite their notes out loud, others rely on tutorials and lectures by content creators. Mike wonders why he assumed that studying involved reading through textbooks, taking notes, and memorizing content in the darkness of his room. "Why was I never taught how to study? Why didn't anyone think to tell me about . . ." Frustrated as he is, he knows better now. He decides to iterate through different methods of studying.

Throughout the week, as he actions his list of To-Dos, Mike reflects. A few important realizations stand out:

▲ Intention is more important than action. Those who mistreat others are often unaware of the harm they impart and the consequences of their actions. Mike learns to verbalize his feelings more often, especially when mistreatment starts to feel like abuse.

▲ Leaving a problem unaddressed almost always leads to an overreaction. And considering how oblivious wrongdoers can be, it's unfair to them if their misconduct is left unaddressed and met instead with accusation and vitriol. Mike knows to bring the issues to light sooner rather than later, even if it makes for an awkward conversation. Being honest about insecurities is always the lesser of two evils.

▲ "You miss 100% of the shots you don't take." If Elly hadn't taken the initiative, Mike knows he would've missed the opportunity. He can't bear to think of what other opportunities he has let slide when they were right there for the taking. He promises himself to find ways to muster up the courage and capitalize on opportunities when they present themselves.

▲ He learns to avoid conflict in public spaces; it will only complicate his sincere attempts. Jimmy might have reacted differently had they been alone. Everyone has an image they are unwilling to compromise to maintain.

▲ Incessantly Distracted with addiction, Mike decides to remain skeptical of infatuation and wary of the risk of cognitive adjustments—always leaving room for doubt. He will remain sensitive to his beliefs by distilling them to their essence and taping the descriptions to his wall. "I believe playing games 8+ hours a week is good for me" *would* have been the statement had he not forcefully admitted himself out of an Unreachable Terminal by Suffering.

And from his Sprint Retrospectives:

▲ Procrastinating the cuts makes them increasingly difficult to action. Mike has to psyche himself up and muster whatever emotional courage he has left for what turn out not to be end-of-the-world actions. However, having a lurking, hairy problem makes it significantly easier to take on other onerous tasks. Moving forward, he continues to harbor a hairy challenge but avoids the need for dramatic provocation by remaining optimistic in worst-case scenarios. "It's *never* really the end of the world" he thinks to himself as he puts up a poster in his room with the expression, "What's the worst that could happen?"

▲ After constructing his RSC, Mike realizes the value of insights from anonymous and public confessions. There are countless videos of individuals suffering from varying addictions and bad habits such substance abuse, malnutrition, poor life choices—you name it! Seeing their long-term effects is much more powerful than hearing or being lectured about them. He will resort to similar publicly available confessions should another comparable issue rise up.

▲ Mike realizes that using his Kanban board offhandedly defeats its purpose. It feels like a chore because he isn't Sprint Planning and breaking down his cards into bite-sized chunks that better suit his limited capacity. He isn't actively moving cards and therefore feels no satisfaction from that step. He isn't adapting the board's tools to what best suits his preferences. Moving forward, if any part of his Kanban use feels redundant, inefficient, or annoying, he will iterate through other ways of achieving the same outcome.

Mike does end up failing three of his six subjects and is forced to retake the exams the next year. But if you think this discouraged his will to persist, you are mistaken. If anything, he feels like it is the best thing that could have happened! Now liberated from distraction and negative influences—and still seeing Elly—he has another year of practice and iteration ahead of him, knowing all too well that he is not yet ready for a tertiary education.

If you're only tracking Mike's journey, skip to page 446.

APPLIED STEP 5: ANDREW

After twisting and turning in bed at night, Andrew hops out of his poorly assembled IKEA bed to take on his list of To-Dos and construct his RSC. He plans to dedicate the entire day to actioning each item, come hell or high water. (See figure 7-35.) He zooms out of his digital canvas and admires his work with pride. It is more than just pixels on a screen; it is his way out, and it starts to feel more real than any chance he's ever had.

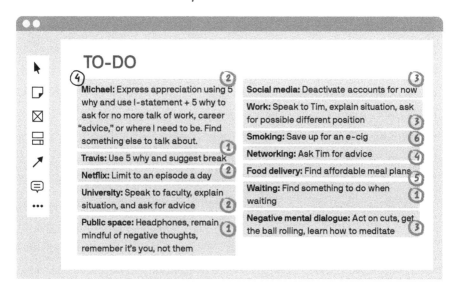

Figure 7-35: Andrew action plan from Five Whys conclusions

The next morning, Andrew arises to the sound of his flip phone's alarm ringtone: Roy Brown's "Mighty, Mighty Man." "Today is the day," he proclaims. He jumps out of bed and goes to work. Something feels different. He can't quite put his finger on it, but all of a sudden, he feels spirited. Freedom is palpable, and things can't get any worse. Whatever happens, he *knows* his freedom is assured, and there is no stopping him. From this moment on, for better or for worse, he tells himself that what happens going forward will be on *his* terms.

From the 7-11 outside his office, he gets his Americano but buys a disposable e-cigarette. Why not? "Hmm, I'm not sure about the flavor, but this isn't as bad as I thought it would be!" He makes his way to Tim's office, more excited than ever, and lays it all out.

"Good heavens, Andrew. Are you sure?" Tim asks worryingly. "And you're doing all this today? What about your clients?" "There's more," says Andrew. Tim pulls up his chair as his expression hardens. "Do you think it's possible if I . . . if I got a chance to try something different? And before you jump to conclusions, I mean within the organization? I'm terrible at networking—you've seen me try—but I want to get better. I want to learn." Perplexed, Tim gives it a think and prods with suspicion, "Are you okay? I mean, one day you're shuffling your feet, the next you're acting like Jim Carrey from that movie . . . what's it called?" *"Yes Man?"* "Yeah, yeah, that's the one. Are you sure about this?" "I've never been more sure," Andrew affirms. "Okay," says Tim. "You've been good with our clients, and since you've done me a few favors already, I think I owe you one back. If you think it's for the better, and it sounds like it is, I'll have a word with the higher ups and see what we can do. How does that sound? Oh, and don't worry about Kylie and the rest. I don't have anything better to do today, anyway. Go and do what you have to do." Ecstatic and energized, Andrew leaves the office and heads to his parents' house.

"Mom, are you th . . ." "Who the hell is Travis?!" she punctuates with a shriek. "A boyfriend? You have a boyfriend? Get out of my house, get out!" "But Mom, I was goi . . ." "Get out!" she roars as she hurls a book in his direction. "Damn it, Jennifer, get a hold of yourself!" Andrew's father chases after him. "She was going to find out eventually, Andrew. Travis called here asking for you. He said you haven't been answering your phone, and your mom was on the one to pick up. I tried to calm her down . . ." Jennifer, now weeping, yells after them. "What have I done to deserve this? After everything we've done for you!" "It's best if you go, Andrew. I love you, I'm not sure why you're not at work, but you need to give her some time."

Andrew runs, tears trickling down his face. Just when he thought he'd be able to turn things around, life throws another curveball his way. He runs not because he's afraid; he runs because it is all he feels he can do. He isn't running away from home, from his mother; he is running away from the world. He doesn't want anything to do with it anymore. He runs until his legs give out and he collapses onto the sidewalk, gasping, sobbing. His dejection turns to enmity, but that shock of adrenaline doesn't last as he gets up and promises himself the freedom he knows he deserves. This is the straw that breaks the camel's back. Andrew's "forces for change" now soar past his "forces against change." He is now Change Receptive.

Still shaken by the incident with his mom, Andrew decides to keep pushing. He doesn't have the energy to think much about what happened and has booked time with a faculty representative at university. Wiping away the last of his tears, he explains his predicament to the rep. She looks worried and asks if everything was okay. Andrew continues. "Look, I . . . I just don't know if this is what I want to major in. I'm not motivated by it; I'm not interested, but I also don't know what else to do." She reassures him that many students feel this way and that he can shift to another major, preferably one where he's be able to transfer credits. She suggests he take a break and think about it, and that he can drop out of the semester and reenroll when he's ready. Andrew doesn't hesitate. "I want to drop out." "Are you sure? You're already halfway through it." "Yes, I'm sure."

Andrew decides to walk back home, about an hour away by foot. On the way, he decides to call Travis. "Where the hell are you? Do I hear cars? Is everything okay, Andrew?" "Travis, do you have any ide—" Andrew stops himself and starts over. "Travis, I'm devastated, I'm pissed, I'm angry, I'm hurt, I'm lonely. And I don't appreciate it when promises are broken, because people get hurt when they do. Mom now knows, and everything is in ruins." "What else was I to do? I was having a really bad day and was worrying about you. I just wanted to check on y—" "I'm sorry, Travis. I've been meaning to talk to you, anyway. I think it's best if we took a break from each other. I just can't . . ." Andrew breaks into tears and hangs up. It feels like his world is crumbling around him. On his way back, a friendly neighborhood cat runs to his legs and purrs. Not in the mood, he shoves it aside, but it returns. No matter what he does, the tabby persists as he walks past strangers. Finally, Andrew turns around, sits with the cat, and cries and cries until his tears run dry, joined by the only living creature whose love feels, for the moment, unconditional.

Andrew spends the weekend in bed, his phone off, his heart heavy and bruised, his mind numb. His roommate Isiah is there to comfort him. He brings in meals and checks in on him every now and again. Sunday night, feeling guilty of depriving Travis of an explanation, Andrew makes the call and confesses. He reads his Five Whys to Travis, back to front. Travis, moved by Andrew's sincerity, thinks it is best as well—a short-lived sentiment. A slew of texts quickly floods Andrew's phone, full of malice, blame, and shame. Andrew quietly reads through them, confident as he looks down at the booklet in hand where his RSC lives. He blocks Travis's number, and just like that, it's over.

The moment Andrew puts his phone down, he realizes how much lighter he feels. Like a cloud burst in a parched desert, he is drenched in relief, the heavy yoke of burden, finally set free. He promises himself to never again take abuse from anyone. He looks back at his RSC and knows what has to be done next. (See figure 7-36.)

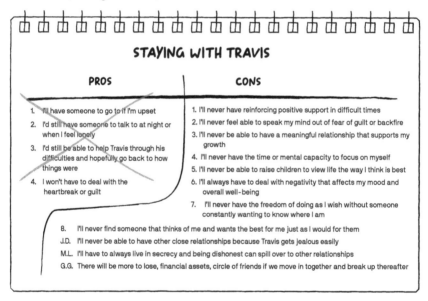

STAYING WITH TRAVIS

PROS	CONS
1. ~~I'll have someone to go to if I'm upset~~	1. I'll never have reinforcing positive support in difficult times
2. ~~I'd still have someone to talk to at night or when I feel lonely~~	2. I'll never feel able to speak my mind out of fear of guilt or backfire
3. ~~I'd still be able to help Travis through his difficulties and hopefully go back to how things were~~	3. I'll never be able to have a meaningful relationship that supports my growth
4. ~~I won't have to deal with the heartbreak or guilt~~	4. I'll never have the time or mental capacity to focus on myself
	5. I'll never be able to raise children to view life the way I think is best
	6. I'll always have to deal with negativity that affects my mood and overall well-being
	7. I'll never have the freedom of doing as I wish without someone constantly wanting to know where I am

8. I'll never find someone that thinks of me and wants the best for me just as I would for them

J.D. I'll never be able to have other close relationships because Travis gets jealous easily

M.L. I'll have to always live in secrecy and being dishonest can spill over to other relationships

G.G. There will be more to lose, financial assets, circle of friends if we move in together and break up thereafter

Figure 7-36: Andrew boyfriend RSC

Throughout the week, as he actions his list of To-Dos, Andrew reflects. A few important realizations stand out:

▲ Having spoken to his mentor, Tim, about networking initiatives and practice, he makes note of how Tim highlighted the financial success he's gained through conversation and curiosity as opposed to research and study. Andrew learns about the lucrative potential of investments, whether it's property, stocks, or other emerging technologies. Tim has nothing to hide, confiding his trust in someone he knows to be authentic.

He goes on to disclose his investment strategies and how in a matter of days he turned a few hundred dollars into more than Andrew makes in a year. At first, the knowledge of what he'd been missing out on demoralizes him. Over time, though, Andrew learns to take initiative and ask for advice in matters that may have previously felt taboo or inappropriate. The prospect of gaining fortune from just a few conversations and a few clicks, seeming to materialize wealth out of thin air, trivializes wealth accumulation and work altogether. It all boils down to risk thresholds—risk versus reward—and *how much is enough.* Relying on a few informed decisions as opposed to slaving away for years, Andrew learns to avoid unfulfilling yet well-paying work and focus his attention on meaningful practices and insightful, diverse conversations with the potential for actionable and profitable realizations.

▲ After all the pain Andrew endured—living in servitude to others, capitulating to their demands and desires, having his sincerity met with contempt and hostility—he regains self-governance and learns to live for no one other than himself. He realizes he needs to stop apologizing for his nature, especially when he hasn't done anything wrong. To apologize when he's in the right is to lie, and that would be living in bad faith.

▲ His father's support reveals the influence of how dogma can make well-intentioned people act in dissonance, fearing consequence and losing what matters most to them—in this case, his wife. This realization provoked a sense of empathy for the oppressed, the indoctrinated, and anyone bound to a rhetoric of fear. Had he been in their shoes, he may very well have harbored the same beliefs and mannerisms and surrendered to peer pressure or love. Andrew knows to rise above it, to value authenticity over anything else. To do otherwise is to stray from the Quasi-Chaotic View, a view he vows to live by.

▲ Invigorated with emotion after making his cuts, Andrew's fire is lit; a blaze of confidence now fills his once-empty shell. He finally realizes the liberating power of saying "no" in rejecting acts of gaslighting, manipulation, or anything that would sway him from his recalibrated moral compass.

▲ Writing out his thoughts and mapping out courses of action seems to suppress the negative feedback loop that kept him up at night. Instead of ruminating through alternative universes, he simply plots out where each decision could take him—knowing all too well not to give any of them much credence. In fact, it becomes his version of counting sheep. The bonus? He is widening his breadth of empathetic consideration and critical thinking!

And from his Sprint Retrospectives:

▲ Andrew recognizes how he unintentionally took on sizable cuts before working his way up to them. The confidence he gains from the chaos that accompanies a "heavy front-load" gives him the courage to take on big cuts, should any arise. He decides to keep visible the cards that detailed his "harrowing" feats of courage to remind him of what is possible when preparing for another potentially jeopardous cut.

▲ While Andrew ought to be proud of what he's accomplished, a sense of indifference quickly manifests. He realizes that, growing up, his accomplishments were never celebrated as he was always compared to others: "Why can't you be more like your brother, Andrew?" The habit remains, and Andrew knows he has to relearn how to celebrate his victories, because he knows he is deserving.

Andrew goes on to deactivate his social media accounts along with his Netflix subscription, browses through ready-made meal packages online, and figures he'll run to work while listening to his favorite Roy Brown album, feeding the tabby cat on the way. He'll keep his sights straight ahead to dampen the distractions and influences of the general public. The realizations from his reflections now recorded, Andrew decides to make another list of lessons from mistakes he promises to never remake. Starting anew, Andrew's commitment deepens; there is no turning back.

If you're only tracking Andrew's journey, skip to page 446.

APPLIED STEP 5: RACHEL

Considering the sensitive nature of her list of To-Dos (see figure 7-37), Rachel is now even more reluctant to bounce her ideas off her friends or lean on them for support. She feels lonelier than ever. She is still hanging on to the false reality that she has a happy, "bent but not broken" family, thinking they are only a few conversations away from fitting that fantastical image she's projected to social media. She decides to prepare a few I-statements and donate her neediest plants to the community garden. At work, she plans to suggest hiring an executive coach to help with team development and to improve overall team meeting productivity.

Figure 7-37: Rachel action plan from Five Whys conclusions

Rachel is starting to feel hopeful. "Hey, I'm actually doing something about it all! It will only get better from here on; I'm sure of it." She has all her problems laid out—an actionable list of expected progress as she works toward an exit.

Drawing from the Five Whys conclusion Rachel had made from questioning a seemingly positive influence—finding peace in the toilet—she discovers it is a highly prioritized negative influence in disguise. She has lost whatever boundaries a wife, a mother, or an individual would expect to have, and is now looking to regain her footing. Rachel is in the process of constructing an RSC until an Informed Perspective suggests professional support before actioning drastic change. Rachel decides to convene a household discussion with her husband and two boys. With her Five-Whys in hand, she begins:

> When I come home from a long day at work, the only place I find peace is in the toilet, and that's mainly because everything outside of the toilet is too much for me to handle. I feel as though I don't have any time to catch a breath and relax, because I'm constantly being asked to do the smallest of things that don't require my attention. I love you all so very much, and as much as I want to stand by you every waking minute of my day, I need some time for myself. But I can't do this if everyone is so dependent on me. I am tired of needing to yell and beg for help. Therefore, I think it's best if we see a family counsellor.

As strong and selfless Rachel is, this confession is terribly difficult to vocalize, let alone admit. And the sensation of finally speaking her mind dissolves her into tears. She's had enough, and her family is now aware of it. "Mom," askes Danny, "what's a family counsellor?" Lewis is more aggressive: "Rachel, you can't be serious. What's come over you? Ever since you've been messing about in that wardrobe of yours, you've been acting strange! Can we just talk about it?" Rachel holds her ground. "I'm done talking, Lewis. I'm done arguing. I'm just done, okay?"

Rachel is now entirely dependent on a family counsellor (who happens to be a trusted family friend), hoping she will make all her problems disappear. Poof! The result: *calamity.* The entire strategy backfires. Off to the counsellor they go, every other week on a Tuesday morning. What always follows is argument after argument, putting Rachel on her heels, defending her feelings.

Who wanted another child? Who did and didn't need a job? Who had a more demanding career? What did he really mean by that one thing he said that one time? It is a deadlock with seemingly no way out. Lewis insists that his expectations of Rachel are justified. He has been working overtime five and sometimes six days a week for years, often with overtime, for a chance at a big promotion—the big break he's dreamed of ever since he graduated. With all the facts laid out, they each iterate and reiterate through precisely how their days transpire, and *still* they can't agree on who is in the right. Weeks turn into months. Neither is willing to give in. Rachel refuses to drop her work, which she finds fulfilling, and the thought of being a housewife is a deal breaker. Lewis refuses to believe her life is harder to manage than his—he's provided so much for the family—and to think he will let all that grueling dedication die in vain is a deal breaker. "Why can't you see, Rachel? I'm doing this for you! For us! I understand it's been difficult, but what about me? What about *my* feelings?"

Rachel is Suffering and knows all too well what it might come down to. She prepares her RSC (see figure 7-38) and keeps it by her side in anticipation of what may be the only way out, but her "forces against change" still outweigh her "forces for change." The only person she feels comfortable opening up to for an Informed Perspective is her mother, as she quickly realizes how emotionally skewed her iteration of her RSC is. Her mom reveals hardships she had faced with her father over the decades and offers her pearls of wisdom. Every morning as she gazes at her Kanban board with the RSC in sight, she sees there is no way around it; she just isn't ready yet. She grows bitter and irritable, rolling her eyes at single women and groups of gals having a good time. There is suddenly a lot more irony, sarcasm, and snide in her remarks as she now resents the life she has—a life every other mother in the neighborhood envies.

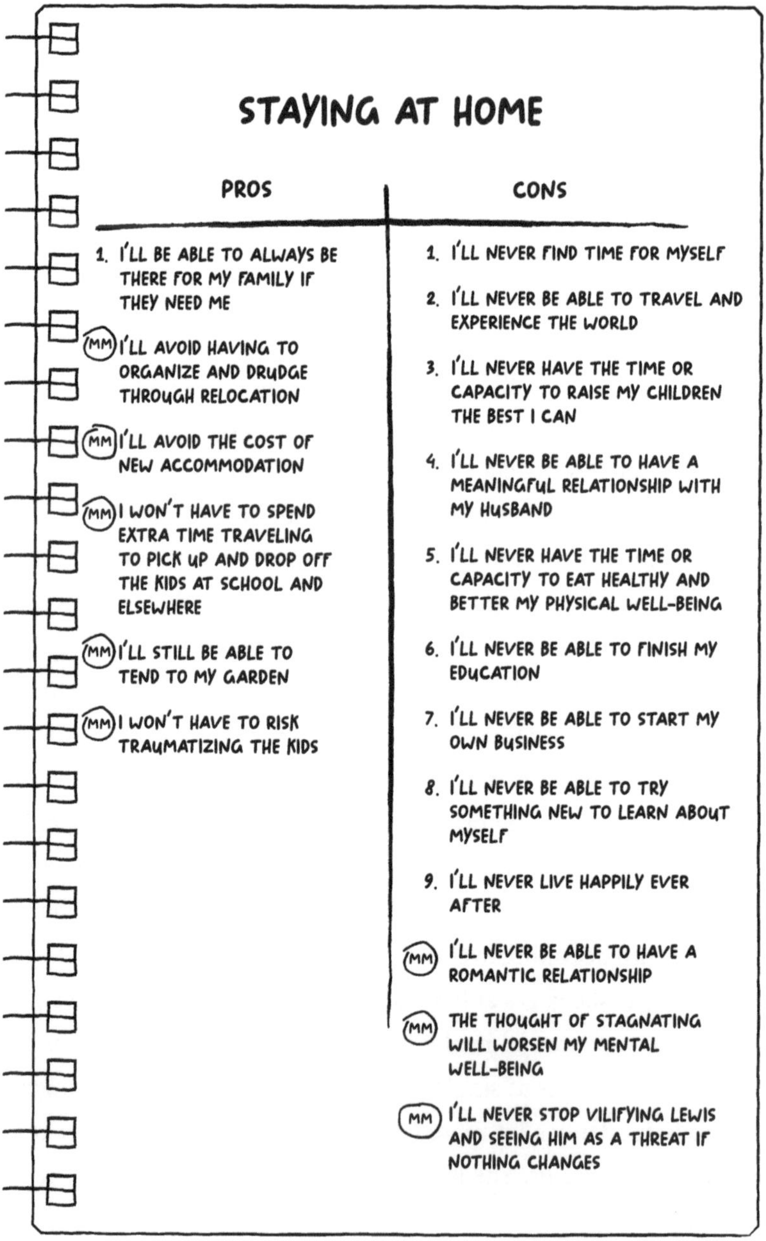

STAYING AT HOME

PROS	CONS
1. I'LL BE ABLE TO ALWAYS BE THERE FOR MY FAMILY IF THEY NEED ME	1. I'LL NEVER FIND TIME FOR MYSELF
(MM) I'LL AVOID HAVING TO ORGANIZE AND DRUDGE THROUGH RELOCATION	2. I'LL NEVER BE ABLE TO TRAVEL AND EXPERIENCE THE WORLD
(MM) I'LL AVOID THE COST OF NEW ACCOMMODATION	3. I'LL NEVER HAVE THE TIME OR CAPACITY TO RAISE MY CHILDREN THE BEST I CAN
(MM) I WON'T HAVE TO SPEND EXTRA TIME TRAVELING TO PICK UP AND DROP OFF THE KIDS AT SCHOOL AND ELSEWHERE	4. I'LL NEVER BE ABLE TO HAVE A MEANINGFUL RELATIONSHIP WITH MY HUSBAND
(MM) I'LL STILL BE ABLE TO TEND TO MY GARDEN	5. I'LL NEVER HAVE THE TIME OR CAPACITY TO EAT HEALTHY AND BETTER MY PHYSICAL WELL-BEING
(MM) I WON'T HAVE TO RISK TRAUMATIZING THE KIDS	6. I'LL NEVER BE ABLE TO FINISH MY EDUCATION
	7. I'LL NEVER BE ABLE TO START MY OWN BUSINESS
	8. I'LL NEVER BE ABLE TO TRY SOMETHING NEW TO LEARN ABOUT MYSELF
	9. I'LL NEVER LIVE HAPPILY EVER AFTER
	(MM) I'LL NEVER BE ABLE TO HAVE A ROMANTIC RELATIONSHIP
	(MM) THE THOUGHT OF STAGNATING WILL WORSEN MY MENTAL WELL-BEING
	(MM) I'LL NEVER STOP VILIFYING LEWIS AND SEEING HIM AS A THREAT IF NOTHING CHANGES

Figure 7-38: Rachel home RSC

Taking her mom's advice, Rachel plans a short getaway, and on the weekend drives to a quiet Airbnb loft in the middle of nowhere, hoping her family will realize how much she's been compromising. She informs them of her plans and suggests they take care of themselves—or at least learn to. Within two hours of leaving, she is bombarded with text messages. "Hey, um, can you tell me how the dishwasher works?" "Which closet are Dewy's nappies in? He's wet the bed again." "That teacher from school called and was wondering whether I . . . I mean, whether you would be able to meet with her again. I think Danny got into another fight." Rachel cranks the radio louder and does her best to ignore her buzzing phone until a surge of calls from a frantic Lewis makes her answer. "Damn it, Rachel, what do you expect me to do? I work six days a week, am close to a promotion, and you've fucked off to who knows where. Stop thinking about yourself for once!" It is the coup de grâce. Rachel hurls her phone at the windscreen, swerves her car, and heads straight back home.

She slams the front door behind her and marches straight to her bedroom, loads up two suitcases, throws in some toiletries. "Where do you think you're going? Rachel? Rachel?!" The only option Rachel has to finally get rid of this primary negative influence is to remove herself entirely from the setting. The decision, she realizes, means she will have to move back to her parents' house. Coldhearted, perhaps? Not given her family's decision not to act on her sincere appeal for support and positive change. The fault isn't hers; her well-being is nonnegotiable. "Lewis is an adult. He can take care of himself and the children just as I've been doing for the last thirteen years." Rachel will spend the next two weeks at her parents'.

Lewis, in complete dismay, strides to her wardrobe and, for the first time, is confronted with her neatly organized Kanban board, in all its detailed glory. "What on Earth . . ." He scans a few cards, the RSC, the Five Whys, and his heart sinks. His first love, his high school darling, the mother of his children, his past, present, and future, has been suffering. Sure, he was aware of her frustrations, but it is the pain she's been experiencing that he has failed to see—that Rachel masked so well with silence and rage. In his hand, he stares at a tear-stained card titled "Lewis: Five Whys." (See figure 7-39.) A tear trickles off his cheek and onto the sticky note meeting hers, and now, so too, does his pain.

Figure 7-39: Rachel husband (positive influence) Five Whys

Difficult as it is, Rachel sleeps through her sorrows and guilt, thinking, missing, reflecting. She thinks long and hard about what was expressed during counselling. Even with all the facts made explicit, "How could Lewis not understand? How is it possible that what seems so obvious to me is neither evident nor important for him? Is this normal? Are we simply incompatible? Was it just bad timing? What am I missing? What could I have done better? The children are at a particularly difficult age. Lewis is on the cusp of a promotion . . ." Her curiosity now taking hold, Rachel dissects any possibility of her being in the wrong. She realizes the need for change. Her family conducted their household practices and responsibilities in one fixed way, never adapting as the kids grew up, while more places and practices were introduced into their lives, such as school and extracurricular activities. But more importantly, she realizes they had been fighting the wrong battles from the get-go. It should have never been her against them; it should have been everyone against the problem. And consequently, arguing to win meant she had already lost.

Rachel sets up a new Kanban board and reconstructs her SOI from memory, though now it is different—no longer focused on who is in the wrong but on all that can be improved. It represents a change in lens, a constructive mindset. What went well, what didn't go well, and what she can do to improve a situation consumes her attention. Though the original negative influences have vanished given that she has (temporarily) cut them all out, she now has a few more to address. Her parents' house, for example, so far from her own, is now associated as a negative influence. It isn't where she feels she belongs.

When she is ready, after two long weeks of shared suffering, she makes her way back home. Expecting the worst, Rachel is in awe of what she walks into. The dishes are stacked, the floor is vacuumed, the kids are already in bed, and a candlelit dinner has been set at the table. "Rachel, I had a look in your wardrobe and I . . . I just wanted to express how much I . . . I just didn't know . . ." "You don't have to say a word," Rachel says. "The state of the house says enough." They wine and dine, and for the first time in seven years, they rekindle their love and rejuvenate their commitment to one another. They are ready and eager to meet each other halfway.

Throughout the week, as she actions her list of To-Dos, Rachel reflects. A few important realizations stand out:

▲ She is ready to let go of the image she so desperately was clinging to. The validation she depended on trivialized, she now knows better than to project a false reality and instead focus her attention on what is real and what it means to live to her fullest potential. For Rachel, it begins with the restoration of her relationship with her husband, with her children, and how the family functions as a whole.

▲ The secrecy within her family needs to stop, and the best way to ensure that is to lead by example. The recital of her Five Whys marked the beginning of what she plans to organize: regular open family discussions where everyone can speak their mind on issues that significantly affect their welfare without the fear of consequence or judgment.

▲ During her visit to the local community garden, Rachel learns the benefits of community garden initiatives. A local representative explains how it brings diverse families together, builds relationships, provides budget savings, and creates healthy habits for youth. This sparks a number of ideas, such as getting her children involved to foster altruism and discipline or osmotically cultivate healthier eating habits.

▲ Suggesting an executive coach at work was met with pushback by management. As much as Rachel loves her work and cares for the company's success and clients, she finds herself demoralized, unnerved, and outraged. Archaic methods and mindsets of authoritative leadership discourage productive initiative and innovation. Rachel realizes how the toxic culture reflects their inadequacies and resistance. They feel threatened by changes instead of appreciating the opportunity to reward potentially profitable initiatives by employees who go the extra mile. Resignation is now a tempting option.

▲ So tumultuous was her family chemistry that Rachel didn't realize she had begun to recoil from any mention of or interaction with them. The authentic conversations that take place with her family after her "time out" feel like a reinvigorating reintroduction to the people she knew she loved and now loves even more. She feels compelled to reacquaint herself with who they are, their interests, and what they feel is missing is their lives, wanting to help develop their autonomy—autonomy she very much wants for herself as well.

And from her Sprint Retrospectives:

▲ Realizing how many of her negative influences are tied to each other, Rachel figures it is a good idea to question potential correlations when navigating her SOIs. She decides to attach a string between sticky notes that might be contingent on one another regardless of how inconspicuous those connections may at first appear to be.

▲ While at her parents, Rachel was in a safe space—she never hid anything from her mother and felt comfortable sharing her reflections. She notices how much easier it was to reflect with someone whom she could bounce ideas off of or whose attentive listening required Rachel to hone her thoughts and clearly and constructively articulate a problems or idea. Rachel decides to visit her parents more often!

Rachel has plans—big plans—for herself and her family. Her proximal people, places, and practices are now primed for change, and so, too, is she.

CHAPTER 35
STEP 6: BULKING

We know not through our intellect but through our experience.

—Maurice JJ Merleau-Ponty, *Phenomenology of Perception*

If you thought our change champions were done, you are mistaken—they have only just begun! Like a hyperbaric oxygen chamber, Mike, Andrew, and Rachel have cultivated an optimal environment for healing, rejuvenation, and rebuilding. Liberated from the noise, *das Gerede*, and negative influences, they can now turn their attention to what matters most for the selves of others and their future selves: their *present* selves.

We have shed the excess and are now ready to *bulk*—to grow our SOI with more people, places, and practices—though, for the moment, it is worth appreciating the peace and how much easier living has become. At times like this, paranoia and habitual pessimism may pop up, followed by immediate relief: "Oh, wait. I don't have to worry about that anymore." It won't be long before the rush of excitement replaces dissonant rumination with the glee of a new beginning—one of many to come, palpable and intoxicating. It's a feeling I wish for us all.

Where does one start? So much to experience, so much to look forward to, so little time. The world is our oyster! The answer is, *anywhere*—much as that might be intimidating for some. Ideation and, contrastingly, option paralysis are problems for those not yet Change Adapted, but rest assured, this is a temporary condition. The point is to do *something*—to act—even if it isn't the "best thing" you could objectively do, for now we know better. If there's anything we've learned about what's "best" for us and what we are made for, it's that the very idea is an illusory fantasy. What will work best for us now is elusive and temporary; what "we're made for" is a socially constructed falsity we must remain conscious of. Remember: the Quasi-Chaotic View advises against long-term commitments and the planning thereof; it's about pursuing and immersing ourselves into what draws our interest *in the moment*, leveraging the novel people, places, and practices we are presented with for Self-Actualizing directives! Again, we are going for quantity, not quality —diverse experiences to feed our growth mindset and Quasi-Chaotic intent.

Exposure to people and places requires a practice, whether it's joining a caravanning group or traveling abroad. It all starts and ends with action. To illustrate how much there is to experience, how much we've been neglecting, and how catastrophically shortsighted we may have become, I will offer an extensive list of practices to consider. Pay attention to the lens through which you examine the list and any connotation you make with what is being proposed.

PRACTICES

Practices encompass "scopes of action"—gateways to people, places, and more practices. The Quasi-Chaotic Lifestyle does not differentiate between work and hobbies. They are one and the same; work can be seen as a hobby, and a hobby can be made profitable and may eventuate into financial security. Practices will therefore only be composed of hobbies (as you will see in the following lists) and all that is needed to sustain them. Hobbies and Sustenance represent all there is to do!

HOBBIES

Skip to page 456 when you've seen enough.

Architecture and Engineering:
Aerospace Engineer/Technician, Agricultural Engineer, Architect, Architectural and Civil Drafter, Landscape Architect, Automotive Engineer, Automotive Technician, Biochemical Engineer, Biomedical Engineer, Cartographer, Photogrammetrist, Chemical Engineer, Civil Engineer, Computer Hardware Engineer, Electrical and Electronic Engineering Technician, Electrical and Electronic Drafter, Electromechanical Technician, Electromechanical Engi-

neering Technologist, Energy Engineer, Environmental Engineer/Technician, Fire-Prevention and -Protection Engineer, Fuel Cell Engineer/Technician, Geodetic Surveyor, Health and Safety Engineer, Human Factors Ergonomist, Industrial Engineering Technician/Technologist, Manufacturing Engineer/Technologist, Mapping Technician, Marine Architect/Engineer, Materials Engineer, Mechanical Engineering Technician/Technologist, Mechatronics Engineer, Microsystems Engineer, Mining and Geological Engineer, Nanosystems Engineer/Technician/Technologist, Nondestructive Testing Specialists, Nuclear Engineer, Petroleum Engineer, Photonics Engineer/Technician, Product Safety Engineer, Radio Frequency Identification Device Specialist, Robotics Engineer/Technician, Solar Energy Systems Engineer, Surveying and Mapping Technician, Transportation Engineer, Validation Engineer, Water/Wastewater Engineer, Wind Energy Engineer.

Arts, Design, Entertainment, Sports, and Media:

Actor/Actress, Art Director, Craft Artist, Painter, Sculptor, Illustrator, Special Effects Artist/Animator, Multimedia Artist/Animator, Audio and Video Equipment Technician, Broadcast News Analyst/Technician, Camera Operator, Choreographer, Scout, Commercial and Industrial Designer, Copywriter, Dancer, Fashion Designer, Floral Designer, Graphic Designer, Interior Designer, Merchandise Displayer, Window Trimmer, Set and Exhibit Designer, Film and Video Editor, Interpreter, Translator, Music Composer/Director, Instrumental Musician (Accordion/Banjo/Bongos/Clarinet/Drums/Flute/Guitar/Handpan/Harmonica/Kazoo/Lyre/Mandolin/Maracas/Ocarina/Piano/Pipe Organ/Recorder/Saxophone/Trumpet/Tuba/Ukulele/Violin/Xylophone), Singer, Photographer, Blogger, Origami Artist, Drink Mixer, Beatboxer, Meditator, Decorator, Homebrewer, Cosplayer, Pole Dancer, Pet Sitter, Aquascaper, Calligrapher, Taxidermist, Wine Taster, Poet, Lyricist, Streamer, Influencer, Circus Performer, Comedian, Filmmaker, Magician, Impressionist, Playwriter, Creative Writer, Producer, Program Director, Public Relations Specialist, Radio/Television Announcer, Radio Operator, Reporter and Correspondent, Sound Engineering Technician, Technical Writers, Umpire, Referee, Sports Official, Competitor in Archery/Kayaking/Parkour/Rock Climbing/Survivalism/Airsoft/Boxing/Knife Throwing/Long-

boarding/Trapshooting/Model Racing/Poker/Jiujitsu/Curling/Backgammon/
Cheerleading/Chess/Handball/Figure Skating/Rowing/Weightlifting/Karate/
Basketball/Baseball/Surfing/Gymnastics/Fencing/Volleyball/Triathlon/
Shooting/Judo/Taekwondo/Rugby/Field Hockey/Sailing/Cricket/BMX
Racing/Canoe/Sprinting/Snowboarding.

Building and Grounds Cleaning and Maintenance:

Housekeeper, Janitor, Landscaper, Lawn Service, Groundskeeper/Grounds
Maintenance Worker, Maid, Pest Control Worker, Pesticide Handler/Sprayer/
Applicator, Tree Trimmer/Pruner.

Business and Financial Operations:

Accountant, Auditor, Artist/Performer/Athlete Agent or Business Manager,
Real Estate Appraiser, Real Estate Assessor, Real Estate Auditor, Budget
Analyst, Business Analyst, Product Owner, Business Continuity Planner,
Buyer's Advocate, Claims Adjuster/Examiner/Investigator, Job Analysis
Specialist, Compliance Officer, Coroner, Cost Estimator, Credit Analyst, Credit
Counsellor, Customs Broker, Energy Auditor, Environmental Compliance
Inspector, Equal Opportunity Representative and Officer, Farm Labor Con-
tractor, Financial Analyst, Fraud Examiner, Fraud Investigator, Fraud Analyst,
Fundraiser, Human Resources Specialist, Insurance Appraiser/Adjuster/
Examiner/Investigator, Insurance Underwriter, Investment Underwriter,
Labor Relations Specialist, Licensing Examiner and Inspector, Loan Counsel-
lor, Loan Officer, Logistics Analyst, Logistics Engineer, Management Analyst,
Market Research Analyst, Meeting/Convention/Event Planner, Online
Merchant, Personal Financial Advisor, Regulatory Affairs Specialist, Risk Man-
agement Specialist, Security Management Specialist, Sustainability Specialist,
Tax Examiner/Collector/Preparer, Training and Development Specialist.

Community and Social Services Occupations:

Child/Family/School Social Worker, Clergy, Community Health Worker,
Educational/Guidance/School/Vocational/Mental Health/Rehabilitation
Counsellor, Health Educator, Healthcare Social Worker, Marriage and Family
Therapist, Mental Health and Substance Abuse Social Worker, Probation Off-
icer, Correctional Treatment Specialist, Social and Human Service Assistant.

Computer and Mathematical:

Actuary, Statistician, Biostatistician, Business Intelligence Analyst, Clinical Data Manager, Computer Scientist, Information Research Scientist, Computer Network Architect, Computer Network Support Specialist, Computer Programmer, Computer Systems Analyst, Computer Systems Engineer/Architect, Computer User Support Specialist, Data Warehousing Specialist, Database Administrator, Database Architect, Document Management Specialist, Geographic Information Systems Technician, Geospatial Information Scientist/Technologist, Informatics Nurse Specialist, Information Security Analyst, Information Technology Project Manager, Mathematical Technician, Mathematician, Network and Computer Systems Administrator, Operations Research Analyst, Search Marketing Strategist, Software Developer (Applications), Software Quality Assurance Engineer and Tester, Telecommunications Engineering Specialist, Video Game Designer, Web Administrator, Web Developer.

Construction and Extraction:

Boilermaker, Brickmason and Blockmason, Carpenter, Carpet Installer, Cement Mason, Concrete Finisher, Construction and Building Inspector, Construction Carpenter, Construction Laborer, Continuous Mining Machine Operator, Derrick Operator (Oil and Gas), Drywall and Ceiling Tile Installer, Earth Driller, Electrician, Elevator Installer and Repairer, Explosives Worker, Ordnance Handling Expert, Fence Erector, First-Line Supervisor of Construction Trades and Extraction Workers, Floor Layer, Floor Sander and Finisher, Glazier, Hazardous Materials Removal Worker, Insulation Worker, Mine Cutting and Channeling Machine Operator, Paper Hanger, Paving, Surfacing, and Tamping Equipment Operator, Pile-Driver Operator, Pipe Fitter and Steamfitter, Pipelayer, Plasterer, Plumber, Rail-Track Laying and Maintenance Equipment Operator, Reinforcing Iron and Rebar Worker, Rock Splitter, Roof Bolter, Roofer, Rotary Drill Operator, Septic Tank Servicer and Sewer Pipe Cleaner, Service Unit Operator, Sheet Metal Worker, Solar Photovoltaic Installer, Solar Thermal Installer and Technician, Stonemason, Taper, Terrazzo Worker and Finisher, Tile and Marble Setter, Weatherization Installer and Technician.

Education, Training, and Library:

Adapted Physical Education Specialist, Adult Basic and Secondary Education and Literacy Teacher/Instructor, Agricultural Sciences Teacher, Anthropology and Archeology Teacher, Architecture Teacher, Archivist, Area/Ethnic/Cultural Studies Teacher, Art/Drama/Music Teacher, Atmospheric/Earth/Marine/Space Sciences Teacher, Audio-Visual/Multimedia Collections Specialist, Biological Science Teacher, Business Teacher, Career/Technical Education Teacher, Chemistry Teacher, Communications Teacher, Computer Science Teacher, Criminal Justice and Law Enforcement Teacher, Curator, Economics Teacher, Education Teacher, Elementary School Teacher, Engineering Teacher, English Language/Literature Teacher, Environmental Science Teacher, Farm/Home Management Advisor, Foreign Language/Literature Teacher, Forestry/Conservation Science Teacher, Geography Teacher, Graduate Teaching Assistant, Health Specialties Teacher, History Teacher, Home Economics Teacher, Instructional Coordinator, Instructional Designer/Technologist, Kindergarten Teacher, Law Teacher, Librarian, Library Science Teacher, Library Technician, Mathematical Science Teacher, Middle School Teacher, Career Guide, Museum Technician/Conservator, Nursing Instructor/Teacher, Philosophy Teacher, Physics Teacher, Political Science Teacher, Postsecondary Teacher, Preschool Teacher, Psychology Teacher, Recreation/Fitness Studies Teacher, Secondary School Teacher, Self-Enrichment Education Teacher, Social Work Teacher, Sociology Teacher, Special Education Teacher, Teacher Assistant, Tutor, Vocational Education Teacher.

Farming, Fishing, and Forestry:

Agricultural Equipment Operator, Agricultural Inspector, Animal Breeder, Faller, Farmworker/Laborer for Crop/Nursery/Greenhouse/Farm/Ranch/Aquacultural Animals, Fisher, Forest and Conservation Worker, Grader and Sorter, Hunter and Trapper, Log Grader and Scaler, Logging Equipment Operator, Nursery Worker.

Food Preparation and Serving Related:

Barista, Bartender, Chef/Head Cook, Fast Food/Cafeteria/Private Household/Restaurant/Short Order Cook, Counter Attendant, Dishwasher, Food Preparation and Serving Worker, Host/Hostess, Waiter/Waitress.

Healthcare Practitioner and Technical:

Acupuncturist, Acute Care Nurse, Advanced Practice Psychiatric Nurse, Allergist/Immunologist, Anesthesiologist, Art Therapist, Athletic Trainer, Audiologist, Cardiovascular Technologist/Technician, Chiropractor, Clinical Nurse Specialist, Critical Care Nurse, Cytotechnologist, Dentist, Dermatologist, Diagnostic Medical Sonographer, Dietetic Technician, Dietitian, Nutritionist, Emergency Medical Technician and Paramedic, Exercise Physiologist, Family/General Practitioner, Genetic Counsellor, Hearing Aid Specialist, Histotechnologist/Histologic Technician, Hospitalist, Internist, Licensed Vocational Nurse, Low Vision Therapist, Orientation/Mobility Specialist, Vision Rehabilitation Therapist, Magnetic Resonance Imaging Technologist, Medical/Clinical Laboratory Technician/Technologist, Medical Records and Health Information Technician, Midwife, Music Therapist, Naturopathic Physician, Neurodiagnostic Technologist, Neurologist, Nuclear Medicine Physician/Technologist, Nurse Anesthetist, Nurse Practitioner, Obstetrician, Gynecologist, Occupational Health and Safety Specialist/Technician, Occupational Therapist, Ophthalmic Medical Technician/Technologist, Ophthalmologist, Optometrist, Oral/Maxillofacial Surgeon, Orthodontist, Orthoptist, Orthotist/Prosthetist, Pathologist, Pediatrician, Pharmacist, Pharmacy Technician, Physical Medicine and Rehabilitation Physician, Physical Therapist, Physician Assistant, Podiatrist, Preventive Medicine Physician, Prosthodontist, Psychiatric Technician, Psychiatrist, Radiation Therapist, Radiologic Technician/Technologist, Radiologist, Recreational Therapist, Respiratory Therapist, Speech-Language Pathologist, Sports Medicine Physician, Surgeon, Surgical Assistant, Surgical Technologist, Urologist, Veterinarian, Veterinary Technologist/Technician, Laboratory Animal Caretaker, Veterinarian.

Installation, Maintenance, and Repair:

Aircraft Mechanic and Service Technician, Automotive Body and Related Repairer, Automotive Glass Installer and Repairer, Automotive Service Technician and Mechanic, Automotive Specialty Technician, Avionics Technician, Bicycle Repairer, Bus and Truck Mechanic and Diesel Engine Specialist, Camera and Photographic Equipment Repairer, Coin/Vending/Amusement Machine Servicer and Repairer, Commercial Diver, Computer/

Automated Teller/Office Machine Repairer, Control and Valve Installer and Repairer, Electric Motor/Power Tool Repairer, Electrical/Electronics Installer and Repairer of Transportation/Industrial/Power Station-Substation/Home Entertainment/Motor Vehicles Equipment, Fabric Mender, Farm Equipment Mechanic and Service Technician, Geothermal Technician, Heating/Air Conditioning/Refrigeration Mechanic and Installer, Home Appliance Repairer, Locksmith and Safe Repairer, Maintenance and Repair Worker, Manufactured Building and Mobile Home Installer, Mechanical Door Repairer, Medical Equipment Repairer, Millwright, Mobile Heavy Equipment Mechanic, Motorboat Mechanic and Service Technician, Motorcycle Mechanic, Musical/ Precision Instrument Repairer and Tuner, Radio Mechanic, Radio/Cellular/ Tower Equipment Installer and Repairer, Rail Car Repairer, Rigger, Security and Fire Alarm Systems Installer, Signal and Track Switch Repairer, Telecommunications Equipment Installer and Repairer, Tire Repairer and Changer, Watch Repairer, Wind Turbine Service Technician.

Life, Physical, and Social Science:
Agricultural and Food Science Technician, Animal Scientist, Anthropologist, Archeologist, Astronomer, Atmospheric/Space Scientist, Biochemist, Biophysicist, Bioinformatics Scientist, Biological Technician, Biologist, Chemical Technician, Chemist, City and Regional Planning Aide, Climate Change Analyst, Clinical Psychologist, School Psychologist, Conservation Scientist, Counselling Psychologist, Economist, Environmental Restoration Planner, Environmental Science and Protection Technician, Environmental Scientist and Specialist, Epidemiologist, Food Science Technician, Food Scientist and Technologist, Forensic Science Technician, Forest and Conservation Technician, Forester, Geneticist, Geographer, Geological and Petroleum Technician, Geological Sample Test Technician, Geophysical Data Technician, Geoscientist, Historian, Hydrologist, Industrial Ecologist, Industrial-Organizational Psychologist, Materials Scientist, Medical Scientist, Microbiologist, Molecular and Cellular Biologist, Neuropsychologist, Nuclear Equipment Operation Technician, Nuclear Monitoring Technician, Park Naturalist, Physicist, Political Scientist, Precision Agriculture Technician, Quality Control Analyst, Range Manager, Remote Sensing Scientist and Technologist, Remote

Sensing Technician, School Psychologist, Social Science Research Assistant, Sociologist, Soil and Plant Scientist, Soil and Water Conservationist, Survey Researcher, Transportation Planner, Urban and Regional Planner, Zoologist, Wildlife Biologist.

Protective and Legal Service:

Animal Control Worker, Bailiff, Correctional Officer/Jailer, Criminal Investigator and Special Agent, Crossing Guard, Detective, Fire Inspector, Fire Inspector and Investigator, Firefighter, First-Line Supervisor of Correctional Officers/Fire Fighting and Prevention Workers/Police and Detectives, Fish and Game Warden, Forest Fire Fighting and Prevention Supervisor/Inspector, Forest Firefighter, Gaming Surveillance Officer and Gaming Investigator, Immigration and Customs Inspector, Intelligence Analyst, Lifeguard, Ski Patrol, Parking Enforcement Worker, Police and Sheriffs Patrol Officer, Police Detective, Police Identification and Records Officer, Police Patrol Officer, Private Detective and Investigator, Retail Loss Prevention Specialist, Security Guard, Sheriff/Deputy Sheriff, Transit/Railroad Police, Transportation Security Screener, Air Crew Member/Officer, Aircraft Launch and Recovery Officer/Specialist, Armored Assault Vehicle Crew Member, Armored Assault Vehicle Officer, Artillery and Missile Crew Member/Officer, Command and Control Center Officer, Infantry, Radar and Sonar Technician, Special Forces, Administrative Law Judge/Adjudicator/Hearing Officer, Arbitrator, Mediator, Conciliator, Court Reporter, Judicial Law Clerk, Lawyer, Paralegal, Title Examiner, Abstractor, Searcher.

Office and Administrative Support:

Bill and Account Collector, Billing/Posting Clerk, Billing/Cost/Rate Clerk, Bioinformatics Technician, Bookkeeper, Accountant, Auditing Clerk, Brokerage Clerk, Cargo and Freight Agent, Correspondence Clerk, Courier/Messenger, Court/Municipal/License Clerk, Credit Authorizer, Credit Checker, Customer Service Representative, Data Entry Keyer, Dispatcher, Eligibility Interviewer, Executive Secretary, Freight Forwarder, Gaming Cage Worker, Hotel/Motel/Resort Desk Clerk, Insurance Claims and Policy Processing Clerk, Legal Secretary, Library Assistant, Mail Clerk and Mail Machine Operator, Medical Secretary, Meter Reader, Municipal Clerk, New Accounts

Clerk, Patient Representative, Payroll and Timekeeping Clerk, Postal Service Clerk/Mail Carrier/Mail Sorter/Processor, Proofreader and Copy Marker, Receptionist/Information Clerk, Reservation/Transportation Ticket Agent/ Travel Clerk.

Sales, Service, and Personal Care:

Amusement/Recreation Attendant, Animal Trainer, Baggage Porter and Bellhop, Barber, Childcare Worker, Concierge, Costume Attendant, Embalmer, Fitness Trainer, Aerobics Instructor, Funeral Attendant, Gaming and Sports Book Writer and Runner, Gaming Dealer, Gaming Supervisor, Hairdresser, Hairstylist, Cosmetologist, Locker Room/Coatroom/Dressing Room Attendant, Makeup Artist, Manicurist and Pedicurist, Mortician, Undertaker, Funeral Director, Motion Picture Projectionist, Nanny, Skincare Specialist, Slot Supervisor, Spa Manager, Tour Guide and Escort, Travel Guide, Usher, Lobby Attendant, Ticket Taker, Advertising Sales Agent, Cashier, Demonstrator and Product Promoter, Energy Broker, Gaming Change Person/Booth Cashier, Insurance Sales Agent, Model, Parts Salesperson, Real Estate Broker, Real Estate Sales Agent, Retail Salesperson, Sales Engineer, Telemarketer, Travel Agent, Investor.

Production:

Adhesive Bonding Machine Operator and Tender, Aircraft Structure/ Surfaces/Rigging/Systems Assembler, Baker, Biofuels Processing Technician, Biomass Plant Technician, Butcher and Meat Cutter, Cabinetmaker and Bench Carpenter, Chemical Equipment Operator and Tender, Chemical Plant and System Operator, Cleaning/Washing/Metal Pickling Equipment Operator and Tender, Coating/Painting/Spraying Machine Setter/Operator/ Tender, Coil Winder, Taper, Finisher, Cooling/Freezing/Crushing/Grinding/ Polishing/Cutting/Slicing Equipment Operator and Tender, Dental Laboratory Technician, Drilling and Boring Machine Tool Setter/Operator/Tender, Electrical/Electronic/Electromechanical/Engine Equipment Assembler, Etcher and Engraver, Fabric/Apparel Patternmaker, Fiberglass Laminator and Fabricator, Food/Tobacco Roasting/Baking/Drying Machine Operator and Tender, Food Batch Maker, Food Cooking Machine Operator and Tender, Foundry Mold and Coremaker, Furniture Finisher, Gas Plant Operator, Gem and Diamond Worker, Glass Blower/Molder/Benders/Finisher, Grinding and Polishing Worker, Hydroelectric Plant Technician, Inspector, Tester, Sorter, Sampler, Weigher, Jeweler, Lathe and Turning Machine Tool Operator, Laundry and Dry-Cleaning Worker, Machinist, Medical Appliance Technician, Metal-Refining Furnace Operator and Tender, Methane/Landfill Gas Generation System Technician, Model Maker, Molder, Shaper, Caster, Ophthalmic Laboratory Technician, Packaging and Filling Machine Operator, Petroleum Pump System Operator, Potter, Pourer, Power Distributor and Dispatcher, Power Plant Operator, Precious Metal Worker, Textile/Garment Presser, Printing Press Operator, Recycling and Reclamation Worker, Shoe and Leather Worker and Repairer, Sewer, Slaughterer and Meat Packer, Solderer and Brazer, Stone Cutter and Carver, Tailor, Dressmaker, Team Assembler, Upholsterer, Welder, Woodworker.

Chances are, you had a quick browse, tried to find your Hobbies, turned the page, turned another, turned back a few, found the page to skip to . . . and here you are! Fact of the matter is, despite the length of these lists, they are expectedly incomplete as new jobs are created on a regular basis, nuanced specializations continue to pop up, and roles that involve a mishmash of skills continue to crop up. You are now either bewildered, annoyed, or anxious. Bewildered by how much there is to experience, annoyed with how much there is to experience, or anxious knowing how much there is to experience. You may even be asking yourself, "How the hell am I supposed to pick, let alone iteratively *work through* them all?!" The choices we make are as arbitrary as our country of birth, religious affiliation, preferences, biases, and present occupations. Recall the argument of free will and how our very being and actions are bound to the influence of causality, whereby the thoughts we think, the values we hold, the decisions we make, and whatever makes you *you* are based on prior experiences and environmental influence. You harbor disparities that shape the path you take—let them, along with your Curiosity, Ambition, and Failure, lead the way while always, always necessitating change.

As for *how* one decides to iterate through (select, change, assess, and adopt) Hobbies, we harken back to what outlines the realm of what's possible:

our respective iron triangles. Whether we dedicate three years to a specific hobby, exploit Angular Momentum and explore the industry we presently work in, taking it as far as we can, or flip the switch and jump ship to a completely unfamiliar industry through Vertical Momentum is ultimately your decision to make.

A slight digression, but please indulge me: Given how foundational the pursuit of a profession, hobby, or practice is, and considering the flagrant absence of comprehensive guidance and methods necessary to excel at them, one is left to question the role of academia. The oldest accounts of education come from ancient Greece, which modeled a form of education that would endure for millennia, unchanged: a focused, tutor-student system of learning, capable of educating the masses. A logistical machine of informational dissemination as opposed to experience. One wonders how much better off we'd be if schools prioritized for excursions in which students were exposed to practitioners from a wide range of industries, professions, specialties, and institutions, or offered experiential "taste-testing" flexible curriculums, or helped students deduce what is most meaningful to them, or, at the very least, alerted young adults to the innumerable, diverse opportunities that await them. One can only lament over how many authentic pursuits each generation is denied, made to believe the pieces will just fall into place and that whatever they happen to find themselves doing is what they ought to do for the rest of their lives. Said prolific writer, philosopher, and activist François-Marie Arouet (known by his nom de plume, Voltaire): "Anyone who can make you believe absurdities can make you commit atrocities." Which includes absurdities of norm and self-condemning atrocities of belief.

You may scoff at the prospect of becoming a party magician or a botanist or anything that doesn't go with "status" or come with a fat salary. Perhaps you ridicule the prospect of drastic change away from a profession you may have naively invested considerable time, resources, and study in. Self-asserted limitations have bound us to what we tell ourselves to be necessary and immutable and yet may be the source of all our angst and unfulfilled wishes. Having drifted far from their essential truths, many believe that work necessitates a cubicle, stapling papers, and putting up with people we would never associate with otherwise—a 9–5 life as a cruel joke. *Why?* Why do we do this to ourselves? Why do we reject the proposition of a professional pivot as a socially disparaging and reputationally suicidal move?

Why do we insist on committing to a field of work we aren't authentically driven to do but believe it's the only way to *be*? Why do we persist, growing miserable and shedding misery on those around us? Just because you may have been forced or gullibly compelled to graduate with a degree that assumes a well-paying job doesn't mean you must follow that path to its often desolate end. It does not. And the sooner you stop telling yourself out of fear or shame that you should stay where you are, the sooner you emancipate yourself of dread and seize a chance to Self-Actualize. Of course, your family wants the best for you, for you to make a living, to live independently, comfortably, and perhaps support them. And yet I ask the question again: How much is enough?

Perhaps the thought of falling behind, letting others get ahead, admitting a misguided choice, or an inability to reconcile a wasted investment is too much to stomach—and what we'd expect of loss aversion. I will reiterate our learnings from the Agile philosophy: Assuming you will or could get the project right the first time is naive and irresponsible. Assuming you *could have gotten* it right the first time is delusional. Of course, others may have stumbled upon a lucrative profession they somewhat enjoy and now have a head start on, but consider what you now know of our everchanging nature, the realities of talent development, and the possibilities that come with a Quasi-Chaotic Lifestyle.

If you're sick of your job, consult HR for other opportunities. You may be able to work alongside a different team or department. Consider a demotion or a lateral move into a different line of work, a new path, even if it means a pay cut or another few months of training. Maybe the industry itself doesn't align with your conscience. Find the time to upskill and explore diverse opportunities; make it a weekly habit until you start receiving offers. It may not happen in a month, but if you want out, persist. Suffer!

Have you considered picking up a trade as a mechanic, electrician, plumber, cleaner, baker, cook, locksmith, hairdresser, gas fitter, roof tiler, sign writer, plasterer, painter, or welder? No? Why not? Would you feel inferior if your family or friends knew you no longer wanted to be a lawyer but intended to become a landscaper because you truly enjoy beautifying a backyard for a loving family of three or because you like spending time outdoors, feeling the soil, and making neighborhoods a better place to live in? If you are to feel ashamed, it should not be for disappointing others but for capitulating to those who don't respect your individualism, passion, or your quest for Self-Actualization.

To live in bad faith is to live inauthentically, yielding to the external pressures of *das Gerede*. Take a stand, make your move, and prove yourself, not for others but for your very own livelihood. Whatever infatuates you, strive to excel, strive for the ideal, take your passion to the levels you dream of. If working for another is what you have identified to be enough to live a life of fulfillment, then do so. Otherwise, pick up the skills and subsequently work your way into entrepreneurship. Become the best landscaper you can be, leverage Osmosis and the people you meet, and when the opportunity arises, hire others and start a business! You choose: six years in a cubicle or two years in backyards doing what you love followed by a thriving business. And take it a step further: be the boss you always wanted. Be loving and caring to those you hire. Build a team you trust and enjoy spending time with!

Imagine a rural lass, grown and raised in a small village atop a Mediterranean mountain, a mother of two at the age of twenty-one, a third nine years later, and twenty-five years after graduating from high school and into housewifery, she decides to finish her education, obtain an MBA, and pursue her newfound passion of handmade jewelry, all while enduring social ridicule and judgment. She ultimately turns this self-taught hobby into a profitable business which she later moves and grows overseas, giving her family the chance to migrate abroad and attain a citizenship they had been longing for for decades. She is now as content and happy as she could be. That's my mother for you. She believed in her dreams, but more importantly, she believed in herself. You believed in a template you sacrificed most of your life for; you can believe in yourself for a minute.

SUSTENANCE

Sustenance involves satisfying our most basic human necessities, enabling us to sustain our Hobbies, develop qualities that warrant merit (the quality of being worthy enough to warrant praise, reward, or an opportunity), and expose ourselves to more people, places, and practices, each with their own rabbit holes of opportunities. We often neglect these needs given First-World privileges, soft structures, and safety nets that permit the negligence of self-autonomy and wellness-related upkeep—to our peril! Both are necessary ingredients for an optimal Quasi-Chaotic Lifestyle.

Cooking:

Boiling, broiling, grilling, roasting, baking, sauteing, poaching, simmering, steaming, braising, stewing, sous vide cooking, slow cooking, meal prepping, or just sticking to raw foods.

The joys and benefits of cooking are incalculable, whether it's the savings we reap and the health benefits we gain compared to the pricey, calory-rich, nutrient-deficient nature of fast food, or simply the practice itself and the sociable opportunities it offers (cooking for others, cooking with others, talking to others about cooking). If you don't enjoy the cleaning, consider one-pot meals. If you're restricted for time, consider slow cooking or sauteing. Did you know there are over one hundred ways to cook an egg? How well are you able to navigate spices? Do you follow recipes, or have you picked up fundamentals through pattern recognition of spice blends, cooking methods, and flavor pairings to the point where you are able to create dishes from whatever you have available?

Cleaning:

Organizing clothes, cutlery, shoes, books, paraphernalia; vacuuming, ironing, sweeping, mopping, treating floors, furniture freshening, dusting, sorting the bins, wiping surfaces down, rinsing, drying, dishwashing, scrubbing, shining, replacing, straightening, folding.

Do you iron your own clothes? Or should you spend a few extra dollars on steam cleaning services? How do you feel about wet wipes, spray bottles, and paper towels? Do you plug the sink and fill it with water and soap to clean the dishes, or do you put dishwashing soap on a sponge directly? Do you have a pull-out spray tap or one of those monstrously designed, low-arching sink taps? Big washing loads or small? Do you separate the colors at a high temperature or leave everything together at a lower temperature? Do you fold your clothes in quarters or have you invested in tight-fitting clothes that straighten themselves out when worn?

Eating:

Ketogenic diet, low-FODMAP diet, liquid diet, gluten-free diet, elimination diet, juice fasting, Atkins diet, Dukan diet, detox diet, paleo, vegan, vegetarian, pescatarian, HCG diet, The Zone diet, raw food diet, intermittent fasting, Mediterranean diet, Weight Watchers diet.

There's a "diet" for everyone, and a *sustainable* diet—one you can sustain without feeling unhealthy or deprived or the need to binge eat—is the best. Do you find yourself forcing certain foods down your throat because you tell yourself masochism is the only path to fitness? Or do you choose a diet that involves all the foods you enjoy in moderation? Butter, bacon, and pork ribs? Go for a ketogenic diet. Fruits, vegetables, and beans? Pick up a vegetarian diet. A diet will discipline your consumption, and any diet will work as long as it gives you the energy, fitness, and health benefits you need to a live a long-lasting and high-octane Quasi-Chaotic Lifestyle!

Sleeping:

Sleeping later; sleeping earlier; a short sleep with a few naps throughout the day; falling to sleep while listening to the sound of rain, fire, a busy street, a dishwasher, crickets, a thunderstorm; falling asleep watching a science of interest, a podcast, Stephen Fry's poetic and melodramatic narration, or perhaps counting sheep or staring at a wall; sleeping in a star position, on your back, or on your side; air conditioning on with extra blankets or with the air conditioning off and butt naked. Would you rather sleep through the day and operate at night? That's certainly possible, and the perk is that it usually comes with a bigger salary!

How rested are you after sleep? How rested can you be with the shortest amount of sleep? The longer we're awake—assuming a sufficient amount of sleep—the more we'll be able to experience! Dreams are fun, but a Quasi-Chaotic reality comes with more control and just as much craziness that dreams have to offer!

Personal care:

Brushing your teeth, showering, bathing, flossing, trimming your nails, managing body odor, managing bad breath, shaving, waxing, styling your hair, cleaning your ears, trimming your nostrils, dressing yourself to suit or to make a statement, getting health checks.

Celebrate your new lifestyle with a new look, a new style, a new you altogether! Get a haircut, maybe some highlights, change your wardrobe and add new accessories. The easiest and quickest taste of change with immediate gratification is to greet a different reflection every morning. Make an effort, get heads turning every time you walk into a room. Get those around you to wonder, "Something's different about her . . ." Even if you don't feel as comfortable or as confident with the new look, remember: *that's not the point!* Nor are you doing it to impress anyone. That may happen, but this is purely for you and you alone, to assure yourself that you have taken the first steps into the world of change. This is a matter to be *proud* of! Have you ever wondered what you'd look like with a little more swagger or completely blacked out from head to toe? Did you know that pleasant scents are scientifically proven to evoke positive, uplifting emotions and memories? You have nothing to lose at this point and everything to gain. Points of conversation, a different impression, a different feel, a different presence. Have at it!

Transport:

What mode of transit works best for you? Cycling, skateboarding, rollerblading, walking, running, skipping, organizing a carpool, catching a cab, taking the train, the tram, the bus, on horseback, transiting alone or with others, listening to positive affirmations with noise cancelling earphones, or eavesdropping on others? Which mode of transport allows you to enjoy or exploit another practice? Which gets you where you need to be the fastest?

Imagine taking a three-hour hike to work and living to tell the tale of your experiences along the way. Such an act reflets discipline, health consciousness, and someone unafraid to take on a challenge. Those around you will have no choice but to shower you with esteem!

Managing expenses:

Do you use spreadsheets, a bookkeeper, an accountant, or all of the above? Do you keep separate accounts for Sustenance and Hobbies, cut corners to save up for a trip, or spend your money and live in the moment? Do you buy everything firsthand, secondhand, or make them yourself? Do you throw away clothes and older items, try to sell them, or give them away to those in need? Do you set an allowance for yourself? Eyeball your account from time to time? Have you considered consulting a financial planner? Do you know how your monthly expenses compare to others?

How much money would you need to sustain the bulk you desire? How expensive are your bulks to begin with? Find out how much is enough and make it happen!

Exercise:

Almost any physically demanding Hobby. Again, it doesn't have to be five sets of twelve reps or the torturous plank or those draining burpees. Consider skipping, hiking, martial arts, walking a dog, goofy dancing to entertain your baby, taking up salsa, enthusiastically and compulsively cleaning your house or your neighbor's house with a focus on squatting or stretching, choosing the stairs over the elevator, avoiding vehicular transport for anything less than a mile away.

Incorporate the physical into your quest for change, and you won't need to restrict your diet as much nor put yourself through the pain of playing catch-up for the rest of your life!

Shopping:

Do you buy everything at full price or wait for sales and stock up? Do you decide what to cook before you shop or let the grocery and its discounts dictate your menu? Do you only shop at supermarkets or visit street markets, conventions, and stalls? Do you only buy clothing in shops, or do you buy them online? Do you ask shopkeepers for advice, or do you scour reviews online before making a purchase?

Convenience stores are exactly that: They are *convenient* and nothing more. So too are online stores. We know better than to live in convenience and comfort. Do your online research and resort to convenience stores when you have no choice. We know by now the importance of increasing the chances of realistic/unrealistic occurrences by getting out of the house. So if our iron triangle permits, dress yourself in confidence and get out there!

Behavior:

Simply put, this is how you conduct yourself. Behaviors dictate outcomes.

If you recall, the reactions of independent entities in complex adaptive systems to imposed conditions lead to unpredictable, and consequently, varying events of emergence. There are times when you have ruminated over what or how you could've, would've, should've said, done, or presented yourself better after a chain of events didn't go your way. And how you moved on from such disgruntlement is often nothing more than the brief solace of a forgettable mental note: "Next time, I'll make sure to . . ."

What we often fail to fully appreciate is how every utterance, every bodily motion, and every action, reaction, and response—both its delivery and interpreted reception—governs how well we are able to capitalize on opportunity. Our ability to communicate articulately, the mental dialogue taking place during an interaction, body language, voice intonation, posture, attitude, eye contact, facial expression—all are subject to change, and all have variations better suited to different people, places, and practices.

Have you developed a distracting tic? Maybe it's time to see a behavioral therapist. Is your vocabulary limited to one and two syllable words? Are you only able to describe the way you're feeling as "good," "bad," or "depressed"? Learn a word a day, read a book, keep cue cards around, and/or surround yourself with others who find pleasure in sesquipedalian discourse to learn to better express yourself and be understood. Do you have an unapproachable "urban scowl" (commonly known as resting b**** face)—coined in the book, *The Like Switch*? Author Jack Schafer, psychologist, behavioral analyst, and ex-FBI agent, suggests using an eyebrow flash (a brief raising of the eyebrows), head tilt, and a warm smile to counteract it. Do you find yourself constantly interrupting others when they speak? Practice mindfulness, bite your tongue, or address the anxiety urging you to contribute.

Contrastingly, which set of behaviors works best for an older demographic or those of a different culture or the cynical, the aggressive, the suspicious, the intimidated? How about in a place of danger or perhaps during stressful work? All of the aforementioned explain why behavior is a Hobby of its own and why we ought to bulk new forms of behavior to adapt to differing situations. If you haven't been consciously making such an effort and found yourself with the social skills of a Victorian brick wall, it just might be the right time to start!

There is no denying that behaviors are deeply tied to personality traits.

So, if you aren't certain which limiting traits or behavioral extremities you ought to be working on, this is the point where our lessons of "the malleable psyche" come to fruition. It advises against completing personality tests when cognitively compromised, such as when you're in a bad mood, depressed, hungry, or ill. Better to undertake a personality test once we've rid ourselves of pressing negative influences to avoid inaccurate results and misguided directives. Rest assured, an "a-ha moment" will be quick to follow once you receive your results—you'll know what needs work once you are presented with descriptions that sound uncannily familiar. So, take the test when its appropriate, address extremities, and then cultivate openness to experience to make change that much more forthcoming!

Set aside your presumptions, skepticism, and cynicism. You don't know what you don't know, so take on "the different" with an open mind. Stuff your Backlog with everything and anything you take interest in, along with the occasional challenge; don't hold back. If a new idea emerges or you take notice of a shortcoming you wish to work on, pop it in there as well! Modify your Backlog using the insights and realizations drawn from Sprint Reviews and Retrospectives to reprioritize cards and add new ones as you go!

Consider pursuing a practice you know or assume you wouldn't enjoy. Is it a practice you really don't enjoy or a story you've been telling yourself for the past eight years because you once got food poisoning from that ethnic cuisine at a subway kiosk? See it as an opportunity to consult with people you already know, or to acquaint yourself with new people to seek advice from, or to share the experience in order to build existing relationships! You may even consider giving hair-raising practices a go to elicit harrowing stories to share or to take advantage of Reinforcing Failure! "Let me tell you about the time I spent forty-five minutes chatting up a bungee-jump assistant to avoid a fifty-foot drop." Don't judge change by scope. Change is change, no matter how benign or ambitious, whether it's just catching up with an old friend or signing up for a two-week Groupon silent retreat. Both are equally, serendipitously profound. The focus is on change!

Also consider the fact that you are changing and so will your palate, your abilities, your motivations, and so on. Still, if you're assuming a particular novel practice isn't for you, leave some room for the contrary *and* make more room for the serendipitous potentialities its novelty and pursuit may present. Either way, give it a proper try. And even if it doesn't quite tickle the cockles of your heart, you can at least reassure yourself that Quidditch still isn't for you!

PEOPLE

Up to this point, you may have been dreading how a Quasi-Chaotic Lifestyle would impact how you interact with strangers. If so, there is nothing to fear. While striking up unsolicited conversations isn't for the fainthearted or those whose social skills and charisma need a little more fine-tuning, it doesn't mean you can't make it easier for yourself. Group/Partnered Accountability, Competitive Ambition, and Pride all facilitate this endeavor: soliciting conversations with purpose and justifying an entrance with an attitude of sincerity makes approaching strangers a little less complicated. Get a wing-woman (or -man) involved. If you both happen to be rolling on a jiujitsu mat, you'll be more worried about your limbs than what the pick-up line ought to be! And wouldn't it make perfect sense to strike up a conversation with the guy who kicked your butt at drone racing, commending them and asking for tips? A justified entrance with the right attitude and body language is all you need to get your foot through the door of social competency. Practice makes perfect. And if what I'm proposing is still a little too much, consider leveraging existing friendships and family; get to know *their* friends and their friends and theirs at gatherings and events. Get the practice that you need!

Have you walked past someone and felt curious enough to imagine a life with them or simply wondered what they do or how they're doing it? Where they got that hat? How they prepare their notes for an exam? What it's like having two kids and a full-time job? What it's like working in a print shop? Exploit Curiosity and remember: most people love talking about themselves, and they love a good listener. Said Dale Carnegie, a pioneer of public speaking: "You can make more friends in two months by becoming interested in other people than you can in two years by trying to get other people interested in you." Offering a genuine compliment or showing interest in what they're doing, wearing, or thinking is a fantastic conversation starter. Don't hesitate. The situation is only as awkward as you make it!

And what about the people you already know? That one friend you've known for years and yet your relationship has grown stale. Change that state of affairs by taking them out in appreciation of all the time you've spent together! Call your distant cousin and ask what they've been up to. Initiate a deep and meaningful conversation with your supervisor. Engage in discussions you've always avoided. There is always something worth noting and being a part of, veiling hidden opportunities where you least expect them. Exposing yourself in different ways to the same people can present chances you never realized existed!

Every person you know and meet is a gateway to everyone they know and so on. Additionally, every person is a gateway to new places and new practices, each of which are gateways to more new people, and on and on it goes. As Arthur Schopenhauer, the renowned nineteenth-century philosopher, once said, "Friends and acquaintances are the surest passport to fortune." A passport we will seek to cover with stamps of fortuity!

PLACES

When we think of "places," what first comes to mind is usually travel, which is always a great and straightforward way to get a change of experience as, quite literally, everything around you is different: the people you meet, the food you eat, the air you breath, the bed in which you sleep, the brand of bubble gum you accidentally step on. However, you don't have to take a European tour to get a taste of change; you don't even have to leave your neighborhood! Take a walk around the block and you'll be surprised to discover what you can find—hidden gems you didn't know existed! A wise man I know whom you'd consider "self-made" insisted on taking a different route any time he went for a walk. Whether in a different country or around the neighborhood, he always met different people whom he often befriended and sometimes became lifelong friends with. He'd walked into shops and up to stalls that piqued his interest. He mingled with people at cafés and always greeted passersby with a smile. He read the posters plastered on bulletin boards. Every now and again, he'd give me a call and insist on introducing me to a stranger he'd just met. He experienced change every single morning, afternoon, and evening, and always had stories to tell. The shortest route isn't always the best route; as much as we value time, pursing opportunity is always time well spent.

Maybe start by moving around all the furniture in your room or home or reorganize your pantry or what you've hung on the wall. Are those light bulbs too dim? Is that chair too squeaky? What if I put up a full-sized stuffed moose in the living room? Is the bed as comfortable as it can be? What if I slept in a hammock? Or maybe I'll sleep in a tent on the balcony tonight—I wonder what that'd be like. If you are starting to think crazy, you are thinking right—a moose on a wall is about as absurd as combing your hair (which really means you're using molded decomposed plants and animals to rake the strings of dead cells that keep your skull safe and warm to impress another mammal whose genitals you want to touch). Strive to be, as Camus coined it, an "absurd hero."

In order to fully demonstrate the utility of our Quasi-Chaotic Tool Kit, tracking our personas' bulks will involve the application of each tool and its subsets. Please note, however, that generating ideas need not be derived in a top-down manner starting with a tool, but I encourage you to begin your first bulk in this manner (as Mike, Andrew, and Rachel will do) to familiarize yourself with the tool kit. In time, you'll be able to naturally default to the right tool for the job as varied feelings, situations, and predicaments arise—a bottom-up approach! Remember to refer to Curiosity when you are uncertain; Osmosis when you feel helpless; Accountability when you are considering surrender; Momentum when you stagnate; Ambition when you're complacent; Failure when facing defeat; and Pride when feeling demoralized.

It is also worth noting that for the sake of succinctness, I will only elaborate on a few of the items that our change champions take on. The rest will be left to your own imagination. Bulking is not a chore; it's a privilege. Cutting grants freedom; freedom enables a bulk. How much more our iron triangle permits dictates the size of our bulk, which is proportionate to Quasi-Chaotic success. The best bulk is a sustainable bulk; take too much on and you are weighed down with excess. Take on too little, and you won't get as far. The capacity you can accommodate is self-determined, but how will you know your capacity if you don't test your limits? In time, you'll learn how much is enough and, in due course, what it means to live to your fullest potential!

Tracking Mike's journey? Read on.

Tracking Andrew's journey? Skip to page 481.

Tracking Rachel's journey? Skip to page 494.

APPLIED STEP 6: MIKE

Mike feels as though the ground beneath him has begun to shift. A sense of overwhelming responsibility showers his thoughts with ideas, each one coupled with anxiety. The idea of taking on the world head-on is scary, but he is excited. He now knows the way.

Mike is determined to make the most of his repeat year. Throughout the weeks, he populates his Backlog with the following items. Some take a little more head-scratching than others, given the unfamiliar angles of prospection—after all, he's been deskbound, "min-maxing" a single form of practice for the most part of his adolescence.

▲ Fallibility Curiosity:

▽ Conscious of how inconspicuous self-deception can be following the unveiling of the cognitive adjustments his video game addiction had provoked, Mike realizes he is susceptible to obsession. He decides to label cards following a thematic pattern and note them as "points of influence" for examination, should a pattern persist. As long as an obsession delivers Self-Actualizing qualities, he'll follow through, though cautiously. Otherwise, he knows better than to let it take control of his life.

▽ When questioning his distaste for expats, Mike quickly learns about cultural competence and ethnocentrism, in which he's been judging other cultures against his own and not considering a contrary perspective—a matter he commits to exploring further.

▽ His relationship with Elly has its ups and downs; after all, it is Mike's first run at being a reliable, caring "other half." His insecurities, inexperience, and emotional instability often lead to misunderstandings and argument. He focuses on himself and seek ways to improve—always a learning experience. And if there is anyone worth the trouble, it's Elly.

▲ Serendipitous Curiosity:

▽ Feeding two birds with one kernel, Mike decides to take the family dog, Hasel, for a walk along a different route every day.

▽ On his walk, he decides it might be worthwhile to examine the local council's notice board and act once each week on whatever is being advertised.

▽ Watching movies, he realizes that the actors who portray self-confidence are fantastic models to emulate and practice. He accrues a repository of movie clips for helping to build his charisma and body language!

▽ He asks to tag along to his mother's place of work during off-peak hours to learn what her colleagues do in different departments!

▲ Developmental Curiosity:

▽ To accelerate his exposure to and understanding of the many practices available to him, Mike makes it his mission to inquire about people's professions: what they involve and why that person decided to pursue and commit to it. In addition, he collects their business cards should he ever feel the need to ask further questions.

▽ After spending a dozen or so hours scouring the internet for study-strain anecdotes, Mike decides to test alternative methods of studying beyond traditional norms. What are all the different ways to consume and retain information?

▽ Nervous, though curious, Mike is ready to take his personality test, given he's finally found himself in the right frame of mind!

▲ Selective Osmosis:

▽ To improve his native tongue, Mike seeks to reacquaint himself with a group he had met during a multicultural school event that happened to share his ethnicity. He also asks his parents to bring him along to local gatherings he had previously opted out of. He figures he'll passively improve his vocabulary in a way that doesn't involve a classroom setting.

▽ Only those who give him time to speak and are genuinely interested in what he has to say remain in his circle; anyone else receives an I-statement and is subsequently cut out if they refuse or ignore his request for civility.

▲ Divergent Osmosis:

▽ Mike decides to make a list of all the traits he feels he lacks: social competence, confidence, industriousness, wittiness, and an adaptive sense of humor. Anyone who exhibits proficiency in any gain his immediate attention.

▽ Conscious of the antagonizing lens through which he has been viewing other cultures, Mike decides to seek invitations to gatherings, celebrations, and events of differing cultures and immerse himself with an open-minded attitude.

▲ Reflective Osmosis:

▽ In his new cohort, Mike notices another student with a stutter. With his ears perked and his eyes focused on those conversing with him, Mike realizes how painful it is to listen to. Difficult as it is, and with his understanding of Pride and its effects, he now realizes how critical it is to iron out his stutter.

▽ Upon being confronted with toxicity online or finding himself in the firing range of an outburst or an unwarranted derogatory insult, Mike knows exactly how to respond: not with vitriol but with empathy and a sincere expression of hurt, as it is almost always a case of projection, and almost never meant with malice.

▲ Self-Accountability:

▽ Mike had developed a knee-jerk habit of blame in response to defeat, the result of an ego of gameplay mastery (How could he ever be at fault of a misplay?) and a fear of failure. With a now palpable urge, he considers diverting that energy into a question he'll ask himself or others (if it's in a group setting): "What could I have done better?"

▽ A quick Google search of "How to hold oneself accountable" inspires him to make a list of his morals—standards of behavior and principles of right and wrong he plasters on his wall and honors when he finds himself facing a thorny decision.

▲ Group Accountability:

▽ Mike decides to search for clubs, social groups, communities, or events that involve a practice he takes interest in and is seeking to pursue. He searches for complementary first sessions and asks his circle if anyone is interested in joining him.

▽ In whatever group-based learning environment he eventually chooses, Mike figures he'll arrive early and hang around afterward for opportunities to mingle and build relationships that might tie him closer to commitment.

▲ Partnered Accountability:

▽ Mike's first accountability partner is his mother. He lets her know what he plans on doing throughout the day, whether sporadic or scheduled, and he promises he'll always get back to her with stories to tell!

▽ To help further ideate challenging Backlog entries, he knows precisely who to go to. A friend of his, who is always able to conjure up the most ridiculous, knee-slapping, creative insults, can surely help him think of new challenges: "Get Lucy to say the word 'tram' ten times without asking her to." "If someone knocks at your door, knock back and see how long it goes on for." And Mike's favorite: "When winter comes, go door to door and try selling your neighbors snow." Not only will it challenge his abilities beyond a point of comfort, but the serendipitous value of the experiences and the stories he'll have to share are incalculable.

▲ Angular Momentum:

▽ No longer driven toward video games out of fear and desperation, nor seeking to remain competitive in the video game he's stood by for years, he figures he'll attempt playing other, less competitive genres with the intention of using the experience as a prize for Self-Accountability.

▽ No matter how boring and uninteresting some of his teachers are at school, he attempts different ways to maintain attention in class, whether it be asking more questions, coming prepared with answers he impresses everyone else with, or assisting others in class—all of which promoted information retention.

▲ Vertical Momentum:

▽ Substituting all the time his video game addiction had consumed with the Quasi-Chaotic Lifestyle, Mike gets a taste of categorical change and wonders which line of work could potentially allow for more of that—perhaps the ability to move across industries when he so desires. He adds it to his list of questions when consulting professionals.

▽ A musical instrument! Mike always loved the sound of the saxophone, so a visit to a music store and a conversation with the store clerks sounds incredibly exciting!

▲ Spontaneous Momentum:

▽ Anticipating the need for pick-me-ups, Mike makes sure to sprinkle his Backlog with simple, arbitrary chores he can do around the house. Whether it's fixing the frame of that picture in the living room, sorting books on a shelf, tidying the garage, or playing a quick game of online chess, his list is ready to be actioned whenever the time called for it.

▽ That pizza brochure still laying around sparks an idea. His father's mate runs a pizza shop. Though it is a few suburbs away, Mike decides to see if he can help make pizzas for a day, free of charge! "And you know what? I'm going to walk my ass all the way there, too."

▲ Competitive Ambition:

▽ Mike's competitiveness is a tool he is primed with and wants to exploit as much as possible. He keeps a board of "records" in his room such as "Most accounts of change in a day," "Fastest time to make the bed," and "Longest time spent studying." He'll show his past selves who's boss!

▽ Surrounding himself with others when attempting the new, Mike figures out who seems to be struggling and offers to support them on their learning journey. While it seems self-serving and petty to contrive a sense of superiority from it, focusing his energy on another keeps him motivated and willing to persist.

▲ Governing Ambition:

▽ Aware of his bad habit of procrastinating by falling into the YouTube black hole of "recommended videos" and online video game streamers, Mike figures he can leverage the opportunity. He permits himself a break once in a while but only if he's on a treadmill. Not only that, but the videos he watches have to involve Hobbies he is unfamiliar with!

▽ He comes across a few orators on YouTube and is impressed with their wit and eloquent responses. If only he knew how to conjure up such sophisticated expressions! He commits to learning one new word a day using sticky notes he slaps in visible spots around his home, e.g., the bathroom mirror, fridge door, the wall behind his monitor.

▲ Contemplative Ambition:

▽ Mike pays attention to those who seem successful at what they do, studying (for example) their posture, physique, eloquence, or knowledge of history, and makes an effort to ask how they arrived at those qualities.

▽ History! Everyone has a past, whether it's Einstein, Bill Gates, or his favorite teacher at school. He thinks he'll look up their pasts and figure out whether those who are regarded as "geniuses" are in fact innately predisposed for greatness or whether environmental influences and chance made them who they are.

▲ Iterative Failure:

▽ Studying is the first practice he feels compelled to iteratively fail at. Mike's competitive nature, in tandem with Competitive Ambition, triggers an "a-ha moment" as he now seeks to better everyone else in this domain. This gives him a fundamental skill that unlocks the holy grail of competitive advantages. "If everyone else can study, you better believe I can do it better!"

▽ His second "a-ha moment" is working through relationship issues with Elly. Mike grows with every argument they have, even though it seems he is doing all the changing. He continues experimenting with ways to make her feel special, making it a quest!

▽ Cooking is an easy pick. Mike tells his parents he'll prepare dinner for them, all on his own, on the weekend and once a week (though they can watch if they desire). He always enjoys the constructive feedback they provide when indulging him in his culinary experiments: "Maybe let the mince cook longer until all the water boils and you start to hear the meat fry." This gives him a sense of progress akin to his online avatar's professions. He is now learning skills in real life!

▲ Reinforcing Failure:

▽ Alfred Pennyworth's quote, "Why do we fall, sir? So, we can learn to pick ourselves back up," sticks with Mike. Learning the art of discipline in a martial arts monastery atop the Tibetan peaks is a little far-fetched, but he knows there won't always be a principal's office to resort to, so he decides to sign up with the local martial arts gym.

▽ He strikes up a conversation with a different student at school once a week to get used to breaking ice, handling rejection and awkward interactions, and maintaining his Pride in the moment.

▲ Opportunistic Failure:

▽ Mike had never finished reading a book until *Necessitating Change*. Needing to review certain sections for encouragement and honing his outlook, he reads them out loud to work on his articulation and stutter.

▽ After struggling with constant interruptions, Mike decides to further work on his stutter by slowing down his speech. It's tricky, but practice makes perfect. He asks his parents to stop him whenever he's speaking too fast or starts to stutter, then he starts over.

▽ He makes an effort to only speak his native tongue at home, which always get his parents laughing—all with good intent, constructive feedback, and positive affirmation!

▲ Lossless Pride:

▽ Mike knows he needs to practice humility. Coming from a cutthroat, competitive, online community, learning to feel comfortable with defeat is a quality worth perfecting. He figures it's best to rehearse a few lines should such a situation call for it. "Was anyone recording? Did you catch that? Wow, I'll add that to my list of things never to do again!"

▽ Wanting to build a thicker skin, Mike agrees to hold "roast battles" with a sarcastic character at school every fortnight during the break. In order to accept and grow comfortable with his temporary short-comings, he figures he needs to learn how to enjoy well-intentioned, self-deprecating humor.

▲ Attractive Pride:

▽ To further boost his confidence and give the impression that what he has to say is important, Mike thinks he should dress the look: an all-black outfit to match the dominant presence he'd like to develop one day. He keeps iterating until it consistently makes a difference!

▽ His poor posture is at the forefront of his attention. He decides to start with a posture brace, remain aware of any slumping, and correct it when he notices.

▲ Reflective Pride:

▽ Mike props up a life-sized photographic cutout of his "old self" in his room as a reminder of where he once was and how far he keeps progressing.

▽ Shocked that he has no pictures or videos of himself, he thinks it's a good idea to record a video every month where he summarizes his day-to-day life. He'll rewatch them months or even years down the line to make the prospect of Reflective Pride that much more impactful!

Mike is convinced he'll never get around to actioning many of these ideas, but he appends his backlog with them all regardless. He feels motivated to do some more than others and decides that's probably where he should start. The anxiety that used to keep Mike awake late at night when void of distraction starts to fade as he can now sleep with a clear conscience, knowing he's actually *doing something* about the problems that plague his well-being.

As for the bulks he goes on to action, a few stand out:

After trialing a few other story-driven, role-playing, and hack-and-slash games, Mike finds himself deeply underwhelmed. His anagnorisis (the moment he discovered the true nature of his own circumstances) leads him to realize that much of his amusement playing video games came from an illusion of accomplishment derived from nothing more than the occasional random number generator (RNG) flukes and the repetition of trivial sequences of clicks followed by congratulatory pixel popups. The justifications of his online community—instilling him with an endless list of cognitive adjustments—were nothing more than the musings of wistful addicts. And given his understanding of the "myth of talent," the only reason anyone else might have bettered him was if they'd spent that many more hours practicing. His own efforts were thus frivolous; he was perfecting motions that led nowhere, in a competition of who was willing to sacrifice more of their life to the game. Sure, the genre did involve some strategy and team coordination, but the fact of the matter was that given how much he'd invested into the game, he received little to nothing in return. In other words, it was Less Permitting. Knowing all this, and after working through the negative influences inciting his urge for escape, his relationship with video games changes forever.

Regarding his study habits, Mike understands that the status quo of reading and writing down notes bores him to the point of disregard, so he begins to appreciate what individuality has to offer. The "min-maxing" approach that is ingrained in his psyche, and his will to have an edge on others, leads him to explore more optimal ways of studying. After hours of research, Mike comes across the work of the nineteenth-century psychologist Herman Ebbinghaus, who demonstrated that there is a predictable and measurable rate at which people forget what they learn, illustrating it through a "forgetting curve." With opportune, spaced-out times to review for long-term retention, Mike decides to find online tools that exploit this fact. He also seeks tools that track his progress with visual indications of incremental progression to spark those hits of dopamine, harkening back to his video gaming days. If he can find a way to gamify studying, the world will be his for the taking!

The visit to his mother's office is eye opening. He is reluctant at first, but his mother assures him that he is free to roam around the building and ask people what they are doing and why. He's met some of them at a Christmas party, so there is less ice to break—and off he goes with his mother's lanyard! He speaks to graphic designers, full-stack developers, the customer support team, the dev-ops team, and the business analytics team. He is fascinated by the open-environment workspace and how everyone is collaborating as equals toward a common goal. He also notices how many of them have hung up game-related memorabilia and posters across the walls. It looks like a lot of fun! What really catches Mike's attention are the technical business analysts. He learns how their work revolves around problem solving and connecting technology with business processes as a means to optimize workflow. He also notices they have strings of notes tied together across the entire room, looking like a scene out of Sherlock Holmes. Even better, they are using Kanban boards that look just like his! He has to write this down; he knows he is on to something. Mike realizes that his urge to formulate an optimal method of studying, alongside his fascination with technology to support a cause, unveiled potential he feels driven to investigate. Mike has learned more about himself in a month than he had throughout his entire life!

One day at the local notice board, Mike finds a brochure pinned to it: "Orientation Day. Learn about our courses!" Mike's eyes widen. He snatches the brochure, picks up Hasel, and runs back home. "Mom, let's go! We're going to miss it!" He attends seminars, presentations, and information sessions that cover course materials and academic tracks with students already enrolled to consult. Of course, it isn't easy for Mike as he is still struggling with social anxiety, but his mother is there for support. Throughout the day, Mike makes a list of courses he took interest in and makes an effort to speak with those working in the field. From there, he and his mother organize meetings with his parents' friends and colleagues that fit these descriptions. Mike gets a chance to ask them what a day in the life of a video-game developer, a therapist, and a marine biologist look like. From this, he realizes two things: First, his mind is still buzzing with the idea of becoming a technical business analyst. Second, therapists don't seem to be as cynical as he once thought. This motivates a sense of action to what his personality test revealed: high levels of neuroticism. All the symptoms were there: low levels of self-esteem, risk-aversion, sensitive to social rejection, easily annoyed and lashing out . . . all which explained some of the problems arising between him and Elly. He decides to start working on one of them, and sooner rather than later!

Speaking of Elly, despite her gripes with Mike's occasional emotional instability and his need to catch up with his social skill set, romantic fluency, and charisma, he is determined to make it work. For example, taking notice of her interest in origami, he spends four weeks learning how to fold the notoriously difficult *kan no mado* dragonfly to show her how much she means to him. Unfortunately, her reception of the intricate paper creation he had invested so much time and care into was disheartening.

Mike's business card collection of people and companies he enjoys, whether a salon, a restaurant, an accountant, or an artist, grows bigger and bigger. He has a repository of recommendations for every occasion at his fingertips. He becomes the person you go to for referral advice!

He asks his physics teacher at school how he ended up with his job, who tells him that it was his way of learning. His teacher figured out that the best way to learn the material was to teach it to his younger siblings, which fueled his desire to make it a lifelong commitment. Mike adds "Experiment with teaching!" to his list of varying ways to study.

His local martial arts gym offers boxing, muay thai, and jiujitsu classes. Mike is most impressed with the belt system in jiujitsu, and his history of video game competitions tilts him toward a "leveling" mentality that has him dreaming about achieving a black belt. It is rough work, and it seems like he'll never get a submission, but Mike enjoys the thought of outsmarting his opponents—someday! Every time he taps, he has an "a-ha moment," impressed with how easily his sparring partner has Mike's limbs at his mercy. Not only that, but given how early he shows up to class each morning, he eventually starts helping his coach with opening-shop activities. After a while, he's offered a job as a part-time receptionist! It's the first job he's ever had, the first dollars he's ever earned, and the first of many steps toward independence and autonomy!

He sticks to his promise of accomplishing at least one NBD every day, ranging from wearing different-colored socks, to brushing his teeth up and down rather than side to side, to performing a somersault in public! He gets more attention out of his mismatching socks than he's ever received. "I like this," Mike thinks to himself. His gums bleed more often than normal when he brushes his teeth differently. "Must be a deficiency of some sort." He tells himself he'll get that checked. And the somersault? He gets a few looks, but the world doesn't come crashing down on him as he thought it would for being so unconventional in public.

His reflections and actions giving rise to further people, places, and practices to explore, Mike has now familiarized himself with the method of sustaining a Quasi-Chaotic Lifestyle. He is still timid, but more decisive; still averse, yet willing.

If you're only tracking Mike's journey, skip to page 508.

APPLIED STEP 6: ANDREW

With all his cuts complete and so little of his past life left, Andrew has a clean canvas to start anew. Given his apprehensive and antisocial nature, his scope of change is composed of mostly proximal changes, but he knows better and decides to throw a few curveballs into his Backlog for much needed, opportunity-rich change.

There isn't much for Andrew to work with except everything that doesn't work. And you know what? That is plenty. Andrew reflects on all that he dislikes, disapproves of, and loathes, deductively identifying directives to action. Much like Mike and over the weeks that followed, Andrew continues populating his Backlog. While his salary isn't anything to brag about, the freedom he has gained more than makes up for it; he has enough time and resources to action a significant scope. That said, and as aggrieved as he is with his mother, he promises his father he will reimburse them for the degree he never completed. The freedom is worth the price.

▲ Fallibility Curiosity:

▽ All that Andrew believed is now in question, including his relationship with his father and his brother. Andrew puts aside his envy, his grudges, and his assumptions and commits to better understanding his family's motives and intentions.

▽ When contemplating items to bulk, Andrew realizes how shortsighted and mundane his ideas were. So conservative had his perspective become that he finds himself imaginatively limited, feeling unable to ideate beyond the mundane. He decides to throw himself in the deep end and take on a prepackaged itinerary for what serves as a real challenge: caving!

▽ Always in fear of social judgment, Andrew questions what others think of him and how they react to what he sees are his insecurities. The best way to find out, he thinks, is to express his fears openly and see what happens: "Just a forewarning: I'm still working on my conversational skills, so you may need to do some of the heavy lifting!"

▲ Serendipitous Curiosity:

▽ Andrew knows all too well that opportunity lies where he least wants to look. To address his social-public negativity, for example, he decides to make more eye contact and smile (even if it feels forced) as opposed to walking with his head down, making quick glances, and associating glimpses of what he perceives as joy with negative connotations. Andrew realizes that to capitalize on opportunity requires him to remain vigilant.

▽ He asks the people he meets how their day *really* is. If he is met with a "Good, yourself?", he goes on to ask another question, such as "How was your drive to work?" or "What did you have for breakfast, if you don't mind me asking?"

▽ He discovers Wim Hof ("The Iceman") when he is watching a video online and commits himself to ice cold showers every day for a week to see how it affects his daily well-being.

▽ If anyone asks for assistance with a matter he is unfamiliar with, he learns it and does it! "Hey Andrew, can you fix this printer?" "You know it!" It tests his resourcefulness and problem-solving skills, whether it involves research, leveraging relationships he already has, or creating new ones by reaching out to professionals for advice!

▲ Developmental Curiosity:

▽ To better address the negative dialogue that afflicts his thoughts, Andrew feels like a helping hand may be necessary. He is still eligible for six sessions of counselling at his university, so he commits to taking advantage of that.

▽ Given his commendable performance at work, Andrew wants to get to the bottom of *why* he does so well. The work does not particularly excite him, but there is a driving force behind his commitment. He wonders if it may have to do with the compassionate impact his work imparts on wholesome and vulnerable individuals, but that isn't quite it . . .

▽ Wanting to understand why he naturally defaults to excessive rumination at night, he decides to give the personality test a shot in search for clues.

▲ Selective Osmosis:

▽ Andrew calls Tim over the weekend and asks how he became such an excellent speaker. To Andrew's surprise, Tim confesses he was part of a public speaking club that is now on top of Andrew's list of To-Dos!

▽ Andrew foresees the need to move out of his flat—not what you'd call an Epicurean community! For as much as he appreciates Isiah's company, Andrew is committed to surrounding himself with ambitious, like-minded, and proactive people. He will still make time to catch up, though!

▲ Divergent Osmosis:

▽ Andrew decides to offer help to someone twice a week no matter what they are doing, and every other week it is someone from a different social class: the homeless, blue collar, white collar, and so on.

▽ Starting small, Andrew decides to get acquainted with the sales department at work. They often have workplace parties and events, so this is a way to start to branch out.

▲ Reflective Osmosis:

▽ There is a waitress at the café where he gets his coffee every morning whose cheerfulness Andrew cannot help but reciprocate when she welcomes him. There is something about the way she carries herself, her commitment to her work, the bow tie that perfectly binds her collarless shirt, that contagious smile—you just wouldn't have it in you to upset her! Whether it is the posture, attire, cordial professionalism, or those bright white teeth, Andrew wants to be treated the way she is, so off he goes to his Backlog!

▽ As Andrew is running a grocery errand one day, he notices a rather antisocial looking teen walking past: a hoodie, a frown, the shuffling of feet. It very much reminds him of himself. From afar, he realizes how unapproachable such a person looks, repelling opportunity. Andrew thinks of listening to a comedic podcast whenever he's in public to provoke a smile and some cheer—even if it marginally attracts opportunity.

▲ Self-Accountability:

▽ At times of adversity or when feeling discouraged, lethargic, or dejected, Andrew's pick-me-up is Travis's last message before he blocked him for good: "You'll never amount to anything." The flame it reignites within is enough to get him through just about anything—though he only uses it as a last resort given how emotionally overwhelmed he becomes revisiting all the pain he unknowingly suppresses.

▽ Andrew comes across a trending weightlifting tournament video on YouTube and notices how the competitors psyche themselves up before a lift. He figures he'll try the same: "When the going gets tough, the tough get going," "You've got this!" and "Let's make it happen, Andrew. Let's do it!" were some of the peps he uses to hype himself up—along with occasional '90s punk rock hits!

▲ Group Accountability:

▽ As much as Andrew still wants to binge-watch TV series, he plans on ensuring that his next set of roommates do not. He also plans on asking them to interrogate his evening plans every now and again and slap him on the wrist if he starts falling back into Incessant Distraction. He is more excited than ever to find his next group of roommates!

▽ As timid as Andrew is, he knows he has to learn how to speak out loud. He plans on inviting his circle out for regular nights of karaoke!

▲ Partnered Accountability:

▽ An obvious choice for Andrew, Tim is the one he relies on to keep him in check. All he'll need is five minutes of his time to share what he plans on doing throughout the week and for Tim to hold him accountable.

▽ He'll ask his new roommates to help ensure he doesn't splurge on takeaways and food delivery. A simple question, once a day or every other day, will suffice.

▲ Angular Momentum:

▽ Apart from trying out a bow tie, Andrew promises to continue changing his look every month to ensure momentum of change, whether it's the sizing of his shirts, wearing a different set of glasses, donning leather gloves—whatever it may be.

▽ Fighting his tobacco cravings, Andrew decides to make a list of mitigation strategies to action whenever they arise. Chewing on a toothpick, munching on a bag of spinach, or leveraging his Backlog of Spontaneous Momentum are a few.

▽ Some of his clients are relatively difficult to work with. Given that his role involves maintaining long-term relationships with clientele, and that some clients are beginning to significantly impact his daily welfare, Andrew seeks to explore other sides of their character. Whether it's finding a topic or trait that interests them both or learning of a grandchild they sometimes speak of or sharing entertaining stories, Andrew makes it his mission to find the good in those he is obligated to work with—making the experience that much more bearable, and potentially serendipitous!

▲ Vertical Momentum:

▽ As much as Andrew enjoys kicking a ball around, he reckons he'll live up to his childhood fantasy and pick up archery, just like his elvish hero!

▽ With half of his weekly obligations freed up and a willingness to improve his social confidence, he figures that working at a local restaurant will be an enjoyable and constructive experience.

▲ Spontaneous Momentum:

▽ After a quick Google search of "random things to do," Andrew finds a nifty site that generates exactly that! He takes note of the first ten things it generates and picks one to do, once a day.

▽ Anytime Andrew feels unmotivated or apathetic to a task he's committed to, he reaches out to a friend and asks how they've been and what they've been up to.

▲ Competitive Ambition:

▽ Andrew is perhaps the least competitive individual you could meet— although that isn't an excuse not to participate. With archery in mind, he promises to record the score of his best group and aim to beat it!

▽ To save on transportation, Andrew decides to rent a bike, and when on the move, he ensures that no other cyclist overtake him. He just peddles faster, building stamina and making the ride that much more exciting while hoping that others will pick up on what he's doing and race him!

▲ Governing Ambition:

▽ He'd always heard about the benefits of meditation, and his inability to find peace in public, along with the demons he still wrestles with, motivate him to give it a chance.

▽ Andrew is always forgetful with names, and so he decides to always ask for the full name of someone he's just met, which he immediately records on his phone.

▽ His distaste for the smell of tobacco caused him to smoke with his nondominant hand. In fact, he had gotten into the habit of using the same hand for anything rancid. He decides to carry out simple tasks such as brushing his teeth, stirring a pot, or scratching an itch with his nondominant hand. Andrew finds the idea of being ambidextrous a fruitful challenge to take on!

▲ Contemplative Ambition:

▽ So fed up is he of expectations, the last of his worries is to console his mother. There is nothing to reconcile, nothing to accept, and nothing to reconsider. Much of his life was dedicated to appeasing family instruction and command, and to be accused of committing a moral evil by his mother or anyone else for fulfilling his sexual destiny, well, that will no longer do.

▽ Confrontation, Andrew realizes, denies him the opportunity of conversation. Whenever he is faced with conflict, Andrew's instinct is to concede, shy away, and circumvent as opposed to standing up for himself—raising persuasive counterpoints and articulating reasonable debate. He figures he'll commit some time to researching argumentation techniques whether it is slowing down, cracking a joke to break the tension, asking questions instead of making statements to demonstrate curiosity (and defuse hostility), or building on an opposing point and turning it against them.

▲ Iterative Failure:

▽ In addition to wanting to recreate his attire and how he's presented, he seeks to rid himself of the top knot he's been rocking for just over four years. He doesn't know which haircut best works for him, so he decides that a buzz cut is a good start. It seems to symbolize his newfound discipline and a direct approach to life. Will it work best for him? There is only one way to find out!

▽ Overthinking and sleep deprivation went hand-in-hand for Andrew. He is only capable of falling asleep when he reaches a point of exhaustion. He decides to tire his mind and his body by reading thirty pages of a book a night followed by a thirty-minute exercise routine that would be different every week.

▽ He's been drinking coffee every day for the past four years; maybe it's time for tea!

▲ Reinforcing Failure:

▽ Andrew hates failing; it reminds him of the punishment he'd receive in his youth, where failure was seen as a moral assault on his parents' successful but hard-earned investments, leaving Andrew hesitant to make his own financial commitments. He decides to maintain a list of all the slipups/accidents/failures/mistakes he knows never to repeat to better accept and live with what is now in the past. He titles it "Remittance of Causality." The bigger the list, the less hardship he'll face!

▽ In his search for work at a restaurant, Andrew decides to do it the old-fashioned way by printing a stack of resumes, walking into diners, bistros, pubs, steak houses, and everything in between, and asking for the manager. He knows his inexperience will lead to rejections, so he should start getting used to it, and he may as well start amassing experience with novel people, places, and practices!

▲ Opportunistic Failure:

▽ Not once did Andrew have it in him to pull an all-nighter. One day, he told himself, he'd find out how long he can stay up and how functional he can be after extended hours of sleep deprivation. You know, just in case.

▽ Andrew sees his financial turmoil as a chance to give up smoking. He also decides to keep a lookout for free and last-minute deals online.

▲ Lossless Pride:

▽ Andrew decides to watch comedians who rely on self-mocking wit. He listens to their tone, watches their body language, and takes note of one-liners he can potentially use!

▽ Rehearsing exits, Andrew thinks, could come in handy. A firm nod of the head, perhaps, maintaining eye contact, maybe a quick smirk. "I'm going to need a bigger mirror for practice."

▲ Attractive Pride:

▽ Andrew is always impressed with people who are able to draw on a wise quote when the opportunity arises, subsequently exhibiting pride of knowledge. He searches for quotes online, writes them on bits of paper with some laminate, hangs them on his keychain, and recites them when killing time in public until they stick!

▽ Tim is probably the only person he feels like he can be himself around, and he's going to need him because Andrew plans on rehearsing a "walk of pride": head high, chest puffed out, and hands that know where they're going. Tim watches, sharing his interpretation of the performance and offering constructive criticism.

▲ Reflective Pride:

▽ Andrew loves a good story. To reflect on his progress, Andrew thinks it'd be worthwhile to ask people he's known for years for descriptions of what he was like when they first met and what they find to be different in him now!

▽ Back in middle school, there was a class where a teacher had the students write an email to their future selves using a website he's forgotten. After a quick search online, Andrew finds a site that does just that! Once a year, he'll send his one-year-older self a summary of what his day-to-day looks like, the issues he's facing, what is on his mind, and what he's looking forward to!

As for the bulks he goes on to action, a few stand out:

After hearing of Andrew's inability to control his negative thinking, his counsellor suggests he look into mindfulness and meditation and give them a go. Given that it is already on his list of things to do, he signs up for a free session and exercises Angular Momentum to endure its practice, whether on the beach, on his roof, or in bed. Still, he finds it difficult to pick up, and figures that he'll save up for a backpacking trip to a Tibetan temple somewhere in the Himalayas.

Further investigating the matter, Andrew completes a personality test and, unsurprisingly, discovers he's exceptionally introverted. However, much to his interest, he discovers he is also excessively agreeable. It is as though he is reading his own story. "They don't like to see other people's feelings get hurt . . . too concerned about the emotional state of others more than themselves," he reads under his breath. "Tend toward submissiveness . . . can be taken advantage of, particularly by disagreeable people . . . lose arguments . . . tend not to be very good at bargaining for themselves . . . have lower salaries and earn less money as a consequence." His eyebrows now raised, he reads on. "Highly agreeable people sacrifice medium- to long-term stability and function for the sake of short-term peace, which means problems that should be solved in the present accumulate counter-productively across time . . . All of this can lead to resentment and hidden anger." It all makes sense and explains so much! What he interpreted as a black cloud following him everywhere he went turns out to be of his own making. The source of much of his daily tribulation is now defined, making his resurgence that more actionable. A quick search online on how to remedy high agreeableness leads him to Dialectical Behavior Therapy (DBT), one he'd endeavor to experiment with!

Calling up his friends at times of stagnation turns out to be impressively serendipitous! Not only do they all express gratitude for his goodwill and compassion for checking in, but he is often invited out or over! It is always a definite yes! During his visits, Andrew always shares his plans for the follow-ing week, instinctively creating accountability partners to answer to when he makes contact again! His curiosity makes him a lot more observant of potential opportunity during these visits, as he inspects the pictures on their walls and asks about their history. He learns of the troubles his friend faces in marriage and what it takes to reconcile. "We decided to give ourselves space every few months. We'd go on separate trips to give ourselves a chance to miss each other. We had to learn how to communicate with one another because we were terrible at it. Being from different cultures and all, we perceived everything differently, so it wasn't anyone's fault." Life advice Andrew is sure to take note of.

You should see Andrew wearing his bow tie. He is absolutely adorable! It isn't the impression he *wanted* for himself, getting pinched on the cheek every other step he takes, but he blushes and pretends like he doesn't really savor the attention. Still, "Definitely a bow tie on a first date," he highlights in his review.

Attempting to better understand his father's mannerisms and intentions, he asks to meet him at a small park. Three months have passed since Andrew wanted anything to do with his family. His father is upset that Andrew hasn't been responding to his texts, underscoring how difficult the situation is. Andrew is nervous though prepared. His father sits waiting on a bench over-looking a quiet lake partially covered with lily pads. There is no greeting from either. Andrew sits down beside him and after a few minutes of silence, he begins. He explains to his father how strenuous his upbringing was, reciting the Five Whys he intended to read to his mother. He goes on to confess that he isn't after an apology but rather answers for why they treat him the way they do. What ensues is a series of Whys. (See figure 7-40.)

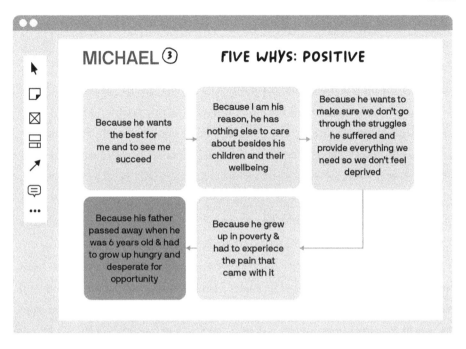

Figure 7-40: Andrew's father (positive influence) Five Whys

His father grew up in a family of nine, in poverty as a result of his own father's passing when he was six. It's a story Andrew is well aware of, but what his father admits next cuts deep. "I never listened to my father. He would always tell me what I should and shouldn't do, but I never listened. Until the day he fell off a tree picking figs and broke his back." His voice begins to crack. "I said, 'I promise, dad; I promise I'll do the things you asked of me.' But it was too late. I wish I had listened. I wish I could have made him proud while he was still around. After that, I had no father. I had no one to look up to. Your grandmother had to care for us nine children. I don't know how to be a father because I never had one. I'm sorry for what you had to go through, but you have to understand, it was from a place of love."

Andrew is quick to embrace his now sobbing father. "I forgive you, dad. All I ever wanted was to make you proud." He goes to explain his plans and how he will reimburse their investment in his education. "No, consider it a gift," his father replies. "I just want you to take care of yourself and to know that I'm proud of you for taking a stand and for being patient with me—with us. Look at you. You've changed so much!"

The following weeks, upon reflection, it finally clicks as to why Andrew makes such an effort at work. Yes, aiding his elderly clients is somewhat fulfilling, but his attention to detail and punctuality come down to the fact that he looks up to Tim. He has come to see *him* as a fatherly figure, wanting to make him proud. Unfortunately, it isn't long before Andrew receives the news that there is no other position in the company he would be eligible for without a tertiary education. He realizes that additional time spent there would be Less Permitting; it wouldn't get him anywhere anytime soon. He'd be missing out on opportunities with Self-Actualizing people, places, and practices he could not concede. Andrew submits his notice of resignation and gives himself a month to find another line of work—Tim is with him every step of the way.

During this time, Andrew moves to a more affordable flat about an hour away from the city central. The other three tenants are like-minded and driven, each focused on their studies and their well-being. One practices journalism, another is an accountant, and the other is a nurse. They are quick to acquaint each other with their pasts, present, and what they see to be their future. He learns about their backpacking years and how they ended up in Melbourne. Fascinated with their adventures and plot twists, Andrew is especially interested in the accountant's trucking days.

It's getting late, and Andrew decides to try an all-nighter. He spends time watching backpacking vlogs, looking up routes and costs. A big sigh of exhaustion is quick to follow as he realizes how much has changed in the past four months. He questions whether it is all worth it and goes out for a stroll at 4 a.m. The moment he sets foot outside, he can't help but stare in awe at the magnificence of the cosmos. The neighborhood he ended up in has minimal light pollution, revealing the galaxy's milky band of light, littered with twinkling gems and brilliance of color. His melancholy fading, Andrew feels at ease, and spends the rest of the morning watching the starlit sky fade and the sun rise.

Authoring a plot twist of his own, Andrew bites the bullet and decides to become a night-shift trucker. It pays well, gives him time to reflect, and every now and then, whenever he faces a hardship, he parks on the side of the road and sets his gaze on the void of space. He sees his temporary financial strain as an opportunity to control his direction of change. Around the house, he begins to help with the cooking—chopping, slicing, grating, and observing. Picking up one recipe and skill set after another, he learns to appreciate the art of mixing and matching ingredients. In his spare time, he takes a few classes on astronomy and is dumbfounded by his eagerness to read on, to take notes. Attempting to visualize the majesty of the cosmos's scale, he finds himself lost in thought and wonder, drowning out his lingering paranoia of being unproductive. Next year, he tells himself, he'll enroll in an astronomy program. His answer lies where his problems dissipate.

If you're only tracking Andrew's journey, skip to page 508.

APPLIED STEP 6: RACHEL

The first few days after Rachel's return felt a little awkward. Despite the apparent transformation, Lewis and the kids are treading carefully, fearful of another abrupt departure. Rachel is quick to address this and explain why she did what she did and her intentions. Her transparency about her initiative encourages everyone else to contribute. It is almost as though they are meeting for the first time!

Most important, however, is everyone's willingness to make it work. The well-being of their family now takes precedent; they are all aligned, and each is eager to make a difference. With the hours that Rachel's respite afforded her, she comes prepared with an action plan. One morning, a delivery truck pulls into their driveway and out comes a nine-by-six-foot whiteboard that Dewy and Danny help carry into their living room. "Alright. We want change, let's make it happen," Rachel declares. She goes on to explain how Kanban boards work, how she adapts it to her particular needs and preferences, what the different sticky notes represent, how to reflect—the whole lot. Rachel does keep her family's board separate from hers; after all, she doesn't want to over-shadow her individuality by cycling everything she does through her family.

▲ Fallibility Curiosity:

▽ Rachel was always under the impression that her children just happened to have difficult personalities, always arguing, always bickering. The blame was always on them. Upon contemplation, it becomes clear that they have picked up some of their habits from the altercations she had with Lewis. She decides to sit down with him and work through different modes of conflict resolution, some of which they exaggerate in front of the kids to demonstrate mature disputation and negotiation. These not only serve as genuine acts of reconciliation but a chance to raise their kids proactively and have fun doing it all together!

▽ Convinced that a 9–5 job is the only way to make a comfortable living, she knows a few moms who work from home, whether it's selling handmade bits and bobs on Etsy or knitted socks on Facebook's marketplace. She decides to reach out and ask for insight.

▲ Serendipitous Curiosity:

▽ A "time out" room! What if they had a room lined with noise cancelling foam? A space for reflection or peace, given how the house's floorboards and walls make it impossible to do anything without the rest of the family hearing it.

▽ On the way back home from work one lazy afternoon, Rachel finds herself driving past an "adult store." Within minutes she is walking back to her car with two bags of exotic creativities with the intention of rejuvenating her marriage's intimacies!

▲ Developmental Curiosity:

▽ As much as conversation with others makes some of her realizations that much more forthcoming, she also knows that some topics are too personal to discuss openly. She decides to try a form of soliloquy (a conversation with herself) by speaking out loud and questioning the next statement to emerge.

▽ No matter how strenuous her workouts are or how long she manages to commit to a healthy diet, Rachel always feels bloated after meals. She figures she'll consult with a nutritionist and get to the bottom of whatever she is doing wrong.

▽ Not expecting much, Rachel decides to complete a personality test on a weekend where she has a little more time to relax and clear her conscience.

▲ Selective Osmosis:

▽ Wanting to find more support, Rachel discovers an online group of struggling mothers offering each other advice. Oh, how relatable their threads are! She knows she's hit gold and populates her Backlog with advice to action. Number 1: the best parenting advice you get is from your kids.

▽ Rachel decides to pass for now on bringing her children to Mary's house. As much as her children enjoy their company, it portrays a false image of what a "healthy household" ought to look like, hindering their behavioral maturation and her family's own ability to cooperate on equal footing. Instead, she acquaints herself with Dewy's and Danny's friends' families, who she knows to be a sophisticated bunch (and who she'd been purposely avoiding, knowing all too well how much worse she'd feel about her own family's circumstances), in the hopes that Dewy's and Danny's norms will return to a healthy baseline. Exposing them to a harmonious family will showcase what they ought to work toward, though Rachel knows better than to conform to an ideal—it serves as merely the beginning!

▲ Divergent Osmosis:

▽ Although her relationship with Lewis has been reinvigorated, his behavior throughout counselling left a bad taste in her mouth; understanding his perspective is difficult. Having immersed herself in the experiences of mothers, Rachel decides to browse through public forums of struggling fathers that may explain Lewis's unwillingness to appreciate her efforts and to compromise.

▽   Still on the topic of obstinacy, Rachel decides to wrap her head around the adamancy of her work's management. She attempts to understand their perspective by assertively consulting one of her colleagues on the board. Why are they so opposed to change? She is going to find out one way or another.

▲ Reflective Osmosis:

▽   Wanting to better understand how parental behavior affects children, she remains vigilant the next time she visits Mary's house to see if she'd be able to connect Vincent's and Mary's eating behaviors to those of their children and whether or not they are aware of it.

▽   With Lewis's endorsement, she sets a video camera atop a bookshelf that overlooks the space where her family spends most of their time. She wants to see for herself what her body language looks like, what she sounds like, and patterns of events that tended to lead to conflict.

▲ Self-Accountability:

▽   Rachel decides to allocate money in a monthly budget which allows her to go on a two-day hiatus once a month, whether it's a night out with her friends, a visit to the hot springs, or a trip to a spa. Anytime she fails to action a task, she deducts $20 from the budget.

▽   One day while listening to an executive coach being interviewed on the radio, Rachel learns about "positive visualization." She figures she'll give it a shot by preparing the email in advance that she'll use to notify her clients and team of a milestone she's soon to accomplish. This allows her to visualize what it will feel and look like ahead of time, bringing the celebrations and rewards closer to where she may be stagnating—the final "umph" to get her through the final stretch.

▲ Group Accountability:

▽   Rachel always wanted to express herself in melody and is seriously considering harp lessons. She decides to ask her family if they want to join in and pick up an instrument of their own! They'd be able to hold each other accountable and practice in the noise-cancelling room Rachel realizes she was making every excuse to install.

▽ Her earlier attempt to learn sign language on her own after hearing that her nephew would be born hard of hearing was short-lived. Still wanting to be a better aunt, she does a quick search online and learns the best way to pick up a language is to actively use it with others. So, she decides to do just that and enroll in a sign language class with others, excited at the opportunities that come with meeting new people and confident that their support will be just what she needs!

▲ Partnered Accountability:

▽ Rachel decides that Dewy will be her accountability partner; she wants to form a stronger bond with her troublesome child—to understand him better and for him to understand her. He stumbles up to her in his goofy way as soon as she arrives from work and immediately bombards her with questions, wanting to know if she's acted on what she said she would earlier in the day and if not, why. "That's not good enough, mom. You're better than that!" he says as he paces back and forth with his arms crossed. Just the cutest.

▽ Rachel overhears one of her work colleagues talking about the fortune she made investing in a plot of land. She brings up the idea with Katie, and the two of them decide to share the risk and invest in their very own plot of land, something affordable in a rural area. Even if it doesn't amount to anything, they'll have a blast doing it and maybe learn a thing or two. "Let's set up a chicken farm on it, Rachel!" "Ha, a plot of cocks. Imagine that. How'd you afford that new car, Katie?" "I'm glad you asked. Two moms and a plot of cocks—that *has* to be on our tombstones when our husbands find out!" They cackle as they embrace the absurd.

▲ Angular Momentum:

▽ Anytime she finds it difficult to get a point across to the boys, Rachel finds another way to convey the message: drawing it out, acting it out, using an example they're familiar with, getting their father to explain it, or getting one of the two to explain it to the other if it managed to click for one of them.

▽ Not wanting the buzz of their date to fade, Rachel makes a list of ideas for date nights, whether it's to the movies, the theater, a picnic, kayaking, or a walk across the beach at sunset. She wants to maintain that lusty momentum!

▲ Vertical Momentum:

▽ Since they've been living in the same house for over fourteen years, Rachel proposes that they move farther out into the outback, away from the buzz of the city and the stress of ceaseless activity.

▽ Rachel contemplates her work. Her family has to come first, but at the same time, she wants to maintain some form of financial independence. Going back to being a housewife is a slippery slope she promises to never revisit. But what if there is another way? She decides to reconstruct her resume, listing the skills and qualities she's gained over the years and figure out what other lines of work could suit.

▲ Spontaneous Momentum:

▽ If Rachel ever wakes up on the wrong side of the bed, not in the mood to action a task, she helps one of the boys with theirs (often much more manageable and equally as fun). This boosts her morale and kick starts the day with the energy of accomplishment!

▽ The clutter in the house is unbearable, the bookshelves stuffed with toys, plates, mugs, batteries, loose papers, souvenirs. And why are all their often-used utensils in such a difficult place to reach?! Another one of her pick-me-ups is to optimize the placement and organization of one cabinet, shelf, and tabletop at a time.

▲ Competitive Ambition:

▽ Every year, Dewy and Danny's school hold an event where high-performing students receive awards. She decides to take on the challenge and mother her children into being one of the few who receive the certificates every parent brags about. How, you may ask? By consulting with the parents of winners, congratulating them, and asking for help if they can manage it. They're definitely doing something right!

▽ At the grocery store one day, Rachel notices how the register screen highlights how much she's saved from buying items on sale. "I'm going to beat that number next time!"

▲ Governing Ambition:

▽ Rachel decides to invest in a second-hand Chinese wok burner! She is always amazed watching chefs toss and stir ingredients at the local Asian restaurant. Aware of how quickly they are able to cook up the tastiest and oftentimes healthiest of foods, it has to be worth trying. The bonus? The boys love to watch and help and they get to cook outside in the sunlight!

▽ Rachel still types with two fingers and is determined to work past her primitive hunt-and-peck technique. She decides to watch online tutorials and play type-racing games that could potentially involve Dewy and Danny!

▲ Contemplative Ambition:

▽ If Rachel is to maintain a healthy diet, she needs to cultivate an environment that encourages it. She has to figure out ways to get her family to enjoy healthy meals, whether it is taste testing, getting them to experiment and cook their own food for fun, or meeting them halfway with a day or two a week of homemade, finger-licking fried chicken!

▽ The sheer number of responsibilities Rachel takes ownership of at home remind her of management problems at work. Poor administration arising from either cynicism, suboptimal delegation of work, or an unwillingness to upskill staff further exacerbated their authoritative conduct and stress-induced misbehavior. Rachel feels no better than them, and decides to upskill her family, delegate responsibility, cut out unnecessary workloads, and relieve the weight bearing her down, freeing up more room for change!

▲ Iterative Failure:

▽ At work, Rachel always looks forward to the days her colleague in sales has to travel interstate. She's always appointed as the substitute, responsible for delivering sales pitches to potential partners. She notices how much she enjoys receiving feedback and how eager she is for advice. She decides to ask her department if it's possible to have two sales consultants.

▽ Rachel never figured out how to tame her curls. She's had to resort to the tedious routine of hair straightening, which often leaves her with a dry, tangled mess of a "do" if she doesn't take her time with it. Apart from Katie and Mary, no one else even knows she has curly hair! She sets out to try different methods of haircare until she can manage those luscious curls like she sees in magazines.

▲ Reinforcing Failure:

▽ Family counselling turns out to be an excellent catalyst of Reinforcing Failure; she repeatedly fails to arrive at the outcome she's imagined! Rachel learns that repeatedly attempting to force her way through a problem with the same approach *is* insane. She has to learn how to *move on* from what isn't working and attempt a different approach, giving others the benefit of the doubt if she knows for a fact that good intent is mutual.

▽ On the topic of moving on, Rachel plans on doing the unthinkable and publicly confessing the true nature of her circumstances on social media. So frequent were her posts of cheerful family/household images and jolly day-to-day summaries portraying a reality she desperately wanted to believe, that she feels she owes every other mother in the neighborhood the truth. If she is going to give up the act, get off her high horse, and enable opportunities of collaboration and support, she needs to get used to the snobby judgments she anticipates.

▲ Opportunistic Failure:

▽ Wanting to expedite the process of building healthy eating habits for her children, Rachel uses this topic as a conversation starter with other mothers. It not only acquaints her with the inner workings of other families; she also finds more items to add to her Backlog! "Have you tried mashing the vegies into patties? If it looks like a burger patty to a kid, it's a burger patty."

▽ Failing to find middle ground during counselling impels Rachel to "reintroduce" herself to Lewis. She plans to ask the same of him. She realizes they have been together for so long that they are now entirely different people.

▲ Lossless Pride:

▽ While Rachel intends to openly admit defeat on social media, she plans on doing it with grace and a constructive outlook, admitting her mistakes, apologizing for projecting a false image, and briefly explaining how she plans to do better.

▽ Rachel remains acutely aware of missteps and misunderstandings and whether she has unintentionally failed to listen with sufficient attention. She decides to get into the habit of using clarifying questions and repeating what she thinks she understands to avoid misinterpretation: "So, what you're saying is . . ."

▲ Attractive Pride:

▽ Rachel already has a wardrobe that shouts "authentic pride," but you always find her running, rushing, and sometimes stumbling, behaviors that suggest a disorganized lifestyle. She decides to refrain from hurry by padding tasks with more time, ensuring graceful movement, and disallowing the stress of tardiness to stir her mood. If she is on track for a late arrival, she plans her apology in transit, admits she had poorly planned her day, and lets them know what she plans on doing differently when they next meet.

▽ She was always self-conscious of her chipped tooth and discolored teeth from all the tobacco she smoked in her teens. She knows it is off-putting to some (though, more so for herself) and is fully aware of the benefits of a bright, shining smile. She books a consultation with a dentist and is ready to pay the price!

▲ Reflective Pride:

▽ The benefits of using sticky notes for tasks facilitates Rachel's aim to appreciate the distances she's traversed. She plans to frame what the first week of her Kanban board looked like, labels and all, and hang it up where her first Kanban board was hidden. By memorializing those early days, she is better equipped to judge her progress—in constant awe of how bad she let her circumstances get. Rachel finds a family photo that was taken on New Year's. It is so canned: the forced smiles, the reluctant hand holding—the embodiment of everything Rachel wants to leave behind. It, too, is framed.

▽ Ruminating over what took place in counselling, Rachel takes note of all that she would have loved to have heard and seen from Lewis. Understanding that they are both facing a similar dilemma with each other, she turns her notes into comments, acts, and gestures she'll use more often: remarks of appreciation, asking if he needs help with anything, genuinely asking how he is feeling and why, taking interest in his work and listening, leaving sweet handwritten messages (as she used to do) in arbitrary locations.

Rachel gives her family a sneak peak of the Kanban board she is perfecting—her pride and joy. The sketches and calligraphy dressed with differently colored sticky notes, the meticulous placement of categorization stickers, and her web of strings that make the entire board intuitively legible—even to her boys—it inspires everyone to match her effort. In working out how their familywide Kanban board will operate, each has a say as they endeavor to find middle ground for what works best for everyone. As for their Backlog that needs populating, Rachel encourages everyone to write out any ideas that come to them, no matter how small, trivial, or grandiose, and hang them up for everyone to see!

The best part of all is how the family is orienting toward freeing up more time for outings. So, the quicker they are able to get their respective tasks done, the more likely they will be able to action grander ventures! Which leads to a lot of great ideas:

▲ Dewy suggests having a two-person team empty the dishwasher where one does the removing and the other places items where they belong.

▲ Danny suggests they get a window wiper so he can polish down the table faster, and a spray gun for . . . reasons.

▲ Lewis suggests they try one-pot recipes to minimize the number of dishes they use.

▲ Rachel suggests they try meal-prepping to avoid cooking every day—a meal-prep that requires all hands on deck twice a week.

▲ Who is the swiftest at unstacking the dishwasher, the quickest to mop the floor, the fastest to fold laundry, the most efficient watering the garden? The boys are determined to beat Rachel's high score!

It is a collective effort as they pack their Backlogs with crazy, sporadic, innovative ideas while attaching cutouts of Marvel avatars they assigned each other to cards they are responsible for.

They decide to track how much time they are collectively saving and to keep building on that number. They celebrate every record they break by revisiting an activity everyone enjoyed. The inclusivity, camaraderie, and competition has Dewy and Danny lose interest in their tablets, as the Kanban board slowly grows to encompass their own personal matters as well. So occupied are they with beating each other's scores that Lewis comes up with the great idea of rewarding milestones with gifts and acknowledgments!

Danny gets the one-month go-kart pass he's always wanted if he manages to achieve a full grade higher for math in his next report card. Dewy gets Danny to do all his chores for him for an entire week if he manages to stay out of trouble for a full academic term. Rachel knows they are on the right track, and she couldn't be happier.

After every completed task, they spend a few minutes reflecting on it and taking note. With a bit of guidance and practice, bad experiences always turn out to be constructive, as everyone is increasingly proficient at garnering positive lessons. What doesn't work for someone always leads to a pivot and to approaches that either validate the incompatibility or rectify the setback. Items that work for everyone are plastered with gold stars and deposited into a special column they revisit on special occasions.

As for the bulks Rachel goes on to action, a few stand out:

Upon consulting the parents of award-winning students, Rachel receives two pearls of wisdom to help Dewy develop discipline, self-control, and respect for others. The first is to enroll him in sports or music lessons where patience, adherence to rules, and teamwork are cultivated. The second is to involve Dewy in the decision-making process. Rachel proceeds to have a one-to-one with Dewy regarding his behavior at school, and after much negotiation, Dewy agrees to enroll in Danny's judo gym. Upon hearing the news, Danny is elated to get his little brother started! The past few months have been an emotional roller-coaster, and watching her two boys finally get along takes her on another ride as tears of joy well up in her eyes. It wasn't long before Dewy's teacher called to ask whether he's been bitten by a radioactive spider with a passion for camaraderie. "One day he's yanking at Patricia's hair, the next, he's bowing and teaching her how to defend herself!"

As Rachel scrolls through her personality test results, skimming through descriptions, one trait stood out from the rest: her orderliness score came back exceptionally high. Pleased with herself, she reads through its accompanying explanation. Her eyes narrow as she rereads a line, gleaning a revealing sign that strikes a chord. "Well, I suppose that explains it!" She learned to disassociate her shortcomings and their consequences from her true self, attributing them to a self that is too preoccupied with details; easily distressed when things don't go *her* way; wanting to control people, tasks, and situations; unable to discard worthless objects; stubborn with inflexible values. Not to mention the clutter, how sensitive she is to mismanagement at work, her unwavering obstinance during counselling, and how everything she had was never good enough. It all starts to make sense as she is now ready to work on this extremity, with a Quasi-Chaotic View as a directive and a baseline self to work from.

Rachel ends up consulting a nutritionist and discovers she is sensitive to FODMAP foods: garlic, onion, asparagus, mango, watermelon, muesli, cashews, cow milk, honey, coconut water . . . the whole lot! No matter how many crunches, meal plans, or hours she spends on a treadmill, she is always bloated. Now she knows why!

After spending most of one evening watching haircare videos online, she comes across the Curly Girl method of maintaining naturally curling hair: cleansing conditioner instead of shampoos, no silicones, no combing or brushing, no terry cloth towels. Scrunching as opposed to rubbing, and hair gel for a cast to break after it's been blow-dried slowly with a diffuser. You should see those gleaming curls! She looks absolutely fabulous, and *no one* fails to comment on it.

Openly admitting the false image she has been projecting on social media is met with compassion and support Rachel did not expect. How brave she is to admit what others do not and actively seek support—for no other reason than to better the livelihood of her family and to live with a clear conscience. It is more important than saving face and turns out to be nothing short of inspiring and influential to other mothers veiling ugly truths they'd otherwise like help with!

Cooking healthier meals for her family, Rachel realizes, turns into a form of love language. The more she focuses on the many different cuisines and forms of cooking they progress through, the more fulfilling it gets! She cooks small meals and asks for a taste test. She secretly disguises ingredients they are normally repelled by in stews and garnishes, and once they realize what they've eaten, their opinions began to turn! And as for "love language," Rachel receives a complimentary book with her purchase called *The Five Love Languages* at that adult shop. It describes five different ways romantic partners express and experience love: words of affirmation, quality time, physical touch, acts of service, and receiving gifts. A serendipitous chain of events then leads to a revelation: Lewis's love language is his service of *providing*, and hers are the compliments, acknowledgments, appreciations, and verbal communication of love! An occasional "I really appreciate your hard work, Rache'. Thank you for making dinner tonight," or "Thank you for helping me with my homework, Mom. You're the best!" makes a world of difference and fills Rachel with the love she so desires. She plans another date night with Lewis to a remote Airbnb cabin she discovers through her monthly hiatuses and looks forward to discussing all she has learned!

It only took a few weeks before they manage to save two hours a day thanks to effective delegation, constructive collaboration, and creative change! Dewy has four winning cards, which he is ever so proud of. He throws a fit every now and then, whining about rules others are bending anytime they came close to breaking his records, but to Rachel's surprise, Danny and Lewis are the first to console and embolden. She is incredibly proud of them all.

After fourteen years of stagnation for nothing more than maintaining what she already had, Rachel finally finds the time to invest in herself and her sense of individuality. In the process, driven with a newfound passion, she finds a cause to pursue. She also realizes that Vincent and Mary are oblivious to their osmotically bad behaviors, resorting to a "Do as I say, not as I do" household ideology. Rachel sits them down and explains the issues she faced in her own household and what she did to turn things around. She spends the next few weeks coaching them through Agile practices and, within two months, manages to get Mary's family on route to their very own Quasi-Chaotic liberation!

In a moment of epiphany, Rachel realizes how supporting mothers in her community and sharing what has worked for her could turn into a part-time career: a family developmental coach! Consulting families with disproportionate contributions to household chores and families struggling to raise their children responsibly in the face of long working hours and financial struggles. *This* is what Rachel wants to do, what she wants to perfect. She can't help the glistening white smile that now beams out from her face.

CHAPTER 36
BRINGING IT ALL TOGETHER

The idea is to be inconsistent, but consistently so.

And that's it! The Quasi-Chaotic Lifestyle. You are now almost entirely equipped with the means to Self-Actualize in an everchanging complex adaptive system with an everchanging self!

Begin by working your way through the Quasi-Chaotic "steps of adoption" (Steps 1–6), get accustomed to the method and the tools, and you'll be ready to hit your Quasi-Chaotic stride as depicted in figure 7-41!

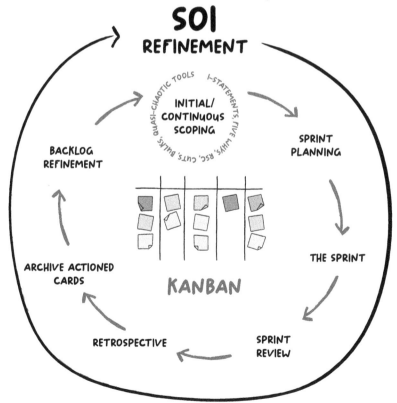

Figure 7-41: The Quasi-Chaotic Lifestyle

Again, it is worth restating how a Quasi-Chaotic Lifestyle does not require strict, procedural execution to work. And I think you know why by now! The order, frequency, and time you spend on Quasi-Chaotic exertion is entirely dependent on your circumstances and capacity. For example, if suited:

▲ You may prefer weeklong Sprints for more room to choose, as opposed to daily Sprints for a more disciplined approach.

▲ You may choose to refine your Backlog as you action a Sprint for efficiency, as opposed to sticking to the standard sequence.

▲ You may decide to exercise the Five Whys on a few items every other week to space out change or periodically all at once to ascertain priority as early as possible.

▲ You may decide to simultaneously cut and bulk gradually to balance heavy losses or allocate a few months a year to each, alternating between Angular Momentum during cuts and Vertical Momentum during bulks to maintain focus and avoid getting overwhelmed, respectively.

▲ You may prepare your cuts and act on them at times that work best for everyone involved as opposed to taking your annual leave from work and ripping the bandages all at once, expediting the cut.

Adapt it as you see fit, as it suits, and if you begin to stray, return to the fundamentals. I recommend that you refine (update and renavigate) your SOI every one-to-three months for any given influence. This is the average number of days it takes to form a new habit and the general rule of thumb when bulking a new person, place, or practice. Give novel points of influence sufficient time and Angular Momentum to leave their mark in order to avoid impulsive and premature judgments.

Upon sustaining a Quasi-Chaotic Lifestyle, especially throughout its adoption, you may find yourself in need of reminders, refreshers, and revision. As stated in the very beginning, I recommend you keep this book close during times of uncertainty and even closer during times of doubt. To that end, and for your convenience, I have compiled a list of references to resources and examples for Quasi-Chaotic processes and definitions you may need to brush up on every now and again. With that said, I cannot stress enough that rereading chapters relevant to the issue you are facing would be the most beneficial:

▲ **Quasi-Chaotic tips:** In living an unconventional lifestyle—a Quasi-Chaotic Lifestyle—you will face unconventional obstacles. Tips for how to overcome them are detailed on page 530 and are well worth a read.

▲ **Quasi-Chaotic Tool Kit Cheat Sheet:** A collection of the Quasi-Chaotic tool summary directive questions can be found on page 543.

▲ **Bulk ideation support:** If you find yourself struggling to ideate initiatives for a bulk, feel free to refer back to pages 447 to 456 for Hobbies, pages 460 to 465 for Sustenance, or, alternatively, you could leverage or adapt what our change champions ideated for themselves in their respective journeys on pages 470, 482, and 494.

▲ **RSC development:** You will find reference to RSC development examples in the list of figures available on page viii. Alternatively, you can revisit the example detailed on page 321.

▲ **Sprint runs:** You can refer back to page 353 where each step is detailed.

▲ **Glossary and index:** Should you require a refresher for any of the Quasi-Chaotic terms and important Self-Actualizing vocabulary, feel free to refer the glossary on page 553 or the index on page 595.

As the saying goes, "Trajectory is more important than position." So far, you've probably lived a life with little sense of authentic direction. You may have been swept up by a passing wave of meaning or a wave of expectation or chance, but it likely didn't last. If you were lucky enough to have had the wave leave you with something worthwhile and are telling yourself you're "set," though, burdened and impatient by unrealized hopes and dreams, you may want to reconsider. What is there to lose besides all that you distaste, dread, are bored of, and roll your eyes at? You won't know what there is to gain if you hang on to what you're afraid to lose. If your current iron triangle permits *some* change, give change a chance. It might be the only chance you get.

The six steps of the Quasi-Chaotic Lifestyle's adoption through the lens of the Quasi-Chaotic View will be the end of a self hijacked by extrinsic influence and the beginning of another self immersed in Self-Actualizing directives, supported by repeating and self-reinforcing cycles of consideration, appreciation, cognizance, informed decision-making, emancipation, transition, accruement, reflection, and growth. As you overcome doubt, uncertainty, insecurity, and inauthenticity, you'll emerge as a beacon of inspiration for those around you. Your transformation will serve as a testament to your ability to chart your own path and shape your destiny.

Now, you may be wondering what became of our change champions. . .

If you were only tracking an individual's journey, I strongly recommend you avoid reading through epilogues of personas you haven't tracked from the beginning. Instead, you can either restart the journey through the lens of another persona, or finish reading the chapter on page 516 after reading through an epilogue!

Mike

Mike ultimately enrolled in a bachelor of IT program, majoring in information systems to pursue his dream job of becoming a technical business analyst. He focused on optimizing methods of study and saw his time at university as a means to further improve his ability to take on and retain information. A programming elective he enrolled in involved the development of a system of his choosing. He went on to develop what he calls a "personal intelligence management system" that centralizes information he leverages for his own Self-Actualizing motives, consisting of multiple productivity modules that he can access anytime and anywhere. One of the modules is a "people management system." It keeps track of those he acquainted himself with options to add notes, contact details, and search filters to facilitate connecting people with one another (which he became known for). He uses it to find Informed Perspectives and Accountability Partners should the need for either arise. Confident of his ability to build such systems on a whim, he decided to pursue a PhD in education with the intent of building software to help identify a learning style that best suits an individual with the intent of influencing pedagogical systems to capitalize on the findings!

He moved out of his parent's house, though not too far away. He pursued sovereignty of responsibility to build character and discipline. Now a blue belt in jiujitsu, Mike was getting ready to compete in a local tournament while also packing for a month-long trip to immerse himself in an overseas culture he once naively looked down on. And you wouldn't know it was Mike you were looking at! He completely transformed his image, his posture, and his articulation, as he now operated with Pride. He was truly a different person. He ended up taking harmonica classes, insisted on maintaining his role at the pizzeria every Sunday, and acquainted himself with almost every store clerk in a two-mile radius from the flat he shared.

And what of the origami incident? Let's just say that Mike learned the true meaning of heartbreak. Elly was a blessing and a curse, for as much as he learned about his shortcomings, the intricacies of a healthy relationship, and what he was looking for from one, the pain of realizing that her list of priorities did not involve him—given all he had sacrificed for her—was difficult to come to terms with. He knew better than to devote 100% of himself to another, deciding he would never settle for anyone discounting his worth, undermining the standard he held himself to, or unwilling to share equal commitment to intrinsic change to make a relationship work. But you should have seen how Mike handled it; he was the quintessential representation of what it means to be a change champion. During a time of reminiscing, he looked back at where he was and then to how far he'd come—the helpless boy he once was, and the capable man he's now become.

Andrew

Andrew ended up setting aside his Kanban board and shifting to a "semi-Quasi-Chaotic Lifestyle." Every now and then, when faced with excessive turmoil, he'd reactivate his Kanban account to straighten out his life. Andrew's fascination with cosmology and his indefatigable willingness to learn more of it had him working through several free online courses between trucking shifts, covering much of the material offered in the first two years of an astronomy degree. Sharpening his social skills and learning to mingle, he acquainted himself with a lecturer at the restaurant where he had worked, a regular customer whom he confided his passion for astronomy to. So impressed was she with his autodidactic (self-taught) grasp of calculus and physics that she invited him to a teaching awards night to meet a few of her colleagues. One thing led to another, and with a letter of recommendation and the stamp of a seal, Andrew committed to a journey that led him to become the talented astronomer he now is, regularly visiting Chilean observatories and immersing himself in worlds too distant for the eye to see.

During one of his visits, he decided to take a tour across Santiago and found himself at a local's home for a cooking class where he met his current loving, like-minded, and supportive partner. Andrew stayed in contact with Tim as he occasionally paid him a visit to cook dinner for his family to express appreciation for being the one who always stood by his side when others didn't. He kept in touch with his father as he promised and mended his relationship with Jeremy, his brother, becoming the best uncle his children could ask for. He rocked a three-piece suit wherever he went: tall, proud, eloquent. In his free time, he volunteered to assist with a mental health program for youth. He has a singing teacher, practices ballroom dancing, and invests his money in emerging technologies—though sparingly. He's never had the same haircut twice, has a pet chameleon, and prefers oolong tea.

One night, after learning of Tim's sudden passing and while mourning in anguish, he received an email from a "distant stranger." It read:

> Right now, I'm enjoying the disaster of a gnocchi I made. I don't know if I'm biting into potato or the crystallized MSG I decided to throw into the mix. I've been reading about neutron stars lately. Did you know that a teaspoon of such a star weighs four billion tons? I think that's pretty cool . . . almost as dense as I'm feeling right now. Seriously, who puts MSG in gnocchi?
>
> It's been difficult, being away from mom and all. I feel lonely from time to time starting everything anew on my own. I feel like I can't get anything right—kind of worthless, you know? But I know I'll figure it out; I know you will have figured it out. I'm learning something new every day, and I remind myself that things can only get better at this pace. They will, right? Tim thinks I'm headed in the right direction, and that's all that matters. Hah! Anyway, I don't know who you are, what you're doing, or what your worries are, but never forget that the pain I'm enduring is for you, because I love you and I know you deserve better.
>
> PS: Write back to me every now and again, will you?

Andrew wanted nothing more than to embrace his past self and tell him that everything was going to be okay. On this day, Andrew would not only bury his lifelong mentor and friend, but his past self and the lingering bitterness that obviated reconciliation with his mother and with former friends who were looking to make peace as well. He couldn't help but recall the words of a polymath astronomer whose qualities separated him from other men of his time and beyond: Galileo Galilei. After torturers forced him to recant his theory that the Earth orbits the Sun, he muttered, "*E pur si muove.*" ("And yet it moves.") Choosing to relinquish the suffering of his past, Andrew could no longer deny ownership of the pain he bitterly held on to as he muttered in tears and melancholy, "*E pur si muove, e pur si muove, e pur si muove . . .*"

Rachel

Disinterested with managerial obstinance, Rachel ended up resigning from her work and pursing a part-time career as a family developmental coach. She spent the other half of the week earning a degree in psychology, working toward a certificate of counselling: specialization—child, youth and family therapy.

Lewis resigned as well, deciding that the prospect of a promotion and the risk and commitment it continued to require wasn't worth it. He now sought work in an organization that would truly value his time and loyalty. Rachel and Lewis formulated a five-step strategy when confronted with a Hard Problem: an open discussion, mapping out pros and cons, constructing a combined RSC, engaging a counsellor if necessary, and capitulating to shared compromise if it came to it. They proactively and periodically visit a family counsellor to keep improving and adapting their conditions when a problem arises as opposed to reactively leaning on external support. They now understand that for their relationship to endure and thrive, they each need to establish a sense of individualism whereby each would have personal projects and self-oriented growth goals: a power couple with two strong individuals who respect each other's iron triangles.

Twice a year, each family member sets off on their own private two-week hiatus, whether it's overseas travel, camping in the outback, or retreating to a resort, always returning to Sprint Reviews and Retrospectives conducted with whomever has the time to assist. On one occasion, during a psychedelic trip to the Amazon she took with Mary, Lawrence, and Katie, Rachel contracted ringworm that led to alopecia. In less than a week, she managed to turn the dread of losing the curls she had put so much time and attention on into what she wished she had done years ago. She shaved her head clean and now had a collection of wigs that she mixed and matched with the dresses she sewed herself! Good ole Rache'.

They moved to a farm in a different state where they lived gracefully, Dewy and Danny each with their own small plot of land they tended with rigor. Danny took on the responsibility of preparing meals, taking interest in a culinary career. Dewy was responsible for organizing meal plans to suit his family's fitness goals, taking interest in a career in nutrition. Their new home was designed to accommodate multiple sizeable whiteboards, and Kanban boards spanned entire corridors, one for each member and one for the whole, as their family had now become!

Rachel blossomed into a symbol of prosperity. From household to household, she cultured gardens of growth from which the fruit of her influence brought peace and cohesion amongst struggling mothers and broken families.

The tribulations Mike, Andrew, and Rachel faced resemble much of what we all face today, in one form or another, in every corner of the globe, whether it's a health crisis, workplace tension, existential dread, friendship struggles, financial crisis, career pressure, unfair treatment, a lack of inner peace, or mental health issues. Each is burdened with an excess of research, studies, books, essays, blogs, coaches, drugs, documentaries, apps, websites, programs, and communities to help find answers, yet we ultimately remain the prime movers of our respective liberties and fate. What came next for our change champions? Well, your guess would be as good as mine, but better to experience such an adventure yourself! Most of their dilemmas were based on real people and real events, how their problems arose, how they were resolved, and the aftermath. The Quasi-Chaotic model offered them a path to freedom, peace, and the means to pursue Self-Actualization. It is now on offer for you.

Take this practical guide to Self-Actualization and fulfill your potential. There are no limits but those you believe there to be.

PART VIII

TRIUMPH

THE FINISH LINE

CHAPTER 37
RECAP

The Traditional Psyche is a way of the past, and it is high time we moved on. Adhering to the status quo, we have been allowing extrinsic stretch goals to dictate what little we are permitted. With complete disregard to our everchanging selves and environment, such a stance has been reliably leading us toward ignorance, apathy, and capitulation to underwhelming and unfulfilled lives. We examined the consequences of twenty-first-century privileges and how its cultural and social suppression of challenge has inhibited our ability to train the mind and overcome prehistoric survival mechanisms that limit our potential. This predicament has been exacerbated by the Traditional Psyche, whose views obfuscate facts of personal development, our capacity to understand what giftedness is and isn't, and how talent development is evidently not exclusive to those with the right genes but a process catalyzed by influence, practice, and change. We quashed views that deny the possibility of intrinsic change and the fact that the traits and characteristics that make us who we are are identifiable, tangible, and malleable toward favorable qualities and away from hindering extremities.

We explored the effects of the social net of hysteria we are so easily swayed into, realizing the need to demagnetize the allure of the viral and the obscene, mainstream stigmas, dogmas, bandwagons, and routines, and Incessant Distraction to afford us the time and nerves to experience and immerse ourselves in authentic growth-catalyzing reality. We denounced evolutionary inclinations—especially a Procreative Predisposition we ought to emancipate ourselves from—knowing better than to ape our origins and to live instead by our own values. We do so to repress the casualness we habitually resort to decisions that we make about restrictive and risky long-term commitments that require the most serious consideration and maturation of the self.

We dove deep into questions of well-being and happiness and scrutinized how such fundamental topics have been woefully neglected, overlooked, and understated as a dialectic matter of priority—so much so that we find ourselves destitute of elementary guidance. Everyone is seemingly swinging in the dark, improvising as they go, living through the motions, and occasionally getting swept up by another way of template living. We learned of Maslow's hierarchy of needs, a pyramid of motivations which offered a foundational structure of directives but more importantly, directives toward an ongoing cycle of self-actualizing experiences that few are aware of, let alone approach. We observed how the lifestyles we inherit herd us toward bottom- or top-heavy pyramids, not knowing how much is enough nor aware of the moving goalposts we parse as abnormality.

For an answer, we turned to the software development industry and the evolving developmental processes it has invested billions to perfecting from which we salvaged pearls of wisdom to leverage. Comparing the limitations of a planning oriented and rigid Waterfall methodology to the flexible building-and-testing-centric Agile philosophy exposed what we've been doing wrong all along: not involving the end user with a project's development, not iterating through quantity to arrive at quality, not minimizing planning given all that is unknown, not taking into account the nature of complex adaptive systems we are all bound to, and not prioritizing value with respect to what is feasible given our iron triangle. Bridging the gap between software development and daily life and drawing upon the nexus of chaos and development, we achieved control of our success through challenge, epiphany, and serendipity—all catalyzed by the essence of the Agile philosophy and the core of the Quasi-Chaotic Lifestyle: change.

We digressed toward a brief yet necessary intermission for those feeling helpless and indifferent. We learned of the evanescent and fortuitous nature of our existence in the vast expanse of the universe—a humbling reality we ought to remain conscious of to keep petty, trivial, and material matters from distracting us from the gift of time and what little of it we are permitted. We experienced a "bait-and-switch," recognizing we may very well be victim of cognitive adjustments, the offender we despise, the wrongdoer to blame, the traitor to abandon. And we arrived at the last resort; having found ourselves at an Unreachable Terminal, we discovered the prime mover of our own undoing. We accept that in order to kindle a spark, our anagnorisis—our true circumstances—our "forces for change" must outweigh our "forces against change," and the only way there is by Suffering, knowing it is we who reject change, realizing that it's time to let go of the hope we cling to and suffer because we are the ones in control. Obligating *Sein-zum-Tode* ("being-toward-death") of authentic perspective and pursuits, we came to terms with what we've become by understanding the illusion of free will, compatibilist outcomes, and the existential freedom of essence we may have been mistakenly tying to our identity.

We united our revealed truths and constructed the Quasi-Chaotic View: a twenty-first-century adapted theory of well-being and happiness that outlines a way of life incorporating all the realizations drawn from what does and doesn't work. A hybrid theory of subjective well-being and happiness, psychic affirmation, and an objective list derived of the Agile Manifesto and Maslow's characteristics of a self-actualized human. We redefined self-actualization as a prime directive that is fixated on a state of being, sensitive to fleeting desires, aware of the angst of stagnation, and seeking opportunities of intertemporal growth by maximizing diversity of experience given what our iron triangle permits. Authenticity, autonomy, informedness, and, above all, change conduct us toward the ten principles that make for a Quasi-Chaotic Self-Actualized individual.

We equipped ourselves with a Quasi-Chaotic Tool Kit to keep us steered, efficient, constructive, and absolute. Through Curiosity we are guided and informed. Through Osmosis we cultivate an environment primed for growth. Through Accountability we muster through challenge. Through Ambition we strive for the ideal. Through Failure we grow. Through Momentum we endure. And through Pride we stride. All of which are the constituents for sustaining a healthy Quasi-Chaotic Lifestyle.

We acknowledged and familiarized ourselves with the nature and inevitability of Hard Problems. We investigated the "three pillars of conviction" and formulated the Quasi-Chaotic Decision-Making Model to enable Self-Actualizing navigation of Hard Problems. Taking into account the shortcomings of our faculties and intuition, the best decision-making models, the

Quasi-Chaotic View, and our proclivities to dissonance and subsequent adjustments, the RSC (the means by which we overcome Hard Problems) engenders confidence over the hairiest of problems that breaking out of the Traditional Psyche will present—and beyond.

And finally, we accustomed ourselves with the Quasi-Chaotic Lifestyle and the six steps that comprise its adoption:

1. **Setting up and practicing the use of our Kanban board:**
   Familiarizing ourselves with the motions of Sprints

2. **Constructing our SOI:**
   Identifying salient points of influence that significantly impact our welfare

3. **Navigating SOI influences:**
   Classifying points of influence to be positive
   and/or negative influences and prioritizing them

4. **Applying the Five Whys to our SOI:**
   Drawing actionable realizations from boiling down
   points of influence to their root causes

5. **Cutting:**
   Ridding ourselves (and SOI) from negative
   and/or Less Permitting influences

6. **Bulking:**
   Engaging with new points of influence to experience, reflect
   upon, and potentially adopt (and amend our SOI with)

We followed the journeys of three separate personas in their attempts to adopt a Quasi-Chaotic Lifestyle, reading through their trials, tribulations, and triumphs to understand how each Quasi-Chaotic tool comes into play and how the Quasi-Chaotic Lifestyle leads to Self-Actualization. Finally, we learned what the cycle of the Quasi-Chaotic Lifestyle would entail after its adoption along with the potential for adaptation. And with that, we are ready to put the theory into practice!

One wonders what the world would look like if everyone adopted a Quasi-Chaotic Lifestyle. Would power grids run and space exploration continue? Would we face a childbirth crisis? Would politicians never come to consensus? Would permanent contracts vanish along with exceptionally specialized talent? Or would an emphasis on Self-Actualization draw more individuals toward their passion, cultivating even more exceptionally specialized talent? Would political initiatives be tested in smaller circles and increasingly bigger groups before bringing consensus into the masses? Would the consequences of bad parenting and ill-informed childbearing become a burden of the past? Would the agility that comes with the privatization of utilities and government responsibilities offer competitive edges (as we have seen from companies such as SpaceX and Relativity Space that place their focus on iteration and Agile development)? These are interesting questions to ponder, but for now, as with Mike, Andrew, and Rachel, we must turn our attention to what matters most for others, our future selves, and most importantly, our *present* selves.

We are here, we are now, and we are present because we are survival machines. Our genes survived because they adapted. We have not yet evolved into our final form—far from it—nor will we ever, but only through further adaptation and change will individuals, societies, and the human race as a whole survive, thrive, and prosper.

CHAPTER 38
GIVING BACK

How often do you hear, "You have to love yourself before you can love someone else" or "You need to help yourself before you can help others"? Again, words that get passed for wisdom often leave us lonelier and more helpless than ever. Do you recall the times your efforts to love or support were brushed off because you didn't "have it all together" yet? The fact of the matter is that loving yourself and helping yourself does not come with a certificate; there is no finish line. Let me be the one to suggest that there is no better impetus for self-improvement and achieving your ambitions than expressing compassion, care, and love for others. Perhaps it's another evolutionary inkling—the gene rewarding its host with a lasting drive through reciprocal kinship. Either way, not only can sayings like these invoke loneliness and isolation and add pressure to the circular fallacy that loving yourself is "all there is," but believing and adhering to such nonsense will prevent a catalyst of growth like no other. Instead, celebrate, if you recall, what Maslow referred to as *gemeinschaftsgefühl* (human kinship)! Help yourself through others, and others can help themselves through you. I could list numerous studies that suggest a significant link between kindness and eudemonic well-being, or how helping others boosts longevity and happiness, reduces chronic pain, lowers blood pressure, and boosts self-esteem and one's sense of optimism. But frankly, it isn't warranted.

How often do others reach out with support that you ignore? I suppose such resistance stems from the ubiquity of inauthenticity or empty words that get passed as etiquette. You would be surprised, however, that many are well aware of how trite this might be yet do so regardless, willing to go the distance. Asking for help or accepting an offer of one is not a sign of weakness but an act of courage and conviction. Giving in and admitting the need for help demonstrates a willingness for resurgence, revival, and renewal—a genuine urge to change your circumstances for the better. Take the offer; *accept* help. The ones who love, care, or look up to you are always eager to lend a hand. It's an opportunity they look forward to, a matter they cherish, an act that is meaningful to them. Do not deny them—or yourself, for that matter—such an experience.

And how often have you been the one to extend the olive branch? What you have to gain from helping another will compel you not only to better yourself but correct your perception of what it means to accept support for yourself. Thus, I say, love others so you can learn to love yourself, and help others so that you can learn to help yourself!

As the proverb goes: "We make a living by what we get. We make a life by what we give." The assurance that comes with regaining control, the realization of liberty, omnipresent opportunity, and living our lives to the fullest as we see fit is a gift. And giving back such a gift to others will make the experience considerably more rewarding and fruitful. That is precisely what it means to pursue experiences that benefit yourself first, but the benefit depends on the benefit to others—which, to reiterate, includes your future selves *and* the future of others, because the totality of influence always returns to your present self-benefit. Doing our small part to help awaken and reinvigorate those who are lost, weary, and in need and then watching them blossom and thrive will be the best mark we can leave in this world and in ourselves—the legacy we *ought* to leave behind.

Where to start? By passing on this book to someone in need of it, whether it's someone you've seen stagnate, give in, give up, fade away, or fall into darkness. You can also conveniently gift them a copy at **NecessitatingChange.com**. "You cannot swim for new horizons until you have courage to lose sight of the shore," said the Nobel laureate writer William Faulkner. Everyone *seems* to want change, but most fear losing sight of the shore. And as you may know, the first step is always the hardest. So, be the one to help with those first few steps and encourage them to return the favor to another. Be the one to influence change!

Said Mahatma Gandhi,

"The best way to find yourself is to lose yourself in the service of others."

The final key that unlocks a life of change is bringing change to those around you. There is no greater catalyst for self-discovery than service to others. It's a gift without a price tag, a gift without expectation, a gift without compromise, a gift with limitless reward, a gift like no other: the gift of change.

You can also join me and the rest of the Giving What We Can community of "effective givers" in bringing change to those in need. Twenty percent of the gross profits Necessitating Change generates will be donated to the most effective charities in the world. Turn to page 547 to learn more about effective altruism, the myth of the self-made man, and how you can make a bigger impact for less.

CHAPTER 39
REBIRTH

In the still of darkness, as the cloud of night culminates, before sunrise, a majestic yellow-and-red-feathered bird ruffles its tethered wings and builds its nest. It places branch, spice, and clove carefully and with intent. It's tired and weary but is not quite finished. As Helios, god of the Sun, rides his shimmering chariot across the morning sky, the bird turns east to face him and trills a farewell song so poignant and beautiful that even Helios stops to listen until it's finished. It's a peal of such utter woe that, for a fleeting instant, the world feels the pang of unrealized wishes and unattainable desires, forgetting the feeble gift of hope, so absolute its sorrow.

The bird begins to beat its wings faster and faster and, with frictive brilliance, bursts into a fiery blaze of divine self-immolation. And then, from the ashes, it emerges once more, rising from the old, a cyclic creature of demise and renewal, beginning and ending and beginning afresh.

This image of the Phoenix is culturally depicted in Egyptian mythology as Bennu, in Jewish mythology as Milcham, in Hindu mythology as Garuda, in Native American mythology as the Thunderbird, and in Slavic Mythology as the Firebird. It symbolizes the nature of rebirth and rejuvenation. Its fire embodies the truth, the light, and the goodness of its reality. What transcends its demise is what keeps it alive. *Sterquiliniis invenitur* ("in filth it shall be found") said the founder of analytic psychology, Carl Jung. What our heart most desires—the truth—is found where we least want to look. Truth brings together the necessary conditions to die to the past and the present knowing that a much more powerful version of ourself will emerge from the remains. And it is only through self-sacrifice that this truth will emerge from our old, incapable, and jaded self.

The regenerative image of the Phoenix is often represented as an eagle with heightened vision and perception, symbolizing the lens through which we view the world with our opinions and biases, our desires and dreams, and how we choose to act on what is permitted. This vision is renewed and restored with every rebirth, generating a different identity of values and aspirations. Each new identity presents its own slew of problems along with additional opportunities to iterate out of and act on. And so in order for us to gain, we must lose ourselves and start again. Live a thousand lives and a thousand more, and with every iteration, we will reemerge more informed, more aware, more confident, more willing, more capable, and more giving. Who are we if we constantly seek out renewal?

Consider the "Ship of Theseus" paradox, the ancient Grecian account that was preserved by Platonist philosopher Plutarch in AD 46. This thought experiment raises the question of whether an object that has had all its components replaced remains the same object. If you change everything about yourself, are you still you? There is something far deeper than traits, talents, and material possession that defines us; that demarcates our individuality from the collective. We are not the idea of who we believe we are and have been but the consequence of the cumulative decisions we have made. We are the product of action, reflection, birth, and rebirth—we are the beginning and the end of who we chose to let go of and become. We are nothing more than what we choose to be now—a choice afforded by all of who we used to be. Said the novelist George R.R. Martin:

> **"Never forget who you were, for surely the world will not.Make it your strength. Then it can never be your weakness. Armor yourself in it, and it will never be used to hurt you."**

Aegis of the past—drawn of experience and introspection—resonating with the momentum of the decisions we make today: decisions of certainty, decisions of action, decisions of progression, decisions of change.

QUASI-CHAOTIC TIPS

GENERAL

▲ Change is good:

You will find that living a Quasi-Chaotic Lifestyle will be noticeable to those around you, and you will inevitably be confronted with a "why" anytime you enact change that goes against the status quo (whether it be the frequency, significance, or level of unconventional change). Responding to that "why" is certainly a conversation worth having. However, you may eventually find it exhausting. Respond succinctly with "Change is good," a phrase that will grow on you and on those asking. You may find yourself contemplating an opportunity and, similarly, tell yourself, "Change is good." Better yet, say it out loud! It's a habit that will always reassure that you are doing what's best, for you!

▲ Premature confession:

Being wary of long-term commitments and always prioritizing for change is likely to scare off potential employers, partners, or anyone seeking certitude of continuity. The novelty of the Quasi-Chaotic Lifestyle and its nuances can be easily misunderstood and misconstrued, especially to those living by the (Traditional Psyche) book—to the detriment of both. Many may assume you to be disloyal or unreliable and grow skeptical or cynical as you try to explain yourself, unaware of your intentions and the level of commitment Angular Momentum and Accountability have to offer. It is for this very reason that we must navigate conversations carefully and avoid haphazardly blurting out our iterative nature. Do so gradually, if necessary, as the relationship matures.

▲ Cruise control:

While suboptimal, one does not necessarily need to maintain an SOI or a Kanban board to fulfill a life of change. Once you get the hang of it and become Change Adapted, the automaticity of Scoping, Sprint Planning, Review, and Retrospectives are possible without them. As long as sufficient thought and time go into reflection and RSC considerations, you will still be able to reap the benefits of a Quasi-Chaotic Lifestyle! However, if you happen to find yourself facing a difficult phase (as one would expect of life and its curve balls), resort to the fundamentals. If you feel like you are beginning to lose control, unpack those sticky notes and markers or reset your digital Kanban account password and get back into the swing of things!

▲ Lose to gain:

The Stoics encourage us to occasionally rehearse worst-case scenarios. In *A Guide to the Good Life: The Ancient Art of Stoic Joy*, Professor William Irvine details how Stoics use negative visualizations to embrace whatever life we happen to have and to extract every bit of delight we can from it. So, periodically, rid yourself of all twenty-first-century luxuries. Get in some dirty rags, sleep on a sidewalk, only eat stale bread, and drink from a dog's bowl. Get ready to revisit your luxuries through a polished and refreshed lens!

▲ Experiences bundled and ready to go:

There are a plethora of online platforms that offer packaged experiences with tour guides and/or groups such as Groupon, Airbnb Experiences, and Kibii. It's the perfect start for Quasi-Chaotic beginners and for those that have yet to find like-minded proponents to experience change with!

▲ Incremental chaos:

Depending on your openness, extraversion, and orderliness scores, I suggest you start with smaller changes that don't involve people (so, practices and places) before you take on a substantial cut or dive headfirst into a chaotic bulk. You will find it surprising how much confidence you can build with a bit of unconventional exercise and a new look! Condition yourself with small changes before making big ones. In time, you will develop the capacity to act on truly life-altering decisions.

▲ Pre-cut prep:

If your agreeableness score is relatively low, I strongly suggest you confront the people you plan to cut with sufficient preparation. Whether it's I-statements or memorizing or simply reading a script you've prepared, it's important to meet confrontation with preparation and compassion. If possible, avoid burning bridges. Remember, it's best if the narrative highlights positive outcomes for you *and* those in question.

▲ Quasi-Chaotic relationships:

"Are you suggesting long-term relationships don't work with a Quasi-Chaotic Lifestyle?" you may be asking. No, they very much do, but long-term stagnant relationships do not, at least for most. Individuals in a relationship who insist on a particular routine, looking the same way, cooking the same food, making the same jokes, and maintaining whatever their déjà-vu-days involve are much more likely to face challenges with the relationship over time. Change helps maintain a fresh and healthy relationship— iterating through methods of conflict resolution, learning and reflecting about one another at an accelerated pace, and ultimately figuring out what works best for each, all while continuously adapting the relationship to suit two everchanging individuals!

▲ Time-boxed chaos:

If your orderliness score is relatively high and you're the type of person who requires routine to operate, consider allocating an hour or two a day to chaos. Use the time to explore new people, places, and practices and consider injecting what worked best into your routine!

▲ Picture perfect:

Adapting to varying people and places, whether its formalities, cultures, or general contextual preferences, primes us for opportunity and its capitalization. A Quasi-Chaotic Lifestyle will consistently have you present yourself differently, whether by your mannerisms, attire, vocabulary, or etiquette, to help identify what works best for you and in certain situations. Take pictures or videos of your setups that you find to be effective and resort back to them when the time calls for it. Not only will it visually represent and reassure you of the distance you're traversing, but it will also reinforce your adaptive mastery!

CURIOSITY

▲ Understanding ourselves:

The personality test suggested in Chapter 5: The Malleable Psyche (see page 59) allows you to connect your results with another's for a relationship report that is made specifically for couples. You will gain access to each other's individual results with a description of what you can both expect from being in a romantic relationship. Take note of extremities, set measures in place, and support each other toward Self-Actualizing ideals!

▲ You, me, what's the difference?:

Social media platforms are a blessing and a curse. Use them strategically to your advantage! Anonymously ask the questions that keep you up at night and ponder what everyone has to say. You'll be amazed to find that most of your questions are already posted or addressed, whether in the form of an article, a book, a post, or a video. Consider also who and where you are asking. Recall considerations that make for an Informed Perspective and choose the platform with an archetype community that is (or were) most similar to you, whether it be age, affiliations, or interests.

▲ Why, but why?:

Revitalize your youthful studiousness. Question everything! Why can't my point be understood? Why did she react the way she did? Why does this matter infuriate me so much? Why does garlic bloat my face? Why do I default to guilt? Why are avocados so bloody expensive? Pursue a seemingly trivial question and commit to finding the answer. Bonus: attempt to find an answer by seeking and asking professionals—real people! (whose contact details can be a resource for future inquiry)—as opposed to looking it up online. It makes for amusing conversations, sets us off on novel paths, and introduces us to new people, places, and practices!

▲ Hidden motives:

Be wary of misinformation! Some questions to ask yourself when consuming information online: Does the headline sound neutral or like clickbait? Does the headline invoke strong emotions like anger, laughter, or sadness? Is there a false connection between the headlines, visuals, or captions and the content? If yes to any, that's a red flag. So read past the headlines. Do a quick search on the author (assuming the author is even mentioned). Are they credible? Are they real? Is their portfolio a parody or designed to invoke outrage or have an obvious agenda with a one-sided theme or narrative? Check the sources behind "studies have shown." What studies? If sources are provided, check on whether their quotes are taken out of context or whether the sources are credible and verifiable. Check the date of publication. Is the content being recycled? Is it old news? Run a search on the topic and look for other publications, other contradictory sentiments. Whatever you do, don't base big decisions on misinformation. Do your homework or face the consequences!

▲ I don't know:

We have been conditioned to feel like gaps in knowledge should be filled at all costs. We are fearful of being anything other than a know-it-all. How many times have you confidently stated an opinion and started believing it as fact because of its repetition? There is nothing wrong with demonstrating conviction in sharing what you think; just remember to acknowledge it for what it is—an opinion. The next time your instinct compels you to blurt the first "opinion" that comes to mind, pause and consider starting with, "I don't know . . . but" or "I'm not entirely sure, but I think . . ." or ending with, "That's what I believe, anyway."

OSMOSIS

▲ Just ask:

A study found that underestimating someone's willingness to comply with a direct request for help can sabotage the likelihood that they actually will by as much as 50% (Flynn and Lake, 2008)! Successful people (in their respective domains) are generally authentically proud of what they've accomplished and are eager to pass their learnings on to others. You need only to ask.

▲ I'll scratch your back if you scratch mine:

Developing relationships is always, initially, a matter of giving and taking. You may want another to share their ways and their insights or support your learning journey, but don't expect everyone to open up if you don't have anything to offer in return. In order to gain, you must give (lose), whether it's praise, good conversation, a laugh, a favor, or perhaps supporting them with their own learning journeys!

▲ Together we are better:

Diversify your circle as much as possible: different cultures, different beliefs, different specializations, different industries, different lifestyles. Cultivate a team of experts in their respective fields to consult when you need it. Surround yourself with expert advice derived of experience. Not only will this assist in procuring Informed Perspectives when required but an entrance to novel people, places, and practices will become that much more accessible and often increasingly serendipitous. Fewer barriers to entry and a guided introduction make Quasi-Chaotic living and change all the more accessible!

▲ Closer, no, closer:

Picking up new habits and desired traits is only possible if we regularly and closely expose ourselves to people who harbor said qualities. We accomplish this by sharing an interest such as a mutual friend, place, or practice. Organize weekly catch-ups, morning runs, or outings you would both enjoy!

▲ Hot potato:

Much of our adult lives are spent in working environments. Another common but deceiving goal we often hear is "work-life balance," a juxtaposition insinuating a "healthy" lifestyle, one that offhandedly assumes work to be daunting, restrictive, stressful, and compromising—and needing to be balanced. We thus strive for higher ground, for Hobbies that need not accompany the monotony and suffering we deride. A career in academia will surround you with the curious. An entrepreneurial career will surround you with the ambitious and extroverted. Does your present job involve a toxic working environment? Do your colleagues blame, procrastinate, talk over each other, patronize enthusiasm over mastery? Keep your resume up to date and keep that potato scorching hot!

ACCOUNTABILITY

▲ Production through obstruction:

Obstruct your areas of frequent use with reminders, illustrations, and notes that present the change or endeavor you seek to fulfill. Sticky notes on the fridge, a large whiteboard leaned up against your wardrobe, or strings tied around your fingers that you will only remove when you see the task through!

▲ Piggy bank:

Try maintaining a piggy bank whereby every time you fail to deliver, such as binge-eating, skipping the gym, or cussing, you deposit ten dollars that you will eventually donate to your preferred effective charity. That extra money can make the difference, and someone is always winning!

▲ No, please, I insist:

When leveraging the utility of Group Accountability, try taking the responsibility of a role. Volunteer to prepare the slides of your orator's club, be responsible to grocery shop for that cooking class, assist your yoga teacher by unloading their car of the mats. Create situations where if you aren't there, you'll let everyone down. That'll get you out of bed and earn you merit to capitalize on!

▲ Ooh, shiny!:

Tempt yourself with the prospect of an exciting novel experience that may come at a higher cost: tickets to an opera, a theme park, or a hot-air balloon ride! Wrap the money in birthday gift paper and hand it to your accountability partner with the condition they never hand it back unless you action a challenge that's been causing you grief!

▲ Lay it out:

Are you procrastinating? Easily distracted? Don't mind the task but for some reason it's taking you forever to get started? Do yourself a favor and make the task accessible! Plan on running? Set your sneakers, shorts, and crop top where you can see them! Need to finish that essay? Keep the document open on your tablet, and place it where it's visible! Need to sort out dinner at some point? Lay the ingredients on your kitchen countertop! You'll have to try it to believe it, but that extra little "umph" will make a world of difference.

MOMENTUM

▲ Midnight craze:

Ask yourself this simple question every night before you go to bed: "What did I do differently today?" The peace of mind that comes with a satisfactory answer makes for a restful slumber. Anticipation of the question makes for spontaneity and serendipitous impetus!

▲ Proliferation of incrementation:

A good habit to pick up is harboring a multitude of practices to develop. On some days you may be in the mood for one instead of another, so it's good to have options. Cycle through your daily selection of hobbies, and you'll never have to force your way through what you know you'd enjoy on some other day!

▲ Igniting a spark:

We sometimes find ourselves in couch-potato mode: drowsy, indifferent, and apathetic. A great way to build back the momentum for change is setting aside what you are telling yourself must be done and take on smaller, achievable, entertaining-yet productive tasks such as playing hide-and-seek with your labradoodle or a brisk walk while listening to a comedic podcast. Kindle the flame and work your way back up to the bigger, more challenging tasks!

▲ Physical over mental:

It's much easier to pick momentum back up through simple physical labor such as cleaning or tidying up the house. If you really can't be bothered acting on anything living in your Sprint, pick up a squeegee and a spray cleaner and get to work. Wipe down those dusty parts of your desk. Put that scrub brush to work and sort the corners of the bathtub you've been cringing at for weeks. It's a sure way to kick-start the engine!

▲ Static progression:

Are there times when you literally have nothing better to do? Are you forced to wait with no one in sight, no reception at hand? Is your Uber Eats order taking forever to arrive? Practice meditation! It is one of the most underutilized, liberating, and practical skills you can develop. You'll never feel unproductive again. The bonus? Mastery of the illusory self!

AMBITION

▲ Contemplative convergence:

We are pattern-seeking animals; it's a cognitive tool that synergizes with Contemplative Ambition to help us identify triggers, connect the dots, and discover Detractors to address. The more we populate our Kanban board, the more data we have to work with. If we come to realize that a particular person, place, or practice is increasingly hindering the movement of cards, it may be time to resort to an RSC. If you're uncertain, use connectors, indicators, or labels to highlight the breadth of correlation.

▲ Good enough? Not on my watch:

Leave a trail of quality behind. Governing Ambition compels us to strive for the ideal. We don't make such an effort for others but for ourselves. Don't settle for good enough. Hold yourself to a higher standard, and the floor of standards of people, places, and practices you will encounter will naturally rise.

▲ Personal best:

How fast are you able to walk a mile, make breakfast, or carry out your morning routine? How fast can you type one hundred words, wash the dishes, tidy your room, burn five hundred calories? Time yourself! It won't take five seconds to pull out your phone, check the starting time, or launch your chronograph. Document your records and strive to beat them! It's fun, it's productive, and besting your past self is as contagious and stimulating as besting others!

▲ Snowballing scope:

A bigger bulk assumes bigger risk. Should life throw a curveball your way, the entirety of your committed scope is at risk. Whether it's stamina, emotional well-being, or other resources you already have tied up, risk may suddenly compromise it all. And when/if it does, it will very much feel like Armageddon, everything going wrong all at once. Pace yourself and remain conscious of the fact that the more you take on, the bigger your attack surface (including all those who may be dependent on you). Recall the Quasi-Chaotic View and strive for simplicity!

▲ Invest in yourself:

Air Jordans are nice, but consider instead investing those thousands of dollars sitting in opaque boxes on the top of your wardrobe in coaches, in yourself, whether it's for music classes, personal finance 101, speech therapy, or working on your public speaking skills. A coach can teach, demonstrate, analyze, encourage, motivate, and instill lifelong skills to proliferate opportunity. It is the biggest Self-Actualizing bang for your buck!

FAILURE

▲ Hard reset:

Some failures may be a little harder to stomach, like flunking a test, repeatedly missing a beat, pencilling in the wrong date of an interview, or binge-eating too many tacos. You may feel inclined to procrastinate or be even harder on yourself in outrage, or perhaps marinate in melancholy and contemplation. Instead, consider dropping what you're doing and choose the next act of change on your list, whether it's visiting an arcade you've never been to or learning to perfect a soufflé! Work those control rods, maintain Momentum, and avoid that thermonuclear meltdown!

▲ Fail-o-meter:

Use a gauge to measure how much you enjoyed failing with any given person, place, or practice. Whether it be stickers to slap onto your sticky notes or a number you prefix your digital cards with, estimate and track your affinities. If that person, place, or practice remained enjoyable throughout failure, imagine how Self-Actualizing it may be with success!

▲ You're messing with my vibe, man:

Consider this: Would you rather pick up a practice with someone who never fails to be overly dramatic about their performance or accompany a bubbly go-getter with a positive attitude and a great sense of humor? Making our way to automaticity of a practice is best pursued with another *übermensch*!

▲ Permission to feel:

A study showed that people who bottled up their emotions increased their chance of premature death from all causes by more than 30%, with their risk of being diagnosed with cancer increasing by 70% (Chapman et al., 2013)! The authors commendably identify the caveat of a potential lack of "confounder control" (a bias-prevention measure) when analyzing the data, so take it with a grain of salt. But it would hardly be shocking to learn that suppressing emotions is harmful. Building resilience to failure takes time, so give yourself time to experience it. Throw your fist out and do your happy skip. Grab that box of tissues and cry your heart out. Let out that "aww" and squirm in place. Give your pal a high five as that chicken parm and fries arrive. Yank that pillow and kick it to the next dimension!

▲ Avoiding absolutes:

Instead of "I'm going to learn to play the sax," consider "I'm going to try and learn to play the sax." In this example, the goal is not to master the saxophone but the very fact that you are attempting the novel. Language is important because you are setting an expectation for yourself and those around you, so make it more about experimentation than obligation!

PRIDE

▲ Humility over hubris:

Did you manage to make a complete fool of yourself? Were you bluntly and publicly rejected as a flirt? Did your joke fall flat? Did you keep tripping on your toe picks while trying to pick up ice skating? What will make matters worse is a whimper or conceding into silence. Take pride in your failure! Brush it off, laugh it off, express how awkward you've made the situation with self-deprecating humor. You will never face an awkward moment again! Easier said than done, but practice makes perfect!

▲ Ownership over excuse:

No one likes excuses, no matter how justified or contextually rational it may be. Tell it how it is, own up to it, but explain how you will seek to improve and then fulfill that mission! Pride is only as good as the power backing it up. Making an excuse makes it easier to make even more. Consider permanently avoiding excuses; it will build your self-confidence and exhibit qualities deeply tied to what it means to be authentically proud!

▲ T-shirts and prophecies:

Print T-shirts with a prophecy you may unfortunately fulfill: "44-year-old trying very hard not to break neck" and wear it proud while learning how to parkour! How about "I'll explain the joke if I have to, but don't make me" or "Breaking records: this year, rejections!" Blunt the pain, fulfill the prophecy, and keep practicing!

▲ Wall of triumph:

Frame your RSCs and hang them on your walls in a space that is visible to you on a daily basis. This helps ward off postdecisional dissonance and alleviates spontaneous angst. Make it a wall of triumph, a gallery of growth, a reminder to hold your head high!

▲ Stooping is self-abusing:

When publicly confronted with insult, patronization, condescension, bigotry, unreasonableness, or immaturity, whether it's your prying neighbors, sneering coworkers, or small-minded in-laws, avoid stooping to their level. You can try diffusing the situation with humor: "Why don't we just thumb wrestle over this—best out of three matches wins?" Or silently confront them by maintaining eye contact and keeping calm with maybe a smile, showing your tormenter that you know what they're doing, which often makes them feel uncomfortable and stop. Alternatively, try stating the obvious with "You're yelling at me" or "You're abusing me" or ask them to repeat themselves with "Excuse me. What did you just call me?" Forcing them to own up to what they said will embarrass almost everyone in the room, compelling them to diffuse the situation for you. And worst-case scenario, you can simply exit the conversation, the room, or the place with a calm smile, bidding everyone a warm farewell, because you know better than to stoop!

QUASI-CHAOTIC TOOL KIT CHEAT SHEET

FALLIBILITY CURIOSITY

AM I UNDER A MISAPPREHENSION?

AM I THE PROBLEM?

HOW DO I VALIDATE A BELIEF OF A POTENTIALLY SELF-ACTUALIZING DIRECTIVE?

DEVELOPMENTAL CURIOSITY

HOW DO I FURTHER MASTERY OF A PRACTICE?

WHY AM I NOT AS ENGAGED & MOTIVATED TO LEARN AS OTHERS?

WHERE IS THIS PROBLEM ARISING FROM?

CURIOSITY
REINING UNCERTAINTY

SERENDIPITOUS CURIOSITY

WHERE TO FROM HERE?

HOW DO I ACQUAINT MYSELF WITH AN UNFAMILIAR SETTING?

HOW DO I DISCOVER A SERENDIPITOUS RABBIT HOLE ENTRANCE?

SELECTIVE OSMOSIS / DIVERGENT OSMOSIS

SELECTIVE OSMOSIS

HOW DO I BREAK BAD HABITS AND BUILD GOOD ONES?

HOW DO I PROLIFERATE SELF-ACTUALIZING OPPORTUNITIES?

HOW CAN I BE MORE LIKE/LESS LIKE THEM?

DIVERGENT OSMOSIS

HOW DO I BROADEN BY PERSPECTIVE?

HOW DO I FIGURE OUT WHAT SELF-ACTUALIZING POTENTIAL I'M MISSING OUT ON?

HOW DO I LEARN TO ADAPT TO DIVERSE SETTINGS AND PEOPLE?

OSMOSIS
PRIMING GROWTH

REFLECTIVE OSMOSIS

HOW DO I CULTIVATE EMPATHY FOR OTHERS?

HOW DO I IMPROVE MY CONFLICT RESOLUTION SKILLS?

HOW CAN I LEARN TO BE MORE PERSONABLE & AGREEABLE?

SELF-ACCOUNTABILITY / GROUP ACCOUNTABILITY

SELF-ACCOUNTABILITY

HOW DO I LEARN TO STOP RELYING ON OTHERS?

HOW DO I TRAIN MYSELF TO BE DISCIPLINED?

HOW DO I BUILD SELF-CONFIDENCE WITH WHAT I SET OUT TO DO?

GROUP ACCOUNTABILITY

HOW DO I SPUR MOTIVATION OF COMMITMENT PASSIVELY?

HOW DO I PERSEVERE THROUGH ONGOING/REGULAR CHALLENGE?

HOW DO I FOSTER A SENSE OF LASTING CAMARADERIE?

ACCOUNTABILITY
DEVELOPING SELF-ASSURANCE

PARTNERED ACCOUNTABILITY

HOW DO I DEMONSTRATE MY CONVICTION FOR OTHERS TO TRUST?

HOW DO I MOTIVATE MYSELF TO TRIUMPH OVER AN INTIMIDATING CHALLENGE?

WHAT DO I DO IF I'M FACED WITH A TASK LACKING INCENTIVE?

ANGULAR MOMENTUM

HOW DO I MAINTAIN PACE OF PROGRESS WITHOUT BURNING MYSELF OUT?

HOW DO I EXPERIENCE A PERSON, PLACE, OR PRACTICE TO THEIR/ITS FULLEST POTENTIAL

HOW DO I ALLEVIATE DRUDGERY OF A NECESSARY TASK?

VERTICAL MOMENTUM

HOW DO I CONSISTENTLY PUSH THE LIMITS OF MY POTENTIAL?

HOW DO I WORK MY WAY UP TO MORE CHALLENGING ENDEAVORS?

HOW DO I ENSURE CAPACITY FOR CHANGE?

MOMENTUM
AVERTING STAGNATION

SPONTANEOUS MOMENTUM

HOW DO I EXERCISE CHANGE ON A WHIM?

WHAT DO I DO IF ALL APPARENT OPPORTUNITIES FOR CHANGE SEEM MONOTONOUSLY PREDICTABLE?

HOW DO I CONTINUOUSLY CREATE LONG-LASTING MEMORABLE EXPERIENCES?

COMPETITIVE AMBITION

WHERE DO I FIND FIERCE MOTIVATION TO EXCEL?

HOW DO I ACCELERATE DEVELOPMENT OF A PRACTICE?

HOW CAN I TURN MUNDANE TASKS INTO EXCITING ONES?

GOVERNING AMBITION

HOW DO I ENSURE I AM PROGRESSING WITH TIME?

HOW DO I CONSISTENCY APPROACH SELF-ACTUALIZATION?

HOW DO I EXPERIENCE THE BEST OF EXPERIENCE?

AMBITION
INFLAMING IMPETUS

CONTEMPLATIVE AMBITION

WHO/WHAT IS HOLDING ME BACK?

HOW DO I UNLEASH MY FULL POTENTIAL?

HOW DO I STOP PLAYING THE VICTIM AND REGAIN CONTROL?

ITERATIVE FAILURE

HOW DO I KNOW WHEN I'VE FOUND A PRACTICE I CAN EXCEL AT?

HOW DO I REGULATE EMOTIONAL REACTIONS TO MISTAKES AND ACCIDENTS?

HOW DO I DEAL WITH GUILT IF I GIVE UP ON COMMITMENT?

REINFORCING FAILURE

HOW DO I BUILD THICKER SKIN?

HOW DO I STOP RUMINATING OVER DEFEAT?

HOW DO I LEARN HOW TO MOVE ON?

FAILURE
CATALYZING SUCCESS

OPPORTUNISTIC FAILURE

HOW DO I MAKE THE MOST OF A BAD SITUATION?

HOW DO I FIND A MOTIF TO APPROACH NEW PEOPLE WITH?

HOW DO I EXPEDITE DEVELOPMENTAL GROWTH?

LOSSLESS PRIDE

HOW DO I EXERCISE THE UNCONVENTIONAL WITHOUT THE ANGST?

HOW DO I BUILD THE COURAGE TO FAIL PUBLICLY?

HOW DO I TURN WHAT WOULD OTHERWISE BE AN EMBARRASSING INCIDENT INTO A REWARDING ONE?

ATTRACTIVE PRIDE

HOW DO I DEVELOP AN ALLURING PRESENCE TO ATTRACT OPPORTUNITY?

HOW DO I GARNER ESTEEM TO BENEFIT FROM EMOTIONALLY?

HOW DO I THWART SUSPICION AND WARINESS OF UNCONVENTIONAL CONDUCT?

PRIDE
REINFORCING DIGNITY

REFLECTIVE PRIDE

HOW DO I PREVENT THE URGE OF COMPARING MY PROGRESS TO PROGRESS OF OTHERS?

HOW DO I LEARN TO EXERCISE SELF-COMPASSION & ACCEPTANCE?

HOW DO I RESIST THE CONSEQUENCES OF HEDONIC ADAPTATION?

EFFECTIVE ALTRUISM AND THE PLEDGE

Although humans are only one chromosome away from the chimpanzee, our morality sets us apart from the rest of the animal kingdom. This is a set of psychological adaptations that allow otherwise selfish individuals to reap the benefits of cooperation, law and order, cultures, traditions, economies, healthcare, art, and all that you know to be good. It is, in short, what makes us human, and much like our desires and temporary selves, morality can become outdated as it, too, constantly changes.

In this book, we've addressed countless moral and ethical considerations and implications, some of which you may have resisted and others you may have outright rejected—even when presented with empirical evidence. Whether morality is subjective or objective—and the possibility for moral *convergence* (a set of morals we can universally agree to)—has been debated for centuries. And despite the necessity of such a convergence for unparalleled human flourishing, it is a consensus we may never realize. In his book *The Moral Landscape*, Sam Harris contends that the only viable moral framework is one where "morally good" things lead to increases in the "well-being of conscious creatures." If you can, at the very least, agree with this, read on.

The force of a Quasi-Chaotic Lifestyle is, as you now know, constrained to our respective iron triangles. These triangles dictate the extent to which we are able to make the most out of a life of change, which depends on the sheer quantity of opportunities we expose ourselves to and our ability to capitalize on them through merit (the quality of being worthy to warrant praise, reward, or an opportunity). We've also assumed that you had *enough* time and resources to have had a fair go at change.

However, there are those who aren't as lucky to be born with:

▲ Time:

From dying young from pregnancy complications, maternal death, neonatal mortality, malaria, parasitic worms, HIV/AIDS, stroke, tuberculosis, etc. Or needing to care for someone suffering from or the loss of someone from the aforementioned. Or being time-poor for having to tend with illness, personal trauma, or family obligations.

▲ Resources:

Not having access to education or other opportunities to learn, grow, and contribute or being impeded by cognitive impairment from birth defects or a childhood of poor nutrition or having been deprived of clean water, sanitation, technology, shelter, teachers, libraries, medicine, or anything that limits one's scope of potential.

▲ Scope:

For the lack of available opportunities within their reach, which for many is close to none.

You could be innately predisposed to being an industrious, agreeable, conscientious, intelligent, creative, and altruistic change champion; contrastingly, you may harbor qualities of the complete opposite but still intend to earnestly exercise positive change. You could be the most deserving of opportunity but denied the chance to grow, thrive, work, contribute, or even survive because of sheer bad luck.

It is this that gives rise to the myth of the "self-made man," an ethically impregnable position that firmly controls the moral principles governing our behavior, attitudes, and decisions. You may like to think that because you weren't born into wealth, you don't owe anyone anything. You may be of the mindset that you'd rather teach others how to fish rather than give them fish. But we refer back to the argument against free will: Did you choose your genome, your family, your privileges, the country, the economy, or the general state of affairs you were born into?

An analogy from the ethical and political philosopher Peter Singer illustrates how we repeatedly fail to live up to our own ideals and principles. Singer asks us to contemplate the following: On the way to work, you pass a small, shallow pond. You find a toddler flailing about and likely soon to drown. You look around but can't find the parents or babysitter or anyone. If you don't wade in, which would ruin your expensive shoes, the toddler dies. What would you do?

You would see it as a moral obligation and view anyone who valued their shoes over a child's life as a moral monster, and yet if you knew you could save a life for a few hundred dollars by donating to a charity that provided mosquito nets in developing countries—and saw a picture of the life you might be saving—you may shrug and say you get approached for such things all the time. As Harris suggests, if it was ever morally defensible to consider people at a distance from us both in space and time as mattering less than those in proximity, it's becoming even less defensible because that distance is shrinking. Through the marvel of technological interconnectedness, the shallow ponds are all in view.

Imagine saving a life by resuscitating someone from certain death. Think of how life-changing and life-defining that moment would be. Imagine if each month you saved a child from drowning or from getting hit by a drunk driver or dying in a burning building, you would live with the conscience of a saint and be a model hero. All of this is possible just by targeting the most effective charities.

Unfortunately, we are easily distracted by dramatic stories and emotions and are unaware of the many others in need who are not brought to our attention. We stand with our noses held high and our arms crossed, unimpressed with modest and honest charity initiatives, capitulating to those with the biggest marketing budget. Instead, those in need often have to rely on our sense of guilty pleasure as we donate to the first homeless person we see to feel better about ourselves.

Also hindering our efforts to help and save lives is concern over the time and effort it would take to vet charities and ensure our money is going to efficacious organizations and not being embezzled or wasted by corruption or incompetence. Getting the most leverage for our donation can be another laborious effort of research. Toby Ord, cofounder of Giving What We Can (GWWC) and a senior research fellow at the Future of Humanity Institute at the University of Oxford, explains: "You could spend forty thousand dollars to restore one person's vision or spend the same amount of money on surgeries for the infectious disease that leads to blindness if left untreated . . . and prevent roughly two thousand from going blind."

William MacAskill is an associate professor of philosophy and a research fellow at the Global Priorities Institute, University of Oxford, who cofounded three nonprofits based on effective altruist principles: Giving What We Can, 80,000 Hours, and the Centre for Effective Altruism. He defines *effective altruism* as a philosophical and social movement that advocates using evidence and reason to figure out how to maximize benefits to others and then taking action on that basis. Most people assume that the best charities are only one and a half to two times more impactful than a typical one. In reality, the differences are much bigger: the best are tens, hundreds, or even thousands of times more impactful. Worse yet, some charities actually do harm. MacAskill asks us to imagine the case of a consumer good like beer in which one store charges one hundred dollars and another ten cents, translating to a 99.9% discount for doing good!

It is also worth noting that improving and saving lives doesn't just avert the direct suffering associated with sickness and death but raises the floor of civilizations, enabling people to participate more fully in education and work; promoting equality, female empowerment, and family planning; improving resource allocation and reducing resource depletion; bolstering economic opportunity; assisting governments in the design and implementation of effective policies; and much, much more.

To be part of this movement of positive change, you don't have to do all the research, vet the charities, or contemplate where your money ought to go. Bed nets, for example, aren't the sexièst story, but dollar for dollar it's the cheapest way to save a life. You don't need to rely on a charity's ability to portray a cause in the most emotionally moving way or pull on your moral intuitions or expose yourself to an endless heartache of tragic stories to feel motivated enough to donate. You can automate the entire process by making a public pledge and donating a percentage of your personal or company's income to funds with strong track records that are driven by cost-effectiveness, transparency, and empirical evidence. Whether its saving lives, fighting extreme poverty, reducing animal suffering, improving long-term futures, or supporting high-impact careers, GWWC and other not-for-profit organizations will do all the work for you.

In addition, many religions have altruistic foundations such as the practice of tithing (giving 10% of one's income) in Christianity and Judaism, Zakat (typically giving 2.5% of one's wealth) in Islam, and Dāna (the general concept of generosity and charity) in Buddhism, Hinduism, and Sikhism. It is therefore not unearthly to suggest the institutionalizing or widespread adoption of moral obligation or, as MacAskill sees it, opportunity. Making such pledges can serve as a form of *Governing-Ambition* and *Self-Accountability* with psychological benefits—better than anything else you can spend money on. There is also empirical evidence that people who spend more money on others report greater happiness and well-being. Considering all of the aforementioned and the fact that wealth and happiness do not have a linear relationship and ever-increasing amounts of wealth have diminishing returns, one can only conclude that a truly moral species acknowledges and acts on these truths through effective giving that helps themselves, their future selves, and the future of others.

In this spirit, Necessitating Change has pledged to donate 20% of its gross profits to the most effective charities. I encourage individuals, communities, and companies to join me in whatever capacity their respective iron triangles can afford.

To learn more about effective altruism, the Giving What We Can pledge, myths about charity, causes to donate to, evidence of any claims made in this section, and more, please visit **www.givingwhatwecan.org**.

GLOSSARY
AND ESSENTIALS

10,000-hour rule:

Popularized by Malcolm Gladwell, it is a rule of thumb suggesting it takes 10,000 hours of intensive practice to achieve mastery of complex skills. Its acknowledgment corrects the confusion one often makes associating thousands of hours of practice with "innate talent," thus discouraging commitment of experience.

absurd hero:

An individual who acknowledges the truth of absurdism and embraces the struggle and freedom of living without purpose.

absurdism:

A belief system positing that inherent value and meaning in life are contradictory to the meaninglessness of the universe.

acceptance criteria:

A set of predefined requirements and test scenarios of a Kanban card that must be met to consider it complete.

Accountability:

A Quasi-Chaotic tool used to minimize surrender and promote perseverance through challenge or what may be a strenuous first few weeks of taking on a new person, place, or practice. Its constituent subtools include Self-Accountability, Group Accountability, and Partnered Accountability.

accountability partner:

An individual (whom one would not want to disappoint) assigned to hold oneself accountable for a commitment made. The accountability partner regularly checks on progress and asks for explanation should one fail to deliver.

Agile philosophy:

An overarching philosophy for software development, the Agile philosophy is a development approach that prioritizes building and testing over planning and maintenance. It emphasizes early, regular, and incremental delivery of value-oriented and working products to end users who are involved throughout development. Agile practices involve solution improvement and flexibility as well as adaptive planning through the collaborative efforts of self-organizing and cross-functional teams. Its values underpin a number of software development frameworks including Kanban and Scrum.

Ambition:

A Quasi-Chaotic tool that cultivates growing efforts and standards to approach Self-Actualization, offering guidance, purpose, and a constant flow of novel challenging experiences to propel one forward. Its constituent subtools include Competitive Ambition, Governing Ambition, and Contemplative Ambition.

amygdala hijack:

An emotional (fight, flight, fawn, or freeze) response that is immediate and overwhelming, triggered by perceived threat.

anagnorisis:

The moment in one's journey—often following Suffering—where one discovers the true nature of their own circumstances.

anchoring bias:

When a judgment or a decision is affected by the first piece of information (the anchor) regarding a given topic or issue.

Angular Momentum:

A Quasi-Chaotic subtool that is used to iterate the means by which a person, place, or practice is interacted with for the sake of exploration, mastery, or leveraging the fuel of change to persevere.

Archive lane:

A Kanban lane that is used as a repository of completed selections of cards from past Sprints for future reference.

Attractive Pride:

A Quasi-Chaotic subtool that is used to refine behavior, posture, and presentation to exhibit attractive authentic pride in order to maximize chances of capitalizing on opportunities.

authentic pride:

Also referred to as "genuine pride," a socially desirable expression of satisfaction derived from one's own efforts of earned achievements, associated with accomplishment and confidence.

automaticity:

The ability to perform a task involuntarily or unconsciously as an innate process, reflex, or habit.

availability bias:

When the frequency and availability of information (whether true or not) is given precedence when making decisions or are seen to be more representative than is actually the case.

Backlog lane:

A Kanban lane that contains an accumulation of cards that require completion for a given project. Cards in the Backlog lane can include "Must Haves," "Could Haves," "Should Haves," ideas to explore, issues to address, and everything in between.

Backlog Refinement:

Also referred to as "Backlog Grooming," it is a practice that involves breaking down backlog items into manageable "chunks," reviewing and clarifying their details, and (re-)prioritizing them.

Big Five personality traits:

A taxonomy of personality traits that consists of Openness to Experience (inventive/curious versus consistent/cautious), Conscientiousness (efficient/organized versus extravagant/careless), Extraversion (outgoing/energetic versus solitary/reserved), Agreeableness (friendly/compassionate versus critical/rational), and Neuroticism (sensitive/nervous versus resilient/confident).

Bulking:

The process of "taking on more" by exposing, introducing, and immersing oneself in novel people, places and practices that influence one's daily welfare—to grow one's SOI.

Change Adaptation/Adapted:

A long-term cognitive transformation of how change is perceived—in which one learns to draw meaning, fulfillment, and pleasure from the act of change itself and not its outcomes. It is identified with automaticity of change.

change capability/capable:

Anything an entity does well that drives meaningful results.

Change Receptive:

The willingness to adapt to altered circumstances. When "forces for change" outweigh "forces against change."

change readiness/ready:

The cognitive precursor to the behaviors of either resistance to, or support for, change effort.

change resistance/resistant:

The refusal or unwillingness to adapt to altered circumstances. When "forces against change" outweigh "forces for change."

cognitive adjustment:

A coping mechanism to reduce or resolve cognitive dissonance. These mental-acrobatics include simple denial, comparing, minimizing, rationalizing, scapegoating, justifying, and grandiosity.

cognitive dissonance:

The mental discomfort resulting of two conflicting beliefs, values, or attitudes.

compatibilism:

The belief that free will and determinism are compatible without being logically inconsistent. Although an individual is free to act on a motive, the nature of that motive is predetermined.

Competitive Ambition:

A Quasi-Chaotic subtool that leverages the excitement and motivations of competition and comradery to generate a will to persevere through what would otherwise be tedious or repetitive but important or necessary challenge.

complex adaptive system:

A system involving a dynamic network of interactions by self-organizing, heterogenous agents, each behaving unpredictably.

Contemplative Ambition:

A Quasi-Chaotic subtool used to reveal Detractors and instill a sensitivity toward people, places, or practices that restrict or prevent change.

Curiosity:

A Quasi-Chaotic tool used to direct one toward individualistic, idiosyncratic, and potentially Self-Actualizing people, places, and practices. Its constituent subtools include Fallibility Curiosity, Serendipitous Curiosity, and Developmental Curiosity.

Cutting:

The process of shedding negative influences (of one's SOI) through constructive and conflict-averse means. Cutting may be challenging or consequential in which the Quasi-Chaotic Decision-Making Model and Quasi-Chaotic tools can be employed to ease what is nonnegotiable.

das Gerede:

German for "the Chatter" and what philosopher Martin Heidegger uses to describe the sum of all trivial matters that distract one from the fact that death and *das Nichts* are inevitable and omnipresent.

das Nichts:

German for "the Nothing" and what philosopher Martin Heidegger uses to refer to the absence of being or oblivion.

determinism:

The philosophical view that all events are determined by previously existing causes. Some philosophers take its implications to argue for the absence of free will.

Detractor:

An individual that negatively questions, restricts, or prevents change.

Developmental Curiosity:

A Quasi-Chaotic subtool used to identify people, places, and practices that spark studiousness and a willingness to learn more—identified to be Self-Actualizing potentialities.

Divergent Osmosis:

A Quasi-Chaotic subtool used to diversify who and what one regularly exposes oneself to, to absorb favorable unique qualities that promote Self-Actualization.

Doing lane:

A Kanban lane containing cards (ideally only one card per Kanban board user at a time) drawn from the To-Do lane that are in the process of being actioned.

Done lane:

A Kanban lane that contains completed Sprint cards.

DSM-5:

Diagnostic and Statistical Manual of Mental Disorders (Fifth Edition). The standard classification of mental disorders used by mental health professionals.

Dunning-Kruger effect:

The cognitive bias whereby people with limited competence in a field overestimate their own competence. The effect also refers to the tendency of those exceptionally competent to underestimate their own competence.

emergence:

When interactions between multiple heterogenous agents in a complex adaptive system result in spontaneous behaviors (opportunities) that would not have been apparent or predictable.

Epicurean community:

A group of people who come together to share the principles of "Epicureanism" and to support each other in living a life that is focused on simple pleasures, friendship, and the pursuit of knowledge.

essentialism:

The belief that all things harbor immutable qualities—qualities that an outside agent cannot will to be different—that makes them what they are.

existentialism:

A philosophical theory which holds that individuals are free agents responsible for determining their own development through their own will.

expectation gap:

The difference between one's expectations of reality and one's experiences of reality—an evaluation that correlates with how happy or unhappy one is.

extinction:

A detrimental effect of stretch goals involving the loss of reinforcement for previously reinforced behavior, which kills motivation.

Failure:

A Quasi-Chaotic tool used to correct one's relationship with failure. Instead of associating negative connotations with failure, as one intuitively perceives it to be a step backward—Failure offers a contrary outlook that asserts the concept to be a core stimulant of growth, a step forward with the right attitude. Its constituent subtools include Iterative Failure, Reinforcing Failure, and Opportunistic Failure.

Fallibility Curiosity:

A Quasi-Chaotic subtool used to arrive at truth. It calls for enduring suspicion and skepticism of all matters trivial and foundational, including our strongest held beliefs, by regularly entertaining the contrary and asking "What if I'm wrong?"

Five Whys:

An iterative interrogative technique of asking and answering the question "Why?" for a given problem five times in an attempt to arrive at the root cause of a particular problem. The Quasi-Chaotic rules of conduct (see page 399) adapt the Five Whys to ensure a course-corrected, self-directed, and blame-free narrative, validating its application in order to produce sufficiently actionable conclusions.

free will:
The idea that individuals have the capacity to make choices that are genuinely their own and free from constraints.

Governing Ambition:
A Quasi-Chaotic subtool used to cultivate a growth mindset that is always centered around progression. Improvements of experience can involve and range from mundane behaviors and mannerisms to people, places, and practices that significantly influence one's welfare.

Group Accountability:
A Quasi-Chaotic subtool used to promote commitment through solidarity in group-based activities.

growth mindset:
The belief that abilities, intelligence, and talents can be developed over time.

Hard Problems:
Refer to costly problems with no clear resolution that necessarily involve negative outcomes regardless of what decision is made.

hedonic treadmill/adaptation:
The tendency of people to return to a stable level of happiness despite significant positive or negative changes in their lives.

Heideggerian journey:
A journey that philosopher Martin Heidegger describes as moving from *Uneigentlichkeit* (or inauthenticity) to *Eigentlichkeit* (or authenticity) remaining aware of our inevitable death and *das Nichts*.

heuristics:
The mental shortcuts derived of evolutionary processes and past experiences that enable one to make judgments and solve problems quickly, efficiently, and in a practical manner that is "good enough."

Hobbies:

An umbrella term that covers practices of work and hobbies as the Quasi-Chaotic Lifestyle does not differentiate between the two; they are one and the same. Work can be seen as a hobby, and a hobby could accompany financial income or eventuate into financial independence.

hubristic pride:

Relates to the expression of egotism and vanity regarding one's achievements, associated with arrogance and conceit.

illusion of self:

Also referred to as the "self-illusion," it refers to the illusion of what one may assume to be a coherent self-identity—which is in fact a figment of one's imagination. Should one cognitively open up to the present moment, one realizes they are nothing more than an observing consciousness and that whatever identity they believe to be true only comes into existence when they think about it and play out that role.

Imagination Gap:

A consequence of hope, it is the obstinate yearning of a goal or vision far too ambitious for one's present capacity. It depicts the hopeless expanse between what is possible and the impossible leading to bereavement, stagnation, and often, an Unreachable Terminal.

Incessant Distraction:

A stagnating state of hypnotic immersion within meaningless routines, expectations, or unproductive/unfulfilling escapes to avoid an underlying pain or truth.

Informed Perspectives:

Individuals who have personal and relevant experience and are willing to provide insight, guidance, and support for one to leverage upon working through a Hard Problem.

Initial Scoping:

An initial general set of guardrails of priorities and outcomes established to ensure they align with defined end user (persona) needs. These are then used to generate cards (that conventionally involve user stories) that populate the Backlog. Within industry practice, this stage is often only exercised once a project commences. Much like its use in software development projects, Initial Scoping is only conducted once, in the beginning, and in the case of a Quasi-Chaotic Lifestyle, once upon commencing its adoption. However, given that the bigger picture (the process of Self-Actualization) is indefinite, cyclical, and consisting of diverse and continuous projects, Initial Scoping is periodically exercised to ensure the Backlog is always updated with tasks that reflect one's everchanging desires and circumstances.

interpersonal gap:

The difference between one's reality and the reality of others—an evaluation that correlates with how happy or unhappy one is.

iron triangle:

Also referred to as the "project triangle" or "triple constraints" of project management, this model depicts how the success of a project is constrained by resources (cost), scope, and time. Changing one constraint without changing others and breaking the iron triangle leads to the quality degradation of scope, underdelivering, delivering late and/or over budget, or cancelling the project all together.

I-statement:

An assertion about one's feelings, beliefs, or values without placing blame on the person in question, coupled with a constructive remedy. It is expressed as a sentence beginning with the word "I" and is contrasted with "You-statements" that begin with "you" and have the following structure: I feel [insert feeling word] when [describe what is causing the feeling]. I would like [what you would prefer to happen instead].

Iterative Failure:

A Quasi-Chaotic subtool used to relieve the discomfort of defeat by encouraging a constructive outlook. It implores the embracement of the fact that mastery; discovering a person, place, or practice one resonates with; and the journey to Self-Actualization itself, necessitate incremental gradations of trial, error, realizations, improvement, and pivots.

Kanban:

A noniterative, "flow-based" management method for a streamlined process of development or production. It aims to maximize efficiency and drive improvement by visualizing workflow using a "board," "lanes" (also referred to as Swim lanes—commonly including Backlog, To-Do, Doing, Done, and Archive lanes), and cards (that encompass chunks of work) amongst other visual cues to improve productivity. The term is also often used in reference to its method of visualization and flow, as its core principles can be used in tandem with other management strategies.

Laplace's demon:

French scholar Pierre-Simon De Laplace's articulation of determinism which suggests that if someone (or a "demon") knew the precise location and momentum of every atom in the universe and had enough computational power, they could calculate the past and future values for any given moment from the laws of classical mechanics.

Less Permitting:

Refers to a person, place, or practice that may harbor favorable potentialities, but is relatively inferior to what other potentially Self-Actualizing people, places, or practices have to offer.

living in bad faith:

The psychological phenomenon whereby individuals act inauthentically by yielding to external pressures of society and adopting false values, surrendering their innate freedom as sentient human beings.

loss aversion:

An intuitive preference of avoiding losses over acquiring equivalent gains.

Lossless Pride:
A Quasi-Chaotic subtool used to void embarrassment, project attractive authentic pride qualities, and promote exposure to opportunities when attempting novel and otherwise potentially-embarrassing experiences publicly.

Manufacturing Success:
The process of developing merit and maximizing realistic and unrealistic occurrences (opportunities) through change to increase the likelihood of Self-Actualizing serendipity.

Maslow's hierarchy of needs:
A motivational theory in psychology proposed by psychologist Abraham Maslow composed of a hierarchical five-tier model of human needs commonly depicted as a pyramid. From the bottom upward, those needs are physiological (food and clothing), safety (job security), love and belonging (friendship), esteem, and self-actualization.

merit:
The quality of being worthy enough to warrant praise, reward, or an opportunity.

Momentum:
A Quasi-Chaotic tool used to prevent stagnation, burnouts, and long-term, uninformed commitments by maintaining momentum of change. Its constituent subtools include Angular Momentum, Vertical Momentum, and Spontaneous Momentum.

MoSCoW (Must Have, Should Have, Could Have, Won't Have):
This is a prioritization technique used in software development to maximize the value delivered to end users.

Navigating SOIs:
The process of identifying and prioritizing positive and negative influences in one's SOI in order of significance of how positively or negatively they impact one's daily welfare.

NBD (Never Been Done):
Refers to activities or actions one has never performed or undertaken.

Opportunistic Failure:
A Quasi-Chaotic subtool that advocates the pursuit of deliberately failure-prone challenges to facilitate interaction with novel people, places, and practices.

Osmosis:
A Quasi-Chaotic tool used to control environmental influences to catalyze one's development. Osmosis emphasizes how who and what we surround ourselves with significantly influence and change our intrinsic nature over time for better or worse. Its constituent subtools include Selective Osmosis, Divergent Osmosis, and Reflective Osmosis.

Partnered Accountability:
A Quasi-Chaotic subtool used to promote commitment by leveraging accountability partners.

Pavlovian conditioning:
Also referred to as "classical conditioning," is a behavioral procedure that involves learning through association, whereby a response becomes more frequent in a given environment as a result of systematic reinforcement from a stimulus designed to produce instinctive behaviors.

persona:
A fictional description of an actual end user archetype developed to ensure that all team members involved with the project's life cycle focus on specific end user considerations: their age, role, interests, hobbies, and technical prowess, daily routines, problems, frustrations—anything and everything that informs design, development, testing, deployment, and future maintenance.

pivoting:
Also referred to as "correcting velocity," it represents a change of direction, trajectory, or level of commitment triggered by a change in circumstances regarding what end users value, often identified in Sprint Reviews.

Pride:

A Quasi-Chaotic tool used to omit the need for external validation, maximize opportunities, and cultivate confidence necessary should one stray off the beaten track by promoting authentic pride, a socially attractive behavior. Its constituent subtools include Lossless Pride, Attractive Pride, and Reflective Pride.

Procreative Predisposition:

Refers to the deeply seated, biologically induced urge to reproduce (by means of intrinsic fulfillment as a reward) to fulfill the gene's sole purpose: survival.

psychic affirmation:

Refers to the emotional evaluation of one's life, the verdict of the psyche or emotional self (an emotional "thumbs-up")—how an agent is disposed emotionally regarding one's life. Under the Emotional State View theory, it involves an agent feeling endorsement (cheerful and joyous), engagement (exuberance and in flow), and attunement (tranquil, confident, and uncompressed).

Quasi-Chaotic Decision-Making Model:

A model used to construct the best possible Self-Actualizing response to a Hard Problem, consisting of the following three stages: realizing, acting on, and living with the decision (see page 320). The product of its application is an RSC.

Quasi-Chaotic Lifestyle:

A lifestyle adapted from the Agile philosophy with change as a core-constant objective, fine-tuned to promote Self-Actualization in increasingly chaotic environments with everchanging selves. It involves the use of Quasi-Chaotic tools, models, and frameworks to maximize and sustain exposure and breadth of experience to and with diverse people, places, and practices, facilitating serendipity, epiphanies, constructive challenge, and catalyze the discovery of Self-Actualizing fronts.

Quasi-Chaotic Tool Kit:

An actionable cognitive and behavioral tool kit for sustaining a healthy

Quasi-Chaotic Lifestyle. It is composed of Curiosity, Osmosis, Accountability, Momentum, Ambition, Failure, and Pride.

Quasi-Chaotic View:

A theory of well-being and happiness that identifies well-being with one's evaluation of their state-of-being toward Self-Actualization and happiness with one's emotional condition as a whole; a state-directive guiding one toward Self-Actualization.

reciprocal altruism:

Behavior in which an individual acts in a manner that is temporarily consequential for the benefit of another with the expectation that the other will act in a similar manner next time.

Reflective Osmosis:

A Quasi-Chaotic subtool used to develop affable modes of interaction through empathetic reflection to maximize scope of opportunity. It is the process of interpreting conflict through the lens of the other, a lens one may be familiar with, and conducting oneself in a manner one would have preferred to have been approached with.

Reflective Pride:

A Quasi-Chaotic subtool used to reassure one of intertemporal progress and prevents susceptibility to feelings of inferiority when comparing oneself to others.

Reinforcing Failure:

A Quasi-Chaotic subtool used to develop cognitive calluses that build resilience and courage to test and take on relatively ambitious change by exposing oneself to purposely challenging change that is likely to end in defeat.

RSC (Receipt of Sufficient Consideration):

The product of the Quasi-Chaotic Decision-Making Model, offering directives and serving as a record of affirmation for an enacted Self-Actualizing response to minimize postdecisional dissonance, grief, and regret.

SAAC (Self-Actualizing Axillary Coefficient):
A rule of thumb used when constructing an RSC. It suggests the RSC should harbor twice as many cons as pros to leverage loss aversion. In addition, the SAAC instructs those without a matter worth compromise to favor decisions that maximize freedom of choice and exposure to diverse opportunities.

Scrum:
An iterative, "interval-based" value-maximizing project management method for developing, delivering, and sustaining outcomes in complex environments. It is composed of ceremonies and practices that enable self-organization, adaptability, and optimization of processes. Work is broken up into multiple Sprints.

Sein-zum-Tode:
German for "being-toward-death" and what philosopher Martin Heidegger describes as a process of growing through the world with the foresight of impending demise that guides an individual with an authentic perspective.

Selective Osmosis:
A Quasi-Chaotic subtool used to build a social milieu imbued with characteristics, behaviors, and knowledge one wants imparted on oneself.

Self-Accountability:
A Quasi-Chaotic subtool used to promote commitment by developing self-sufficient habits and strategies to cultivate responsibility and taking ownership of opportunities to grow.

self-actualization:
Regarding Maslow's hierarchy of needs, it refers to the highest level of psychological development where personal potential is fully realized, activated, and expressed.

(Existential) Self-Actualization:
An adapted version of Maslow's self-actualization, (Existential) Self-Actualization is the cyclical process of creating, testing, and potentially flourishing off an identity toward psychic affirmation and maintaining the state by regularly recreating the identity. To be Self-Actualized would be to live to one's

fullest self-desired potentialities, maximizing opportunities of self-growth one's iron triangle permits.

Serendipitous Curiosity:

A Quasi-Chaotic subtool used to produce serendipitous rabbit holes potentially involving Self-Actualizing people, places, or practices by pursuing arbitrary motives as they emerge.

SOI (Scope of Influence):

Encompasses all that significantly influences our daily welfare, namely people, places, and practices. People entries must necessarily refer to individuals; places can be areas, rooms, environments, situations, etc.; practices involve Hobbies and Sustenance.

Spontaneous Momentum:

A Quasi-Chaotic subtool used to maintain momentum of change by exercising change on a whim if it has been too long since one has attempted an NBD.

Sprint:

The basic unit of development in Scrum of a short and fixed length that involves several phases including:
Initial Scoping, Sprint Planning, Stand-Up meetings, Sprint Reviews, Backlog Refinement, and Sprint Retrospectives.

Sprint Planning:

The kickoff to a Sprint involving the selection of the highest-priority actionable, valuecentric cards that are feasible with respect to the project's (one's) iron triangle and the allotted time frame of the Sprint.

Sprint Retrospective:

A short ceremony in which the methods and processes by which tasks are being completed are reviewed and optimized. Motivations, opinions, ideas, and action plans are discussed (reflected upon) and implemented in following Sprints.

Sprint Review:

A short ceremony involving the review of completed work as well as discussions (reflection) and note-taking of the problems faced, how they were resolved, and what was learned about particular tasks actioned throughout the Sprint.

Stand-Up meeting:
Also referred to as a daily Scrum, a ten to fifteen-minute meeting that takes place each day during a Sprint and before the day's development begins when individuals briefly summarize their day's commitments, roadblocks, and their previous day's accomplishments.

stretch goal:
A high-effort and often long-term goal whose chance of attainment is less than 10% with a high risk of extinction.

Suffer:
The process of cultivating Change Reception upon arriving at an Unreachable Terminal by knowingly and willingly allowing degradation of one's circumstances by refusing change, sustaining a detrimental way of life, enduring increasingly overwhelming angst.

survivorship bias:
The logical error of focusing on those who've succeeded and overlooking those who did not because of their lack of information, awareness, or availability of the entire perspective, which may lead to risky and uninformed decision-making.

Sustenance:
Refers to all one needs to sustain their Hobbies including cooking, cleaning, eating, sleeping, personal care, transport, managing expenses, exercise, shopping, and behavior.

Therefore Check:
A troubleshooter used to check the logical flow of the chain of answers produced using the Five Whys. It involves reading through the answers in reverse chronological order separating each statement with "therefore." The Therefore Check can be used as means to communicate negative influences with Detractors with sincerity should they remain unconvinced after using an I-statement.

To-Do lane:

A Kanban lane consisting of a selection of cards drawn from the Backlog that are "up next" to action for a given Sprint. Cards in the To-Do lane must include a sufficient level of detail to be actionable, measurable, and small enough to be accomplished in 2-4 hours or less. The addition of acceptance criteria is ideal to ensure an understanding of what is required to determine the card complete.

Traditional Psyche:

Refers to the rigid, linear, familiar, and mundane lifestyle and aspirational templates passed down from generations or inherited from social norms.

Unreachable Terminal:

A state of self-delusion and obstinance of an Imagination Gap resulting in perpetual dissonance, entrenching Change Resistance, and preventing Change Reception.

Vertical Momentum:

A Quasi-Chaotic subtool used to test and reassure the possibility of higher modes of experience by periodically exerting significant change in the people, places, or practices we regularly come in contact with.

Waterfall methodology:

A sequential project management approach to software development broken up into linear phases, each of which cannot be commenced until its preceding phase is completed in its entirety. Emphasis is placed on the first phase, which involves comprehensive stakeholder and customer requirement–gathering and meticulous documentation, making pivots difficult to implement without reengineering premade plans. Design, Implementation, Verification, and Maintenance are the remaining phases.

REFERENCES

Part I: Breaking Bad Habits
CHAPTER 1: THE TRADITIONAL PSYCHE

Bourdieu, P. Outline of a Theory of Practice. Translated by R. Nice. Cambridge: Cambridge University Press, 1977.

Parker, Erica. "LEGO Group Kicks Off Global Program to Inspire the Next Generation of Space Explorers as NASA Celebrates 50 Years of Moon Landing." The Harris Poll (2019). https://theharrispoll.com/briefs/lego-group-kicks-off-global-program-to-inspire-the-next-generation-of-space-explorers-as-nasa-celebrates-50-years-of-moon-landing/.

Akande, G. "Influencer Career Desires for 17% of Kids." Awin.com (February 8, 2019). https://www.awin.com/gb/news-and-events/awin-news/nearly-one-fifth-of-british-children-aspire-to-be-social-media-influencers.

"This Is What Kids in 2015 Want to Be When They Grow Up." Fatherly (November 19, 2015). https://www.fatherly.com/news/what-kids-want-to-be-when-they-grow-up/.

Mazzuca, J. "Teen Career Picks: The More Things Change . . ." Gallup.com (May 13, 2003). https://news.gallup.com/poll/8371/teen-career-picks-more-things-change.aspx.

"From the Archive, 9 November 1950: What Children Want to be When They Grow Up." Guardian (November 9, 2012). https://www.theguardian.com/theguardian/2012/nov/09/children-careers-film-archive-1950.

Patalay, P., and S.H. Gage. "Changes in Millennial Adolescent Mental Health and Health-Related Behaviours Over 10 Years: A Population Cohort Comparison Study." International Journal of Epidemiology 48, no. 5 (2019). https://doi.org/10.1093/ije/dyz006.

The Health of America—Major Depression: The Impact on Overall Health. Blue Cross Blue Shield (2018). https://www.bcbs.com/sites/default/files/file-attachments/download-infographic/health-of-america-report/HoA_Major_Depression_Infographic_0.pdf.

Reinert, M., D. Fritze, and T. Nguyen. "The State of Mental Health in America 2022." Mental Health America (October 2021). https://mhanational.org/issues/state-mental-health-america.

"Causes of Death, Australia, 2019." Australian Bureau of Statistics, Catalogue No. 3303.0 (October 23, 2020). https://www.abs.gov.au/statistics/health/causes-death/causes-death-australia/2019.

Curran, T. and A.P. Hill. "Young People's Perceptions of Their Parents' Expectations and Criticism Are Increasing Over Time: Implications for Perfectionism." Psychological Bulletin 148, nos. 1-2 (2022): 107–28. https://doi.org/10.1037/bul0000347.

Twenge, J. M., A. B. Cooper, T. E. Joiner, M. E. Duffy, and S.G. Binau. "Age, Period, and Cohort Trends in Mood Disorder Indicators and Suicide-Related Outcomes in a Nationally Representative Dataset, 2005–2017." Journal of Abnormal Psychology 128, no. 3 (2019): 85–199. https://doi.org/10.1037/abn0000410.

Giattino, C., E. Ortiz-Ospina, and M. Roser. Working Hours. Our World in Data, 2013. https://ourworldindata.org/working-hours.

Park, A., C. Bryson, E. Clery, J. Curtice, and M. Philips, eds. British Social Attitudes 30. NatCen Social Research (2013). https://www.bsa.natcen.ac.uk/media/38723/bsa30_full_report_final.pdf.

Smith, T. W., M. Hout, M., and P. V. Marsden. General Social Survey, 1972–2014 [Cumulative File]. Inter-university Consortium for Political and Social Research [distributor], National Opinion Research Center [distributor] (March 14, 2016). https://doi.org/10.3886/ICPSR36319.v2.

Smith, T. W. General Social Survey, 2018. Association of Religion Data Archives (March 4, 2020). https://doi.org/10.17605/OSF.IO/7JF94.

CHAPTER 2: PESTILENTIAL GOAL SETTING

Gary, M. S., M. M. Yang, P. W. Yetton, and J. D. Sterman. "Stretch Goals and the Distribution of Organizational Performance." Organization Science 28, no. 3 (2017): 395–410. https://doi.org/10.1287/orsc.2017.1131.

Kerr, S. and S. Landauer. "Using Stretch Goals to Promote Organizational Effectiveness and Personal Growth: General Electric and Goldman Sachs." Academy of Management Executive (1993–2005) 18, no. 4 (2004): 134–38. https://www.jstor.org/stable/4166134.

Fisher, J., S. Peffer, and G. Sprinkle. "Budget-Based Contracts, Budget Levels, and Group Performance." Journal of Management Accounting 15 (2003): 51-74. 10.2308/jmar.2003.15.1.51.

Chow, C., T. Lindquist, T., and A. Wu. "National Culture and the Implementation of High-Stretch Performance Standards: An Exploratory Study." Behavioral Research in Accounting 1 (2001): 85–109. 10.2308/bria.2001.13.1.85.

Ordóñez, L., M. Schweitzer, A. Galinsky, and M. Bazerman. "Goals Gone Wild: The Systematic Side Effects of Over-Prescribing Goal Setting." Academy of Management Perspectives 23 (2009). 10.2139/ssrn.1332071.

Sitkin, S., K. See, C. Miller, M. Lawless, and A. Carton. "The Paradox of Stretch Goals: Organizations in Pursuit of the Seemingly Impossible." Academy of Management Review 36 (2010). 10.5465/AMR.2011.61031811.

Mossholder, K. W. "Effects of Externally Mediated Goal Setting on Intrinsic Motivation: A Laboratory Experiment." Journal of Applied Psychology 65, no. 2(1980): 202–10. https://doi.org/10.1037/0021-9010.65.2.202.

Rawsthorne, L. J., and A. J. Elliot. "Achievement Goals and Intrinsic Motivation: A Meta-Analytic Review." Personality and Social Psychology Review 3, no. 4 (1999): 326–44. https://doi.org/10.1207/s15327957pspr0304_3.

Shalley, C. E., G. R. Oldham. "Effects of Goal Difficulty and Expected External Evaluation on Intrinsic Motivation: A Laboratory Study." Academy of Management Journal 28, no. 3 (1985): 628–40. https://doi.org/10.2307/256118.

MacCrimmon, K. R., D. A. Wehrung, and W. T. Stanbury. Taking Risks: The Management of Uncertainty. New York: Free Press, 1986.

Earley, P., T. Connolly, and G. Ekegren, G. "Goals, Strategy Development, and Task Performance: Some Limits on the Efficacy of Goal Setting." Journal of Applied Psychology 74 (1989): 24–33. 10.1037/0021-9010.74.1.24.

Wood, R., A. Mento, and E. Locke, E. "Task Complexity as a Moderator of Goal Effects: A Meta-Analysis." Journal of Applied Psychology 72 (1987): 416–25. 10.1037/0021-9010.72.3.416.

Nesse R. M. "Natural Selection and the Elusiveness of Happiness." Philosophical Transactions of the Royal Society of London. Series B, Biological Sciences 359, no. 1449 (2004): 1333–47. https://doi.org/10.1098/rstb.2004.1511.

King, L. A., and C. M. Burton. "The Hazards of Goal Pursuit." In Virtue, Vice, and Personality: The Complexity of Behavior, edited by E. C. Chang and L. J. Sanna, 53–69. American Psychological Association, 2003. https://doi.org/10.1037/10614-004.

CHAPTER 3: THE TWENTY-FIRST-CENTURY DILEMMA

Middeldorp, C. M., A. J. Birley, D. C. Cath, N. A. Gillespie, G. Willemsen, D. J. Statham, E. J. C. de Geus, J. G. Andrews, R. van Dyck, A. L. Beem, P. F. Sullivan, N. G. Martin, and D. I. Boomsma. "Familial Clustering of Major Depression and Anxiety Disorders in Australian and Dutch Twins and Siblings." Twin Research and Human Genetics 8, no. 6 (2005): 609–15. https://doi.org/10.1375/twin.8.6.609.

Bredehoft, D., J. Clarke, and C. Dawson. "Relationships Between Childhood Overindulgence and Parenting Attributes: Implications for Family Life Educators." Paper presented at the 2002 National Council on Family Relations Annual Meeting, Houston, TX, November 4, 2002.

Blake, S. "Students Sliding Because 'Too Soft' Schools and Parents Never Let Them Fail: WHY Are Our Kids Failing to Keep Up with the Best Students in the World? Some Experts Blame Parents and Schools for Being 'Too Soft.'" News Corp Australia Network. (August 16, 2013). https://www.news.com.au/lifestyle/parenting/students-sliding-because-8216too-soft8217-schools-and-parents-never-let-them-fail/news-story/d864dd4fe6f73701deaa529fb520934b.

Lawton, A. "Schools Must Stop Lowering Standards." Toronto Sun (November 26, 2015). https://torontosun.com/2015/11/26/schools-must-stop-lowering-standards.

Sheppard, J. "Exam Thresholds Lowered to Prevent Grades Plummeting after Test Reform." Daily Mail (online edition) (August 13, 2017). https://www.dailymail.co.uk/news/article-4786360/Exam-thresholds-lowered-prevent-grades-plummeting.html.

Williams, O., R. Ellis, and B. Kesslen. "Move to End Standardized Testing in High Schools Draws Both Praise and Concern." NBC News (November 7, 2021). https://www.nbcnews.com/news/us-news/move-end-standardized-testing-high-schools-draws-both-praise-concern-n1282657.

Mueller, C. M., and C. S. Dweck. "Praise for Intelligence Can Undermine Children's Motivation and Performance." Journal of Personality and Social Psychology 75, no. 1 (1998): 33–52. https://doi.org/10.1037/0022-3514.75.1.33.

Lee, H. I., Y. H. Kim, P. Kesebir, and D. E. Han. "Understanding When Parental Praise Leads to Optimal Child Outcomes." Social Psychological and Personality Science 8, no. 6 (2016): 679–88. https://doi.org/10.1177/1948550616683020.

Haidt, J. The Coddling of the American Mind. New York: Penguin Books, 2018.

"Depression." Better Health Channel (July 24, 2018). https://www.betterhealth.vic.gov.au/health/conditionsandtreatments/depression.

Carswell, A., and P. Michael. "Job Snobs: Aussie Dole Bludgers Too Lazy to Pick Up $250 a Day Picking Fruit." Daily Mail (January 23, 2015). https://www.dailytelegraph.com.au/news/nsw/job-snobs-aussie-dole-bludgers-too-lazy-to- pick-up-250-a-day-picking-fruit/news-story/7d5483abad48a4c0e3e8b4fdde966995.

Banarjee, A., R. Hanna, G. Kreindler, and B. A. Olken. "Debunking the Stereotype of the Lazy Welfare Recipient." Working paper no. 308, Center for International Development at Harvard University (October 2015). https://www.hks.harvard.edu/centers/cid/publications/faculty-working-papers/debunking-stereotype-lazy-welfare-recipient.

CHAPTER 4: SELF-LIMITING RELUCTANCY

K. Anders Ericsson, R. T. Krampe, and C. Tesch-Römer. "The Role of Deliberate Practice in the Acquisition of Expert Performance." Psychological Review 100, no. 3 (1993): 363–406. https://doi.org/10.1037//0033-295x.100.3.363.

Lehman, H. C. Age and Achievement. Princeton, NJ: Princeton University Press, 1953.

Simonton, D. K. Scientific Genius: A Psychology of Science. Cambridge: Cambridge University Press, 1988.

Kalinowski, A. G. "The Development of Olympic Swimmers." In Developing Talent in Young People, edited by B. S. Bloom, 139–92. New York: Ballantine Books, 1985.

Monsaas, J. A. "Learning to Be a World-Class Tennis Player." In Developing Talent in Young People, edited by B. S. Bloom, 211–69. New York: Ballantine Books, 1985.

Wallingford, R. "Long Distance Running." In The Scientific Aspects of Sports Training, edited by A. W. Tayler and F. Landry, 118–30. Springfield, IL: Charles C. Thomas, 1975.

Gustin, W C. "The Development of Exceptional Research Mathematicians." In Developing Talent in Young People, edited by B. S. Bloom, 270–331. New York: Ballantine Books, 1985.

"New documentary on the Polgar family." Chess Base (August 28, 2012). https://en.chessbase.com/post/new-documentary-on-the-polgar-family.

Sternberg, R. J. "The Cost of Expertise." In The Road to Excellence: The Acquisition of Expert Performance in the Arts and Sciences, Sports, and Games, edited by A. K. Ericsson, 347–54. Psychology Press, 1996.

Anderson, J. R. Learning and Memory: An Integrated Approach. Wiley, 2000.

Marcus, G. F. Guitar Zero: The Science of Becoming Musical at Any Age. New York: Penguin Books, 2012.

Gagné, F. "Predictably, an Unconvincing Second Attempt." High Ability Studies 18, no. 1 (2007): 67–69. https://doi.org/10.1080/13598130701350742.

Howe, M., J. Davidson, and Sloboda. "Innate Talents: Reality or Myth?" Behavioral and Brain Sciences 21, no. 3 (1998): 399–407, doi:10.1017/S0140525X9800123X.

Ericsson, K., K. Nandagopal, and R. Roring, "Giftedness Viewed from the Expert-Performance Perspective." Journal for the Education of the Gifted 28 (2005): 287–311. https://doi.org/10.4219/jeg-2005-335.

Gagné, F. "Motivation within the DMGT 2.0 Framework." High Ability Studies 21 (2010): 81–99. https://doi.org/10.1080/13598139.2010.525341.

Gagné, Françoys. "SIX YouTube presentations on the DMGT." dmgt-mddt (blog), n.d. https://gagnefrancoys.wixsite.com/dmgt-mddt/the-dmgt-on-youtube.

Gagné, F. "The DMGT: Changes Within, Beneath, and Beyond." Talent Development and Excellence 5 (2013): 5–19.

Gagné, F. "Yes, Giftedness (AKA 'Innate' Talent) Does Exist!" (May 22, 2013). DOI:10.1093/ACPROF:OSO/9780199794003.003.0010.

Anastasi, A. Abilities and the measurement of achievement. In New Directions for Testing and Measurement, edited by W. B. Schrader, 1–10. Jossey-Boss, 1980.

Galton, F. Hereditary Genius: An Inquiry into Its Laws and Consequences. Prometheus Books, 2006.

Colangelo, N., S. G. Assouline, and C. Belin. Talent Development IV: Proceedings from the 1998 Henry B. and Jocelyn Wallace National Research Symposium on Talent Development. Great Potential Press, 2001.

Jensen, A. "Galton's Legacy to Research on Intelligence." Journal of Biosocial Science 34 (2002): 145–72. https//doi.org/10.1017/S0021932002001451.

Frank, R. H. Success and Luck: Good Fortune and the Myth of Meritocracy. Princeton University Press, 2017.

Deaner, R. O., A. Lowen, and S. Cobley. "Born at the Wrong Time: Selection Bias in the NHL Draft." PLoS ONE 8, no. 2 (2013): e57753. https://doi.org/10.1371/journal.pone.0057753.

Ericsson, K. A., R. W. Roring, and K. Nandagopal. "Giftedness and Evidence for Reproducibly Superior Performance: An Account Based on the Expert Performance Framework." High Ability Studies 18, no. 1 (2007): 3–56. https://doi.org/10.1080/13598130701350593.

Malina, R. M., C. Bouchard, and E. Or. Sport and Human Genetics. Human Kinetics, 1986.

Guth, L. M., and S. M. Roth. "Genetic Influence on Athletic Performance." Current Opinion in Pediatrics 25, no. 6 (2013): 653–58. https://doi.org/10.1097/mop.0b013e3283659087.

Gladwell, M. Outliers: The Story of Success. New York: Back Bay Books, 2008.

Macnamara, B. N., D. Z. Hambrick, and F. L. Oswald. "Deliberate Practice and Performance in Music, Games, Sports, Education, and Professions: A Meta-Analysis." Psychological Science 25 no. 8 (2014): 1608–18. https://doi.org/10.1177/0956797614535810.

Ericsson, A. K., and K. W. Harwell. "Deliberate Practice and Proposed Limits on the Effects of Practice on the Acquisition of Expert Performance: Why the Original Definition Matters and Recommendations for Future Research. Frontiers." Frontiers in Psychology 25 (Oct 2019). https://www.frontiersin.org/articles/10.3389/fpsyg.2019.02396/full.

Simon, H. A., and W. G. Chase. "Skill in Chess." American Scientist 61, no. 4 (1973): 394–403.

Petanjek, Z., M. Judaš, G. Šimić, M. R. Rašin, H. B. M. Uylings, P. Rakic, and I. Kostović. "Extraordinary Neoteny of Synaptic Spines in the Human Prefrontal Cortex." Proceedings of the National Academy of Sciences 108, no. 32 (2011): 13281–86. https://doi.org/10.1073/pnas.1105108108.

Fair, D. A., A. L. Cohen, J. D. Power, N. U. F. Dosenbach, J. A. Church, F. M. Miezin, B. L. Schlaggar, and S. E. Petersen. "Functional Brain Networks Develop from a 'Local to Distributed' Organization." PLOS Computational Biology 5, no. 5 (2009): e1000381. https://doi.org/10.1371/journal.pcbi.1000381.

Drachman D. A. "Do We Have Brain to Spare?" Neurology 64, no. 12 (2004–2005). https://doi.org/10.1212/01.WNL.0000166914.38327.BB.

Craik, F. I., and E. Bialystok. "Cognition Through the Lifespan: Mechanisms of Change." Trends in Cognitive Sciences 10, no. 3 (2006): 131–38. https://doi.org/10.1016/j.tics.2006.01.007.

Fingas, J. "Sorry, Folks: Study Says Musical Talent Mostly Comes from Your Genes." Engadget (July 7, 2014). https://www.engadget.com/2014-07-07-study-says-musical-talent-is-genetic.html?guccounter=1&guce.

Beard, A. "Your Success Is Shaped by Your Genes." Harvard Business Review (January 1, 2017). hbr.org/2017/01/your-success-is-shaped-by-your-genes.

Planning for student diversity. ACARA (2021). https://www.australiancurriculum.edu.au/resources/student-diversity/planning-for-student-diversity/.

Harris, S. Lying. Four Elephants Press, 2013.

CHAPTER 5: THE MALLEABLE PSYCHE

Tupes, E. C., and R. E. Christal. "Recurrent Personality Factors Based on Trait Ratings." Journal of Personality 60, no. 2 (1992): 225–51. https://doi.org/10.1111/j.1467-6494.1992.tb00973.x.

Goldberg, L. R. "The structure of phenotypic personality traits." American Psychologist 48, no. 1 (1993): 26–34. https://doi.org/10.1037//0003-066x.48.1.26.

Menner, R. J., G. W. Allport, and H. S. Odbert. "Trait-Names, a Psycho-Lexical Study." American Speech 11, no. 3 (1936): 259. https://doi.org/10.2307/452250.

Cattell, R. B. (1943). "The Description of Personality: Basic Traits Resolved into Clusters." The Journal of Abnormal and Social Psychology 38, no. 4 (1943): 476–506. https://doi.org/10.1037/h0054116.

DeYoung, C. G., L. C. Quilty, and J. B. Peterson. "Between Facets and Domains: 10 Aspects of the Big Five." Journal of Personality and Social Psychology 93, no. 5 (2007): 880–96. https://doi.org/10.1037/0022-3514.93.5.880.

"Understand Myself—What You Need to Know." www.understandmyself.com (n.d.). https://www.understandmyself.com/.

Bouchard, T.A., Jr., D. T. Lykken, M. McGue, N. L. Segert, and A.Tellegen. Sources of Human Psychological Differences: The Minnesota Study of Twins Reared Apart (2005). http://web.missouri.edu/~segerti/1000H/Bouchard.pdf.

Jang, K. L., W. J. Livesley, and P. A. Vernon. "Heritability of the Big Five Personality Dimensions and Their Facets: A Twin Study." Journal of Personality 64, no. 3 (1996): 577–91. https://doi.org/10.1111/j.1467-6494.1996.tb00522.

Bouchard, T. J., and M. McGue. "Genetic and Environmental Influences on Human Psychological Differences." Journal of Neurobiology 54, no. 1 (2002): 4–45. https://doi.org/10.1002/neu.10160.

Vernon, P. A., R. A. Martin, J. A. Schermer, and A. Mackie. "A Behavioral Genetic Investigation of Humor Styles and Their Correlations with The Big-5 Personality Dimensions." Personality and Individual Differences 44, no. 5 (2008): 1116–25. https://doi.org/10.1016/j.paid.2007.11.003.

Joseph, J. Twenty-Two Invalidating Aspects of the Minnesota Study of Twins Reared Apart (MISTRA), abridged version, (2018). https://www.madinamerica.com/wp-content/uploads/2018/11/Twenty-Two-Invalidating-Aspects-of-the-MISTRA-by-Jay-Joseph-Abridged-Version-1.pdf.

Power, R., and M. Pluess. "Heritability Estimates of the Big Five Personality Traits Based on Common Genetic Variants." Translational Psychiatry 5 (2015): e604. 10.1038/tp.2015.96.

Roberts, B. W., and D. Mroczek. "Personality Trait Change in Adulthood." Current Directions in Psychological Science 17, no. 1 (2008): 31–35. https://doi.org/10.1111/j.1467-8721.2008.00543.x.

Srivastava, S., O. P. John, S. D. Gosling, and J. Potter. "Development of Personality in Early and Middle Adulthood: Set Like Plaster or Persistent Change?" Journal of Personality and Social Psychology 84, no. 5 (2003): 1041–53. https://doi.org/10.1037/0022-3514.84.5.1041.

Mroczek, D., and A. Spiro. "Modeling Intraindividual Change in Personality Traits: Findings from the Normative Aging Study." Journals of Gerontology, Series B, Psychological Sciences and Social Sciences 58 (2003): 153–65. 10.1093/geronb/58.3.P153.

Roberts, B. W., K. E. Walton, and W. Viechtbauer. "Patterns of Mean-Level Change in Personality Traits Across the Life Course: A Meta-Analysis of Longitudinal Studies." Psychological Bulletin 132, no. 1 (2006): 1–25. https://doi.org/10.1037/0033-2909.132.1.1.

Soto, C., O. John, S. Gosling, and J. Potter. "Age Differences in Personality Traits From 10 to 65: Big Five Domains and Facets in a Large Cross-Sectional Sample." Journal of Personality and Social Psychology 100 (2011): 330–348. 10.1037/a0021717.

Lodi-Smith, J., and B. W. Roberts. "Social Investment and Personality: A Meta-Analytic Analysis of the Relationship of Personality Traits to Investment in Work, Family, Religion, and Volunteerism." Personality and Social Psychology Review 11, no. 1 (2007): 68–86. doi:10.1177/1088868306294590.

Hudson, N. W., B. W. Roberts, and J. Lodi-Smith. "Personality Trait Development and Social Investment at Work." Journal of Research in Personality 46, no. 3 (2012): 334–44. https://doi.org/10.1016/j.jrp.2012.03.002.

Nye, C. D., and B. W. Roberts. A developmental perspective on the importance of personality for understanding workplace behavior. In Handbook of Personality at Work, edited by N. D. Christiansen and R. P. Tett , 796–818. Routledge, 2013.

Hudson, N. W., and R. C. Fraley. "Volitional Personality Trait Change: Can People Choose to Change Their Personality Traits?" Journal of Personality and Social Psychology 109, no. 3 (2015): 490–507. https://doi.org/10.1037/pspp0000021.

Hudson, N. W., D. A. Briley, W. J. Chopik, and J. Derringer. "You Have to Follow Through: Attaining Behavioral Change Goals Predicts Volitional Personality Change." Journal of Personality and Social Psychology 117, no. 4 (2019): 839–57. https://doi.org/10.1037/pspp0000221.

Jacques-Hamilton, R., J. Sun, J., and L. D. Smillie. "Costs and Benefits of Acting Extraverted: A Randomized Controlled Trial." Journal of Experimental Psychology: General (2018). https://doi.org/10.1037/xge0000516.

Hudson, N. W. "Does Successfully Changing Personality Traits via Intervention Require That Participants Be Autonomously Motivated to Change?" Journal of Research in Personality 95 (2021): 104160. https://doi.org/10.1016/j.jrp.2021.104160.

Roberts, B. W., J. Luo, D. A. Briley, P. I. Chow, R. Su, and P. L. Hill. "A Systematic Review of Personality Trait Change through Intervention." Psychological Bulletin 143, no. 2 (2017): 117–41. https://doi.org/10.1037/bul0000088.

Bleidorn, W., P. Hill, M. D. Back, J. J. A. Denissen, M. Hennecke, C. J. Hopwood, M. Jokela, C. Kandler, R. E. Lucas, M. Luhmann, U. Orth, J. Wagner, C. Wrzus, J. Zimmermann, and B. Roberts. "The Policy Relevance of Personality Traits." American Psychologist 74, no. 9 (2019): 1056–67. https://doi.org/10.1037/amp0000503.

CHAPTER 6: INCESSANT DISTRACTION

Wilson, T. D., D. A. Reinhard, E. C. Westgate, D. T. Gilbert, N. Ellerbeck, C. Hahn, C. L. Brown, and A. Shaked. "Just Think: The Challenges of the Disengaged Mind." Science 345, no. 6192 (2014): 75–77. https://doi.org/10.1126/science.1250830.

Lorenz-Spreen, P., B. M. Mønsted, P. Hövel, P., and S. Lehmann. "Accelerating Dynamics of Collective Attention." Nature Communications 10, no. 1 (2019): 1–9. https://doi.org/10.1038/s41467-019-09311-w.

"Abundance of Information Narrows Our Collective Attention Span." ScienceDaily (n.d.). https://www.sciencedaily.com/releases/2019/04/190415081959.htm.

Watt, J. D., and S. J. Vodanovich. "Boredom Proneness and Psychosocial Development." The Journal of Psychology 133, no. 3 (1999): 303–14. https://doi.org/10.1080/00223989909599743.

Ingraham, Christopher. "Screen Time Is Rising, Reading Is Falling, and It's Not Young People's Fault." Washington Post, June 21, 2019. https://www.washingtonpost.com/business/2019/06/21/screen-time-is-rising-reading-is-falling-its-not-young-peoples-fault/.

Salim, Saima. "How Much Time Do You Spend on Social Media? Research Says 142 Minutes per Day." Digital Information World, January 4, 2019. https://www.digitalinformationworld.com/2019/01/how-much-time-do-people-spend-social-media-infographic.html.

Gumm, Emily. "Screen Time Trends and What You Can Do." GattiHR, n.d. https://www.gattihr.com/screen-time-trends-and-what-you-can-do/.

Newman, Nic. "Executive Summary and Key Findings of the 2020 Report." Digital News Report, n.d. https://www.digitalnewsreport.org/survey/2020/overview-key-findings-2020/.

Wheelwright, Trevor. "2022 Cell Phone Usage Statistics: How Obsessed Are We?" Reviews.org, January 24, 2022. https://www.reviews.org/mobile/cell-phone-addiction/.

Baird, B., J. Smallwood, and J. W. Schooler. "Back to the Future: Autobiographical Planning and the Functionality of Mind-Wandering." Consciousness and Cognition 20, no. 4 (2011): 1604–11. https://doi.org/10.1016/j.concog.2011.08.007.

Mann, S., and R. Cadman. "Does Being Bored Make Us More Creative?" Creativity Research Journal 26, no. 2 (2014): 165–73. https://doi.org/10.1080/10400419.2014.901073.

Oishi, Y., Q. Xu, L. Wang, B.-J. Zhang, K. Takahashi, Y. Takata, Y.-J. Luo, Y. Cherasse, S. N. Schiffmann, A. de Kerchove d'Exaerde, Y. Urade, W.-M. Qu, Z.-L. Huang, and M. Lazarus. "Slow-Wave Sleep Is Controlled by a Subset of Nucleus Accumbens Core Neurons in Mice." Nature Communications 8, no. 1 (September 29, 2017). https://doi.org/10.1038/s41467-017-00781-4.

Grafe, L. A., and S. Bhatnagar. "Orexins and Stress." Frontiers in Neuroendocrinology 51 (2018):132–145. https://doi.org/10.1016/j.yfrne.2018.06.003.

Beutel, M. E., E. M. Klein, S. Aufenanger, E. Brähler, M. Dreier, K. W. Müller, O. Quiring, L. Reinecke, G. Schmutzer, B. Stark, and K. Wölfling. "Procrastination, Distress and Life Satisfaction across the Age Range – A German Representative Community Study." PLOS ONE 11, no. 2 (2016): e0148054. https://doi.org/10.1371/journal.pone.0148054.

CHAPTER 7: PROCREATIVE PREDISPOSITION

Trump-Steele, R., C. Nittrouer, M. Hebl, and L. Ashburn-Nardo. "The Inevitable Stigma for Childbearing-Aged Women in the Workplace: Five Perspectives on the Pregnancy-Work Intersection." In Research Perspectives on Work and the Transition to Motherhood. Springer, 2016. 10.1007/978-3-319-41121-7_5.

Bodin, M., L. Plantin, and E. Elmerstig. "A Wonderful Experience or a Frightening Commitment? An Exploration of Men's Reasons to (Not) Have Children." Reproductive Biomedicine & Society Online 9 (2016). 10.1016/j.rbms.2019.11.002.

Margolis, R., and M. Myrskylä. "Parental Well-being Surrounding First Birth as a Determinant of Further Parity Progression." Demography 52 (2015): 1147–66. https://doi.org/10.1007/s13524-015-0413-2.

Wolfinger, N.H. Does Having Children Make People Happier in the Long Run? Institute for Family Studies (2018). https://ifstudies.org/blog/does-having-children-make-people-happier-in-the-long-run.

Health and Retirement Study. 2016 HRS Core (December 2019). https://hrsdata.isr.umich.edu/data-products/2016-hrs-core.

Stern, G.M. "The Long-Term Realities of Being Childless." Next Avenue (December 9, 2020). https://www.nextavenue.org/the-long-term-realities-of-being-childless/.

Aarssen, L. W., and S. T. Altman. "Fertility Preference Inversely Related to 'Legacy Drive' in Women, but Not in Men: Interpreting the Evolutionary Roots, and Future, of the 'Childfree' Culture." Open Behavioral Science Journal 6, no 1 (2012). https://benthamopen.com/ABSTRACT/TOBSJ-6-37.

Glass, J., R. W. Simon, and M. A. Andersson. "Parenthood and Happiness: Effects of Work-Family Reconciliation Policies in 22 OECD Countries." American Journal of Sociology 122, no. 3 (2016): 886–929. https://doi.org/10.1086/688892.

Evenson, R. J., R. W. Simon. "Clarifying the Relationship Between Parenthood and Depression." Journal of Health and Social Behavior 46, no. 4 (2005): 341–58. https://doi.org/10.1177/002214650504600403.

Koropeckyj-Cox, T. "Beyond Parental Status: Psychological Well-Being in Middle and Old Age." Journal of Marriage and Family 64, no. 4 (2002): 957–71. https://www.jstor.org/stable/3599995.

Deaton, A., and A. A. Stone. "Evaluative and Hedonic Wellbeing Among Those with and without Children at Home." Proceedings of the National Academy of Sciences 111, no. 4 (2014): 1328–33. https://doi.org/10.1073/pnas.1311600111.

Expenditures on Children by Families Reports—All Years. US Department of Agriculture, Food and Nutrition Service (2011). https://www.fns.usda.gov/resource/expenditures-children-families-reports-all-years.

Blanchflower, D., and A. Clark. NBER Working Paper Series: Children, Unhappiness and Family Finances: Evidence from One Million Europeans. (2019). https://www.nber.org/system/files/working_papers/w25597/w25597.pdf.

Russia: Marriage and Divorce Rates 2000–2017. Statista (2017). https://www.statista.com/statistics/1009719/russia-marriage-and-divorce-rate/.

Marriage and Divorce Statistics. Ec.europa.eu (n.d.). https://ec.europa.eu/eurostat/statistics-explained/index.php?title=Marriage_and_divorce_statistics.

NVSS—Marriages and Divorces. Center for Disease Control and Prevention (2019). https://www.cdc.gov/nchs/nvss/marriage-divorce.htm.

Marriages and Divorces, Australia, 2020. Australian Bureau of Statistics (November 24, 2021). https://www.abs.gov.au/statistics/people/people-and-communities/marriages-and-divorces-australia/2020.

CHAPTER 8: A CURSED GRAIL

Seligman, M. E. P. Authentic Happiness: Using the New Positive Psychology to Realize Your Potential for Lasting Fulfillment. Free Press, 2013.

Gilbert, D.T. Stumbling on Happiness. New York: Vintage, 2007.

Achor, S. The Happiness Advantage: How a Positive Brain Fuels Success in Work and Life. Currency, 2018.

Peale, N.V. The Power of Positive Thinking. New York: Touchstone/Simon & Schuster, 2015.

Byrne, R. The Secret: The 10th Anniversary Edition. Atria Books, 2016.

Pinker, S.A. Enlightenment Now: The Case for Reason, Science, Humanism, and Progress. New York: Viking, 2018.

Schwarz, N., and F. Strack. "Reports of Subjective Well-Being: Judgmental Processes and Their Methodological Implications." In Well-being: The Foundations of Hedonic Psychology, edited by D. Kahneman, E. Diener, and N. Schwarz, 61–84. Russell Sage Foundation, 1999.

Kahneman, D., E. Diener, and N. Schwarz, eds. Well-Being: The Foundations of Hedonic Psychology. Russell Sage Foundation, 1999.

Changing World Happiness. Worldhappiness.report (2019). https://worldhappiness.report/ed/2019/changing-world-happiness/.

Fredrickson, B. L. "What Good Are Positive Emotions?" Review of General Psychology 2, no. 3 (1998): 300–319. https://doi.org/10.1037/1089-2680.2.3.300.

Bentham, J., and J. S. Mill. The Utilitarians: An Introduction to the Principles of Morals and Legislation. New York: Doubleday, 1973.

Hippel, W.V. The social leap: The New Evolutionary Science of Who We Are, Where We Come From, and What Makes Us Happy. New York: Harper Wave/HarperCollins, 2018.

Brickman, C., and D. T. Campbell. "Hedonic Relativism and Planning the Good Society." In Adaptation-Level Theory: Based on a Symposium on Adaptation-Level Theory, Held at the University of Massachusetts at Amherst, May 1970, edited by M.H. Appley, 287–302. Academic Press, 1971.

Brickman, P., D. Coates, D., and R. Janoff-Bulman. "Lottery Winners and Accident Victims: Is Happiness Relative?" Journal of Personality and Social Psychology 36, no. 8 (1978): 917–927. https://doi.org/10.1037/0022-3514.36.8.917.

Kahneman, D., B. L. Fredrickson, C. A. Schreiber, and D. A. Redelmeier. "When More Pain Is Preferred to Less: Adding a Better End." Psychological Science 4, no. 6 (1993): 401–405. https://doi.org/10.1111/j.1467-9280.1993.tb00589.x.

Strijbosch, W., O. Mitas, M. van Gisbergen, M. Doicaru, J. Gelissen, and M. Bastiaansen.. From Experience to Memory: On the Robustness of the Peak-and-End-Rule for Complex, Heterogeneous Experiences. Frontiers, 2019. https://www.frontiersin.org/articles/10.3389/fpsyg.2019.01705/full.

Harris, S. (Host). "The Map of Misunderstanding: A Conversation with Daniel Kahneman." Making Sense podcast, episode no. 150 (March 12, 2019). https://www.samharris.org/podcasts/making-sense-episodes/150-map-misunderstanding.

"Why We're Unhappy—The Expectation Gap." Nat Ware | TEDxKlagenfurt—closed TED | Amara (n.d.). https://amara.org/en/videos/ag3uxbdDCadg/en/1908889/.

Carver, C. S., and M. F. Scheier. Attention and Self-Regulation. New York: Springer, 1981. https://doi.org/10.1007/978-1-4612-5887-2.

Horowitz, D. Happier?: The History of a Cultural Movement that Aspired to Transform America. Oxford University Press, 2018.

Tamir, M., S. H. Schwartz, S. Oishi, and M. Y. Kim. "The Secret to Happiness: Feeling Good or Feeling Right?" Journal of Experimental Psychology: General 146, no. 10 (2017): 1448–59. https://doi.org/10.1037/xge0000303.

Kesebir, P., and E. Diener. "In Pursuit of Happiness: Empirical Answers to Philosophical Questions." Perspectives on Psychological Science 3, no. 2 (2018): 117–25. https://doi.org/10.1111/j.1745-6916.2008.00069.x.

Wiese, B. S. "Successful Pursuit of Personal Goals and Subjective Well-Being." In Personal Project Pursuit: Goals, Action, and Human Flourishing, edited by B. R. Little, K. Salmela-Aro, & S. D. Phillips, 301–328. Lawrence Erlbaum Associates Publishers, 2007.

Mauss, I. B., M. Tamir, C. L. Anderson, and N. S. Savino. "Can Seeking Happiness Make People Unhappy? Paradoxical Effects of Valuing Happiness." Emotion 11, no. 4 (2011): 807–15. https://doi.org/10.1037/a0022010.

Schafer, J. "Happiness Without Sadness Has No Meaning." Psychologytoday.com (Australia) (November 29, 2016). https://www.psychologytoday.com/au/blog/let-their-words-do-the-talking/201611/happiness-without-sadness-has-no-meaning.

Bentham, J. The Principles of Morals and Legislation. Prometheus Books, 1988.

Haybron, D. M. The Pursuit of Unhappiness: The Elusive Psychology of Well-Being. Oxford University Press, 2010.

Csikszentmihalyi, M. R. Flow: The Psychology of Optimal Experience. New York: Harper and Row, 1990.

Griffin, J. Well-Being: Its Meaning, Measurement and Moral Importance. Clarendon, 1986.

Sobel, D. "Full Information Accounts of Well-Being." Ethics 104, no. 4 (1994): 784–810. https://doi.org/10.1086/293655.

Rawls, J. A Theory of Justice: Revised Edition. The Belknap Press of Harvard University Press, 1999.

Nussbaum, M. C. "Human Functioning and Social Justice: In Defense of Aristotelian Essentialism." Political Theory 20, no 2 (1992): 202–46. http://www.jstor.org/stable/192002.

Nussbaum, M.C. Creating Capabilities: The Human Development Approach, 33–34. Harvard University Press, 2011.

Willand, N., B. Middha, and G. Walker. "Using the Capability Approach to Evaluate Energy Vulnerability Policies and Initiatives in Victoria, Australia." Local Environment 26, no. 9 (2021): 1109–1127. https://doi.org/10.1080/13549839.2021.1962830.

Klein, E. "The Curious Case of Using the Capability Approach in Australian Indigenous Policy". Journal of Human Development and Capabilities 17, no. 2 (2016): 245–59. https://doi.org/10.1080/19452829.2016.1145199.

Skourdoumbis, A. "Distorted Representations of the "Capability Approach" in Australian School Education." The Curriculum Journal 26, no. 1 (2015): 24–38. https://doi.org/10.1080/09585176.2014.955512.

Diener, E., R. A. Emmons, R. J. Larsen, and S. Griffin. "The Satisfaction with Life Scale." Journal of Personality Assessment 49, no. 1 (1985): 71–75. https://doi.org/10.1207/s15327752jpa4901_13.

Sumner, L. W. Welfare, Happiness, and Ethics. Clarendon, 1996.

Brandt, R. B. "Two Concepts of Utility." In The Limits of Utilitarianism, edited by H. B. Miller and W. H. Williams, 169–85. University of Minnesota Press, 1982.

Harris, R. The Happiness Trap: How to Stop Struggling and Start Living. Trumpeter, 2008.

CHAPTER 9: SHORT-SIGHTED LIMITS

Maslow, A. H. "A Theory of Human Motivation. Psychological Review 50, no. 4 (1943): 370–96. https://doi.org/10.1037/h0054346.

Maslow, A. H. Religions, Values, and Peak-Experiences. Penguin Books, 1964.

Kenrick, D. T., V. Griskevicius, S. L. Neuberg, and M. Schaller. "Renovating the Pyramid of Needs." Perspectives on Psychological Science 5, no. 3 (2010): 292–314. https://doi.org/10.1177/1745691610369469.

Kahneman, D., and A. Deaton. "High Income Improves Evaluation of Life but Not Emotional Well-Being." Proceedings of the National Academy of Sciences 107, no. 38 (2010): 16489–93. https://doi.org/10.1073/pnas.1011492107.

Killingsworth, M. A. "Experienced Well-Being Rises with Income, Even Above $75,000 Per Year." Proceedings of the National Academy of Sciences 118, no. 4 (2010). https://doi.org/10.1073/pnas.2016976118.

Jebb, A. T., L. Tay, E. Diener, and S. Oishi. "Happiness, Income Satiation and Turning Points Around the World." Nature Human Behaviour 21, no. 1 (2018): 33–38. https://doi.org/10.1038/s41562-017-0277-0.

Armson, P. D. Enough? How Much Money Do You Need for the Rest of Your Life? Inspiring Authors Limited—Createspace Independent Publishing Platform, 2016.

Part II: Revelations of Promise
CHAPTER 10: THE WATERFALL METHODOLOGY

Royce, W. W. Managing the Development of Large Software Systems: Concepts and Techniques. Undefined (2017). https://www.semanticscholar.org/paper/Managing-the-Development-of-Large-Software-Systems%3A-Royce/4afe47371b891778c6cc6fa401bfc1673ea0d63f.

Operational Effectiveness of the Myki Ticketing System. Victorian Auditor-General's Office (n.d.). https://www.audit.vic.gov.au/report/operational-effectiveness-myki-ticketing-system?section=#:~:text=Conclusion.

Dowling, J. "Myki 'Main Cause of Complaints' to Public Transport Watchdog." The Age. (February 13, 2014). https://www.theage.com.au/national/victoria/myki-main-cause-of-complaints-to-public-transport-watchdog-20140213-32nde.html.

2013 IT Project Success Rates Survey Results. Ambysoft.com (2013). http://www.ambysoft.com/surveys/success2013.html.

Chaos Report 2015. The Standish Group International (2015). https://www.standishgroup.com/sample_research_files/CHAOSReport2015-Final.pdf.

PMI Pulse of the Profession® 2017. Pmi.org, 2017. https://www.pmi.org/learning/thought-leadership/pulse/pulse-of-the-profession-2017.

VersionOne 11th Annual State of Agile Report. VersionOne Inc. (2017). https://www.agile247.pl/wp-content/uploads/2017/04/versionone-11th-annual-state-of-agile-report.pdf.

Agile Project Delivery Confidence: Mitigate Project Risks and Deliver Value to Your Business. PricewaterhouseCoopers LLC (2017). https://www.pwc.com/gx/en/actuarial-insurance-services/assets/agile-project-delivery-confidence.pdf.

"Survey Data Shows That Many Companies Are Still Not Truly Agile—Sponsor Content from CA TECHNOLOGIES." Harvard Business Review (March 22, 2018). https://hbr.org/sponsored/2018/03/survey-data-shows-that-many-companies-are-still-not-truly-agile.

CHAPTER 11: THE AGILE PHILOSOPHY

Turner, J. R., and R. Baker, R. "Just Doing the Do: A Case Study Testing Creativity and Innovative Processes as Complex Adaptive Systems." New Horizons in Adult Education and Human Resource Development 32, no. 2 (2020): 40–61. https://doi.org/10.1002/nha3.20283.

Agile Manifesto for Software Development Agile Alliance (December 12, 2018). https://www.agilealliance.org/agile101/the-agile-manifesto/.

Hirotaka Takeuchi and Nonaka Ikujiro "The New New Product Development Game: Stop Running the Relay Race and Take Up Rugby." Harvard Business Review (January 1986). https://hbr.org/1986/01/the-new-new-product-development-game.

CHAPTER 14: SHADES OF SERENDIPITY

Pluchino, A., A. E. Biondo, and A. Rapisarda. "Talent Versus Luck: The Role of Randomness in Success and Failure." Advances in Complex Systems 21, no. 03n04 (2018): 1850014. https://doi.org/10.1142/s0219525918500145.

Mauboussin, M. J. The Success Equation: Untangling Skill and Luck in Business, Sports, and Investing. Harvard Business Review Press, 2012.

Taleb, N.N. Fooled by Randomness: The Hidden Role of Chance in Life and in the Markets. Random House, 2016.

Taleb, N.N. Black Swan: The Impact of the Highly Improbable. Taylor And Francis, 2017.

Frank, R. H. Success and Luck: Good Fortune and the Myth of Meritocracy. Princeton University Press, 2017.

Part III: Desperate Measures
CHAPTER 17: SUFFER

Blaise, P., and A. J. Krailsheimer. Pensées. Penguin Books, 1995.

Frahm, J. Conversations of Change: A Guide to Implementing Workplace Change. Jennifer Frahm Collaborations Pty Ltd., 2017.

Lewin, K., and Dorwin Cartwright, eds. Field Theory in Social Science: Selected Theoretical Papers. Harper, 1951.

Camus, A. The Myth of Sisyphus. Vintage Books, 2018.

Laplace, S.-P. A Philosophical essay on probabilities. Dover Publications, 1995.

"We Stop Celebrating Our Birthday Aged 37 . . . and Start Lying About Our Age." The Argus, Dec 19, 2019. https://www.theargus.co.uk/news/national/uk-today/18112375.stop-celebrating-birthday-aged-37-start-lying-age/.

Part IV: Direction
CHAPTER 18: THE QUASI-CHAOTIC VIEW

Tiberius, V. "Recipes for a Good Life: Eudaimonism and the Contribution of Philosophy." In The Best Within Us: Positive Psychology Perspectives on Eudaimonia, edited by A. S. Waterman: 19–38. American Psychological Association, 2013. https://doi.org/10.1037/14092-002.

Thorburn, M. "Theoretical Constructs of Well-Being and Their Implications for Education." British Educational Research Journal 41, no. 4 (2015): 650–65. https://doi.org/10.1002/berj.3169.

Maslow, A. H., B. Maslow, and R. Lowry. The Journals of A.H. Maslow. Brooks/Cole, 1979.

Maslow, A. H. The Farther Reaches of Human Nature. Viking Press, 1971.

Winston, C. N. "Points of Convergence and Divergence Between Existential and Humanistic Psychology: A Few Observations." The Humanistic Psychologist 43, no. 1 (2015): 40–53. https://doi.org/10.1080/0887 3267.2014.993067.

Maslow, A. H. Motivation and Personality (3rd ed.). Harper & Row, 1987.

Heidegger, M. Being and Time. Translated by J. Macquarrie and E. Robinson. Harperperennial/Modern Thought, 2008.

Diogenes, L. "The Stoics: Persaeus." In "Zeno." Translated by Robert Drew Hicks. In Lives of the Eminent Philosophers, vol 2:7. Harvard University Press, 1979.

Graham, D. W. Heraclitus. PhilPapers; Oxford University Press, 2008. https://philpapers.org/rec/GRAH.

Heraclitus, E., and C. H. Kahn. The Art and Thought of Heraclitus: An Edition of the Fragments with Translation and Commentary. Cambridge University Press, 1979.

Lefrançois, G. R., G. Leclerc, M. Dubé, R. Hébert, and P. Gaulin, P. "The Development and Validation of a Self-Report Measure of Self-Actualization." Social Behavior and Personality: An International Journal 25, no. 4 (1997): 353–65. https://doi.org/10.2224/sbp.1997.25.4.353.

Piedmont, R. L., M. F. Sherman, N. C. Sherman. "Maladaptively High and Low Openness: The Case for Experiential Permeability." Journal of Personality 80, no. 6 (2012): 1641–68. https://doi.org/10.1111/j.1467-6494.2012.00777.x.

Murphy, M. C. Natural Law and Practical Rationality. Cambridge University Press, 2001.

Parfit, D. A. Reasons and Persons. Oxford University Press, 1984.

Part V: The Tool Kit
CHAPTER 19: CURIOSITY

Lucas, C. G., S. Bridgers, T. L. Griffiths, and A. Gopnik. "When Children Are Better (or at Least More Open-Minded) Learners Than Adults: Developmental Differences in Learning the Forms Of Causal Relationships." Cognition 131, no. 2 (2014): 284–99. https://doi.org/10.1016/j.cognition.2013.12.010.

Thompson-Schill, S. L., M. Ramscar, and E. G. Chrysikou. "Cognition Without Control." Current Directions in Psychological Science 18, no. 5 (2009): 259–63. https://doi.org/10.1111/j.1467-8721.2009.01648.x.

Ainsworth-Land, G. T., and B. Jarman. Breakpoint and Beyond: Mastering the Future—Today. Harper Business, 1993.

Fazio, R. H., J. R. Eiser, and N. J. Shook. "Attitude Formation through Exploration: Valence Asymmetries." Journal of Personality and Social Psychology 87, no. 3 (2004): 293–311. https://doi.org/10.1037/0022-3514.87.3.293.

Rich, A. S., and T. M. Gureckis. "The Limits of Learning: Exploration, Generalization, and the Development of Learning Traps." Journal of Experimental Psychology: General 147, no. 11 (2018): 1553–70. https://doi.org/10.1037/xge0000466.

Liquin, E. G., and A. Gopnik. "Children Are More Exploratory and Learn More than Adults in an Approach-Avoid Task." Cognition 218 (2022): 104940. https://doi.org/10.1016/j.cognition.2021.104940.

Kashdan, T., D. Disabato, F. Goodman, and P. Mcknight. "The Five-Dimensional Curiosity Scale Revised (5DCR): Briefer Subscales While Separating Overt and Covert Social Curiosity." Personality and Individual Differences 157 (2020): 109836. 10.1016/j.paid.2020.109836.

Millon, T. Personality Disorders in Modern Life. Wiley, 2004.

Gruber, M. J., and C. Ranganath. "How Curiosity Enhances Hippocampus-Dependent Memory: The Prediction, Appraisal, Curiosity, and Exploration (PACE) Framework." Trends in Cognitive Sciences 23, no. 12 (2019): 1014–25. https://doi.org/10.1016/j.tics.2019.10.003.

CHAPTER 20: OSMOSIS

Lakin, J. L., V. E. Jefferis, C. M. Cheng, and T. L. Chartrand. "The Chameleon Effect as Social Glue: Evidence for the Evolutionary Significance of Nonconscious Mimicry." Journal of Nonverbal Behavior 27, no. 3 (2003): 145–62. https://doi.org/10.1023/a:1025389814290.

Lakin, J. L., and T. L. Chartrand. "Using Nonconscious Behavioral Mimicry to Create Affiliation and Rapport." Psychological Science 14, no. 4 (2003): 334–9. https://doi.org/10.1111/1467-9280.14481.

Shan, X., and U. Zölitz. Peers Affect Personality Development. Papers.ssrn.com, 2002. https://papers.ssrn.com/sol3/papers.cfm?abstract_id=4121424.

Chartrand, T. L., and J. A. Bargh. "The Chameleon Effect: The Perception–Behavior Link and Social Interaction." Journal of Personality and Social Psychology 76, no. 6 (1999): 893–910. https://doi.org/10.1037/0022-3514.76.6.893.

Kosse, F., T. Deckers, P. Pinger, H. Schildberg-Hörisch, and A. Falk. "The Formation of Prosociality: Causal Evidence on the Role of Social Environment." Journal of Political Economy 128, no. 2 (2020): 434–67. https://doi.org/10.1086/704386.

Abeler, J., A. Falk, and F. Kosse. Malleability of Preferences for Honesty. Papers.ssrn.com. (2021). https://papers.ssrn.com/sol3/papers.cfm?abstract_id=3886585.

Boneva, T., T. Buser, A. Falk, and F. Kosse, F. The Origins of Gender Differences in Competitiveness and Earnings Expectations: Causal Evidence from a Mentoring Intervention. www.iza.org. (2021). https://www.iza.org/publications/dp/14800/the-origins-of-gender-differences-in-competitiveness-and-earnings-expectations-causal-evidence-from-a-mentoring-intervention.

Sorrenti, G., U. Zölitz, E. Ribeaud, and M. Eisner, M. The Causal Impact of Socio-Emotional Skills Training on Educational Success. www.iza.org (2020). https://www.iza.org/publications/dp/13087/the-causal-impact-of-socio-emotional-skills-training-on-educational-success#:~:text=IZA%20DP%20No.

Stieger, M., C. Flückiger, D. Rüegger, T. Kowatsch, B. W. Roberts, and M. Allemand. "Changing Personality Traits with the Help of a Digital Personality Change Intervention." Proceedings of the National Academy of Sciences 118, no. 8 (2021): e2017548118. https://doi.org/10.1073/pnas.2017548118.

Dahmann, S. C., and S. Anger. Cross-Fertilizing Gains or Crowding Out? Schooling Intensity and Noncognitive Skills. Human Capital and Economic Opportunity Global Working Group (2018). https://hceconomics.uchicago.edu/research/working-paper/cross-fertilizing-gains-or-crowding-out-schooling-intensity-and-noncognitive.

CHAPTER 21: ACCOUNTABILITY

Lally, P., C. H. M. van Jaarsveld, H. Potts, and J. Wardle. "How Are Habits Formed: Modelling Habit Formation in the Real World." European Journal of Social Psychology 40, no. 6 (2009): 998–1009. https://doi.org/10.1002/ejsp.674.

Fast, N. J., and L. Z. Tiedens. "Blame Contagion: The Automatic Transmission of Self-Serving Attributions." Journal of Experimental Social Psychology 46, no. 1 (2010): 97–106. https://doi.org/10.1016/j.jesp.2009.10.007.

Carr, P. B., and G. M. Walton. "Cues of Working Together Fuel Intrinsic Motivation." Journal of Experimental Social Psychology 53 (2014): 169–84. https://doi.org/10.1016/j.jesp.2014.03.015.

CHAPTER 23: AMBITION

El Baroudi, S., C. Fleisher, S. N. Khapova, P. Jansen, and J. Richardson. "Ambition at Work and Career Satisfaction: The Mediating Role of Taking Charge Behavior and the Moderating Role of Pay." Career Development International 22, no. 1 (2017): 87–102. https://doi.org/10.1108/cdi-07-2016-0124.

Judge, T. A., D. M. Cable, J. W. Boudreau, and R. D. Bretz. "An Empirical Investigation of the Predictors of Executive Career Success." Personnel Psychology 48, no. 3 (1995): 485–519. https://doi.org/10.1111/j.1744-6570.1995.tb01767.x.

Zimmerman, R. D., W. R. Boswell, A. J. Shipp, D. B. Dunford, and J. W. Boudreau. "Explaining the Pathways Between Approach-Avoidance Personality Traits and Employees' Job Search Behavior." Journal of Management 38, no. 5 (2011): 1450–75. https://doi.org/10.1177/0149206310396376.

Ashby, J. S., and I. Schoon. "Career success: The Role of Teenage Career Aspirations, Ambition Value and Gender in Predicting Adult Social Status and Earnings." Journal of Vocational Behavior 77, no. 3 (2010): 350–60. https://doi.org/10.1016/j.jvb.2010.06.006.

Ng, T. W. H., and D. C. Feldman. "A Conservation of Resources Perspective on Career Hurdles and Salary Attainment." Journal of Vocational Behavior 85, no. 1 (2014): 156–68. https://doi.org/10.1016/j.jvb.2014.05.008.

Hirschi, A., and D. Spurk. "Striving for Success: Towards a Refined Understanding and Measurement of Ambition." Journal of Vocational Behavior (2021): 103577. https://doi.org/10.1016/j.jvb.2021.103577.

Judge, T. A., J. D. Kammeyer-Mueller. "On the Value of Aiming High: The Causes and Consequences of Ambition." Journal of Applied Psychology 97, no. 4 (2012): 758–75. https://doi.org/10.1037/a0028084.

CHAPTER 24: FAILURE

Yin, Y., Y. Wang, J. A. Evans, and D. Wang. "Quantifying the Dynamics of Failure Across Science, Startups and Security." Nature 575, no. 7781 (2019): 190–94. https://doi.org/10.1038/s41586-019-1725-y.

Noonan, D. "Failure Found to Be an 'Essential Prerequisite' for Success." Scientific American (October 30, 2019). https://www.scientificamerican.com/article/failure-found-to-be-an-essential-prerequisite-for-success/.

CHAPTER 25: PRIDE

Lazarus, R. S. Emotion and Adaptation. New York: Oxford University Press, 1991.

Leary, M. R., and D. L. Downs. "Interpersonal Functions of the Self-Esteem Motive." Efficacy, Agency, and Self-Esteem (1995): 123–44. https://doi.org/10.1007/978-1-4899-1280-0_7.

Tracy, J. L. Pride: The Secret of Success. Mariner Books, 2017.

Eskreis-Winkler, L., and A. Fishbach. "Not Learning from Failure—the Greatest Failure of All." Psychological Science (2019): 095679761988113. https://doi.org/10.1177/0956797619881133.

Smith, R. H. The Joy of Pain: Schadenfreude and the Dark Side of Human Nature. Oxford University Press, 2014.

Hill, S., and D. Buss. "The Evolutionary Psychology of Envy." Envy: Theory and Research. (2010): 60–70. 10.1093/acprof:oso/9780195327953.003.0004.

Kalma, A. "Hierarchisation and Dominance Assessment at First Glance." European Journal of Social Psychology 21, no. 2 (1991): 165–81. https://doi.org/10.1002/ejsp.2420210206.

Mazur, A., and A. Booth. "The Biosociality of Testosterone in Men." In Mind, Brain, and Society: Toward a Neurosociology of Emotion: Vol. 5. Social Perspectives on Emotions, edited by D. D. Franks and T. S. Smith. Stamford, CT: Jai Press, 1991.

Festinger, L. "A Theory of Social Comparison Processes." Human Relations 7, no. 2 (1954): 117–40. https://doi.org/10.1177/001872675400700202.

Part VI: Decisions
CHAPTER 26: HARD PROBLEMS

Pink, D. H. World Regret Survey. Worldregretsurvey.com (n.d.). https://worldregretsurvey.com/.

Pink, D. H. The Power of Regret: How Looking Backward Moves Us Forward. Riverhead Books, 2022.

Bauer, I., and C. Wrosch. "Making Up for Lost Opportunities: The Protective Role of Downward Social Comparisons for Coping with Regrets Across Adulthood." Personality and Social Psychology Bulletin 37, no. 2 (2011): 215–28. https://doi.org/10.1177/0146167210393256.

Das, N., and A. H. Kerr. "'Woulda, Coulda, Shoulda': A Conceptual Examination of the Sources of Postpurchase Regret." Journal of Marketing Theory and Practice 18 no. 2 (2010): 171–80. https://doi.org/10.2753/mtp1069-6679180205.

Zeelenberg, M., K. van den Bos, E. van Dijk, E., and R. Pieters. "The Inaction Effect in the Psychology Of Regret." Journal of Personality and Social Psychology 82, no. 3 (2002): 314–27. https://doi.org/10.1037/0022-3514.82.3.314.

Bar-Eli, M., O. H. Azar, I. Ritov, Y. Keidar-Levin, and G. Schein, G. "Action Bias Among Elite Soccer Goalkeepers: The Case of Penalty Kicks." Journal of Economic Psychology 28, no. 5 (2007): 606–21. https://doi.org/10.1016/j.joep.2006.12.001.

Miller, D. T., and B. R. Taylor. "Counterfactual Thinking, Regret, and Superstition: How To Avoid Kicking Yourself." In What Might Have Been: The Social Psychology of Counterfactual Thinking, edited by N. J. Roese and J. M. Olson, 305–31. Eribaum, 1995.

N'gbala, A., and N. R. Branscombe. "When Does Action Elicit More Regret Than Inaction and Is Counter-factual Mutation the Mediator of This Effect?" Journal of Experimental Social Psychology 33, no. 3 (1997): 324–43. https://doi.org/10.1006/jesp.1996.1322.

Gilovich, T., and V. H. Medvec. "The Experience of Regret: What, When, and Why." Psychological Review 102, no. 2 (1995): 379–95. https://doi.org/10.1037/0033-295X.102.2.379.

Higgins, E. T. "Beyond Pleasure and Pain." American Psychologist 52, no. 12 (1997): 1280–1300. https://doi.org/10.1037/0003-066X.52.12.1280.

Higgins, E. T. "Promotion and Prevention: Regulatory Focus as a Motivational Principle." Advances in Experimental Social Psychology, 30 (1998): 1–46. https://doi.org/10.1016/s0065-2601(08)60381-0.

Itzkin, A., D. Dijk, D., and O. Azar. "At Least I Tried: The Relationship Between Regulatory Focus and Regret Following Action vs. Inaction." Frontiers in Psychology (2016). https://doi.org/ 10.3389/fpsyg.2016.01684.

Van Dijk, D., T. Seger-Guttmann, and D. Heller, D. "Life-Threatening Event Reduces Subjective Well-Being through Activating Avoidance Motivation: A Longitudinal Study." Emotion (Washington, D.C.) 13, no. 2 (2013): 216–25. https://doi.org/10.1037/a0029973.

Davidai, S., and T. Gilovich. "The Ideal Road Not Taken: The Self-Discrepancies Involved in People's Most Enduring Regrets." Emotion 18, no. 3 (2018): 439–52. https://doi.org/10.1037/emo0000326.

Friedman, R. S., and J. Förster. "The Effects of Promotion and Prevention Cues on Creativity." Journal of Personality and Social Psychology 81, no. 6 (2001): 1001–13. https://doi.org/10.1037/0022-3514.81.6.1001.

Vaughn, L. A., J. Baumann, and C. Klemann. "Openness to Experience and Regulatory Focus: Evidence of Motivation from Fit." Journal of Research in Personality 42, no. 4 (2008): 886–94. https://doi.org/10.1016/j.jrp.2007.11.008.

Groeneveld, D. Big Five, Regulatory Focus and The Dual Pathway to Creativity Model. Feb.studenttheses.ub.rug.nl (2012). https://feb.studenttheses.ub.rug.nl/7699/.

Levitt, J.T., T. A. Brown, S. M. Orsillo, and D. H. Barlow. "The Effects of Acceptance Versus Suppression of Emotion on Subjective and Psychophysiological Response to Carbon Dioxide Challenge in Patients with Panic Disorder." Behavior Therapy 35 (2004): 747–66. https://contextualscience.org/system/files/Levitt_etal,2004.pdf.

Tull, M. T., K. L. Gratz, K. Salters, and L. Roemer. "The Role of Experiential Avoidance in Posttraumatic Stress Symptoms and Symptoms of Depression, Anxiety, and Somatization." Journal of Nervous and Mental Disease 192, no. 11 (2004): 754–61. https://doi.org/10.1097/01.nmd.0000144694.30121.89.

Roemer, L., K. Salters, S. D. Raffa, and S. M. Orsillo. "Fear and Avoidance of Internal Experiences in GAD: Preliminary Tests of a Conceptual Model." Cognitive Therapy and Research 29 no. 1 (2005): 71–88. https://doi.org/10.1007/s10608-005-1650-2.

Kashdan, T. B., N. Morina, and S. Priebe. "Post-Traumatic Stress Disorder, Social Anxiety Disorder, and Depression in Survivors of the Kosovo War: Experiential Avoidance as a Contributor to Distress and Quality of Life." Journal of Anxiety Disorders 23 no. 2 (2009): 185–96. https://doi.org/10.1016/j.janxdis.2008.06.006.

Shallcross, A. J., A. S. Troy, M. Boland, and I. B. Mauss, I. B. "Let It Be: Accepting Negative Emotional Experiences Predicts Decreased Negative Affect and Depressive Symptoms." Behaviour Research and Therapy 48, no. 9 (2010): 921–29. https://doi.org/10.1016/j.brat.2010.05.025.

Arimitsu, K., and S. G. Hofmann. "Effects of Compassionate Thinking on Negative Emotions." Cognition and Emotion 31 no. 1 (2015): 160–67. https://doi.org/10.1080/02699931.2015.1078292.

Weiss, R. S. "Grief, bonds, and relationships." In Handbook of Bereavement Research: Consequences, Coping, and Care, edited by M. S. Stroebe, R. O. Hansson, W. Stroebe, and H. Schut, 47–62. American Psychological Association (2001). https://doi.org/10.1037/10436-002.

Bonanno, G. A., and I. R. Galatzer-Levy. "Beyond Normality in the Study of Bereavement: Heterogeneity in Depression Outcomes Following Loss in Older Adults." Social Science & Medicine 74, no 12 (2012): 1987–94. https://doi.org/10.1016/j.socscimed.2012.02.022.

Nesse, R. "Spousal Bereavement in Late Life." In An Evolutionary Framework for Understanding Grief, edited by D. Carr, R. Nesse, and C. Wortman, 195–226. Springer, 2005.

CHAPTER 27: THE THREE PILLARS OF CONVICTION

Boudon, R. "Beyond Rational Choice Theory." Annual Review of Sociology 29, no. 1 (2003): 1–21. https://doi.org/10.1146/annurev.soc.29.010202.100213.

Vroom, V.H., and P. W. Yetton. Leadership and Decision-Making. University Of Pittsburgh Press, 1973.

Klein, G. A. Sources of Power: How People Make Decisions. MIT Press, 2017.

Argyris, C., and D. A. Schön. Theory in Practice: Increasing Professional Effectiveness. Jossey-Bass, 1992.

Burke, L. A., and M. K. Miller. "Taking the Mystery Out of Intuitive Decision Making." Academy of Management Perspectives 13, no. 4 (1999): 91–99. https://doi.org/10.5465/ame.1999.2570557.

Schwarz, N. "Emotion, Cognition, and Decision Making." Cognition and Emotion 14, no. 4 (2000): 433–40. https://doi.org/10.1080/026999300402745.

Böhm, G., and W. Brun. "Introduction to the Special Issue: Intuition and Affect in Risk Perception and Decision Making." Judgment and Decision Making 3 (2008): 1–4.

Lerner, J. S., Y. Li, P. Valdesolo, and K. S. Kassam. Emotion and Decision Making. Annual Review of Psychology 66, no. 1 (2015): 799–823. https://doi.org/10.1146/annurev-psych-010213-115043.

Sinclair, M. Handbook of Research Methods on Intuition. Edward Elgar Publishing, 2016.

Von Neumann, J., and O. Morgenstein. Theory of Games and Economic Behaviour. Princeton University Press, 1953.

Friedman, M. Essays in Positive Economics. University Of Chicago Press, 1953.

Wilson, T. D., and D. T. Gilbert. "Affective Forecasting." In Advances in Experimental Social Psychology 35, edited by M. P. Zanna, 345–411. Elsevier Academic Press, 2003. https://doi.org/10.1016/S0065-2601(03)01006-2.

Dunning, D. "Self-Image Motives and Consumer Behavior: How Sacrosanct Self-Beliefs Sway Preferences in the Marketplace." Journal of Consumer Psychology 17, no 4 (2007): 237–49. https://doi.org/10.1016/s1057-7408(07)70033-5.

Buehler, R., D. Griffin, and J. Peetz. "The Planning Fallacy: Cognitive, Motivational, and Social Origins." In Advances in Experimental Social Psychology 43, edited M. P. Zanna and J. M. Olson, 1–62. Academic Press, 2010. https://doi.org/10.1016/S0065-2601(10)43001-4.

Peetz, J., and R. Buehler. "Is There a Budget Fallacy? The Role of Savings Goals in the Prediction of Personal Spending." Personality and Social Psychology Bulletin 35, no. 12 (2009): 1579–91. https://doi.org/10.1177/0146167209345160.

MacDonald, T. K., and M. Ross. "Assessing the Accuracy of Predictions about Dating Relationships: How and Why Do Lovers' Predictions Differ from Those Made By Observers?" Personality and Social Psychology Bulletin 25, no. 11 (1999): 1417–29. https://doi.org/10.1177/0146167299259007.

Lipkus, I., and J. Shepperd. "College Smokers' Estimates of Their Probabilities of Remaining a Smoker in the Near Future." Journal of Health Psychology 14, no. 4 (2009): 547–55. https://doi.org/10.1177/1359105309103574.

Helzer, E. G., and D. Dunning. "Why and When Peer Prediction Is Superior to Self-Prediction: The Weight Given to Future Aspiration Versus Past Achievement." Journal of Personality and Social Psychology 103, no 1 (2012): 38–53. https://doi.org/10.1037/a0028124.

Hilbig, B. E., S. G. Scholl, and R. F. Pohl. "Think or Blink—Is the Recognition Heuristic an 'Intuitive' Strategy?" Judgment and Decision Making 5, no. 4 (2010): 300–9.

Kirkebøen, G. Intuitive Choices Lead to Intensified Positive Emotions: An Overlooked Reason for "Intuition Bias"? Frontiers, 2017. https://www.frontiersin.org/articles/10.3389/fpsyg.2017.01942/full.

Tversky, A. N., and D. Kahneman. Advances in Prospect Theory: Cumulative Representation of Uncertainty. Journal of Risk and Uncertainty 5, no. 4 (1992), 297–323. https://doi.org/10.1007/bf00122574.

Putler, D. S. "Incorporating Reference Price Effects into a Theory of Consumer Choice." Marketing Science 11, no. 3 (1992): 287–309. https://doi.org/10.1287/mksc.11.3.287.

Tversky, A. N., and D. Kahneman. "Judgment Under Uncertainty: Heuristics and Biases." Science 185, no. 4157 (1974): 1124–31.

Roser, M., E. Ortiz-Ospina, and H. Ritchie. Life Expectancy. Our World in Data, 2013. https://ourworldindata.org/life-expectancy.

Roser, M. The Short History of Global Living Conditions and Why It Matters That We Know It. Our World in Data, 2013. https://ourworldindata.org/a-history-of-global-living-conditions-in-5-charts.

Levy, J. S., and W. R. Thompson. Causes of War. Wiley-Blackwell, 2010.

UCDP—Uppsala Conflict Data Program (2019). Ucdp.uu.se. https://ucdp.uu.se/.

Marshall, M., Gurr, T., and K. Jaggers. POLITY™ IV PROJECT Political Regime Characteristics and Transitions, 1800–2016 Dataset Users' Manual (n.d.). https://www.systemicpeace.org/inscr/p4manualv2016.pdf.

Wiltermuth, S. and L. Tiedens. "Incidental Anger and the Desire to Evaluate." Organizational Behavior and Human Decision Processes 116 (2011): 55–65. https://doi.org/10.1016/j.obhdp.2011.03.007.

Lerner, J. S., Y. Li, P. Valdesolo, and K. S. Kassam. "Emotion and Decision Making." Annual Review of Psychology 66, no. 1 (2015): 799–823. https://doi.org/10.1146/annurev-psych-010213-115043.

Gino, F., and M. E. Schweitzer. "Blinded By Anger or Feeling the Love: How Emotions Influence Advice Taking." The Journal of Applied Psychology 93, no. 5 (2008); 1165–73. https://doi.org/10.1037/0021-9010.93.5.1165.

PREQUEL TO PART VII: EXECUTION

Ross, L., M. R. Lepper, and M. Hubbard. "Perseverance in Self-Perception and Social Perception: Biased Attributional Processes in the Debriefing Paradigm." Journal of Personality and Social Psychology 32, no. 5 (1975): 880–92. https://doi.org/10.1037/0022-3514.32.5.880.

Part VII: Execution
CHAPTER 33: FIVE WHYS

Richard Feynman: Fun to Imagine. BBC (n.d.). https://www.bbc.co.uk/programmes/p0198zc1.

CHAPTER 35: BULKING

Schafer, J., and M. Karlins. The Like Switch: An Ex-FBI Agent's Guide to Influencing, Attracting, and Winning People Over. Atria, 2019.

QUASI-CHAOTIC TIPS

Flynn, F. J., & Lake, V. K. (2008). "If you need help, just ask": Underestimating compliance with direct requests for help. Journal of Personality and Social Psychology, 95(1), 128-143. https://doi.org/10.1037/0022-3514.95.1.128

Chapman, B. P., Fiscella, K., Kawachi, I., Duberstein, P., & Muennig, P. (2013). Emotion suppression and mortality risk over a 12-year follow-up. Journal of Psychosomatic Research, 75(4), 381–385. https://doi.org/10.1016/j.jpsychores.2013.07.012"

INDEX

Milton Keynes UK
Ingram Content Group UK Ltd.
UKHW010745180923
428890UK00003B/153